Hugh Johnson's
Pocket Wine Book
98

MITCHELL BEAZLEY

Acknowledgments

This store of detailed recommendations comes partly from my own notes and partly from those of a great number of kind friends. Without the generous help and cooperation of innumerable winemakers, merchants and critics, I could not attempt it. I particularly want to thank the following for help with research or in the areas of their special knowledge.

Colin Anderson MW
Fritz Ascher
Martyn Assirati
Jean-Claude Berrouet
Gregory Bowden
Lucy Bridgers
Michael Broadbent MW
Jim Budd
Michael Cooper
John Cossart
Michael Edwards
Len Evans
Dereck Foster
Jacqueline Friedrich
Rosemary George MW
Howard G Goldberg
James Halliday
Shirley Jones
Gabriel Lachmann
Tony Laithwaite
John Livingstone-Learmonth
Andreas März
Richard Mayson
Maggie McNie MW
Adam Montefiori
Vladimir Moskvan
Christian Moueix
Richard Neill
Judy Peterson-Nedry
Stuart Pigott
John and Erica Platter
Carlos Read
Jan and Maite Read
Michael, Prinz zu Salm
Joanna Simon
Stephen Skelton
Paul Strang
Marguerite Thomas
Bob Thompson
Peter Vinding-Diers
Julia Wilkinson
Simon Woods
Hilary Wright

Hugh Johnson's Pocket Wine Book 1998

21st Anniversary Limited Edition

Published by Mitchell Beazley, an imprint of Reed International Books Limited, Michelin House, 81 Fulham Road, London SW3 6RB and Auckland and Melbourne

First edition published 1977
Revised editions published 1978, 1979, 1980, 1981, 1982, 1983, 1984, 1985, 1986, 1987, 1988, 1989, 1990, 1991, 1992, 1993, 1994, 1995, 1996, 1997

A CIP record for this book is available from the British Library.

ISBN 1 84000 0368

Commissioning Editor: Sue Jamieson
Executive Art Editor: Fiona Knowles
Editor: Lucy Bridgers
Production: Rachel Lynch

Printed and bound in China

Contents

Foreword

The first edition of this little book appeared in 1977. Twenty-one years later it has twice as many pages and details four times as many wines. But numbers are not the only things that have changed in the wine world.

Surveying the near-third of my life since I first started this exercise in compression, it seems to me that the biggest change is in the consumer: in expectations, knowledge, demands and willingness to pay more for better wine. In 1977, the wine-countries of Europe were gross drinkers with, frankly, only the sketchiest knowledge. Britain was still mired in Edwardian attitudes; hardly anything beyond 'the classics' was considered worth investigation. America and Australia were just waking up to wine.

They (America and Australia) became its motors. Their uninhibited experiments made science-based winemaking first possible, then the norm, in every country that could afford it. Their influence brought first Italy, then Spain and Portugal, into the modern wine world, and has now so permeated France that it almost passes without comment there.

Without geographical traditions and stylistic conventions, the New World coined varietalism, giving the grape variety pride of place. What started as a sales tool became an invaluable learning aid as millions learned the tastes of Cabernet and Chardonnay and Pinot Noir. They also learned the taste of oak, universally adopted as seasoning for fruit flavours that were often a bit too plain.

Varietalism was a direct challenge to the concept of terroir, the notion that each situation and its soil gives a wine a specific character – and that some are inherently better (for the appropriate grapes) than others.

This rivalry has now been pretty much played out, as experience has shown that the effects of terroir are inescapable, and winemakers and grape-growers of the New World are discovering the secrets of their own. The consumer, therefore, is being offered the best of both worlds, in all senses. There has never been a better time to enjoy wine in all its variety.

There is, of course, a hitch. Enthusiasm for wines that are expressive of grape, place and vintage is outpacing the supply. There has always been (and probably always will be) a surplus of bulk wine expressive of nothing but desperation. But competition for fine wines, especially for well-known names, is now almost worldwide. It is reds that are particularly affected. The news has reached the Far East that red wines are good for you, and with surprising haste, the dedicated cognac-drinkers of China and Japan are switching to Bordeaux and Burgundy.

The proprietors of their favourite wines (naturally the most expensive) are in a dilemma. Is this a passing fad, or a long-term new market? Traditional European customers are being frightened by global famine prices. It is the kind of boom that can easily be followed by bust.

The switch in medical opinion affects us all. Non-Prohibitionist attitudes, especially in the US, seemed immovable until doctors finally made the unsurprising announcement that wine-drinking in moderation is moderately good for you. Now, absurdly, it is only the French government with its preposterous 'Loi Evin' that forbids the advertising of alcohol. Whether wine comes out of current research as being substantially different from other forms of alcohol is less clear – though it may be better for your figure. Laying aside the broader issues, though, this micro-encyclopedia looks closely at the present position in this fast-changing world. Even readers who bought the last edition (others, I'm afraid, only come back to the well at intervals of two or three) will find thousands of changes of detail, emphasis and evaluation.

This is intended to be a practical guide; theory has little place here. In essence, it compresses all the useful information you can't possibly carry in your head – and neither can I. My information is gleaned, as ever, from many sources, from tastings, visits and never-ending correspondence. Revision is a continuing process. Before you read this I will have a much scribbled-on proof for next year's edition.

The book is designed to take the panic out of buying. You are faced with a daunting restaurant wine list, or mind-numbing shelves of bottles in a store. Your mind goes blank. Out comes your little book. You can start with what you propose to eat, by turning to the wines for food section on pages 14–27, or where you are by turning up a national section, or a grape variety you like. Just establish which country a wine comes from, then look up the principal words on the label in that country's section. You should find enough information to guide your choice – and often a great deal more: the cross-references are there to help you delve further. Even after 20 editions I find I can browse for hours...

How to use this book

The top line of most entries consists of the following information:

❶	❷	❸	❹
Aglianico del Vulture Bas	r dr (s/sw sp)	★★★	87 88 **90** 91 92 93 94 (95) (96)

❶ **Wine name and the region the wine comes from.**

❷ **Whether it is red, rosé or white (or brown/amber), dry, sweet or sparkling, or several of these (and which is most important):**

r	red
p	rosé
w	white
br	brown
dr	dry*
sw	sweet
s/sw	semi-sweet
sp	sparkling

( ) brackets here denote a less important wine
*assume wine is dry when **dr** or **sw** are not indicated

❸ **Its general standing as to quality: a necessarily rough and ready guide based on its current reputation as reflected in its prices:**

★	plain, everyday quality
★★	above average
★★★	well known, highly reputed
★★★★	grand, prestigious, expensive

So much is more or less objective. Additionally there is a subjective rating:

★ etc Stars are coloured purple for any wine which in my experience is usually especially good within its price range. There are good everyday wines as well as good luxury wines. This system helps you find them.

❹ **Vintage information: which of the recent vintages that may still be available can be recommended; of these, which are ready to drink this year, and which will probably improve with keeping. Your choice for current drinking should be one of the vintage years printed in bold type. Buy light-type years for further maturing.**

95 etc	recommended years which may be currently available
90' etc	vintage regarded as particularly successful for the property in question
87 etc	years in **bold** should be ready for drinking (the others should be kept)
89 etc	vintages in colour are the ones to choose first for drinking in '98 – they should be à point. (See also Bordeaux introduction, page 78.)
(93) etc	provisional rating

The German vintages work on a different principle again: see page 136.

Other abbreviations

DYA	drink the youngest available
NV	vintage not normally shown on label; in Champagne, means a blend of several vintages for continuity
CHABLIS	properties, areas or terms cross-referred within the section

A quick-reference vintage chart appears on page 280

Grape Varieties

In the past 15 years a radical change has come about in all except the most long-established wine countries: the names of a handful of grape varieties have become the ready reference to wine. In senior wine countries, above all France and Italy (between them producing nearly half the world's wine), more complex traditions prevail. Wine is known by its origin, not just the particular fruit-juice that fermented.

For the present the two notions are in rivalry. Eventually the primacy of place over fruit will become obvious, at least for wines of quality. But for now, for most people, grape tastes are the easy reference-point – despite the fact that they are often confused by the added taste of oak. If grape flavours were really all that mattered this would be a very short book.

But of course they do matter, and a knowledge of them both guides you to flavours you enjoy and helps comparisons between regions. Hence the originally Californian term 'varietal wine' – meaning, in principle, one grape variety.

At least seven varieties – Cabernet, Pinot Noir, Riesling, Sauvignon Blanc, Chardonnay, Gewürztraminer and Muscat – have tastes and smells distinct and memorable enough to form international categories of wine. To these you can add Merlot, Malbec, Syrah, Sémillon, Chenin Blanc, Pinots Blanc and Gris, Sylvaner, Viognier, Nebbiolo, Sangiovese, Tempranillo… The following are the best and/or commonest wine grapes. Abbreviations used in the text are in brackets.

Grapes for white wine

Albariño
The Spanish name for N Portugal's Alvarinho, emerging as excellently fresh and fragrant wine in Galicia.

Aligoté
Burgundy's second-rank white grape. Crisp (often sharp) wine, needs drinking in 1–3 yrs. Perfect for mixing with cassis (blackcurrant liqueur) to make a 'Kir'. Widely planted in E Europe, esp Russia.

Arinto
White central Portuguese grape for crisp, fragrant dry whites.

Blanc Fumé
Alias of SAUV BL, referring to its reputedly 'smoky' smell, particularly from the Loire (Sancerre and Pouilly). In California used for oak-aged Sauv and reversed to 'Fumé Blanc'. But the smoke is oak.

Bual
Makes top-quality sweet Madeira wines.

Chardonnay (Chard)
The white burgundy grape, the white champagne grape, and the best white grape of the New World, partly because it is one of the easiest to grow and vinify. All regions are trying it, mostly aged (or, better, fermented) in oak to reproduce the flavours of burgundy. Australia and California make classics. Those of Italy, Spain, New Zealand, South Africa, New York State, Chile, Hungary and the Midi are all coming on strong. Called Morillon in Austria.

Chasselas
Prolific early-ripening grape with little aroma, mainly grown for eating. AKA Fendant in Switzerland (where it is supreme), Gutedel in Germany.

Chenin Blanc (Chenin Bl)
Great white grape of the middle Loire (Vouvray, Layon etc). Wine can be dry or sweet (or very sweet), but with plenty of acidity – hence its long life and use in warmer climates (eg California). See also Steen.

Clairette
A low-acid grape formerly widely used in the S of France as a vermouth base. Being revived.

Colombard
Slightly fruity, nicely sharp grape, hugely popular in California, now gaining ground in SW France, South Africa, California etc.

Fendant See Chasselas.

Folle Blanche
High acid/little flavour make this ideal for brandy. Called Gros Plant in Brittany, Picpoul in Armagnac. Respectable in California.

Fumé Blanc (Fumé Bl) See Blanc Fumé.

Furmint
A grape of great character: the trademark of Hungary both as the principal grape in Tokay and as vivid vigorous table wine with an appley flavour. Called Sipon in Slovenia. Some grown in Austria.

Gewürztraminer, alias Traminer (Gewürz)
One of the most pungent grapes, distinctively spicy with aromas like rose petals and grapefruit. Wines are often rich and soft, even when fully dry. Best in Alsace; also good in Germany, E Europe, Australia, California, Pacific NW, New Zealand.

Grauburgunder See Pinot Gris.

Grechetto or Greco
Ancient grape of central and S Italy: vitality and style.

Grüner Veltliner
Austria's favourite (planted in almost half her vineyards). Around Vienna and in the Wachau and Weinviertel (also in Moravia) it can be delicious: light but dry and lively. The best age 5 years or so.

Hárslevelü
The other grape of Tokay (with FURMINT).

Italian Riesling
Grown in N Italy and E Europe. Much inferior to Rhine RIES, with lower acidity, best in sweet wines. Alias Welschriesling, Olaszrizling (no longer legally labelled simply 'Riesling').

Kéknyelü
Low-yielding, flavourful grape giving one of Hungary's best whites. Has the potential for fieriness and spice. To be watched.

Kerner
The most successful of many recent German varieties, mostly made by crossing RIES and SILVANER, but in this case Ries x (red) Trollinger. Early-ripening flowery (but often too blatant) wine with good acidity. Popular in Pfalz, Rheinhessen etc.

Loureiro
The best and most fragrant Vinho Verde variety in Portugal.

Macabeo
The workhorse white grape of N Spain, widespread in Rioja (alias Viura) and in Catalan cava country.

Malvasia
Known as Malmsey in Madeira, Malvasia in Italy, Malvoisie in France. Alias Vermentino (esp in Corsica). Also grown in Greece, Spain, W Australia, E Europe. Makes rich brown wines or soft whites, ageing magnificently with superb potential not often realized.

Marsanne
Principal white grape (with Roussanne) of the N Rhône (eg in Hermitage, St-Joseph, St-Péray). Also good in Australia, California and (as Ermitage Blanc) the Valais. Soft full wines that age v well.

Müller-Thurgau (Müller-T)
Dominant in Germany's Rheinhessen and Pfalz and too common on the Mosel; a cross between RIESLING and SILVANER. Ripens early to make soft aromatic wines for drinking young. Makes good sweet wines but usually dull, often coarse, dry ones.

Muscadelle
Adds aroma to many white Bordeaux, esp Sauternes. Also the base for Australian Liqueur Tokay.

Muscadet, alias Melon de Bourgogne
Makes light, refreshing, very dry wines with a seaside tang round Nantes in Brittany. (California 'Pinot Bl' is this grape.)

Muscat
(Many varieties; the best is Muscat Blanc à Petits Grains.) Universally grown, easily recognized, pungent grapes, mostly made into perfumed sweet wines, often fortified (as in France's vins doux naturels). Superb in Australia. Rarely (eg Alsace) made dry.

Palomino, alias Listan
Makes all the best sherry but poor table wine.

Pedro Ximénez, alias PX
Makes very strong wine in Montilla and Málaga. Used in blending sweet sherries. Also grown in Argentina, the Canaries, Australia, California, South Africa.

Pinot Blanc (Pinot Bl)
A cousin of PINOT N; not related to CHARD, but with a similar, milder character: light, fresh, fruity, not aromatic, to drink young; eg good for Italian spumante. Grown in Alsace, N Italy, S Germany, E Europe. Weissburgunder in Germany. See also Muscadet.

Pinot Gris (Pinot Gr)
At best makes rather heavy, even 'thick', full-bodied whites with a certain spicy style. Known (formerly) as Tokay in Alsace; Ruländer (sweet) or Grauburgunder (dry) in Germany; Tocai or Pinot Grigio in Italy and Slovenia (but much thinner wine).

Pinot Noir (Pinot N)
Superlative black grape (See Grapes for red wine) used in Champagne and occasionally elsewhere (eg California, Australia) for making white, sparkling, or very pale pink 'vin gris'.

Riesling (Ries)
Germany's great grape, and at present the world's most underrated. Wine of brilliant sweet/acid balance, either dry or sweet, flowery in youth but maturing to subtle oily scents and flavours. Unlike CHARD it does not need high alcohol for character. Very good (usually dry) in Alsace (but absurdly nowhere else in France), Austria, Australia (widely grown), Pacific NW, Ontario, California, South Africa. Often called White-, Johannisberg- or Rhine-Riesling. Subject to 'noble rot'.

Ruländer
German name for PINOT GRIS used for sweeter wines.

Sauvignon Blanc (Sauv Bl)
Makes v distinctive aromatic grassy – or gooseberry – sometimes rank-smelling wines; best in Sancerre. Blended with SEM in Bordeaux. Can be austere or buxom. Pungent success in New Zealand, now overplanted everywhere. Also called Fumé Blanc or vice versa.

Savagnin
The grape of Vin Jaune of Savoie related to TRAMINER?

Scheurebe
Spicy-flavoured German RIES x SYLVANER, very successful in Pfalz, esp for Auslesen. Can be weedy in dry wines.

Sémillon (Sém or Sem)
Contributes the lusciousness to Sauternes; subject to 'noble rot' in the right conditions but increasingly important for Graves and dry white Bordeaux, too. Grassy if not fully ripe, but can make soft dry wine of great ageing potential. Formerly called 'Riesling' in parts of Australia. Old Hunter Valley Sem can be great wine.

Sercial
Makes the driest Madeira (where myth says it is really RIESLING).

Seyval Blanc (Seyval Bl)
French-made hybrid of French and American vines. V hardy and attractively fruity. Popular and reasonably successful in eastern States and England but banned by EC from 'quality' wines.

Steen
South Africa's most popular white grape: good lively fruity wine. Said to be the CHENIN BL of the Loire.

Silvaner, alias Sylvaner
Germany's former workhorse grape: wine rarely fine except in Franken where it is savoury and ages admirably, and in Rheinhessen and the Pfalz, where it is enjoying a renaissance. Good in the Italian Tyrol and useful in Alsace. Very good (and powerful) as 'Johannisberg' in the Valais, Switzerland.

Tokay
See Pinot Gris. Also a table grape in California and a supposedly Hungarian grape in Australia. The wine Tokay (Tokaji) is made of FURMINT.

Torrontes
Aromatic, MUSCAT-like Argentine grape, usually made dry.

Traminer See Gewürztraminer.

Trebbiano
Important but mediocre grape of central Italy, used in Orvieto, Chianti, Soave etc. Also grown in S France as Ugni Bl, and Cognac as St-Emilion. Mostly thin, neutral wine; really needs blending.

Ugni Blanc (Ugni Bl) See Trebbiano.

Verdejo
The grape of Rueda in Castile, potentially fine and long-lived.

Verdelho
Madeira grape making excellent medium-sweet wine; in Australia, fresh soft dry wine of great character.

Verdicchio
Gives its name to good dry wine in central-eastern Italy.

Vermentino See Malvasia.

Vernaccia
Grape grown in central and S Italy and Sardinia for strong smooth lively wine, sometimes inclining towards sherry.

Viognier
Rare grape of the Rhône, grown at Condrieu for v fine fragrant wine. Much in vogue in the Midi, California etc, but still only a trickle.

Viura See Macabeo.

Weissburgunder See Pinot Blanc.

Welschriesling See Italian Riesling.

Grapes for red wine

Aleatico
Dark Muscat variety, alias Aglianico, used the length of W Italy for fragrant sweet wines.

Baga
The standard red of Bairrada in central Portugal. Dark, tannic – potentially vg.

Barbera
Most popular of many productive grapes of N Italy, esp Piedmont, giving dark, fruity, often sharp wine. Gaining prestige in California.

Brunello
South Tuscan form of SANGIOVESE, splendid at Montalcino.

Cabernet Franc, alias Bouchet (Cab F)
The lesser of two sorts of Cab grown in Bordeaux but dominant (as 'Bouchet') in St-Emilion. The Cab of the Loire, making Chinon, Saumur etc, and rosé.

Cabernet Sauvignon (Cab S)
Grape of great character: spicy, herby, tannic, with characteristic 'blackcurrant' aroma. The first grape of the Médoc; also makes most of the best California, S American and E European reds. Vies with Shiraz in Australia. Its wine almost always needs ageing; usually benefiting from blending with eg MERLOT, CAB F or SYRAH. Makes very aromatic rosé.

Cannonau
Grenache in its Sardinian manifestation: can be v fine, potent.

Carignan
By far the commonest grape of France, covering hundreds of thousands of acres. Prolific with dull but harmless wine. Best from old vines in Corbières. Also common in N Africa, Spain, California.

Cinsaut
Common bulk-producing grape of S France; in S Africa crossed with PINOT N to make PINOTAGE. Pale wine, but quality potential.

Dolcetto
Source of soft seductive dry red in Piedmont. Now high fashion.

Gamay
The Beaujolais grape: light, very fragrant wines, at their best young. Makes even lighter wine in the Loire Valley, in central France, and in Switzerland and Savoie. Known as 'Napa Gamay' in California.

Gamay Beaujolais
Not GAMAY but a poor variety of PINOT N in California.

Grenache, alias Garnacha, Alicante, Cannonau
Useful grape for strong fruity but pale wine: good rosé and vin doux naturel. Esp in S France, Spain, California. Old-vine versions are currently prized in S Australia. Usually blended (eg in Châteauneuf-du-Pape).

Grignolino
Makes one of the good everyday table wines of Piedmont.

Kadarka, alias Gamza
Makes healthy, sound, agreeable reds in Hungary, Bulgaria etc.

Kékfrankos
Hungarian Blaufränkisch, said to be related to Gamay and producing similar light red wines.

Lambrusco
Productive grape of the lower Po Valley, giving quintessentially Italian, cheerful sweet and fizzy red.

Malbec, alias Cot
Minor in Bordeaux, major in Cahors (alias Auxerrois) and esp Argentina. Dark, dense and tannic wine capable of real quality.

Merlot
Adaptable grape making the great fragrant and plummy wines of Pomerol and (with CAB F) St-Emilion, an important element in Médoc reds, soft and strong (and à la mode) in California, Washington, a useful adjunct in Australia, lighter but often good in N Italy, Italian Switzerland, Slovenia, Argentina etc.

Montepulciano
Confusingly, a major central-eastern Italian grape of high quality, as well as a town in Tuscany.

Mourvèdre, alias Mataro
Excellent dark aromatic tannic grape used mainly for blending in Provence (but solo in Bandol) and the Midi. Enjoying new interest in eg S Australia, California.

Nebbiolo, alias Spanna and Chiavennasca
One of Italy's best red grapes; makes Barolo, Barbaresco, Gattinara, Valtellina. Intense, nobly fruity and perfumed wine but very tannic, taking years to mature.

Periquita
Ubiquitous in Portugal for firm-flavoured reds. Often blended with Cabernet Sauvignon and also known as Castelão Francês.

Petit Verdot
Excellent but awkward Médoc grape now largely superseded.

Pinot Noir (Pinot N)
The glory of Burgundy's Côte d'Or, with scent, flavour, and texture unmatched anywhere. Less happy elsewhere; makes light wines rarely of much distinction in Germany, Switzerland, Austria, Hungary. The great challenge to California and Australia (and recently S Africa). Shows exciting promise in California's Carneros and Central Coast, Oregon, Ontario, Yarra Valley, Adelaide Hills, Tasmania and NZ.

Pinotage
Singular S African grape (PINOT N x CINSAUT). Can be very fruity and can age interestingly, but often jammy.

Refosco
Possibly a synomym for Mondeuse of Savoie. Produces deep, flavoursome age-worthy wines esp in warmer climates.

Saint-Laurent
Dark, smooth and full-flavoured Austrian speciality. Also a little in the Pfalz.

Sangiovese (or Sangioveto)
The main red grape of Chianti and much of central Italy. BRUNELLO is the Sangiovese Grosso.

Saperavi
Makes good sharp very long-lived wine in Georgia, Ukraine etc. Blends very well with CABERNET (eg in Moldova).

Spätburgunder
German for PINOT N, but a very pale shadow of burgundy.

Syrah or Petite Sirah, alias Shiraz
The great Rhône red grape, giving tannic purple peppery wine which can mature superbly. Very important as Shiraz in Australia, increasingly successful in the Midi, S Africa and California. Has a growing fan club.

Tannat
Raspberry-perfumed, highly tannic force behind Madiran, Tursan and other firm-structured reds from southwest France. Also for rosé.

Tempranillo
The pale aromatic fine Rioja grape, called Ull de Lebre in Catalonia, Cencibel in La Mancha. Early ripening.

Touriga Nacional
Top port and Douro grape, travelling further afield in Portugal for full-bodied reds.

Zinfandel (Zin)
Fruity adaptable grape peculiar to California with blackberry-like, and sometimes metallic, flavour. Can be gloriously lush, but also makes 'blush' white wine.

Wine & Food

The dilemma is most acute in restaurants. Four people have chosen different dishes. The host calculates. A bottle of white and then one of red is conventional, regardless of the food. The formula works. But it can be refined – or replaced with something more original, something to really bring out the savours of both food and wine.

Remarkably little ink has been spilt on this byway of knowledge, but 20 years of experiment and the ideas of many friends have gone into making this list. It is perhaps most useful for menu-planning at home. But used with the rest of the book, it may ease menu-stress in restaurants too. At the very least, it will broaden your mind.

Before the meal – aperitifs

The conventional aperitif wines are either sparkling (epitomized by champagne) or fortified (epitomized by sherry in Britain, port in France, vermouth in Italy etc). A glass of white or rosé (or in France red) table wine before eating is presently in vogue. It calls for something light and stimulating, fairly dry but not acid, with a degree of character; rather Riesling or Chenin Blanc than Chardonnay.

Warning: Avoid peanuts; they destroy wine flavours.

Olives are also too piquant for most wines; they need sherry or a Martini. Eat almonds, pistachios or walnuts, plain crisps or cheese straws instead.

First courses

Aïoli
A thirst-quencher is needed for its garlic heat. Rhône (★→★★), Provence rosé, Minervois, Verdicchio. And marc, too, for courage.

Antipasto in Italy
Dry or med white (★★): Italian (Arneis, Soave, Pinot Grigio, Greco di Tufo) or Muscadet sur lie; light red (Dolcetto, Franciacorta, ★★ young Chianti).

Artichoke vinaigrette
Young red (★): Bordeaux, Côtes du Rhône; or an incisive dry white, eg NZ Sauv Bl or a modern Greek.
hollandaise Full-bodied slightly crisp dry white (★ or ★★): Pouilly Fuissé, Pfalz Spätlese, or a Carneros or Yarra Valley Chardonnay (★★).

Asparagus
A difficult flavour for wine, being slightly bitter, so the wine needs plenty of its own. Sauv Bl echoes the flavour. Sémillon beats Chardonnay, esp from Australia, but Chard works well with melted butter. Alsace Pinot Gris, even dry Muscat can be good, or Jurançon Sec. With eg a feuilleté try sweet wine: Sauternes, Loire or Tokay.

Aubergine purée (Melitzanosalata)
Crisp New World Sauv Bl eg from Chile or NZ, or modern Greek or Sicilian dry white. Or Bardolino red or Chiaretto.

Avocado with prawns, crab etc
Dry to medium or slightly sharp white (★★→★★★): Rheingau or Pfalz Kabinett, Sancerre, Pinot Grigio; Sonoma or Australian Chard or Sauvignon, Cape Steen, or dry rosé. Or Chablis.
vinaigrette Light red (★), N Italian Enfer d'Arvier, or manzanilla sherry.

Bisques
Dry white with plenty of body (★★): Pinot Gris, Chard. Fino or dry amontillado sherry, or Montilla. West Australian Sem.

Boudin (blood sausage)
Local Sauv Bl or Chenin – esp in the Loire. Or Beaujolais Cru esp Morgon.

Bouillabaisse
Herby dry white (★→★★), Roussette de Savoie or Provence, Corsican or Spanish rosé, or Cassis, Verdicchio, California Blanc Fumé.

Caesar Salad
California (Central Coast) Chardonnay.

Carpaccio, beef
Seems to work well with the flavour of most wines, incl ★★★ reds. Top Tuscan vino da tavola is appropriate, but fine Chards are good. So are vintage and pink champagnes. (See also Carpaccio under fish.)
salmon Chardonnay (★★→★★★), or champagne.

Caviar
Iced vodka. Champagne, if you must, full-bodied (eg Bollinger, Krug).

Ceviche
Australian Riesling or Verdelho (★★), Chile or NZ Sauvignon Bl.

Charcuterie
Young Beaujolais-Villages or ★★ Bordeaux Blanc, Loire reds such as Bourgueil, Swiss or Oregon Pinot N. Young Argentine or Italian reds.

Cheese fondue
Dry white (★★): Valais Fendant or any other Swiss Chasselas, Grüner Veltliner, Alsace Ries or Pinot Gris.

Chowders
Big-scale white (★★), not necessarily bone dry: Pinot Gris, Rhine Spätlese, Australian Sem, buttery Chard. Or fino sherry, dry Madeira or Marsala.

Consommé
Medium-dry amontillado sherry (★★→★★★), Sercial Madeira.

Crostini
Morellino di Scansano, Montepulciano d'Abruzzo, Valpolicella.

Crudités
Light red or rosé (★→★★, no more): Côtes du Rhône, Minervois, Chianti Okanagan Pinot Noir; or fino sherry. Or Alsace Sylvaner or Pinot Gris.

Dim-Sum
Classically, China tea. For fun: **fried Dim-Sum**: Pinot Grigio or Riesling; **steamed**: light red (Bardolino or Beaujolais-Villages). Or NV champagne.

Eggs See also Soufflés.
These present difficulties: they clash with most wines and spoil good ones. So ★→★★ of whatever is going. Try Pinot Bl or straightforward, not too oaky Chardonnay. As a last resort I can bring myself to drink champagne with scrambled eggs.
Quail's eggs Blanc de Blancs champagne.

Escargots
Rhône reds (Gigondas, Vacqueyras), or St-Véran or Aligoté. In the Midi, vg Petits-Gris go with local white, rosé or red. In Alsace, Pinot Bl or Muscat.

Fish terrine
Pfalz Ries Spätlese Trocken, Chablis, Washington Sém, Clare Valley Ries, Sonoma Chard; or fino sherry.

Foie gras
White (★★★→★★★★). In Bordeaux they drink Sauternes. Others prefer a late-harvest Pinot Gris, Riesling (incl New World) or Gewürz. Tokay Aszú is the new Lucullan choice. Old dry amontillado can be sublime. But not Chard.

Gazpacho
A glass of fino before and after. Or Sauvignon Bl.

Goat's cheese, grilled or fried (warm salad)
Sancerre, Pouilly-Fumé or New World Sauvignon Bl. Chilled Chinon or Saumur-Champigny or Provence rosé. Or strong red: Château Musar, Greek, Turkish, sparkling Shiraz.

Gravlax
Akvavit or iced sake. Or Grand Cru Chablis, or ★★★ California, Washington or Margaret River Chardonnay, or Mosel Spätlese (not Trocken).

Guacamole
California Chardonnay (★★), Riesling Kabinett, dry Muscat or NV champagne. Or Mexican beer.

Haddock, smoked, mousse of
A wonderful dish for showing off any stylish full-bodied white, incl Grand Cru Chablis or NZ Chardonnay.

Ham, raw or cured See also Prosciutto.
Alsace Grand Cru Pinot Gris or good, crisp Italian Collio white.

Herrings, raw or pickled
Dutch gin (young, not aged) or Scandinavian akvavit, and cold beer. If wine essential, try Muscadet.

Hors d'oeuvres See also Antipasto.
Clean, fruity, sharp white (★→★★): Sancerre or any Sauvignon Bl, Grüner Veltliner, Vinho Verde, Cape Steen; or young light red Bordeaux, Rhône or Corbières. Or fino sherry.

Houmous
Pungent, spicy dry white, eg Hungarian or Retsina.

Mackerel, smoked
An oily wine-destroyer. Manzanilla sherry, proper dry Vinho Verde or schnapps, peppered or bison-grass vodka. Or good lager.

Mayonnaise
Adds richness that calls for a contrasting bite in the wine. Côte Chalonnaise whites (eg Rully) are good. Try NZ Sauvignon Bl, Verdicchio or a Spätlese Trocken from the Pfalz.

Melon
Strong sweet wine (if any): port (★★), Bual Madeira, Muscat de Frontignan or vin doux naturel; or dry, perfumed Viognier or Australian Marsanne.

Minestrone
Red (★): Grignolino, Chianti, Zinfandel, Rhône Syrah etc. Or fino.

Mushrooms à la Grecque
Greek Verdea or Mantinia, or any hefty dry white, or fresh young red.

Omelettes See Eggs.

Oyster stew
California, Long Island or S Australian ★★ Chardonnay.

Oysters
White (★★→★★★): NV champagne, Chablis or (better still) Chablis Premier Cru, Muscadet, white Graves, Sancerre. Guinness or Scotch and water.

Pasta
Red or white (★→★★) according to the sauce or trimmings:
cream sauce Orvieto, Frascati, Alto Adige Chardonnay.
meat sauce Montepulciano d'Abruzzo, Salice Salentino, Merlot.
pesto (basil) sauce Barbera, Sicilian Torbato, NZ Sauvignon Bl, Hungarian Hárslevelü or Furmint.
seafood sauce (eg vongole) Verdicchio, Soave, Pomino, Sauv Bl.
tomato sauce Sauvignon Bl, Barbera, S Italian red, Zinfandel, S Australian Grenache.

Pâté
According to constituents and quality:
chicken livers Call for pungent white (Alsace Pinot Gris or Marsanne), a smooth red like a light Pomerol or Volnay, or even amontillado sherry.
with simple pâté A dry white ★★: Good vin de pays, Graves, Fumé Blanc.
with duck pâté Châteauneuf-du-Pape, Cornas, Chianti Classico or Franciacorta.

Peperonata
Dry Australian Riesling, W Australian Semillon or NZ Sauvignon Bl. Tempranillo or Beaujolais.

Pipérade
Navarra rosado, Béarn or Irouléguy rosés. Or dry Australian Riesling.

Pimentos, roasted
NZ Sauvignon, Spanish Chardonnay, or Valdepeñas.

Pizza
Any dry Italian red ★★ or Rioja ★★, Australian Shiraz or California Sangiovese. Corbières, Coteaux d'Aix-en-Provence or red Bairrada.

Prawns or shrimps
Fine dry white (★★→★★★): burgundy, Graves, NZ Chard, Washington Riesling – even fine mature champagne.
Indian-, Thai- or Chinese-style rich Australian Hunter Valley Chardonnay. ('Cocktail sauce' kills wine, and I suspect, in time, people.)

Prosciutto (also with melon, pears or figs)
Full-bodied dry or medium white (★★→★★★): Orvieto, Gambellara, Pomino, Fendant or Grüner Veltliner, Alsace or California Gewürztraminer, Australian Semillon or Jurançon Sec.

Quiches
Dry white with body (★→★★): Alsace, Graves, a Sauvignon, or dry Rheingau; or try young red (Beaujolais-Villages, Chilean Pinot Noir), according to the ingredients. Never a fine-wine dish.

Ravioli See pasta.
with wild mushrooms Dolcetto or Nebbiolo d'Alba, Oregon Pinot Noir, red Rioja crianza.

Saffron sauces (eg on fish)
Pungent or full-bodied white (esp Chardonnay) or Provence rosé.

Salade niçoise
Very dry, ★★, not too light or flowery white or rosé: Provençal, Rhône or Corsican; Catalan white; Fernão Pires, Sauv Bl or Hungarian dry white.

Salads
As a first course, especially with blue cheese dressing, any dry and appetizing white wine. After a main course: no wine.
NB Vinegar in salad dressings destroys the flavour of wine. If you want salad at a meal with fine wine, dress the salad with wine or a little lemon juice instead of vinegar.

Salami
Barbera, top Valpolicella, young Zinfandel, Tavel or Ajaccio rosé, Vacqueyras, young Bordeaux, Chilean Cab Sauv or New World Gamay.

Salmon, smoked
A dry but pungent white: fino sherry, Alsace Pinot Gris, Chablis Grand Cru, Pouilly-Fumé, Pfalz Ries Spätlese, vintage champagne. If you must have red try a lighter one such as Barbera. Vodka, schnapps or akvavit.

Seafood salad
Fresh N Italian Chard or Pinot Grigio. Australian Verdelho or Clare Ries.

Shark's fin soup
Add a teaspoon of cognac. Sip amontillado.

Soufflés
As show dishes these deserve ★★→★★★ wines.
fish Dry white: ★★★ burgundy, Bordeaux, Alsace, Chardonnay etc.
cheese ★★★ Red burgundy or Bordeaux, Cabernet Sauvignon etc.
spinach (tougher on wine) Mâcon-Villages, St-Véran, Valpolicella.

Tapenade
Manzanilla or fino, or any sharpish dry white or rosé.

Taramasalata
A rustic southern white with personality; not necessarily Retsina. Fino sherry works well. Try Arbois or white Rioja. The bland supermarket version goes well with fine delicate whites or champagne.

Terrine
As for pâté, or equivalent red: Mercurey, St-Amour or Beaujolais-Villages, fairly young St-Emilion (★★), California Syrah or Sangiovese, Bulgarian or Chilean Cabernet.

Thai-style dishes (seasoned with lemon-grass, coconut milk, ginger etc)
Pungent Sauv Bl eg Loire, Styrian, NZ or South African, or Riesling Spätlese (Pfalz or Austrian).Or Gewürz.

Tortilla
Rioja crianza. Or white Mâcon-Villages.

Trout, smoked
Sancerre, California or South African Sauvignon Bl. Rully or Bourgogne Aligoté, Chablis or champagne.

Vegetable terrine
Not a great help to fine wine, but California, Chilean or South African Chardonnays make a fashionable marriage.

Fish

Abalone
Dry or medium white (★★→★★★): Sauvignon Blanc, Côte de Beaune blanc, Pinot Grigio, Muscadet sur lie.

Anchovies
A robust wine: red, white or rosé – try Rioja.

Bass, striped or sea
Weissburgunder from Baden or Pfalz. Vg for any fine/delicate white, eg Coonawarra dry Riesling, Chablis.

Beurre blanc, fish with
A top-notch Muscadet sur lie, a Sauvignon/ Sémillon blend, Chablis or a Rheingau Charta wine.

Brandade
Chablis Premier Cru or Sancerre Rouge.

Carpaccio of salmon or tuna See also First courses.
Puligny-Montrachet, Condrieu or (★★★) Australian Chardonnay.

Cod
Good neutral background for fine dry/medium whites: ★★→★★★ Chablis, Meursault, Corton-Charlemagne, cru classé Graves, dry Vouvray; German Kabinett or dry Spätlesen, or a good light red, eg Beaune.

Crab, cioppino
Sauvignon Blanc; but West Coast friends say Zinfandel.
cold, with salad Alsace Riesling or Muscat, dry California or Australian Riesling, or Viognier from Condrieu.
softshell ★★★ Chardonnay or top-quality German Riesling Spätlese.
Chinese, baked with ginger and onion
German Riesling Kabinett or Spätlese Halbtrocken. Hungarian Furmint, Gewürz. **with Black Bean sauce** A big Barossa Shiraz or Syrah.

Eel, jellied
NV champagne or a nice cup of (Ceylon) tea.
smoked Strong/sharp wine: fino sherry, Bourgogne Aligoté. Schnapps.

Fish and chips, fritto misto (or tempura)
Chablis, ★★ white Bordeaux, Sauv Bl, Arneis, Fino, Montilla, Koshu, tea...

Fish pie (with creamy sauce)
Napa Chardonnay, Pinot Gris d'Alsace.

Haddock
Rich dry white (★★→★★★): Meursault, California or NZ Chard, Marsanne.

Hake
Sauv Bl or any freshly fruity white: Pacherenc, Tursan, white Navarra.

Herrings
Need a white with some acidity to cut their richness. Bourgogne Aligoté, Gros Plant from Brittany, dry Sauvignon Bl. Or cider.

Kedgeree
Full white, still or sparkling: Mâcon-Villages, South African Chard or champagne.

Kippers
A good cup of tea, preferably Ceylon (milk, no sugar). Scotch? Manzanilla if you must drink wine.

Lamproie à la Bordelaise
5-yr-old St-Emilion or Fronsac: ★★→★★★.

Lobster, richly sauced
Vintage champagne, fine white burgundy, cru classé Graves, California Chard or Australian Ries, Pfalz Spätlese.

salad White (★★→★★★★): NV champagne, Alsace Riesling, Chablis Premier Cru, Condrieu, Mosel Spätlese, Penedès Chard.

Mackerel
Hard or sharp white (★★): Sauvignon Blanc from Touraine, Gaillac, Gros Plant, Vinho Verde, white Rioja. Or Guinness.

Mullet, red
A chameleon, adaptable to good white or red, esp Pinot Noir.

Mussels
Muscadet sur lie, Chablis Premier Cru, ★★★ Chardonnay.
stuffed, with garlic See Escargots.

Perch, Sandre
Exquisite fishes for finest wines: top white burgundy or noble Mosels. Or try top Swiss Fendant or Johannisberg.

Salmon, fresh
Fine white burgundy (★★★): Puligny- or Chassagne-Montrachet, Meursault, Corton-Charlemagne, Chablis Grand Cru; Condrieu, California, Idaho or NZ Chard, Rheingau Kabinett/Spätlese, Australian Ries. Young Pinot N can be perfect, too – Merlot or claret not bad.

Sardines, fresh grilled
Very dry white (★→★★): Vinho Verde, Soave, Muscadet, modern Greek.

Sashimi
If you are prepared to forego the wasabi, sparkling wines will go, or Washington or Tasmanian Chardonnay, Chablis Grand Cru, Rheingau Riesling Halbtrocken, English Seyval Bl. Otherwise, iced sake or beer.

Scallops
An inherently slightly sweet dish, best with medium-dry whites.
in cream sauces German Spätlese (★★★) a -Montrachet or top Australian Chardonnay.
grilled or fried Hermitage Blanc, Gewürztraminer, Grüner Veltliner, ★★ Entre-Deux-Mers, Australian Riesling or champagne.

Shad
White Graves (★★→★★★) or Meursault or Hunter Semillon.

Shellfish
Dry (★★★) white with plain boiled shellfish, richer wines with richer sauces.

Shrimps, potted
Fino sherry, (★★★) Chablis, Gavi or Long Island Chardonnay.

Skate with black butter
White (★★) with some pungency (eg Menetou-Salon), or a clean straightforward one like Muscadet or Arneis.

Snapper
Serious Sauvignon Blanc country.

Sole, plaice etc: plain, grilled or fried
Perfect with fine wines: ★★★→★★★★ white burgundy, or its equivalent.
with sauce Depending on the ingredients: sharp dry wine for tomato sauce, fairly rich for sole véronique etc.

Sushi
Hot wasabi is usually hidden in every piece. German QbA trocken wines or simple Chablis or NV brut champagne. Or, of course, sake or beer.

Swordfish
Full-bodied dry (★★) white. Nothing grand.

Trout
Delicate white wine, eg ★★★ Mosel (esp from Saar), Alsace Pinot Bl.
smoked See first courses.

Tuna, grilled
White, red or rosé (★★) of fairly fruity character; a top St-Véran or white Hermitage, or Côtes du Rhône would be fine. Pinot Noir and Merlot are the best reds.

Turbot
Your best rich dry white: ★★★ Meursault or Chassagne-Montrachet, mature Chablis or its California, Australian or NZ equivalent. Condrieu. Mature Rheingau, Mosel or Nahe Spätlese or Auslese (not trocken).

Whitebait
Crisp dry whites: Muscadet, Touraine Sauvignon Bl or Verdicchio.

Meat, poultry etc

Barbecues
Red (★★) with a slight rasp, therefore young: Shiraz, Chianti, Navarra, Zinfandel, Turkish Buzbag. Bandol for a real treat.

Beef, boiled
Red (★★): Bordeaux (Bourg or Fronsac), Roussillon, Australian Shiraz. Gevrey-Chambertin, Côte Rôtie. Or top-notch beer.
roast An ideal partner for fine red wine: ★★→★★★★ red of any kind.

Beef stew
Sturdy red (★★→★★★): Pomerol or St-Emilion, Hermitage, Cornas, Barbera, Shiraz, Napa Cabernet, Torres Gran Coronas.

Beef Stroganoff
Dramatic red (★★→★★★): Barolo, Valpolicella Amarone, Cahors, Hermitage, late-harvest Zin – even Moldovan Negru de Purkar.

> **Warning notice:**
> Tomatoes (with anything): the acidity of tomatoes is no friend to fine wines. Sauvignon Blanc is their only friend. For reds try Chianti.

Boudin Blanc
Loire Chenin Bl (★★→★★★) esp when served with apples: Dry Vouvray, Saumur, Savennières. Mature red Côtes de Beaune, if without apple.

Cabbage, stuffed
Hungarian Cab Franc/Kadarka, Squinzano and other spicy S Italian reds.

Cajun food
Fleurie, Brouilly or Sauv Bl. With gumbo: amontillado or Mexican beer.

Cassoulet
Red (★★) from SW France (Côtes du Frontonnais, Cahors, Madiran), or Shiraz. But best of all Beaujolais Cru or young red Navarra.

Chicken/turkey/guinea fowl, roast
Virtually any wine, incl very best bottles of dry/med white and finest old reds (esp burgundy). The meat of fowl can be adapted with sauces to match almost any fine wine (eg coq au vin: with red burgundy). Try sparkling Shiraz with strong, sweet or spicy stuffings and trimmings. Avoid sauces which include tomato if you want to taste any good bottles.

Chicken casserole
Lirac, St-Joseph, or ★★ Bordeaux or Chilean Pinot Noir.
Kiev Alsace Riesling, Collio, Chardonnay, Bergerac Rouge.

Chilli con carne
Young red (★→★★): Gattinara, Beaujolais, Navarra, Zinfandel, Argentine Malbec.

Chinese food, Canton or Peking style
Dry to med-dry white (★★→★★★) – Mosel Ries Kabinett – can be good throughout a Chinese banquet. Many like Gewürz. Dry or off-dry sparkling (esp cava) cuts the oil and matches sweetness. Eschew sweet/sour dishes but try an 89/90 St-Emilion ★★ (or Le Pin?), New World Pinot N, or Châteauneuf-du-Pape with duck. I often serve both white and red wines concurrently during Chinese meals.
Szechuan style Muscadet, Alsace Pinot Blanc or v cold beer.

Choucroute garni
Alsace, Pinot Blanc, Pinot Gris or Riesling or beer.

Cold meats
Generally better with full-flavoured white than red. Mosel Spätlese or Hochheimer and Côte Chalonnaise are very good. And so is Beaujolais.

Confit d'oie/de canard
Young tannic red Bordeaux Cru Bourgeois (★★→★★★) California Cabernet and Merlot, and Priorato help cut the richness. Alsace Tokay-Pinot Gris or Gewürztraminer matches it.

Coq au vin
Red burgundy (★★→★★★★). In an ideal world one bottle of Chambertin in the dish, two on the table.

Curry
Medium-sweet white (★→★★), very cold: Orvieto abboccato, California Chenin Bl, Slovenian Traminer, Indian sparkling. Or emphasize the heat with a tannic Barolo or Barbaresco, or deep-flavoured reds such as St-Emilion, Cornas, Shiraz-Cabernet or Valpolicella Amarone.

Duck or goose
Rather rich white (★★★): Pfalz Spätlese or Alsace réserve exceptionelle; or mature gamey red: Morey-St-Denis or Côte Rôtie, or ★★★ Bordeaux or burgundy. With oranges or peaches, the Sauternais propose drinking Sauternes, others Monbazillac or Auslese.
Peking See Chinese food.
wild duck Big-scale red (★★★): Hermitage, Bandol, California or S African Cab, Australian Shiraz – Grange if you can find it.
with olives Top-notch Chianti or Tuscan VdT.

Frankfurters
German (★→★★), NY Riesling, Beaujolais, light Pinot Noir. Or Budweiser.

Game birds, young birds plain-roasted
The best red wine you can afford.
older birds in casseroles ★★→★★★ Red (Gevrey-Chambertin, Pommard, Santenay or Grand Cru St-Emilion, Napa Valley Cabernet or Rhône).
well-hung game Vega Sicilia, great red Rhône, Chateau Musar.
cold game Mature vintage champagne.

Game pie
hot Red (★★★): Oregon Pinot Noir.
cold Equivalent white or champagne.

Goulash
Flavoursome young red (★★): Zinfandel, Bulgarian Cabernet or Mavrud, Hungarian Kadarka, young Australian Shiraz, Copertino.

Grouse See Game birds – but push the boat right out.

Haggis
Fruity red, eg young claret, New World Cabernet or Châteauneuf-du-Pape. Or of course malt whisky.

Ham
Softer red burgundies (★★→★★★): Volnay, Savigny, Beaune; Chinon or Bourgueil; slightly sweet German white (Rhine Spätlese); Czech Müller-Thurgau; lightish Cabernet (eg Chilean), or California Pinot Noir.

Hamburger
Young red (★→★★): Beaujolais or Bulgarian Cabernet, Chianti, Zinfandel, Kadarka from Hungary. Or Coke or Pepsi.

Hare
Jugged hare calls for ★★→★★★ flavourful red: not-too-old burgundy or Bordeaux, Rhône (eg Gigondas), Bandol, Barbaresco or a Rioja reserva. The same for saddle. Australia's Grange would be an experience.

Heart, stuffed
Full-bodied tannic red: Shiraz-Cabernet, Dão, Cornas.

Kebabs
Vigorous red (★★): Greek Nemea or Naoussa, Turkish Buzbag, Chilean Cabernet, Zinfandel or Barossa Shiraz.

Kidneys
Red (★★→★★★): St-Emilion or earthier versions: Nuits-St-Georges, Cornas, Barbaresco, Rioja, Spanish or Australian Cabernet, Portuguese Bairrada.

Lamb, cutlets or chops
As for roast lamb, but a little less grand.
roast One of the traditional and best partners for very good red Bordeaux – or its Cabernet equivalents from the New World. In Spain, the partner of the finest old Rioja reservas.

Liver
Young red (★★): Beaujolais-Villages, St-Joseph, Médoc, Italian Merlot, Breganze Cabernet, Zinfandel, Portuguese Bairrada.
Calf's Red Rioja crianza, Salice Salentino Riserva, Fleurie.

Meatballs
Tangy medium-bodied red (★★→★★★): Mercurey, Crozes-Hermitage, Madiran, Rubesco, Dão, Zinfandel or Cabernet.
Spicy Indian style Dry Muscat; even Viognier.

Moussaka
Red or rosé (★→★★): Naoussa from Greece, Chianti, Corbières, Côtes de Provence, Ajaccio or Patrimonio, Chilean Pinot Noir.

Osso buco
Low tannin, supple red, eg Dolcetto d'Alba or Pinot Noir.

Oxtail
Rather rich red (★★→★★★): St-Emilion, Pomerol, Pommard, Nuits-St-Georges, Barolo or Rioja reserva, California or Coonawarra Cabernet, Châteauneuf-du-Pape; or a dry Rheingau Riesling Spätlese.

Paella
Young Spanish red (★★), dry white or rosé: Penedès or Rioja.

Pigeons or squab
Lively reds (★★→★★★): Savigny, Chambolle-Musigny; Crozes-Hermitage, Chianti Classico or California Pinot. Or try Franken Silvaner Spätlese.

Pork, roast
A good rich neutral background to a fairly light red or rich white. It deserves ★★★ treatment – Médoc is fine. Portugal's famous sucking pig is eaten with Bairrada garrafeira, Chinese is good with Pinot Noir.

Quail As for pigeon. Carmignano, Rioja Reserva, mature claret, Pinot N.

Rabbit
Lively medium-bodied young Italian red (★→★★★) or Aglianico del Vulture, or Chiroubles, Chinon, Saumur-Champigny or Rhône rosé.

Risotto
Pinot Gr from Friuli, Gavi, youngish Sém, Dolcetto or Barbera d'Alba.
with mushrooms Cahors, Madiran, Barbera.
with fungi porcini Finest mature Barolo or Barbaresco.

Satay
Australia's McLaren Vale Shiraz or Alsace or NZ Gewürztraminer.

Sauerkraut
Lager or stout. (But see also Choucroute garni.)

Sausages See also Frankfurters, Salami.
The British banger requires a 2½-yr-old NE Italian Merlot (or a red wine, anyway).

Shepherd's pie
Rough-and-ready red (★→★★) seems most appropriate, eg Barbera, but beer or dry cider is the real McCoy.

Steak, au poivre
A fairly young ★★★ Rhône red or Cabernet.
tartare Vodka or ★★ light young red: Beaujolais, Bergerac, Valpolicella.
Korean Yuk Whe (the world's best steak tartare) Sake.
filet or tournedos Any ★★★ red (but not old wines with béarnaise sauce).
T-bone Reds of similar bone structure (★★→★★★): Barolo, Hermitage, Australian Cabernet or Shiraz.
fiorentina (bistecca) Chianti Classico Riserva or Brunello.

Steak and kidney pie or pudding
Red Rioja reserva or mature ★★→★★★ B'x.

Stews and casseroles
★★★ Burgundy such as Chambolle-Musigny or Bonnes-Mares if fairly simple; otherwise lusty full-flavoured red: young Côtes du Rhône, Toro, Corbières, Barbera, Shiraz, Zinfandel etc.

Sweetbreads
A grand dish, so grand wine: Rhine Riesling (★★★) or Franken Silvaner Spätlese, Alsace Grand Cru Pinot Gris or Condrieu, depending on sauce.

Tandoori chicken
Sauvignon Blanc, or young ★★ red Bordeaux or light N Italian red served cool.

Thai food
Ginger and lemon grass call for Sauvignon Bl.
coconut curries Hunter Valley and other ripe, oaked Chards; Alsace Pinot Bl for refreshment.

Tongue
Good for any red or white of abundant character, esp Italian. Also Beaujolais, Loire reds and full dry rosés.

Tripe
Red (★→★★), eg Corbières, Roussillon or rather sweet white (eg German Spätlese). Better: W Australian Sem-Chard, or cut with pungent dry white such as Pouilly-Fumé or fresh red eg Saumur-Champigny.

Veal, roast
A good neutral background dish for any fine old red which may have faded with age (eg a Rioja reserva) or a ★★★ German or Austrian Riesling or Vouvray or Alsace Pinot-Gris.

Venison
Big-scale red (★★★) incl Mourvèdre (Mataro) solo as in Bandol, or in blends, Rhône, Bordeaux or California Cab of a mature vintage; or rather rich white (Pfalz Spätlese or Alsace Tokay-Pinot Gr).

Vitello tonnato
Full-bodied white esp Chard; light red (eg Valpolicella) served cool.

Urgent notice: sherry, port, Madeira and food
By a quirk of fashion, the wines of Jerez, Madeira and to some extent the ports of the Douro Valley are currently being left on the sidelines by a world increasingly hypnotized by a limited range of 'varietal' wines. Yet all three regions include wines of every quality of 'greatness', and far more gastronomic possibilities than anyone seems to remember. It is notorious that for the price of a bottle of top-class white burgundy you can buy three of the very finest fino sherry, which with many dishes (see above) will make an equally exciting accompaniment. Mature Madeiras give the most lingering farewell of any wine to a splendid dinner. Tawny port is a wine of many uses, especially wonderful at sea. Perhaps it is because the New World cannot rival these Old World classics that they are left out of the headlines.

Vegetarian dishes

Bean and vegetable stew with herb dumplings
Bairrada from Portugal, Toro from Spain.

Bubble-and-squeak
Beer, stout, or Beaujolais Nouveau.

Cauliflower cheese with gratin topping
Crisp aromatic white: Sancerre, Riesling Spätlese, Muscat.

Couscous with spiced vegetables
Young red with a bite: Shiraz, Corbières, Minervois etc.

Fennel-based dishes
Sauvignon Bl: Pouilly-Fumé or one from NZ; Beaujolais.

Grilled Mediterranean vegetables
Brouilly, Barbera or Cab-Shiraz.

Kidney bean and roast vegetable salad
Red Rioja reserva, New World Merlot, Provence red such as Bandol.

'Meaty' aubergine, lentil or mushroom bakes
Corbières, Zinfandel, Shiraz-Cabernet.

Mushrooms (in most contexts)
Fleshy red; eg★★★ Pomerol, California Merlot, Rioja reserva or Vega Sicilia.
on toast Your best claret.
wild mushroom risotto (ceps are best for wine) Ribera del Duero, Barolo or Chianti Rufina, or top claret: Pauillac or St-Estèphe.

Onion/leek tart
Fruity off-dry or dry white (★→★★★): Alsace Pinot Gr or Gewürz. Jurançon, Australian Ries. Or Beaujolais or Loire red.

Peppers or aubergines (eggplant), stuffed
Vigorous red wine(★★): Nemea, Italian Chianti or Dolcetto, California Zinfandel, Bandol, Vacqueyras.

Pumpkin/Squash ravioli or risotto
Full-bodied fruity dry or off-dry white: white Rhône (Viognier or Marsanne); demi-sec Vouvray or South African Chenin.

Ratatouille
Vigorous young red (★★): Chianti, Bulgarian Cabernet or Merlot, young red Bordeaux or Gigondas or Coteaux du Languedoc.

Spinach, ricotta and pasta bake
Valpolicella (its bitterness helps); Greco di Molise, or Sicilian/Sardinian white.

Desserts

Apple pie, strudel or Tarte Tatin
Sweet (★★→★★★) German, Austrian, Hungarian or Loire white.

Apples, Cox's Orange Pippins
Vintage port (**55 60 63 66 70 75 82**).

Bread and butter pudding
Fine 10-yr-old Barsac, Tokay or Australian botrytised Sem.

Cakes and gâteaux see also chocolate, coffee, ginger, rum
Bual or Malmsey Madeira, oloroso or cream sherry.

Cheesecake
Sweet white: Vouvray or Anjou, refreshing but nothing special.

Chocolate flavours
Generally only powerful flavours can compete. Bual, California orange Muscat, Beaumes-de-Venise, Australian liqueur Muscat, 10-yr-old tawny port; Asti for light, fluffy mousses. Experiment with rich, ripe reds: Syrah, Zinfandel even sparkling Shiraz. Or a tot of good rum.

Christmas pudding, mince pies
Tawny port, cream sherry, Asti or Banyuls.

Coffee flavours
Sweet Muscat incl Australia liqueur Muscats or Tokay Aszú.

Creams, custards, fools see also chocolate, coffee, ginger, rum
Sauternes, Loupiac, Ste-Croix-du-Mont, Monbazillac.

Crème brûlée
★★★→★★ Sauternes or Rhine Beerenauslese, best Madeira or Tokay. (With concealed fruit, a more modest sweet wine.)

Crêpes Suzette
Sweet champagne or Asti spumante.

Fruit
fresh Sweet Coteaux du Layon, light sweet or liqueur Muscat.
stewed, ie apricots, pears etc Sweet Muscatel: try Muscat de Beaumes-de-Venise, Moscato di Pantelleria or Spanish dessert Tarragona.
dried fruit (and compotes) Banyuls, Rivesaltes, Maury.
flans and tarts Sauternes, Monbazillac or sweet Vouvray or Anjou: ★★★.
salads, orange salad
A fine sweet sherry, or any Muscat-based wine.

Ginger flavours
Sweet Muscats, New World botrytised Riesling and Semillon.

Ice-cream and sorbet
Fortified wine (Australian liqueur Muscat, Banyuls); sweet Asti spumante or sparkling Moscato. Amaretto liqueur with vanilla; rum with chocolate.

Meringues
Recioto di Soave, Asti or champagne doux.

Mille Feuille
Delicate sweet sparkling white eg Moscato d'Asti, demi-sec champagne.

Nuts
Finest oloroso sherry, Madeira, vintage or tawny port (nature's match for walnuts), Vin Santo, Setúbal Moscatel.

Oranges, caramelized
Experiment with old Sauternes or California Orange Muscat.

Panettone
Jurançon moelleux, late-harvest Riesling, Barsac, Tokay Azsu.

Pears in red wine
A pause before the port. Or try Rivesaltes, Banyuls or Ries Beerenauslese.

Pecan Pie
Orange Muscat or liqueur Muscat.

Raspberries (no cream, little sugar)
Excellent with fine reds that themselves taste of raspberries: young Juliénas, Regnié.

Rum flavours (Baba, mousses, ice-cream)
Muscat – from Asti to Australian liqueur, according to weight of dish.

Strawberries, wild (no cream)
Serve with ★★★ red Bordeaux (most exquisitely Margaux) poured over.

Strawberries and cream
Sauternes (★★★) or similar sweet Bordeaux, or Vouvray Moelleux (1990).

Summer pudding
Fairly young Sauternes of a good vintage (82 83 85 86).

Sweet soufflés
Sauternes or Vouvray moelleux. Sweet (or rich) champagne.

Tiramisú
Vin Santo, young tawny port, Beaumes-de-Venise or Sauternes.

Trifle
Should be sufficiently vibrant with its internal sherry.

Zabaglione
Light gold Marsala or Australian botrytised Semillon or Asti.

Wine & Cheese

The notion that wine and cheese were married in heaven is not born out by experience. Fine red wines are slaughtered by strong cheeses: only sharp or sweet white wines survive.

Principles to remember, despite exceptions, are first: the harder the cheese the more tannin the wine can have. And the creamier it is the more acidity is needed in the wine. The main exception constitutes a third principle: wines and cheeses of a region usually go together.

Cheese is classified by its texture and the nature of its rind, so its appearance is a guide to the type of wine to match it. Individual cheeses mentioned below are only examples taken from the hundreds sold in good cheese shops.

Fresh, no rind – cream cheese, crème fraîche, Mozzarella, Mascarpone (not layered with blue)
Light crisp white – Côtes de Duras, Bergerac, Vinho Verde; or pink – Anjou, Rhône; or very light, v young, v fresh red Bordeaux, Bardolino or Beaujolais.

Hard cheeses, waxed or oiled, often showing marks from cheesecloth – Gruyère family, Manchego and many other Spanish cheeses, Parmesan, Cantal, old Gouda, Cheddar and most 'traditional' English cheeses
Particularly hard to generalize here; Gouda, Gruyère, some Spanish and a few English cheeses complement fine claret or Cab and great Shiraz/Syrah wines, but strong cheeses need less refined wines, preferably local. Sugary, granular old Dutch red Mimolette is perhaps the best of all for finest mature Bordeaux. Also for Tokay Aszú.

Blue cheeses
Roquefort can be wonderful with Sauternes, but don't extend the idea to other blues. It is the sweetness of Sauternes, especially old, which complements the saltiness. Stilton and port, preferably tawny, is a classic. Intensely flavoured old oloroso, amontillado, Madeira, Marsala and other fortified wines go with most blues.

Natural rind (mostly goat's cheese) with bluish-grey mould (the rind becomes wrinkled when mature, s'times dusted with ash – St-Marcellin
Sancerre, Valençay, light fresh Sauv, Jurançon, Savoy, Soave, Italian Chard.

Bloomy rind soft cheeses, pure white rind if pasteurized, or dotted with red: Brie, Camembert, Chaource, Bougon (goat's milk 'Camembert')
Full dry white burgundy or Rhône if cheese is white, immature; powerful, fruity St-Emilion, E European Pinot, young Australian (or Rhône) Shiraz/Syrah if mature.

Washed-rind soft cheeses, with rather sticky orange-red rind – Langres, mature Epoisses, Maroilles, Carré de l'Est, Milleens
Local reds, especially for Burgundy cheeses; vigorous Languedoc, Cahors, Côtes du Frontonnais, Corsican, southern Italian, Sicilian, Bairrada.

Semi-soft cheeses, grey-pink thickish rind – Livarot, Pont l'Evêque, Reblochon, Tomme de Savoie, St-Nectaire
Powerful white Bordeaux, Chardonnay, Alsace Pinot Gris, dryish Riesling, southern Italian and Sicilian white, aged white Rioja, dry oloroso sherry. But the strongest of these cheeses kill most wines.

Food & Finest Wine

With very special bottles, the wine sometimes guides the choice of food rather than the usual way round. The following suggestions are largely based on the gastronomic conventions of the wine regions producing these treasures, plus diligent research. They should help bring out the best in your best wines.

Red wines

Red Bordeaux and other Cabernet Sauvignon-based wines

(very old, light and delicate: eg pre-59, with exceptions such as 45)
Leg or rack of young lamb, roast with a hint of herbs (but not garlic); entrecôte; roast partridge or grouse, sweetbreads; or cheese soufflé after the meat has been served.

Fully mature great vintages (eg Bordeaux 59 61)
Shoulder or saddle of lamb, roast with a touch of garlic, roast ribs or grilled rump of beef.

Mature but still vigorous (eg 78 70 66)
Shoulder or saddle of lamb (incl kidneys) with rich sauce, eg béarnaise. Fillet of beef marchand de vin (with wine and bone-marrow). Avoid Beef Wellington: pastry dulls the palate.

Merlot-based Bordeaux (Pomerol, St-Emilion)
Beef as above (fillet is richest) or venison.

Côte d'Or red burgundy

(Consider the weight and texture, which grow lighter/more velvety with age. Also the character of the wine: Nuits is earthy, Musigny flowery, great Romanées can be exotic, Pommard renowned for its four-squareness etc.) Roast chicken, or better, capon, is safe standard with red burgundy; guinea-fowl for slightly stronger wines, then partridge, grouse or woodcock for those progressively more rich and pungent. Hare and venison (chevreuil) are alternatives.

Great old reds
The classic Burgundian formula is cheese: Epoisses (unfermented). It is a terrible waste of fine old wines.

Vigorous younger burgundy
Duck or goose roasted to minimize fat.

Great Syrahs: Hermitage, Côte Rôtie, Grange; or Vega Sicilia

Beef, venison, well-hung game; bone-marrow on toast; English cheese (esp best farm Cheddar).

Rioja Gran Reserva, Pesquera...

Richly flavoured roasts: wild boar, mutton.

Barolo, Barbaresco

Cheese risotto with white truffles; pasta with game sauce (eg pappardelle alle lepre); porcini mushrooms; Parmesan.

White wines

Very good Chablis, white burgundy, other top quality Chardonnays

White fish simply grilled or meunière with Doria garnish of sautéed cucumber. Dover sole, turbot, Rex sole are best. (Seabass is too delicate; salmon passes but does little for fine wine.)

Supreme white burgundy (Le Montrachet, Corton-Charlemagne) or equivalent Graves

Roast veal, capon or sweetbreads; richly sauced white fish or scallops as above. Or lobster or wild salmon.

Condrieu, Château Grillet or Hermitage Blanc

Very light pasta scented with herbs and tiny peas or broad beans.

Grand Cru Alsace, Riesling

Truite au bleu, smoked salmon or choucroute garni.
Pinot Gris Roast or grilled veal.
Gewürztraminer Cheese soufflé (Munster cheese).
Vendange Tardive Foie gras or Tarte Tatin.

Sauternes

Simple crisp buttery biscuits (eg Langue-de-Chat), white peaches, nectarines, strawberries (without cream). Not tropical fruit. Pan-fried foie-gras. Experiment with cheeses.

Supreme Vouvray moelleux etc

Buttery biscuits, apples, apple tart.

Beerenauslese/TBA

Biscuits, peaches, greengages.

Tokay Aszú (4–6 putts)

Foie gras is thoroughly recommended. Fruit desserts, cream desserts, even chocolate can be wonderful.

Finest old amontillado/oloroso

Pecans.

Great vintage port or Madeira

Walnuts or pecans. A Cox's Orange Pippin and a digestive biscuit is a classic English accompaniment.

Old vintage champagne (not Blanc de Blancs)

As aperitif, or with cold partridge, grouse or woodcock.

The 1996 Vintage

The rain came and went, and came again. August was cool, September bright over France as a whole. But 1996 was a year when the further north you went, the happier the harvesters were.

In Champagne, furthest north, they brought in what some describe as a superlative vintage. The Loire Valley, from Muscadet to Sancerre and Pouilly, is even more pleased with '96 than its its excellent '95s. The great sweet Chenin Blanc wines of Touraine and Anjou may be classics. Alsace did what nature designed it to do: make intense, dry wines of wonderful aroma and acidity. Lack of botrytis meant less sweet wines than some would have liked.

In mid-France, in Burgundy, no rain fell in September and grapes came steadily to powerful readings of both sugar and acidity. Both reds and whites look exceptional, but such healthy conditions could result in an excessive crop. This makes two potentially excellent burgundy years in a row. In Chablis, though, the best vineyards were hit by hail. Shortage here usually leads to run-away prices.

The Bordeaux vintage is reported on page 79. Above all it will be remembered for great Cabernet-led Médocs and excellent whites. In the Rhône Valley too the white wine vintage was exceptional, but an unusually cool, damp August reined back the reds; the further south, the wetter and less promising. Châteauneuf-du-Pape had a disappointing harvest, a pattern repeated over most of the south of France, from Provence through the Languedoc to Roussillon.

It rained in northern Spain and northern Italy, too, but not enough to prevent Piedmont and Rioja from claiming success. Ribera del Duero went further, claiming triumph. Tuscany saw unusual amounts of rain but made satisfactory to very fine wines, especially in Montalcino. Plentiful rain brought Portugal a useful big harvest, but probably not a vintage port year. The German harvest was delayed by the cool weather, but an Indian summer gave the late-ripening Riesling perfect conditions for intense, classic wines, though without enough botrytis for many Ausleses. The Middle Mosel had severe summer hail. The Rheingau and Pfalz have model wines to show. Further east in Europe the normal vintage was seriously rained on. Botrytis came late to Tokaji, but just in time for fine Aszú wines.

Northern California, battling with phylloxera, was disappointed by rain at flowering time, further reducing the crop. Summer was then hot, and the small harvest over too quickly for many. The same was true in Washington: a serious grape shortage. Oregon's problem was harvest rain. California's Central Coast, though, had a good flowering and a fine vintage, and made plenty of good wine.

Australia's 1996 vintage broke records for quantity, producing excellent wines, especially in South Australia. 1997 was less prolific and more plenty. South Africa recorded its biggest vintage ever, despite summer starting late and staying relatively cool, and some problems with fungal diseases. White wines are notable and fresh and quality reds full of colour and flavour. As for New Zealand, whose international profile is out of all proportion to its size, 1996 was thoroughly satisfactory and 1997 looks even better.

France

Heavier shaded areas are the wine growing regions

The following abbreviations of regional names are used in the text:

Al	Alsace
Beauj	Beaujolais
Burg	Burgundy
B'x	Bordeaux
Champ	Champagne
Lo	Loire
Prov	Provence
Pyr	Pyrenees
N/S Rh	North/South Rhône
SW	Southwest

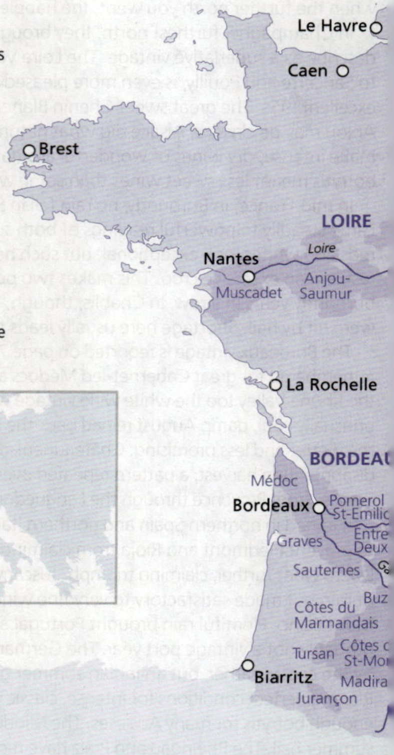

France's best wines set the standards by which all the world's finest are judged. At the aspirational level, too, whether with simple varietal wines or the renaissance of almost-forgotten local specialities, France has little to learn. But as more and more countries and regions raise their game to challenge France her age-old complacency begins to look ill-judged.

Sadly, the French government's own attitude to the Appellations Controlées which were her pride has become cynically commercial. It was revealed in 1996 that the INAO, the body governing Appellations, nods through over 97% of all wines submitted. This is not to say that they are bad wines; simply that the *fonctionnaires* no longer believe it matters.

Appellations remain the key to French wine. An appellation defines a type. It may apply to a single small vineyard or to a large

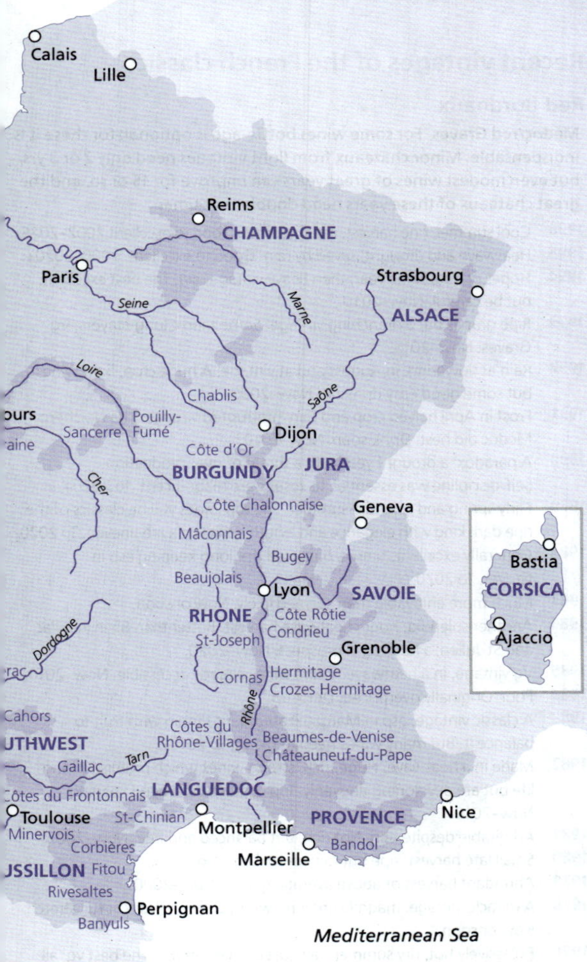

district. Burgundy on the whole has the most precise and smallest appellations, Bordeaux the widest and most general. An appellation is the first thing to look for on a label. But more important is the name of the maker The best growers' and merchants' names are a vital ingredient of these pages. Regions without the overall quality and traditions required for an appellation can be ranked as vins délimités de qualité supérieure (VDQS), a shrinking category as its members gain AC status. Their place is being taken by the relatively new and highly successful vins de pays. Vins de pays are almost always worth trying. They include some brilliant originals and often offer France's best value for money – which still (and even with an over-valued franc) means the world's.

Recent vintages of the French classics

Red Bordeaux

Médoc/red Graves For some wines bottle-age is optional: for these it is indispensable. Minor châteaux from light vintages need only 2 or 3 yrs, but even modest wines of great years can improve for 15 or so, and the great châteaux of these years need double that time.

1996 Cool summer, fine harvest, esp Cabernet. Good to excellent 2002–2025.
1995 Heatwave and drought; saved by rain. Good to excellent. 2000–2020+.
1994 Hopes of a supreme year; then heavy vintage rain. The best excellent, but be careful. Now–2010.
1993 Ripe grapes but a drenching vintage. Some tannic long-stayers. Vg Graves. Now–2015.
1992 Rain at flowering, in August and at vintage. A huge crop; light wines, but some good easy drinking. Now–2005.
1991 Frost in April halved crop and rain interrupted vintage. The Northern Médoc did best. Drink soon. Now–2010?
1990 A paradox: a drought year with a threat of over-production. Self-discipline was essential. Its results are magnificent. To 2020+.
1989 Early spring and splendid summer. The top wines will be classics of the ripe dark kind with elegance and length. Small ch'x are uneven. To 2020.
1988 Generally excellent; tannic, balanced, for long keeping esp in Graves. To 2020.
1987 Much more enjoyable than seemed likely. Now or soon.
1986 Another splendid, huge, heatwave harvest. Better than 85 in Pauillac and St-Julien; a long-term prospect. Now–2020.
1985 Vg vintage, in a heatwave. V fine wines already accessible. Now–2010.
1984 Poor. Originally overpriced. Drink up.
1983 A classic vintage, esp in Margaux: abundant tannin with fruit to balance it. But many wines need drinking. To 2010?
1982 Made in a heatwave. Huge, rich, strong wines which promise a long life but are developing unevenly. Top châteaux still need keeping. Now–2010.
1981 Admirable despite rain. Not rich, but balanced and fine. Now–2005.
1980 Small late harvest: ripe but rained-on. Drink up.
1979 Abundant harvest of above average quality. Now–2000.
1978 A miracle vintage: magnificent long warm autumn. Now at full stretch. Now or soon.
1976 Excessively hot, dry summer; rain just before vintage. The best vg; all now ready.
1975 A v fine vintage but excess of tannin is *still* the problem. Time to drink.
1970 Big, excellent vintage with scarcely a failure. Now–2005.

Older fine vintages: 66 62 61 59 55 53 52 50 49 48 47 45 29 28.

St-Emilion/Pomerol

1996 Cool fine summer, vintage rain on Merlot. Less consistent than Médoc. 2002–2020.
1995 Perhaps even better than Médoc/Graves. 1999–2015.
1994 Less compromised by rain than Médoc. Very good, especially Pomerol. 1999–2015.
1993 As in the Médoc, but probably better, esp in Pomerol; good despite terrible vintage weather.
1992 Exceptionally dilute but some charming wines to drink quickly. Drink now or soon.

1991 A sad story. Many wines not released.
1990 Another chance to make great wine or a lot of wine. Now–2020.
1989 Large, ripe, early harvest; an overall triumph. To 2020.
1988 Generally excellent; ideal conditions. But some châteaux overproduced. Pomerol best. Now–2000+.
1987 Some v adequate wines (esp in Pomerol). Drink soon.
1986 A prolific vintage; but top St-Emilions have long life ahead.
1985 One of the great yrs, with a long future. To 2010.
1984 A sad story. Most of the crop wiped out in spring. Avoid.
1983 Less impressive than it seemed. Drink soon.
1982 Enormously rich and concentrated wines, most excellent. Now–2000+.
1981 A vg vintage, if not as great as it first seemed. Now or soon.
1979 A rival to 78, but not developing as well as hoped. Now or soon.
1978 Fine wines, but some lack flesh. Drink soon.
1976 V hot, dry summer, but vintage rain. Some excellent. Drink soon.
1975 Most St-Emilions good, the best are superb. Pomerol made splendid wine. Now–2000.
1971 On the whole better than Médocs, but now ready.
1970 Beautiful wines with great fruit and strength. V big crop. Now.

Older fine vintages: 67 66 64 61 59 53 52 49 47 45.

Red burgundy

Côte d'Or Côte de Beaune reds generally mature sooner than the bigger wines of the Côte de Nuits. Earliest drinking dates are for lighter commune wines, eg Volnay, Beaune; latest for the biggest wines of eg Chambertin, Romanée. But even the best burgundies are much more attractive young than the equivalent red Bordeaux.

1996 Fine summer and vintage. Intense ripe wines for keeping. 2002–2020.
1995 Small, excellent crop, despite vintage rains. Grapes were very ripe.
1994 Ripe grapes compromised by vintage rain. Côte de Nuits better. Generally lean, but exceptions in Côte de Nuits. Now–2005.
1993 An excellent vintage – concentrated; for keeping 1999–2010.
1992 Ripe, plump, pleasing. No great concentration. Now–2005.
1991 Very small harvest; some wines v tannic. Côte de Nuits best. Now–2010.
1990 A great vintage: perfect weather compromised only by drought on some slopes and over-production in some vineyards. Long life ahead but start to enjoy. To 2020.
1989 A year of great charm, not necessarily for very long maturing, but will age. Now–2015.
1988 Very good but tannic. Now–2020 (but only the best).
1987 Small crop with ripe fruit flavours, esp in Côte de Beaune. Now–2010.
1986 Aromatic but rather dry wines: generally lack flesh. Drink now–2000.
1985 At best a great vintage. Concentrated wines are splendid. Now–2010.
1984 Lacks natural ripeness; tends to be dry and/or watery. Now – if at all.
1983 Powerful, vigorous, tannic and attractive vintage dreadfully compromised by rot. Be very careful. Now–2005.
1982 Big vintage, pale but round and charming. Côte de Beaune best. Drink up.
1981 A small crop, ripe but picked in rain.
1980 A wet year, but v attractive wines from best growers who avoided rot. Côte de Nuits best. Drink.
1979 Big, generally good, ripe vintage with weak spots. Drink up.
1978 A small vintage of outstanding quality. The best will live to 2000+.

Older fine vintages: 71 69 66 64 62 61 59 (all mature).

White burgundy

Côte de Beaune Well-made wines of good vintages with plenty of acidity as well as fruit will improve and gain depth and richness for some years – anything up to 10. Lesser wines from lighter vintages are ready for drinking after 2 or 3 years.

1996 Excellent crop; excellent potential 2000–2020.
1995 A potentially great vintage, diluted in places.
1994 Patchy; top growers made v fine potent wines – but not for long keeping. 1998–2005.
1993 September rain on ripe grapes. Easy wines, pleasant young but far behind reds. Now–2000.
1992 Ripe, aromatic and charming. Will develop beautifully. Now–2010.
1991 Mostly lack substance. Frost problems. For early drinking. Now.
1990 Very good, even great, but with a tendency to fatness. Now–2000+.
1989 Revealing itself as a model. At best ripe, tense, structured and long. Now–2010.
1988 Extremely good, some great wines but others rather dilute. Drink soon.
1987 V disappointing, though a few exceptions have emerged. Avoid.
1986 Powerful wines; most with better acidity/balance than 85. Now–2000.
1985 V ripe; those that still have balance are ageing v well. Now–2000.
1984 Most lean or hollow. Avoid.
1983 Potent wines; some faulty, but the best splendid. Drink soon.

The white wines of the Mâconnais (Pouilly-Fuissé, St-Véran, Mâcon-Villages) follow a similar pattern, but do not last as long. They are more appreciated for their freshness than their richness.

Chablis Grand Cru Chablis of vintages with both strength and acidity can age superbly for up to 10 years; Premiers Crus proportionately less.

1996 Ideal harvest but hail on top v'yds. 1999–2015.
1995 Potentially an outstanding vintage. 1998 Now–2010.
1994 Downpours on a ripe vintage. Delicious easy wines to 2000+.
1993 Fair to good quality; nothing great. Now–2001.
1992 Ripe and charming wines. Grands Crus splendid. Now–2005 at least.
1991 Generally better than Côte d'Or. Useful wines. Now.
1990 Grands Crus will be magnificent; other wines may lack intensity and acidity. Now–2000.
1989 Excellent vintage of potent character. Now–2000.
1988 Almost a model: great pleasure now. Now–2000.
1986 A splendid big vintage. Drink up.

Beaujolais 96: v satisfactory, but not for long keeping; 95: excellent. 94 vg; to drink soon. 93: Fine Crus to drink. 92: avoid now. 91: drink up. 90 drink top Crus. Older wines should be finished.

Alsace 96 excellent for dry wines, but not much Gewürz. 95 has mixed results – late-harvest Riesling best. 94 was a general success, if not a triumph. 93 was good, fruity, not for long keeping. 92 was splendid; 91 admirable. 90 was the third outstanding vintage in succession. 89 and 88 both made wines of top quality (though rain spoiled some 88s). 87s should be drunk soon and 86s finished. Top 85s and 83s are ready to drink up.

Abel-Lepitre Brut NV; Brut 85 **86 88** 90; Cuvée 134 Bl de Blancs NV; Réserve CREMANT BL DE BLANCS CUVEE 'C' **83** 85 **86 88** 90; Rosé **83** 85 **86 88** 90 Middle-rank CHAMP house, also owning GOULET, PHILIPPONNAT and St-Marceaux. Luxury Cuvée: Cuvée Reserve Abel-Lepitre 85.

Abymes Savoie w ★ DYA Hilly little area nr Chambéry; light mild Vin de Savoie AC from the Jacquère grape has alpine charm.

Ackerman-Laurance Classic-method sparkling house of the Loire, oldest in SAUMUR. Improving still wines under guidance of Jacques Lurton.

Agenais SW France r p (w) ★ DYA VDP of Lot-et-Garonne, mostly based on coops at Goulens,Donzac, Monflanquin and Mézin.

Ajaccio Corsica r p w ★→★★ 91 92 **93** 94 95 96 The capital of CORSICA. AC for some vg SCIACARELLO reds. Top grower: Peraldi.

Aligoté Second-rank burgundy white grape and its wine. Should be pleasantly tart and fruity with local character when young. BOUZERON is the one commune to have an all-Aligoté appellation. Its wine is richer, but try others from good growers. NB PERNAND-VERGELESSES.

Aloxe-Corton Burg r w ★★→★★★ **78'** 85' **87 88'** 89' 90' **91 92** 93' 94 95 96 Village at N end of COTE DE BEAUNE famous for its two GRANDS CRUS: CORTON (red), CORTON-CHARLEMAGNE (white). Village wines much lighter but to try.

Alsace Al w (r sp) ★★→★★★ **85' 88 89 90' 92 93 94** 95 96 Region comprising the eastern foothills of Vosges Mts, esp between Strasbourg and Mulhouse, producing unique wines: aromatic, fruity, full-strength, usually dry and expressive of each grape variety. Some sw wines also made; see Vendange Tardive and Sélection des Grains Nobles. Mostly sold by grape variety (PINOT BL, RIES, GEWURZ etc). Matures well (except Pinot Bl and MUSCAT) up to 5, even 10 yrs; GRAND CRU even longer. Also gd-quality and -value CREMANT. PINOT N often has gd varietal character but not widely sold outside region. (See below.)

Fifteen good Alsace producers

Among many good growers offering reliability, value for money and tastes varying from scintillating to sumptuous, NB Léon Beyer, Marcel Deiss, Dopff 'Au Moulin', Hugel (Special cuvées), Marc Kreydenweiss, Kuentz-Bas, Albert Mann, Muré-Clos St-Landelin, Rolly-Gassmann, Charles Schleret, Dom Schoffit, Doms Schlumberger, Dom Trimbach, Dom Weinbach, Zind-Humbrecht.

Alsace Grand Cru w ★★★→★★★★ **76 85 88 89' 90 91 92 93** 94 95 96 AC restricted to 50 of the best named v'yds (approx 4,000 acres, 1,680 in production) and four noble grapes (RIES, PINOT GR ('Tokay'), GEWURZ and MUSCAT). Not without controversy but generally vg and expressive of terroir.

Ampeau, Robert Exceptional grower and specialist in VOLNAY; also POMMARD etc. Perhaps unique in only releasing long-matured bottles.

André, Pierre Négociant with growing reputation at Ch Corton-André, ALOXE-CORTON; 95 acres of v'yds in CORTON, SAVIGNY, GEVREY-CHAMBERTIN etc. Also owns REINE PEDAUQUE.

d'Angerville, Marquis Top burgundy grower with immaculate 30-acre estate in VOLNAY. Top wines: Champans and CLOS des Ducs.

Anjou Lo p r w (sw dr sp) ★→★★★★ Both region and Loire AC embracing wide spectrum of styles – light reds incl AC Anjou GAMAY; improving dry whites. Esp good red (CAB) ANJOU-VILLAGES, strong dry SAVENNIERES; luscious COTEAUX DU LAYON CHENIN whites.

France entries also cross-refer to Châteaux of Bordeaux section, pages 78–103.

Anjou-Coteaux de la Loire Lo w s/sw sw ★★→★★★ **89' 90' 93 94 95'** 96 Tiny AC for some forceful CHENIN whites. Demi-sec or sw not as rich as COTEAUX DU LAYON, esp Musset-Roullier, Ch de Putille, Doms du Fresche, du Putille.

Anjou-Villages Lo r ★→★★ **89 90 93** 95 96 Superior AC for red wines (majority CAB F, some CAB S) from central ANJOU. Potentially juicy, quite tannic young but gd value esp from Bablut, RICHOU, Rochelles, Pierre-Bise, Ch de Coulaine, Ogereau, Montigilet, Ch de Tigné (Gérard Dépardieu's domaine).

Appellation Contrôlée (AC or AOC) Government control of origin and production of all the best French wines (see France Introduction).

Apremont Savoie w ★★ DYA One of the best villages of SAVOIE for pale delicate whites, mainly from Jacquère grapes, but recently incl CHARD.

Arbin Savoie r ★★ Deep-coloured lively red from MONDEUSE grapes, rather like a good LOIRE CABERNET. Ideal après-ski wine. Drink at 1–2 yrs.

Arbois Jura r p w (sp) ★★→★★★ Various good and original light but tasty wines; speciality is VIN JAUNE. On the whole DYA.

l'Ardèche, Coteaux de Central France r p (w) ★→★★ DYA Area W of Rhône given impetus by G DUBOEUF of BEAUJOLAIS. Bargain fresh country reds; best from pure SYRAH, GAMAY, CAB. Powerful, almost burgundian CHARD 'Ardèche' by LOUIS LATOUR (keep 1–3 yrs). (Choose this rather than his too-oaky 'Grand Ardèche'.)

l'Arlot, Domaine de Outstanding producer of supreme NUITS-ST-GEORGES, esp CLOS de l'Arlot, red and white. Owned by AXA Insurance.

Armagnac Region of SW France and its often excellent brandy; more rustic and peppery than COGNAC. Top names: Samalens, Dartigalongue, Laberdolive, Boignères. Table wines: COTES DE GASCOGNE.

Aube Southern extension of CHAMP region. See Bar-sur-Aube.

Aujoux, J-M Substantial grower/merchant of BEAUJOLAIS. Swiss-owned.

Auxey-Duresses Burg r w ★★→★★★ **85 87 88 89 90' 91 92** 93 94 95 96 Second-rank (but v pretty) COTE DE BEAUNE village: affinities with VOLNAY, MEURSAULT. Best estates: Diconne, HOSPICES DE BEAUNE (Cuvée Boillot), LEROY, M Prunier, R Thévenin. Drink whites in 4–5 yrs. Top white: Leroy's Les Boutonniers.

Avize Champ ★★★★ One of the top Côte des Blancs villages. All CHARDONNAY.

Aÿ Champ ★★★★ One of the best PINOT N-growing villages of CHAMP.

Ayala NV; Demi-Sec NV; Brut **89 90**; Château d'Aÿ **82 83 85**; Grande Cuvée **82 85 88 90**; Blanc de Blancs **88 92**; Brut Rosé NV Once-famous Aÿ-based old-style CHAMP firm. Deserves more notice for its fresh appley wines.

Bahuaud, Donatien ★★→★★★ Leading Loire wine merchant. Le Master de Donatien is the top MUSCADET Ch de la Cassemichère also good.

Bandol Prov r p (w) ★★★ **79 82 83 85' 86 87' 88 89 90 91** 92 93 94 95 96 Little coastal region near Toulon producing Provence's best wines; splendid vigorous tannic reds predominantly from MOURVEDRE; esp DOM OTT, Dom de Pibarnon, Ch Pradeaux, Mas de la Rouvière, DOM TEMPIER, Ch Vannières.

Banyuls Pyr br sw ★★→★★★ One of the best VINS DOUX NATURELS, made chiefly of GRENACHE (a Banyuls GRAND CRU is made from over 75% GRENACHE, aged for 2 yrs+). In fact, a distant relation of port. The best wines are RANCIOS eg those from Domaine des Hospices, Domaine du Mas Blanc (★★★), Domaine Vial Magnères (Blanc), at 10–15 yrs old. Cheap NV wines end up in bars.

Bar-sur-Aube Champ w (p) ★★ Important secondary CHAMP region 100 miles SE of R Marne, Epernay etc. Some gd lighter wines. Excellent ROSE DES RICEYS.

Barancourt Brut Réserve NV; Rosé NV; Bouzy Grand Cru **81 83 85**; Rosé GC **85** Grower at BOUZY making full-bodied CHAMP. New owners Champ VRANKEN; now esp Bouzy Rouge and Rosé GRAND CRU.

Barrique The Bordeaux (and Cognac) term for an oak barrel holding 225 litres (eventually 300 bottles). Barrique-ageing to flavour almost any wine with oak was the craze of the late '80s, with some sad results.

Barsac B'x w sw ★★→ ★★★★ **70 71' 75 76' 78 79' 80' 81 82 83' 85 86'** 88' **89'** 90' 91 93 95 96 Neighbour of SAUTERNES with similar superb golden wines, generally less rich and more racy. Richly repays long ageing. Top ch'x: CLIMENS, COUTET, DOISY-DAENE, DOISY-VEDRINES.

Barton & Guestier BORDEAUX shipper since 18th C, now owned by Seagram.

Bâtard-Montrachet Burg w ★★★★ **78 79 85** 86' **88 89'** 90' **91** 92 93 94 95 96 Larger (55-acre) neighbour of M'RACHET. Should be v long-lived with intense flavours and rich texture. Bienvenues-Bâtard-M is a separate adjacent 9-acre GRAND CRU with 15 owners, thus no substantial bottlings and very rare. Top growers incl BOUCHARD PERE, J-M Boillot, CARILLON, DROUHIN, Gagnard, LOUIS LATOUR, LEFLAIVE, Lequin-Roussot, MOREY, RAMONET, SAUZET.

Baumard, Domaine des ★★→★★★ Leading grower of ANJOU wine, esp SAVENNIERES, COTEAUX DU LAYON (CLOS Ste-Catherine) and QUARTS DE CHAUME.

Baux-en-Provence, Coteaux des Prov r p ★→ ★★★ Neighbour of COTEAUX D'AIX, also gathering speed, but now declassified to VDP for boring technical reasons. NB the excellent DOM DE TREVALLON (CAB and SYRAH) and Mas de Gourgonnier.

Béarn SW France r p w ★→★★ DYA 93 **94** Low-key Basque AC centred on coop at Bellocq. Also Dom de Guilhémas. JURANCON red and MADIRAN rosé (★★) must be sold as Béarn.

Confusingly, the best wines of the Beaujolais region are not identified as Beaujolais at all on their labels despite the fact that they exhibit all the best characteristics of the region. They are known simply by the names of their 'crus': Brouilly, Chénas, Chiroubles, Côte de Brouilly, Fleurie, Juliénas, Morgon, Moulin-à-Vent, Regnié, Saint-Amour. See entries for each of these. They are some of the best-value wines in France.

Beaujolais Beauj r (p w) ★ DYA Simple AC of the v big Beaujolais region: light short-lived fruity red of GAMAY grapes. Beaujolais Supérieur is little different.

Beaujolais de l'année The BEAUJOLAIS of the latest vintage, until the next.

Beaujolais Primeur (or Nouveau) Same as above, made in a hurry (often only 4–5 days fermenting) for release at midnight on the third Wednesday in November. Ideally soft, pungent, fruity and tempting; often crude, sharp, too alcoholic. BEAUJ-VILLAGES should be a better bet.

Beaujolais-Villages Beauj r ★★ **95 96** Wines from better (N) half of BEAUJOLAIS; should be much tastier than plain BEAUJOLAIS. The 10 (easily) best 'villages' are the 'CRUS': FLEURIE etc (see note above). Of the 30 others the best lie around Beaujeu. Crus cannot be released EN PRIMEUR before December 15th. Best kept until spring (or considerably longer).

Beaumes-de-Venise S Rh br (r p) ★★→★★★ DYA Regarded as France's best dessert MUSCAT, from S COTES DU RHONE; can be highly flavoured, subtle, lingering (eg from CHAPOUTIER, Dom de Coyeux, Dom Durban, JABOULET, VIDAL-FLEURY). Red and rosé from Ch Redortier and the coop are also good.

Beaune Burg r (w) ★★★ 78' 85' **88 89'** 90' **91** 92 93 94 95 96 The historic wine capital of Burgundy, a walled town, hollow with cellars. Wines are classic burgundy – but no GRAND CRU. Many fine growers. Négociants' CLOS wines (usually PREMIER CRU) are often best; eg DROUHIN'S superb CLOS des Mouches, JADOT'S CLOS des Ursules. Beaune du Château is a BOUCHARD PERE brand. Best v'yds: Bressandes, Fèves, Grèves, Marconnets, Teurons.

Becker, Caves J Proud old family firm at Zellenberg, ALSACE. Classic RIESLING Hagenschlauf and GRAND CRU Froehn MUSCAT. Second label: Gaston Beck.

FRANCE

Bellet Prov p r w ★★★ Fashionable much above average local wines from nr Nice. Serious producers: Ch'x de Bellet and CREMAT. Pricey.

Bergerac Dordogne r w p dr sw ★★→★★★ **89 90' 91 92 93 94** 95' 96 Effectively, but not politically, eastward extension of Bordeaux. Top properties incl La Tour des Gendres, Doms de Gouyat, de Jaubertie, Ch'x Grinou, de la Mallevieille, les Marais, le Paradis, le Raz, la Tour de Grangemont and CLOS des Verdots. See also MONTBAZILLAC, MONTRAVEL, ROSETTE, SAUSSIGNAC and PECHARMANT.

Besserat de Bellefon Grande Tradition NV; Cuvée des Moines Brut and Rosé NV; Grande Cuvée NV; Brut and Rosé **85 89** Reims CHAMP house for fine light wines. Owned by MARNE ET CHAMPAGNE.

Beyer, Léon Ancient ALSACE family firm at Eguisheim making forceful dry wines that need ageing at least 3–5 yrs. Comtes d'Eguisheim GEWURZ is renowned, and 'Cuvée Particulière' RIES of GRAND CRU Pfersigberg is esp fine. Beyer is militant against Grand Cru restrictions.

Bichot, Maison Albert One of BEAUNE's biggest growers and merchants. V'yds (32-acre Dom du CLOS Frantin: excellent): CHAMBERTIN, RICHEBOURG, CLOS DE VOUGEOT etc; Dom Long-Depaquit in CHABLIS; also many other brand names.

Billecart-Salmon NV; Rosé NV; Brut **85 86 88 89**; Bl de Blancs **83 85 86 88 89**; Grande Cuvée **82 85** One of the very best CHAMP houses, founded in 1818, still family-owned. Fresh-flavoured wines incl a v tasty rosé. CUVEES: Nicolas François Billecart (**88**), Elisabeth Salmon Rosé (**88 89**).

Bize, Simon Admirable red burgundy grower with 35 acres at SAVIGNY-LES-BEAUNE. Usually model wines, racy and elegant.

Blagny Burg r w ★★→★★★ (w) **85 86' 88 89 90' 91 92** 93 94 95 96 Hamlet between MEURSAULT and PULIGNY-M'RACHET: whites have affinities with both (sold under each AC), reds with VOLNAY (sold as AC Blagny). Good ones need age; esp AMPEAU, Jobard, LATOUR, LEFLAIVE, Matrot, G Thomas.

Blanc de Blancs Any white wine made from white grapes only, esp CHAMP (usually both red and white). Not an indication of quality.

Blanc de Noirs White (or slightly pink or 'blush') wine from red grapes.

Blanck, Paul et Fils Versatile ALSACE grower at Kientzheim. Good PINOT BL, and GRANDS CRUS Furstentum (GEWURZ, PINOT GR, esp RIES), Schlossberg (Ries).

Blanquette de Limoux Midi w sp ★★ Good bargain sparkler from near Carcassonne with long local history. V dry and clean; increasingly tasty as more CHARD and Chenin are added, esp in more recent AC CREMANT de Limoux. Normally NV but some top vintage CUVEES.

Blaye B'x r w ★ **88 89 90 93 94** 95 96 Your daily BORDEAUX from E of the Gironde. PREMIERES COTES DE BLAYE is the AC of the better wines.

Boillot, J-M POMMARD-based domaine: v fine PULIGNY-M'RACHET, BATARD-M etc.

Boisset, Jean-Claude Far and away the biggest burgundy merchant and grower, based in NUITS-ST-GEORGES. Owner of Bouchard-Aîné, Lionel Bruck, F Chauvenet, Delaunay, JAFFELIN, Morin Père et Fils, de Marcilly, Pierre Ponnelle, Thomas-Bassot, VIENOT. New acquisitions incl CELLIER DES SAMSONS (BEAUJOLAIS) and a share in MOMMESSIN. Generally high commercial standards.

Bollinger NV 'Special Cuvée'; Grande Année **76 79 82 83 85 88 89 90**; Rosé **81 82 83 85 88** Top CHAMP house, at AY. Dry, very full-flavoured style, needs ageing. Luxury wines: RD (**73 75 76 79 81 82 85**), VIELLES VIGNES Françaises (75 79 80 81 82 85 88 89) from ungrafted Pinot vines. Pioneered Charter of Quality ('91). Investor in Petaluma, Australia.

Bonneau du Martray, Domaine Biggest grower (with 22 acres) of CORTON-CHARLEMAGNE of highest quality; also red GRAND CRU CORTON all on a high since '90. Cellars at PERNAND-VERGELESSES. White wines have often outlived reds.

NB Vintages in colour are those you should choose first for drinking in 1998.

Bonnes-Mares Burg r ★★★→★★★★ **78' 79 80 85' 87 88 89** 90' 91 **92** 93 94 95 96 37-acre GRAND CRU between CHAMBOLLE-MUSIGNY and MOREY-ST-DENIS. V sturdy long-lived wines, less fragrant than MUSIGNY; can rival CHAMBERTIN. Top growers: DUJAC, Groffier, JADOT, MUGNIER, ROUMIER, DOM DES VAROILLES, DE VOGUE.

Bonnezeaux Lo w sw ★★★→★★★★ **76' 78 81 83 85' 86 88' 89' 90' 93'** 94 95' Velvety, structured and complex sweet wine from CHENIN grapes, potentially the best of COTEAUX DU LAYON. Esp Angeli, Ch de Fesles, Dom du Petit Val. Ages well – but v tempting young.

Bordeaux B'x r w (p) ★ **90 93 94 95 96** (for ch'x see pages 78–103) Catch-all AC for low-strength B'x wine. Not to be despised: it may be light but its flavour cannot be imitated. If I had to choose one simple daily wine this would be it.

Bordeaux Supérieur ★→★★ As above, with slightly more alcohol.

Borie-Manoux Admirable BORDEAUX shipper and château-owner, owned by the Castéja family. Ch'x incl BATAILLEY, BEAU-SITE, DOMAINE DE L'EGLISE, HAUT-BAGES-MONPELOU, TROTTEVIEILLE.

Bouchard Père et Fils Important burgundy shipper (est 1731) and grower with 209 acres of excellent v'yds, mainly in the COTE DE BEAUNE, and cellars at the Château de Beaune. Controlled since '95 by HENRIOT, who has taken radical steps to upgrade quality and image.

Bouches-du-Rhône Prov r p w ★ VINS DE PAYS from Marseille environs. Robust reds from southern varieties, CAB S, SYRAH and Merlot.

Bourg B'x r (w) ★★ **86' 88' 89' 90' 93** 94 95 96 Un-fancy claret from E of the Gironde. For ch'x see Côtes de Bourg.

Bourgeois, Henri Leading SANCERRE grower/merchant in Chavignol; also own Laporte. Also POUILLY-FUME. Top wines incl: MD de Bourgeois, La Bourgeoise.

Bourgogne Burg r w (p) ★★ **90' 92 93** 94 95 96 Catch-all Burgundy AC, with higher standards than basic B'X. Light, often gd flavour, best at 2–4 yrs. Top growers make bargain beauties from fringes of COTE D'OR villages; do not despise. BEAUJOLAIS CRUS can also be labelled Bourgogne.

Bourgogne Grand Ordinaire Burg r (w) ★ DYA Lowest B'y AC, also allowing GAMAY. Rare. White may incl ALIGOTE, PINOT BL, Melon de Bourgogne.

Bourgogne Passe-Tout-Grains Burg r (p) ★ Age 1–2 yrs, junior burgundy: minimum 33% PINOT N, the balance GAMAY, mixed in the vat. Often enjoyable. Not as heady as BEAUJOLAIS.

Bourgueil Lo r (p) ★★→★★★(★) **76' 85 86' 88 89' 90' 93'** 95' 96 Normally delicate fruity mainly CAB F red from TOURAINE. Deep-flavoured, long-lasting in best yrs, ageing like Bordeaux. ST-NICOLAS-DE-BOURGUEIL often lighter. Esp from Amirault, Audebert, Billet, Breton, Caslot, Cognard, Delaunay, Druet, Gambier, Lamé-Delille-Boucard, Mailloches.

Bouvet-Ladubay The major producer of sp SAUMUR, controlled by TAITTINGER. Wines incl brut 'Saphir' CREMANT 'Excellence' and oak-fermented deluxe 'Trésor' (white, rosé), with 2 yrs age. Also good sw Grand Vin de Dessert.

Bouzeron Village of the COTE CHALONNAISE distinguished for the only single-village AC ALIGOTE. Top grower: de Villaine. Also NB BOUCHARD PERE.

Bouzy Rouge Champ r ★★★ **85 88 89 90 91** Still red of famous CHAMP PINOT village. Like v light burgundy, ageing early but can last well.

Brand ALSACE GRAND CRU hot spot nr Turkheim. Tokay-PINOT GRIS does extremely well here; also excellent GEWURZ from ZIND-HUMBRECHT.

Brédif, Marc One of the most important growers and traders of VOUVRAY, esp sparkling (METHODE TRADITIONELLE and PETILLANT). Owned by LADOUCETTE.

Bricout Brut NV (Rés, Prestige, Cuvée Spéciale Arthur Bricout); Rosé NV; Brut **85 89** Sm CHAMP house at AVIZE: light CHARD-led wines. Excellent Cuvée Prestige.

Brocard, J-M CHABLIS grower to note for fine value, crisp and typical wines, incl Montmains, Montée de Tonnèrre. A confirmed terroiriste.

Brouilly Beauj r ★★**94 95 96** Biggest of the 10 CRUS of BEAUJOLAIS: fruity, round, refreshing wine, can age 3–4 yrs. CH DE LA CHAIZE is largest estate. Top growers: Michaud, Dom de Combillaty, Dom des Grandes Vignes.

Bruno Paillard Brut Première Cuvée NV; Rosé Première Cuvée NV; CHARD Réserve Privée NV, Brut **85 8990** Small but prestigious young CHAMP house: excellent silky vintage and NV; fair prices.

Brut Term for the dry classic wines of CHAMP. Brut Ultra/Zéro: a recent term for bone-dry wines.

Buisse, Paul Quality Montrichard merchant: range of Loire, esp TOURAINE wines.

Bugey Savoie r p w sp ★→★★DYA VDQS for light sp, still or half-sp wines from Roussette (or Roussanne) and CHARD (gd). Best from Cerdon and Montagnieu.

Buxy Burg w ★★ Village in AC MONTAGNY with gd coop for CHARD.

Buzet SW France r (w p) ★★ **89' 90'91 92' 93 94** 95 96 Region just SE of B'X with similar wines, but prunier. Dynamic coop has bulk of production, incl some single properties (eg Ch de Gueyze). More local character from Dom de Pech, Dom de Versailles Ch'x du Frandat and Sauvagnères.

Cabardès Midi r (p w) ★→★★ **88 89 90 91** 92 **93 94** 95 96 In line for AC. Region north of Carcassonne, CORBIERES, etc. MIDI and BORDEAUX grapes show promise at Ch Rivals, Ch Rayssac, Ch Ventenac, Coop de Conques sur Orbiel.

Cabernet See Grapes for red wine (pages 11–13).

Cabernet d'Anjou Lo p s/sw ★→★★ DYA Delicate, grapey, med-sw rosé. Traditionally: sw, age-worthy; a few venerable bottles survive. Esp from Bablut.

Cabrières Midi p (r) ★★DYA COTEAUX DU LANGUEDOC.

Cahors SW France r ★→★★**82 83 85 86' 88 89' 90' 92'** 93 94 95' 96 Historically 'black' and tannic from Malbec grapes, still long-lived, full-bodied wines (a newer style of VIN DE L'ANNEE not is typical). Best incl CLOS de Gamot and Coutale, Ch'x du Cayrou, La Caminade, Pech de Jammes, La Reyne, du Cèdre, Les Ifs and Latuc, Doms de Paillas, Pineraie, Savarines and Eugénie.

Cairanne S Rh r p w ★★**88 89 90'92 93** 94 95' 96 One of best COTES DU RHONE-VILLAGES: solid, robust esp from Doms B Alary, Ameillaud, Brusset, l'Oratoire St-Martin, Rabasse-Charavin, Richaud. Some improving whites.

Calvet Famous old shippers of BORDEAUX and burgundy, now owned by Allied-Domecq. Some reliable standard wines, esp from Bordeaux.

Canard-Duchêne Brut NV; Demi-Sec NV; Rosé NV; Charles VII NV; Brut **85 88 90** CHAMP house connected with VEUVE-CLICQUOT, ie, same group as MOET-Hennessy. Fair prices for lively, PINOT-tasting wines. Improved quality recently.

Canon-Fronsac B'x r ★★→★★★ **82 83' 85' 86 88 89' 90' 92** 93 94 95 96 Full tannic reds of increasing quality from small area W of POMEROL. Need less age than formerly. Eg Ch'x: CANON, CANON DE BREM, CANON-MOUEIX, Coustolle, La Dauphine, La Fleur Caillou, Junayme, Mazeris-Bellevue, Moulin-Pey-Labrie, Toumalin, La Truffière, Vraye-Canon-Boyer. See also Fronsac.

Cantenac B'x r ★★★ Village of HAUT-MEDOC entitled to the AC MARGAUX. Top ch'x include BRANE-CANTENAC, PALMER etc.

Cap Corse Corsica w br ★★→★★★ CORSICA'S wild N cape. Splendid MUSCAT from CLOS Nicrosi, Rogliano, and rare soft dry Vermentino white. Vaut le détour, if not le voyage.

Caramany Pyr r (w) ★ **90 91** 92 **93 94** 95 96 Notionally superior AC for single-village COTES DU ROUSSILLON-VILLAGES.

Carillon, Louis Leading PULIGNY-M domaine now in top league. Esp PREMIER CRU Referts, Perrières and a tiny amount of GRAND CRU Bienvenues-Bâtard.

Cassis Prov w (r p) ★★ DYA Seaside village E of Marseille known for lively dry white wine – one of the best in PROVENCE (eg Dom du Paternel). Not to be confused with cassis, a blackcurrant liqueur made in Dijon.

Cave Cellar, or any wine establishment.

Cave coopérative Wine-growers' cooperative winery; 55% of all French production. Almost all now well-run, well-equipped and their wine fair value.

Cellier des Samsons BEAUJOLAIS/MACONNAIS coop at Quincié with 2,000 grower-members. Wines widely distributed; now under ownership of BOISSET.

Cépage Variety of vine, eg CHARDONNAY, Merlot.

Cérons B'x w dr sw ★★ **83' 85' 86' 88' 89' 90** 91 **92** 93 94 95 96 Neighbour of SAUTERNES with some good sweet wine ch'x, eg de Cérons et de Calvimont, Grand Enclos, Haura. Ch Archambeau makes vg dry GRAVES.

Chablis

There is no better expression of the all-conquering Chardonnay than the full but tense, limpid but stony wines it makes on the heavy limestone soils of Chablis. Chablis terroir divides cleanly into 3 quality levels with remarkable consistency. Best makers use v little or no new oak to mask the precise definition of variety and terroir. They include: Billand-Simon, J-M Brocard, J Collet, D Dampf, R Dauvissat, B, D et E, and J Defaix, Droin, Drouhin, Durup, Fèvre, Geoffroy, J-P Grossot, Lamblin, Laroche, Long-Depaquit, Dom des Malandes, Michel, Pic, Pupillon, Raveneau, G Robin, Tribut. Simple unqualified 'Chablis' may be thin; best is premier or grand cru (see below). Coop, La Chablisienne, has high standards and many different labels (it makes 1 in every 3 bottles).

Chablis Burg w ★★→★★★ **90 92 93 94** 95 96 Unique full-flavoured dry minerally wine of N Burgundy, CHARD only, from 10,000 acres (doubled since '85).

Chablis Grand Cru Burg w ★★★→★★★★ **78 83 85 86 88 89 90 91 92** 93 94 95 96 In maturity a match for greatest white burgundy: forceful but often dumb in youth, at best with age has hint of SAUTERNES. 7 v'yds: Blanchots, Bougros, CLOS, Grenouilles, Preuses, Valmur, Vaudésir. See also Moutonne.

Chablis Premier Cru Burg w ★★★ **85 86 88 89 90 91 92 93** 94 95 96 Technically second-rank but at best excellent, more typical of CHABLIS than its GRANDS CRUS. Often outclasses more expensive MEURSAULT and other COTE DE BEAUNES. Best vineyards include Côte de Léchet, Fourchaume, Mont de Milieu, Montée de Tonnerre, Montmains, Vaillons. See above for producers.

Chai Building for storing and maturing wine, esp in BORDEAUX.

Chambertin Burg r ★★★★ **78' 79 80 83 85' 87 88 89** 90' 91 **92** 93 94 95 96 32-acre GRAND CRU for some of the meatiest, most enduring, best red burgundy, 15 growers, incl BOUCHARD, Camus, Damoy, DROUHIN, MORTET, PONSOT, Rebourseau, Rossignol-Trapet, ROUSSEAU, Tortochot, TRAPET.

Chambertin-Clos de Bèze Burg r ★★★★ **78' 79 80 83 85 87 88 89** 90' 91 **92** 93 94 95 96 37-acre neighbour of CHAMBERTIN. Similarly splendid wines. May legally be sold as Chambertin. 10 growers incl B CLAIR, CLAIR-DAU, Damoy, DROUHIN, Drouhin-Laroze, FAIVELEY, JADOT, ROUSSEAU.

Chambolle-Musigny Burg r (w) ★★★→★★★★ **78' 85' 87 88 89 90'** 91 **92** 93 94 95 96 420-acre COTE DE NUITS village: fabulously fragrant, complex, never heavy wine. Best v'yds: Les Amoureuses, part of BONNES-MARES, Les Charmes, MUSIGNY. Growers to note: Barthod, DROUHIN, FAIVELEY, Hudelot-Noëllat, JADOT, Moine-Hudelot, Mugneret, MUGNIER, RION, ROUMIER, Serveau, DE VOGUE.

Champagne Sparkling wine of PINOTS NOIR and MEUNIER and/or CHARD, and its region (70,000+ acres 90 miles E of Paris); made by METHODE TRADITIONELLE. Bubbles from elsewhere, however good, cannot be champagne.

Champy Père et Cie Oldest burgundy négociant, in BEAUNE, rejuvenated by Meurgey family (also brokers 'DIVA'). Range of v well-chosen wines.

Chandon de Briailles, Domaine Small burgundy estate at SAVIGNY. Makes wonderful CORTON (and Corton Blanc) and vg PERNAND-VERGELESSES.

Chanson Père et Fils Old grower-NEGOCIANT family co at BEAUNE (125 acres). Esp BEAUNE CLOS des Fèves, SAVIGNY, PERNAND-VERGELESSES, CORTON. Fine quality.

Chapelle-Chambertin Burg r ★★★ **78' 85 87 88 89'** 90' 91 **92** 93 94 95 96 13-acre neighbour of CHAMBERTIN. Wine more 'nervous', not so meaty. Top producers: Damoy, JADOT, Rossignol-Trapet, TRAPET.

Chapoutier Long-est'd grower and trader of full-bodied Rhônes produced on bio-dynamic principles. Best are special CUVEES CHATEAUNEUF Barbe Rac (100% GRENACHE), red HERMITAGE Le Pavillon, white Hermitage Cuvée d'Orée (100% Marsanne, late-picked), also CROZES red Les Varonniers (since '94).

Chardonnay See Grapes for white wine (pages 7–11). Also the name of a MACON-VILLAGES commune. Hence Mâcon-Chardonnay.

Charmes-Chambertin Burg r ★★★ **78' 85' 87** 88 **89'** 90' 91 **92** 93 94 95 96 76-acre CHAMBERTIN neighbour, incl AC MAZOYERES-C. 'Suppler', rounder wines; esp from Bachelet, Castagnier, DROUHIN, DUJAC, LEROY, ROTY, ROUMIER, ROUSSEAU.

Chartron & Trebuchet Young NEGOCIANT co (founded '84): some delicate harmonious white burgundies, esp Dom Chartron's PULIGNY-M'RACHET, CLOS de la Pucelle. Also BATARD- and CHEVALIER-M'RACHET. Good ALIGOTE too.

Chassagne-Montrachet Burg r w ★★★→★★★★ r (★★★) **78' 85 87** 88 **89' 90'** 91 **92** 93 94; w **78' 83 85 86 88 89' 90 91** 92 93 94 95 96 750-acre COTE DE BEAUNE village with excellent rich dry whites and sterling hefty reds. Whites rarely have the extreme finesse of PULIGNY next door but often cost less. Best vineyards include part of M'RACHET, BATARD-M'RACHET, Boudriottes (r w), Caillerets, CRIOTS-BATARD-M'RACHET, Morgeot (r w), Ruchottes, CLOS ST-JEAN (r). Growers include Amiot-Bonfils, Blain-Gagnard, Colin-Deleger, Delagrange-Bachelet, DROUHIN, J-N Gagnard, GAGNARD-DELAGRANGE, Lamy-Pillot, MAGENTA, Ch de la Maltroye, MOREY, Niellon, RAMONET-PRUDHON.

> **Château**
> **Means an estate, big or small, good or indifferent, particularly in Bordeaux (see pages 78–103). Elsewhere in France château tends to mean, literally, castle or great house, as in most of the following entries. In Burgundy 'Domaine' is the usual term.**

Château d'Arlay Major JURA estate; 160 acres in skilful hands with wines incl vg VIN JAUNE, VIN DE PAILLE, PINOT N and MACVIN.

Château de Beaucastel S Rh r w ★★★ **78' 79 81' 83 85 86' 87 88 89' 90' 92** 93' 94' 95' 96 One of the biggest (173 acres), best-run CHATEAUNEUF-DU-PAPE estates. Deep-hued, complex wines from unusual varietal mix incl ⅓ MOURVEDRE. Small amount of wonderful Roussanne white to keep 5–10 yrs. Also leading COTES DU RHONE Coudoulet de Beaucastel (red and white). New interest: Beaucastel Estate, Paso Robles, California.

Château de la Chaize Beauj r ★★★ **93 94** 95 Best-known BROUILLY estate.

Château Corton-Grancey Burg r ★★★ **78 85 88 89** 90 91 92 93 95 96 Famous ALOXE-CORTON estate; property of LOUIS LATOUR: benchmark wines.

Château de Crémat Prov r p w ★★→★★★ Prestigious little estate in BELLET, nr Nice. Light but long-lived reds, adequate rosés, excellent original whites.

Château Fortia S Rh r (w) ★★★ **78' 79 81 83 84 85 86 88 89 90** 93 94 95 96 Trad 72-acre CHATEAUNEUF property. Owner's father, Baron Le Roy, also fathered the APPELLATION CONTROLEE system in the '20s. Good, but not at v top today.

Château Fuissé Burg w ★★★ The ultimate POUILLY-FUISSE estate. The Vincent's Pouilly-F VIEILLES VIGNES is ★★★★, and sumptuous with age; though recent wines have needed less time. Also ST-VERAN, MACON-VILLAGES (value).

Château de la Jaubertie English- (Rystone) owned top BERGERAC estate. Sumptuous luxury SAUV BL, Cuvée Mirabelle. Equally fine Réserve red.

Château de Meursault Burg r w ★★★ 100-acre estate owned by PATRIARCHE, with good v'yds and wines in BEAUNE, MEURSAULT, POMMARD, VOLNAY. Splendid cellars open to the public for tasting.

Château de Mille Prov r p w ★★ Leading star of advancing COTES DU LUBERON AC.

Château de Montaigne Dordogne w (sw) ★★ Home of the great philosopher Michel de M (outside HAUT-MONTRAVEL), now making sweet COTES DE MONTRAVEL, also sharing a part-owner with CH PALMER (MARGAUX).

Château La Nerthe S Rh r (w) ★★★ **78'** 79 **81' 85 86 88 89' 90'** 93 94 95' 96 Renowned imposing 222-acre CHATEAUNEUF estate. Solid modern-style wines, esp special CUVEES Cadettes (r) and Beauvenir (w).

Château Rayas S Rh r (w) ★★★ **78' 79 81'** 83 85 **86 88' 89 90'** 91 93 94' 95 96 Famous old-style property of only 37 acres in CHATEAUNEUF-DU-PAPE. Talented, eccentric owner Jacques Reynaud died in 1997. Concentrated wines are entirely GRENACHE, yet can age superbly. Pignan is second label. Also vg Ch Fonsalette, COTES DU RHONE (NB Cuvée SYRAH and long-lived whites).

Château Routas Prov r p w ★★ Recent blends incl SYRAH, CAB S, CHARD-Viognier have been outstanding for the Var region.

Château de Selle Prov r p w ★★→★★★ 100-acre estate of OTT family nr Cotignac, Var. Pace-setters for PROVENCE. Cuvée Spéciale is largely CAB S.

Château Simone Prov r p w ★★ Age 2–6 yrs. Famous old property almost synonymous with AC PALETTE, nr Aix-en-Provence. The red is best: smooth but herby and spicy. White is catching up.

Château Val-Joanis Prov r p w ★★★ Impressive estate making full-blooded COTES DU LUBERON.

Château Vignelaure Prov r ★★★ **82' 83' 85 86 87** 88 89 90 **91** 92 93 94 95 96 135-acre Provençal estate nr Aix: exceptional more-or-less B'x-style wine with CAB S, SYRAH and GRENACHE grapes. Bought in '94 by Rystone Co.

Château-Chalon Jura w ★★★ Not CHATEAU but AC: unique dry yellow wine, like sharpish fino sherry. Usually ready when bottled (at circa 6 yrs). A curiosity.

Château-Grillet N Rh w ★★★★ **89' 90 92 94** 95 96 9-acre terraced v'yd of Viognier; one of France's smallest ACS. Intense, fragrant, absurdly over-expensive, but showing signs of revival in the '90s. Drink young; any oxidation spoils it.

Châteaumeillant Lo r p ★→★★ DYA Tiny VDQS area nr SANCERRE. GAMAY and PINOT N for light reds and rosés.

Châteauneuf-du-Pape S Rh r (w) ★★★ **78'** 79 **81' 83** 85 **86 88 89' 90'** 93 94 95' 96 8,200 acres near Avignon with core of 30 or so domaines for very fine wines (quality more variable over remaining 90) mix of up to 13 varieties led by GRENACHE, SYRAH, MOURVEDRE. The best are dark, strong, exceptionally long-lived. Whites either fruity and zesty or rather heavy: mostly now 'DYA'. Top growers incl Ch'x DE BEAUCASTEL, FORTIA, Gardine, MONT-REDON, LA NERTHE, RAYAS; Doms de Beaurenard, Le Bosquet des Papes, Les Cailloux, Font-de-Michelle, Grand Tinel, VIEUX TELEGRAPHE; Henri Bonneau, CLOS du Mont-Olivet, CLOS des Papes, CLOS St-Jean etc.

Châtillon-en-Diois Rh r p w ★ DYA Small AC of mid-Rhône. Adequate largely GAMAY reds; white (some ALIGOTE) mostly made into CLAIRETTE DE DIE.

Chave, Gérard To many the superstar grower (with his son Jean-Louis) of HERMITAGE, with 25 acres red, 12 acres white – spread over 9 hillside v'yds. V long-lived red and white (esp vg red ST-JOSEPH), and also VIN DE PAILLE.

To decipher codes, please refer to 'Key to symbols' on front flap of jacket, or to 'How to use this book' on page 6.

Chavignol Village of SANCERRE with famous v'yd, Les Monts Damnés. Chalky soil gives vivid wines that age 4–5 yrs; esp from BOURGEOIS and Cotat.

Chénas Beauj r ★★★ **90 91 92** 93 94 95 96 Smallest BEAUJOLAIS CRU and one of the weightiest; neighbour to MOULIN-A-VENT and JULIENAS. Growers incl Benon, Champagnon, Charvet, Ch Chèvres, DUBOEUF, Lapièrre, Robin, Trichard, coop.

Chenin Blanc See Grapes for white wine (pages 7–11).

Chenonceau, Ch de Lo ★★ Architectural jewel of Loire makes good to v good AC Touraine SAUV BL, CAB and CHENIN, still and sparkling.

Chéreau Carré Makers of some of top domaine MUSCADETS (esp Ch'x du Chasseloir, du Coing).

Chevalier-Montrachet Burg w ★★★★ 78 **83 85' 86 88 89' 90** 91 **92** 93 95 96 17-acre neighbour of M'RACHET making similar luxurious wine, perhaps less powerful. Incl 2.5-acre Les Demoiselles. Growers incl LATOUR, JADOT, BOUCHARD PERE, CHARTRON, Deleger, LEFLAIVE, Niellon, PRIEUR.

Cheverny Lo r p w ★→★★ Loire AC nr Chambord. Dry crisp whites from SAUV BL and CHARD. Also GAMAY, PINOT N or CAB reds; generally light but tasty. 'Cour Cheverny' uses the local Romorantin grape. Sparkling wines use CREMANT DE LOIRE AC. Esp Cazin, Huards, OISLY ET THESEE, Dom de la Soucherie.

Chevillon, R 32-acre estate at NUITS-ST-GEORGES; outstanding winemaking.

Chignin Savoie w ★ DYA Light soft white from Jacquère grapes for alpine summers. Chignin-Bergeron is best and liveliest.

Chinon Lo r (p w) ★★→★★★ 76 **85 86' 88 89' 90' 93'** 95' 96 Juicy, variably rich CAB F from TOURAINE. Drink cool, young; treat exceptional yrs like B'X. Small quantity of crisp dry white from CHENIN. Top growers: Bernard Baudry, Alliet, COULY-DUTHEIL (CLOS de l'Echo), Druet, Ch de la Grille, Joguet, Raffault.

Chiroubles Beauj r ★★★ **94 95 96** Good but tiny BEAUJOLAIS CRU next to FLEURIE; freshly fruity silky wine for early drinking (1–3 yrs). Growers incl Bouillard, Cheysson, DUBOEUF, Fourneau, Passot, Raousset, coop.

Chorey-lès-Beaune Burg r (w) ★★ **85 87 88 89 90' 91 92** 93 94 95 96 Minor AC on flat land N of BEAUNE: 3 fine growers: Arnoux, Germain (Ch de Chorey), TOLLOT-BEAUT.

Chusclan S Rh r p w ★→★★ **89 90' 92 93** 94 95' 96 Village of COTES DU RHONE-VILLAGES with able coop. Labels incl Cuvée de Marcoule, Seigneurie de Gicon. Also Dom des Lindas and special CUVEES from André Roux.

Cissac HAUT-MEDOC village just west of PAUILLAC.

Clair, Bruno Recent domaine at MARSANNAY. Vg wines from there and GEVREY-CHAMBERTIN (esp CLOS DE BEZE), FIXIN, MOREY-ST-DENIS, SAVIGNY.

Clairet Very light red wine, almost rosé. Bordeaux Clairet is an AC.

Clairette Traditional white grape of the MIDI. Its low-acid wine was a vermouth base. Revival by Terrasses de Landoc is full and zesty.

Clairette de Bellegarde Midi w ★ DYA AC nr Nîmes: plain neutral white.

Clairette de Die Rh w dr s/sw sp ★★ NV Popular dry or (better) semi-sweet MUSCAT-flavoured sparkling wine from pre-Alps in E Rhône; or straight dry CLAIRETTE white, surprisingly ageing well 3–4 yrs. Worth trying.

Clairette du Languedoc Midi w ★ DYA Neutral white from nr Montpellier, but watch for improvements. Ch La Condamine Bertrand looking good.

Clape, La Midi r p w★→★★ Cru to note of AC COTEAUX DU LANGUEDOC. Full-bodied wines from limestone hills between Narbonne and the sea. Red gains character after 2–3 yrs, Bourboulenc white after even longer. Vg rosé. Esp from Ch'x Rouquette-sur-Mer, Pech-Redon, Dom de l'Hospitalet, La Rivière-Haute.

Claret Traditional English term for red BORDEAUX.

Climat Burgundian word for individually named v'yd, eg BEAUNE Grèves.

Clos A term carrying some prestige, reserved for distinct (walled) v'yds, often in one ownership (esp Burgundy and ALSACE). Les CLOS is CHABLIS' Grandest Cru.

Clos de Bèze See Chambertin-CLOS de Bèze.

Clos des Lambrays Burg r ★★★ 15-acre GRAND CRU vineyard at MOREY-ST-DENIS. Changed hands *again* in '96.

Clos des Mouches Burg r w★★★ Splendid PREMIER CRU BEAUNE v'yd, largely owned by DROUHIN. White and red, spicy and memorable – and consistent.

Clos de la Roche Burg r★★★ **78' 82**85' **86 87** 88 **89'** 90 91**92** 93' 94 95 96 MOREY-ST-DENIS GRAND CRU (38-acres). Powerful complex, like CHAMBERTIN. Esp BOUCHARD PERE, BOUREE, CASTAGNIER, DUJAC, Lignier, PONSOT, REMY, ROUSSEAU.

Clos du Roi Burg r ★★★ Part of GRAND CRU CORTON. Also a BEAUNE PREMIER CRU.

Clos Rougeard Lo r (sw) Controversial SAUMUR-CHAMPIGNY with cult following. Intense wines that age in new (or nearly new) Bordeaux barrels. Also tiny amount of luscious COTEAUX DE SAUMUR.

Clos St-Denis Burg r★★★ **78 79 82**85' **87** 88 **89'** 90' 91 **92** 93' 94 95 96 16-acre GRAND CRU at MOREY-ST-DENIS. Splendid sturdy wine growing silky with age. Growers incl DUJAC, Lignier, PONSOT.

Clos Ste-Hune Al w★★★★ V fine austere RIES from TRIMBACH; perhaps ALSACE'S best. Needs 5+ yrs age; doesn't need GRAND CRU status.

Clos St-Jacques Burg r ★★★78' **82 83**85' **86 87** 88 **89'** 90' 91 **92** 93' 94 95 96 17-acre GEVREY-CHAMBERTIN PREMIER CRU. Excellent powerful velvety long-ager, often better (and dearer) than some GRANDS CRUS esp by Esmonin and ROUSSEAU.

Clos St-Jean Burg r★★★ **78 85'** 88**89' 90'** 91 **92** 93 **94** 95 96 36-acre PREMIER CRU of CHASSAGNE-M'RACHET. Vg red, more solid than subtle, from eg Ch de la Maltroye. NB Domaine RAMONET.

Clos de Tart Burg r ★★★85' **87** 88'**89' 90' 92** 93 94 95 96 GRAND CRU at MOREY-ST-DENIS, owned by MOMMESSIN. At best wonderfully fragrant, young or old.

Clos de Vougeot Burg r ★★★78 85' **87** 88**89' 90' 91**92 93 94 95 96 124-acre COTE DE NUITS GRAND CRU with many owners. Variable, occasionally sublime. Maturity depends on the grower's philosophy, technique and position on hill. Top growers incl CLAIR-DAU, DROUHIN, ENGEL, FAIVELEY, GRIVOT, GROS, Hudelot-Noëllat, JADOT, LEROY, Chantal Lescure, MEO-CAMUZET, Mugneret, ROUMIER.

Coche-Dury 21-acre MEURSAULT domaine (and 1 acre+ of CORTON-CHARLEMAGNE) with high reputation for oak-perfumed wines. Also vg ALIGOTE.

Cognac Town and region of the Charentes, W France, and its brandy.

Collines Rhodaniennes S Rh r w p ★ Popular Rhône VIN DE PAYS. Mainly reds: Merlot, SYRAH, GAMAY. Some Viognier and CHARD in white.

Collioure Pyr r★★ **85 86 88**89 90 91 92 93 94 95' 96 Strong dry red from BANYULS area. Tiny production. Top growers incl Cellier des Templiers, Les CLOS de Paulilles, Cave L'Etoile, Doms du Mas Blanc, de la Rectorie, La Tour Vieille, Vial-Magnères.

Comté Tolosan SW r p w ★→★★ DYA Covers multitude of sins and whole of southwest. Mostly coop wines. Dom de Ribonnet (Christian Gerber, S of Toulouse) for range of varietal wines, reds **90** and earlier.

Condrieu N Rh w ★★★★ DYA Soft fragrant white of great character (and price) from VIOGNIER. Can be outstanding but rapid growth of v'yd (now 250 acres worked by 90 growers) has made quality outside few top names variable. Increased use of young oak (eg GUIGAL'S Doriane CUVEE and Cuilleron) is a doubtful move. Best growers: Y Cuilleron, DELAS, GUIGAL, André Perret, Niéro-Pinchon, Vernay (esp Coteau de Vernon), Villard. CHATEAU-GRILLET: similar. Don't try ageing it.

Corbières Midi r (p w)★★→★★★ **88 89 90**91 92**93 94 95'** 96 Vigorous bargain red wines. Best growers incl Ch'x Aiguilloux, Lastours, des Ollieux, Les Palais, de la Voulte Gasparet, Doms de Fontsainte, du Vieux Parc, de Villemajou, and coops de Embrès et Castelmaure, Camplong, St-Laurent-Cabrerisse etc.

Cordier, Ets D Important BORDEAUX shipper and château-owner with wonderful track-record, now owned by Groupe Suez. Over 600 acres. Incl Ch'x CANTEMERLE, CLOS DES JACOBINS, GRUAUD-LAROSE, LAFAURIE-PEYRAGUEY, MEYNEY etc.

Cornas N Rh r ★★→★★★ **78' 79 80 81 83' 85' 86 88 89' 90'** 91' 93 94' 95' 96 Sturdy v dark SYRAH wine from 215-acre steep granite v'yds S of HERMITAGE. Needs to age 5–15 yrs. Top: Allemand, de Barjac, Colombo (beware: new oak), Clape, Courbis, DELAS, Juge, Lionnet, JABOULET (esp St-Pierre CUVEE) N Verset.

Corrèze Dordogne r ★ DYA VDP from Coop de Branceilles, between Brive and Beaulieu. Also Dom de la Mégénie.

Corsica (Corse) Strong wines of all colours. ACS are: AJACCIO, CAP CORSE, PATRIMONIO and better crus Cap Corse and Sartène. VIN DE PAYS: ILE DE BEAUTE.

Corton Burg r ★★★→★★★★ **78' 85' 87** 88 **89'** 90' 91 92 93 94 95 96 The only GRAND CRU red of the COTE DE BEAUNE. 200 acres in ALOXE-C incl CLOS DU ROI, Les Bressandes. Rich and powerful, should age well. Many good growers.

Corton-Charlemagne Burg w ★★★★ **78' 79 82 83 85' 86' 87 88 89'** 90' **91** 92 93 94 95 96 The white section (one third) of CORTON. Rich spicy lingering and ages magnificently. Top growers: BONNEAU DU MARTRAY, Chapuis, COCHE-DURY, Delarche, Dubreuil-Fontaine, FAIVELEY, HOSPICES DE BEAUNE, JADOT, LATOUR, Rapet.

Costières de Nîmes S Rh r p w ★→★★ DYA Large new AC of improving quality from Rhône delta. Formerly Costières du Gard. NB Ch'x de Campuget, Mourgues du Gres, de Nages, de la Tuilerie, Mas des Bressades.

> **Côte(s)**
> **Means hillside; generally a superior v'yd to those on the plain. Many ACs are prefixed by 'Côtes' or 'Coteaux', meaning the same. In St-Emilion distinguishes valley slopes from higher plateau.**

Côte de Beaune Burg r w ★★→★★★★ Used geographically: the southern half of the COTE D'OR. Applies as an AC only to parts of BEAUNE itself.

Côte de Beaune-Villages Burg r w ★★ **85 88 89' 90' 91 92** 93 94 95 96 Regional APPELLATION for secondary wines of classic area. Cannot be labelled 'Côte de Beaune' without either '-Villages' or village name appended.

Côte de Brouilly Beauj r ★★ **91 93 94 95 96** Fruity rich vigorous BEAUJOLAIS CRU. One of best. Esp from: Dom de Chavanne, G Cotton, Ch Delachanel, J-C Nesme, Ch Thivin.

Côte Chalonnaise Burg r w sp ★★ V'yd area between BEAUNE and MACON. See also Givry, Mercurey, Montagny, Rully. Alias 'Région de Mercurey'.

Côte de Nuits Burg r (w) ★★→★★★★ N half of COTE D'OR. Mostly red wine.

Côte de Nuits-Villages Burg r (w) ★★ **88 89 90 91 92** 93 94 95 96 A junior AC for extreme N and S ends of Côte; well worth investigating for bargains.

Côte d'Or Département name applied to the central and principal Burgundy v'yd slopes: COTE DE BEAUNE and COTE DE NUITS. The name is not used on labels.

Côte Roannaise Central France r p ★→★★ DYA Recent ('94) AC west of Lyon. Silky, focussed GAMAY. Demon, Lapandéry, Dom du Pavillon.

Côte Rôtie N Rh r ★★★→★★★★ **78 79 80 82 83' 85' 86 87 88' 89' 90'** 91' 94' 95' 96 Potentially finest Rhône red, from S of Vienne, mainly SYRAH; can achieve rich, complex softness and finesse with age (esp 5 to 10+ years). Top growers incl Barge, Bernard, Burgaud, Champet, CHAPOUTIER, Clusel-Roch (improving fast), DELAS, J-M Gérin, GUIGAL (long oak-ageing, different and fuller), JABOULET, Jamet, Jasmin, Ogier, ROSTAING (elegant, cask-influenced), VIDAL-FLEURY.

Coteaux d'Affreux Aspiring to VDP status. Should perhaps use grapes as base.

Coteaux d'Aix-en-Provence Prov r p w ★→★★★ AC on the move. Est'd CH VIGNELAURE now challenged by Ch'x Commanderie de la Bargemone and Fonscolombe. See also Baux-en-Provence.

Coteaux d'Ancenis Lo r p w (sw) ★ DYA VDQS E Of Nantes for light GAMAY reds and rosés, sharpish dry whites from CHENIN, and semi-sweet from Malvoisie (ages well). Esp Guindon (Malvoisie).

Coteaux de l'Ardèche See l'Ardèche.

Coteaux de l'Aubance Lo w sw ★★→★★★ **88' 89' 90' 93'** 94' 95' 96 Similar to COTEAUX DU LAYON, improving sweet wines from CHENIN. A few SELECTION DES GRAINS NOBLES. Esp from Bablut, Montgilet, RICHOU, Rochelles.

Coteaux des Baronnies S Rh r p w ★ Rhône VIN DE PAYS. SYRAH, Merlot, CAB S, CHARD, plus trad grapes. Promising. Dom du Rieu-Frais (incl gd Viognier) and Dom Rosière (incl gd SYRAH) worth noting.

Côteaux de Chalosse SW France r p w ★ DYA. Good country wines from coop at Mugron (Landes).

Coteaux Champenois Champ r w (p) ★★★ DYA (whites) AC for non-sp CHAMP. Vintages (if mentioned) follow those for champ. Not worth inflated prices.

Coteaux du Giennois Lo r p w ★ DYA Sm VDQS N of POUILLY about to become AC. Light GAMAY, PINOT, SAUV à la SANCERRE. Top growers: Balland-Chapuis, Paulat.

Coteaux de Glanes SW France r ★ DYA Lively VDP from nr Bretenoux. Coop only producer.

Coteaux du Languedoc Midi r p w ★★ Scattered well-above-ordinary MIDI AC areas. Best reds (eg CABRIERES, LA CLAPE, FAUGERES, St-Georges-d'Orques, Quatourze, ST-CHINIAN, St-Saturnin) age for 2–4 yrs. Now also some good whites. Standards rising dizzily.

Champagne: a handful of good small houses

Jacques Selosse – in Avize, specializes in Blanc de Blancs
Ployez Jacquemart – excellent NV and vintage, based in Ludes on the Montagne de Reims
Vilmart – in the centre of Rilly-la-Montagne, tiny amounts, high quality
Napoléon – exceptionally fine vintage wines
R & I Legras – Chouilly house with complete range, incl Blanc de Blancs and a Coteaux Champenois
Boizel – Epernay house; champagnes noted for their fruit
Gardet & Cie – rich well-aged wines with high Pinot Noir element
Daniel Dumont – in Rilly-la-Montagne; well-aged Grande Réserve and fine Demi-Sec
Pierre Gimmonet – Cuis; extensive holdings on Côte des Blancs; vinous, subtle Cuvée Gastronome
Larmandier-Bernier – Vertus; top flight Blanc de Blancs wines esp Cramant Grand Cru
Tarlant – Oeuilly; oak-fermented wines incl Krug-like Cuvée Louis

Coteaux du Layon Lo w s/sw sw ★★→★★★★ **75 76 85' 86** 88' 89' 90' 93' 94 95 96 The heart of ANJOU, S of Angers: sw CHENIN with admirable acidity, ageing almost forever, excellent aperitif, or goes with rich creamy main courses or fruit dessert. Introducing new AC SELECTION DES GRAINS NOBLES; cf ALSACE. 7 villages can add name to AC. Top ACS: BONNEZEAUX, C du Layon-Chaume, QUARTS DE CHAUME. Growers incl esp BAUMARD, Cady, Delesvaux, Dom de l'Echalier, des Forges, Ogereau, Papin (Pierre-Bise), Jo Pithon, Robineau, Yves Soulez (Genaiserie), P-Y Tijou (Soucherie).

Coteaux du Loir Lo r p w dr sw ★→★★★ **76 85 88' 89' 90' 92 93'** 95 96 Small region N of Tours, incl JASNIERES. Occasionally fine CHENIN, GAMAY, Pineau d'Aunis, CAB. Top growers: Aubert de Rycke, Fresneau, Gigou. The Loir is a tributary of the Loire.

Coteaux de la Loire See Anjou-Coteaux de la Loire.

Coteaux du Lyonnais Beauj r p (w) ★ DYA Junior BEAUJOLAIS. Best EN PRIMEUR.

Coteaux de Peyriac Midi r p ★ DYA One of the most-used VIN DE PAYS names of the Aude département. Huge quantities.

Coteaux de Pierrevert S Rh r p w sp ★ DYA Minor southern VDQS nr Manosque. Well-made coop wine, mostly rosé, with fresh whites.

Coteaux du Quercy SW France r ★ DYA Area s of Cahors. Good with local cuisine. Private growers work alongside excellent coop near Monpezat.

Coteaux de Saumur Lo w sw ★★→★★★ **89 90 93** 95' 96 Rare potentially fine s/sw CHENIN. VOUVRAY-like sw (MOELLEUX) best. Esp CLOS ROUGEARD, Legrand, Vatan.

Coteaux et Terrasses de Montauban SW France r p ★→★★ Dominated by coop at LAVILLEDIEU-LE-TEMPLE. Also Dom de Montels.

Coteaux du Tricastin S Rh r p w ★★ **88 89 90' 92** 94 95' 96 Fringe COTES DU RHONE of increasing quality. Attractive red can age 8 yrs. Dom de Grangeneuve, Dom de Montine, Dom St-Luc and Ch La Décelle among the best.

Coteaux Varois Prov r p w ★→★★ Substantial new AC zone: California-style Dom de St-Jean de Villecroze makes vg red.

Coteaux du Vendômois Lo r p w ★→★★ DYA Fringe Loire VDQS west of Vendôme. Reds, incl CAB, increasing; CHENIN also important.

Côtes d'Auvergne Central France r p (w) ★→★★ DYA Flourishing small VDQS. Red (at best) a little like BEAUJOLAIS. Mainly GAMAY, but also PINOT NOIR and CHARDONNAY. Boulin-Constant, Bellard, Cave St-Verny.

Côtes de Blaye B'x w ★ DYA Run-of-the-mill BORDEAUX white from BLAYE.

Côtes de Bordeaux St-Macaire B'x w dr sw ★ DYA Everyday BORDEAUX white from E of SAUTERNES.

Côtes de Bourg B'x r ★→★★ **82' 83 85' 86' 88' 89' 90** 92 93 94 95 96 Appellation used for many of the better reds of BOURG. Ch'x incl DE BARBE, La Barde, DU BOUSQUET, Brûlesécaille, La Croix de Millorit, Falfas, Font Guilhem, Grand-Jour, de la Grave, La Grolet, Guerry, Guionne, Haut-Maco, Lalibarde, Lamothe, Mendoce, Peychaud, Rousset, Tayac, de Thau.

Côtes du Brulhois SW France r p (w) ★→★★ Nr Agen. Mostly centred on Goulens and Donzac coops. Also Dom de Coujétou-Peyret.

Côtes de Castillon B'x r ★→★★ **86' 88' 89' 90' 92 93 94** 95 96 Flourishing region just E of ST-EMILION. Similar but lighter wines. Best ch'x incl Beauséjour, La Clarière-Laithwaite, Fonds-Rondes, Haut-Tuquet, Lartigue, Moulin-Rouge, PITRAY, Rocher-Bellevue, Ste-Colombe, Thibaud-Bellevue.

Côtes de Duras Dordogne r w p ★→★★ **90' 92 93 94** 95 96 BORDEAUX satellite; mostly lighter wines. Doms de Laulan (gd Sauv), de Durand, Amblard, Ch'x Lafon et La Grave Béchade are better than Berticot and Landerrouat coops.

Côtes de Forez Lo r p (sp) ★ DYA Uppermost Loire VDQS (GAMAY), around Boën, N of St-Etienne: juicy easy-drinking wines. Esp Vignerons Foreziens.

Côtes de Francs B'x r w ★★ **85 86' 88' 89' 90' 92 93** 94 95 96 Fringe BORDEAUX from E of ST-EMILION. Increasingly attractive tasty wines, esp from Ch'x de Belcier, La Claverie, de Francs, Lauriol, PUYGUERAUD, La Prade.

Côtes du Frontonnais SW France r p ★★ Sometimes called 'Beaujolais of Toulouse'. Mostly DYA, but some reds with CAB need longer. Good growers like Doms de Joliet, Caze, du Roc and Ch'x Bellevue-la-Forêt and Plaisance give the good coop a hard time keeping up.

Côtes de Gascogne SW w (r p) ★ DYA VIN DE PAYS branch of ARMAGNAC. Remarkably popular, led by Plaimont coop and Grassa family. Best-known for fresh, fruity whites based on the Colombard grape, often with some SAUV BL. Also Doms de Papolle, Bergerayre.

Côtes du Jura Jura r p w (sp) ★ DYA Various light tints/tastes. ARBOIS is better.

For key to grape variety abbreviations, see pages 7–13.

Côtes du Lubéron Prov r p w sp ★→★★ **88 89 90 93** 94 95' 96 Spectacularly improved country wines from N PROVENCE. Actors and media-magnates among owners. Stars are CH DE MILLE, CH VAL-JOANIS, with vg largely SYRAH red, and whites as well. Others incl good coop and Ch de la Canorgue.

Côtes de la Malepère Midi r ★ DYA Rising star VDQS on frontier of MIDI and SW, nr Limoux using grape varieties from both. Watch for fresh eager reds.

Côtes du Marmandais Dordogne r p w ★ DYA Light wines. Cocumont coop better than Beaupuy. Ch de Beaulieu and Dom des Geais better still.

Côtes de Montravel Dordogne w dr sw ★ DYA Part of BERGERAC; traditionally med-sw, now often quite dry. Gd from Ch Laroque and Dom de Libarde. Montravel Sec is dry, HAUT MONTRAVEL SW.

Côtes de Provence Prov r p w ★→★★★ Wines of Provence; revolutionized by new attitudes and investment. Dom Bernarde, Castel Roubine, Commanderie de Peyrassol, Dom de la Courtade, DOM OTT, Dom des Planes, Dom Rabiéga, Dom Richeaume are leaders. 60% is rosé, 30% red. See also Coteaux d'Aix, Côtes de Lubéron, Bandol etc.

Côtes du Rhône S Rh r p w ★→★★ **90' 93 94 95'** 96 Basic AC of the Rhône Valley. Best drunk young – even as PRIMEUR. Wide variations of quality due to grape ripeness: tending to rise with alcohol %. See Côtes du Rhône-Villages.

> **Top Côtes du Rhône producers:** Ch'x La Courançonne, l'Estagnol, Fonsalette, Montfaucon, St-Esteve and Trignon (incl Viognier white); CLOS Simian; Coops Chantecotes (Ste-Cécile-les-Vignes), Villedieu (esp white); Doms Coudoulet de Beaucastel (red and white), Gramenon (GRENACHE, Viognier), Janasse, Jaume, Réméjeanne, Vieux Chêne; Guigal, Jaboulet.

Côtes du Rhône-Villages S Rh r p w ★→★★ **88 89' 90' 93 94** 95' 96 Wine of the 17 best S Rhône villages. Substantial and, on the whole, reliable. S'times delicious. See Beaumes-de-Venise, Cairanne, Chusclan, Laudun, Rasteau, Sablet, Séguret, St-Gervais etc. Sub-category with non-specified village name: gd value eg Doms Cabotte, Montbayon, Rabasse-Charavin, Renjarde.

Côtes du Roussillon Pyr r p w ★→★★ **88 89 90 91 93 94** 95 96 E Pyrenees AC. Hefty CARIGNAN r best, can be v tasty (eg Gauby). Some w: sharp VINS VERTS.

Côtes du Roussillon-Villages Pyr r ★★→★★★ **86 88 89 90 91 92 93 94** 95 96 The region's best reds, from 28 communes including CARAMANY, LATOUR DE FRANCE, LESQUERDE. Best labels are Coop Baixas, Cazes Frères, Dom des Chênes, Gauby (incl full, exotic white), Château de Jau, Coop Lesquerde, Dom Piquemal, Coop Les Vignerons Catalans. Some now choose to renounce AC status and make varietal VINS DE PAYS.

Côtes de St-Mont SW France r w p ★★ Promising Gers VDQS. seeking AC status, imitating MADIRAN and PACHERENC. Coop Plaimont all-powerful (Hauts de Bergelle range and Ch de Sabazan). Private growers incl Ch de Bergalasse.

Côtes du Tarn SW France r p w ★ DYA overlaps GAILLAC; from same growers esp coops.

Côtes de Thongue Midi r w ★ DYA Popular VIN DE PAYS from the HERAULT. Some gd wines especially from Doms Arjolle, COUSSERGUES, Croix Belle, Montmarin.

Côtes de Toul E France p r w ★ DYA Very light VDQS wines from Lorraine; mainly VIN GRIS (rosé).

Côtes du Ventoux S Rh r p (w) ★★ **90' 93 94** 95 96 Booming (15,000-acre) AC between the Rhône and PROVENCE for tasty reds (from café-style to much deeper flavours) and easy rosés. La Vieille Ferme, owned by J-P Perrin of CH DE BEAUCASTEL, is top producer; Coop Villes-St-Auzon, Domaine Anges, Ch'x Pesquié and Valcombe and PAUL JABOULET are good too.

Côtes du Vivarais S Rh r p w ★ DYA Ardèche VDQS. 2,500 acres across several villages on W bank S of ST-PERAY. Improving, more substantial reds. Best producers: Boulle, Gallety, Dom de Belvezet.

Coulée de Serrant Lo w dr sw ★★★★ **73 76' 78 79' 81 82 83' 85' 86** 88 **89'** 90' 91 **92** 93 95' 96 16-acre CHENIN v'yd on Loire's N bank at SAVENNIERES run on ferociously organic principles. Intense strong fruity/sharp wine, good aperitif and with fish. Ages almost for ever.

Couly-Dutheil Lo r p w ★★ Largest grower and merchant in CHINON; range of reliable wines – CLOS d'Olive and l'Echo are top wines.

Coussergues, Domaine de Midi r w p ★ DYA Large estate in formerly notorious territory nr Beziers. CHARD, SYRAH etc are bargains.

Crémant In CHAMP means 'creaming' (half-sparkling). Since '75 an AC for quality classic-method sparkling from ALSACE, Loire, BOURGOGNE and most recently LIMOUX – often a bargain. Term phasing out in Champ.

Crémant de Loire w sp ★★→★★★ NV High-quality sparkling wine from ANJOU, especially SAUMUR and TOURAINE. Esp BAUMARD Berger, Delhumeau, LANGLOIS-CHATEAU, Nerleux, OISLY ET THESEE, Passavant.

Crépy Savoie w ★★ DYA Light soft Swiss-style white from S shore of Lake Geneva. 'Crépitant' has been coined for its faint fizz.

Criots-Bâtard-Montrachet Burg w ★★★ **78' 79 85 86 88 89 90 91** 92 **93** 94 95 96 4-acre neighbour to BATARD-M. Similar wine without extreme pungency.

Crozes-Hermitage N Rh r (w) ★★ **85' 86 88 89 90' 91' 92** 94 95 96 Nr HERMITAGE: larger v'yds, SYRAH wine with fewer dimensions. Some is fruity, early-drinking (drink at 2+ yrs); some cask-aged (wait 5–8 yrs). Good examples from Belle, Ch Curson, Dom du Colombier, Combier, Desmeure, Dom des Entrefaux, CHAPOUTIER, Fayolle et Fils, Alain Graillot, Dom du Pavillon, Dom de Thalabert of JABOULET. Jaboulet's Mule Blanche is good white.

Cruse et Fils Frères Senior BORDEAUX shipper. Now owned by Pernod-Ricard. The Cruse family (not the company) owns CH D'ISSAN.

Cunac SW France ★ r DYA Part of GAILLAC area. Light fruity quaffable reds for summer drinking.

Cussac Village S of ST-JULIEN. (AC HAUT-MEDOC.) Top ch'x: BEAUMONT, LANESSAN.

Cuve Close Short-cut method of making sparkling wine in a tank. Sparkle dies away in glass much quicker than with METHODE TRADITIONELLE wine.

Cuvée Wine contained in a cuve or vat. A word of many uses, including synonym for 'blend' and first-press wines (as in CHAMP); in Burgundy interchangeable with 'CRU'. Often just refers to a 'lot' of wine.

Dagueneau, Didier ★★★→★★★★ Top POUILLY-FUME producer. Pouilly's enfant terrible has created new benchmarks for the AC and for SAUV. Top cuvée is barrel-fermented Silex. Serge D, another top producer, is Didier's uncle.

Daumas Gassac See Mas de Daumas Gassac.

De Castellane Brut NV; Brut **85 89 90**; Cuvée Royale **82 88 89**; Prestige Florens de Castellane **82 86 88**; Cuvée Commodore Brut **85 88 89** Long-est'd Epernay CHAMP house, part-owned by LAURENT-PERRIER. Gd rather light wines.

De Luze, A & Fils BORDEAUX shipper owned by Rémy-Martin of COGNAC.

Degré alcoolique Degrees of alcohol, ie percent by volume.

Deiss, Domaine Marcel Fine ALSACE grower at Bergheim with 50 acres, wide range incl splendid RIES (GRAND CRU Schoenenberg), GEWURZ (Altenburg at Bergheim), good SELECTION DES GRAINS NOBLES and VIN DE PAILLE.

Delamotte Brut; Bl de Blancs (**90**); Cuvée Nicolas Delamotte Fine small CHARD-dominated CHAMP house at Le Mesnil, owned by LAURENT-PERRIER.

Delas Frères Old and worthy firm of Rhône wine specialists with vineyards at CONDRIEU, COTE ROTIE, HERMITAGE. Top wines: Condrieu, Marquise de Tourette Hermitage (red and white). Owned by ROEDERER.

Delbeck Small fine CHAMP house reborn '91. Plenty of PINOT N in blend. Excellent vintage wines (**85**).

Delorme, André Leading COTE CHALONNAISE merchants and growers. Specialists in CREMANT DE BOURGOGNE and excellent RULLY etc.

Demi-Sec Half-dry: in practice more than half sweet. (Eg of CHAMP.)

Deutz Deutz Brut Classic NV; Rosé NV; Brut **79 81 82 85 88 90**; Rosé **85 88**; Bl de Bls **81 82 85 88 89 90** One of top sm CHAMP houses, bought in '95 by ROEDERER. Flavoursome wines. Luxury brands: Cuvée William Deutz (**79 82 85 88**), Rosé (**85**). V successful branches in California, NZ. Also Sekt in Germany.

Dirler, Jean-Pierre ALSACE producer of GRAND CRUS Kessler, Saering and Spiegel; esp for RIES.

Dom Pérignon, Cuvée 71 73 75' 76' 78 82' 83 85' 88 90; Rosé **78 82 85 88** Luxury CUVEE of MOET & CHANDON (launched 1936), named after the legendary abbey cellarmaster who first blended (still) CHAMP. Astonishing consistent quality and character, esp with 10–15 yrs bottle-age.

Domaine Property, particularly in Burgundy and the south.

Dopff & Irion Another excellent Riquewihr (ALSACE) business. Esp MUSCAT les Amandiers, RIES Les Murailles, GEWURZ Les Sorcières, PINOT GR Les Maquisards: long-lived. Good CREMANT d'Alsace.

Dopff au Moulin Ancient top-class family wine house at Riquewihr, ALSACE. Best: GEWURZ: GRAND CRUS BRAND and Sporen, RIES SCHOENENBOURG, Sylvaner de Riquewihr. Pioneers of Alsace sp wine; good cuvées: Bartholdi and Julien.

Doudet-Naudin SAVIGNY merchant and grower. V'yds incl BEAUNE-CLOS DU ROI, Redrescul. Dark long-lived wines, supplied to Berry Bros & Rudd of London, eventually come good. Lighter style recently.

Dourthe Frères B'X merchant with wide range: good CRUS BOURGEOIS, incl BELGRAVE, MAUCAILLOU, TRONQUOY-LALANDE. Beau-Mayne is well-made brand.

Doux Sweet.

Drappier, André Leading Aube region CHAMP house, esp for Bl de Noirs. Family-run. Tasty crisp NV, Brut Zéro Signature Bl de Bl **88**, Grande Sendrée (rosé) **83 89**.

DRC See Romanée-Conti, Domaine de la.

Drouhin, J & Cie Deservedly prestigious burgundy grower (150 acres) and merchant with highest standards. Cellars in BEAUNE; v'yds in Beaune, CHABLIS, CLOS DE VOUGEOT, MUSIGNY, etc, and Oregon, USA. Top wines incl (esp) BEAUNE-CLOS DES MOUCHES, CHABLIS LES CLOS, CORTON-CHARLEMAGNE, GRIOTTE-CHAMBERTIN, PULIGNY-M'RACHET-Les Folatières. Majority share now held by Tokyo co.

Duboeuf, Georges The Grand Fromage of BEAUJOLAIS. Top-class merchant at Romanèche-Thorin. Leader of the region in every sense, with a huge range of admirable wines. Also MOULIN-A-VENT untypically aged in new oak, and white MACONNAIS, etc.

Dubos High-level BORDEAUX NEGOCIANT.

Duclot BORDEAUX NEGOCIANT; top-growth specialist. Linked with J-P MOUEIX.

Dujac, Domaine Burgundy grower (Jacques Seysses) at MOREY-ST-DENIS with vineyards in that village and BONNES-MARES, ECHEZEAUX, GEVREY-CHAMBERTIN etc. Splendidly vivid and long-lived wines. Now also buying grapes in MEURSAULT, and new venture with CAB in COTEAUX VAROIS.

Dulong Highly competent BORDEAUX merchant. Breaking all the rules with unorthodox Rebelle blends. Also VIN DE PAYS.

Durup, Jean One of the biggest CHABLIS growers with 375 acres, including Domaine de l'Eglantière and admirable Ch de Maligny.

Duval-Leroy Coteaux Champ r w; Brut; Bl de Blancs Brut **90**; Fleur de Champagne Brut NV and Rosé NV; Cuvée des Rois Rosé NV; Fleur de C Brut **88**; Cuvée des Rois Brut **86**. Large progressive Vertus house; v high standards.

FRANCE

Echezeaux Burg r ★★★ **78' 82** 85' **87** 88 **89'** 90' 91 92 93 94 95 96 74-acre GRAND CRU between VOSNE-ROMANEE and CLOS DE VOUGEOT. Can be superlative, fragrant, without great weight, eg Confuron-Cotetidot, ENGEL, Gouroux, Grivot, A F GROS, MONGEARD-MUGNERET, Mugneret, DRC.

Edelzwicker Alsace w ★ DYA Modest blended light white.

Eguisheim, Cave Vinicole d' Vg ALSACE coop: fine GRAND CRUS Hatschbourg, Hengst, Ollwiller and Spiegel. Owns WILLM. Top label: Wolfberger (65% of production). Best ranges: Grande Réserve and Sigillé. Good CREMANT and PINOT.

Eichberg Eguisheim (ALSACE) GRAND CRU. Another warm patch, with the lowest rainfall in Colmar area: good for vg KUENTZ-BAS VENDANGE TARDIVE.

Engel, R Top-class grower of CL DE VOUGEOT, ECHEZEAUX, GRANDS-ECH'X, VOSNE-ROM.

Entraygues SW p w DYA ★ Fragrant, bone-dry country VDQS. Esp F Avallon's.

Entre-Deux-Mers B'x w ★→★★ DYA Improving standard dry white BORDEAUX from between the Rivers Garonne and Dordogne (aka E-2-M). Often a good buy as techniques improve. Esp Ch'x BONNET, Gournin, Latour-Laguens, Moulin de Launay, Séguin, Thieuley, Turcaud etc.

Estaing SW r p w ★ DYA Neighbour of ENTRAYGUES and similar in style.

L'Estandon The everyday wine of Nice (AC COTES DE PROVENCE) in all colours.

l'Etoile Jura w dr sp (sw) ★★ Subregion of the Jura known for stylish whites, incl VIN JAUNE, similar to CHATEAU-CHALON; good sparkling.

Faiveley, J Family-owned growers and merchants at NUITS-ST-GEORGES, with v'yds (270 acres) in CHAMBERTIN-CLOS DE BEZE, CHAMBOLLE-MUSIGNY, CORTON, MERCUREY, NUITS (74 acres). Consistent high quality rather than charm.

Faller, Théo Top ALSACE grower at Domaine Weinbach, Kaysersberg. Makes concentrated firm dry wines needing unusually long ageing, up to 10 yrs. Esp GRAND CRUS SCHLOSSBERG (RIES), Kirchberg de Ribeauvillé (GEWURZ).

Faugères Midi r (p w) ★★★ **88 89 90 91** 92 93 94 95 96 Isolated COTEAUX DU LANGUEDOC village with above-average wine and exceptional terroir. Gained AC status '82. Esp Dom Alquier, Dom des Estanilles, Ch La Liquière.

Fessy, Sylvain Dynamic BEAUJOLAIS merchant with wide range.

Fèvre, William Excellent CHABLIS grower with the biggest GRAND CRU holding (40 acres). But spoils some of his top wines with new oak. One whimsy wine he calls Napa Vallée de France. His label is Dom de la Maladière.

Fiefs Vendéens Lo r p w ★ DYA Up-and-coming VDQS for light wines from the Vendée, just S of MUSCADET on the Atlantic coast. Wines from CHARD, CHENIN, Colombard, Grolleau, Melon (whites), CAB, PINOT N and GAMAY for reds and rosés. Esp Coirier, Ferme des Ardillers.

Filliatreau, Domaine Lo r ★★→★★★ Paul Filliatreau put SAUMUR-CHAMPIGNY on map and in Paris restaurants. Supple, fruity drinkable Jeunes Vignes. Other cuvées aged 2 to 5 years (Vieille Vignes and La Grande Vignolle).

Fitou Midi r ★★ **85 86** 88 **89** 90 91 92 93 94 95 96 Superior CORBIERES-style red wines; powerful, ageing well. Best from coops at Cascastel, Paziols and Tuchan. Interesting experiments with Mourvèdre grapes in Leucate.

Fixin Burg r ★★ **78' 85'** 88' **89'** 90' **91 92** 93 94 95 96 Worthy and under-valued northern neighbour of GEVREY-CHAMBERTIN. Often splendid reds. Best v'yds: CLOS du Chapitre, Les Hervelets, CLOS Napoléon. Growers incl Bertheau, R Bouvrier, CLAIR, FAIVELEY, Gelin, Gelin-Molin, Guyard.

Fleurie Beauj r ★★★ **90** 91 **92 93** 94 95 **96** The epitome of a BEAUJOLAIS CRU: fruity, scented, silky, racy wines. Esp from Chapelle des Bois, Chignard, Depardon, Després, DUBOEUF, Ch de Fleurie, the coop.

Floc de Gascogne r p w ARMAGNAC'S answer to PINEAU DES CHARENTES. Unfermented grape juice blended with Armagnac.

Fortant de France Midi r p w ★→★★ VDP D'OC brand (dressed to kill) of remarkable quality single-grape wines from Sète neighbourhood. See Skalli.

Frais Fresh or cool.
Frappé Ice-cold.
Froid Cold.
Fronsac B'x r ★→★★★ **82 83 85' 86' 88' 89' 90' 92** 93 94 95 96 Picturesque area of increasingly fine tannic reds just W of ST-EMILION. Ch'x incl de Carles, DALEM, LA DAUPHINE, Fontenil, Mayne-Vieil, Moulin-Haut-Laroque, LA RIVIERE, La Rousselle, La Valade, La Vieille Cure, Villars. Give them time. See also smaller Canon-Fronsac.
Frontignan Midi br sw ★→★★ NV Strong sweet liquorous MUSCAT of ancient repute. Best growers: Ch'x Stony and La Peyrade.
Gagnard-Delagrange, Jacques Estimable small (13-acre) grower of CHASSAGNE-M'RACHET, including some M'RACHET. Look out also for his daughter's estate, Blain-Gagnard and Fontaine-Gagnard.
Gaillac SW France r p w dr sw sp ★→★★(★) mostly DYA except oaked reds (94 95). White slightly fizzy 'perlé' (Dom de Salmes and coops at Labastide and Rabastens) and fully sp sw and dr local specialities (Robert Plageoles). Red primeurs often beat Beaujolais for medals (vg Dom. de Labarthe). Sw 95 whites excellent (Ch de Mayragues and Doms de Long Pech and Bicary). Good all-rounders: Dom de Labarthe, Mas Pignou, Mas d'Aurel, above coops and Cave Técou (best of the three, esp 'Passion' range).
Gamay See Grapes for red wine (pages 11–13).
Gard, Vin de Pays du The Gard département at the mouth of the Rhône is a centre of gd VINS DE PAYS production. These incl Coteaux Flaviens, Pont du Gard, SABLES DU GOLFE DU LION, Salaves, Uzège and Vaunage. To follow, eg Dom de Baruel (incl SYRAH).
Geisweiler et Fils Big Burgundy merchant and grower. Now owned by the Rehs of the Mosel. Cellars and 50 acres at NUITS-ST-GEORGES, also 150 acres at Bevy in HAUTES-COTES DE NUITS and 30 in the COTE CHALONNAISE.
Gers r w p ★ DYA Indistinguishable from adjoining COTES DE GASCOGNE.
Gevrey-Chambertin Burg r ★★★ **78 85' 87** 88 **89'** 90' 91 **92** 93 94 95 96 The village containing the great CHAMBERTIN and its GRAND CRU cousins and many other noble v'yds (eg PREMIERS CRUS Cazetiers, Combe aux Moines, CLOS ST-JACQUES, CLOS des Varoilles), as well as much more commonplace land. Growers incl Boillot, Damoy, DROUHIN, Dugat, Esmonin, FAIVELEY, Dom Harmand-Geoffroy, JADOT, LECLERC, LEROY, MORTET, ROTY, ROUMIER, ROUSSEAU, Serafin, TRAPET, VAROILLES.
Gewürztraminer Speciality grape of ALSACE: one of 4 allowed for specified GRAND CRU wines. The most aromatic of Alsace grapes: spicy or floral on nose, grapefruit or lychees on palate.
Gigondas S Rh r p ★★→★★★ **78 79 81' 83 85 86 88 89' 90'** 93 94 95' 96 Worthy neighbour to CHATEAUNEUF-DU-PAPE. Strong, full-bodied, sometimes peppery wine, largely GRENACHE; eg Ch de Montmirail, Dom du Cayron, Les Font-Sane, Goubert, Gour de Chaule, Grapillon d'Or, Les Pallieroudas, Doms du Pesquier, les Pallières, Raspail-Aÿ, Sta-Duc, St-Gayan, des Travers, du Trignon.
Ginestet Long-established B'x négociant now owned by Jacques Merlaut, said to be second in turnover. Merlaut's empire incl Ch'x CHASSE-SPLEEN, HAUT-BAGES-LIBERAL, LA GURGUE, FERRIERE.
Gisselbrecht, Louis High-quality ALSACE growers and merchants at Dambach-la-Ville. RIES and GEWURZ best. Cousin Willy Gisselbrecht's wines are v competitive.
Givry Burg r w ★★ **85' 88' 89' 90'** 91 **92** 93 94 95 96 Underrated COTE CHALONNAISE village: light but tasty and typical burgundy from eg DELORME, Dom Joblot, L LATOUR, T Lespinasse, CLOS Salomon, BARON THENARD.
Gorges et Côtes de Millau SW France r p w ★ DYA Locally popular country wines. Reds best. Coop at Aguessac dominant .

FRANCE

Gosset Brut NV; Brut **81 82 83 85 88 90**; Grande Réserve; Grand Millésime Brut **79 82 83 85**; Grand Rosé **85 88** Sm, v old CHAMP house at AY. Excellent full-bodied wine (esp Grand Millésime). Gosset Celebris is prestige CUVEE, launched '95 by quality-conscious new owners, Cointreau family of Frapin-Cognac.

Goulaine, Château de The ceremonial showplace of MUSCADET; a noble family estate and its wine. Adequately good rather than excellent.

Goût Taste, eg goût anglais: as the English like it (ie, dry, or, differently for CHAMP, well-aged).

Grand Cru One of top Burgundy vineyards with its own APPELLATION CONTROLEE. Similar meaning in recent ALSACE law, but more vague elsewhere. In ST-EMILION the third rank of ch'x incl about 200 properties.

Grande Champagne The AC of the best area of COGNAC.

Grande Rue, La Burg r ★★★ **89' 90'** 91 92 93 94 95 96 Recently promoted GRAND CRU in VOSNE-ROMANEE, neighbour to ROMANEE-CONTI. Owned by Dom Lamarche (itself recently sold).

Grands-Echezeaux Burg r ★★★★ **78' 82 85' 87** 88' **89'** 90' 91' 92 93 94 95 96 Superlative 22-acre GRAND CRU next to CLOS DE VOUGEOT. Wines not weighty but aromatic. Viz: DROUHIN, ENGEL, MONGEARD-MUGNERET, DOM DE LA ROMANEE-CONTI.

Gratien, Alfred and Gratien & Meyer Brut NV; Cuvée Paradis Brut; Cuvée Paradis Rosé; Brut **79 82 83 85' 88** Excellent smaller family CHAMP house with top traditional standards. Fine v dry long-lasting wine is made in barrels. Gratien & Meyer is counterpart at SAUMUR. (Vg Cuvée Flamme.)

Graves B'x r w ★★→★★★★ Region S of B'x city with excellent soft earthy reds, dry whites (SAUV-Sém) reasserting star status. PESSAC-LEOGNAN is inner zone.

Graves de Vayres B'x r w ★ DYA Part of ENTRE-D-M; no special character.

Grenache See grapes for red and white wine (pages 7–13).

Griotte-Chambertin Burg r ★★★★ **78' 85' 87 88' 89'** 90' 91 92 93 94 95 96 14-acre GRAND CRU adjoining CHAMBERTIN. Similar wine, but less masculine, more 'tender'. Growers incl DROUHIN, PONSOT.

Grivot, Jean 31-acre COTE DE NUITS domaine, in 5 ACS incl RICHEBOURG, NUITS PREMIERS CRUS, VOSNE-ROMANEE, CLOS DE VOUGEOT etc. Top-quality.

Gros, Domaines An excellent family of vignerons in VOSNE-ROMANEE comprising (at least) Domaines Jean, Michel, Anne et François, Anne-François Gros and Gros Frère et Soeur. This burgundy is being parcelled out.

Gros Plant du Pays Nantais Lo w ★ DYA Junior VDQS cousin of MUSCADET, sharper, lighter; from the COGNAC grape, aka Folle Blanche, Ugni Bl etc.

Guffens-Heynen Belgian POUILLY-FUISSE grower. Minute quantity, fine quality. Also heady GAMAY and COTE D'OR wine from bought-in grapes under the Verget label. To follow.

Guigal, Ets E Celebrated grower (COTE ROTIE) and merchant of CONDRIEU, Côte Rôtie and HERMITAGE. Since '85 owner of VIDAL-FLEURY. By ageing single-vineyard Côte Rôtie (La Landonne, La Mouline and La Turque) for 42 months in new oak Guigal breaks local tradition to please (esp) American palates. His standard wines are good value, especially the red COTES DU RHONE. Special CONDRIEU CUVEE La Doriane (since '95) – full, oaky.

Guyon, Antonin Considerable domaine at ALOXE-CORTON with adequate wines from CHAMBOLLE-MUSIGNY, CORTON etc, and HAUTES-COTES DE NUITS.

Haut-Poitou Lo w r ★→★★ DYA Up-and-coming VDQS S of ANJOU. Vg whites (CHARD, SAUV, CHENIN) from Cave, now linked with DUBOEUF. Improving reds from GAMAY and CAB, best will age 4–5 yrs. Has rejected restrictions of AC status for freedom of choice.

Haut-Benauge B'x w ★ DYA AC for a limited area in ENTRE-DEUX-MERS.

NB Vintages in colour are those you should choose first for drinking in 1998.

Haut-Médoc B'x r ★★→★★★ **70 75 78 81' 82' 83' 85' 86' 87** 88' 89' **90' 92** 93 94 95 96 Big AC including all the best parts of the MEDOC. Most of the zone has communal ACS (eg MARGAUX, PAUILLAC). Some excellent ch'x (eg LA LAGUNE) are simply AC HAUT-MEDOC.

Haut-Montravel Dordogne w sw ★ **90' 93** 95 96 Rare BERGERAC sweet white; rather like MONBAZILLAC.

Hautes-Côtes de Beaune Burg r w ★★ **85 88 89' 90' 91 92** 93 94 95 96 AC for a dozen villages in the hills behind the COTE DE BEAUNE. Light wines, worth investigating. Top growers: Cornu, Mazilly.

Hautes-Côtes de Nuits Burg r w ★★ **85 88 89' 90' 91 92** 93 94 95 96 As above, for COTE DE NUITS. An area on the way up. Top growers: C Cornu, Jayer-Gilles, M GROS. Also has large BEAUNE coop; good esp from GEISWEILER.

Heidsieck, Charles Brut Réserve NV; Brut **79 81 83 85 89 90**; Rosé **81 83 85** Major Reims CHAMP house, now controlled by Rémy Martin; also incl Trouillard, de Venoge. Luxury brand Bl des Millénaires (**83 85 89**). Fine quality recently; NV a real bargain. See also Piper-Heidsieck.

Heidsieck, Monopole Brut NV Important CHAMP merchant and Reims grower owned by Champ Vranken since '95. Luxury brands of note: Diamant Bleu (**76 79 82 85 89**), Diamant Rosé (**82 85 88**).

Hengst Wintzenheim (ALSACE) GRAND CRU. Excels with top-notch GEWURZ from Albert Mann; also Pinot-Auxerrois, Chasselas (esp JOSMEYER'S) and pinot noir (esp A Mann's) with no GC status.

Henriot Brut Souverain NV; Blanc de Blancs de CHARD NV; Brut **79 82 85 88 89**; Brut Rosé **81 83 85 88**; Luxury Cuvée: Cuvée des Enchanteleurs **85** Old family CHAMP house; regained independence in '94. V fine fresh creamy style. Also owns BOUCHARD PERE (since '95).

Hérault Midi Biggest v'yd département in France: 980,000 acres of vines. Chiefly VIN DE TABLE but some gd AC COTEAUX DU LANGUEDOC and pioneering Vins de Pays de l'Hérault.

Hermitage N Rh r w ★★★→★★★★ **61 66 70 72 78' 79 80 82 83' 84 85 86 87 88** 89' 90' 91' 94 95' 96' By tradition, the 'manliest' wine of France: dark powerful and profound. Truest example of the SYRAH grape from 312 hillside acres on E bank of Rhône, largely granite. Needs long ageing. White (Marsanne, some Roussanne) is heady and golden; now usually made for early drinking, though best wines mature for up to 25 yrs; can be better than red (eg 93).Top makers: CHAPOUTIER, CHAVE, DELAS, Faurie, Grippat, GUIGAL, JABOULET, Sorrel. TAIN coop also useful.

Hospices de Beaune Historic hospital and charitable institution in BEAUNE, with excellent v'yds (known by 'CUVEE' names) in BEAUNE, CORTON, MEURSAULT, POMMARD, VOLNAY. Wines are auctioned on the third Sunday of each November.

Huet **47' 59' 76' 85' 88'** 89' **90'** 93 95' 96 Leading top-quality estate in VOUVRAY, run on biodynamic principles. Often austere wines need long ageing.

Hugel et Fils The best-known ALSACE growers and merchants; founded at Riquewihr in 1639 and still in the family. 'Johnny' H (ret'd '94) is the region's beloved spokesman. Quality escalates with Cuvée Tradition and then Jubilée Réserve ranges. SELECTIONS DES GRAINS NOBLES: Hugel pioneered this style in Alsace and still makes some of finest examples. Also occasionally VIN DE PAILLE.

Hureau, Ch de ★★→★★★ Dynamic SAUMUR estate: quality SAUMUR-CHAMPIGNY, Saumur Blanc, COTEAUX DE SAUMUR.

Ile de Beauté Name given to VINS DE PAYS from CORSICA. Mostly red.

Impériale BORDEAUX bottle holding 8.5 normal bottles (6.4 litres).

Irancy ('Bourgogne Irancy') Burg r (p) ★★ **85 88 89 90 91 92 93** 94 95 96 Good light red made nr CHABLIS from PINOT N and the local César. The best vintages are long-lived and mature well. To watch. Growers incl Colinot.

Irouléguy SW France r p (w) ★★ DYA Agreeable local wines of the Basque country. Mainly rosé; also dark dense Tannat/CAB reds to keep 5 yrs+. Gd from Doms Ilarria, Brana, Peio Espil, Riouspeyrous and coop. A future MADIRAN?

Jaboulet Aîné, Paul Old family firm at Tain, leading grower of HERMITAGE (esp La Chapelle ★★★★), Crozes Thalabert (vg value) and merchant of other Rhône wines – esp CORNAS, COTES DU RHONE Parallèle 45.

Jacquart Brut NV, Brut Rosé NV (Carte Blanche and Cuvée Spéciale); Brut **85 89 90** Relatively new ('62) coop-based CHAMP marque; in quantity the sixth-largest. Fair quality. Luxury brands: Cuvée Nominée Blanc **85**, CN Rosé **85**. Vg Mosaïque Bl de Blancs **90**, Mosaïque Rosé **90**.

Jacquesson Sm excellent Dizy CHAMP house. Superb vintage Bl de Blancs (**90**); exquisite barrel-fermented Signature luxury CUVEES: both w (**88**) and rosé (**89**).

Jadot, Louis Much-respected top-quality burgundy merchant house with v'yds (150 acres) in BEAUNE, CORTON etc. Incl former Clair-Dau. Wines to bank on.

Jaffelin Independent quality NEGOCIANT, bought in '92 from DROUHIN by BOISSET.

Jardin de la France Lo w r p DYA One of France's four regional VINS DE PAYS. Covers Loire Valley: mostly single grape (esp CHARD, GAMAY, SAUV). Top Vin de Pays de zone: Marches de Bretagne.

Jasnières Lo w dr (sw) ★★★ **76 78 79 83 85 86 88' 89' 90' 92** 93' 95' 96 Rare and almost immortal dry VOUVRAY-like wine (CHENIN) of N TOURAINE. Esp Aubert de Rycke, Boulay, Gigou.

Jayer, Henri See Rouget, Emmanuel.

Jeroboam In BORDEAUX a 6-bottle bottle (holding 4.5 litres) or triple magnum; in CHAMP a double magnum.

Joseph Perrier Cuvée Royale Brut NV; Cuvée Royale Bl de Blancs NV; Cuvée Royale Rosé NV; Brut **76 79 82 83 85 89** Family-run CHAMP house with considerable v'yds at Châlons-en-Champagne. Vinous fruity style, best in great prestige Cuvée Joséphine **82 85**.

JosMeyer Family house at Wintzenheim, ALSACE. Vg long-ageing wines, esp GEWURZ and Pinot Bl. Fine RIES from Hengst GRAND CRU. Wide range of grape varieties, labels and locations.

Juliénas Beauj r ★★★ **93 94 95** 96 Leading CRU of BEAUJOLAIS: vigorous fruity wine to keep 2–3 yrs. Growers incl Ch'x du Bois de la Salle, des Capitans, de Juliénas, des Vignes; Dom Bottière, Dom R Monnet, coop.

Jura See Côtes de Jura.

Jurançon SW France w sw dr ★★→★★★ **78 82 83 85' 86 88' 89'** 90' 91 93 94 95' 96 Rare high-flavoured long-lived speciality of Pau in Pyrenean foothills, at best like wildflower SAUTERNES. Not to be missed. Both sw and dr should age. Top growers: Dom du Bellegarde, Barrère, Dom Cauhapé, Gaillot, Guirouilh, Lamouroux, Lapeyre, Larredya, de Rousse, Jean Schaetzel. Also coop's dry Grain Sauvage, Brut d'Ocean and Peyre d'Or.

Kaefferkopf Alsace w dr sw ★★★ Ammerschwihr v'yd famous for blends rather than single-variety wines and denied GRAND CRU status for this reason.

Kientzheim-Kayserberg, Cave Vinicole de Important ALSACE coop for quality as well as style. Esp GEWURZ, RIES GRAND CRU Schlossberg and CREMANT.

Kientzler, André Fine ALSACE RIESLING specialist in Geisburg GRAND CRU, esp the VENDANGE TARDIVE and SELECTION DES GRAINS NOBLES. Equally good from GCs Kirchberg de Ribeauvillé for GEWURZ and Osterberg for occasional 'vins de glaces' (Eisweins). Also makes vg Auxerrois and Chasselas.

Kreydenweiss Fine ALSACE grower: 24 acres at Andlau, esp for PINOT GR (vg GRAND CRU Moenchberg), PINOT BL and RIES. Top wine: Kastelberg (RIES ages 20 yrs+); also fine Auxerrois 'Kritt Klevner' and gd VENDANGE TARDIVE. One of first in Alsace to use new oak. Good RIES-PINOT GR blend 'CLOS du Val d'Eléon'.

Kriter Popular sparkler processed in Burgundy by PATRIARCHE.

Krug Grande Cuvée; Vintage **79 81 82** 85; Rosé; CLOS du Mesnil (Bl de Blancs) **79 80 81 82 83 85**; Krug Collection **62 64 66 69 71 73 76** Small but supremely prestigious CHAMP house. Dense full-bodied v dry wines for long ageing, superlative quality. Owned by Rémy-Cointreau (but no one would know).

Kuentz-Bas Top-quality ALSACE grower/merchant at Husseren-les-Châteaux, esp for Tokay-PINOT GR, GEWURZ. Also good VENDANGES TARDIVES.

Labouré-Roi Outstandingly reliable merchant at NUITS. Mostly whites. Many fine domaine wines, esp René Manuel's MEURSAULT, Chantal Lescure's Nuits, CLOS DE VOUGEOT. Vg CHABLIS. Also VOLNAY-SANTENOTS.

Ladoix-Serrigny Burg r (w) ★★ Northernmost village of COTE DE BEAUNE below hills of CORTON. To watch for bargains.

A warning to visitors to France

France's retail wine trade is not an example to the world. Do not expect to find either good quality or value. Anyone shopping for wine even close to famous vineyards will find high prices and generally poor-to-awful quality. Most supermarkets buy purely on name and price and épiceries (sometimes the only local wine retailers) only on price. The destiny of fine wines is principally the restaurant trade (where they are outrageously marked-up).

The French buy largely direct from producers. Very many have a cousin whose wine, rightly or wrongly, they believe in. No country has a wine trade more on the ball than Great Britain.

Ladoucette, de ★★→★★★ Leading producer of POUILLY-FUME, based at Ch de Nozet. Luxury brand: Baron de L can be wonderful (but at a price). Also SANCERRE Comte Lafond and La Poussie (and PIC CHABLIS).

Lafarge, Michel 25-acre COTE DE BEAUNE estate with VOLNAYS.

Lafon, Domaine des Comtes 34-acre top burgundy estate in MEURSAULT, LE M'RACHET, VOLNAY. Glorious intense whites; extraordinary dark reds.

Laguiche, Marquis de Largest owner of LE M'RACHET. Magnificent wines made by DROUHIN.

Lalande de Pomerol B'x r ★★ **82 85 86' 88' 89' 90' 92 93** 94 95 96 Neighbour to POMEROL. Wines similar, but less mellow. Top ch'x: Les Annereaux, DE BEL-AIR, Belles-Graves, Bertineau-St-Vincent, La Croix Bellevue, La Croix-St-André, Hauts-Conseillants, Hauts-Tuileries, Moncets, SIAURAC, TOURNEFEUILLE. To try.

Langlois-Château One of top SAUMUR sp house (esp CREMANT). Controlled by BOLLINGER. Also range of Loire still wines, esp Saumur Bl VIEILLES VIGNES.

Lanson Père & Fils Black Label NV; Rosé NV; Brut **88 89 90** Imp't improving CHAMP house with cellars at Reims. Long-lived luxury brand: Noble Cuvée (**81 85** 88). Black Label is reliable fresh (s'times thin) NV. New CUVEE: Bl de Bls **83** 89.

Laroche Important grower (242 acres) and dynamic CHABLIS merchant, incl Domaines La Jouchère and Laroche. Top wines: Blanchots (esp Réserve de l'Obédiencerie ★★★★) and CLOS VIEILLE VIGNES. Also blends good non-regional CHARD and now ambitious MIDI range, Dom La Chevalière.

Latour, Louis Famous burgundy merchant and grower with v'yds (120 acres) in BEAUNE, CORTON, etc. Among the v best for white: CHEVALIER-M'RACHET Les Demoiselles, CORTON-CHARLEMAGNE, M'RACHET, good-value MONTAGNY and ARDECHE CHARD etc. Also PINOT N Valmoissine from the Var.

Latour de France r (w) ★→★★ **88 89 90 91 92 93** 94 95 96 Supposedly superior village in AC COTES DE ROUSSILLON-VILLAGES.

Latricières-Chambertin Burg r ★★★ **78' 83 85'** 88' **89'** 90' 91 92 93 94 95 96 17-acre GRAND CRU neighbour of CHAMBERTIN. Similar wine but lighter and 'prettier' eg from FAIVELEY, LEROY, PONSOT, TRAPET.

Laudun S Rh w r p ★ Village of COTES DU RHONE-VILLAGES (west bank). Attractive wines from the coop incl fresh whites. Dom Pelaquié is best, esp white.

Laurent-Perrier Brut NV; Rosé NV; Brut **78 79 81 82 85 88 90** Dynamic highly successful family-owned CHAMP house at Tours-sur-Marne. Excellent luxury brands: Cuvée Grande Siècle (NV and **85 88**), CGS Alexandra Brut Rosé (**85 88**). Also Ultra Brut. Owns SALON, DELAMOTTE, DE CASTELLANE.

Lavilledieu-du-Temple SW France r p w ★ DYA Fruity wines from coop nr Montauban. Also produces VDP from COTEAUX DU QUERCY, COTEAUX ET TERRACES DE MONTAUBAN.

Leflaive, Domaine Sometimes considered the best of all white burgundy growers, at PULIGNY-M'RACHET. Best v'yds: Bienvenues- and Chevalier-M'rachet, Clavoillons, Pucelles and (since '91) Le M'rachet. Increasingly organic methods; ever-finer wines.

Leflaive, Olivier Négociant at PULIGNY-M'RACHET since '84, nephew of the above, now with 25 acres of his own. Reliable whites and reds, incl less famous ACS, have upgraded seriously since '90. Now ★★★.

Léognan B'x r w ★★★→★★★★ Top village of GRAVES with its own AC: PESSAC-LEOGNAN. Best ch'x: DOM DE CHEVALIER, HAUT-BAILLY, MALARTIC-LAGRAVIERE.

Leroy The ultimate NEGOCIANT-ELEVEUR at AUXEY-DURESSES with a growing domaine and the finest stocks of old wines in Burgundy. Part-owners of DOM DE LA ROMANEE-CONTI. In '88 bought the 35-acre Noëllat estate in CLOS VOUGEOT, NUITS, ROMANEE-ST-VIVANT, SAVIGNY etc. Leroy's whole range (from AUXEY whites to CHAMBERTIN and neighbours) is simply magnificent. ★★★★ all round.

Lesquerde ★★ **90 91** 92 **93 94** 95 96 New superior AC village of COTES DU ROUSSILLON-VILLAGES.

Lichine, Alexis & Cie BORDEAUX merchants (once of the late Alexis Lichine). No connection with CH PRIEURE-LICHINE.

Lie, sur On the lees. MUSCADET is often bottled straight from the vat, for maximum freshness and character.

Limoux Pyr r w ★★ Burgeoning AC, formerly for BLANQUETTE DE LIMOUX sparkling, now good for CREMANT de Limoux, CHARD and PINOT N VDP as well as traditional grapes. Also a gd claret-like red from coop: Anne des Joyeuses.

Liquoreux Term for a very sweet wine: eg SAUTERNES, top VOUVRAY, JURANCON etc.

Lirac S Rh r p w ★★ **89' 90' 91 93** 94 95' 96 Next to TAVEL. Approachable soft red (best needs 5 yrs age). Red is overtaking rosé, esp Doms Cantegril-Verda, Devoy-Martine, Maby (Fermade), André Méjan, de la Mordorée, Sabon, St-Roch, Ch de Ségriès. Gd whites too.

Listel Midi r p w ★→★★ DYA Vast (4,000-acre+) historic estate on sandy beaches of the Golfe du Lion. Owned by giant Salins du Midi salt co and VAL D'ORBIEU group. Pleasant light 'vins des sables' incl sparkling. Dom du Bosquet-Canet is a fruity CAB, Dom de Villeroy fresh BLANC DE BLANCS SUR LIE, and CHARD since '89. Also fruity almost non-alcoholic PETILLANT, Ch de Malijay COTES DU RHONE, Abbaye de Ste-Hilaire COTEAUX VAROIS, Ch La Gordonne COTES DE PROVENCE.

Listrac-Médoc B'x r ★★→★★★ Village of HAUT-MEDOC next to MOULIS. Best ch'x: CLARKE, FONREAUD, FOURCAS-DUPRE, FOURCAS-HOSTEN.

Livinière, La Midi r (p w) ★→★★ High-quality MINERVOIS village. Best growers: Abbaye de Tholomies, Combe Blanche, Ch de Gourgazaud, Laville Bertrou, Doms Maris, Ste-Eulalie, Vallière, Coop La Livinière.

Long-Depaquit Vg CHABLIS domaine (esp MOUTONNE), owned by BICHOT.

Lorentz, Gustave (Sous marque Jerome Lorentz) ALSACE grower and merchant at Bergheim. Esp GEWURZ and RIES from GRAND CRUS Altenberg de Bergheim and Kanzlerberg.

Loron & Fils Big-scale grower and merchant at Pontanevaux; specialist in BEAUJOLAIS and sound VINS DE TABLE.

Loupiac B'x w sw ★★ **76 79' 83 85 86' 88' 89 90 91** 93 95 96 Across River Garonne from SAUTERNES. Top ch'x: CLOS-Jean, Haut-Loupiac, LOUPIAC-GAUDIET, RICAUD, Rondillon.

Lugny See Mâcon-Lugny.

Lussac-St-Emilion B'x r ★★ **82 85 86' 88' 89' 90'** 92 93 94 95 96 NE neighbour to ST-EMILION. Top ch'x incl Barbe Blanche, BEL AIR, DU LYONNAT, Tour de Grenat, Villadière. Coop (at PUISSEGUIN) makes pleasant Roc de Lussac.

Macération carbonique Traditional fermentation technique: whole bunches of unbroken grapes in a closed vat. Fermentation inside each grape eventually bursts it, giving vivid fruity mild wine, not for ageing. Esp in BEAUJOLAIS; now much used in the MIDI and elsewhere, even CHATEAUNEUF DU PAPE.

The Mâconnais

The hilly zone just north of Beaujolais has outcrops of limestone where Chardonnay gives full, if not fine, wines. The village of Chardonnay here may (or may not) be the home of the variety. Granite soils give strong Gamay reds. The top Mâconnais AC is Pouilly-Fuissé, then St-Véran, then Mâcon-Villages with a village name. The potential is here to produce lower-priced, richly typical Chardonnays to out-do the New World (and indeed the south of France). Currently most wines are less than extraordinary.

Mâcon Burg r w (p) ★★ **90' 91 92 93 94** 95 96 Sound, usually unremarkable reds (GAMAY best), tasty dry (CHARD) whites. Almost DYA.

Mâcon-Lugny Burg r w sp ★★ **90 91 92 93 94** 95 96 Village next to VIRE with huge and vg coop (4M bottles). Les Genevrières is sold by LOUIS LATOUR.

Mâcon-Villages Burg w ★★→★★★ **90 91 92 93 94** 95 96 Increasingly well-made typical white burgundies (when not over-produced). Named for their villages, eg M-CHARDONNAY, -Clessé, -Lugny, -Prissé, -Viré, -Uchizy. Best coop is probably Prissé, biggest Lugny. Top growers: Vincent (Fuissé), Thévenet (Clessé), Bonhomme (Viré), Merlin (La Roche Vineuse).

Mâcon-Viré Burg w ★★ **90 91 92 93 94** 95 96 One of the best white wine villages of MACON. Esp A Bonhomme, CLOS du Chapitre, JADOT, Ch de Viré, coop.

Macvin Jura w sw ★★ AC for 'traditional' MARC and grape juice aperitif.

Madiran SW France r ★★→★★★ **82 85' 86' 88 89' 90'** 92 93 94 95' 96 Dark vigorous red from ARMAGNAC, like hard but fruity MEDOC with a fluid elegance of its own. Need keeping. Ch'x Montus, Bouscassé, Doms. Berthoumieu, Laplace (Ch d'Aydie), Chapelle Lenclos, Labranche-Laffont, Pichard, Laffitte-Teston, Capmartin and coop's Ch Crouseilles. White is AC PACHERENC DU VIC BILH.

Magenta, Duc de Recently revamped Burgundy estate (30 acres), half red, half white, based at CHASSAGNE-M'RACHET, managed by JADOT.

Magnum A double bottle (1.5 litres).

Mähler-Besse First-class Dutch NEGOCIANT in B'X. Has share in CH PALMER and owns Ch Michel de Montaigne. Brands incl Cheval Noir. (Total: 250 acres)

Mailly-Champagne Top CHAMP coop. Luxury wine: Cuvée des Echansons.

Maire, Henri The biggest grower/merchant of JURA wines, with half of the entire AC. Some top wines, many cheerfully commercial. Fun to visit.

Maranges Burg r ★★ New ('89) AC for 600-odd acres of S COTE DE BEAUNE, beyond SANTENAY: one-third PREMIER CRU. Top NEGOCIANTS: DROUHIN, JAFFELIN.

Marc Grape skins after pressing; also the strong-smelling brandy made from them (see Italian 'Grappa').

Marcillac SW France r p ★→★★ DYA Became AC in '90. Violet-hued with grassy red-fruit character. Good from coop Cave de Valady (rustic), Dom du Cros and Jean-Luc Matha.

FRANCE

Margaux B'x r ★★→★★★★ **70 78 79 81** **82' 83' 85 86' 87** 88' 89 **90'** 92 93 94 95 96 Village of HAUT-MEDOC. Some of most 'elegant' and fragrant red BORDEAUX. AC incl CANTENAC and several other villages. Top ch'x incl MARGAUX, RAUSAN-SEGLA, LASCOMBES etc.

Marionnet, Henry Leading TOURAINE property specializing in GAMAY and Sauv. Top cuvée Le M de Marionnet. Now making wine in Chile: Terra Noble.

Marne et Champagne Recent but huge-scale CHAMP house, owner (since '91) of LANSON and many smaller brands, incl BESSERAT DE BELLEFON. Alfred Rothschild brand v gd CHARD-based wines.

Marque déposée Trademark.

Marsannay Burg p w (r) ★★★ **85 88' 89' 90'** 91 **92** 93 95 96 (rosé DYA) Village with fine light red and delicate PINOT N rosé. Incl villages of Chenôve, Couchey. Growers: Charlopin, CLAIR, Dijon University, JADOT, ROTY, TRAPET.

Mas de Daumas Gassac Midi r w p ★★★ **82 83 85 86 87 88 89 90** 91 92 93 94' 95 96 The one 'first-growth' estate of the LANGUEDOC, producing potent largely CAB S on apparently unique soil. Sensational quality. Also Rosé Frisant and a sumptuous white of blended CHARD, Viognier, Petit Manseng etc to drink at 2–3 yrs. Now also a vg quick-drinking red, Les Terrasses de Guilhem, from a nearby coop and trad Languedoc varietals (Clairette, Cinsaut, Aramon etc) from v old vines under Terrasses de Landoc label. VIN DE PAYS status. New fun fizz: Terrasses du Lido.

Maury Pyr r sw ★★ NV Red VIN DOUX NATUREL of GRENACHE from ROUSSILLON. Taste the terroir. Much recent improvement, esp at Mas Amiel.

Mazis (or Mazy) Chambertin Burg r ★★★ **78' 83 85' 87 88' 89'** 90' 91 92 93 94 95 96 30-acre GRAND CRU neighbour of CHAMBERTIN, s'times equally potent. Best from FAIVELEY, HOSPICES DE BEAUNE, LEROY, Maume, ROTY.

Mazoyères-Chambertin See Charmes-Chambertin.

Médoc B'x r ★★ **82' 83 85 86' 88' 89' 90' 92 93** 94 95 96 AC for reds of the less-good (northern) part of BORDEAUX's biggest and best district. Flavours tend to earthiness. HAUT-MEDOC is much better. Top ch'x include LA CARDONNE, GREYSAC, LOUDENNE, LES ORMES-SORBET, POTENSAC, LA TOUR-DE-BY.

Meffre, Gabriel The biggest S Rhône estate, based at GIGONDAS. Variable quality. Often in French supermarkets. Also bottles and sells for small CHATEAUNEUF-DU-PAPE domaines, eg Guy Jullian, Dom de Baban.

Mellot, Alphonse ★★→★★★ Leading SANCERRE grower and merchant. Especially for La Moussière and wood-aged Cuvée Edmond; also MENETOU-SALON.

Menetou-Salon Lo r p w ★★(★) DYA Increasingly attractive similar wines from W of SANCERRE: SAUV BL white, PINOT N red. Top growers: Clément, Henri Pellé, Jean-Max Roger.

Méo-Camuzet V fine domaine in CLOS DE VOUGEOT, NUITS, RICHEBOURG, VOSNE-ROMANEE. HENRI JAYER inspires winemaking. Esp: V-R Cros Parantoux.

Mesnil-sur-Oger, Le Champ ★★★★ One of top Côtes des Blancs villages; Structured CHARD for v long ageing.

Mercier & Cie, Champagne Brut NV; Brut Rosé NV; Brut **85 88 90** One of the biggest CHAMP houses at Epernay. Controlled by MOET & CHANDON. Good commercial quality, sold mainly in France. Bulle d'Or and Réserve de l'Empereur CUVEES no longer produced.

Mercurey Burg r w ★★→★★★ **85 88' 89' 90' 91 92** 93 94 95 96 Leading red wine village of COTE CHALONNAISE. Good middle-rank burgundy incl more and improving whites. Growers incl Ch de Chamirey, Chanzy, FAIVELEY, M Juillot, Dom de Suremain.

Mercurey, Région de The up-to-date name for the COTE CHALONNAISE.

Métaireau, Louis ★★→★★★ The ringleader of a group of top MUSCADET growers. Expensive well-finished wines: Number One and Cuvée LM.

Méthode champenoise The traditional laborious method of putting bubbles into CHAMP by refermenting the wine in its bottle. Must be referred to as 'classic method' or 'méthode traditionelle' when used outside the region. Not mentioned on champ labels.

Méthode traditionelle See entry above.

Meursault Burg w (r) ★★★→★★★★ **78' 83 85 86 88 89' 90' 91 92 93** 94 95 96 COTE DE BEAUNE village with some of the world's very greatest whites: savoury, dry but nutty and mellow. Best v'yds: Charmes, Genevrières, Perrières; also: Goutte d'Or, Meursault-Blagny, Poruzots, Narvaux, Tillets. Producers incl AMPEAU, J-M Boillot, M Bouzereau, Boyer-Martenot, CH DE MEURSAULT, COCHE-DURY, Fichet, Grivault, P Javillier, Jobard, LAFON, LATOUR, O Leflaive, LEROY, Manuel, Matrot, Michelot-Buisson, P MOREY, G ROULOT, Tesson. See also neighbouring Blagny.

Meursault-Blagny See Blagny.

Michel, Louis CHABLIS domaine with model, unoaked, v long-lived wines, incl superb LES CLOS, vg Montmains, MONTEE DE TONNERRE.

Midi General term for the south of France west of the Rhône delta. Improving reputation; brilliant promise. Many top wines based on grape variety rather than APPELLATION. A melting-pot.

Minervois Midi r (p w) br sw ★→★★ **86 88 89 90 91 92 93 94** 95 96 Hilly AC region for good MIDI wines: lively, full of flavour, esp from Ch du Donjon, Fabas, Dom Laurent Fabre, LA LIVINIERE, de Peyriac, Coop Pouzols, La Tour Boisée, de Violet, CLOS Centeilles. See also St-Jean de Minervois.

Mis en bouteille au château/domaine Bottled at the château, property or estate. NB 'dans nos caves' (in our cellars) or 'dans la région de production' (in the area of production) are often used but mean little.

Moelleux 'With marrow': creamy sweet. Used of the sw wines of VOUVRAY, COTEAUX DU LAYON etc.

Moët & Chandon Brut NV; Rosé **81 82 85 86 88 90** 92; Brut Imperial **76 78 81 82 83 85 86 88 90** 92 Much the biggest CHAMP merchant and grower, with cellars in Epernay, and branches in Argentina, Australia, Brazil, California, Germany and Spain. Consistent high quality, esp in vintage wines. Coteaux Champenois 'Saran' is still wine. Prestige CUVEE: DOM PERIGNON. Links with CLICQUOT, MERCIER, POMMERY, RUINART etc and Cognac Hennessy.

Moillard Big family firm (Domaine Thomas-Moillard) of growers and merchants in NUITS-ST-GEORGES, making full range incl dark and v tasty wines, eg CLOS DU ROI, CLOS DE VOUGEOT, CORTON etc.

Mommessin, J Major BEAUJOLAIS merchant, merged with THORIN. Owner of CLOS DE TART. White wines less successful than red.

Monbazillac Dordogne w sw ★★→★★★ **75 76 79 83' 85 86' 88' 89' 90'** 92 93 95' 96 Golden SAUTERNES-style wine from BERGERAC, gradually gaining typicité. Can age well. L'Ancienne Cure, Ch'x de Belingard-Chayne, La Borderie, Treuil-de-Nailhac, Le Fagé, Haut-Bernasse, Poulvère, Theulet, Tirecul-la-Gravière, Dom de la Haute-Brie et du Caillou, CLOS Fontindoule stand out among 120 growers. Also Coop de Monbazillac (Ch de Monbazillac and Ch Septy).

Mondeuse Savoie r ★★ DYA Red grape of SAVOIE. Good vigorous deep-coloured wine. Perhaps the same as NE Italy's Refosco.

Mongeard-Mugneret 50-acre VOSNE-ROMANEE estate. Very fine ECHEZEAUX, RICHEBOURG, SAVIGNY, VOSNE PREMIER CRU, VOUGEOT etc.

Monopole V'yd under single ownership.

Mont-Redon, Ch de S Rh r w ★★★ **78' 81' 85 86 88 89 90'** 93' 94' 95' 96 Outstanding 235-acre CHATEAUNEUF-DU-PAPE estate. Fine complex reds and vg aromatic but substantial (eg **94**) whites.

Montagne-St-Emilion B'x r ★★ **82' 83** 85 86' 88' 89' 90' 93 94 95 96 NE neighbour and largest 'satellite' of ST-EMILION: similar wines and AC regulations; becoming more important each year. Top ch'x: Calon, Faizeau, Haut-Gillet, Roudier, St-André-Corbin, Teyssier, DES TOURS, VIEUX-CH-ST-ANDRE.

Montagny Burg w (r) ★★ **89' 90** 92 93 94 95 96 COTE CHALONNAISE village. Between MACON and MEURSAULT, both geographically and gastronomically. Top producers: Cave Coop de Buxy, LOUIS LATOUR, Michel, Ch de la Saule.

Montée de Tonnerre Burg w ★★★ **86 88 89** 90 91 92 93 94 95 Famous excellent CHABLIS PREMIER CRU. Esp from BROCARD, Duplessis, L MICHEL, Raveneau, Robin.

Monthelie Burg r (w) ★★→★★★ **85** 88' 89' 90' 91 92 93 94 95 96 Little-known VOLNAY neighbour, s'times almost equal. Excellent fragrant reds. Esp BOUCHARD PERE, COCHE-DURY, COMTE LAFON, DROUHIN, Garaudet, Ch de Monthelie (Suremain).

Montlouis Lo w dr sw (sp) ★★→★★★ **75 76 78 85'** 88' 89 90' 93' 95' 96 Neighbour of VOUVRAY. Similar sweet, or long-lived dry wines; also sparkling. Top growers: Berger, Chidaine, Deletang, Moyer, Taille aux Loups.

Montrachet Burg w ★★★★ **71** 78 79 82 83 85' 86' 88 89' 90 91 92 93 94 95 96 (Both 't's in the name are silent.) 19-acre GRAND CRU V'yd in both PULIGNY- and CHASSAGNE-M'RACHET. Potentially the greatest white burgundy: strong, perfumed, intense, dry yet luscious. Top wines from LAFON, LAGUICHE (DROUHIN), LEFLAIVE, RAMONET, DOM DE LA ROMANEE-CONTI, THENARD.

Montravel Dordogne ★★→★★★ w DYA. Similar to dry white BERGERAC. Good examples from Doms de Krevel, Gouyat, Ch Péchaurieux. Separate AOCs for semi sw Côtes de Montravel esp Dom de Golse, Ch de Montaigne, Ch Pique-Sègue and sw Haut-Montravel (Dom de Libarde, Ch Laroque).

Moreau & Fils CHABLIS merchant and grower with 100 acres. Also major table wine producer. Best wine: CLOS des Hospices (GRAND CRU).

Morey, Domaines 50 acres in CHASSAGNE-M'RACHET. Vg wines made by family members, esp Bernard, incl BATARD-M'RACHET.

Morey-St-Denis Burg r ★★★ **78** 85' 87 88 89' 90' 91 92 93 94 95 96 Small village with four GRANDS CRUS between GEVREY-CHAMBERTIN and CHAMBOLLE-MUSIGNY. Glorious wine often overlooked. Incl Amiot, Castagnier, DUJAC, Groffier, Lignier, Moillard-Grivot, Perrot-Minot, PONSOT, ROUSSEAU, Serveau.

Morgon Beauj r ★★★ **89 90** 91 93 94 95 96 The 'firmest' CRU of BEAUJOLAIS, needing time to develop its rich, savoury flavour. Growers incl Aucoeur, Ch de Bellevue, Desvignes, Lapièrre, Ch de Pizay. DUBOEUF excellent.

Mortet, Denis The new kid on the GEVREY block. Super wines since '93 incl a range of village Gevreys.

Moueix, J-P et Cie Legendary leading proprietor and merchant of ST-EMILION, POMEROL and FRONSAC. Ch'x incl LA FLEUR-PETRUS, MAGDELAINE and part of PETRUS. Also in California: see Dominus.

Moulin-à-Vent Beauj r ★★★ **85** 89 90 91 93 94 95 96 The 'biggest' and potentially best wine of BEAUJOLAIS; can be powerful, meaty and long-lived, eventually can even taste like fine Rhône or burgundy. Many good growers, esp Ch du Moulin-à-Vent, Ch des Jacques, Dom des Hospices, Janodet.

Moulis B'x r ★★→★★★ H-MEDOC village with several CRUS EXCEPTIONNELS: CHASSE-SPLEEN, MAUCAILLOU, POUJEAUX (THEIL) etc. Good hunting ground.

Mourvèdre See grapes for red wine pages 11-13.

Mousseux Sparkling.

Mouton Cadet Popular brand of blended red and white BORDEAUX.

Moutonne CHABLIS GRAND CRU honoris causa (between Vaudésir and Preuses), owned by BICHOT.

France entries also cross-refer to Châteaux of Bordeaux section, pages 78–103.

Mugnier, J-F 10-acre Ch de Chambolle estate with first-class delicate CHAMBOLLE-MUSIGNY Les Amoureuses and MUSIGNY. Also BONNES-MARES.

Mumm, G H & Cie Cordon Rouge NV; Mumm de Cramant NV; Cordon Rouge **79 82 85 88 89**; Rosé NV Major CHAMP grower and merchant owned by Seagram. Luxury brands: René Lalou (**79 82** 85), Grand Cordon (85; launched '91). Also in Napa, California; Chile ('96 first yr), Argentina, South Africa ('Cape Mumm').

Muré, Clos St-Landelin Fine ALSACE grower and merchant at Rouffach with v'yds in GRAND CRU Vorbourg. Full-bodied wines: ripe (unusual) PINOT N, big RIES and MUSCAT VENDANGES TARDIVES.

Muscadet Lo w ★★→★★★ DYA Popular, good-value, often delicious v dry wine from around Nantes at the mouth of the Loire. Should never be sharp but should have an iodine tang (like the bilge of a trawler). Perfect with fish dishes. The best are from zonal appellations: COTEAUX DE LA LOIRE, COTES DE GRAND LIEU, SEVRE ET MAINE. Choose a SUR LIE – on the lees. Good generic Muscadet from Ch de la Preuille.

Muscadet Côtes de Grand Lieu New zonal AC ('95) for MUSCADET around the eponymous lake. Best are SUR LIE, from eg Bâtard, Luc Choblet, Malidain.

Muscadet Coteaux de la Loire Lo w Small MUSCADET zone E of Nantes, best are SUR LIE, esp Guindon, Luneau-Papin, Les Vignerons de la Noëlle.

Muscadet de Sèvre-et-Maine Wine from the central (best) part of the area. Top growers include Guy Bossard, Chéreau-Carré, Doillard, Landron, Luneau-Papin, METAIREAU.

Muscat Distinctively perfumed grape and its (usually sweet) wine, often fortified as VIN DOUX NATUREL. Made dry in ALSACE.

Muscat de Beaumes-de-Venise See Beaumes-de-Venise.

Muscat de Frontignan Midi br sw ★★ DYA Sweet MIDI MUSCAT. Quality improving – esp from Ch'x Gres St-Paul, Tour de Farges, Coop du MUSCAT DE LUNEL. See Frontignan.

Muscat de Lunel Midi br sw ★★ NV Ditto. A small area but good, making real recent progress. Look for Dom CLOS Bellevue.

Muscat de Mireval Midi br sw ★★ NV Ditto, from nr Montpellier.

Muscat de Rivesaltes Midi br sw ★★ NV Sweet MUSCAT wine from large zone near Perpignan. Especially good from Cazes Frères, Château de Jau.

Musigny Burg r (w) ★★★★ 78 **79 82** 85' **86 87** 88' 89' 90' 91 92 93 94 95 96 25-acre GRAND CRU in CHAMBOLLE-MUSIGNY. Can be the most beautiful, if not the most powerful, of all red burgundies (and a little white). Best growers: DROUHIN, JADOT, LEROY, MUGNIER, ROUMIER, DE VOGUE.

Nature Natural or unprocessed – esp of still CHAMP.

Négociant-éleveur Merchant who 'brings up' (ie matures) the wine.

Nicolas, Ets Paris-based wholesale and retail wine merchants controlled by Castel Frères. One of the biggest in France and one of the best.

Noble Joué p ★→★★ Ancient but recently revived rosé from three Pinots (Gris, Meunier, Noir) just S of Tours. Esp from Rousseau and Sard.

Nuits-St-Georges Burg r ★★→★★★ 78' **82 83** 85' **86 87** 88' 89' 90' 91 92 93 94 95 96 Important wine town: wines of all qualities, typically sturdy and relatively tannic, needing time. Name often shortened to 'Nuits'. Best v'yds incl Les Cailles, CLOS des Corvées, Les Pruliers, Les St-Georges, Vaucrains etc. Many growers and merchants esp DOM DE L'ARLOT, Ambroise, J Chauvenet, Chevillon, Confuron, FAIVELEY, GRIVOT, Lechemeaut, LEROY, MACHARD DE GRAMONT, Michelot, RION.

d'Oc Midi r p w ★→★★ Regional VIN DE PAYS for Languedoc and ROUSSILLON. Esp single-grape wines and VINS DE PAYS PRIMEURS. Tremendous technical advances recently. Top growers: VAL D'ORBIEU, SKALLI, Jeanjean.

Oisly & Thesée, Vignerons de ★★ Go-ahead coop in E TOURAINE (Loire), with good SAUV BL (esp Cuvée Excellence), CAB, GAMAY, Cot and CHARD. Blends labelled Baronnie d'Aignan and good domaine wines. Value.

Orléanais, Vin de l' Lo r p w ★ DYA Small VDQS for light but fruity wines, based on Pinots Meunier and Noir, CAB and CHARD. Esp CLOS St-Fiacre.

Ostertag Little ALSACE domaine at Epfig. Uses new oak for good PINOT N and makes the best RIES and Pinot Gr of GRAND CRU Muenchberg. GEWURZ from lieu-dit Fronholz is worth ageing.

Ott, Domaines Top high-quality producer of PROVENCE, incl CH DE SELLE (rosé, red), CLOS Mireille (white), BANDOL and Ch de Romassan.

Pacherenc du Vic-Bilh SW France w dr sw ★★ DYA The white wine of MADIRAN in three styles: dry, sw unwooded (both DYA) and sw oaked (allow to age for 5 years). Ch Laffitte-Teston often best, but MADIRAN producers are generally all good.

Palette Prov r p w ★★ Near Aix-en-Provence. Full-bodied reds, solid rosés and fragrant whites from CHATEAU SIMONE.

Parigot-Richard Producer of vg CREMANT DE BOURGOGNE at SAVIGNY.

Pasquier-Desvignes V old firm of BEAUJOLAIS merchants nr BROUILLY.

Patriarche One of the bigger firms of burgundy merchants. Cellars in BEAUNE; also owns CH DE MEURSAULT (100 acres), sparkling KRITER etc.

Patrimonio Corsica r w p ★★→★★★ **91 92 93 94** 95 96 Wide range from dramatic chalk hills in N CORSICA. Fragrant reds from Nielluccio, crisp whites. Top growers: Gentile, Leccia, Arena.

Pauillac B'x r ★★→★★★★ **66' 70' 75 78' 79 81' 82' 83' 85' 86' 87** 88' 89' **90'** 91 **92** 93 94 95' 96 The only BORDEAUX (HAUT-MEDOC) village with 3 first growths (CH'X LAFITE, LATOUR, MOUTON) and many other fine ones, famous for high flavour; v varied in style.

Pécharmant Dordogne r ★★→★★★ **85 88 90 93 94** 95' 96 Inner AC for best BERGERAC reds, needing ageing. Best: La Métairie, Dom du Haut-Pécharmant, Ch Champarel, Dom des Bertranoux and Ch de Tiregand.

Pelure d'oignon 'Onion skin' – tawny tint of certain rosés.

Perlant or Perlé Very slightly sparkling.

Pernand-Vergelesses Burg r (w) ★★★ **78' 85 87 88' 89'** 90 91 **92** 93 94 95 96 Village next to ALOXE-CORTON containing part of the great CORTON and CORTON-CHARLEMAGNE v'yds and one other top v'yd: Ile des Vergelesses. Growers incl BONNEAU DU MARTRAY, CHANDON DE BRIAILLES, CHANSON, Delarche, Dubreuil-Fontaine, JADOT, LATOUR, Rapet.

Perrier-Jouët Brut NV; Blason de France NV; Blason de France Rosé NV; Brut **76 79 82 85 88 90** Excellent CHAMP grower at Epernay, the first to make dry champagne and once the smartest name of all, now owned by Seagram. Luxury brands: Belle Epoque (**79 82 83 85 86 88 89**) in a painted bottle. Also Belle Epoque Rosé (**79 82 85 88**).

Pessac-Léognan B'x Relatively recent AC for the best part of N GRAVES, incl the area of most of the GRANDS CRUS.

Pétillant Normally means slightly sparkling; but half-sparkling speciality in TOURAINE esp VOUVRAY and MONTLOUIS.

Petit Chablis Burg w ★★ DYA Wine from fourth-rank CHABLIS v'yds. Not much character but can be pleasantly fresh. Best: coop La Chablisienne.

Pfaffenheim Top ALSACE coop with 500 acres. Strongly individual wines of all varieties incl good Sylvaner and vg PINOTS (N, GR, BL). GRANDS CRUS: Goldert, Steinert and Hatschbourg. Hartenberger Crémant d'Alsace is vg.

Pfersigberg Eguisheim (ALSACE) GRAND CRU with two parcels; v aromatic wines. GEWURZ does v well. RIES esp Paul Ginglinger and LEON BEYER Cuvée Particulière. Top grower: KUENTZ-BAS.

Philipponnat NV; Rosé NV; Réserve Spéciale **82 85 88**; Grand Blanc Vintage **76 81 82 85 88 89**; CLOS des Goisses **76 78 79 82 85 86** Small family-run CHAMP house: well-structured, wines, esp remarkable single-v'yd CLOS des Goisses, charming rosé. Owned by Marie Brizard. Since '92 also Le Reflet Brut NV.

Piat Père & Fils Big-scale merchant of BEAUJOLAIS and MACON wines at Mâcon, now controlled by Grand Met. V'yds in MOULIN-A-VENT, also CLOS DE VOUGEOT. BEAUJOLAIS, MACON-VIRE in special Piat bottles maintain a fair standard. Piat d'Or is something else.

Pic, Albert Fine CHABLIS producer, controlled by DE LADOUCETTE.

Picpoul de Pinet Midi w ★→★★ Improving AC exclusively for the old variety Picpoul. Best growers: Dom Gaujal, Coop Pomérols.

Pineau des Charentes Strong sweet aperitif made from white grape juice and COGNAC.

Pinot See Grapes for white and red wine (pages 7–13).

Piper-Heidsieck Brut NV; Brut Rosé NV; Brut **76 79 82 85 89 90** CHAMP-makers of old repute at Reims, now owned by Rémy-Cointreau. Rare (**76 79 85 88**) and Brut Sauvage (**79 82 85**) are far ahead of their other, rather light wines. See also Piper Sonoma, California.

Pol Roger Brut White Foil NV; Brut **75 76 79 82 85 88 90**; Rosé **75 79 82 85 88**; Blanc de CHARDONNAY **79 82 85 88** Top-ranking family-owned CHAMP house at Epernay, much-loved in Britain. Esp good NV White Foil, Rosé, Réserve PR (**88**) and CHARD. Sumptuous luxury CUVEE: 'Sir Winston Churchill' (**75 79 82 85 86**).

Burgundy: growers and merchants
The image of Burgundy négociants' wines is the family car/ Detroit end of the business. In contrast, buying growers' wines can feel like driving a sports car. There are arguments for both.

Pomerol B'x r ★★→★★★★ **70 75' 81' 82' 83 85 86 88** 89' **90' 92 93** 94 95 96 Next village to ST-EMILION: similar but more plummy and creamy wines, often maturing sooner, reliable, delicious. Top ch'x: CERTAN-DE-MAY, L'EVANGILE, LA FLEUR, LA FLEUR-PETRUS, LATOUR-A-POMEROL, PETRUS, LE PIN, TROTANOY, VIEUX CH CERTAN etc.

Pommard Burg r ★★★ **78' 85' 86 87 88' 89'** 90 91 **92** 93 94 95 96 The biggest COTE D'OR village. Few superlative wines, but many potent and distinguished ones to age 10 yrs+. Best v'yds: Epenots, HOSPICES DE BEAUNE CUVEES, Rugiens. Growers incl Comte Armand, G Billard, Billard-Gonnet, J-M Boillot, de Courcel, Gaunoux, LEROY, Machard de Gramont, de Montille, A Mussy, Ch de Pommard, Pothier-Rieusset.

Pommery Brut NV; Rosé NV; Brut **82 83 85 87 88 89** Very big CHAMP grower and merchant at Reims, bought by MOET-Hennessy in '91. Wines are much improved. The luxury Louise Pommery (**81 82 83 85 87 88**) is outstanding. Louise Pommery Rosé (**82 83 85 88 89**).

Ponsot, J M 25-acre MOREY-ST-DENIS estate. Many GRANDS CRUS incl CHAMBERTIN, CHAPELLE-C, LATRICIERES-C, CLOS DE LA ROCHE, CLOS ST-DENIS. V high quality.

Pouilly-Fuissé Burg w ★★→★★★ **89' 90' 91 92** 93 94 95 96 The best white of the MACON region. At its best (eg Ch Fuissé VIEILLES VIGNES) outstanding, but usually over-priced compared with (eg) CHABLIS. Top growers: Ferret, Forest, GUFFENS-HEYNEN, Luquet, Noblet, Valette, Vincent.

Pouilly-Fumé Lo w ★★→★★★ **90' 91' 92' 93' 94 95' 96** 'Gun-flinty', fruity, often sharp white from upper Loire, nr SANCERRE. Grapes must be SAUV BL. Best CUVEES can improve 5–6 yrs. Top growers incl Cailbourin, Chatelain, DAGUENEAU, Ch de Favray, Edmond and André Figeat, LADOUCETTE, Masson-Blondelet, Redde, Tinel Blondelet, Cave de Pouilly-sur-Loire.

FRANCE

Pouilly-Loché Burg w ★★ POUILLY-FUISSE's neighbour. Similar, much cheaper, but scarce.

Pouilly-sur-Loire Lo w ★ DYA Neutral wine from the same v'yds as POUILLY-FUME but different grapes (Chasselas). Rarely seen today.

Pouilly-Vinzelles Burg w ★★ **90 91 92** 93 94 95 96 Neighbour of POUILLY-FUISSE. Similar wine, worth looking for. Value.

Pousse d'Or, Domaine de la 32-acre estate in POMMARD, SANTENAY and esp VOLNAY, where its MONOPOLES Bousse d'Or and CLOS des 60 Ouvrées are powerful, tannic, and justly famous.

Premier Cru First growth in BORDEAUX, but the second rank of v'yds (after GRAND CRU) in Burgundy incl CHABLIS.

Premières Côtes de Blaye B'x r w ★→★★ **82 85 86 88' 89' 90' 92** 93 94 95 96 Restricted AC for better wines of BLAYE; greater emphasis on reds. Ch'x incl Barbé, LE BOURDIEU, Charron, l'Escadre, Haut-Sociondo, Le Menaudat, La Rose-Bellevue, Segonzac, La Tonnelle.

Premières Côtes de Bordeaux B'x r w (p) dr sw ★→★★ Large hilly area east of GRAVES across the River Garonne: a good bet for quality and value, upgrading sharply. Largely Merlot. Ch'x incl Bertinerie (esp), Carsin, La Croix de Roche, Fayau, Fontenil, Gardera, HAUT-BRIGNON, du Juge, Laffitte (sic), Lamothe, Peyrat, Plaisance, REYNON, Tanesse. An area to watch, esp in good vintages.

Prieur, Domaine Jacques Splendid 40-acre estate all in top Burgundy sites, incl PREMIER CRU MEURSAULT, VOLNAY, PULIGNY- and even LE M'RACHET. Now 50% owned by RODET and quality rejuvenated, esp since '89.

Primeur 'Early' wine for refreshment and uplift; esp from BEAUJOLAIS; VINS DE PAYS too. Wine sold 'En Primeur' is offered for sale still in barrel for future delivery.

Prissé See Mâcon-Villages.

Propriétaire-récoltant Owner-manager.

Provence See Côtes de Provence.

Puisseguin St-Emilion B'x r ★★ **82 85 86 88' 89' 90' 92** 93 94 95 96 E neighbour of ST-EMILION, its smallest 'satellite'; wines similar – not so fine or weighty but often value. Ch'x incl La Croix de Berny, LAURETS, Puisseguin, Soleil, Teyssier, Vieux-Ch-Guibeau. Also Roc de Puisseguin from coop.

Puligny-Montrachet Burg w (r) ★★★★ **85' 86' 88 89' 90' 91 92** 93 94 95 96 Bigger neighbour of CHASSAGNE-M'RACHET: potentially even finer, more vital and complex rich dr w. Apparent finesse can also be the result of over-production. Best v'yds: BATARD-M'RACHET, Bienvenues-Bâtard-M'rachet, Caillerets, Champ-Canet, CHEVALIER-M'RACHET, Clavoillon, Les Combettes, M'RACHET, Pucelles etc. Top growers incl Amiot-Bonfils, AMPEAU, J-M BOILLOT, BOUCHARD PERE, L CARILLON, CHARTRON, H Clerc, DROUHIN, JADOT, LATOUR, DOM LEFLAIVE, O LEFLAIVE, Pernot, SAUZET.

Quarts de Chaume Lo w sw ★★★→★★★★ **75 76 78' 79' 82 85' 86 88'** 89' **90'** 91 92 93' 94 95 96 Famous COTEAUX DU LAYON plot. CHENIN grapes grown for immensely long-lived intense rich golden wine. Esp from BAUMARD, Bellerive, Claude Papin, Suronde.

Quatourze Midi r w (p) ★ **91 92 93 94** 95 96 Minor cru of COTEAUX DE LANGUEDOC. Best wines from Dom Notre Dame du Quatourze.

Quincy Lo w ★→★★ DYA Small area: v dry SANCERRE-style wine of SAUV BL. Worth trying. Growers: Domaine Mardon, Sorbe.

Ramonet, Domaine Leading estate in CHASSAGNE-M'RACHET with 34 acres, incl some M'RACHET. Vg whites, and red CLOS ST-JEAN.

Rancio Term for the much-appreciated nutty tang of brown wood-aged fortified wine, esp BANYULS and other VDN. A fault in table wines.

Rangen V high-class ALSACE GRAND CRU in Thann and Vieux Thann. Owes much of its reputation to ZIND-HUMBRECHT. Esp for PINOT GR, GEWURZ, RIES.

Rasteau S Rh r br sw (p w dr) ★★ 85' 86 88 89 90' 93 94 95' 96 Village for sound, robust reds, especially Beaurenard, Cave des Vignerons, Ch du Trignon, Doms Didier Charavin, Rabasse-Charavin, Girasols, St-Gayan, Soumade. Strong sweet GRENACHE dessert wine is (declining) speciality.

Ratafia de Champagne Sweet aperitif made in CHAMP of 67% grape juice and 33% brandy. Not unlike PINEAU DES CHARENTES.

Récolte Crop or vintage.

Regnié Beauj r ★★ 94 95 96 BEAUJ village between MORGON and BROUILLY, promoted to CRU in '88. About 1,800 acres. Try DUBOEUF's or Aucoeur's.

Reine Pédauque, La Long-established burgundy grower and merchant at ALOXE-CORTON with growing reputation, esp in duty-free. V'yds in ALOXE-CORTON, SAVIGNY etc, and COTES DU RHONE. Owned by PIERRE ANDRE.

Remoissenet Père & Fils Fine burgundy merchant (esp for whites) with a tiny BEAUNE estate (6 acres). Give his reds time. Also broker for NICOLAS wine shops. Some of his best wines are from THENARD.

Rémy Pannier Important Loire wine merchant at SAUMUR.

Reuilly Lo w (r p) ★★ Neighbour of QUINCY with similar whites, gaining in reputation. Also rosés (Pinot Gris, pinot noir) and reds (PN). Esp from Claude Lafond, Beurdin, Sorbe and Vincent.

Riceys, Rosé des Champ p ★★★ DYA Minute AC in S CHAMP for a notable PINOT N rosé. Principal producers: A Bonnet, Jacques Defrance.

Richebourg Burg r ★★★★ 78' 80' 82 83 85' 87 88' 89' 90' 91 92 93' 94 95 96 19-acre VOSNE-ROMANEE GRAND CRU. Powerful perfumed fabulously expensive wine, among Burgundy's very best. Top growers: BICHOT, GRIVOT, J GROS, LEROY, MEO-CAMUZET, DOM DE LA ROMANEE-CONTI.

Richou, Dom Long-est'd quality ANJOU estate for wide range of wines, esp ANJOU-VILLAGES VIEILLES VIGNES, COTEAUX DE L'AUBANCE Les Trois Demoiselles.

Riesling See Grapes for white wine (pages 7–11).

Rion, Daniel et Fils 46-acre domaine in Prémeaux (NUITS). Excellent VOSNE-ROMANEE (Les Chaumes, Les Beaumonts), Nuits PREMIER CRU Les Vignes Rondes and CHAMBOLLE-MUSIGNY-Les Charmes. NB Also Patrice Rion.

Rivesaltes Midi r w br dr sw ★★ NV Fortified wine of east Pyrenees. A tradition v much alive, if struggling these days. Top producers: Château de Calce, Dom Cazes, Château de Jau.

Roche-aux-Moines, La Lo w sw ★★★→★★★★ 75 76' 78 79 82 83 85 86 88' 89' 90' 93' 94 95' 96 60-acre v'yd in SAVENNIERES, ANJOU. Intense strong fruity/sharp wine, needs long ageing or drinking fresh.

Rodet, Antonin Substantial quality burgundy merchant with large (332-acre) estate, esp in MERCUREY (Ch de Chamirey). See also Prieur. Now owned by LAURENT-PERRIER.

Roederer, Louis Brut Premier NV; Rich NV; Brut 71 73 75 76 78 79 81 83 85 86 88 89 90; Blanc de Blancs 88 90; Brut Rosé 75 83 85 86 88 91 One of the best CHAMP-growers and merchants at Reims. Vanilla-rich NV with plenty of flavour. Luxury brands: velvety Cristal Brut (79 82 83 85 86 88 89 90) and Cristal Rosé (88) in white glass bottles need time. Also owns champ house DEUTZ and CHATEAU DE PEZ in Bordeaux. See also California, Australia (Tasmania).

Rolly Gassman Distinguished ALSACE grower at Rorschwihr esp for Auxerrois and MUSCAT from lieu-dit Moenchreben.

Romanée, La Burg r ★★★★ 78' 82 85' 87' 88' 89' 90' 91 92 93 94 95 96 2-acre GRAND CRU in VOSNE-ROMANEE, just uphill from ROMANEE-CONTI. Monopole of Liger-Belair, sold by BOUCHARD PERE.

To decipher codes, please refer to 'Key to symbols' on front flap of jacket, or to 'How to use this book' on page 6.

FRANCE

Romanée-Conti Burg r ★★★★ **66' 76 78' 80' 82 83 85' 86** 87 88' 89' 90' 91 92 93' 94 95 96 4.3-acre MONOPOLE GRAND CRU in VOSNE-ROMANEE; 450 cases pa. The most celebrated and expensive red wine in the world, with reserves of flavour beyond imagination. See next entry.

Romanée-Conti, Domaine de la (DRC) The grandest estate in Burgundy. Incl whole of ROMANEE-CONTI and LA TACHE and major parts of ECHEZEAUX, GRANDS ECH'X, RICHEBOURG and ROMANEE-ST-VIVANT. Also v sm parts of M'RACHET and VOSNE-ROMANEE. Crown-jewel prices. Keep top DRC vintages for decades.

Romanée-St-Vivant Burg r ★★★★ **78' 80' 82 85' 87** 88' **89'** 90' 91 92 93' 95 96 23-acre GRAND CRU in VOSNE-ROMANEE. Similar to ROMANEE-CONTI but lighter and less sumptuous. Top growers: DRC and LEROY.

Ropiteau Burgundy growers in MEURSAULT. Merchant business was bought in '94 by BOISSET.

Rosé d'Anjou Lo p ★ DYA Pale slightly sw rosé. CAB D'ANJOU should be better.

Rosé de Loire Lo p ★→★★ DYA Wide-ranging AC for dr Loire rosé (ANJOU is sw).

Rosette Dordogne w s/sw ★★ DYA Pocket-sized AC for charming apéritif wines, eg CLOS Romain and Ch Puypezat- Rosette.

Rostaing Growing 17-acre COTE ROTIE estate with prime plots, notably La Blonde (soft, elegant wines) and fuller, firmer La Viaillère and La Landonne (15–20 years). Style is polished, some new oak.

Roty, Joseph Small grower of classic GEVREY-CHAMBERTIN, esp CHARMES- and MAZIS-CHAMBERTIN. Long-lived wines.

Rouget, Emmanuel Inheritor (nephew) of the legendary 13-acre estate of Henri Jayer in ECHEZEAUX, NUITS-SAINT-GEORGES and VOSNE-ROMANEE. Top wine: Vosne-Romanée-Cros Parantoux. Jayer (who retired '88) still consults here and at DOM MEO-CAMUZET.

Roumier, Georges 35-acre domaine with exceptional wines from BONNES-MARES, CHAMBOLLE-MUSIGNY-Amoureuses, MUSIGNY etc. High standards. Long-lasting reds.

Rousseau, Domaine A Major burgundy grower famous for CHAMBERTIN etc, of v highest quality. Wines are intense, long-lived and mostly GRAND CRU.

Roussette de Savoie Savoie w ★★ DYA Tastiest of the fresh whites from S of Lake Geneva.

Roussillon Midi Top region for VINS DOUX NATURELS. Lighter MUSCATS are taking over from darker heavier wines. See Côtes du Roussillon for table wines.

Ruchottes-Chambertin Burg r ★★★ **78' 85' 87** 88' **89'** 90' 91 92 93' 94 95 96 7.5-acre GRAND CRU neighbour of CHAMBERTIN. Similar splendid lasting wine of great finesse. Top growers: LEROY, Mugneret, ROUMIER, ROUSSEAU.

Ruinart Père & Fils 'R' de Ruinart Brut NV; 'R' de Ruinart Rosé NV; 'R' de Ruinart Brut **86 88 90** The oldest CHAMP house, now owned by MOET-Hennessy, with notably fine crisp wines, esp the luxury brands: Dom Ruinart Blanc de Blancs (**81 82 83 85 86 88**), Dom Ruinart Rosé (**81 82 83 85 86**). NB the vg mature Rosé. Notable value.

Rully Burg r w (sp) ★★ **89' 90' 91 92** 93 94 95 96 COTE CHALONNAISE village famous for CREMANT. Still white and red are light but tasty, good value, esp whites. Growers incl DELORME, FAIVELEY, Dom de la Folie, Jacquesson, A RODET.

Sables du Golfe du Lion Midi p r w ★ DYA VIN DE PAYS from Mediterranean sand-dunes: especially GRIS DE GRIS from Carignan, GRENACHE and Cinsaut. Dominated by LISTEL.

Sablet S Rh r w (p) ★★ **89 90' 93** 94 95' 96 Admirable, improving COTES DU RHONE village, esp Dom de Boissan, Les Goubert, Piaugier, Ch du Trignon, Dom de Verquière. Whites to try too.

St-Amour Beauj r ★★ **93 94 95 96** Northernmost CRU of BEAUJOLAIS: light, fruity, irresistible. Growers to try: Janin, Patissier, Revillon.

St-André-de-Cubzac B'x r w ★→★★ **88' 89' 90' 92' 93 94** 95 96 Town 15 miles NE of BORDEAUX, centre of the minor Cubzaguais region. Sound reds have AC B'X SUPERIEUR. Incl: Dom de Beychevelle, Ch du Bouilh, CH DE TERREFORT-QUANCARD, CH TIMBERLAY.

St-Aubin Burg w (r) ★★ **88 89' 90 91 92** 93 94 95 96 Little-known neighbour of CHASSAGNE-M'RACHET, up a side-valley. Several PREMIERS CRUS for light firm quite stylish wines at fair prices. Also sold as COTE DE BEAUNE-VILLAGES. Top growers incl Clerget, JADOT, J Lamy, LAMY-PILLOT, H Prudhon, Roux and Thomas.

St-Bris Burg w (r) ★ DYA Village west of CHABLIS known for fruity ALIGOTE, but chiefly for SAUVIGNON DE ST-BRIS. Also good CREMANT.

St-Chinian Midi r ★→★★ **89 90 91 92 93 94** 95 96 Hilly area of growing reputation in COTEAUX DU LANGUEDOC. AC since '82. Tasty southern reds, esp at Berlou and Roquebrun, and from Ch de Viranel.

St-Emilion B'x r ★★→★★★★ **70' 75 79' 81 82' 83' 85' 86' 88 89' 90' 92** 93 94 95 96 The biggest top-quality BORDEAUX district (13,000 acres); solid rich tasty wines from hundreds of ch'x, incl AUSONE, CANON, CHEVAL BLANC, FIGEAC, MAGDELAINE etc. Also a good coop.

St-Estèphe B'x r ★★→★★★★ **75 78' 81 82' 83' 85' 86 87** 88' **89' 90'** 91 92 93 94 95' 96 N village of HAUT-MEDOC. Solid, structured, sometimes superlative wines. Top ch'x: COS D'ESTOURNEL, MONTROSE, CALON-SEGUR, etc, and more notable CRUS BOURGEOIS than any other HAUT-MEDOC commune.

St-Gall Brut NV; Extra Brut NV; Brut Blanc de Blancs NV; Brut Rosé NV; Brut Blanc de Blancs **90**; Cuvée Orpale **85** Brand name used by Union-Champagne: vg CHAMP growers' coop at AVIZE. Style is usually softer than true BRUT.

St-Georges-St-Emilion B'x r ★★ **82 83' 85' 86' 88' 89' 90' 92** 93 94 95 96 Part of MONTAGNE-ST-EM with high standards. Best ch'x: Belair-Montaiguillon, Marquis-St-G, ST-GEORGES, Tour du Pas-St-G.

St-Gervais S Rh r (w) ★ West bank S Rhône village. Sound coop, excellent Dom Ste-Anne reds (marked MOURVEDRE flavours); whites incl a Viognier.

St-Jean de Minervois Min w sw ★★→★★★ Perhaps top French MUSCAT: sw and fine. Much recent progress esp Dom de Barroubio, Michel Sige, coop.

St-Joseph N Rh r (p w) ★★ **85 86 88' 89 90' 91** 94' 95' 96 AC stretching the whole length of N Rhône (40 miles). Delicious, fruit-packed wines at its core, around Tournon; elsewhere quality variable. Often better, more structure than CROZES-HERMITAGE, esp from CHAPOUTIER, CHAVE, Chèze, Coursodon, Faury, Gaillard, B Gripa, Grippat, JABOULET, Marsanne, Paret, Perret, Trollat. Good whites too (mainly Marsanne grape).

St-Julien B'x r ★★★→★★★★ **70' 75 78' 79 81' 82' 83' 85' 86' 87 88'** 89' **90' 91 92** 93 94 95' 96 Mid-MEDOC village with a dozen of BORDEAUX's best ch'x, incl three LEOVILLES, BEYCHEVELLE, DUCRU-BEAUCAILLOU, GRUAUD-LAROSE, etc. The epitome of well-balanced, fragrant and savoury red wine.

St-Nicolas-de-Bourgueil Lo r p ★★→★★★ **85' 86 88 89' 90'** 92 **93'** 95' 96 The next village to BOURGUEIL: the same lively and fruity CAB F red. Top growers: Amirault, Cognard, Mabileau, Taluau.

St-Péray N Rh w sp ★★ NV Rather heavy w Rhône, much of it sp. A curiosity worth trying once. Top names are J-F Chaboud, B Gripa (still wine), J-L Thiers.

St-Pourçain-sur-Sioule Central France r p w ★→★★ DYA Red and rosé made from GAMAY and/or Pinot, white from Tressalier and/or CHARD (increasingly popular) or SAUV. Recent vintages improved but too pricey. Top growers: Ray, Dom de Bellevue and good coop.

St-Romain Burg r w ★★ (w) **88 89' 90' 91 92** 93 94 95 96 Overlooked village just behind the COTE DE BEAUNE. Value, especially for firm fresh whites. The reds have a clean 'cut'. Top growers: FEVRE, Jean Germain, Gras, LATOUR, LEROY, Thévenin-Monthelie.

FRANCE

St-Véran Burg w ★★ **90 91** 92 **93** 94 95 96 Next-door AC to POUILLY-FUISSE. Similar wines but better value, with real character from the best slopes of MACON-VILLAGES. Try DUBOEUF'S, Domaine des Deux Roches, Demessey, CH FUISSE and Dom des Valanges.

Ste-Croix-du-Mont B'x w sw ★★ **75 76' 82 83** 86' 88' **89** 90 **91 92** 93 95' 96 Neighbour to SAUTERNES with similar golden wine. No superlatives but well worth trying, esp CLOS des Coulinats, Ch Loubens, Ch Lousteau Vieil, Ch du Mont. Often a bargain, esp with age.

Salon 71 73 76 79 82 83 The original BLANC DE BLANCS CHAMP, from Le Mesnil in the Côte de Blancs. Superlative intense v dry wine with long keeping qualities in tiny quantities. Bought in '88 by LAURENT-PERRIER.

Sancerre Lo w (r p) ★★→★★★ **89 90' 93' 95' 96** Very fragrant and fresh SAUV BL, almost indistinguishable from POUILLY-FUME, its neighbour across River Loire. Top wines can age 5 yrs+. Also light PINOT N red (best drunk at 2–3 yrs) and rosé (do not over-chill). Occasional vg VENDANGES TARDIVES. Top growers incl BOURGEOIS, Cotat Frères, Lucien Crochet, André Dezat, Jolivet, MELLOT, Vincent Pinard, Roger, Vacheron.

Santenay Burg r (w) ★★★ **78' 85' 87 88' 89' 90 91 92** 93 94 95 Sturdy reds from village S of CHASSAGNE. Best v'yds: La Comme, Les Gravières, CLOS de Tavannes. Top growers: Lequin-Roussot, MOREY, POUSSE D'OR.

Saumur Lo r w p sp ★→★★★ Fresh fruity whites plus a few more serious, vg CREMANT and Saumur Mousseaux (producers incl BOUVET-LADUBAY, Cave des Vignerons de Saumur, GRATIEN ET MEYER, LANGLOIS-CHATEAU), pale rosés and increasingly good CAB F (see next entry).

Saumur-Champigny Lo r ★★→★★★ **82 85 86' 88 89' 90' 93'** 95' 96 Flourishing nine-commune AC for fresh CAB F ageing remarkably in sunny years. Look for CH DU HUREAU, Ch de Villeneuve, domaines FILLIATREAU, Legrand, Nerleux, Roches Neuves, Val Brun, CLOS ROUGEARD, coop St-Cyr.

Saussignac Dordogne w sw ★★→★★★ MONBAZILLAC-style age-worthy wines. Producers of new ultra-sw style incl Ch des Miaudoux and Dom de Richard.

Sauternes B'x w sw ★★→★★★★ **67' 71' 75 76' 78 79' 80 81 82** 83' **85** 86' 88' **89'** 90' 91 92 95' 96 District of 5 villages (incl BARSAC) which make France's best sw wine, strong (14%+ alcohol), luscious and golden, demanding to be aged. Top ch'x are D'YQUEM, CLIMENS, COUTET, GUIRAUD, SUDUIRAUT etc. Dry wines cannot be sold as Sauternes.

Sauvignon Blanc See Grapes for white wine (pages 7–11).

Sauvignon de St-Bris Burg w ★★ DYA A baby VDQS cousin of SANCERRE, from nr CHABLIS. To try. 'Dom Saint Prix' from Dom Bersan is good.

Sauvion & Fils Ambitious and well-run MUSCADET house, based at the Ch de Cléray. Top wine: Cardinal Richard.

Sauzet, Etienne Top-quality white burgundy estate at PULIGNY-M'RACHET. Clearly-defined, well-bred wines, at best superb.

Savennières Lo w dr sw ★★★→★★★★ **75 76' 78' 82 83** 85 86' 88 **89' 90'** 93 95' 96 Small ANJOU district of pungent long-lived whites, incl Baumard, Ch de Chambboureau, Ch de Coulaine, Closel, Ch d'Epiré. Top sites: COULEE DE SERRANT, ROCHE-AUX-MOINES, CLOS du Papillon.

Savigny-lès-Beaune Burg r (w) ★★★ **85' 87 88' 89' 90' 91** 92 **93** 94 95 96 Important village next to BEAUNE; similar balanced mid-weight wines, often deliciously lively, fruity. Top v'yds: Dominode, Les Guettes, Marconnets, Serpentières, Vergelesses; growers: BIZE, Camus, CHANDON DE BRIAILLES, CLAIR, Ecard, Girard-Vollot, LEROY, Pavelot, TOLLOT-BEAUT.

Savoie E France r w sp ★★ DYA Alpine area with light dry wines like some Swiss or minor Loires. APREMONT, CREPY and SEYSSEL are best-known whites, ROUSSETTE is more interesting. Also good MONDEUSE red.

Schaller, Edgard ALSACE grower (dry style wines) in Mandelburg GRAND CRU, Mittelwihr; esp for RIES 'Mambourg VIELLES VIGNES' (needs time) and 'Les Amandiers' (younger-drinking).

Schlossberg V successful ALSACE GRAND CRU for RIESLING. Divided into two parts: Kientzheim and small section at Kayserberg.

Schlumberger, Domaines ALSACE growers at Guebwiller. Unusually rich wines incl luscious GEWURZ GRAND CRUS Kessler and Kitterlé (also SGN and VT). Fine RIES from GRAND CRUS Kitterlé and Saering. Also good PINOT GR.

Schlumberger, Robert de SAUMUR sparkling wine made by Austrian method: fruity and delicate.

Schoffit, Domaine Colmar ALSACE house with GRAND CRU RANGEN PINOT GR, GEWURZ of top-quality. Chasselas is unusual daily delight.

Schröder & Schÿler Old BORDEAUX merchant, co-owner of CH KIRWAN.

Schoenenbourg V rich successful Riquewihr GRAND CRU (ALSACE): RIESLING, Tokay-PINOT GR, v fine VT and SGN. Esp from MARCEL DEISS and DOPFF AU MOULIN. Also vg MUSCAT.

Apples into milk

Malolactic (or secondary) fermentation sometimes happens after the first (alcoholic) fermentation. It is the natural conversion of excess malic (sharp) acid in the wine into (milder) lactic acid. It is generally desirable in cool, high-acid wine regions, not in warm regions where a touch of sharpness is a balancing attribute. It can be encouraged or prevented. Where the acidity can be spared, 'malo' adds 'complexity' to flavours.

Sciacarello Red grape of CORSICA'S best red and rosé, eg AJACCIO, Sartène.

Sec Literally means dry, though CHAMP so-called is medium-sweet (and better at breakfast, tea-time and weddings than BRUT).

Séguret S Rh r w ★ Good S Rhône village nr GIGONDAS. Peppery, quite full red, rounded clean white. Esp Ch La Courançonne, Dom de Cabasse.

Sélection des Grains Nobles (SGN) Description coined by HUGEL for ALSACE equivalent to German Beerenauslese. Grains nobles are individual grapes with 'noble rot' (see page 100).

Sèvre-et-Maine The delimited zone containing the best v'yds of MUSCADET.

Seyssel Savoie w sp ★★ NV Delicate pale dry Alpine white, making very pleasant sparkling wine.

Sichel & Co Two famous merchant houses. In BORDEAUX Peter A Sichel runs Maison Sichel and owns CH D'ANGLUDET and part of CH PALMER, with interests in CORBIERES. In Germany, Peter M F Sichel (of New York) runs Sichel Söhne, makers of BLUE NUN and respected merchants.

Silvaner See Grapes for white wine (pages 7–11).

Sipp, Jean and Louis ALSACE growers in Riquewihr. Both produce vg RIES GRAND CRU Kirchberg, Jean's: youthful elegance (smaller v'yd, own vines only); Louis': firmer when mature. Louis also makes vg GEWURZ esp Grand Cru Osterburg.

Sirius Serious oak-aged blended BORDEAUX from Maison SICHEL.

Skalli Revolutionary producer of top VINS DE PAYS D'OC from CAB S, Merlot, CHARD etc, at Sète in the Languedoc. FORTANT DE FRANCE is standard brand. Style and value.

Sparr, Pierre Sigolsheim ALSACE grower/producer, as good at CUVEES of several grapes (eg Symphonie) as rich GRANDS CRUS.

Sur Lie See Lie and Muscadet.

Syrah See Grapes for red wine (pages 11–13).

FRANCE

Tâche, La Burg r ★★★★ **78' 80' 82 83 85' 86 87** 88' **89'** 90' 91 92 93' 94 95 96 15-acre (1,500 case) GRAND CRU of VOSNE-ROMANEE and one of best v'yds on earth: dark perfumed luxurious wine. See DOM DE LA ROMANEE-CONTI.

Tain, Cave Coopérative de, 450-members. Making increasingly good red HERMITAGE since '91. Good value.

Taittinger Brut NV; Rosé NV; Brut **73 75 76 78 79 80 82 83 85 86 88 89 90**; Collection Brut **78 81 82 83 85 86 88** Fashionable Reims CHAMP grower and merchant making wines with a distinctive silky flowery touch. Luxury brand: Comtes de Champagne BLANC DE BLANCS (**79 81 82 83 85 86 88**), also vg Rosé (**79 83 85 86**). Also owns Champagne Irroy. See also Domaine Carneros, California.

Tastevin, Confrèrie des Chevaliers du Burgundy's colourful successful promotion society. Wine with their Tastevinage label has been approved by them and is usually of a fair standard. A tastevin is the traditional shallow silver wine-tasting cup of Burgundy.

Tavel Rh p ★★★ DYA France's most famous, though not her best, rosé: strong and dry. Best growers: Ch d'Aquéria, Bernard, Dom Corne-Loup, Maby, Dom de la Mordorée, Prieuré de Montézargues, Ch de Trinquevedel.

Tempier, Domaine ★★★★ The top grower of BANDOL: noble reds and rosé.

Terroirs Landais Gascony r p w ★ VDP an extension in the département of Landes of the COTES DE GASCOGNE. Domaine de Laballe is most seen example.

Thénard, Domaine The major grower of the GIVRY appellation, but best known for his substantial portion (4+ acres) of LE M'RACHET. Could still try harder with this jewel.

Thézac-Perricard SW France r p ★ West of Cahors. Same grapes but lighter style. Best at three years' old. All made by coop at Thézac.

Thorin, J Grower and major merchant of BEAUJOLAIS, owner of the Château des Jacques, MOULIN-A-VENT.

Thouarsais, Vin de Lo w r p ★ DYA Light CHENIN (20% CHARD permitted), GAMAY and CAB from tiny VDQS S of SAUMUR. Esp Gigon.

Tokay d'Alsace Old name for PINOT GRIS. Now banned as real (Hungarian) Tokay (qv) owns the name. Tokay-Pinot Gris or simply Pinot Gris used.

Tollot-Beaut Stylish burgundy grower with 50 acres in the COTE DE BEAUNE, including v'yds at Beaune Grèves, CORTON, SAVIGNY- (Les Champs Chevrey) and at his CHOREY-LES-BEAUNE base.

Touchais, Moulin Proprietory name of a selected COTEAUX DU LAYON released onto the market after about 10 years' cellaring. Vintages back to the '20s are like creamy honey and not over-priced.

Touraine Lo r p w dr sw sp ★→★★★★ Big mid-Loire region with immense range, includes dry white SAUV BL, dry and sweet CHENIN (eg VOUVRAY), red CHINON and BOURGUEIL. Also large AC with light CAB F, GAMAYS, gutsy Cot, or increasing a blend of these; grassy Sauv Bl and MOUSSEUX; often bargains. Amboise, Azay-le-Rideau and Mesland are sub-sections of the AC.

Trévallon, Domaine de Provence r w ★★★ **83 84 85 86 87 88 89 90 91** 92 93 94 95 96 Highly fashionable estate at LES BAUX. Rich intense CAB-SYRAH blend to age.

Trimbach, F E Distinguished ALSACE grower and merchant at Ribeauvillé with supremely elegant if at times austere house style. Best wines incl RIES CLOS STE-HUNE, Cuvée Frédéric-Emile (grapes mostly from GRAND CRU Osterberg). Also GEWURZ.

Turckheim, Cave Vinicole de Perhaps the best coop in ALSACE. Many fine wines incl GRANDS CRUS from 790 acres, eg vg PINOT GR from GC Hengst.

For key to grape variety abbreviations, see pages 7–13.

Tursan SW France r p w ★ VDQS aspiring to AOC. Easy drinking holiday-style wines. Mostly from coop at Geaune, but Ch de Bachen (★★) belongs to master-chef Michel Guérard, who makes one-off atypical whites in the New-World style.

Vacqueyras S Rh r ★★ **85 86 88' 89' 90'** 93 94 95 96 Full, peppery GRENACHE-based neighbour to GIGONDAS and often cheaper. Try JABOULET's version, Ch de Montmirail, Ch des Tours, Dom Archimbaud-Vache, La Fourmone, Montvac, Pascal Frères, Ricard, Le Sang des Cailloux.

Val d'Orbieu, Vignerons du Association of some 200 top growers and coops in CORBIERES, COTEAUX DU LANGUEDOC, MINERVOIS, ROUSSILLON etc, marketing a first-class range of selected MIDI AC and VDP wines.

Valençay Lo r p w ★ DYA VDQS in E TOURAINE, S of Cher; light easy-drinking s'times sharpish wines from similar range of grapes as Touraine, esp SAUV BL.

Vallée du Paradis Midi r w p ★ Popular VINS DE PAYS of local red varieties.

Vallouit, Louis de N Rhône family co mixing v'yd ownership (biggest in COTE ROTIE: esp Les Roziers, ST-JOSEPH Les Anges) with NEGOCIANT business.

Valréas S Rh r (p w) ★★ **88 90' 93** 94 95' 96 COTES DU RHONE village with big coop. Good mid-weight reds (more sap than Cairanne, Rasteau), improving whites. Esp Romain Bouchard, Dom des Grands Devers.

Varichon & Clerc Principal makers and shippers of SAVOIE sparkling wines.

Varoilles, Domaine des Burgundy estate of 30 acres, principally in GEVREY-CHAMBERTIN. Tannic wines with long life expectancies.

The vin de pays revolution

The junior rank of country wines. No one should overlook this category, the most dynamic in France today. More than 140 vins de pays names have come into active use recently, mainly in the Midi. They fall into three categories: regional (eg Vin de Pays d'Oc for the whole Midi); departmental (eg Vin de Pays du Gard for the Gard département near the mouth of the Rhône), and vins de pays de zone, the most precise, usually with the highest standards. Single-grape vins de pays and vins de pays primeurs (reds and whites, all released on the third Thursday in November) are especially popular. Well-known zonal vins de pays include Coteaux de l'Uzège, Côtes de Gascogne, Val d'Orbieu. Don't hesitate. There are some real gems among them, and a great many charming trinkets.

Vaudésir Burg w ★★★★ **78' 83' 85' 86 88 89' 90 91 92** 93 94 95 96 Arguably the best of seven CHABLIS GRANDS CRUS (but then so are the others).

VDQS Vin Délimité de Qualité Supérieure (see page 33).

Vendange Harvest.

Vendange Tardive Late harvest. ALSACE equivalent to German Auslese, but stronger.

Veuve Clicquot Yellow label NV; White Label Demi-Sec NV; Gold Label **76 78 79 82 83** (since '85 called Vintage Réserve: **85 88 89**); Rosé Reserve **83 85 88** Historic CHAMP house of highest standing, now owned by LVMH. Full-bodied, almost rich: one of Champ's surest things. Cellars at Reims. Luxury brands: La Grande Dame (**79 83 85 88 89**), new Rich Réserve (**89**) released '95 and La Grande Dame Rosé (**88**), launched '97.

Veuve Devaux Premium brand of powerful Union Auboise coop in Bar-sur-Seine. Excellent well-aged Grande Réserve NV and Oeil de Perdrix Rosé.

Vidal-Fleury, J Long-established shipper of top Rhône wines and grower of COTE ROTIE. Bought in '85 by GUIGAL.

FRANCE

Vieille Ferme, La S Rh r w ★★ Vg brand of COTES DU VENTOUX (red) and COTES DU LUBERON (white) made by the Perrins, owners of CH DE BEAUCASTEL

Vieilles Vignes Old vines – therefore the best wine. Used by many, esp by BOLLINGER, DE VOGUE and CH FUISSE.

Vieux Télégraphe, Domaine du S Rh r (w) ★★★ **78' 79 81'** 82 83 85 **86 88 89' 90 92** 93 94 95' 96 A leader in fine, vigorous, modern red CHATEAUNEUF-DU-PAPE, and usually fresh whites (robust 95), which age well in lesser yrs. New second wine: Vieux Mas des Papes. Second dom: de la Roquette.

Vignoble Area of vineyards.

Vin de l'année This year's wine. See Beaujolais, Beaujolais-Villages.

Some vins de pays for 1998

1 **Vin de Pays d'Oc** – A great diversity of grapes for some of the best value vins de pays: some traditional (Carignan, Grenache, Syrah), some new to the region (Chardonnay, Viognier, Cabernet, Merlot), and usually mentioned on label.
2 **Vin de Pays du Jardin de la France** – Loire Valley. Main grapes: Sauvignon, Chardonnay and Chenin whites; Gamay, Grolleau and Cabernet for light reds.
3 **Vin de Pays du Comté Tolosan** – A wider area of the Southwest for red wine from Cabernets, Merlot, Tannat (and there are whites from Sauvignon, Sémillon and others).
4 **Vin de pays des Côtes du Tarn** – For crisp, dry white wine of the Tarn département in the Massif Central: made from the Mauzac grape and others; also a little rustic red.
5 **Vin de Pays de l'Ardèche** – Covers the Ardèche département in the Rhône Valley: Louis Latour's pioneer Chardonnay, and Gamay and Syrah single-variety reds are the ones to look for.
6 **Vin de Pays de l'Hérault** – Some of the best and worst vins de pays are from this large Midi wine area; a demonstration of the extremes of tradition and innovation both in grape varieties and technique. You may be lucky.
7 **Mas de Daumas Gassac** – The Grand Cru vin de pays: serious Cabernet Sauvignon red; also look for white Viognier-Chardonnay blend, and a lightly sparkling rosé.
8 **Vin de Pays des Côtes de Gascogne** – Decline in sales of armagnac has been to the benefit of the local table wines: fragrant dry Colombard and Ugni Blanc are refreshing but perhaps less interesting than experiments with the local Gros and Petit Manseng.
9 **Vin de Pays des Sables du Golfe de Lion** – Pioneering Salins du Midi is virtually the sole producer here on S coast, renowned for its rosé, Listel.
10 **Vin de Pays de l'Yonne** – A useful outlet for wine from young Chablis vines – good value Chardonnays.

Vin Doux Naturel (VDN) Sweet wine fortified with wine alcohol, so the sweetness is 'natural', not the strength. The speciality of ROUSSILLON. A vin doux liquoreux is several degrees stronger.

Vin de garde Wine that will improve with keeping. The serious stuff.

Vin Gris 'Grey' wine is v pale pink, made of red grapes pressed before fermentation begins, unlike rosé which ferments briefly before pressing. Oeil de Perdrix means much the same; so does 'blush'.

Vin Jaune Jura w ★★★ Speciality of ARBOIS: odd yellow wine like fino sherry. Normally ready when bottled (at at least 7 yrs old). Best is CH-CHALON.

Vin nouveau See Beaujolais Nouveau.

Vin de paille Wine from grapes dried on straw mats, consequently v sweet, like Italian passito. Esp in the JURA. See also Chave.

Vin de Table Standard everyday table wine, not subject to particular regulations about grapes and origin. Choose VINS DE PAYS instead.

Vin Vert Very light acidic refreshing white wine, a speciality of ROUSSILLON (and v necessary in summer in those torrid parts).

Vinsobres S Rh r (p w) ★★ 85 **86 88** 89 **90' 93** 94 95' 96 Contradictory name of gd S Rhône village. Potentially substantial reds, rounded fruitness, but many ordinary. Best producers incl Dom les Aussellons, Bicarelle, Dom du Moulin.

Viré See Mâcon-Viré.

Visan S Rh r p w ★★ **88 89 90** 93 94 95 96 Village for far better reds than whites. Note: Dom des Grands Devers.

Viticulteur Wine-grower.

Vogüé, Comte Georges de ('Dom les Musigny') First-class 30-acre BONNES-MARES and MUSIGNY dom at CHAMBOLLE-MUSIGNY. At best: the ultimate examples.

Volnay Burg r ★★★ 78 85' **87 88' 89'** 90' **91 92** 93 94 95 96 Village between POMMARD and MEURSAULT: often the best reds of the COTE DE BEAUNE, not dark or heavy but structured and silky. Best v'yds: Caillerets, Champans, CLOS des Chênes, CLOS des Ducs etc. Best growers: D'ANGERVILLE, J Boillot, HOSPICES DE BEAUNE, LAFARGE, LAFON, de Montille, POUSSE D'OR, Rossignol-Changarnier.

Volnay-Santenots Burg r ★★★ Excellent red wine from MEURSAULT is sold under this name. Indistinguishable from other PREMIER CRU VOLNAY. Best growers: AMPEAU, LAFON, LEROY.

Vosne-Romanée Burg r ★★★→★★★★ 78' 85' **87** 88' **89'** 90' 91 **92** 93 94 95 96 Village with Burgundy's grandest CRUS (ROMANEE-CONTI, LA TACHE etc). There are (or should be) no common wines in Vosne. Many good growers include Arnoux, Castagnier, CHEVIGNY, DRC, ENGEL, GRIVOT, GROS, JAYER, LATOUR, LEROY, MEO-CAMUZET, MONGEARD-MUGNERET, Mugneret, RION.

Vougeot See Clos de Vougeot.

Vouvray Lo w dr sw sp ★★→★★★★ 76' **79 82 83 85' 86** 88' 89' **90'** 93 95' 96 4,350-acre AC just E of Tours: v variable wines, increasingly gd, reliable. DEMI-SEC is classic style but in great years MOELLEUX can be intensely sw, almost immortal. Gd dry sp – look out for PETILLANT. Best producers: Allias, Champalou, Foreau, Fouquet, Ch Gaudrelle, HUET, Pinon, Poniatowski, Vigneau-Chevreau.

Vranken, Champagne With impressive Epernay HQ: ever more powerful CHAMP group created in '76 by Belgian marketing man. CHARD-led wines of fair quality. Leading brand Demoiselle. Acquired HEIDSIECK MONOPOLE in '96.

Wolfberger Principal label of Eguisheim coop. Exceptional quality for such a large-scale producer.

'Y' (pronounced 'ygrec') **78' 79' 80' 84 85 86 87 88 89 90 94** Dry wine produced occasionally at CH D'YQUEM. Most interesting with age.

Ziltener, André Swiss burgundy grower/mail-order merchant with entertaining cellars at Ch Ziltener, CHAMBOLLE MUSIGNY. Wide range.

Zind-Humbrecht, Domaine 64-acre ALSACE estate in Thann, Turckheim, Wintzenheim. First-rate single-v'yd wines (esp CLOS St-Urbain), and v fine from GRANDS CRUS Goldert (GEWURZ and MUSCAT), HENGST and RANGEN.

NB Vintages in colour are those you should choose first for drinking in 1998.

Châteaux of Bordeaux

The following abbreviations of regional names are used in the text:

B'x	Bordeaux
E-Deux-Mers	Entre-Deux-Mers
H-Méd	Haut-Médoc
Mar	Margaux
Méd	Médoc
Pau	Pauillac
Pessac-L	Pessac-Léognan
Pom	Pomerol
St-Em	St-Emilion
St-Est	St-Estèphe
St-Jul	St-Julien
Saut	Sauternes

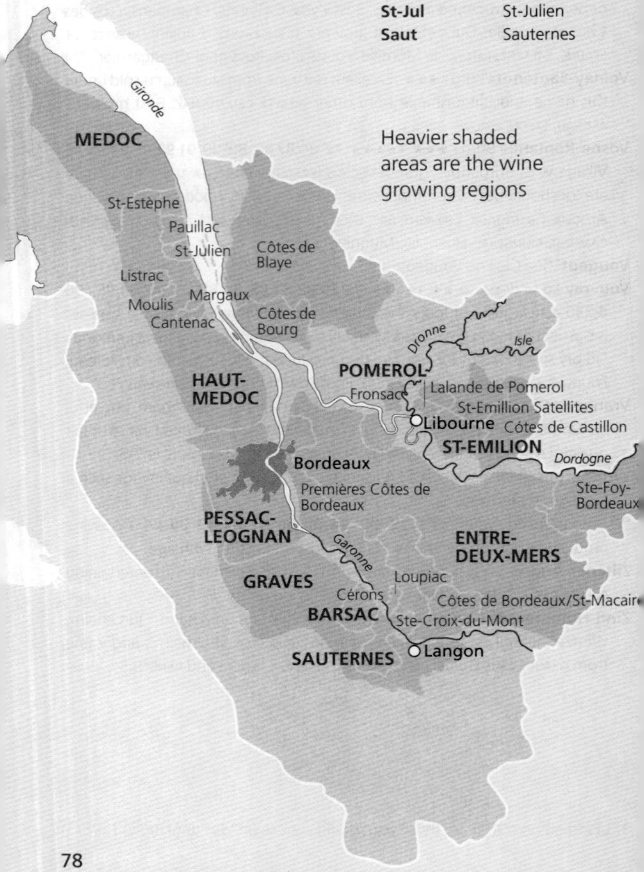

Heavier shaded areas are the wine growing regions

You could be forgiven for thinking that the vintages in Bordeaux have taken to a new pattern – almost a biblical one. Three fat years (88, 89, 90), three lean years (91, 92, 93), then three fat ones again: 94, 95, 96. Of course it is not that simple, even within the limits of Bordeaux, but it does help to make it memorable. 94 was not famously good (but it is generally better than its reputation); 95 is famously good, an immediate sell-out – whatever the future may hold; 96 is a splendid follow-up and a certain long-term rival.

It was a cliff-hanger of a summer, cool and damp in August, then cool and dry in September, turning stormy, then drying and warming again. Many Merlot vineyards, sadly, were caught in the late September rains. Cabernet, though, came through triumphantly. The Médoc, and especially its northern half, has a vintage to rival, and in some properties surpass, 95. The best growers of St-Emilion and Pomerol were able to make good wine, but wish it were better.

In this listing I have picked out in colour the vintages which proprietors themselves will be serving this year as their first choices: their own wines in the state of maturity they prefer. Their choices, for older or younger wines or both, remind us that there are no absolutes – least of all in the glorious diversity of Bordeaux.

d'Agassac H-Méd r ★★ **82' 83' 85' 86 88 89' 90'** 91 92 93 94 95 96 Sleeping Beauty 14th-C moated fort. 86 acres v nr Bordeaux suburbs. Wine popular in Holland. Same owners as CHATEAU CALON-SEGUR.

d'Alesme Mar r ★★ **82 83 85 86** 88' 89 **90** 94 95 96 Tiny (17-acre) third-growth, formerly 'Marquis-d'Alesme'. A lost CRU CLASSE, once highly regarded. Potential here.

Andron-Blanquet St-Est r ★★ **82 85' 86 88** 89' 90 92 93 94 95 96 Sister château to COS-LABORY. 40 acres. Wines showing more charm.

L'Angélus St-Em r ★★★ **81 82 83' 85' 86 87** 88 89' 90' 91 92 93' 94' 95 96 57-acre classed-growth on ST-EMILION COTES. A recent star with some sumptuous wines and promoted to Premier Grand Cru Classé status in '96.

d'Angludet Cantenac-Mar r ★★★ **70' 76' 78' 79 81' 82 83 85** 86 **87 88'** 89' 90 **91 92** 93 94 95 96 75-acre CRU EXCEPTIONNEL of classed-growth quality owned by PETER A SICHEL. Lively fragrant MARGAUX of great style. Value.

d'Archambeau Graves r w dr (sw) ★★ (r) **85 86 88 89 90 91 92 93 94** 95 96 (w) **88 90' 92'** 93 **95** 96 Up-to-date 54-acre property at Illats. Vg fruity dry white; since '85 fragrant barrel-aged reds (¾ of v'yd).

d'Arche Saut w sw ★★ **81 82 83' 85 86' 88' 89'** 90 **91 93** 94 **95** 96 Classed-growth of 88 acres rejuvenated since '80. Modern methods. Rich juicy wines.

d'Arcins Central Méd r ★★ **86 88 89 90** 93 94 95 96 185-acre Castel family property (Castelvin is a famous VIN DE TABLE). Sister to next-door Barreyres (160 acres).

Vintages shown in light type should only be opened now out of curiosity to gauge their future. Vintages shown in bold type are deemed (usually by their makers) to be ready for drinking. Remember though that the French tend to enjoy the vigour of young wines, and that many 82s, 83s, 85s and 86s have at least another decade of development in front of them. Vintages marked thus' are regarded as particularly successful for the property in question. Vintages in colour are the first choice for '98.

d'Armailhac Pau r ★★★ **78' 81** 82' **83** 85 86' **88** 89 90' **91** 92 93 94' 95 96 New name ('91) for CH MOUTON-BARONNE-PHILIPPE. Substantial fifth growth nurtured by the late Baron Philippe de Rothschild. 125 acres: wine less rich and luscious than MOUTON-ROTHSCHILD, but outstanding in its class.

l'Arrosée St-Em r ★★★ **79 81** 82 83 85' **86'** 88 **89'** 90' 92 93 94' 95 96 24-acre COTES estate. Name means diluted, but wine is top-flight: opulent, structured. Modern cuvier; 100% new barrels.

Ausone St-Em r ★★★★ **75 76 78' 79** 81 82' 83' 85 **86'** 88 89 90 92 93 94 95 96 First growth with 17 acres (about 2,500 cases) in the best position on the COTES with famous rock-hewn cellars. The most expensive ST-EMILION, but for a long time behind CHEVAL BLANC or FIGEAC in performance. Partial change of owners in '97: new broom?

Bahans-Haut-Brion Graves r ★★★ NV and **82 83 85 86' 87 88 89' 90 91 92** 93 94 95 96 The second-quality wine of CH HAUT-BRION. Worthy of its noble origin; softly earthy yet intense.

Balestard-la-Tonnelle St-Em r ★★ **81** 83 **85 86' 87** 88' **89 90'** 92 93 94 95 96 Historic 30-acre classed growth on the plateau. Big flavour; more finesse since '85. New chai in '95 and further investment in '96.

de Barbe Côtes de Bourg r (w) ★★ **85 86 88 89 90 92** 93 94 95 96 The biggest (148 acres), best-known château of BOURG. Light fruity Merlot.

Baret Pessac-L r w ★★ (r) **85 86 88** 89' 90' 95 96 Famous name recovered from a lull. Now run by BORIE-MANOUX. White well-made too.

Bastor-Lamontagne Saut w sw ★★ **76 79 82** 83 85 **86 87 88'** 89' 90' 94 95 96 Large Bourgeois Preignac sister-château to CH BEAUREGARD. Classed-growth quality; excellent rich wines. Second label: Les Remparts de Bastor (92 93). Also Ch St-Robert at Pujols: red and white GRAVES. 10,000 cases.

Batailley Pau r ★★★ **70 75' 78'** 81 82' **83'** 85' 86 **88'** 89' **90' 91** 92 93 94 95 96 The bigger of the famous pair of fifth growths (with HAUT-BATAILLEY) on the borders of PAUILLAC and ST-JULIEN. 110 acres. Fine, firm, strong-flavoured wine, to age. Home of the Castéja family of BORIE-MANOUX.

Beaumont Cussac (Haut-Méd) r ★★ **82 85 86'** 88 89' 90' **91** 92 **93' 94** 95 96 200-acre+ CRU BOURGEOIS, well known in France for easily enjoyable and improving wines from maturing vines. Second label: Ch Moulin d'Arvigny. 35,000 cases. In the same hands as CH BEYCHEVELLE.

Beauregard Pom r ★★★ **82'** 83 85 **86** 88 **89' 90' 92** 93 94' 95 96 42-acre v'yd; fine 17th-C château nr LA CONSEILLANTE owned by a bank. Top-rank rich wines. Advice from M Rolland; cellar extended and re-equipped '96. Second label: Benjamin de Beauregard.

Beau-Séjour-Bécot St-Em r ★★★→★★★★ **70 78 82'** 83 85 **86'** 88' **89'** 90' 92 93 94 95 96 Other half of BEAUSEJOUR-DUFFAU-LAGAROSSE; 45 acres. Controversially demoted in class in '85 but re-promoted to 1er Grand Cru Classé in '96. The Bécots also own CH GRAND-PONTET. Now also La Gomerie: 1,000 cases, 100% Merlot.

Beau-Site St-Est r ★★ **81 82 83** 85 86' **88** 89' **90** 92 93 95 96 55-acre CRU BOURGEOIS EXCEPTIONNEL in same hands as CH BATAILLEY etc. Quality and substance typical of ST-ESTEPHE.

Beauséjour-Duffau St-Em r ★★★ **82** 83 85 86 88 **89'** 90' **92** 93' 94 95 96 Part of the old Beau-Séjour Premier Grand Cru estate on W slope of the COTES. 17 acres in old family hands; firm-structured, concentrated, hedonistic.

de Bel-Air Lalande de Pom r ★★ **81 82'** 85 **86** 88' **89' 90 92** 93 94' 95 96 The best-known estate of L de P, just N of POMEROL. Similar wine. 37 acres.

Bel-Air-Marquis-d'Aligre Soussans-Mar r ★★ **81 82' 85** 86 88 89 90 95 96 Organically run CRU EXCEPTIONNEL with 42 acres of old vines giving only 3,500 cases. The owner likes gutsy wine.

Bel-Orme-Tronquoy-de-Lalande St-Seurin-de-Cadourne (H-Méd) r ★★ **81 82 83 85** 86 88 89 90 **91** 92 **93** 94 95 96 60-acre CRU BOURGEOIS N of ST-ESTEPHE. Old v'yd producing tannic wines. More effort since new manager.

Belair St-Em r ★★★ 75' **78 79' 82'** 83' 85' **86'** 88' 89' 90' **92** 93 94 95 96 Neighbour of AUSONE. Wine considerably easier, less tight. Also NV Roc-Blanquant (magnums only).

Belgrave St-Laurent r ★★ 82 **83** 85 86' 88 89 90' 93 94 95 96 Obscure fifth growth in ST-JULIEN's back-country. 107 acres. Managed by DOURTHE since '79. Second label: Diane de Belgrave.

Bellegrave Listrac r ★★ 82 **83 85** 86 88 89 90 **92** 93 94 95 96 38-acre CRU BOURGEOIS making full-flavoured wine with advice from PICHON-LALANDE.

Berliquet St-Em r ★★ 82 83 **85 86** 88 89' 90 **91 92** 93 94 95 96 23-acre Grand Cru Classé recently v well run.

Bertineau St-Vincent Lalande de Pom r ★★ 10 acres owned by top oenologist Michel Rolland (see also Le Bon Pasteur).

Beychevelle St-Jul r ★★★→★★★★ **70' 78 81** 82' **83** 85 86' 88 89' **90** 91 **92** 93 94' 95 96 170-acre fourth growth with MEDOC's finest mansion. Owned by an insurance company since '85. Wine of elegance and power, just below top-flight ST-JULIEN. Second wine: Amiral de Beychevelle.

Biston-Brillette Moulis r ★★ Another attractive MOULIS. 7,000 cases.

Le Bon Pasteur Pom r ★★★ 70 75 76 81 82 83 85 86' 87 **88** 89' 90' 92 93' 94' 95 96 Excellent small property on ST-EM boundary, owned by consultant oenologist Michel Rolland. Concentrated, sometimes even creamy wines.

Bonalgue Pom r ★★ Ambitious 2,500-case estate to watch. Les Hautes-Tuileries is sister château. Wines age 5-10 yrs.

Bonnet E-Deux-Mers r w ★★ (r) **90** 92 93 94 95 96 (w) DYA Owned by Lurton family. Big-scale producer (600 acres!) of some of the best ENTRE-DEUX-MERS.

Le Boscq St-Est r ★★ 82 **83** 85 86 88 89' 90 92 93 95 96 Leading CRU BOURGEOIS giving excellent value in tasty ST-ESTEPHE.

Le Bourdieu-Vertheuil H-Méd r ★★ **82** 83 85 86 **88 89** 90' 92 93' 94 95 96 Vertheuil CRU BOURGEOIS with sister-château Victoria (134 acres in all); ST-ESTEPHE-style wines. New owners, equipment and effort since '90.

Bourgneuf Pom r ★★ **82 83** 85' **86** 88 89' 90 92 95 96 22-acre v'yd on chalky clay soil, its best wines fairly rich with typically plummy POMEROL perfume. 5,000 cases. Alias Bourgneuf-Vayron.

Bouscaut Graves r w ★★ 82' **83** 85 **86' 88 89 90** 92 93 95 96 Classed growth at Cadaujac bought in '80 by Lucien Lurton of BRANE-CANTENAC etc. 75 acres red (largely Merlot); 15 white. Never yet brilliant, but slowly getting there.

du Bousquet Côtes de Bourg r ★★ 82 **83** 85 **86** 88 89 90' 92 93 95 96 Reliable estate with 148 acres making attractive solid wine.

Boyd-Cantenac Mar r ★★★ 78' 81 82' **83'** 85 86' **88 89 90 91** 92 93 94' 95 96 44-acre third growth often producing attractive wine, full of flavour, if not of third-growth class. See also Ch Pouget.

Branaire-Ducru St-Jul r ★★★ 79' 81 82' **83 85 86 88** 89' 90' **91 92** 93 94 95 96 Fourth growth of 125 acres. Notably spicy and flavoury wine in the '70s. Late '80s saw a full-scale revival. New owners in '88. Second label: Duluc.

Brane-Cantenac Cantenac-Mar r ★★★ **78' 81** 82' **83 85** 86' 88 89 90 94 95 96 Big (211-acre) second growth. At (rare) best rich, even gamey wines of strong character. Same owners as CH'X BOUSCAUT, CLIMENS, DURFORT-VIVENS, VILLEGEORGE etc. Second labels: ch'x Baron de Brane, Notton.

du Breuil Cissac r ★★ **88 89 90** 92 93 95 96 Abandoned historic château bought by owners of CISSAC and restored. To follow.

Brillette Moulis r ★★ **82 83** 85' **86** 88 **89'** 90 91 92 93 95 96 70-acre CRU BOURGEOIS. Reliable and attractive. Second label: Berthault Brillette.

BORDEAUX

La Cabanne Pom r ★★ **82' 83 85 86 88' 89' 90' 92 93** 94 95 96 Well-regarded 25-acre property nr the great TROTANOY. Recently modernized. Second wine: Dom de Compostelle. See also CH HAUT-MAILLET.

Cadet-Piola St-Em r ★★ **75' 79 81 82 83' 85' 86 88 89'** 90 **92** 93' 94' 95 96 Distinguished little property (17.5 acres) just N of the town of ST-EMILION. 3,000 cases of tannic wine. CH FAURIE-DE-SOUCHARD has the same owner; less robust.

Caillou Saut w sw ★★ **75 76 78 81 82 83 85 86 87** 88' 89' 90' 91 92 94 95 96 Well-run second-rank 37-acre BARSAC v'yd for firm fruity wine. Private Cuvée (81 83 85 86 88 89') is a top selection. After ten-year legal battle JB Bravo has lost control of château to his sister. To follow...

Calon-Ségur St-Est r ★★★ **78 81 82' 83 85' 86 88'** 89' 90 91 93 94 95 96 Big (123-acre) third growth of great reputation for fruity hearty wines; less stylish than very top ST-ESTEPHES but currently on good form. Second label: Marquis de Ségur.

Cambon-la-Pelouse H-Méd r ★★ **82 85 86 87 88** 89 90 **91 92 93** 95 96 Big accessible CRU BOURGEOIS. A sure bet for fresh typical MEDOC without wood-ageing. Change of ownership '96.

Camensac St-Laurent r ★★ **82' 85 86' 88 89 90** 91 **92 93** 94' 95 96 149-acre fifth growth. Quite lively if not exactly classic wines. New vat-house in '94. Second label: La Closerie de Camensac.

Canon Canon-Fronsac r ★★→★★★ **82 83 85 86'** 88 89' 90 **92** 93 94 95 96 Tiny property of CHRISTIAN MOUEIX. Long-ageing wine.

Canon St-Em r ★★★ **79' 81 82' 83 85' 86 87 88' 89' 90'** 92 93' 94' 95 96 Famous first-classed-growth with 44+ acres on the plateau west of the town bought in '96 by (Chanel) owners of RAUSAN-SEGLA. Conservative methods, modern kit: v impressive wine, among ST-EMILION'S best. Second label (in '91): Clos J Kanon.

Canon-de-Brem Canon-Fronsac r ★★ **81 82' 83 85 86 88 89' 90 92** 93 94 95 96 One of the top FRONSAC v'yds for vigorous wine. MOUEIX property.

Canon-la-Gaffelière St-Em r ★★★ **82 83 85 86' 87** 88' 89 90' **92** 93' 94 95 96 47-acre classed growth on lower slopes of COTES. German owners. Total renovation in '85. Stylish, up-front impressive wines.

Canon-Moueix Canon-Fronsac r ★★ **81 82 83 85 86 87 88 89' 90 92** 93 94 95 96 The latest MOUEIX investment in this rising AC. V stylish wine. NB also sister-châteaux CANON-DE-BREM, Canon-Milary.

Cantegril Graves r ★★ **88 89 90** 95 96 Good earthy red from CH DOISY-DAENE.

Cantemerle Macau r ★★★ **61 81 82 83' 85** 88 89' 90 **91 92** 93 94 95 96 Romantic southern MEDOC estate, a château in a wood with 150 acres of vines. Fifth growth capable of great things (eg 89). Problems in the late '70s, but since '81 CORDIER management has restored to potential. New cellars and oak vats introduced in '90. Second label: Villeneuve de Cantemerle.

Cantenac-Brown Cantenac-Mar r ★★→★★★ **70 81 82 83 85 86' 88 89** 90' 92 93 94 95 96 Formerly old-fashioned 77-acre third growth. New owners (same as PICHON-LONGUEVILLE) investing heavily; direction from J-M Cazes and promising since '94. Tannic wines. 2nd label: Canuet.

Cap-de-Mourlin St-Em r ★★ **79' 81 82' 83 85 86** 88 89 90 **92** 93 **94** 95 96 Well-known 37-acre property of the Cap-de-Mourlin family, owners of CH BALESTARD and CH ROUDIER, MONTAGNE-ST-EM. Rich tasty ST-EMILION.

Capbern-Gasqueton St-Est r ★★ **82 83 85 86** 88 89 90 92 93 94 95 96 Good 85-acre CRU BOURGEOIS; same owner as CALON-SEGUR.

Châteaux entries also cross-refer to France section, pages 32–77.

Carbonnieux Graves r w ★★★ **82 83** 85 86' **88** 89' 90' 91 92 93 94 95 96 Historic estate at LEOGNAN for sterling red and white. The whites, 50% Sémillon (eg **88 89** 90 91 92' 93 94'), have the structure to age 10 yrs. Ch'x Le Pape and Le Sartre are also in the family. Second label: La Tour-Léognan.

Cardaillan Graves r ★★ The trusty red wine of the distinguished CHATEAU DE MALLE (SAUTERNES).

La Cardonne Blaignan (Méd) r ★★ 86 **88** 89 90 91 **92 93** 94 95 96 Fairly large (125 acre) CRU BOURGEOIS of northern MEDOC. Rothschild-owned 1973–90. Big changes since. Fairly simple Médoc, best young.

de Carles Fronsac r ★★ 90 92 93 94 95 96 Steadily well-made quite juicy FRONSACS.

Les Carmes-Haut-Brion Graves r ★★ **81' 82' 83** 85 **86** 88' 89 90' 91 92 93' 94 95 96 Small (11-acre) neighbour of HAUT-BRION with higher-than-Bourgeois standards. Old vintages show its potential. Only 1,500 cases.

Caronne-Ste-Gemme St-Laurent r ★★→★★★ **81 82' 83** 85 86 88 **89' 90** 91 92 93' 94' 95 96 CRU BOURGEOIS EXCEPTIONNEL (100 acres). Steady stylish quality repays patience. At minor CRU CLASSE level.

Carsin Premières Côtes r w ★★ Ambitious Australian enterprise. V attractive wines. To follow.

Carteau-Côtes-Daugay St-Em ★★ Emerging 5,000-case GRAND CRU; to follow for full-flavoured wines maturing fairly early.

du Castéra Méd r ★★ **85 86** 88 89 90' 91 **92 93** 94' 95 96 Historic property at St-Germain (N MEDOC). Recent investment; tasty but not tannic wine.

Certan-Giraud Pom r ★★ 75 **81** 82 83' **85 86 88 89' 90'** 92 93' 94 95 96 Small (17-acre) property next to PETRUS. Steady, but could it be better?

Certan-de-May Pom r ★★★ **75** 78 79 81 **82'** 83' 85' **86 87** 88' 89' 90' 92 93 94 95 96 Neighbour of VIEUX CHATEAU CERTAN. Tiny property (1,800 cases) with full-bodied, rich, tannic wine, consistently flying v high.

Chambert-Marbuzet St-Est r ★★ **70 76 78 79 81 82** 83 **85 86 87** 88 89' 90' **91 92 93** 94' 95 96 Tiny (20-acre) sister ch of HAUT-MARBUZET. Vg predominantly Cab, aged v tastily in new oak. Owner, M Duboscq, likes wines well hung.

Chantegrive Graves r w ★★ 89 90 91 92 93 94 95 96 215-acre estate, half white, half red; modern GRAVES of v fair quality. Cuvée Caroline is top white selection (89 90 **92 93** 94 95 96), Cuvée Edouard top red (**82 83 85 87 88** 89 90). Other labels incl Mayne-Lévêque, Bon-Dieu-des-Vignes.

Chasse-Spleen Moulis r ★★★ **70 75'** 78' **79** 81' **82'** 83' **85 86** 87 **88 89' 90' 91 92** 93 94 95 96 180-acre CRU EXCEPTIONNEL at classed-growth level. Consistently good, often outstanding, long-maturing wine. Second label: Ermitage de C-S. One of the surest things in Bordeaux. See also La Gurgue and Haute-Bages-Libéral.

Causpaude, La St Em r ★★ Another to watch. Modern methods and full-flavoured wine.

Chauvin St Em r ★★ Steady performer with a certain following.

Chéret-Pitres Graves r w ★→★★ Substantial estate in the up-and-coming village of Portets. Drink young or keep.

Cheval Blanc St-Em r ★★★★ **75' 76** 78 **79 81'** 82' **83'** 85' 86 87 88 89 90' 92 93 94' 95 96 This and AUSONE are the 'first growths' of ST-EMILION. Cheval Bl is consistently richer, more full-blooded, intensely vigorous and perfumed, from 100 acres. Delicious young; lasts a generation. 2nd wine: Le Petit Cheval.

Chevalier, Domaine de Graves r w ★★★★ 66' 70' 78' **79** 81' 83' 85 86' 87 88' 89' 90' **91 92** 93 94' 95 96 Superb estate of 94 acres at LEOGNAN. The red is stern at first, softly earthy with age. The white matures slowly to rich flavours (**83' 85' 87'** 88 89 90' 91 92 93' 94 95 96). Also the Domaine de la Solitude, PESSAC-LEOGNAN.

Cissac Cissac-Médoc r ★★ **70' 75' 78' 81 82'** 83' **85** 86' 88 **89** 90 91 92 93 94' 95 96 Pillar of the bourgeoisie. 80-acre CRU GRAND BOURGEOIS EXCEPTIONNEL: steady record for tasty, v long-lived wine. Second wine: Les Reflets du Ch Cissac. Also, since '87, CH DU BREUIL.

Citran Avensan (H-Méd) r ★★ **82 85 86 87** 88 89' 90' **91** 92 **93 94'** 95 96 CRU EXCEPTIONNEL of 178 acres, back in possession of Villar-Merlaut family since '96 after a Japanese interlude of dark, tannic wines. Major works. Second label is Moulins de Citran. To watch.

Clarke Listrac r (p w) ★★ 82 **83** 85' 86' **87 88** 89' **90'** 91 **92** 93 94 95 96 Huge (350-acre) CRU BOURGEOIS Rothschild development, incl visitor facilities and neighbouring ch'x Malmaison and Peyrelebade. Also a unique sweet white 'Le Merle Blanc du Ch Clarke'.

Clerc-Milon Pau r ★★★ **81** 82' 83 85 **86' 87** 88 89' 90' 91 92 93 94 95 96 Once-forgotten fifth growth bought by the late Baron Philippe de Rothschild in '70. Now 73 acres. Not thrilling in the '70s (except **70**), but vg 85, 86 (esp), and now a top performer, weightier than ARMAILHAC.

Climens Saut w sw ★★★★ **71' 75' 76 78 79** 80' **81 82** 83' **85' 86'** 88' 89 90' 95 96 74-acre BARSAC classed growth making some of the world's most stylish wine (but not the v sweetest) for a good 10 yrs' maturing. (Occasional) second label: Les Cyprès. Same owner as CH BRANE-CANTENAC etc.

Clinet Pom r ★★★★ 82 83 85 86 88' 89' 90' 91 92 93' 94 95 96 17-acre property in central POMEROL making intense sumptuous wines from old vines. Since '88 one of the models for POMEROL.

Clos l'Eglise Pom r ★★★ **75 81 83 85 86** 88 89 90' **92** 93 94 95 96 14-acre v'yd on one of the best sites in POMEROL. Fine wine without great muscle or flesh. The same family owns CH PLINCE.

Clos Floridène Graves r w ★★ (r) **90' 91** 92 **93'** 94 95 96 (w) **89' 90 92** 93 94 94 95 96 A sure thing from one of the best white winemakers of Bordeaux, Denis Dubourdieu. Oak-fermented Sauv-Sém to keep 5 yrs, and fruity red. See also Ch Reynon.

Clos Fourtet St-Em r ★★★ **78 79 81** 82' 83 85 86 88 89 90 **92** 93 94 95 96 Well-placed 42-acre first growth on the plateau, cellars almost in town. Back on form after a middling patch: André Lurton is now winemaker; more changes to come. Same owners as BRANE-CANTENAC, CLIMENS etc. Second label: Dom de Martialis.

Clos Haut-Peyraguey Saut w sw ★★ **75 76 79 80 83 85** 86' **87** 88' **89** 90' 93 94 95 96 Tiny production of excellent medium-rich wine. Haut-Bommes is the second label.

Clos des Jacobins St-Em r ★★ **75' 78 79 81** 82' 83' **85 86 87** 88' 89' 90' 92 93 94 95 96 Well-known and well-run little (18-acre) classed growth owned by CORDIER. Wines of roundness and style.

Clos du Marquis St-Jul r ★★→★★★ **81** 82 **83** 85 **86' 87** 88 89' 90 91 92 93 94 95 96 The second wine of LEOVILLE-LAS-CASES, cut from the same cloth and regularly a match for many classed growths.

Clos de l'Oratoire St-Em r ★★ Steady performer on the plateau nr CH FIGEAC.

Clos René Pom r ★★ **75 81** 82' 83 85 **86 87** 88 89 90 **91 92 93** 94 95 96 Leading château west of POMEROL. 38 acres. Increasingly concentrated wines. New vats in '96. Alias Ch Moulinet-Lasserre.

La Closerie-Grand-Poujeaux Moulis r ★★ 85 86 88 89 90 91 92 93 94' 95 96 Small but respected middle-MEDOC property modernized in '92/'93. Also owners of neighbouring ch'x Bel-Air-Lagrave and Haut-Franquet.

La Clotte St-Em r ★★ **82 83' 85 86 88 89** 90' **92 93' 94** 95 96 Tiny COTES GRAND CRU: pungent supple wine. Drink at owners' restaurant, Logis de la Cadène, in ST-EM. Second label: Clos Bergat Bosson (**91 93** 94 95 96).

Colombier-Monpelou Pau r ★★ 82 **83 85** 86' **88** 89 90' **91** 92 **92** 93 94 95 96 Reliable small CRU BOURGEOIS made to a fair standard.

La Conseillante Pom r ★★★★ **70'** 75' **76 79** 81' 82' **83 84** 85 **86 87** 88 **89** 90' **91** 92 93 94 95 96 29-acre historic property on the plateau between PETRUS and CHEVAL BLANC. Some of the noblest and most fragrant POMEROL, worthy of its superb position; drinks well young or old.

Corbin (Giraud) St-Em r ★★ **75 79 81** 82' 83 **85** 86 **88 89 90'** 92 93 94 95 96 28-acre classed growth in N ST-EMILION where a cluster of Corbins occupy the plateau edge. Top vintages are v rich. Same owner as CERTAN-GIRAUD.

Corbin-Michotte St-Em r ★★ **81 82 83 85 88** 89' 90 93 94' 95 96 Well-run modernized 19-acre property; 'generous' POMEROL-like wine.

Cordeillan-Bages Pau r ★★ A mere 1,000 cases of rather lean PAUILLAC from the château-hotel of J-M Cazes (see Lynch-Bages).

Cos-d'Estournel St-Est r ★★★★ 75' 79 81' 82' 83' 85' 86' 87 88' **89'** 90' **91 92** 93' 94 95 96 140-acre second growth with eccentric chinoiserie tower overlooking CH LAFITE. The most refined ST-ESTEPHE and regularly one of best wines in the MEDOC. Second label: Les Pagodes de Cos-d'Estournel.

Cos-Labory St-Est r ★★ 82 **83** 85 **86** 88 89' 90' 91 92 93 94 95 96 Little-known fifth-growth neighbour of COS-D'ESTOURNEL with 37 acres. Efforts since '85 have raised it steadily to classed-growth form (esp since '90). ANDRON-BLANQUET is sister château.

Coufran St-Seurin-de-Cadourne (H-Méd) r ★★ **81** 82' **83** 85 **86'** 87 **88** 89 90 91 92 **93** 94 95 96 Coufran and CH VERDIGNAN, in the extreme N of the HAUT-MEDOC, are co-owned. Coufran is mainly Merlot for supple wine. 148 acres. CH SOUDARS is another, smaller sister.

Couhins-Lurton Graves w ★★→★★★ **85 86' 88** 89 90 91 92 93 94 95 96 Tiny quantity of v fine oaky Sauv Bl for maturing. Classed growth château being restored.

Coutet Saut w sw ★★★ **71' 75'** 76 81' **82** 83' **85** 86' 87 88' **89'** 90' (no 93 94) 95 96 Traditional rival to CH CLIMENS; 91 acres in BARSAC. Usually slightly less rich; at its best equally fine. Cuvée Madame is a v rich selection in the best vintages. A dry GRAVES is sold under the same name.

Couvent des Jacobins St-Em r ★★→★★★ 82' 83 85 86 **87 88 89 90** 92 93 94 95 96 Well-known 22-acre v'yd on E edge of town. Among the best of its kind. Splendid cellars. Second label: Ch Beau-Mayne.

Le Crock St-Est r ★★ **81** 82 **83** 85 86 88 89 90' 92 93 95 96 Outstanding CRU BOURGEOIS of 74 acres in the same family as CH LEOVILLE-POYFERRE. Among the best Crus Bourgeois of the commune.

La Croix Pom r ★★ **75'** 79' **81** 82 **83** 85' **86 88** 89 90 91 92 **93** 94 95 96 Well-reputed property of 32 acres. Appealing plummy POMEROL. Also La C-St-Georges, La C-Toulifaut, Castelot, Clos des Litanies and HAUT-SARPE (St-Em).

La Croix-de-Gay Pom r ★★★ 81 82' 83' 85 86 88' **89 90 91 92 93 94'** 95 96 30 acres in best part of the commune. Recently on fine form. Has underground cellars (rare in POMEROL). LA FLEUR-DE-GAY is the best selection.

La Croix du Casse Pom r ★★ 89 90 92 93 94 95 96 Up-and-coming property to look out for.

Croizet-Bages Pau r ★★ **82' 83 85** 86 **88** 89 90' 91 92 93 94 95 96 52-acre fifth growth (lacking a château or a reputation). Same owners as CH RAUZAN-GASSIES. Only a flicker of life, but new manager in '94.

Croque-Michotte St-Em r ★★ 75 78 **81** 82' **83 85 86 87** 88 89' 90' **91** 93 94 95 96 35-acre classed growth on the POMEROL border. New equipment.

To decipher codes, please refer to 'Key to symbols' on front flap of jacket, or to 'How to use this book' on page 6.

de Cruzeau Graves r w ★★ (r) **86** 88 89 **90** 91 **92** 93 94 95 96 100-acre GRAVES-LEOGNAN v'yd recently developed by André Lurton of LA LOUVIERE etc. V high standards; to try. Oak-fermented white keeps 2–5 years.

Curé-Bon-la-Madeleine St-Em r ★★ **75 78 81** 82' 83 85 **86** 88 89 90 94 95 96 Tiny little-known (12-acre) property between AUSONE and CANON.

Dalem Fronsac r ★★ **82 83 85 86 87 88 89 90 91** 92 93 94 95 96 Leading full-blooded FRONSAC. 36 acres: 85% Merlot.

Dassault St-Em r ★★ **82 83 85 86 88 89 90 92 93** 94 95 96 Consistent, early-maturing middle-weight GRAND CRU. 58 acres.

La Dauphine Fronsac ★★ **82** 85 86 **87** 88 **89' 90' 92 93** 94 95 96 Old star rejuvenated by J-P MOUEIX.

Dauzac Labarde-Mar r ★★→★★★ **82' 83 85 86** 88' 89' 90' 92 93' 94 95 96 120-acre fifth growth nr the river south of MARGAUX; underachiever for many years. New owner (insurance company) in '89; direction since '92 by André Lurton. New cuvier in '94. Second wine: La Bastide Dauzac.

Desmirail Mar r ★★ **82** 83' 85 86 88 89 90 94 95 96 Third growth, now 45 acres. A long-defunct name revived in '81 by Lucien Lurton of BRANE-CANTENAC. So far wines for drinking fairly young.

Doisy-Daëne Barsac w (r) sw dr ★★★ **76' 78 79** 80 **81 82** 83 85 **86 88' 89' 90' 91** 94 95 96 Forward-looking, even experimental, 34-acre estate for crisp oaky dry white and red CH CANTEGRIL as well as notably fine (and long-lived) sweet BARSAC. L'Extravagance (90) was a super-cuvée.

Doisy-Dubroca Barsac w sw ★★ **75' 76 78 79 81** 83 **85 86 87 88'** 89 90' 95 96 Tiny (8.5-acre) BARSAC classed growth allied to CH CLIMENS.

Doisy-Védrines Saut w sw ★★★ **70** 75' 76' **78 79 80 81** 82' 83' **85** 86 88' 89' 90 92 93 95 96 50-acre classed growth at BARSAC, nr CLIMENS and COUTET, recently re-equipped. Delicious, sturdy, rich: for keeping. NB the 89.

La Dominique St-Em r ★★★ **78 79 81** 82' 83 **86' 87** 88' **89' 90' 92** 93 94 95 96 45-acre classed growth next to CH CHEVAL BLANC for fruity, nose-catching wines. Second label: St Paul de Dominique (91). Under new ownership (97).

Ducluzeau Listrac r ★★ Tiny sister property of DUCRU-BEAUCAILLOU. 10 acres, unusually 90% Merlot.

Ducru-Beaucaillou St-Jul r ★★★★ **61 62 66'** 70' 75' 76 78' **79 80 81 82'** 83' 85' 86' **87** 88 89 90 **91** 92 93 94 95 96 Outstanding second growth; 120 acres overlooking the river in stone cellar under château. M Borie makes classic cedar-scented claret for long ageing. See also Grand-Puy-Lacoste, Haut-Batailley, Lalande-Borie.

Duhart-Milon-Rothschild Pau r ★★★ **78 79** 81 82' **83** 85 86 **87** 88 89 90 91 92 93 95 96 Fourth-growth neighbour of LAFITE, under same management. Maturing vines; increasingly fine quality and reputation. 110 acres. Second label: Moulin de Duhart.

Duplessis-Fabre Moulis r ★★ **82 83 85 86 87** 88' 89 90 92 93 95 96 Former sister château of FOURCAS-DUPRE; since '89 owned by DOURTHE.

Durfort-Vivens Mar r ★★★ **78' 79' 81** 82' **83** 85' 86 **87** 88' 89' 90 95 96 Relatively small (49-acre) second growth owned by M Lurton of BRANE-CANTENAC. Recent wines have structure (lots of Cab S) and class.

Dutruch-Grand-Poujeaux Moulis r ★★ **75 79 81** 82' 83 85 **86** 87 **88** 89 **90** 91 92 93 94 95 96 One of the leaders of MOULIS making full-bodied and tannic wines. 60 acres.

de l'Eglise, Domaine Pom r ★★ **79' 81** 82' **83** 85 86 **88** 89 90 92 93 95 96 Small property: stylish resonant wine distributed by BORIE-MANOUX.

L'Eglise-Clinet Pom r ★★★ **70** 71' **75 76 78 79 81** 82' 83' 84 85' 86 87 88' **89** 90' 91 92 93' 94 95 96 11 acres. Ranked v nr top; full fleshy wine. Changed hands in '82; 86 90 noble. 1,700 cases. Second label: La Petite Eglise.

L'Enclos Pom r ★★★ **70 75 79 82' 83 85 86 87 88 89' 90' 91 92 93 94** 95 96 Respected 26-acre property on west side of POMEROL, nr CLOS RENE. Usually big well-made long-flavoured wine.

L'Evangile Pom r ★★★★ **75' 78 79 82' 83' 85' 86 87** 88' 89' 90' 92 93 95 96 33 acres between PETRUS and CHEVAL BLANC. Deep-veined but elegant style in a POMEROL classic. In the same area and class as LA CONSEILLANTE. Bought in '90 by Domaines (LAFITE) Rothschild.

de Fargues Saut w sw ★★★ **70' 71' 75' 76' 78 79 80 81 83 85' 86 87** 88 89 90 95 96 25-acre v'yd by ruined château in same ownership as CH D'YQUEM. Fruity and extremely elegant wines, maturing earlier than Yquem.

Faurie-de-Souchard St-Em r ★★ **82 83 85 86 88** 89 90 91 92 93 94 95 96 Small GRAND CRU CLASSE château on the COTES, now tightening its grip. See also Château Cadet-Piola.

de Ferrand St-Em ★★→★★★ **85** 86 **87** 88 89 90' 92 93' 95 96 Big (75-acre) plateau estate. Rich oaky wines, with plenty of tannin.

Ferrand-Lartigue St-Em ★★ New perfectionist 5-acre property. First wine (93) v promising in dense rich style.

Ferrande Graves r (w) ★★ **81 82 83 85 86 88** 89 90 91 **92** 93 94 95 96 Major estate of Castres: 100+ acres. Easy enjoyable red and good white wine, at their best at 1–4 yrs.

Ferrière Mar r ★★ **89 90 91 92 93 94** 95 96 Up until '92 a phantom third growth; only 20 acres; part of LASCOMBES. Now in same capable hands as CHASSE-SPLEEN.

Feytit-Clinet Pom r ★★ **81 82' 83 85' 86 87 88' 89' 90' 92** 93 94 95 96 Little property near LATOUR-A-POMEROL. At best fine lightish wines. Managed by J-P MOUEIX.

Fieuzal Graves r (w) ★★★ **75 79 81 82' 83 85' 86' 87** 88 89 90' 91 92 93 94 95 96 75-acre classed growth at LEOGNAN. Finely made, memorable wines of both colours esp since '84. Classic whites since '85 are 4–10-yr keepers (esp **85 88 89 90**). New owners took over in '94. Ch Le Bonnat is sister château vinified at Fieuzal.

Figeac St-Em r ★★★★ **64 70' 75 76 81 82' 83 84 85' 86' 87 88 89' 90' 92** 93 94' 95 96 First growth neighbour of CHEVAL BLANC. 98-acre gravelly vineyard gives one of Bordeaux's most stylish, rich but elegant wines, lovely to drink relatively quickly but lasting indefinitely. Second label: Grangeneuve.

Filhot Saut w sw dr ★★ **75 76' 82' 83' 85 86' 87 88' 89 90'** 91 92 93 94 95 96 Second-rank classed growth with splendid château, 148-acre v'yd. Lightish rather simple (Sauv) sweet wines for fairly early drinking, a little dry, and red. Vg 'Crème de Tête' (**90** extremely rich).

La Fleur St-Em r ★★ **81 82' 83 85 86 88 89' 90'** 92 93 94 95 96 16-acre COTES estate; increasingly fruity wines. Now managed by J-P MOUEIX.

La Fleur-de-Gay Pom r ★★★★ 1,000-case super-CUVEE of CH LA CROIX DE GAY.

La Fleur-Pétrus Pom r ★★★★ **70 75' 78 79 81' 82 83' 85 86 87 88' 89' 90'** 92 95 96 18-acre v'yd flanking PETRUS and under same management. Exceedingly fine densely plummy wines; POMEROL at its most stylish and expensive.

Fombrauge St-Em r ★★ **81 82' 83 85 86 87 88' 89** 90 92 93 94' 95 96 120 acres at St-Christophe-des-Bardes, E of ST-EMILION; Danish connections. Reliable mainstream St-Emilion making great efforts. Second label: Ch Maurens.

Fonbadet Pau r ★★ **70 76 78 79 80 81' 82' 83 85 86 87** 88 89 90' 91 92 93 94 95 96 CRU BOURGEOIS of solid reputation. 38 acres next to PONTET-CANET. Old vines; wine needs long bottle-age. Recent building work. Value.

Fonplégade St-Em r ★★ **75 78 81 82' 83 85 86 87** 88 **89** 90' 93 94 95 96 48-acre Grand Cru Classé on the COTES W of ST-EMILION in the Antoine Moueix group. Firm and long-lasting.

BORDEAUX

Fonréaud Listrac r ★★ **78' 79 81 82' 83 85' 86' 87 88 89** 90 91 92 93 94 95 96 One of the bigger (96 acres) and better CRUS BOURGEOIS of its area. New broom (and barrels) since '83. Now also 5 acres of white: Le Cygne, barrel-fermented. See also Ch Lestage.

Fonroque St-Em r ★★★ **70 75' 78 79 81 82 83' 85' 86 87 88 89' 90' 92** 93 94 95 96 48 acres on the plateau N of ST-EMILION. J-P MOUEIX property. Big deep dark wine: drink or (better) keep.

Les Forts de Latour Pau r ★★★ **70' 75 78' 79 80 81 82' 83 84 85 86' 87** 88 90' 91 92 93 94 95 96 The second wine of CH LATOUR; the authentic flavour in (slightly) lighter format. For a long time unique in being bottle-aged at least 3 yrs before release; since '90 offered EN PRIMEUR as well.

Fourcas-Dupré Listrac r ★★ **70' 78' 81 82' 83' 85' 86'** 88 89' 90 91 92 94 95 96 Top-class 100-acre CRU BOURGEOIS EXCEPTIONNEL making consistent wine in the tight LISTRAC style. To follow. Second label: Ch Bellevue-Laffont.

Fourcas-Hosten Listrac r ★★→★★★ **70 75 78' 81 82' 83' 85** 86' **87** 88 89 90 91 92 94 95 96 96-acre CRU BOURGEOIS currently considered the best of its (underestimated) commune. Firm wine with a long life.

Franc-Mayne St-Em r ★★ **85 86 87 88 89' 90' 91** 92 93 94 95 96 '89 acquisition of AXA Insurance. 18 acres run by J-M Cazes (LYNCH-BAGES). Ch'x La Fleur-Pourret and Petit-Figeac (19 acres) are in same stable.

de France Pessac-L r w ★★ Well-known GRAVES property: 65 acres red, 10 white, recently replanted. Try a top vintage.

La Gaffelière St-Em r ★★★ **70 82' 83' 85 86' 87** 88' 89' 90' 92 93 94 95 96 61-acre first growth at the foot of the COTES below CH BEL-AIR. Elegant, not rich wines; worth its rank since '82, after a bad patch.

Galius St-Em r ★★★ **85 86** 88 89 90 92 93 94 95 96 Oak-aged selection from ST-EMILION coop, to a high standard. Formerly Haut Quercus.

La Garde Graves r (w) ★★ **81 82' 83' 84 85 86** 88 **89 90** 91 **92** 93 94 95 96 Substantial property for reliable red. Réserve du Château is grand stuff.

Le Gay Pom r ★★★ **70 75' 76' 78 79 82' 83' 85** 86 88 89' 90' 92 95 96 Fine 14-acre v'yd on N edge of POMEROL. Same owner as CH LAFLEUR; under J-P MOUEIX management since '85. Impressive tannic wines.

Gazin Pom r ★★★ **81 82 83 85 86 87' 88** 89' 90' 92 93 94' 95 96 Large property (for POMEROL): 58 acres next to PETRUS. Inconsistent up to '85; now back on magnificent form. Distributed by J-P MOUEIX. Second label: Ch l'Hospitalet.

Gilette Saut w sw ★★★ **37 49 53 55 59 61 62 70** Extraordinary small Preignac château stores its sumptuous wines in cask to a great age. Only about 5,000 bottles of each. Ch Les Justices is the sister château (83 85 86).

Giscours Labarde-Mar r ★★★ **70 71' 75' 76 78' 79' 81' 82 83 85 86 87 88** 89' 90 91 **92'** 93 94 95 96 Splendid 182-acre third growth south of CANTENAC. Excellent vigorous wine in '70s; '80s v wobbly; revival in '90s. Recently purchased by Mr Albada-Jelgersma. Second labels: ch'x Cantelaude, Grand Goucsirs (!) and La Sirène de Giscours. Ch La Houringue is baby sister.

du Glana St-Jul r ★★ **81 82' 83 85 86** 88 89 90 91 92 **93 94** 95 96 Big CRU BOURGEOIS. Undemanding; undramatic; value. Second wine: Ch Sirène.

Gloria St-Jul r ★★→★★★ **70' 75 76 78 79 81 82 83 85 86 88 89** 90 92 93 94 95 96 CRU BOURGEOIS with wine of vigour. 110 acres. In '82 the owner bought ST-PIERRE. Recent return to long-maturing style. 2nd label: Peymartin.

Grand-Barrail-Lamarzelle-Figeac St-Em r ★★ **82' 83 85 86** 88 **89 90** 91 **92** 93 94 95 96 48-acre property S of FIGEAC, incl Ch La Marzelle. Well-reputed and popular, if scarcely exciting. Now also a smart hotel.

NB The vintages printed in colour are the ones you should choose first for drinking in 1998.

Grand-Corbin-Despagne St-Em r ★★→★★★ 70 75 76 **78** 79 **81** 82' 83 **85** 86 88 89 90' 91 92 93 94 95 96 One of biggest and best GRANDS CRUS on CORBIN plateau. A new generation (of the founding Despagne family, since 1812) in '93. Also Ch Maison Blanche, MONTAGNE ST-EM.

Grand-Mayne St-Em ★★→★★★ 82 83 85 **86 87** 88 89' 90' 93 94 95 96 40-acre GRAND CRU CLASSE on W COTES. Wonderfully rich tasty wines recently.

Grand-Pontet St-Em r ★★ 82' 83 85 86' **87** 88 **89** 90' 92 93 94 95 96 35 acres beside CH BEAU-SEJOUR-BECOT; both revitalized since '85. To follow.

Why do the Châteaux of Bordeaux have such a large section of this book devoted to them? The reason is simple: collectively they form by far the largest supply of high-quality wine on earth. A single typical Médoc château with 150 acres (some have far more) makes approximately 26,000 dozen bottles of identifiable wine each year – the production of two or three California 'boutique' wineries. Moreover between the extremes of plummy Pomerol, grainy Graves and tight, restrained Médocs – not to mention crisp dry whites and unctuous golden ones – Bordeaux offers a wider range of tastes than any other region.

The tendency over the last two decades has been to buy more land. Many classed growths have expanded quite considerably since their classification in 1855. The majority have also raised their sights and invested their recent profits in better technology.

Grand-Puy-Ducasse Pau r ★★★ **79** 81 82' **83** 85 **86 87 88 89' 90 91** 92 93 94 95 96 Fifth growth enlarged to 90 acres under expert management, but remains way behind the next entry. Second label: Ch Artiges-Arnaud.

Grand-Puy-Lacoste Pau r ★★★ 70' **75** 78' **79'** 81' 82' 83 85' 86' **87** 88' 89' 90' 91 92 93 94 95 96 Leading fifth growth famous for excellent full-bodied vigorous PAUILLAC. 110 acres among the 'Bages' châteaux, owned by the Borie family of DUCRU-BEAUCAILLOU. Second label: Lacoste-Borie.

Gravas Saut w sw ★★ **83' 85 86** 88 89' 90' **91** 92 93 94 95 96 Small BARSAC property; impressive firm sweet wine. NB Cuvée Spéciale.

La Grave, Domaine Graves r w ★★ 89' 90' 91 92 93 94 95 96 Innovative little estate with lively reds and delicious oak-fermented whites (w 91 92 93 94 95 96). Made at CH DE LANDIRAS by Peter Vinding-Diers.

La Grave à Pomerol Pom r ★★★ 75' 76' 78 79 81' 82' 83 85 **86'** 87 88 89' 90 **92** 93 94 95 96 Verdant château with small but first-class v'yd owned by CHRISTIAN MOUEIX. Beautifully structured lightish POMEROL.

Gressier-Grand-Poujeaux Moulis r ★★→★★★ **70 75' 78 79' 81 82 83' 85** 86 **87 88 89** 90 **91** 92 93 94 95 96 Vg CRU BOURGEOIS, neighbour of CHASSE-SPLEEN. Fine firm wine with good track record. Repays patient cellaring.

Greysac Méd r ★★ 81' 82 83 85 86 **88 89 90 91** 92 93 94 95 96 Elegant 140-acre property. Easy early-maturing wines popular in US.

Gruaud-Larose St-Jul r ★★★ **61 70 75 78' 79 81** 82' 83' 85 **86' 87** 88' 89 90' **91** 92 93 94 95 96 One of the biggest and best-loved second growths. 189 acres. Smooth rich stylish claret, year after year; ages for 20+ years. Bought '94 by Alcatel Co but same CORDIER management. New equipment '94 and '96. Vg second wine: Sarget de Gruaud-Larose.

Guadet-St-Julien St-Em ★★ **81 82 83 85 86 87** 88 **89** 90' 92 93 95 96 Extremely well-made wines from v small GRAND CRU CLASSE.

Guiraud Saut w (r) sw (dr) ★★★ 67 **79 80 81 82** 83' **84** 85 86' **87** 88' 89' 90' 92 93 94 95 96 Restored classed growth of top quality. 250+ acres. At best excellent sweet wine of great finesse; also small amount of red and dry white.

Guiteronde du Hayot Saut ★★ 75-acres in BARSAC; known for finesse, value.

La Gurgue Mar r ★★ **81 82 83' 85' 86 87** 88 **89' 90 91 92** 93 94 95 96 Small, well-placed 25-acre property, for MARGAUX of the fruitier sort. From owners of CHASSE-SPLEEN and HAUT-BAGES-LIBERAL. To watch.

Hanteillan Cissac r ★★ **82' 83 85' 86 87 88' 89 90' 91** 92 **93** 94 95 96 Huge vineyard: v fair Bourgeois wine, conscientiously made. Ch Laborde is the second label.

Haut-Bages-Averous Pau r ★★ **81 82' 83 85' 86 87 88** 89' **90** 91 92 93 94 95 96 The second wine of CH LYNCH BAGES. Should be tasty drinking.

Haut-Bages-Libéral Pau r ★★ **75' 82' 83 85 86' 87 88 89 90' 91 92 93** 94' 95 96 Lesser-known fifth growth of 70 acres (next to LATOUR) in same stable as CHASSE-SPLEEN. Results are excellent, full of PAUILLAC vitality.

Haut-Bages-Monpelou Pauillac r ★★ **81 82' 83 85 86 88** 89' 90 91 92 93 95 96 25-acre CRU BOURGEOIS stable-mate of CH BATAILLEY on former DUHART-MILON land. Good minor PAUILLAC.

Haut-Bailly Graves r ★★★ **70' 78 79' 81' 82 83 85' 86 87 88'** 89' 90' 92 93' 94 95 96 70-acres+ at LEOGNAN, Belgian-owned. Since '79 some of the best savoury, round, intelligently made red GRAVES have come from this château. Second label is La Parde de Haut-Bailly.

Haut-Batailley Pau r ★★★ **66 70' 75' 78 79 81 82' 83 85** 86 **87** 88 89' 90' 91 92 93 94 95 96 Smaller part of divided fifth growth BATAILLEY: 49 acres. Gentler than sister château GRAND-PUY-LACOSTE. Second wine: La Tour-d'Aspic.

Haut-Bergey Pessac-L r ★★ 40 acres, largely Cab; fragrant delicate GRAVES.

Haut-Bommes See Clos Haut-Peyraguey.

Haut-Brion Pessac (Graves) r (w) ★★★★ **61 64 70' 71' 75' 76 78' 79' 80 81** 82' **83' 84** 85' 86' **87** 88' 89' 90' 91 92 93 94 95 96 The oldest great château of BORDEAUX and the only non-MEDOC first growth of 1855. 108 acres. Deeply harmonious, never-aggressive wine with endless soft earthy complexity. Consistently great (and modestly priced) since '75. A little full dry white in **78 81 82 83 85 87 88** 89' **90 91** 92 93 94 95. See Bahans-Haut-Brion, La Mission-Haut-Brion.

Haut-Maillet Pom ★★ **82 83 85 86 88 89 90** 91 **92 93** 95 96 12-acre sister château of LA CABANNE. Well-made gentle wines.

Haut-Marbuzet St-Est r ★★→★★★ **70 75' 76 78' 81 82' 83' 85' 86' 87 88 89' 90'** 91 **92** 93' 94 95 96 The best of many good ST-ESTEPHE CRUS BOURGEOIS. Monsieur Dubosq has reassembled the ancient Dom de Marbuzet, in total 175 acres. Haut-M is 60% Merlot. See also CHAMBERT-MARBUZET, MACCARTHY, MacCarthy-Moula, Tour de Marbuzet. New oak gives them a distinctive, if not subtle, style of great appeal.

Haut-Pontet St-Em r ★★ Reliable 12-acre v'yd of the COTES deserving its GRAND CRU status. 2,500 cases.

Haut-Sarpe St-Em r ★★ **79 81 82 83' 85 86 87 88 89 90' 91 92 93 94 95** 96 GRAND CRU CLASSE (6,000 cases) with elegant château and park, 70% Merlot. Same owner as CH LA CROIX, POMEROL.

Hortevie St-Jul r ★★ **81 82 83 85' 86 87 88 89'** 90' 91 **92 93** 94 95 96 One of the few ST-JULIEN CRUS BOURGEOIS. This tiny v'yd and its bigger sister TERREY-GROS-CAILLOU are shining examples. Now hand-harvesting only.

Houissant St-Est r ★★ **82 83 85** 86 **87 88 89' 90'** 91 **92** 93 94 95 96 Typical robust well-balanced ST-ESTEPHE CRU BOURGEOIS also called Ch Leyssac; well-known in Denmark.

d'Issan Cantenac-Mar r ★★★ **70 75' 78 79 81 82' 83' 85 86 87 88 89** 90' **91** 92 93 94 95 96 Beautifully restored moated château nr the Garonne with 75-acre third growth vineyard; but recent vintages lack what it takes. Second label: Ch de Candale.

Kirwan Cantenac-Mar r ★★★ 70 **78** 79 81 **82' 83' 85** 86 **87 88** 89' 90' 91 92 93' 94 95 96 86-acre third growth; majority owned by insurance company La Gan. Mature v'yds recently giving tastier wines. New consultant (M Rolland) since '92.

Labégorce Mar r ★★ **75' 78 79** 81' **82'** 83' 85 86 **87 88** 89' 90' 91 **92** 93 94 95 96 Substantial 69-acre property N of MARGAUX; long-lived wines of true Margaux quality. New owner since '89; re-equipped '96.

Labégorce-Zédé Mar r ★★→★★★ **75' 78** 81' 82' **83' 85 86' 87** 88 89' 90' 91 92 93 94 95 96 CRU BOURGEOIS on road N from MARGAUX. 62 acres. Typically delicate, fragrant; truly classic since '81. Same family as VIEUX CH CERTAN. Second label: Dom Zédé. Also 23 acres of AC Bordeaux: 'Z'.

Lacoste-Borie The second wine of CH GRAND-PUY-LACOSTE.

Lafaurie-Peyraguey Saut w sw ★★★ **78 80 81' 82 83' 85 86' 87** 88' 89' 90' 95 96 Fine classed growth of only 49 acres at Bommes, belonging to CORDIER. Now one of best buys in Sauternes.

Lafite-Rothschild Pau r ★★★★ **59 75' 76' 78 79** 81' **82'** 83 **84** 85 86' 87 88' 89' 90' 91 92 93 94 95 96 First growth of famous elusive perfume and style in its great vintages, which keep for decades. Resplendent since '76. Amazing circular cellars opened '87. Joint ventures in Chile ('88), California ('89), Portugal ('92). Second wine: Carruades de Lafite. 225 acres. Also owns CH'X DUHART-MILON, L'EVANGILE, RIEUSSEC.

Lafleur Pom r ★★★★ 70' 75' **78** 79' 81 82' **83 85'** 86' 88' 89' 90' 92 93 94 95 96 Superb 12-acre property just N of PETRUS. Resounding wine of the turbo-charged, tannic, less 'fleshy' kind for long maturing/investment. Same owner as LE GAY. Second wine: Les Pensées de Lafleur.

Lafleur-Gazin Pom r ★★ **75' 79** 81 82' **83** 85' 86 **87** 88' 89 90 92 93 94 95 96 Distinguished small J-P MOUEIX estate on the NE border of POMEROL.

Lafon-Rochet St-Est r ★★ **70' 81** 82 83' 85 **86** 87 **88' 89' 90' 91 92** 93 94 95 96 Fourth-growth neighbour of COS D'ESTOURNEL, restored in '60s and again recently. 110 acres. Good hard full-bodied ST-ESTEPHE, slow to 'give'. New cellar equipment '96. Same owner as CH PONTET-CANET. Second label: Numéro 2.

Lagrange Pom r ★★ **70'** 75' 78 81 82' 83 85' 86 **87 88 89' 90'** 92 93 94 95 96 20-acre vineyard in the centre of POMEROL run by the ubiquitous house of J-P MOUEIX. Rising profile for flavour/value.

Lagrange St-Jul r ★★★ 70 **79 81** 82 83 84 85' 86' 87 88' 89' 90' 91 **92** 93 94 95 96 Formerly neglected third growth inland from ST-JULIEN, bought by Suntory ('83). 280 acres now in tiptop condition with wines to match (and lots of oak). Second wine: Les Fiefs de Lagrange (**83** 85 86 87 88 **89** 90 91 **92** 93 94 95 96).

La Lagune Ludon r ★★★ **70' 75' 76' 78' 79 81** 82' 83' **85** 86' 87 88' **89' 90'** 91 92 93 94 95 96 Ultra-modern 160-acre third growth in southernmost MEDOC. Attractively rich wines with marked oak; steadily high quality. Owned by AYALA.

Lalande-Borie St-Jul r ★★ **81** 82 83 85 **86** 87 88 89 90' 91 92 93 94 95 96 A baby brother of the great DUCRU-BEAUCAILLOU created from part of the former v'yd of CH LAGRANGE. Gracious, easy drinking.

Lamarque Lamarque (H-Méd) r ★★ **82 83' 85** 86' **87 88** 89 90' 91 92 93 94 95 96 Splendid medieval fortress in central MEDOC with 113 acres giving admirable wine of high Bourgeois standard. Second wine: Donjon de L.

Lamothe Bergeron H-Méd r ★★ 88 89 150 acres at CUSSAC making 25,000 cases of reliable claret. Run by GRAND-PUY-DUCASSE.

Landiras Graves w r ★★→★★★ (w) **90** 91 92' 93' 94 95' 96 Medieval ruin in S GRAVES replanted in '80s. 50 acres Sém, 15 red (88 **89** 90' **91** 92 93 94 95). See also Domaine La Grave. Second label: Notre Dame de Landiras (AC B'x).

BORDEAUX

Lanessan Cussac (H-Méd) r ★★→★★★ **78' 79 81 82 83 85 86' 87 88' 89' 90' 91 92** 93 94 95 96 Distinguished 108-acre CRU BOURGEOIS EXCEPTIONNEL just S of ST-JULIEN. Fine rather than burly but ages v well. Same family owns châteaux de Ste-Gemme, Lachesnaye, La Providence.

Langoa-Barton St-Jul r ★★★ **70' 75' 76 78' 79 81 82' 83** 85 86' **87** 88' 89' 90' 91 92 93 94' 95 96 49-acre third growth sister-château to LEOVILLE-BARTON. V old Barton-family estate with impeccable standards and generous value. Second wine: Lady Langoa.

Larcis-Ducasse St-Em r ★★ **66 78 79 81 82' 83 84 85 86 87 88'** 89' 90' 91 92 93 94 95 96 Top property of St-Laurent, eastern neighbour of ST-EMILION, on COTES next to CH PAVIE. 30 acres in a fine situation; wines medium.

Larmande St-Em r ★★★ **75' 78 79 81 82 83' 85 86 87** 88' 89' 90' 92 93 94 95 96 Substantial 54-acre property related to CAP-DE-MOURLIN. Replanted, re-equipped and now making rich strikingly scented wine. Second label: Ch des Templiers.

Laroque St-Em r ★★→★★★ **75' 81 82' 83 85 86 88 89 90 91 92 93** 94 95 96 Important 108-acre v'yd on the ST-EMILION COTES in St-Christophe. Promoted to GRAND CRU CLASSE in '96.

Larose-Trintaudon St-Laurent r ★★ **82 85 86 87 88 89 90' 91 92 93** 94' 95 96 The biggest v'yd in the MEDOC: 425 acres. Modern methods make reliable fruity and charming CRU BOURGEOIS wine to drink young. New management in '89 and second label Larose St-Laurent.

Laroze St-Em r ★★ **82 83 85 86 87 88' 89 90' 91 92** 93 94 95 96 Large v'yd (74 acres) on western COTES. Fine fairly light wines from sandy soils; approachable when young.

Larrivet-Haut-Brion Graves r (w) ★★ **75' 81 82' 83** 85 **86 87 88 89 90** 91 **92** 93 94 95 96 Little LEOGNAN property with perfectionist standards. Also 500 cases of fine barrel-fermented white (**87 88 89 90 91 92 93** 94 95 96).

Lascombes Mar r (p) ★★★ **70' 75' 82 83 85 86 87 88'** 89' 90' **91 92** 93 94 95 96 240-acre second growth owned by British brewers Bass-Charrington; lavishly restored. Has reemerged as a serious contender since '86 with robust vigorous wines. Second wine: Ch Segonnes.

Latour Pau r ★★★★ **59 61 62 64 66 67** 70' **71 73 75' 76 78' 79 80 81** 82' **83 84 85** 86' **87** 88' 89' 90' 91' 92 93' 94' 95' 96 First growth considered the grandest statement of the MEDOC. Rich, intense, almost immortal wines in great yrs; classical, perfumed and pleasing even in weak ones. 150 acres sloping to R Gironde. Latour always needs time to show its hand. British-owned from '63 to '93, now again in (private) French hands. 2nd wine: LES FORTS DE LATOUR; 3rd, Pauillac.

Latour-Martillac Graves r w ★★ (r) **82' 83 85' 86 87 88'** 89 90 91 92 93 94 95 96 Small but serious property at Martillac. 10 acres of white grapes; 37 of black. The white can age admirably (86 87 88 89 90 91 92 93' 94' 95 96). The owner is resurrecting the neighbouring Ch Lespault.

Latour-à-Pomerol Pom r ★★★★ **61 70' 76 79 81 82 83 85' 86 87 88' 89' 90'** 92 93 94 95 96 Top growth of 19 acres under MOUEIX management. POMEROL of great power and perfume, yet also ravishing finesse.

des Laurets St-Em r ★★ **82 83 85 86 88 89'** 90' **92 93** 94 95 96 Major property in PUISSEGUIN-ST-EMILION and MONTAGNE-ST-EMILION (to the E) with 160 acres of v'yd on the COTES (40,000 cases). Sterling wines sold by J-P MOUEIX.

Laville-Haut-Brion Graves w ★★★★ **82 85' 86 87' 88** 89' 90 92 93' 94 95 96 A tiny production of the v best white GRAVES for long succulent maturing, made at CH LA MISSION-HAUT-BRION. The 89 is off the dial.

Châteaux entries also cross-refer to France section, pages 32–77.

Léoville-Barton St-Jul r ★★★→★★★★ 70' 75' 76 78' 81 82' 83 85' 86' 87 88' 89' 90' 91 92 93 94' 95 96 90-acre portion of the great second growth LEOVILLE v'yd in Anglo-Irish hands of the Barton family for over 150 years. Powerful classic claret; traditional methods, v fair prices. Major investment has raised already high standards to 'super-second'. See also Langoa-Barton.

Léoville-Las-Cases St-Jul r ★★★★ 66' 75' 76 78' 79 81' 82' 83' 84 85' 86' 87 88 89' 90' 91 92 93' 94 95 96 Largest LEOVILLE. Next to LATOUR; 210 acres. One of the highest reputations in Bordeaux. Elegant complex powerful austere wines, for immortality. Second label CLOS DU MARQUIS also outstanding.

Léoville-Poyferré St-Jul r ★★★ 81 82' 83' 84 85 86' 87 88 89' 90' 91 92 93 94 95 96 For years the least outstanding of the LEOVILLES; since '80 again living up to the great name. Michel Rolland now makes the wine; cellar re-equipped '96. 156 acres. Second label: Ch Moulin-Riche.

Lestage Listrac r ★★ 82' 83 85 86' 87 88 89' 90' 91 92 93 94 95 96 130-acre CRU BOURGEOIS in same hands as CH FONREAUD. Light, quite stylish wine aged in oak since '85. Second wine: Ch Caroline. Also white: La Mouette.

Lilian-Ladouys St-Est ★★ 89 90 91 92 93 94 95 96 Recent creation: a 50-acre CRU BOURGEOIS with high ambitions and early promise. To watch.

Liot Barsac w sw ★★ 75' 76 82 83 85 86 88 89' 90' 92 94 95 96 Consistent fairly light golden wines from 50 acres.

Liversan St-Sauveur r ★★ 82' 83 85 86' 87 88' 89' 90' 91 92 93 94 95 96 116-acre Grand Cru Bourgeois inland from PAUILLAC. Since '84 the Polignac family have had steadily high standards. Now managed by owners of PATACHE D'AUX. Second wine: Ch Fonpiqueyre.

Livran Méd r ★★ 82' 83 85 86 88' 89' 90' 91 92 93 94' 95 96 Big CRU BOURGEOIS at St-Germain in the N MEDOC. Consistent round wines (half Merlot).

Médoc: the class system

The Médoc has 60 crus classés, ranked in 1855 in five classes. In a separate classification it has 18 Crus Grands Bourgeois Exceptionnels, 41 Crus Grands Bourgeois (which must age their wine in barrels), and 68 Crus Bourgeois. (The old terms Grand Bourgeois and Exceptionnel – like so many traditional and useful things – are not acceptable to the EC, and are therefore no longer used on labels.)

Apart from the first growths, the five classes of 1855 are now hopelessly jumbled in quality, with some second growths at fifth growth level and vice versa. They also overlap in quality with the Crus Exceptionnels. (Besides the official 18, another 13 châteaux are unofficially acknowledged as belonging to this category.) The French always do things logically.

Loudenne St-Yzans (Méd) r ★★ 82' 83 85 86' 87' 88 89' 90 91 92 93 95 96 Beautiful riverside château owned by Gilbeys since 1875. Well-made CRU BOURGEOIS red and increasingly delicious dry Sauvignon white from 120 acres. The white is best at 2–4 yrs (90 91 92' 93 94 95 96). Re-equipped '96

Loupiac-Gaudiet Loupiac w sw ★★ 85 86 87 88 89 90 91 92 93 94 95 96 Reliable source of good-value 'almost-SAUTERNES', just across R Garonne.

La Louvière Graves r w ★★★ (r) 81 82' 83 85 86' 87 88' 89' 90' 91 92 93' 94' 95 96 (w) 86 88 89' 90' 91 92 93' 94 95 96 Noble 135-acre LEOGNAN estate restored by the ubiquitous Lurton family. Excellent white; red wine of classed growth standard.

de Lussac St-Em r ★★ 82 83 85 86 88 89' 90 91 92 93 94 95 96 One of the best estates in LUSSAC-ST-EMILION (to the NE).

Lynch-Bages Pau r (w) ★★★→★★★★ **61' 66 70 75' 78' 81** 82' **83' 84** 85' **86' 87 88' 89'** 90' **91 92** 93' 94 95 96 Always popular, now a regular star. 200 acres. Rich robust wine: deliciously dense, brambly; aspiring to greatness. See also Haut-Bages-Averous. From '90, intense oaky white. Owner J-M Cazes also directs CH PICHON-LONGUEVILLE etc for AXA Insurance.

Lynch-Moussas Pau r ★★ **80 81** 82 **83** 85 86 **87 88** 89 90' 91 92 93 94 95 96 Fifth growth restored by the director of CH BATAILLEY since '69. Now 60+ acres are making serious wine, gaining depth as the vines age.

du Lyonnat Lussac-St-Em r ★★ 82 83 85 86' 88 **89** 90' **91** 92 93 94 95 96 120-acre estate with well-distributed reliable wine.

MacCarthy St-Est r ★★ **88 89 90** 91 92 93 94 95 96 The second label of CHATEAU CHAMBERT-MARBUZET.

Macquin-St-Georges St-Em r ★★ 85 86' 88 89 90' 91 92 93 94 95 96 Steady producer of delicious 'satellite' ST-EMILION at ST-GEORGES.

Magdelaine St-Em r ★★★ 70' 71' 75 78 **81** 82' 83' 85 **86 88 89' 90'** 92 93 94 95 96 Leading COTES first growth: 28 acres next to AUSONE owned by J-P MOUEIX. Beautifully balanced subtle wine: recently powerful and fine. Substantial rebuilding ('92) promises even better things.

Magence Graves r w ★★ Go-ahead 93-acre property in S GRAVES. Sauv Bl-flavoured dry white and fruity red. Both age well 2–6 yrs.

Malartic-Lagravière Graves r (w) ★★★ (r) 81 82' 83 85 **86' 87 88 89 90' 91 92 93'** 94 95 96 (w) 85 87' 88 **89** 90 91 92 **93** 94 95 96 LEOGNAN classed growth of 53 acres. Rather hard red wine and a little long-ageing Sauvignon Blanc white. Austere wines that need cellaring. New owner: AA Bonnie, a Belgian industrialist ('96).

Malescasse Lamarque (H-Méd) r ★★ **82 83 85 86 88 89 90 91 92** 93' 94 95' 96 Renovated CRU BOURGEOIS with 100 well-situated acres. Second label: Le Tana de M. Same owners as GRUAUD-LAROSE; ex-PICHON-LALANDE director. To watch.

Malescot-St-Exupéry Mar r ★★★ 70 75 **82' 83' 85 86** 88 89 90' 91 92 93 94 95 96 Third growth of 84 acres. Often tough when young, eventually fragrant MARGAUX. New consultant from '90 augurs well.

de Malle Saut w r sw dr ★★★ (w sw) **75 76 78 79 80 81' 82' 83 85 86' 87** 88 **89'** 90' 91 94 95 96 Beautiful château with Italian gardens at Preignac. 124 acres. Vg SAUTERNES (second label: Ste Hélène 90 93 95 96); also dry white (90 94 95 96) and red (GRAVES) CH DU CARDAILLAN (★★) (**88** 89 **90** 93 **95** 96).

de Malleret H-Méd r ★★ **82 83 85** 86 88 89' **90** 92 93 94 95 96 The Marquis du Vivier makes 25,000 cases of fine gentlemanly claret at Le Pian, among forests just N of Bordeaux.

de Marbuzet St-Est r ★★ Second label of COS-D'ESTOURNEL until '94 when it became a Cru Bourgeois in its own right.

Margaux Mar r (w) ★★★★ **53 61' 78' 79 80 81' 82'** 83' **84** 85' 86' **87** 88' **89' 90'** 91 **92** 93' 94 95 96 First growth (209 acres), the most seductive and fabulously perfumed of all in its (v frequent) best vintages. Pavillon Rouge (**81 82' 83 85** 86 **87** 88 89 90' 91 92 93 94 95 96) is second wine. Pavillon Blanc is best white (Sauv) of MEDOC (85 86 87 88 **89** 90 **91** 92 93 94 95 96).

Marquis-d'Alesme See d'Alesme.

Marquis-de-Terme Mar r ★★→★★★ **81' 82** 83' 85 86' **87** 88' 89' 90' 91 92 93 95 96 Renovated fourth growth of 84 acres. Fragrant, fairly lean style has developed since '85, with more Cab S and more flesh.

Martinens Mar r ★★ **81 82 83** 85 86 88 **89** 90 **91** 92 93 94' 95 96 Worthy 75-acre CRU BOURGEOIS of the mayor of CANTENAC; new barrels since '89.

Maucaillou Moulis r ★★ **75' 79 81 82 83' 85'** 86' **87 88' 89' 90'** 91 92 93 94' 95 96 130-acre CRU BOURGEOIS with high standards, property of DOURTHE family. Richly fruity Cap de Haut-Maucaillou is second wine.

Mazeyres Pom r ★★ Consistent, useful, improving lesser POMEROL. (50 acres.)

Méaume B'x Supérieur r ★★ An Englishman's domaine, N of POMEROL. Since '80 has built solid reputation for vg daily claret to age 4–5 yrs. 7,500 cases.

Meyney St-Est r ★★→★★★ **75' 78' 79** 81 82' **83** 85 86' **87** 88' 89' 90' 91 92 93 94 95 96 Big (125-acre) riverside property next door to CH MONTROSE in a superb situation; one of the best of many steady CRUS BOURGEOIS in ST-ESTEPHE. Owned by CORDIER. Second label: Prieur de Meyney.

Millet Graves r w (p) ★★ (r) **82 83 85 86 88** 89 90' **92 93** 94 95 96 Useful GRAVES. Second label, Clos Renon: drink young. Cuvée Henri: new oak-aged white.

La Mission-Haut-Brion Graves r ★★★★ **59 61 64 66' 75' 78' 79 80** 81 82' **83 84 85' 86 87** 88 89' 90' 91 92 93 94' 95 96 Neighbour and long-time rival to CH HAUT-BRION; since '84 in same hands. New equipment in '87. Consistently grand-scale full-blooded wine for long maturing; even 'bigger' wine than H-B. 30 acres. Second label is La Chapelle de la Mission. White is LAVILLE-H-B.

Monbousquet St-Em r ★★ **78' 79'** 81 82 83 **85'** 86 88' 89' 90' 93 94 95 96 Attractive early-maturing wine from deep gravel soil: lasts well. Second label: Ch Caperot 91 92'.

Monbrison Arsac-Mar r ★★→★★★ 81 82 83 **84 85 86** 87 **88' 89' 90** 91 **92** 93 94 95 96 A new name to watch. Top Bourgeois standards (plus new oak). 4,000 cases and 2,000 of second label, Ch Cordet.

Montrose St-Est r ★★★→★★★★ 61 64 **66 70' 75'** 76 78 81 82' **83 84** 85 **86' 87** 88 89' 90' 91 92 93 94 95 96 158-acre family-run second growth famous for deeply coloured forceful old-style claret. Vintages 79–85 (except 82) were lighter, but recent Montrose is almost ST-ESTEPHE'S answer to CH LATOUR. Second wine: La Dame de Montrose.

Moulin du Cadet St-Em r p ★★ 81 82' **83** 85 **86 88** 89' **90' 92** 93 95 96 Little v'yd on the COTES, owned by J-P MOUEIX. Fragrant medium-bodied wines.

Moulin-Pey-Labrie Canon-Fronsac r ★★ Increasingly well-made drinker-friendly Fronsac.

Moulin-à-Vent Moulis r ★★ **81 82' 83** 85' **86 87** 88 **89 90'** 91 92 93 94 95 96 60-acre property in the forefront of this booming AC. Lively forceful wine. LA TOUR-BLANCHE (MEDOC) has the same owners.

Moulinet Pom r ★★ **82 83** 85 **86** 87 88 89' **90** 92 93 94 95 96 One of POMEROL'S bigger châteaux; 45 acres on lightish soil, wine lightish too.

Mouton-Baronne-Philippe See d'Armailhac.

Mouton-Rothschild Pau r (w) ★★★★ **59 61 62' 66' 70' 75'** 76 78 81 82' 83' 85' 86' **87** 88' 89' 90' 91 92 93' 94 95' 96 Officially a first growth only since '73, though for 40 yrs worthy of the title. 175 acres (87% Cab S) make majestic rich wine, often MEDOC'S most opulent (also, from '91, white Aile d'Argent). Artists' labels and the world's greatest museum of art relating to wine. Baron Philippe, the foremost champion of the MEDOC, died in '88. His daughter Philippine now reigns. See also Opus One, California.

Nairac Saut w sw ★★ 73 75 76' 79 **80 81** 82 **83' 85** 86' **87 88 89 90'** 91 92 93 94 95 96 Perfectionist BARSAC classed growth. Wines to lay down for a decade.

Nenin Pom r ★★ **70' 75' 76 78 82 83 85'** 86 **87** 88' 89 90 **93'** 94 95 96 Well-known 66-acre estate; on a (v necessary) but slow upswing since '85 (esp 93, 94).

d'Olivier Graves r w ★★★ (r) 82 83 **84** 85 86 87 88 89' 90' 91 92 93 94 95 96 (w) **87** 88 89 90 **91 92** 93 94 95 96 90-acre classed growth, surrounding a moated castle at LEOGNAN. 9,000 cases red, 6,000 white. New broom since '89 is upgrading flavour (with more oak).

Les Ormes-de-Pez St-Est r ★★→★★★ 75' **78 79** 81' 82' 83' 85 **86' 87** 88 89' 90' 91 92 94 95 96 Outstanding 72-acre CRU BOURGEOIS owned by CH LYNCH-BAGES. Increasingly notable full-flavoured ST-ESTEPHE.

BORDEAUX

Les Ormes-Sorbet Méd r ★★ **78 81 82' 83** 85' 86' **87 88** 89 **90'** 91 92 **93** 94 95 96 Emerging 10,000-case producer of good stylish red aged in new oak at Couquèques. A leader of the N MEDOC. Second label: Ch de Conques.

Palmer Cantenac-Mar r ★★★★ **61' 62 66' 70 71' 75' 76 78' 79' 80 81 82 83' 84** 85 86' **87** 88' 89 90 91 92 93 94 95 96 The star of CANTENAC: a third growth that can achieve first-growth quality. Wine of power, flesh, delicacy and much Merlot. New steel vat-room in '95. 110 acres with Dutch, British (PETER A SICHEL) and French owners. Second wine: Réserve du Général.

Pape-Clément Graves r (w) ★★★ **70 75' 82** 83 85 86' 87 **88' 89' 90' 92 93'** 94' 95 96 Ancient v'yd at PESSAC with record of seductive, scented, not ponderous reds. Early '80s not so good: dramatic new quality (and more white) since '85.

de Parenchère r (w) ★★ **89** 90 93 94 95 Steady supply of useful AC Ste-Foy Bordeaux from handsome château with 125 acres.

Patâche d'Aux Bégadan (Méd) r ★★ **82' 83'** 85 86 88 89' 90' 91 **92** 93 94 95 96 90-acre CRU BOURGEOIS of the N MEDOC. Fragrant largely Cab wine with the earthy quality of its area. See also Ch Liversan.

Paveil (de Luze) Mar r ★★ **81 82'** 83' 85 86' **87** 88' 89' 90 91 92 93 94 95 96 Old family estate at SOUSSANS. Small but highly regarded. Investment '97.

Pavie St-Em r ★★★ **78 79'** 81 82' 83' **85** 86' 87 **88'** 89' 90' 91 **92** 93' 94 95 96 Splendidly-sited first growth; 92 acres mid-slope on the COTES. Rich and tasty and on top form since '82. PAVIE-DECESSE and La Clusière in same family.

Pavie-Decesse St-Em r ★★→★★★ **82 83 85 86 87** 88 89 90 92 93 94 95 96 24 acres seriously challenging their big brother (above).

Pavie-Macquin St-Em r ★★→★★★ **82 83 85' 86 87** 88 89' 90' **92** 94 95 96 Another PAVIE challenge; this time the neighbours up the hill. 25-acre COTES v'yd E of ST-EMILION. Fine organic winemaking by a son of VIEUX CH CERTAN. Second label: Les Chênes.

Pavillon Rouge (Blanc) du Château Margaux See Ch Margaux.

Pedesclaux Pau r ★★ **81 82' 83 85 86 87** 88 89 90' 91 92 93 94 95 96 50-acre fifth growth on the level of a good CRU BOURGEOIS. Solid strong wines that Belgians love. Second labels: Bellerose, Grand-Duroc-Milon.

Petit-Village Pom r ★★★ **75' 78 79 81** 82' 83 **85'** 86 **87** 88 89' 90' **91 92** 93 94 95 96 Top property revived. 26 acres next to VIEUX CHATEAU CERTAN, same owner (AXA) as CH PICHON-LONGUEVILLE since '89. Powerful plummy wine.

Pétrus Pom r ★★★★ **61 62 64 66 67 70' 71' 73 75' 76 78 79' 80 81 82' 83 84 85' 86 87 88' 89' 90** 92 93 94 95 96 The unchallenged (though unofficial) first growth of POMEROL. 28 acres of gravelly clay giving (400 bottles of) massively rich and concentrated wine, on allocation to the world's millionaires. 95% Merlot vines. Each vintage adds lustre (NB no 91).

Peyrabon St-Sauveur r ★★ **79 81 82' 83 85 86' 87 88 89'** 90' 91 92 93 94 95 96 Serious 132-acre CRU BOURGEOIS popular in the Low Countries. Also La Fleur-Peyrabon (only 12 acres).

Peyre-Labade r p Listrac ★★ Second label of CH CLARKE.

Peyreau St-Em r ★★ Sister-château of CLOS DE L'ORATOIRE.

de Pez St-Est r ★★★ **64 70' 75' 76 78' 79 81 82'** 83 **85** 86' **87** 88 89 90' 91 92 **93' 94** 95 96 Outstanding CRU BOURGEOIS of 60 acres. As reliable as any of the classed growths of the village if not as fine. Direction from CHAMPAGNE house ROEDERER in Reims.

Phélan-Ségur St-Est r ★★→★★★ **75' 81** 82' **85 86 87** 88' 89' 90' **91 92** 93 94 95 96 Big and important CRU BOURGEOIS (125 acres): some fine old vintages. No 83 or 84 vintages, but from '86 has gone from strength to strength.

Pibran Pau r ★★ **87 88** 89' 90' 91 92 93 94 95 Small CRU BOURGEOIS allied to PICHON-LONGUEVILLE. Classy wine with PAUILLAC drive.

Pichon-Lalande (formerly Pichon-Longueville, Comtesse de Lalande) Pau r ★★★★ 61 62 66 **70' 75' 76** 78' 79' 81 **82'** 83' **84** 85' 86' 87 88' 89' 90' 91 92 93 94 95 96 'Super-second'-growth neighbour to CH LATOUR. 148 acres. Consistently among v top performers; long-lived wine of fabulous breed for those who like it luscious, even in lesser yrs. Second wine: Réserve de la Comtesse. Rivalry across the road (next entry) is well worth watching.

Pichon-Longueville (formerly Baron de Pichon-Longueville) Pau r ★★★★ 78 79' **81** 82' 83 85 86' 87 88' 89' 90' 91 92 93 94' 95 96 77-acre second growth: wines have varied widely. Since '87 owned by AXA Insurance, run by J-M Cazes (LYNCH-BAGES). Revitalized winemaking matches aggressive new buildings. Second label: Les Tourelles de Longueville.

Le Pin Pom r ★★★★ 81 82 83 **85** 86 87 88 89 90' 92 93 94 95 96 A mere 500 cases of Merlot, with same owners as VIEUX-CHATEAU-CERTAN. A perfectionist miniature, but prices well beyond PETRUS are ridiculous.

Pindefleurs St-Em r ★★ **82' 83 85 86** 88 89 90' 92 **93'** 94 95 96 Steady 23-acre v'yd on light soil. Second label: Clos Lescure.

Pique-Caillou Graves r (w dr) ★★ 85' **86 88'** 89 90' 91 92 93 94 95 96 Refurbished property nr Bordeaux airport. Some seductive GRAVES, and white since '93. Also next-door Ch Chênevert. Plans for new road ('97) through estate being fiercely contested: watch this space...

de Pitray Castillon r ★★ **82** 83 85 86 **87 88** 89 90 91 92 93 94 95 96 Large (62-acre) v'yd on COTES DE CASTILLON E of ST-EM. Flavoursome chewy wines.

> **St-Emilion: the class system**
>
> **St-Emilion has its own class system, last revised in 1996. At the top are two Premiers Grands Crus Classés 'A': Châteaux Ausone and Cheval Blanc. Then come 11 Premiers Grands Crus Classés 'B'. 55 châteaux were elected as Grands Crus Classés. Another 170-odd are classed simply as Grands Crus, a rank renewable each year after official tastings. St-Emilion Grand Cru is therefore the very approximate equivalent of Médoc Crus Bourgeois and Grand Bourgeois.**

Plagnac Méd r ★★ **82 83** 85 86 88 **89'** 90' **91** 92 93 94 95 96 CRU BOURGEOIS at Bégadan in N MEDOC restored by CORDIER. To follow.

Plince Pom r ★★ **75 79 81 82 83 85** 86 88 89' 90 92 93 **94 95** 96 Reputable 20-acre property nr Libourne. Lightish wine from sandy soil.

La Pointe Pom r ★★→★★★ 82 83' 85 **86** 88 89' 90' 92 93 94 95 96 Prominent 63-acre estate; well-made wines, but relatively spare of flesh. LA SERRE is in the same hands.

Pontac-Monplaisir Graves r (w) ★★ **87** 89 90 91 92 93 94 95 96 Another GRAVES property offering delicious white and fragrant light red.

Pontet-Canet Pau r ★★★ **81 82'** 83 85 86' 87 **88 89' 90' 91 92** 93 94' 95 96 182-acre neighbour to MOUTON-ROTHSCHILD. Dragged its feet for many yrs. Owners (same as LAFON-ROCHET) have done better since '85. Should make v fine wines, but hardness is an old problem. '90 vintages promise well. New investment in '96. Second label: Les Hauts de Pontet.

Pontoise-Cabarrus H-Méd r ★★ Useful and improving 60-acre CRU BOURGEOIS at ST-SEURIN. Wines need 5–6 yrs.

Potensac Méd r ★★ 78' 81' 82' 83 85' 86 87 88 89' 90' 91 92 **93** 94 95 96 Best-known CRU BOURGEOIS of N MEDOC. Neighbouring ch'x Lassalle, Gallais-Bellevue and super-second LEOVILLE-LAS-CASES all owned by Delon family. Class shows.

Pouget Mar ★★ **78 81 82' 83 85 86 87** 88 **89** 90 **91** 92 93 94 95 96 19 acres attached to BOYD-CANTENAC. Sharing owners since 1906. Similar, lighter wines.

Poujeaux (Theil) Moulis r ★★ **70' 75' 76 78 79' 81 82' 83' 85' 86 87 88' 89' 90'** 91 92 **93'** 94' 95 96 Family-run CRU EXCEPTIONNEL of 120 acres. 20,000-odd cases of characterful tannic and concentrated wine for a long life. Second label: La Salle de Poujeaux. Also Ch Arnauld.

Prieuré-Lichine Cantenac-Mar r ★★★ **70 75 78' 82' 83' 85 86' 87** 88 89' **90' 91 92** 93' 94' 95 96 143-acre fourth growth brought to the fore by the late Alexis Lichine, now advised by Michel Rolland. Full fragrant MARGAUX currently on form. Second wine: Clairefont. Now producing a good Bordeaux Blanc.

Puy-Blanquet St-Em r ★★ **75' 82' 83 85 86 88** 89' 90' 92 **93 94** 95 96 The major property of St-Etienne-de-Lisse, E of ST-EMILION, with over 50 acres.

Puygueraud Côte de Francs r ★★ **85 86 88 89' 90 92** 93 94 95 96 Leading château of this rising district. Wood-aged wines of surprising class. Ch Laclaverie and Les Charmes-Godard follow the same lines.

Rabaud-Promis Saut w sw ★★→★★★ **83' 85 86' 87 88'** 89' 90 95 96 74-acre classed growth at Bommes. Since '86 near top rank. Rich stuff.

Rahoul Graves r w ★★ (r) **82 83 85 86 88 89' 90' 91 92** 93 94 95 96 37-acre v'yd at Portets making particularly good wine from maturing vines; 80% red. White (90 91 **94** 95 96) also oak-aged.

Ramage-la-Bâtisse H-Méd r ★★ **82 83' 85 86 88 89' 90 91 92** 93 94 95 96 Potentially outstanding CRU BOURGEOIS of 130 acres at ST-SAUVEUR, N of PAUILLAC. Increasingly good since '85. Ch Tourteran is second wine.

Rausan-Ségla Mar r ★★★→★★★★ **70' 82 83' 84 85 86'** 88' **89'** 90' **91** 92 93 94' 95 96 106-acre second growth famous for its fragrance; a great MEDOC name since '82 trying successfully to regain its rank. New owners in '94 have invested heavily. Second wine: Ségla. This should be the top second growth of all. Ancient vintages can be superb.

Rauzan-Gassies Mar r ★★ **75' 79 82 83 85 86 88 89' 90' 91** 92 **93** 94 95 96 75-acre second-growth neighbour of the last with little excitement to report for two decades. But '96 looks like new leaf.

Raymond-Lafon Saut w sw ★★★ **75' 76 78 79 80' 81 82 83' 85 86' 87 88** 89' 90' 91 92 93 94 95 96 Serious SAUTERNES estate of 44 acres now run by the ex-manager of YQUEM. Splendid wines for prolonged ageing. Ranks among the v top Sauternes.

de Rayne-Vigneau Saut w sw ★★ **76' 83 85 86' 88' 89** 90' **91 92** 94 95 96 164-acre classed growth at Bommes. Standard sweet wine and dry Rayne Sec.

Respide-Médeville Graves w (r) ★★ (w) **87 88 89 90 91** 92' 93 94 95 96 One of the better unclassified white wine châteaux. Full-flavoured wines for ageing. (NB Cuvée Kauffman.) Drink the reds at 4–6 yrs.

Reynon Premières Côtes r w ★★→★★★ 100 acres for fragrant white from old Sauv vines (VIEILLES VIGNES) (**92 93' 94 95 96**); also serious red (**85 86 88' 89 90 91 92 93 94 95** 96). Second wine (red): Ch Reynon-Peyrat. See also Clos Floridène.

Reysson Vertheuil (H-Méd) r ★★ **82' 83 85 86 87** 88 **89'** 90' 95 96 Recently replanted 120-acre CRU BOURGEOIS in Japanese hands.

Ricaud Loupiac w sw (r dr) ★★ (w) **81 82 83' 85 86' 88** 89 90 91 92 94 95 96 Substantial grower of almost SAUTERNES-like wine just across the river. New owners are working hard. It ages well.

Rieussec Saut w sw ★★★★ **67 71' 75' 79 81 82 83' 85 86' 87** 88' 89' 90' 91 92 93 94 95 96 Worthy neighbour of CH D'YQUEM with 136 acres in Fargues, bought in '84 by the (LAFITE) Rothschilds. Can be exquisitely fine. Also dry 'R' and super-wine Crème de Tête.

Smaller Bordeaux châteaux to watch for:

The detailed list of Bordeaux châteaux on these pages is limited to the prestigious classified parts of the vast Bordeaux region. But this huge vineyard by the Atlantic works on many levels. Standard Bordeaux appellation wine is claret at its most basic – but it is still recognizable. The areas listed on this page with some of their leading châteaux are a more important resource; they are potentially distinct and worthwhile variations on the claret theme to be investigated and enjoyed.

Bordeaux Supérieur Château Dôme Ile de Margaux

Canon-Fronsac Châteaux Coustolle, La Fleur Caillou, Junayme, Mazeris-Bellevue, Toumalin, La Truffière, Vraye-Canon-Boyer

Côtes de Bourg Châteaux La Barde, Brûlesécaille, Falfas (try 89 90 91 92 93 94 in '98, esp 89 90), Font Guilhem, Grand-Jour, de la Grave, La Grolet, Guerry, Guionne, Haut-Maco, Lalibarde, Lamothe, Mendoce, Peychaud (89 90 ready for '98 drinking), Roc des Combes, Rousset, Tayac, de Thau

Côtes de Castillon Châteaux Beauséjour, Belcier (92 90 89 are to try in '98), La Clarière-Laithwaite, Côte Montpezat (best in '98: 94 and 95), Fonds-Rondes, Haut-Tuquet, Lartigue, Moulin-Rouge, Rocher-Bellevue, Ste-Colombe, Thibaud-Bellevue

Côtes de Francs Châteaux de Belcier, Les Charmes Godard, La Claverie, de Francs, Lauriol, La Prade

Entre-Deux-Mers Châteaux Gournin, Latour-Laguens, Moulin de Launay, Séguin, Turcaud

Fronsac Châteaux Fontenil, Mayne-Vieil, Moulin-Haut-Laroque, La Rousselle, La Valade, La Vieille Cure, Villars (82 85 86 88 89 best in '98)

Lalande de Pomerol Châteaux Les Annereaux, Belles-Graves, La Croix Bellevue, La Croix-St-André, Les Hauts Conseillants (86 89 90 92 will be good in '98) and châteaux Les Hauts-Tuileries, Moncets

Lussac St-Emilion Châteaux Barbe Blanche, Bel Air, Du Courlat (89 90 92 ready in '98, also cuvée Jean-Baptiste), Tour de Grenat, Villadière

Montagne St-Emilion Châteaux Calon, Faizeau, Haut-Gillet, Maison Blanche, Roudier, Teyssier (esp 94 95 for '98)

Premières Côtes de Blaye Châteaux Bertinerie (89 90 92 93 94 reds, 91 92 93 Haut-Bertinerie white ready in '98), Barbé, Charron, l'Escadre, Haut-Sociando, Le Menaudat, Peybonhomme Les Tours (95 and prior for drinking in '98, esp 91 92), La Rose-Bellevue, Segonzac (93 and 94 ready in '98), La Tonnelle

Premières Côtes de Bordeaux Château Bertinerie (vg), Carsin, La Croix de Roche, Fayau, Fontenil, Gardera, du Juge, Laffitte (sic), Lamothe, Peyrat, Plaisance, Tanesse, Suau (91 93 94 95 will be ready for '98 drinking), Lafitte-Laguens

Sainte-Croix du Mont Châteaux Clos des Coulinats, Loubens, Lousteau-Vieil, du Mont

For key to grape variety abbreviations, see pages 7–13.

Ripeau St-Em r ★★ **81 82 83 85 86 87 88 89 90** 93 94 95 96 Steady GRAND CRU in the centre of the plateau. 40 acres.

La Rivière Fronsac r ★★ **82 83 85' 86 87** 88' **89** 90 95 96 The biggest and most impressive FRONSAC property with a Wagnerian castle. Tannic but juicy wines win prizes in youth and stay young for a decade.

de Rochemorin Graves r (w) ★★→★★★ **82 83 85 86 87 88 89' 90' 91 92 93** 95 96 An important restoration at Martillac by the Lurtons of CH LA LOUVIERE: 165 acres of maturing vines promise great things. Oaky whites to keep 4–5 yrs.

Romer Saut w sw Classed growth with its name under legal dispute.

de Roquetaillade-la-Grange Graves r w ★★ **86 88 89 90** 91 **92** 93 **94 95** 96 Substantial estate: fine red (southern) GRAVES and well-made white. See Cap de Mourlin.

Rouget Pom r ★★ **75' 76' 78 79 81 82' 83 85' 86 88 89' 90** 92 93 94 95 96 Attractive old estate on the N edge of POMEROL. Good, without polish.

Royal St-Emilion Brand name of the important and dynamic growers' coop. See also Berliquet, Galius.

Ruat-Petit-Poujeaux Moulis r ★★ **82 85 86 88 89 90** 91 **92** 93 94 95 96 45-acre v'yd gaining in reputation for vigorous wine, to drink in 5–6 yrs.

St-André-Corbin St-Em r ★★ **81 82' 83 85' 86** 88 **89** 90 **92** 93 94 95 96 54-acre estate in MONTAGNE- and ST-GEORGES-ST-EMILION: above-average wines.

St-Bonnet Méd r ★★ **82 85 86 88** 89 90 **91 92** 93 94 95 96 Big N MEDOC estate at St-Christoly. V flavoursome wine.

St-Estèphe, Marquis de St-Est r ★ **82 86 88 89 90** 93 94 95 96 The growers' coop; bigger but not as interesting as formerly.

St-Georges St-Georges-St-Em r ★★ **82 83 85' 86 87 88' 89' 90'** 92 93 94 95 96 Noble 18th-C château overlooking the ST-EMILION plateau from the hill to the north. 125 acres. Vg wine sold direct to the public.

St-Georges-Côte-Pavie St-Em r ★★ **82 83' 85' 86 88' 89'** 90' 92 93 94 95 96 Perfectly placed little v'yd on the COTES. Run with dedication.

St-Pierre St-Jul r ★★★ **70' 78' 81' 82' 83' 85** 86' 88' 89' 90' 91 92 93 94 95 96 Small (42-acre) fourth growth bought in '82 by the late Henri Martin of CH GLORIA. V stylish and consistent classic ST-JULIEN.

de St-Pierre Graves w (r) ★★ Main-line white of notable character and flavour to drink young or keep. Also red.

> **Rotting with style**
> Botrytis cinerea (French pourriture noble, German Edelfäule, English noble rot) is a form of mould that attacks the skins of ripe grapes in certain vineyards in warm and misty autumn weather.
>
> Its effect, instead of rotting the grapes, is to wither them. The skin grows soft and flaccid, the juice evaporates through it, and what is left is a super-sweet concentration of everything in the grape except its water content.
>
> The world's best sweet table wines are all made of 'nobly rotten' grapes. They occur in good vintages in Sauternes, the Rhine and the Mosel (where wine made from them is called Trockenbeerenauslese), in Tokaji in Hungary, in Burgenland in Austria, and elsewhere – California and Australia included. The danger is rain on pulpy grapes already far gone in botrytis. All too often the growers' hopes are dashed by the weather.

de Sales Pom r ★★★ **75' 82' 83 85 86** 88 89' 90' 92 93 94 95 96 Biggest v'yd of POMEROL (116 acres), attached to grandest château. Not poetry, but some good prose. Second labels: ch'x Chantalouette, du Delias.

Saransot-Dupré Listrac r (w) ★★ 86 88 89 90 92 93 94 95 96 Small property performing well since '86. Also one of LISTRAC's growing band of whites.

Sénéjac H-Méd r (w) ★★ **78 82' 83'** 85 **86' 87** 88 89' 90' 91 92 93 94 95 96 60-acre CRU BOURGEOIS in S MEDOC. Unusual all-Sém white, to age (90 91 92 93 94 95 96). Second label: Artigue de Sénéjac.

La Serre St-Em r ★★ **75 81** 82 **83** 85 **86** 88' 89 90 **92** 93 94 95 96 Small GRAND CRU, same owner as LA POINTE. Increasingly tasty.

Siaurac Lalande de Pom r ★★ Substantial, consistent; nr POMEROL. 57 acres.

Sigalas-Rabaud Saut w sw ★★★ **76'** 79 80 81 82 **83** 85 86 **87** 88' 89' 90' 91 92 95 96 The smaller part of the former RABAUD estate: 34 acres in Bommes making fine sweet wine in a rich grapey style.

Siran Labarde-Mar r ★★ **70 75'** 78' **81** 82' **83 85** 86 **88** 89' **90'** 93 94 95 96 77-acre property approaching CRU CLASSE quality. Recent investment. To follow for full-flavoured wines to age.

Smith-Haut-Lafitte Graves r (w p) ★★★ (red) **82' 85 86 89'** 90' 91 92 93 94 95 96, (white) 92 **93 94** 95 96 Classed growth at Martillac: 122 acres (14 acres planted to white grape varieties). Ambitious new owners (since '90) have spent hugely to spectacular effect. Second label: Les Hauts de Smith.

Sociando-Mallet H-Méd r ★★ 82' **83** 85' 86' 88' 89' 90' 91 92 93 94 95 96 Splendid CRU GRAND BOURGEOIS at ST-SEURIN. 65 acres. Conservative big-boned wines to lay down for yrs. Second wine: Demoiselles de Sociando.

Soudars H-Méd r ★★ **86** 89 90 **93** 94 95 96 Sister to COUFRAN; new CRU BOURGEOIS doing v well.

Soutard St-Em r ★★★ 70' 71 78' **79** 81 **82'** 83 **85'** 86 87 88' 89' **90'** 91 92 93 94 95 96 Excellent 48-acre classed growth, 60% Merlot. Potent wines: long-lived for Anglo-Saxon drinking; exciting young to French palates. Second label: Clos de la Tonnelle.

Suduiraut Saut w sw ★★★★ 67 70 75 76' **78 79' 81** 82' 83' **84 85 86** 88' 89' 90' 94 95 96 One of the best SAUTERNES, in its best vintages supremely luscious. 173 acres potentially of top class. Now in AXA control. See Pichon-Longueville. Sélection Cuvée Madame (**82 83 86** 89).

du Tailhas Pom r ★★ 5,000 cases. POMEROL of the lighter kind, near FIGEAC.

Taillefer Pom r ★★ **82** 83 85 86 **88'** 89 **90** 92 **93** 94 95 96 28-acres on the edge of POMEROL in the Antoine Moueix family (see also Fonplégade).

Talbot St-Jul r (w) ★★★ 78' **79 81** 82' 83' **84 85'** 86' 87 88' 89' 90 92 93 94 95 96 Important 240-acre fourth growth, sister to GRUAUD-LAROSE. Wine similarly attractive: rich, satisfying, reliable; gd value. Vg second label: Connétable Talbot. White: 'Caillou Blanc'. Oenologist also oversees TOUR DE MONS.

Tayac Soussans-Mar r ★★ **82** 83 85 86 **87** 88 89 90 92 93 94 95 96 MARGAUX'S biggest CRU BOURGEOIS. Reliable if not noteworthy.

de Terrefort-Quancard B'x r w ★★ **89 90 91** 92 93 94 95 96 Huge producer of good-value wines at ST-ANDRE-DE-CUBZAC on the road to Paris. Rocky subsoil contributes to very drinkable quality. 33,000 cases. Drink at 5–10 yrs. Several other châteaux owned by Cheval-Quancard.

Terrey-Gros-Caillou St-Jul ★★ 82' **83 85** 86' 88 89 90 91 92 93 94 95 96 Sister-château to HORTEVIE; at best, equally noteworthy and stylish.

du Tertre Arsac-Mar r ★★ **70' 79' 81** 82' **83'** 85 86 88' 89' 90' 91 92 93 94 95 96 Fifth growth isolated S of MARGAUX; restored by the owner of CALON-SEGUR. Formerly fragrant and long-lived. To watch in hope.

Tertre-Daugay St-Em r ★★★ 82' 83' 85 86 88' 89' 90' 92 93 94 95 96 Small, spectacularly sited GRAND CRU. Restored to good order by owner of LA GAFFELIERE.

Le Tertre-Rôteboeuf St-Em ★★★ 85 86 87 88' 89' 90' 91 92 93 94 95 96 A new star making concentrated, even dramatic, largely Merlot wine since '83. The 'roast beef' of the name gives the right idea.

Thieuley E-Deux-Mers r p w ★★ Substantial supplier esp of clairet (rosé) and grapey Sauv. But reds are aged in oak.

Timberlay B'x r (w) ★ **92 93 94** 95 96 185 acres at ST-ANDRE-DE-CUBZAC. Pleasant light wines to age 2–5 yrs. Same owners as VILLEMAURINE.

Toumilon Graves r w ★★ Little château in St-Pierre-de-Mons to note. Fresh and charming red and white.

La Tour-Blanche Saut w (r) sw ★★★ **81' 82 83' 85 86 87** 88' **89' 90'** 91 92 **93** 94 95 96 Historic leader of SAUTERNES, now a gov't wine college. Coasted in '70s; hit historic form again in '88.

La Tour-de-By Bégadan (Méd) r ★★ **81 82' 83 85' 86 87 88' 89' 90' 91 92** 93 94 95 96 V well-run 182-acre CRU BOURGEOIS in N MEDOC increasing its reputation for attractive sturdy wine.

La Tour-Carnet St-Laurent r ★★ **82 83 85 86 88 89' 90 91 92** 93' 94' 95 96 Fourth growth with medieval fortress, long neglected. Light wine; slightly bolder since '86. Second wine: Sire de Comin.

La Tour-Figeac St-Em r ★★ **79 81 82' 83 85 86 87 88 89' 90'** 93 94' 95 96 34-acre GRAND CRU CLASSE between CH FIGEAC, POMEROL. California-style ideas since '94.

La Tour-Haut-Brion Graves r ★★★ **70 78 79 81 82' 83 85 87 88** 89 90 91 92 93 94 95 96 Formerly second label of CH LA MISSION-HAUT-BRION. Up to '83 a plainer, v tannic wine. Now a separate v'yd: wines more fun to drink.

La Tour-Haut-Caussan Méd r ★★ Ambitious small (23-acre) estate at Blaignan to watch.

La Tour-du-Haut-Moulin Cussac (H-Méd) r ★★ **75 76 81 82' 83 84 85'** 86' **87** 88' 89' 90' 91 92 93 94 95 96 Conservative grower: intense top CRU BOURGEOIS.

La Tour-de-Mons Soussans-Mar r ★★ **70' 82' 83 85 86'** 88' 89' 90' 91 92 93 94 95 96 Famous CRU BOURGEOIS of 87 acres, 3 centuries in the same family. A long dull patch but new ('95) TALBOT-influence means wines look better.

Tour du Pas St-Georges St-Em r ★★ Wine from 40 acres of ST-GEORGES-ST-EMILION made by AUSONE winemaker. V stylish; to follow.

La Tour-du-Pin-Figeac St-Em r ★★ 26-acre GRAND CRU worthy of restoration.

La Tour-du-Pin-Figeac-Moueix St-Em r ★★ **81 82 83 85 86** 88' 89' 90' 92 93 94 95 96 Another 26-acre section of the same old property, owned by the Armand Moueix family. Splendid site; powerful wines.

La Tour-St-Bonnet Méd r ★★ **82' 83 85 86 87** 88 **89' 90' 91 92 93** 94 95 96 Consistently well-made potent N MEDOC from St-Christoly. 100 acres.

Tournefeuille Lalande de Pom r ★★ **81' 82' 83' 85 86 88 89 90'** 91 92 93 94 95 96 Best-known château of NEAC. 43 acres; sound wine. Also Ch de Bourg.

des Tours Montagne-St-Em r ★★ **82 85 86 88 89 90 92 93 94 95** 96 Spectacular château with modern 170-acre v'yd. Sound easy wine.

Toutigeac, Domaine de E-Deux-Mers r (w) ★ **89 90'** 91 92 93 **94' 95** 96 Enormous producer of useful Bordeaux at Targon.

Tronquoy-Lalande St-Est r ★★ **70 79 81 82' 83 85 86 88 89 90** 92 93 94 95 96 40-acre CRU BOURGEOIS estate: typical high-coloured, ageworthy wines. DOURTHE-distributed.

Troplong-Mondot St-Em r ★★★ **82' 83 85'** 86 **87 88' 89' 90' 91 92** 93 94 95 96 70 acres well-sited on the COTES above CH PAVIE (and in same family). Now run with passion and new barrels. To follow. Second wine: Mondot.

Trotanoy Pom r ★★★★ **61' 70' 71' 75' 76' 78 79 81 82 83 84 85'** 86 **87 88 89 90'** 92 93 94 95 96 Potentially the second POMEROL, after PETRUS, from the same stable. Only 27 acres; but at best (eg 82) a glorious fleshy perfumed wine. Ten wobbly years since; now resurgence.

Trottevieille St-Em r ★★★ **79' 81 82' 83 85' 86 87 88 89' 90** 92 93 94 95 96 GRAND CRU of 27 acres on the COTES. Dragged its feet for yrs. Same owners as BATAILLEY have raised their sights since '85.

Le Tuquet Graves r w ★★ (r) **93 94 95** 96 (w) **93 94 95 96** Big estate at Beautiran. Light fruity wines to drink young; the white better. (Cuvée Spéciale oak-aged.)

Valandraud St-Em r ★★★ 91 92 93 94 95 96 Brand-new micro-château with aspirations to glory. Already silly prices.

Verdignan Méd r ★★ **81 82 83 85 86 87 88 89' 90** 91 92 95 96 Substantial Bourgeois sister to CH COUFRAN. More Cab than Coufran.

Vieux-Château-Certan Pom r ★★★ **78 79 81 82' 83' 85** 86' **87 88'** 89 90' 92 93 94 95 96 Traditionally rated close to PETRUS in quality, but totally different in style; almost HAUT-BRION build. 34 acres. Same (Belgian) family owns LABEGORCE-ZEDE and tiny POMEROL, LE PIN. See also Château Puygueraud.

Vieux-Château-St-André St-Em r ★★ **81 82' 83 85' 86 87 88' 89' 90' 91** 92 93' 94' 95 Small v'yd in MONTAGNE-ST-EMILION owned by the winemaker of PETRUS. To follow. 2,500 cases.

Villegeorge Avensan r ★★ **82 83' 85 86 87' 88** 89 90 92 93 94 95 96 24-acre CRU BOURGEOIS N of MARGAUX; same owner as BRANE-CANTENAC. Enjoyable rather tannic wine. Sister-château: Duplessis (Hauchecorne).

Villemaurine St-Em r ★★ **82' 83 85' 86 87 88** 89 90 **91** 92 93 94 95 96 Small GRAND CRU with splendid cellars (some new investment '96) well-sited on the COTES by the town. Firm wine with a high proportion of Cab.

Vray-Croix-de-Gay Pom ★★ **75' 82' 83 85 86 87 88 89 90 92 93 94 95** 96 V small ideally situated v'yd in the best part of POMEROL. Needs devotion.

Yon-Figeac St-Em r ★★ **81 82 83 85 86 88 89 90 92** 93 94 95 96 59-acre GRAND CRU to follow for savoury supple wine.

d'Yquem Saut w sw (dr) ★★★★ **67' 71' 73 75' 76' 77 78 79 80' 81' 82' 83' 84 85 86' 87** 88' 89' 90' (91 93 94 95 to come) The world's most famous sweet-wine estate. 250 acres; only 500 bottles per acre of v strong intense luscious wine, kept 4 yrs in barrel. Most vintages improve for 15 yrs+. Also makes dry Ygrec ('Y') in 78 79 80 84 85 (86 v little) 87 88 89 91 92 95.

More Bordeaux châteaux are listed under Canon-Fronsac, Côtes de Bourg, Côtes de Castillon, Côtes de Francs, Fronsac, Lalande de Pomerol, Loupiac, Premières Côtes de Blaye, Premières Côtes de Bordeaux, St-André-de-Cubzac, Ste-Croix-du-Mont in the A–Z of France, pages 32–77.

Italy

Heavier shaded areas are
the wine growing regions

The following abbreviations are used in the text:

Ab	Abruzzi	Pie	Piedmont
Ap	Apulia	Sar	Sardinia
Bas	Basilicata	Si	Sicily
Cal	Calabria	T-AA	Trentino-Alto Adige
Cam	Campania	Tus	Tuscany
E-R	Emilia-Romagna	Umb	Umbria
F-VG	Friuli-Venezia Giulia	VdA	Valle d'Aosta
Lat	Latium	Ven	Veneto
Lig	Liguria		
Lom	Lombardy	fz	frizzante
Mar	Marches	pa	passito

Italy's genius tends to be of a private and idiosyncratic nature, revealing itself in beauty amongst ugliness, kindness and wit among people with little to spare. It also rears its head in the steady defiance with which wine growers raise their personal stakes despite the inefficiencies of the legislation around them.

When the 1992 Wine Law was introduced I suggested that it would eventually make everything orderly and intelligible. I outlined its 'pyramid' system with the (officially) humble vino da tavola at the bottom, narrowing to the lofty and exclusive Vigna wine from a DOCG zone at the top. Yet after half a dozen years the law seems to have changed almost nothing.

It clearly was never going to increase the skill and dedication of the very best growers and makers – predictably following their own instincts, and in many cases with stunning results. The finest Italian red wines rank among the best in the world.

Italians may well disagree with me, but their country is not the source of fine white wines. Although at once I can think of dozens of exceptions, starting in the northeast in Friuli and running down through the peninsula as far south as Campania and even further in Sicily. It is fairer to say that the average Italian's taste in white wine remains devoted to neutral dryness, avoiding those lovely hints of fruit that would be there if they didn't strip them out. This is even the case in Piedmont and Tuscany – Italy's greatest wine regions. Neither produces white wines to compare with their reds.

But their reds are so original and glorious that they distract attention from many other regions with their striking and memorable flavours. For example, value-seekers should continue

looking closely at the eastern side of the country – especially from the Abruzzi down to Apulia, Italy's heel. Collectively this may be the biggest vineyard in the world – and yet until the past few years it has remained virtually anonymous; its wines leaving home in tankers to unknown destinies in the north.

Sloppy winemakers in the famous regions have the luxury of names to ride on. Emerging regions have an entirely different ethos. Montepulciano d'Abruzzo, Salice Salentino... these and dozens of other debutante Adriatic DOCs are worth careful study.

Abbazia di Rosazzo ★★★ Major estate of the COLLI ORIENTALI. White Ronco delle Acacie and Ronco di Corte and red Ronco dei Roseti are all vg single-v'yd wines.

Abboccato Semi-sweet.

Adami ★★→★★★ Producers of top PROSECCO DI CONEGLIANO-VALDOBBIADENE (Vigneto Giardino).

Adanti ★★→★★★ Umbrian producer of pleasant red SAGRANTINO DI MONTEFALCO, VINO DA TAVOLA BIANCO D'ARQUATA and Rosso d'Arquata (a vg blend of BARBERA, Canaiolo and MERLOT). Also gd CABERNET SAUVIGNON reds. Good value.

Aglianico del Vulture Bas DOC r dr (s/sw sp) ★★★ **87 88 90** 91 92 93 94 (95) (96) Among the best wines of S Italy. Ages well to rich aromas. Called VECCHIO after 3 yrs, RISERVA after 5. Top growers: D'ANGELO (also makes vg pure Aglianico VDT Canneto) and PATERNOSTER.

Alba Major wine city of PIEDMONT, on River Tanaro, S of Turin.

Albana di Romagna E-R DOCG w dr s/sw (sp) ★★(★) DYA Italy's first DOCG for white wine, though it is hard to see why. Albana is the (undistinguished) grape. FATTORIA PARADISO makes some of the best. AMABILE is usually better than dry. ZERBINA's botrytis-sweet PASSITO (Scacco Matto) is outstanding.

Alcamo Si DOC w ★ Soft neutral whites. Rapitalà is the best brand.

Aleatico Excellent red Muscat-flavoured grape for sweet aromatic strong wines, chiefly of the S. Aleatico di Puglia DOC (best grower is CANDIDO) is better and more famous than Aleatico di Gradoli (Latium) DOC.

Alezio Ap DOC p (r) ★★ DYA Recent DOC at Salento, especially for delicate rosé. Top grower is Calò Michele (who also makes good barrel-aged NEGROAMARO VDT, Vigna Spano is ★★★).

Allegrini ★★★ Top-quality producer of Veronese wines, incl fine VALPOLICELLA from prime new v'yds and vg AMARONE.

Altare, Elio ★★★ Small producer of good, v modern BAROLO. Look for Barolo Vigna Arborina and BARBERA VDT Vigna Larigi.

Altesino ★★ Producer of BRUNELLO DI MONTALCINO and VDT Palazzo Altesi.

Alto Adige T-AA DOC r p w dr sw sp ★→★★★ DOC covering 20 different wines, usually named by their grapes, in 33 German-speaking villages around Bolzano. Whites are best. Region often called Südtirol.

Ama, Castello di, (or Fattoria di Ama) ★★★→★★★★ One of the best, most consistent modern CHIANTI CLASSICO estates, nr Gaiole. La Casuccia and Bellavista are top single-v'yd wines. Also good VDTS, CHARD, SAUV, MERLOT (Vigna L'Apparita), PINOT N (Il Chiuso).

Amabile Means semi-sweet, but usually sweeter than ABBOCCATO.

Amaro Bitter. When prominent on label, contents are not wine but 'bitters'.

Amarone della Valpolicella (formerly Recioto della Valpolicella Amarone) Ven DOC r ★★★→★★★★ **83 85 86 88 90** 91 93 (94) 95 (96) Dry version of RECIOTO DELLA VALPOLICELLA: potent, concentrated, long-lived and very impressive; from air-dried grapes. Best are from the following growers: Serègo Alighieri, ALLEGRINI, ANTONELLI, BERTANI, BRIGALDARA, Brunelli, Corte Sant Alda, Aleardo Ferrari, DAL FORNO, GUERRIERI-RIZZARDI, LE RAGOSE, MASI, QUINTARELLI, SAN RUSTICO, LE SALETTE, Speri, TEDESCHI, Villa Spinosa. NB alcohol content is high.

Anghelu Ruju ★★★ ('Red Angel') Port-like version of Sardinian CANNONAU wine from SELLA & MOSCA. Well worth trying.

Anselmi, Roberto ★★★ A leader in SOAVE with his single-vineyard Capitel Foscarino and exceptional sweet dessert RECIOTO dei Capitelli.

NB Vintages in colour are those you should choose first for drinking in 1998.

Antinori, Marchesi L & P ★→★★★ Immensely influential long-established Florentine house of the highest repute, now wholly owned by Piero A, who shares the management with his daughters. Famous for first-rate CHIANTI CLASSICO (esp PEPPOLI, Tenute Marchese Antinori, Villa Antinori and Badia a Passignano), Umbrian (CASTELLO DELLA SALA) and PIEDMONT (PRUNOTTO) wines. The first pioneer of new VDT, eg TIGNANELLO, SOLAIA (Tuscany), CERVARO DELLA SALA (Umbria). Marchese Piero A was the Voice of Italy in world wine circles in the '70s and '80s. Recent acquisitions in S Tuscan Maremma, MONTEPULCIANO, MONTALCINO, Pitigliano and in PIEDMONT in ASTI (for BARBERA). See also Prunotto.

Antonelli ★★→★★★ Vg DOCG SAGRANTINO and ROSSO DI MONTEFALCO.

Apulia Puglia. Italy's heel, producing almost a fifth of all Italian wine, but mostly bottled in North Italy/France. Best DOC: SALICE SALENTINO. Producers are: Botromagno, Calò Michele, CANDIDO, Coop Copertino, Coppi, LEONE DE CASTRIS, Masseria Monaci, RIVERA, ROSA DEL GOLFO, TAURINO, Vallone.

Aquileia F-VG DOC r w ★→★★ (r) **93 94 95** 12 single-grape wines from around the town of Aquileia on the Slovenian border. Good REFOSCO.

Argiano ★★★ Top MONTALCINO producer.

Argiolas, Antonio ★★→★★★ Important Sardinian producer making wines of astonishing quality. Very good: CANNONAU, NURAGUS, VERMENTINO and red VINO DA TAVOLA Turriga (★★★).

Armani ★★→★★★ Vg DOC VALDADIGE and TRENTINO CHARD.

Arneis Pie w ★★ DYA At last a fairly good white from BAROLO country: the revival of an ancient grape to make fragrant light wine. DOC: Roero Arneis, a zone N of Alba, and LANGHE Arneis. Good from Almondo, Bel Colle, Correggia, Deltetto, BRUNO GIACOSA, Malvirà, Negro, Rabino and Gianni Voerzio (Roero A); Castello di Neive (Langhe A). Often too expensive.

Artimino Tusc r ★★★ Ancient hill-town W of Florence. Fattoria di Artimino produces top DOCG CARMIGNANO.

Assisi Umb r (w) ★→★★ DYA IGT Rosso and Bianco di Assisi: v attractive. Try drinking them cool.

Asti Major wine centre of PIEDMONT.

Asti (Spumante) Pie DOCG w sp ★→★★ NV Immensely popular sweet and v fruity Muscat sparkling wine, now updated to DOCG without perceptible improvement. V low in alcohol; can be delicious with dessert. Producers incl BERA WALTER, Dogliotti-Caudrina, Cascina Fonda, Vignaioli di Santo Stefano.

Attems, Conti Famous old COLLIO estate with wide range of good typical wines (esp PINOT GRIGIO). Now run by Collavini.

Avignonesi ★★★→★★★★ Noble MONTEPULCIANO house with very fine range: VINO NOBILE, blended red Grifi, top CHARDONNAY, SAUVIGNON, MERLOT and superlative VIN SANTO.

Azienda agricola/agraria A farm producing crops, often incl wine.

Azienda/casa vinicola Wine firm using bought-in grapes and/or wines.

Azienda vitivinicola A (specialized) wine estate.

Badia a Coltibuono ★★→★★★ Fine CHIANTI-maker in an old abbey at Gaiole with a restaurant and collection of old vintages. Also VDT SANGIOVETO.

Banfi (Castello or Villa) ★★→★★★ Space-age CANTINA of biggest US importer of Italian wine. Huge plantings at MONTALCINO, mostly SANGIOVESE, but also Syrah, PINOT NOIR, CABERNET SAUVIGNON, CHARDONNAY, SAUVIGNON etc, are part of a drive for quality plus quantity. BRUNELLO is good but 'Poggio all'Oro' is ★★★★. Centine is ROSSO DI MONTALCINO. In PIEDMONT Banfi produces vg sparkling Banfi Brut, Principessa GAVI, BRACCHETO D'ACQUI, PINOT GRIS. See also Eastern States USA.

Banti Eric ★★ One of the best DOC MORELLINO DI SCANSANO.

ITALY

Barbacarlo Lom r dr sw sp ★→★★ Traditional light wines with typical bitter-almond taste, from OLTREPO PAVESE.

Barbaresco Pie DOCG r ★★→★★★★ **85' 88' 89' 90'** 93 94 (95) (96) Neighbour of BAROLO; the other great NEBBIOLO wine. Perhaps marginally less sturdy. At best palate-cleansing, deep, subtle and fine. At 4 yrs becomes RISERVA. Producers incl CERETTO, CIGLIUTI, GAJA, BRUNO GIACOSA, Marchesi di Gresy, MOCCAGATTA, Fiorenzo Nada, Giorgio Pelissero, PIO CESARE, Produttori del B, PRUNOTTO, Alfredo Roagna, BRUNO ROCCA, Sottimano.

Barbatella, Cascina La ★★★ Top producer of BARBERA D'ASTI: excellent single-v'yd Sonvico and dell'Angelo.

> **Barbera**
> Dark acidic red grape, the second most planted in Italy after SANGIOVESE; a speciality of PIEDMONT also used in Lombardy, Emilia-Romagna and other northern provinces. Its best wines follow...

Barbera d'Alba Pie DOC r ★★→★★★ **85' 88' 89' 90' 93'** 94 95 96 Tasty tannic fragrant red. SUPERIORE can age 7+ yrs. Round ALBA, NEBBIOLO is sometimes added to make a VDT (some barrique-aged 100% BARBERA is also vdt). Top producers: CIGLIUTI, CLERICO, Elvio Cogno, A and G CONTERNO, CONTERNO-FANTINO, E GRASSO, Silvio Grasso, Manzone, G MASCARELLO, OBERTO, PARUSSO, Pianpolvere Soprana, PRUNOTTO, BRUNO ROCCA, Scavino, Aldo Vajra, Eraldo Viberti, VIETTI, Gianni Voerzio, R VOERZIO.

Barbera d'Asti Pie DOC r ★★→★★★ **85' 88' 89' 90' 91 93'** 94 95 96 For real BARBERA-lovers: Barbera alone, tangy and appetizing, drunk young or aged up to 7–10 yrs or longer. Top growers: La Barbatella, Bava, BOFFA, BRAIDA, Bricco Mondalino, Cantina Sociale Vinchio e Vaglio, CASCINA CASTLET, Michele Chiarlo, Colle Manora, COPPO, Livio Pavese, Marchesi Alfieri, Martinetti, Neirano, Occhetti, Rovero, La Tenaglia, TERRE DA VINO, Trinchero, Viarengo.

Barbera del Monferrato Pie DOC r ★→★★ DYA Easy-drinking BARBERA from Alessandria and ASTI. Pleasant, slightly fizzy, s'times sweetish. Delimited area is almost identical to BARBERA D'ASTI, but regulations are more relaxed.

Barberani ★★→★★★ Leading ORVIETO producer; Calcaia is botrytis-sweet wine.

Barbi, Fattoria dei ★★ Traditional producer of BRUNELLO DI MONTALCINO.

Barco Reale Tus DOC r ★★ DOC for junior wine of CARMIGNANO; same grapes.

Bardolino Ven DOC r (p) ★★ DYA Pale summery slightly bitter red from E shore of Lake Garda. Bardolino CHIARETTO is even paler and lighter. Top makers: GUERRIERI-RIZZARDI, Le Vigne di San Pietro, Villabella, Zenato, Fratelli Zeni.

> **A Barole of honour**
> **The giants of Barolo:** Bruno Giacosa, Aldo Conterno, Giacomo Conterno, Bartolo Mascarello, Giuseppe Mascarello, Vietti.
> **A promising new generation of classic Barolos:** Renato Corino, Elio Grasso, Rocche dei Manzoni, G D Vajra, Gianni Voerzio, Roberto Voerzio.
> **Successful experimental/fashionable Barolos:** Elio Alterno, Domenico Cerico, Conterno-Fantino, Angelo Gaja, Luciano Sandrone, Paolo Scavino.

Barolo Pie DOCG r ★★★→★★★★ **82' 85' 88' 89' 90'** 93 95 (96) Small area S of ALBA with one of Italy's supreme reds: rich, tannic, alcoholic (min 13%), dry but wonderfully deep and fragrant (also crisp and clean) in the mouth. From NEBBIOLO grapes. Ages for up to 15 yrs (RISERVA after 5).

Bellavista ★★★ FRANCIACORTA estate with brisk SPUMANTE (Gran Cuvée Franciacorta is top). Also Crémant. Good VDT reds from CAB and PINOT N.

Bera, Walter ★★→★★★ Sm estate nr BARBARESCO. Vg MOSCATO D'ASTI and ASTI.

Berlucchi, Guido Italy's biggest producer of sparkling METODO CLASSICO, at FRANCIACORTA. Quality steady.

Bertani ★★→★★★ Well-known producer of quality Veronese wines (VALPOLICELLA, AMARONE, SOAVE, etc).

Bertelli ★★ Good small PIEDMONT producer: BARBERA D'ASTI, VDT CAB, CHARD.

Biancara, La ★★★ Top-quality GAMBELLARAS: vg RECIOTO and late-harvest VENDEMMIA TARDIVA. (ZONIN is number one in quantity.)

Bianco White.

Bianco d'Arquata Umb w ★★ DYA See Adanti.

Bianco di Custoza Ven DOC w (sp) ★→★★ DYA Twin of SOAVE from the other side (west) of Verona. Good from Corte Sant'Arcadio, Le Tende, Le Vigne di San Pietro, MONTRESOR.

Bianco di Pitigliano Tus DOC w ★ DYA Dull dry white from nr Grosseto.

Bigi Famous producer of ORVIETO and other wines of Umbria and TUSCANY. Bigi's TORRICELLA v'yd produces vg dry Orvieto.

Biondi-Santi ★★→★★★★ The original producer of BRUNELLO DI MONTALCINO, from 45-acre Il Greppo v'yd. Prices are absurd, but the v old vintages are unique.

Bisol ★★→★★★ Vg PROSECCO DI VALDOBBIADENE. Also top MET CLASS SPUMANTE.

Boca Pie DOC r ★★ **85 88 89 90** 93 95 Another NEBBIOLO from N of PIEDMONT. Look for Poderi ai Valloni (Vigneto Cristiana ★★★).

Boffa, Alfiero ★★→★★★ Sm property: top BARBERA D'ASTI. Esp single-v'yd wines.

Bolgheri Tus DOC r p w (sw) ★★→★★★★ On the coast south of Livorno. Incl 7 types of wine: BIANCO, VERMENTINO, SAUVIGNON BLANC, ROSSO, ROSATO, VIN SANTO OCCHIO DI PERNICE and (since '94) SASSICAIA (★★★★). Top producers are Le Macchiole (Il Paleo ★★★★), ORNELLAIA (Masseto and Ornellaia, both ★★★★), SAN GUIDO (Sassicaia ★★★★). Also Michele Satta.

Bolla ★★ Famous Verona firm for VALPOLICELLA, SOAVE, etc. Top wines: Castellaro (one of the v best SOAVES), Creso (red and white), Jago.

Bonarda Minor red grape (alias Croatina) widely grown in PIEDMONT, Lombardy, Emilia-Romagna and blended with BARBERA.

Bonarda Lom DOC r ★★ Soft fresh often red FRIZZANTE from S of Pavia.

Borgo del Tiglio ★★★ FRIULI estate for one of NE Italy's top MERLOTS: VDT Rosso della Centa; also good are COLLIO CHARD, TOCAI and BIANCO.

Boscaini Ven Verona producer of VALPOLICELLA, AMARONE, SOAVE.

Boscarelli, Poderi ★★★ Small estate with vg VINO NOBILE DI MONTEPULCIANO, barrel-aged VDT Boscarelli and good ROSSO DI M.

Brachetto d'Acqui Pie DOCG r sw (sp) ★★ DYA Sweet sparkling red with enticing Muscat scent. Much better than it sounds. Best producer: BANFI.

Braida ★★★ Estate for top BARBERA D'ASTI (Bricco della Bigotta and Barbera VDT BRICCO DELL'UCCELLONE).

Bramaterra Pie DOC r ★★ **85 88 89 90** 93 95 (96) Neighbour to GATTINARA. NEBBIOLO grapes predominate in a blend. Good producers: Perazzi, SELLA.

Breganze Ven DOC ★→★★★ (r) **90 91** 93 94 95 (96) A catch-all for many varieties around Vicenza. CABERNET and PINOT BL are best. Top producers: B Bartolomeo, MACULAN.

Bricco Term for a high (and by implication vg) -ridge v'yd in PIEDMONT.

Bricco Manzoni Pie r ★★★ **82' 85' 88' 89' 90'** 91 92 93 (94) 95 (96) V successful blend of NEBBIOLO and BARBERA from Monforte d'Alba.

Bricco dell'Uccellone Pie r ★★★ **88' 89' 90' 91 92 93'** 94 95 (96) Barrique-aged BARBERA from the firm of the late Giacomo Bologna. Bricco della Bigotta and Ai Suma are others.

Brigaldara ★★→★★★ Small VALPOLICELLA producer. Top AMARONE and RECIOTO.

Brindisi Ap DOC r ★★ Strong NEGROAMARO. Esp Patriglione (★★★) from TAURINO.

Brolio, Castello di ★★→★★★ After a sad period under foreign ownership, the Ricasoli family has taken this legendary estate in hand again. The first results are very promising. More to come...

Brunelli ★★★ Improving quality of AMARONE and VALPOLICELLA (esp Pa'Riondo).

Brunello di Montalcino Tus DOCG r ★★★→★★★★ **82' 85' 86 88'** 90' 91 (93) (94) 95' (96) With BAROLO, Italy's most celebrated red: strong, full-bodied, high-flavoured, tannic and long-lived. 4 yrs' ageing; after 5 becomes RISERVA. Quality ever-improving. Montalcino is 25 miles S of Siena.

> **Good Brunello di Montalcino producers include:** Altesino, Argiano, Banfi, Barbi, Biondi-Santi, Campogiovanni, Capanna-Cencioni, Caparzo, Casanova di Neri, Case Basse, Castelgiocondo, Cerbaiona, Col d'Orcia, Costanti, Eredi Fuligni, Gorelli, Lisini, Mastrojanni, Siro Pacenti, Pacenti Franco e Rosildo, Il Palazzone, Ciacci Piccolomini, Pieve di Santa Restituta, Poggio Antico, Poggione, Salvioni-Cerbaiola, San Giorgio, Talenti. See also Rosso di Montalcino (value).

Brusco dei Barbi Tus r ★★ **88 90 91** 93 (94) 95 96 Lively variant on BRUNELLO using old CHIANTI GOVERNO method from Fattoria dei Barbi.

Bukkuram Si br ★★★ Celebrated MOSCATO DI PANTELLERIA from De Bartoli.

Ca'del Bosco ★★★→★★★★ FRANCIACORTA estate making some of Italy's v best sparkling wine, CHARD, and excellent reds (see Zanella).

Cabernet Sauvignon Much used in NE Italy and now (esp in VDT) in TUSCANY, PIEDMONT and the south.

Cacchiano, Castello di ★★★ First-rate CHIANTI CLASSICO estate at Gaiole, owned by RICASOLI cousins. Outstanding RISERVA 'Millennio'.

Cafaggio, Villa ★★ CHIANTI CLASSICO estate. Solid red VDT: Solatio Basilica.

Caldaro (Lago di Caldaro) T-AA DOC r ★ DYA Alias KALTERERSEE. Light soft bitter-almond red from SCHIAVA grapes. From a huge area. CLASSICO from a smaller area is better.

Calò, Michele ★★★ Top producer of Salento wines; look for DOC ALEZIO ROSSO and vdt Vigna Spano.

Caluso Passito Pie DOC w sw (fz) ★★ Made from Erbaluce grapes; delicate scent, velvety taste. Tiny production. Best from Bianco, Ferrando.

Candido, F ★★★ Top grower of Salento, APULIA; gd reds: Duca d'Aragona, Cappello del Prete, SALICE SALENTINO; also vg dessert wine: ALEATICO DI PUGLIA.

Canevel ★★→★★★ Vg producer of PROSECCO DI CONEGLIANO-VALDOBBIADENE.

Cannonau di Sardegna Sar DOC r (p) dr s/sw ★★ **90 91 92** 93 94 95 Cannonau (Grenache) is S's basic red grape. Ranges from v potent to fine and mellow: Arcadu Tonino, CS di Jerzu, Giuseppe Gabbas, Alberto Loi, SELLA & MOSCA.

Cantalupo, Antichi Vigneti di ★★→★★★ Top GHEMME wines – especially single-vineyard Breclemae and Carellae.

Cantina Cellar or winery.

Cantina Sociale (CS) Growers' coop.

Capannelle ★★★ Good producer of VDT (formerly CHIANTI CLASSICO), nr Gaiole.

Caparzo, Tenuta ★★★ MONTALCINO estate with excellent BRUNELLO La Casa; also vg ROSSO DI MONTALCINO (look for La Caduta), red blend Ca'del Pazzo and white blend Le Grance.

Capezzana, Tenuta di (or Villa) ★★→★★★ The Tuscan estate (W of Florence) of the Contini Bonacossi family. Excellent CHIANTI Montalbano and CARMIGNANO. Also vg Bordeaux-style red, GHIAIE DELLA FURBA.

Caprai ★★★ Top DOCG SAGRANTINO and vg ROSSO DI MONTEFALCO.

Capri Cam DOC r p w ★→★★ Legendary island with widely abused name. Only interesting wines are from La Caprense.

Cardizze Famous, frequently too expensive and too sweet DOC PROSECCO of top v'yd nr VALDOBBIADENE.

Carema Pie DOC r ★★→★★★ **85' 88' 89' 90'** 91 93 95 (96) Old speciality of N PIEDMONT. Best from Luigi Ferrando (or the CANTINA SOCIALE).

Carignano del Sulcis Sar DOC r p ★★→★★★ **90 91** 93 94 95 96 Well-structured red wine with capacity for ageing. The best is Terre Brune from CANTINA SOCIALE di Santadi.

Carmignano Tus DOCG r ★★★ **85' 86 88' 90' 91** 93 94 95 96 Region W of Florence. CHIANTI grapes plus 10% CABERNET S make distinctive, reliable, even excellent reds. Best incl Ambra, ARTIMINO, CAPEZZANA, Farnete and Poggiolo.

Carpenè Malvolti Leading producer of classic PROSECCO and other sparkling wines at Conegliano, Veneto.

Carpineto ★★ Producer of CHIANTI CLASSICO in N part of region.

Carso F-VG DOC r w ★★→★★★ (r) **90 93** 94 95 96 DOC nr Trieste incl good MALVASIA. Terrano del C is a REFOSCO red. Top grower: Edi Kante.

Casa fondata nel... Firm founded in...

Casalte, Fattoria Le ★★★ Good VINO NOBILE DI MONTEPULCIANO; also ROSSO and white VDT Celius.

Casanova di Neri ★★★ BRUNELLO DI MONTALCINO (and vg ROSSO DI M) from the Neri family; better every year.

Case Basse ★★★ Small estate with v impressive BRUNELLO and VDT Intistieti.

Case Bianche, Le ★★ Reliable estate nr Conegliano (Ven) for PROSECCO, SAUV and surprising red Wildbacher (from ancient Austrian grape).

Castel del Monte Ap DOC r p w ★★ (r) **92 93** 94 Dry fresh well-balanced southern wines. The red is RISERVA after 3 yrs. Rosé most widely known. RIVERA'S Il Falcone stands out.

Castelgiocondo ★★★ FRESCOBALDI estate in MONTALCINO: vg BRUNELLO; gd vdt MERLOT Lamaïone.

Castell'in Villa ★★★ Vg CHIANTI CLASSICO estate.

Castellare ★★→★★★ Small but admired CHIANTI CLASSICO producer with first-rate SANGIOVESE VDT I Sodi di San Niccoló and sprightly GOVERNO del Castellare: old-style CHIANTI updated.

Castello Castle. (See under name: eg Albola, Castello d'.)

Castelluccio ★★→★★★ Best SANGIOVESE of Emilia-Romagna: VDT Ronco dei Cigliegi and Ronco della Simia.

Castlet, Cascina ★★→★★★ Producers of concentrated BARBERA PASSITO, VDT Passum, vg BARBERA D'ASTI.

Caudrina-Dogliotti Redento ★★★ Top MOSCATO D'ASTI: La Galeisa and Caudrina.

Cavalleri ★★→★★★ Vg and reliable producer of FRANCIACORTA wines. Sparkling are the best.

Cavallotto ★★→★★★ Reliable BAROLO estate: esp Barolo Vigna San Giuseppe.

Cavicchioli Large Emilia-Romagna producer of LAMBRUSCO and other sparkling: Lambrusco di Sorbara Vigna del Cristo is best.

Ca'Vit (Cantina Viticoltori) Group of quality coops near Trento. Wines include MARZEMINO, CAB, PINOTS N, BL and GR, NOSIOLA. Top wines: Brume di Monte (red and white) and sparkling Graal and Firmato.

Cecchi Large-scale producer and bottler of Tuscan wines.

Cerasuolo Ab DOC p ★★ The ROSATO version of MONTEPULCIANO D'ABRUZZO.

Ceretto ★★★ Vg grower of BARBARESCO (Bricco Asili), BAROLO (Bricco Rocche), top BARBERA D'ALBA (Piana), CHARD (La Bernardina), DOLCETTO and ARNEIS. Also vg METHODO CLASSICO SPUMANTE La Bernardina.

To decipher codes, please refer to 'Key to symbols' on front flap of jacket, or to 'How to use this book' on page 6.

Cervaro See Castello della Sala.

Chardonnay Has recently joined permitted varieties for several N Italian DOCs (eg T-AA, FRANCIACORTA, F-VG, PIEDMONT). Some of the best (eg from ANTINORI, FELSINA, GAJA, LUNGAROTTI) are still only VDT.

Chianti Tus DOCG r ★→★★ **93 94'** 95 96 The lively local wine of Florence and Siena. At best fresh fruity and tangy, still sometimes sold in straw-covered flasks. Mostly made to drink young. Of the subdistricts, RUFINA (★★→★★★) and Colli Fiorentini (★→★★★) can make CLASSICO-style RISERVAS. Montalbano, COLLI Senesi, Aretini and Pisani make lighter wines.

Chianti Classico Tus DOCG r ★★→★★★★ **90 91 93 94** 95 96 (Riserva) **85 86 88 90** 93 (95) (96) Senior CHIANTI from central area. Its old pale astringent style is now rarer as top estates opt for either darker tannic wines or softer and fruitier ones. Some are among the best wines of Italy. Members of the Consorzio use the badge of a black rooster, but several top firms do not belong.

Outstanding Chianti Classico producers include: Ama, Antinori, Bibbiano, Brolio, Cacchiano, Carobbio, Casa Emma, Castel Ruggero, Castellare, Castell'in Villa, Le Cinciole, Coltibuono, Felsina, Le Filigare, Fonterutoli, Fontodi, Isole e Olena, Querciabella, Lilliano, La Massa, Le Masse di San Leolino, Nittardi, Palazzino, Paneretta, Poggerino, Rampolla, Rodano, San Felice, San Giusto, Valtellina, Vecchie Terre di Montefili, Verrazzano, Viticcio, Volpaia.

Chianti Putto Tus DOCG r ★→★★ DYA From a league of producers outside the CLASSICO zone. The neck-label, a pink cherub, is now rarely seen.

Chiarli Producer of Modena LAMBRUSCO (look for Generale Cialdini label).

Chiarlo, Michele ★★ Good PIEDMONT producer. (BAROLOS Cerequio, Cannubi, GAVI and BARBERA D'ASTI are vg.)

Chiaretto Rosé (the word means 'claret') produced esp around Lake Garda. See Bardolino, Riviera del Garda.

Chiesa di Santa Restituta See Pieve di Santa Restituta.

Chionetti ★★→★★★ Makes best DOLCETTO DI DOGLIANI (look for Briccolero).

Ciacci Piccolomini ★★★ Vg BRUNELLO DI MONTALCINO (best is Vigna di Pianrosso) and ROSSO DI M.

Cigliuti, Renato ★★★ Small-high quality estate for BARBARESCO.

Cinqueterre Lig DOC w dr sw pa ★★ Fragrant fruity white from steep coast nr La Spezia. PASSITO is known as SCIACCHETRA (★★→★★★). Good from De Batte, Coop Agricola di Cinqueterre, Forlini & Cappellini, F Giusti.

Cinzano Major Vermouth company also known for its ASTI from PIEDMONT and Florio MARSALA. Now owned by Grand Met.

Cirò Cal DOC r (p w) ★→★★ **88 89 90'** 91 92 93 94 (95) (96) V strong red from Gaglioppo grapes; fruity white (DYA). Best: LIBRANDI (Duca San Felice ★★★), San Francesco (Donna Madda, Ronco dei Quattroventi), Caparra & Siciliani.

Classico Term for wines from a restricted area within the limits of a DOC. By implication, and often in practice, the best of the district. Applied to sparkling wines it denotes the classic method (as for champagne).

Clerico, Domenico ★★★ Constantly evolving PIEDMONT wines; the aim is for international flavour. Esp good for BAROLO.

Cocci Grifoni ★★→★★★ Vg DOC ROSSO PICENO (look for Vigna Messieri).

Col d'Orcia ★★★ Top estate of MONTALCINO with interesting VDT. Best wine is BRUNELLO (look for Poggio al Vento).

Colle Picchioni ★★ Estate S of Rome making the best MARINO white; also red (CAB-MERLOT) VDT, Vigna del Vassallo, perhaps Latium's best.

Colli Hills. Occurs in many wine-names.

Colli Berici Ven DOC r p w ★★ Hills S of Vicenza. CAB is the best wine. Top producer is Villa Dal Ferro.

Colli Bolognesi E-R DOC r p w ★★ (w) DYA SW of Bologna. 8 wines, 5 grape varieties. TERRE ROSSE is top estate (★★★). Other good producers are Tenuta Bonzara and Santarosa (look for VDT Giò Rosso).

Colli Euganei Ven DOC r w dr s/sw (sp) ★→★★ DYA A DOC SW of Padua for 7 wines. Red is adequate; white and sparkling soft and pleasant. Best producers: Vignalta, Cà Lustra.

Colli Orientali del Friuli F-VG DOC r w dr sw ★★→★★★★ (r) **88 90** 93 94 (95) (96) 20 different wines (18 named after their grapes) on hills E of Udine. Whites esp are vg. Top producers: ABBAZIA DI ROSAZZO, BORGO DEL TIGLIO, DORIGO, Le Viarte, LIVIO FELLUGA, LIVON, Ronchi di Cialla, RONCO DEL GNEMIZ, Torre Rosazza, Rubini, Specogna.

Colli Piacentini E-R DOC r p w ★→★★ DYA DOC incl traditional GUTTURNIO and Monterosso Val d'Arda among 11 types grown S of Piacenza. Good fizzy MALVASIA. Most wines FRIZZANTE. New French and local reds: La Stoppa, La Tosa, Marchese Malaspina, Villa Peirano.

Colli Romani The wooded hills S of Rome: ancient summer resort and source of FRASCATI etc.

Colli del Trasimeno Um DOC r w ★→★★ **93 94** 95 96 Often lively wines from Perugia. Best: Casale dei Cucchi (formerly Morolli), Marella, Pieve del Vescovo.

Colline Novaresi Pie DOC r w ★→★★ New DOC for old region in Novara province. 7 different wines: BIANCO, ROSSO, NEBBIOLO, BONARDA, Vespolina, Croatina and BARBERA. Incl declassified BOCA, GHEMME, FARA and SIZZANO.

Collio F-VG DOC r w ★★→★★★★ **88 90** 93 94 (95) (96) 19 wines, 17 named after their grapes, from a small area on the Slovenian border. Vg whites, esp SAUV, PINOT BIANCO and PINOT GRIGIO. Best from: BORGO DEL TIGLIO, La Castellada, GRAVNER, JERMANN, Primosic, Princic, Radikon, Ronco dei Tassi, RUSSIZ SUPERIORE, SCHIOPETTO, Venica & Venica, VILLA RUSSIZ.

Coltassala Tus r ★★★ Notable VDT red of SANGIOVESE from the ancient CHIANTI CLASSICO estate of CASTELLO DI VOLPAIA at Radda.

Conterno, Aldo ★★★★ Legendary grower of BAROLO etc, at Monforte d'Alba. Good GRIGNOLINO, FREISA, vg CHARD 'Printanier' and 'Bussia d'Oro'. Best BAROLOS are Cicala and Colonello. Barrel-aged NEBBIOLO VDT 'Favot' vg.

Conterno, Giacomo ★★★★ Top grower of BAROLO etc at Monforte d'Alba. Monfortino Barolo is long-aged, rare, outstanding.

Conterno-Fantino ★★★ 3 young families for vg BAROLO etc at Monforte d'Alba.

Contini, Attilio ★→★★★ Famous producer of VERNACCIA DI ORISTANO; best is vintage blend 'Antico Gregori'.

Contucci, Conti ★★→★★★ Ancient esteemed makers of VINO NOBILE DI MONT.

Copertino Ap DOC r (p) ★★ **92 93 94** 95 96 Savoury ageable red of NEGROAMARO from the heel of Italy. Look for CANTINA SOCIALE'S RISERVA and Tenuta Monaci.

Coppo ★★ Ambitious producers of BARBERA D'ASTI (eg 'Pomorosso').

Cordero di Montezemolo-Monfalletto ★★ Tiny maker of good BAROLO.

Cortese di Gavi See Gavi. (Cortese is the grape.)

Corzano & Paterno, Fattoria di ★★→★★★ Dynamic CHIANTI COLLI Fiorentini estate. Vg RISERVA, red VDT Corzano and outstanding VIN SANTO.

COS ★★★ Tiny estate: 3 friends making top Sicilian wines esp VDT Vigne di Cos white (CHARD) and red (CAB).

Costanti, Conti ★★★ Tiny estate for top-quality BRUNELLO DI MONTALCINO.

D'Ambra ★★ Top producer of ISCHIA wines, esp excellent white DOC Biancolella ('Piellero' and single-v'yd 'Frassitelli').

D'Angelo ★★→★★★ Leading producers of admirable DOC AGLIANICO DEL VULTURE. Barrel-aged Aglianico VDT Canneto also vg.

Dal Forno, Romano ★★★→★★★★ Very high-quality VALPOLICELLA and AMARONE from perfectionist grower, bottling only best: 14,000 bottles from 20 acres.

Darmagi Pie r ★★★★ **82' 85' 88' 89' 90'** 91 93 (94) 95 (96) CAB S from GAJA in BARBARESCO is one of PIEDMONT'S most discussed (and expensive) VDT reds.

Denominazione di Origine Controllata (DOC) Means the same as Appellation d'Origine Contrôlée (qv France).

Denominazione di Origine Controllata e Garantita (DOCG) Like DOC but with an official guarantee of origin indicated by a neck-label on the bottle.

Decugnano dei Barbi ★★ Top ORVIETO estate with an ABBOCCATO known as 'Pourriture Noble', and a good red VDT.

Di Majo Norante ★★→★★★ Lone star of Molise on the Adriatic with vg Biferno DOC MONTEPULCIANO and white Falanghina 'Ramitello'. Also lighter, more aromatic Molí. To watch for new ideas.

DOC, DOCG See Denominazione di Origine Controllata (e Garantita).

Italy's DOCG wines: the complete list
Albana di Romagna, Asti and Moscato d'Asti, Barbaresco, Barolo, Brachetto d'Acqui, Brunello di Montalcino, Carmignano, Chianti, Chianti Classico, Franciacorta, Gattinara, Ghemme, Montefalco, Sagrantino, Taurasi, Torgiano, Vernacchia di San Gimignano, Vino Nobile di Montepulciano

Dolce Sweet.

Dolceacqua See Rossese di Dolceacqua.

Dolcetto ★→★★★ PIEDMONT'S earliest-ripening grape, for v attractive everyday wines: dry young-drinking fruity fresh with deep purple colour. Gives its name to several DOCs: D d'Acqui, D d'Asti, D delle Langhe Monregalesi, D di Diano d'Alba (also Diano DOC), D di Dogliani (CHIONETTI and Pecchenino are top growers) and D di Ovada (best from Abbazia di Vallechiara). Dolcetto d'Alba is made by most BAROLO and BARBARESCO growers.

Donnafugata Si r w ★ Zesty Sicilian whites (best are Vigna di Gabri, Damaskino). Also sound red. Was VDT, now in DOC Contessa Entellina.

Donnaz VdA DOC ★★ **93** 95 (96) Mountain NEBBIOLO: fragrant pale, faintly bitter. Aged for a statutory 3 yrs. Now part of VALLE D'AOSTA regional DOC.

Dorigo, Girolamo ★★★→★★★★ Top COLLI ORIENTALI DEL FRIULI producer for outstanding white VDT 'Ronc di Juri', CHARD, dessert VERDUZZO and PICOLIT, red Pignolo (★★★★), REFOSCO, Schioppettino, and VDT Montsclapade.

Duca Enrico See Duca di Salaparuta.

Duca di Salaparuta ★★ Popular Sicilian wines. Sound dry reds, pleasant soft whites. Excellent barrique red Duca Enrico (★★★) is one of Sicily's best. Valguarnera is premium oak-aged white.

Elba Tus r w (sp) ★ DYA The island's white is drinkable with fish. Keep a look out for the 'Acquabona'.

Enfer d'Arvier V dA DOC r ★★ **93** 95 (96) Alpine speciality; a pale pleasantly bitter light red.

Enoteca Wine library. There are many, the impressive original being the Enoteca Italiana of Siena. Also used for wine shops or restaurants.

Erbaluce di Caluso See Caluso Passito.

Eredi Fuligni ★★★ Vg producer of BRUNELLO and ROSSO DI MONTALCINO.

Est! Est!! Est!!! Lat DOC w dr s/sw ★ DYA Unextraordinary white from Montefiascone, N of Rome. Trades on its oddball name.

Etna Si DOC r p w ★→★★ (r) **93 94** 95 96 Wine from volcanic slopes. Red is warm, full, balanced and can age well; white is distinctly grapey. Top producers: Russo Vincezo, Scammacca.

Falchini ★★→★★★ Producer of good DOCG VERNACCIA DI SAN GIMIGNANO and the best reds of the district, eg VDT Campora (★★★).

Falerno del Massico Cam DOC r w ★★ (r) **90 92 93 94** 95 96 As in Falernum, the best-known wine of ancient times. Times change. Strong red from AGLIANICO, fruity white from Falanghina. Good producer: VILLA MATILDE.

An Italian choice for 1998

Barbera d'Asti Vigna del Sole M Chiarlo, Calamandrana (Piedmont)
Gattinara Riserva Travaglini, Gattinara (Piedmont)
Brut Franciacorta Ca'del Bosco, Erbusco (Lombady)
Amarone della Valpolicella Il Sestante, San Pietro in Cariano (Veneto)
Extra Brut Riserva Spumante Vivaldi, Mölten (Alto Adige)
Chianti Classico Rodano, Castellina in Chianti (Tuscany)
Vino Nobile di Montepulciano Dei, Montepulciano (Tuscany)
Verdicchio Macrina Garofoli, Loreto (Marches)
Rosso del Conte Tasca d'Almerits, Regaleali (Sicily)

Fara Pie DOC r ★★ **90'** 93 95' (96) Good NEBBIOLO from Novara, N PIEDMONT. Fragrant; worth ageing; esp Dessilani's Caramino.

Farneta, Tenuta ★★→★★★ Nr Siena but outside CHIANTI CLASSICO, an estate for pure SANGIOVESE VDT: eg Bongoverno (★★★) and Bentivoglio (★★★).

Farnetella, Castello di ★★ Estate nr MONTEPULCIANO where Giuseppe Mazzocolin of FELSINA makes vg SAUV and CHIANTI COLLI Senesi.

Fattoria Tuscan term for a wine-growing property, traditionally noble.

Favorita Pie w ★→★★ DYA Dry fruity white making friends in BAROLO country.

Fazi-Battaglia ★→★★ Well-known producer of VERDICCHIO, etc. White Le Moie VDT is pleasant. Also owns Fassati (producer of VINO NOBILE DI MONTEPULCIANO).

Felluga ★★★ Brothers Livio and Marco (RUSSIZ SUPERIORE) have separate companies in COLLIO and COLLI ORIENTALI. Both are highly esteemed.

Felsina-Berardenga ★★★→★★★★ CHIANTI CLASSICO estate with famous RISERVA Vigna Rancia and VDT Fontalloro.

Ferrari ★→★★★ Cellars making some of Italy's best dry sparkling wines nr Trento, TRENTINO-ALTO ADIGE. Giulio Ferrari RISERVA is best.

Fiano di Avellino Cam w ★★→★★★ (DYA) Considered the best white of Campania, esp from new VIGNADORA estate. Also good from MASTROBERARDINO, Vadiaperti, Feudi di S Gregorio, Struzziero, Vega.

Florio The major volume producer of MARSALA, controlled by CINZANO.

Foianeghe T-AA vdt r (w) ★★ **90 93** 95 (96) Brand of Conti Bossi Fedrigotti. TRENTINO CAB-MERLOT red to age 7–10 yrs. White is PINOT BL-CHARD-TRAMINER.

Folonari Large run-of-the-mill merchant of Lombardy. See also GIV.

Fontana Candida ★→★★ One of the biggest producers of FRASCATI. Single-v'yd Santa Teresa stands out. See also GIV.

Fontanafredda ★★ Big historic producer of PIEDMONT wines on former royal estates, incl BAROLO from single v'yds and a range of ALBA DOCS. Also very good DOCG ASTI and SPUMANTE Brut (esp ★★★ Vigna Gattinera).

Fonterutoli ★★★ Historic CHIANTI CLASSICO estate at Castellina with noted VDT Concerto and splendid RISERVA Ser Lapo.

Le Fonti, Fattoria ★★ CHIANTI estate of 30 acres at Panzano. Still uses ancient 'promiscuo' mixed cultivation.

Fontodi ★★★→★★★★ Top Panzano CHIANTI CLASSICO estate for highly regarded RISERVA, red VDT Flaccianello, white vdt 'Meriggio' (PINOT BIANCO-SAUV-TRAMINER).

Foradori ★★★ Elizabetta F makes very best TEROLDEGO (Morel, Sgarzon). Also oak-aged TEROLDEGO Granato, vg CHARD.

Forteto della Luja ★★★ Number 1 for LOAZZOLO.

ITALY

Franciacorta Lom DOC w (p) sp ★★→★★★★ Small sparkling wine centre fast growing in quality and renown. Wines exclusively bottle-fermented. CA'DEL BOSCO and BELLAVISTA outstanding. Also vg: Castelfaglia, Castellino-Bonomi, CAVALLERI, Faccoli, Gatti, Guarischi, Mirabella, Monte Rossa, Ricci-Curbastro, Uberti and Villa. For whites and reds see Terre di Franciacorta.

Frascati Lat DOC w dr s/sw sw (sp) ★→★★ DYA Best-known wine of Roman hills: should be soft, limpid, golden, tasting of whole grapes. Most is disappointingly neutral today: look for Conte Zandotti, Villa Simone, or Santa Teresa from FONTANA CANDIDA. Sweet is known as Cannellino.

Freisa Pie r dr s/sw sw (sp) ★★ DYA Usually v dry (except nr Turin), often FRIZZANTE red, said to taste of raspberries and roses. With enough acidity it can be highly appetizing, especially with salami. Good wines come from CIGLIUTI, CONTERNO, Cozzo, Gilli, PARUSSO, Pecchenino, Pelissero, Sebaste, Trinchero, VAJRA and VOERZIO.

Frescobaldi ★★★ Ancient noble family, leading pioneers of CHIANTI at NIPOZZANO, E of Florence. Also white POMINO and PREDICATO SAUV BL (Vergena) and CAB (Mormoreto). See also Montesodi. Now also owns Castelgiocondo (★★★), a big MONTALCINO estate for BRUNELLO and vg VDT MERLOT Lamaïone. From '97: a joint Tuscan venture with Mondavi of California.

Friuli-Venezia Giulia The NE region on the Slovenian border. Many wines; the DOCs COLLIO and COLLI ORIENTALI include most of the best.

Friuli vintages

1996 Rains from mid-August to mid-October. Whites have surprising body and aroma; reds: not bad, but wait and see...

1995 Promising year, then heavy rains in August and September. Light whites, better reds.

1994 Wet spring and September, hot between. Whites can lack acidity; reds better.

1993 A windy vintage reduced quantities but produced highly concentrated healthy grapes. Top-quality whites, but harvest rains compromised the reds.

1992 August rains not so bad in Friuli – an excellent year for whites, and good reds too.

Frizzante (fz) Semi-sparkling. Used to describe wines such as LAMBRUSCO.

Gaja ★★★★ Old family firm at BARBARESCO under meteoric direction of Angelo G. Top-quality – and price – PIEDMONT wines, esp BARBARESCO (single v'yds SORI Tildin, Sorì San Lorenzo, Costa Russi) and BAROLO Sperss (since '88). Also setting trends with excellent CHARD (Gaja & Rey) and CAB DARMAGI. Latest acquisition: Marengo-Marenda estate (BAROLO) commercial Gromis label, and control of PIEVE DI SANTA RESTITUTA (BRUNELLO).

Galestro Tus w ★ V light white from eponymous shaley soil in CHIANTI country. Current moves to upgrade (v necessary).

Gambellara Ven DOC w dr s/sw (sp) ★→★★ DYA Neighbour of SOAVE. Dry wine similar. Sweet (known as RECIOTO DI GAMBELLARA) nicely fruity. Also VIN SANTO. Outstanding producer: LA BIANCARA (★★★).

Gancia Famous ASTI house also producing vermouth and dry sparkling. New Torrebianco estate in APULIA is making good VDT whites: CHARD, SAUV, PINOT BL, also vg single-v'yd BAROLO, 'Cannubi' (★★★), since '89.

Garganega Principal white grape of SOAVE and GAMBELLARA.

Garofoli, Gioacchino ★★→★★★ Quality leader of the Marches (nr Ancona). Notable style in VERDICCHIO Macrina and Serra Fiorese; also vg sparkling. ROSSO CONERO Piancarda and vg Grosso Agontano (★★★).

Gattinara Pie DOCG r ★★★ **82' 85' 88' 89' 90'** 93 95 (96) V tasty BAROLO-type red (from NEBBIOLO, locally known as Spanna). Best are single-v'yd wines from Antoniolo. Others incl Bianchi, Le Colline-Monsecco, Nervi.

Gavi (or Cortese di Gavi) Pie w ★★→★★★ DYA At (rare) best, subtle dry white of CORTESE grapes. LA SCOLCA is best known, vg are BANFI (watch for Vigna Regale), Castellari Bergaglio, TERRE DA VINO. La Giustiniana, Tenuta San Pietro, Castello di Tassarolo and Villa Sparina are v fair; also fair: CHIARLO, Podere Saulino, Cascina degli Ulivi, La Zerba.

Ghemme Pie DOCG r ★★→★★★ **85' 86 88' 89 90'** 93 95 (96) Neighbour of GATTINARA but not as good. Best is Antichi Vigneti di Cantalupo.

Ghiaie della Furba Tus r ★★★ **88 90** 93 95 (96) Bordeaux-style VDT CAB blend from the admirable TENUTA DI CAPEZZANA, CARMIGNANO.

Giacosa, Bruno ★★★★ Inspired loner: outstanding BARBARESCO, BAROLO and PIEDMONT wines at Neive. Remarkable ARNEIS white and PINOT N sparkling.

GIV (Gruppo Italiano Vini) Complex of coops and wineries, apparently Europe's largest (60 million bottles). Sells 12% of Italian wine, incl BIGI, Conti Serristori, FOLONARI, FONTANA CANDIDA, LAMBERTI, Macchiavelli, MELINI, Negri, Santi...

Goldmuskateller Aromatic ALTO ADIGE grape made into irresistible dry white, esp by TIEFENBRUNNER.

Governo Old Tuscan custom, enjoying mild revival with some producers, in which dried grapes or must are added to young wine to induce second fermentation and give a slight prickle – sometimes instead of using must concentrate to increase alcohol.

Gradi Degrees (of alcohol), ie percent by volume.

Grappa Pungent spirit made from grape pomace (skins etc after pressing).

Grasso, Elio ★★★ Hard-working, reliable quality producer at Monforte d'Alba: outstanding BAROLO (look for Gavarini and Casa Maté), potent barrel-aged BARBERA D'ALBA Vigna Martina, DOLCETTO, etc.

Grattamacco ★★★ Top Tuscan producer on coast outside classic centres (nr SASSICAIA S of Bolgheri). Vg Grattamacco SANGIOVESE-CAB blend.

Grave del Friuli F-VG DOC r w ★★ (r) **88 90 93** 94 95 96 DOC covering 15 different wines, 14 named after their grapes, from nr the Slovenian border. Good MERLOT and CAB. Best producers: Borgo Magredo, Di Lenardo, Le Fredis, PIGHIN, Teresa Raiz, Vigneti Le Monde.

Gravner, Josko ★★★→★★★★ Together with MARIO SCHIOPETTO, spiritual leader of COLLIO: estate with range of excellent whites, led by CHARD and SAUV.

Grechetto White grape with more flavour than the ubiquitous TREBBIANO, increasingly used in Umbria.

Greco di Bianco Cal DOC w sw ★★ An original smooth and fragrant dessert wine from Italy's toe; worth ageing. Best from Ceratti. See Mantonico.

Greco di Tufo Cam DOC w (sp) ★★→★★★ (DYA) One of the best white wines from the S of the country: fruity and slightly 'wild' in flavour. A character. Best: Vignadangelo by MASTROBERARDINO and VIGNADORA-MASTROBERARDINO. Also vg from Vadiaperti, Di Meo, Feudi di S Gregorio, Vega.

Gresy, Marchesi de (Cisa Asinari) ★★★ Consistent producer of fine BARBARESCO; also vg SAUV and CHARD.

Grevepesa Reliable CHIANTI CLASSICO coop.

Grignolino d'Asti Pie DOC r ★ DYA Lively standard light red of PIEDMONT.

Guerrieri-Gonzaga ★★→★★★ Top producer in TRENTINO; esp VINO DA TAVOLA San Leonardo, a ★★★ CAB-MERLOT blend.

Guerrieri-Rizzardi ★★→★★★ Top producer of AMARONE, BARDOLINO, SOAVE and VALPOLICELLA from various family estates.

Gutturnio dei Colli Piacentini E-R DOC r dr ★→★★ DYA BARBERA-BONARDA blend from the hills of Piacenza, often FRIZZANTE.

Haas, Franz ★★→★★★ Very good ALTO ADIGE MERLOT and PINOT NERO.

Hofstätter ★★★ Südtirol producer of top Italian PINOT NOIR; look for S Urbano.

IGT (Indicazione Geografica Tipica) New category: between VDT and DOC.

Ischia Cam DOC w (r) ★→★★ DYA Wine of the island off Naples. Slightly sharp white SUPERIORE is the best of the DOC. Top producer D'AMBRA makes single v'yd DOC Biancolella: Piellero and excellent Frassitelli.

Isole e Olena ★★★→★★★★ Top CHIANTI CLASSICO estate of great beauty with fine red VDT Cepparello. Vg VIN SANTO, CAB, CHARD, and L'Eremo Syrah.

Isonzo F-VG DOC r w ★★★ (r) **88 90** 93 94 DOC covering 19 wines (17 varietals) in the NE. Best whites and CAB compare with neighbouring COLLIO wines. Best from Borgo Conventi, Francesco Pecorari, Pierpaolo Pecorari, Ronco del Gelso, VIE DI ROMANS, Villanova.

Jermann, Silvio ★★★→★★★★ Family estate in COLLIO: top white VDT, incl singular VINTAGE TUNINA oak-aged white blend and lighter Vinnae. Also fresh Capo Martino (**91**) and CHARD. 'WHERE THE DREAMS HAVE NO END...'

Kalterersee German (and local) name for LAGO DI CALDARO.

Kante, Edi ★★★ Lone star of CARSO with outstanding DOC CHARD, SAUV, MALVASIA and vg red Terrano.

Lacryma (or Lacrima) Christi del Vesuvio Cam r p w dr (sw fz) ★→★★ DYA Famous but ordinary range of wines in great variety from Vesuvius. (DOC Vesuvio.) MASTROBERARDINO produces the only good example.

Lageder, Alois ★→★★★ The lion of Bolzano (ALTO A). DOCs: SANTA MADDALENA, etc. Exciting wines, incl oak-aged CHARD and CAB Löwengang. Single-v'yd SAUV is Lehenhof, PINOT BL Haberlehof, PINOT GR Benefizium Porer.

Lago di Caldaro See Caldaro.

Lagrein, Südtiroler, T-AA DOC r p ★★→★★★ **85 88 90** 94 95 96 A Tyrolean grape with a bitter twist. Good fruity wine – at best very appetizing. The rosé is 'Kretzer', the dark 'Dunkel'. Best from Gojer, Gries, Kössler, Maddalena, Niedermayr, Rottensteiner, Schwanburg.

Lamberti ★→★★ Large producers of SOAVE, VALPOLICELLA, BARDOLINO, etc at Lazise on the E shore of Lake Garda. NB LUGANA and VDT Turà. See also GIV.

Lambrusco E-R DOC (or not) r p dr s/sw ★→★★ DYA Popular fizzy red, best known in industrial s/sw version. Best is SECCO, traditional is with second fermentation in bottle (yeast sediment on bottom). DOCs are L Grasparossa di Castelvetro, L Salamino di Santa Croce and, perhaps best, L di Sorbara. Best from: Barbolini, Bellei, Casali, CAVICCHIOLI, Franco Ferrari, Graziano, Rinaldo Rinaldini.

Langhe The hills of central PIEDMONT, home of BAROLO, BARBARESCO, etc. Has become name for recent DOC (r w ★★→★★★) for 8 different wines: ROSSO, BIANCO, NEBBIOLO, DOLCETTO, FREISA, ARNEIS, FAVORITA and CHARDONNAY. Barolo and Barbaresco can now be declassified to DOC Langhe (Nebbiolo previously only allowed VDT status).

La Scolca ★★→★★★ Famous estate in GAVI for top Gavi and SPUMANTE (look for Extra Brut Soldati La Scolca).

Latisana F-VG DOC r w ★→★★ (r) **94** 95 (96) DOC for 13 varietal wines from 50 miles NE of Venice. Esp good TOCAI FRIULANO.

Le Pupille ★★★ Top producer of MORELLINO DI SCANSANO. outstanding VDT Cab-Merlot blend Saffredi.

Le Salette ★★★ Small VALPOLICELLA producer: look for vg AMARONE La Marega and RECIOTO Le Traversagne.

Leone de Castris ★★ Large producer of APULIAN wines. Estate at SALICE SALENTINO, near Lecce.

Lessona Pie DOC r ★★ **88 89 90** 93 94 95 (96) Soft dry claret-like wine from the province of Vercelli. NEBBIOLO, Vespolina and BONARDA grapes.

Librandi ★★→★★★ Top Calabria producer. Vg red CIRO (RISERVA Duca San Felice is ★★★) and VDT Gravello (interesting value CAB-Gaglioppo blend).

Lilliano, Castello di ★★★ Old CHIANTI CLASSICO estate pulling its weight again.

Liquoroso Means strong, usually sweet and always fortified.

Lisini ★★★ Small estate for some of the finest recent vintages of BRUNELLO.

Livon ★★★ Top producer of COLLI ORIENTALI.

Loazzolo Pie DOC w sw ★★★ **90 91 93** 94 95 (96) New DOC for MOSCATO dessert wine from botrytised air-dried grapes: expensive and sweet. Esp from Borgo Maragliano, Borgo Moncalvo, Borgo Sambui, Bricchi Mej, Luja.

Locorotondo Ap DOC w (sp) ★ DYA Pleasantly fresh southern white. To try.

Lugana Lom and Ven DOC w (sp) ★★→★★★ DYA Whites of S Lake Garda: can be fragrant, smooth, full of body and flavour. Good from Ca'dei Frati, Ottella, Roveglia, Zenato.

Lungarotti ★★→★★★ The leading producer of TORGIANO wine, with cellars, hotel and wine museum nr Perugia. Also some of Italy's best CHARD (Miralduolo and Vigna I Palazzi) and PINOT GR. See Torgiano.

Maculan ★★→★★★ The top producer of DOC BREGANZE. Also Torcolato, dessert VDT (★★★) and Prato di Canzio (CHARD, PINOT BL and PINOT GR).

Malvasia

An important underrated grape of chameleon character: white or red wines, sparkling or still, strong or mild, sweet or dry, aromatic or rather neutral, often as VDT, sometimes as DOC. White, dry to sweet, strong concentrated: **M di Cagliari** Sar DOC ★★ (eg Meloni); red fragrant grapey sweet, sometimes sparkling: **M di Casorzo d'Asti** Pie DOC ★★ (eg Bricco Mondalino); red aromatic sparkling: **M di Castelnuovo Don Bosco** Pie DOC ★★ (eg Gilli); white rich strong, long-living: **M delle Lipari** Si DOC ★★★ (eg Colosi); white dry to semi-sweet, deep bouquet, long-lived: **M de Nus** VdA DOC ★★★ (eg La Crotta de Vignerons). Always worth trying.

Manduria (Primitivo di) Ap DOC r s/sw (dr sw fz) ★★ **90 91 92** 93 94 95 96 Heady red, naturally strong but often fortified. From nr Taranto. Especially Vinicola Savese's.

Mantonico Cal w dr sw fz ★★ **89 90 91** 92 93 94 95 Fruity deep amber dessert wine from Reggio Calabria. Can age remarkably well. Good from Ceratti. See also Greco di Bianco.

Marchesi di Barolo ★★ Important ALBA wines: BAROLO, BARBARESCO, DOLCETTO and GAVI.

Marino Lat DOC w dr s/sw (sp) ★→★★ DYA A neighbour of FRASCATI with similar wine; often a better buy. Look for COLLE PICCHIONI brand.

Marsala Si DOC br dr s/sw sw fz ★★→★★★ NV Sicily's sherry-type wine, invented by the Woodhouse Bros from Liverpool in 1773; excellent aperitif or for dessert, but mostly used in the kitchen for zabaglione etc. The dry ('virgin'), sometimes made by the solera system, must be 5 yrs old. Top producers: FLORIO, Pellegrino, Rallo, VECCHIO SAMPERI. V special old vintages ★★★★.

Martini & Rossi Vermouth and sparkling wine house (now controlled by Bacardi group. (Has a fine wine-history museum in Pessione, nr Turin.)

Marzemino (Trentino) T-AA DOC r ★→★★ **93 94** 95 96 Pleasant local red. Fruity, slightly bitter. Esp from Bossi Fedrigotti, Casata Monfort, CA'VIT, De Tarczal, Gaierhof, Letrari, Simoncelli, Vallarom, Vallis Agri.

NB Vintages in colour are those you should choose first for drinking in 1998.

Mascarello The name of two top producers of BAROLO etc: Bartolo M and Giuseppe M & Figli. Look for the latter's BAROLO Monprivato (★★★★).

Masi ★★→★★★ Well-known, conscientious and reliable specialist producers of VALPOLICELLA, AMARONE (★★★), RECIOTO, SOAVE etc, incl fine red Campo Fiorin. Also look for excellent barrel-aged red VDT Toar.

Mastroberardino ★★→★★★ Campania's leading wine producing family has split into two parts: M and VIGNADORA-M but with v few changes. Wines incl FIANO DI AVELLINO, GRECO DI TUFO, LACRYMA CHRISTI and TAURASI (look for Radici).

Melini ★★ Long-est'd producers of CHIANTI CLASSICO at Poggibonsi. Good quality/price; look for single-v'yd C Classico Selvanella. See also GIV.

Meranese di Collina T-AA DOC r ★ DYA Light red of Merano, known in German as Meraner Hügel.

Merlot Adaptable red B'x grape widely grown in N (esp) and central Italy. Merlot DOCs are abundant. Best growers are: HAAS, SCHRECKBICHL and Baron Widman in T-AA, Torre Rosazza (L'Altromerlot) and BORGO DEL TIGLIO in F-VG and the Tuscan Super-VDTS of AMA (L'Apparita), AVIGNONESI, ORNELLAIA (Masseto) and FRESCOBALDI (Lamaïone).

Metodo classico or tradizionale Now the mandatory terms to identify classic method sparkling wines. 'Metodo Champenois' banned since '94 and now illegal. (See also Classico.)

Mezzacorona Huge TRENTINO coop with gd DOC TEROLDEGO and MC sp Rotari.

Moccagatta ★★→★★★ Specialist in impressive single-v'yd BARBARESCO: Basarin, Bric Balin (★★★) and Vigna Cole.

Monacesca, La ★★★ Top producer of vg VERDICCHIO DI MATELICA. Top wine: Mirus.

Moncaro MARCHES coop: good VERDICCHIO DEI CASTELLI DI JESI.

Monferrato Pie DOC r w sw p ★★ The hills between the River Po and the Apennines give their name to a new DOC; incl ROSSO, BIANCO, CHIARETTO, DOLCETTO, Casalese and FREISA CORTESE.

Monica di Sardegna Sar DOC r ★ DYA Monica is the grape of light dry red.

Monsanto ★★→★★★ Esteemed CHIANTI CLASSICO estate, esp for Il Poggio v'yd.

Montalcino Small town in the province of Siena, TUSCANY, famous for its deep red BRUNELLO and younger ROSSO DI MONTALCINO.

Monte Vertine ★★★→★★★★ Top estate at Radda in CHIANTI. VDT Le Pergole Torte (100% SANGIOVESE) is one of TUSCANY's best. Also Sodaccio (Sangioveto plus Canaiolo) and fine VIN SANTO.

Montecarlo Tus DOC w r ★★ DYA (w) White wine area in N TUSCANY: smooth neutral blend of TREBBIANO with a range of better grapes. Now applies to a CHIANTI-style red too. Good producers: Buonamico (esp VDT 'Il Fortino'), Carmignani (vg VDT 'For Duke'), Michi.

Montefalco (Rosso di) Umb DOC r ★★ **91 93** 95 96 SANGIOVESE-TREBBIANO-SAGRANTINO blend. ADANTI's Rosso d'Arquata VDT stands out.

Montefalco Sagrantino Umb DOCG r dr (sw) ★★★ **90 91 92** 93 95 96 Strong, v interesting SECCO or sweet PASSITO red from Sagrantino grapes only. Good from: ADANTI, Antonelli, Caprai-Val di Maggio, Colpetrone.

Montellori, Fattoria di ★★→★★★ Tuscan producer making admirable SANGIOVESE-CAB VDT blend 'Castelrapiti Rosso', Viognier VDT 'Bonfiglio', CHARD VDT 'Castelrapiti Bianco' and vg MC SPUMANTE.

Montepulciano An important red grape of central-east Italy as well as the famous Tuscan town (see next entries).

Montepulciano d'Abruzzo Ab DOC r p ★→★★★ **90 91 92 93 94** 95 96 Happens rarely, but at best one of Italy's tastiest reds, full of flavour and warmth, from Adriatic coast nr Pescara. Best: VALENTINI, Barone Cornacchia, Bosco Nestore, Filomusi-Guelfi, Illuminati, Cataldi Madonna, Masciarelli, Montori, Nicodemi, Tenuta del Priore and Zaccagnini. See also Cerasuolo.

Montepulciano, Vino Nobile di See Vino Nobile di Montepulciano.

Montescudaio Tus DOC r w ★→★★ New DOC nr Pisa. Terriccio is good producer, esp of VDT MERLOT-CAB SAUV blends Lupicaia and Tassinaia.

Montesodi Tus r ★★★→★★★★ **85 86 88 90 91** 93 94 95 96 Tip-top CHIANTI RUFINA RISERVA from FRESCOBALDI.

Montresor ★★ VERONA winehouse: good LUGANA, BIANCO DI CUSTOZA, VALPOLICELLA.

Morellino di Scansano Tus DOC r ★★→★★★ **88' 90' 91 93** 94 95 96 Local SANGIOVESE of the Maremma, the S Tuscan coast; enjoying vogue as it finds focus on more modern flavours. Cherry-red, lively and tasty young or matured. Fattorie LE PUPILLE, MORIS FARMS, E Banti are best.

Moris Farms ★★★ Top producer of MORELLINO DI SCANSANO; look for RISERVA and super-concentrated CAB S-Morellino blend Avvoltore.

Moscadello di Montalcino Tus DOC w sw (sp) ★★ DYA Traditional wine of MONTALCINO, much older than BRUNELLO. Sweet white fizzy, and sweet to high-octane PASSITO MOSCATO. Good producers: BANFI, POGGIONE.

ITALY

Moscato

Fruitily fragrant ubiquitous grape for a diverse range of wines: sparkling or still, light or full-bodied, but always sweet. Most famous is **M d'Asti** Pie DOCG (★★→★★★): light, aromatic, sparkling and delicious from BERA, CAUDRINA-DOGLIOTTI, Grimaldi, Icardi, La Morandina, Marenco, Perrone, RIVETTI, Saracco and Vignaioli di Santo Stefano. Italy's best is from the island of Pantelleria off the Tunisian coast, with top wines from De Bartoli, Murana. And rare but prestigious is **Moscato di Trani** (sometimes fortified), best from Nugnes.

Müller-Thurgau Makes wine to be reckoned with in TRENTINO-ALTO ADIGE and FRIULI, esp TIEFENBRUNNER's Feldmarschall.

Murana, Salvatore ★★→★★★ Vg Moscato di PANTELLERIA and PASSITO di P.

Nasco di Cagliari Sar DOC w dr sw (fz) ★★ Sardinian speciality with light bitter taste, high alcohol content. Good from Meloni.

Nebbiolo The best red grape of PIEDMONT and Lombardy.

Nebbiolo d'Alba Pie DOC r dr (s/sw sp) ★★ **88 89 90 93** 95 From ALBA (but not BAROLO, BARBARESCO). Sometimes like lightweight BAROLO; can be easier to enjoy than the powerful classic wine. Best from Correggia, MASCARELLO, PRUNOTTO, RATTI, Roagna. See also Roero.

Negroamaro Literally 'black bitter'; APULIAN red grape with potential for quality. See Copertino and Salice Salentino.

Nepente di Oliena Sar r ★★ Strong fragrant CANNONAU red; a touch bitter. Good from Arcadu Tonino.

Nipozzano, Castello di ★★★ FRESCOBALDI estate east of Florence making MONTESODI CHIANTI. The most important outside the CLASSICO zone.

Nittardi ★★★ Up-and-coming little CHIANTI CLASSICO estate.

Nosiola (Trentino) T-AA DOC w dr sw ★★ DYA Light fruity white from dried Nosiola grapes. Also good VIN SANTO. Best from Pravis: Le Frate.

Nozzole ★★→★★★ Famous estate, owned by RUFFINO, in the heart of CHIANTI CLASSICO, N of Greve. Also good CAB.

Nuragus di Cagliari Sar DOC w ★ DYA Lively Sardinian white.

Oberto, Andrea ★★ Small La Morra producer: top BAROLO and BARBERA D'ALBA.

Oltrepò Pavese Lom DOC r w dr sw sp ★→★★★ DOC applicable to 14 wines produced in the province of Pavia, mostly named after their grapes. PINOT NERO and METODO-CLASSICO-SPUMANTE can sometimes be astonishing. Top growers incl Anteo, Cabanon, Doria, La Versa, Le Fracce, Luciano Brega, Monsupello, Montelio, Vercesi del Castellazzo.

Ornellaia Tus ★★★→★★★★ New 130-acre estate of LODOVICO ANTINORI nr Bolgheri on the Tuscan coast. Watch for VDT Ornellaia (CAB-MERLOT), vg straight VDT Masseto (MERLOT) and vg VDT SAUV Poggio delle Gazze.

Orvieto Umb DOC w dr s/sw ★→★★★ DYA The classical Umbrian golden white: smooth and substantial; formerly very dull but recently more interesting, esp in sweet versions. Orvieto CLASSICO is better. Only the finest examples (eg BARBERANI, BIGI, DECUGANO DEI BARBI) age well. But see Castello della Sala.

Pacenti, Siro ★★★ Vg BRUNELLO DI MONTALCINO and ROSSO DI M.

Pagadebit di Romagna E-R DOC w dr s/sw ★ DYA Pleasant traditional 'payer of debts' from around Bertinoro.

Palazzino, Podere Il ★★★ Small estate with admirable CHIANTI CLASSICO and VDT Grosso Sanese.

Panaretta, Castello della ★★→★★★ To follow for fine CHIANTI CLASSICO.

Pancrazi, Marchese ★★→★★★ Estate nr Florence: some of Italy's top PINOT NERO.

Panizzi ★★ Makes top-class VERNACCIA DI SAN GIMIGNANO.

Pantelleria See Moscato.

Paradiso, Fattoria ★★→★★★ Old family estate near Bertinoro (E-R). Good ALBANA and PAGADEBIT and unique red Barbarossa. Vg SANGIOVESE.

Parrina Tus r w ★★ **94** 95 Grand estate nr the classy resorts of Argentario, S TUSCANY. Light red and white from Maremma coast, S TUSCANY.

Parusso ★★★ Tiziana and Marco Parusso make top-level BAROLO (eg single-v'yd Bussia, Mariondino), also vg BARBERA D'ALBA and DOLCETTO etc.

Pasolini Dall'Onda Noble family with estates in CHIANTI COLLI Fiorentini and Romagna, producing traditional-style wines.

Pasqua, Fratelli ★★ Good level producer and bottler of Verona wines: VALPOLICELLA, AMARONE, SOAVE.

Passito (pa) Strong sweet wine from grapes dried on the vine or indoors.

Paternoster ★★→★★★ Top AGLIANICO DEL VULTURE producer.

Pecorari, Pierpaolo ★★→★★★ Vg DOC ISONZO wines; best are CHARD and SAUV.

Pelaverga Pie r ★★ (DYA) Pale red with spicy perfume, from Verduno. Good producers: Alessandria, Bel Colle, Castello di Verduno.

Peppoli ★★★ Estate owned by ANTINORI, producing excellent CHIANTI CLASSICO in a full round youthful style.

Per'e Palummo Cam r ★ Appetizing light tannic red from island of ISCHIA.

Perrone, Elio ★★→★★★ Small estate for one of best MOSCATO D'ASTIS.

Piave Ven DOC r w ★→★★ (r) **94** 95 96 (w) DYA Flourishing DOC NW of Venice covering 8 wines, 4 red and 4 white, named after their grapes. CAB, MERLOT and RABOSO reds can all age. Good from Molon-Traverso.

Picolit (Colli Orientali del Friuli) F-VG DOC w s/sw sw ★★→★★★ **93 94** 95 96 Delicate dessert wine; exaggerated reputation. A little like Jurançon. Ages up to 6 yrs, but wildly overpriced. Best: DORIGO, Dri, LIVIO FELLUGA, Graziano Specogna.

Piedmont (Piemonte) The most important Italian region for top-quality wine. Turin is the capital, ASTI and ALBA the wine centres. See Barbaresco, Barbera, Barolo, Dolcetto, Grignolino, Moscato etc.

Piemonte Pie DOC r w p (sp) ★→★★★ New all-PIEDMONT blanket-DOC incl Piemonte BARBERA, P BONARDA, P BRACHETTO, P CORTESE, P GRIGNOLINO, P CHARD, P SPUMANTE, P MOSCATO.

Pieropan ★★★ Outstanding SOAVE and RECIOTO: for once deserving its fame.

Pieve di Santa Restituta ★★★ Estate for admirable BRUNELLO DI MONTALCINO, vg ROSSO DI M and red VDT Pian de Cerri. Links with GAJA.

Pigato Lig DOC w ★★ DOC under Riviera Ligure di Ponente. Often out-classes VERMENTINO as Liguria's finest white, with rich texture and structure. Good from: Anfossi, COLLE dei Bardellini, Feipu, Lupi, TERRE ROSSE, Vio.

Piedmont vintages

1996 Again promising, despite a month's rainfall before a fine-weather harvest. Quality of Barbera and Nebbiolo is v high: vintage could turn out to be better than '95.

1995 V promising vintage, then incessant autumn rains: average quality white, Dolcetto, Barbera. Some excellent Barolos, but only where harvested mid-October or later when warm and dry.

1994 Hot summer; but vintage rains prevented excellence.

1993 Hot summer, good Dolcetto and Barbera, but September rains disrupted Nebbiolo harvest and severe selection was necessary for Barolo and Barbaresco.

1992 An extremely difficult year due to incessant rainfall. Whites good. Nebbiolo wines not so lucky.

1991 Cold April and suddenly v hot in July, harvest then interrupted by rain: some elegant Barolo, Barbaresco and Barbera. Dolcetto and whites fine.

Pighin, Fratelli Solid producers of COLLIO and GRAVE DEL FRIULI.

Pinot Bianco (Pinot Bl) Popular grape in NE for many DOC wines, generally bland and dry. Best from ALTO ADIGE ★★ (top growers: CS St-Michael, LAGEDER, Elena Walch), COLLIO ★★ (vg from Keber, Mangilli, Picech, Princic) and COLLI ORIENTALI ★★→★★★ (best from Rodaro and VIGNE DAL LEON).

Pinot Grigio (Pinot Gr) Tasty low-acid white grape popular in NE. Best from DOCs ALTO ADIGE (LAGEDER, Kloster Muri-Gries, Schwanburg) and COLLIO (Caccese, SCHIOPETTO). AMA in TUSCANY makes vg VDT Pinot Gr.

Pinot Nero (Pinot Noir) Planted in much of NE Italy. DOC status in ALTO ADIGE (HAAS, SCHRECKBICHL, St-Michael-Eppan coop, Niedrist, Hofstätter, coop Girlan, coop Kurtatsch, coop Kaltern, Niedermayr, LAGEDER) and in OLTREPO PAVESE (Vercesi del Castellazzo, Ruiz de Cardenas). Promising trials elsewhere eg Tuscany (BANFI, FONTODI, AMA, Pancranzi, RUFFINO). Also fine sparkling wines from several regions: TRENTINO (Maso Cantanghel, POJER & SANDRI), Lombady (CA'DEL BOSCO).

Pio Cesare ★★→★★★ Long-established PIEDMONT producer. All red, incl BAROLO.

Podere Tuscan term for a wine-farm; smaller than a FATTORIA.

Poggio Antico (Montalcino) ★★★ Admirably consistent top-level BRUNELLO, ROSSO and red VDT Altero.

Poggione, Tenuta Il ★★★ Perhaps the most reliable estate for BRUNELLO and ROSSO DI MONTALCINO.

Pojer & Sandri ★★★ Top TRENTINO producers: reds and whites, incl SPUMANTE.

Poliziano ★★★ Federico Carletti makes vg VINO NOBILE DI MONT (esp Asinone, Caggiole), VDT Elegia (CAB, SANGIOVESE) and wonderful VIN SANTO. Vg value.

Pomino Tus DOC w (r br) ★★★ **93' 94** 95 96 Fine white, partly CHARD (esp Il Benefizio), and a SANGIOVESE-CAB-MERLOT-PINOT N blend. Also VIN SANTO. Esp from FRESCOBALDI and SELVAPIANA.

Predicato Name for 4 kinds of VDT from central TUSCANY, illustrating the current headlong rush from tradition. P del Muschio is CHARD and PINOT BL; P del Selvante is SAUV BL; P di Biturica is CAB with SANGIOVESE; P di Cardisco is Sangiovese straight. Esp RUFFINO's Cabreo brand wines.

Primitivo Vg red grape of far S, now identified with California's Zinfandel. Of few producers, Coppi, Sava, Savese are best.

Primitivo di Apulia See Manduria.

Produttori del Barbaresco ★★→★★★ Coop and one of DOCG's most reliable producers. Often outstanding single-v'yd wines (Ovello, Rabajà, Pajé etc).

Prosecco White grape making light very dry sparkling wine popular in Venice. The next is better.

Prosecco di Conegliano-Valdobbiàdene Ven DOC w s/sw sp (dr) ★★ DYA Slight fruity bouquet, the dry pleasantly bitter, the sweet fruity; the sweetest (and most expensive) are known as Superiore di Cartizze. CARPENE-MALVOLTI is best-known producer, now challenged by ADAMI, Bisol, Bortolotti, Canevel, CASE BIANCHE, Collalto, Nino Franco, Foss Marai, Ruggeri.

Prunotto, Alfredo ★★★ Very serious ALBA company with top BARBARESCO (esp Montestefano, ★★★★), BAROLO (esp ★★★★ single-v'yd Bussia and Cannubi), NEBBIOLO, etc. Now controlled by ANTINORI.

Querciabella ★★★ Up-and-coming CHIANTI CLASSICO estate with excellent red VDT Camartina and a dream of a white VDT, Bâtard Pinot (P BL and GR).

Quintarelli, Giuseppe ★★★★ True artisan producer of VALPOLICELLA, RECIOTO and AMARONE, at the top in both quality and price.

Raboso del Piave (now DOC) Ven r ★★ **93 94** 95 (96) Powerful sharp interesting country red; needs age. Look for Molon-Traverso.

Ragose, Le ★★★ Family estate, one of VALPOLICELLA's best. AMARONE and RECIOTO top quality; CAB and Valpolicella vg too.

Ramandolo See Verduzzo Colli Orientali del Friuli.

Ramitello See Di Majo Norante.

Rampolla, Castello dei ★★★ Fine CHIANTI CLASSICO estate at Panzano; also excellent CAB-based VDT Sammarco.

Ratti, Renato ★★→★★★ Maker of vg BAROLO and other ALBA wines. The late Signor Ratti (d '88) was a highly respected local wine-scene leader.

> **Recioto**
> Wine made of half-dried grapes. Speciality of Veneto since the days of the Venetian empire; has roots in classical Roman wine, Raeticus. Always sweet, sometimes sparkling: sp is to drink young; sweet, concentrated, can be kept for a long time.

Recioto di Gambellara Ven DOC w sw (sp s/sw DYA) ★ Mostly half-sparkling and industrial. Best is strong and sweet. Look for LA BIANCARA (★★★).

Recioto di Soave Ven DOC w s/sw (sp) ★★★ **90 91 92** 93 95 96 SOAVE made from selected half-dried grapes: sweet fruity fresh, slightly almondy; high alcohol. Outstanding from ANSELMI and PIEROPAN.

Recioto della Valpolicella Ven DOC r s/sw ★★→★★★ **88 90** 93 95' Strong late-harvest red. Vg from Accordini, ALLEGRINI, BRIGALDARA, Corte Sant'Alda, DAL FORNO, Degani, Nicolis, Serègo Alighieri, LE RAGOSE, LE SALETTE, SAN RUSTICO, Speri, TEDESCHI.

Recioto della Valpolicella Amarone See Amarone.

Refosco r ★★ **90 93** 94 95 (96) Interesting full-bodied dark tannic red, needs ageing. The same grape as the Mondeuse of Savoie (France)? It tastes like it. Best comes from F-VG DOC COLLI ORIENTALI, GRAVE and CARSO (where known as Terrano). Vg from Bosco Romagno, Villa Belvedere, DORIGO, EDI KANTE, Le Fredis, LIVON, VOLPE PASINI. Often value.

Regaleali ★★★ Owned by the noble family Tasca D'Almerita, perhaps the best Sicilian producer; situated between Palermo and Caltanissetta to the SE. Vg VDT red, white and pink 'Regaleali', red 'Rosso del Conte' (★★★) and CAB. Also impressive CHARD (★★★).

Ribolla (Colli Orientali del Friuli and Collio) F-VG DOC w ★→★★ DYA Thin NE white. The best comes from COLLIO. Top estates: La Castellada, GRAVNER, Krapez, Radikon, Venica & Venica, VILLA RUSSIZ.

Ricasoli ★→★★★ Famous Tuscan family, 'inventors' of CHIANTI, whose CHIANTI CLASSICO is named after their BROLIO estate and castle.

Riecine Tus r (w) ★★→★★★ First-class CHIANTI CLASSICO estate at Gaiole, created by its English owner, John Dunkley. Also VDT La Gioia SANGIOVESE.

Riesling Formerly used to mean Italian Ries (Ries Italico or Welschriesling). German (Rhine) Ries, now ascendant, is called Ries Renano. Best are DOC ALTO ADIGE ★★ (esp coop Kurtatsch, Ignaz Niedrist, coop La Vis, Elena Walch) and DOC OLTREPO PAVESE Lom ★★ (Brega, Cabanon, Doria, Frecciarossa, coop La Versa), also astonishing from RONCO del Gelso (DOC ISONZO).

Ripasso VALPOLICELLA re-fermented on AMARONE grape skins to make a more complex, longer-lived and fuller wine. Best is MASI's Campo Fiorin.

Riserva Wine aged for a statutory period, usually in barrels.

Riunite One of the world's largest coop cellars, nr Reggio Emilia, producing huge quantities of LAMBRUSCO and other wines.

Rivera ★★ Reliable winemakers at Andria, near Bari (APULIA), with good red Il Falcone and CASTEL DEL MONTE rosé. Also Vigna al Monte label.

Rivetti, Giorgio (La Spinetta) ★★★ First success with MOSCATO, then with reds. Top Moscato d'Asti, vg BARBERA, v interesting VDT Pin (Barbera-NEBBIOLO).

Riviera del Garda Bresciano Lom DOC w p r (sp) ★→★★ Simple, sometimes charming cherry-pink CHIARETTO and neutral white from SW Garda. Good producers: Ca'dei Frati, Comincioli, Costaripa, Monte Cigogna.

Rocca, Bruno ★★★ Young producer with admirable BARBARESCO (Rabajà).

Rocca di Castagnoli ★★→★★★ Recent producer of vg CHIANTI CLASSICO (best: Capraia, RISERVA Poggio a'Frati), also vg VDT Stielle and Buriano (blends of CAB and SANGIOVESE).

Rocca delle Macìe ★→★★ Large CHIANTI CLASSICO winemaker nr Castellina.

Rocche dei Manzoni, Podere ★★★ Go-ahead estate at Monforte d'Alba. Excellent BAROLO (best: Vigna Big), BRICCO MANZONI (outstanding NEBBIOLO-BARBERA blend VINO DA TAVOLA), ALBA wines, CHARD (L'Angelica) and Valentino Brut sparkling.

Rodano ★★★ Enrico Pozzesi makes mild but typical CHIANTI CLASSICO at Castellina. Both Annata and RISERVA vg.

Roero Pie DOC r ★★ **93 94** 95 96 Evolving former drink-me-quick NEBBIOLO from Roeri hills nr ALBA. Can be delicious. Best: Correggia, Deltetto, Malabaila, Malvirà.

Roero Arneis Pie DOC r ★★ DYA Mellow, light white from the hills around Roeri; usually too expensive. Good from: Almondo, BRUNO GIACOSA, Correggia, Deltetto, Malabaila, Malvirà, VIETTI, Gianni Voerzio.

Ronco Term for a hillside v'yd in FRIULI-VENEZIA GIULIA.

Ronco del Gnemiz ★★★ Tiny property with outstanding COLLI ORIENTALI DOCs and VDT CHARD.

Rosa del Golfo ★★→★★★ Mino Calò's ROSATO DEL SALENTO is one of the best. Also vg red VDT Portulano.

Rosato Rosé.

Rosato del Salento Ap p ★★ DYA From nr BRINDISI and v like Brindisi, COPERTINO and SALICE SALENTINO ROSATOS; can be strong, but often really juicy and good. See Brindisi, Copertino, Salice Salentino for producers.

Rossese di Dolceacqua Lig DOC r ★★ DYA Well-known fragrant light red of the Riviera. Good from Giuncheo, Guglielmi, Lupi, Perrino, Terre Bianche.

Rosso Red.

Rosso Cònero Mar DOC r ★★→★★★ **88 90 92 93** 94 95 (96) Some of the best MONTEPULCIANO (varietal) reds of Italy, eg GAROFOLI's Grosso Agontano, Moroder's RC Dorico, UMANI RONCHI's Cumaro and San Lorenzo. Also vg from Conte Dittajuti, E Lanari Leardo, Le Terrazze, Marchetti.

Rosso di Montalcino Tus DOC r ★★→★★★ **90 93** 94 95 96 DOC for younger wines from BRUNELLO grapes. Still variable but potentially a winner if the many good producers are not greedy over prices. For growers see Brunello di Montalcino.

Rosso di Montepulciano Tus DOC r ★★ **93 94** 95 96 Equivalent of the last for junior VINO NOBILE, recently introduced and yet to establish a style. For growers see Vino Nobile di M.

Rosso Piceno Mar DOC r ★★ **90 91 93** 94 95 (96) Stylish Adriatic red. SUPERIORE from classic zone near Ascoli. Best include Cocci Grifoni, Velenosi Ercole, Saladini Pilastri, Villamagna.

Rubesco ★★ The excellent popular red of LUNGAROTTI; see Torgiano.

Ruchè (also Rouchè or Rouchet) A rare old grape (French origin) giving fruity, fresh, rich bouqueted red wine (s/sw). Ruchè di Castagnole Monferrato is recent DOC, with Piero Bruno best producer. Rouchet Briccorosa is dry and excellent (★★★) from SCARPA.

Ruffino ★→★★★ Well known CHIANTI merchants, at Pontassieve. RISERVA Ducale Oro and Santedame are the top wines. NB new PREDICATO wines (red and white Cabreo) and CAB Il Pareto.

Rufina ★→★★★ Important subregion of CHIANTI in the hills E of Florence. Best wines from Basciano, Castello Nipozzano (FRESCOBALDI), SELVAPIANA.

Russiz Superiore (Collio) See Felluga, Marco.

Sagrantino di Montefalco See Montefalco.

St-Michael-Eppan Top SUDTIROL coop: look for St-Valentin (★★★), SAUV, vg SPUMANTE, PINOT N, PINOT BIANCO, Gewürz and even vg RIES Renano.

Sala, Castello della ★★→★★★ ANTINORI's estate at ORVIETO. Borro is the regular white. Top wine is Cervaro della Sala: CHARD and GRECHETTO aged in oak. Muffato della S is one of Italy's best botrytis wines.

Salice Salentino Ap DOC r ★★→★★★ **88 89 90 93** 94 95 (96) Resonant but clean and quenching red from NEGROAMARO grapes. RISERVA after 2 years. Top makers: CANDIDO, De Castris, TAURINO, Vallone.

San Felice ★★→★★★ Rising star in CHIANTI with fine CLASSICO Poggio Rosso. Also red VDT Vigorello and PREDICATO di Biturica.

San Gimigniano Famous TUSCAN city of towers and its dry white VERNACCIA.

San Giusto a Rentennano One of the best CHIANTI CLASSICO producers (★★★). Delicious but v rare VIN SANTO. Excellent VDT red Percarlo.

San Guido, Tenuta ★★★★ See Sassicaia.

San Polo in Rosso, Castello di ★★★ CHIANTI CLASSICO estate with first-rate red VDT Cetinaia (aged in big casks, not barriques).

San Rustico ★★ Small VALPOLICELLA estate; vg AMARONE Vigneti del Gaso.

Sandrone, Luciano ★★★ Exponent of new-style BAROLO vogue with vg B Cannubi Boschis, DOLCETTO and BARBERA.

Sangiovese (Sangioveto) Principal red grape of Italy. Top performance only in TUSCANY, where its many forms incl CHIANTI, VINO NOBILE, BRUNELLO, MORELLINO etc. Very popular is S di Romagna (E-R DOC r ★→★★), a pleasant standard red. Vg from PARADISO, Trerè, ZERBINA. Outstanding ★★★ VDTS RONCO dei Cigliegi, R delle Ginestre from CASTELLUCCIO. Sometimes gd from ROSSO PICENO (Marches).

Santa Maddalena (or St-Magdalener) T-AA DOC r ★ DYA Typical SCHIAVA Tyrolean red, lightish with bitter aftertaste. Best from: Cantina Sociale St-Magdalena, CS Girlan, Gojer, Thurnhof.

Santa Margherita Large Veneto (Portogruaro) merchants: Veneto (Torresella), ALTO-ADIGE (Kettmeir), Tuscan (Lamole di Lamole), Lombardy (CA'DEL BOSCO).

Saracco, Paolo ★★★ Small estate with top MOSCATO D'ASTI.

Sartarelli ★★→★★★ One of top VERDICCHIO DEI CASTELLI DI JESI producers, (Tralivio), outstanding, rare Verdicchio VENDEMMIA Tardiva (Contrada Balciana).

Sassicaia Tus r ★★★★ **83' 85' 88' 89** 90' **91** 92' 93 94 95 (96) Outstanding pioneer CAB, Italy's best, from the Tenuta San Guido of the Incisa family, at Bolgheri nr Livorno. 'Promoted' from SUPER-TUSCAN VDT to DOC BOLGHERI in '94.

Sauvignon Sauvignon Blanc is working v well in the northeast, best from DOCs ALTO ADIGE, COLLIO, COLLI ORIENTALI, ISONZO and TERLANO.

Sauvignon (Colli Orientali del Friuli) F-VG DOC w ★★→★★★ **93 94** 96 Best from: Aquila del Torre, RONCO DEL GNEMIZ, Torre Rosazza.

Sauvignon Collio F-VG DOC w ★★→★★★ **93 94** 96 Best wines from La Castellada, GRAVNER, Renato Keber, Komjanc, Primosic, SCHIOPETTO, VILLA RUSSIZ.

Sauvignon Isonzo F-VG DOC w ★★→★★★ **93 94** 96 V full fruity white, increasingly good quality. Top producers: Pecorari, Lis Neris, VIE DI ROMANS.

Savuto Cal DOC r p ★★ **93 94** 95 96 Fragrant juicy wine from the provinces of Cosenza and Catanzaro. Best producer is Odoardi.

Scarpa ★★→★★★ Old-fashioned house with full-bodied smooth BARBERA D'ASTI (La Bogliona), rare Rouchet, vg DOLCETTO, BAROLO, BARBARESCO.

Scavino, Paul ★★★ Successful modern-style BAROLO producer. Sought-after single-v'yd wines: Bric del Fiasc and Cannubi; also oak-aged BARBERA.

Schiava High-yielding red grape of TRENTINO-ALTO ADIGE with characteristic bitter aftertaste, used for LAGO DI CALDARO, SANTA MADDALENA etc.

Schiopetto, Mario ★★★→★★★★ Legendary COLLIO pioneer with brand-new 20,000-case winery; vg DOC SAUV, PINOT GR, TOCAI, VDT blend 'Bl de Rosis' etc.

Schreckbichl (or Colterenzio CS) No 1 SUDTIROL CANTINA SOCIALE. Admirable ALTO ADIGE CAB S, Gewürz, PINOT N (look for Schwarzhaus RISERVA), CHARD, PINOT BL, PINOT GR, SAUV (look for Lafoa), red VDT Cornelius etc.

Sciacchetrà See Cinqueterre.

Secco Dry.

Sella & Mosca ★★ Major Sardinian growers and merchants at Alghero. Their port-like Anghelu Ruju (★★★) is excellent. Also pleasant white TORBATO and delicious light fruity VERMENTINO Cala Viola (DYA).

Selvapiana ★★★ Top CHIANTI RUFINA estate. Best wine is RISERVA Bucerchiale.

Sforzato See Valtellina.

Sizzano Pie DOC r ★★ **90 93** 95 (96) Full-bodied red from Sizzano, (Novara); mostly NEBBIOLO. Ages up to 10 yrs. Esp from: Bianchi, Dessilani.

Soave Ven DOC w ★→★★★ DYA Famous mass-produced Veronese white. Should be fresh with smooth, limpid texture. Standards are rising (at last). S CLASSICO is more restricted and better. Esp from ANSELMI, PIEROPAN; also Gini, GUERRIERI-RIZZARDI, Inama, Pra, Suavia, TEDESCHI.

Solaia Tus r ★★★★ **85' 88' 90 91** 93 94 95 (96) V fine Bordeaux-style VDT of CAB S and a little SANGIOVESE from ANTINORI; first made in '78. Extraordinarily influential in shaping VDT (and Italian) philosophy.

Solopaca Cam DOC r w ★★ **95** 96 Rather sharp red; soft dry white from nr Benevento. Some promise: esp Antica Masseria Venditti.

Sorì Term for a high S, SE or SW oriented v'yd in PIEDMONT.

Spanna See Gattinara.

Spumante Sparkling, as in sweet ASTI or many good dry wines, incl both METODO CLASSICO (best from TRENTINO, A ADIGE, FRANCIACORTA, PIEDMONT, some vg also from TUSCANY and Veneto) and tank-made cheapos.

Stravecchio Very old.

Südtirol The local name of German-speaking ALTO ADIGE.

Super-Tuscans Term coined for high-price novelties from TUSCANY, usually involving CAB, barriques, and frequently fancy bottles and prices.

Superiore Wine that has undergone more ageing than normal DOC and contains 0.5–1% more alcohol.

Tasca d'Almerita See Regaleali.

Taurasi Cam DOCG r ★★★ **90 92** 93 94 95 96 The best Campanian red, from MASTROBERARDINO of Avellino. Harsh when young. RISERVA after 4 yrs. Radici (since '86) is Mastroberardino's top estate bottling.

> **Italy's best bubbles**
> **Alto Adige**: Kössler, Vivaldi; **Franciacorta**: Bellavista, Ca'del Bosco, Cavalleri, Faccoli, Gatti, Guarischi, Uberti, Villa; **Trentino**: Ferrari's Riserva del Fondatore, Letrari, Mezzacorona's Rotari, Pojer & Sandri; **Piedmont**: Bruno Giacosa, Rocche dei Manzoni, Fontanafredda's Gattinera, Martini & Rossi's Montelera; **Oltrepò Pavese**: Anteo's Selezione del Gourmet; **Veneto**: Bisol

Taurino, Cosimo ★★★ Tip-top producer of Salento-APULIA, vg SALICE SALENTINO, VDT Notarpanoro and BRINDISI Patriglione (s'times even ★★★★).

Tedeschi, Fratelli ★★★ V reliable and vg producer of VALPOLICELLA, AMARONE, RECIOTO and SOAVE. Vg Capitel San Rocco red and white VDT.

Terlano T-AA DOC w ★★→★★★ DYA DOC for 8 BOLZANO varietal whites, esp SAUV. Terlaner in German. Esp from CS Andrian, CS Terlan, LAGEDER, Niedrist.

Teroldego Rotaliano T-AA DOC r p ★★→★★★ **90 91 92 93 94** 95 96 Attractive blackberry-scented red; slightly bitter aftertaste; can age very well. Esp FORADORI's. Also good from CA'VIT, Dorigati, Sebastiani.

Terre di Franciacorta Lom DOC r w ★★ Usually lightish, sometimes v pleasant reds (blends of CAB, BARBERA, NEBBIOLO, MERLOT); quite fruity and balanced whites (CHARD, PINOTS BIANCO NERO).

Terre di Ginestra Si w ★★→★★★ Good VDT from SW of Palermo, esp Pelavet.

Terre Rosse ★★★ Distinguished small estate nr Bologna. Its CAB, CHARD, SAUV, PINOT GR, RIES, even Viognier etc, are the best of the region.

Terre da Vino ★★→★★★ Association of 27 PIEDMONT coops and private estates selecting and selling best produce: incl most local DOCs. Best: BARBERA D'ASTI La Luna e i Falo and GAVI Ca' da Boslo.

Teruzzi & Puthod (Fattoria Ponte a Rondolino) ★★→★★★ Innovative producers of SAN GIMIGNANO with vg VERNACCIA DI SAN G, white VDTS 'Terre di Tufi' and 'Carmen'.

Tiefenbrunner ★★ Leading grower of some of the very best ALTO ADIGE white and red wines at Schloss Turmhof, Kurtatsch (Cortaccio).

Tignanello Tus r ★★★→★★★★ **85 88 90** 93 94 95 (96) Pioneer and still leader of the new style of Bordeaux-inspired Tuscan reds, made by ANTINORI.

Tocai Mild smooth white (no relation of Hungarian Tokay) of NE. DOC also in Ven and Lom (★→★★), but producers are most proud of it in F-VG (esp COLLIO and COLLI ORIENTALI): (★★→★★★). Best producers: BORGO DEL TIGLIO, Keber, Picech, Princic, Raccaro, RONCO del Gelso, RONCO DI GNEMIZ, SCHIOPETTO, Scubla, Specogna, Castello di Spessa, Toros, Venica & Venica, VILLA RUSSIZ, VOLPE PASINI.

Torbato di Alghero Sar w (pa) ★★ DYA Good N Sardinian table wine. Leading brand is SELLA & MOSCA.

Torgiano Umb DOC r w p (sp) ★★→★★★ and **Torgiano, Rosso Riserva** Umb DOCG r ★★★ **85 88 90** 93 94 95 (96) (3 yrs ageing) Top red from nr Perugia, comparable with best CHIANTI CL. Rubesco: standard. RISERVA Vigna Monticchio: ★★★★; keep 10 yrs. VDT San Giorgio incl CAB to splendid effect. White Torre di Giano (TREBBIANO and GRECHETTO) also ages well. See also Lungarotti.

Toscana See Tuscany.

Traminer Aromatico T-AA DOC w ★★→★★★ DYA (German: Gewürztraminer) Delicate, aromatic, soft. Best from: Cantina Sociale Girlan/Cornaiano, CS St-Michael, CS SCHRECKBICHL/COLTERENZIO, Hofkellerei, HOFSTATTER, Laimburg, Plattenhof, Stiftskellerei Neustift.

Trebbiano Principal white grape of TUSCANY, found all over Italy. Ugni Blanc in French. Sadly a waste of good v'yd space, with v rare exceptions.

Trebbiano d'Abruzzo Ab DOC w ★→★★ DYA Gentle, neutral, slightly tannic white from round Pescara. VALENTINI is much the best producer (also making MONTEPULCIANO D'ABRUZZO).

Trentino T-AA DOC r w dr sw ★→★★★ DOC for as many as 20 different wines, mostly named after their grapes. Best are CHARD, PINOT BL, MARZEMINO, TEROLDEGO. The region's capital is Trento.

Triacca Vg producer of VALTELLINA; also owns estates in TUSCANY (CHIANTI CLASSICO: La Madonnina; MONTEPULCIANO: Santavenere).

Tuscany (Toscana) Italy's central wine region, incl DOCs CHIANTI, MONTALCINO, MONTEPULCIANO etc.

Tuscany vintages

1996 Some autumn rain fell after a fine summer; despite this, grapes ripened quite well (esp those whose growers held out longest before picking). Result: a relatively good vintage for reds.

1995 Much autumn rain, worse even than 1992. The top estates made good wines if they waited for a warm, dry October. Otherwise, dull quality.

1994 Dry summer, showers in September; good to very good wines.

1993 A hot summer was followed by heavy October rains; despite these Chianti Classico generally good, Brunello and Vino Nobile di Montepulciano vg.

1992 Promise of a top-quality vintage dispelled for reds by rain. The whites had better luck and are vg.

1991 A difficult vintage: wines to drink quickly, without many positive surprises.

Umani Ronchi ★→★★★ Leading merchant of quality wines of the Marches; notably VERDICCHIO (Casal di Serra and Villa Bianchi) and ROSSO CONERO (Cumaro and San Lorenzo).

Uzzano, Castello di Famous old CHIANTI CLASSICO estate at Greve. Currently performing below par.

Vajra, Giuseppe Domenico ★★★ Vg consistent BAROLO producer, esp for BARBERA, BAROLO, DOLCETTO etc. Also an interesting (not fizzy) FREISA.

Val di Cornia Tus DOC r p w ★→★★ New DOC nr Livorno; some good producers: Ambrosini, Tua Rita, Graziani, Gualdo del Re.

Valcalepio Lom DOC r w ★→★★ From nr Bergamo. Pleasant red; lightly scented fresh white. Good from Bonaldi, Il Calepino and Tenuta Castello.

Valdadige T-AA DOC r w dr s/sw ★→★★ Name for the simple wines of the ADIGE VALLEY – in German 'Etschtaler'. Best producer: Armani.

Valentini, Edoardo ★★★→★★★★ Perhaps the best traditionalist maker of TREBBIANO and MONTEPULCIANO D'ABRUZZO.

Valgella See Valtellina.

Valle d'Aosta VdA DOC ★★→★★★ Regional DOC for 15 Alpine wines incl DONNAZ. A mixed bag. Vg from monastery-run Institut Agricole Régional, Charrère, Crote de Vignerons, Grosjean.

Valle Isarco (Eisacktal) T-AA DOC w ★★ DYA A DOC applicable to 5 varietal wines made NE of Bolzano. Good MULLER-T, Silvaner. Top producers are CS Eisacktaler, Kloster Neustift and Kuenhof.

Vallechiara, Abbazia di ★★→★★★ Young PIEDMONT estate, owned by actress Ornella Muti, with astonishingly good wines, eg DOC Dolcetto di Ovada and DOLCETTO-based VDTS Due Donne and Torre Albarola.

Valpolicella Ven DOC r ★→★★★ **93 94** 95 96 Attractive light red from nr Verona; best young. Quality improvement over last few yrs. V best can be conc, complex and merit higher prices. Delicate nutty scent, slightly bitter taste. (None of this is true of junk Valpolicella sold in litre and bigger bottles.) CLASSICO more restricted; SUPERIORE has 12% alcohol and 1 yr of age. Good esp from ALLEGRINI, BRIGALDARA, Brunelli, Corte Sant Alda, A FERRARI, Fornaser, GUERRIERI-RIZZARDI, LE RAGOSE, MASI, LE SALETTE, SAN RUSTICO, Speri, TEDESCHI, Tommasi. DAL FORNO and QUINTARELLI make the best (★★★). Interesting VDTS on the way to a new Valpolicella style are Toar (★★★) from MASI, La Poja (★★★) from ALLEGRINI.

Valtellina Lom DOC r ★★→★★★ **88 89 90** 93 95 (96) DOC for tannic wines: mainly from Chiavennasca (NEBBIOLO) grapes in Alpine Sondrio province, N Lombardy. V SUPERIORE: Grumello, Inferno, Sassella, Valgella. Best from: Conti Sertoli-Salis, Fay, TRIACCA, Nera, Arturo Pelizzatti Perego, Nino Negri. Sforzato is most concentrated type of Valtellina; equivalent to RECIOTO AMARONE.

Vecchio Old.

Vecchio Samperi Si ★★★ MARSALA-like VDT from outstanding estate. The best is barrel-aged 20 years, not unlike amontillado sherry. The owner, Marco De Bartoli, also makes the best DOC Marsalas.

Vendemmia Harvest or vintage.

Venegazzù Ven r w sp ★★→★★★ **88 89 90** 93 94 95 (96) Remarkable rustic Bordeaux-style red produced from CABERNET grapes near Treviso. Rich bouquet and soft warm taste. 'Della Casa' and 'Capo di Stato' are best quality. Also makes v fair sparkling.

Verdicchio dei Castelli di Jesi Mar DOC w (sp) ★→★★★ DYA Ancient pleasant fresh pale white from nr Ancona, dating back to the Etruscans. Also CLASSICO. Trad in amphora-shaped bottles. Esp from Belelli, Bonci-Vallerosa, Brunori, Bucci, Coroncino, GAROFOLI, Mancinelli, MONCARO, Monteschiavo, SARTARELLI, UMANI RONCHI, Zaccagnini; also FAZI-BATTAGLIA.

Verdicchio di Matelica Mar DOC w (sp) ★★ DYA Similar to the last, smaller and less well-known. Especially from Belisario, Castiglioni-Bisci and La Monacesca (outstanding).

Verona Capital of the Veneto region (home of VALPOLICELLA, BARDOLINO, SOAVE etc) and seat of Italy's splendid annual April Wine fair 'Vinitaly'.

Verduzzo (Colli Orientali del Friuli) F-VG DOC w dr s/sw sw ★★→★★★ **91 92 93** 94 (96) Full-bodied white from a native grape. The best sweet is called Ramandolo. Top makers: Dario Coos, DORIGO, Giovanni Dri.

Verduzzo (del Piave) Ven DOC w ★ DYA A dull little white wine.

Vermentino Lig w ★★ DYA Best seafood white wine of Riviera: esp from Pietra Ligure and San Remo. DOC is Riviera Ligure di Ponente. See Pigato. Particularly gd from Anfossi, Colle dei Bardellini, Lambruschi, Lupi, Cascina dei Peri.

Vermentino di Gallura Sar DOC w ★★→★★★ DYA Soft dry strong white of N Sardinia. Especially from CS di Gallura, CS Del Vermentino, Capichera.

Vernaccia di Oristano Sar DOC w dr (sw fz) ★→★★★ **78' 81 83 85' 87 88** 91 92 93 94 95 96 Sardinian speciality, like light sherry, a touch bitter, full-bodied and interesting. SUPERIORE with 15.5% alcohol and 3 yrs of age. Top producer CONTINI also makes ancient solera wine Antico Gregori.

Vernaccia di San Gimignano Tus DOCG w ★→★★ DYA Once Michelangelo's favourite, then ordinary tourist wine. Much improvement in last few yrs, now newly DOCG with tougher production laws. Best from FALCHINI, Montenidoli, Palagetto, PANIZZI, Rampa di Fugnano, TERUZZI & PUTHOD, Vagnoni.

Vernatsch German for SCHIAVA.

Verrazzano, Castello di ★★★ Outstanding CHIANTI CLASSICO estate near Greve.

Vicchiomaggio CHIANTI CLASSICO estate near Greve.

VIDE An association of better-class Italian producers for marketing their estate wines from many parts of Italy.

Vie di Romans ★★★→★★★★ A young wine genius, Gianfranco Gallo, has built up his father's ISONZO estate to top FRIULI status within a few years. Unforgettable CHARD and SAUV; excellent TOCAI and PINOT GR.

Vietti Excellent (★★★→★★★★) producer of characterful PIEDMONT wines, including BAROLO and BARBARESCO, at Castiglione Falletto in BAROLO region.

Vigna A single vineyard.

Vignadora ★★★ Founded after recent split of famous MASTROBERARDINO family estate. Walter M and sons make FIANO and GRECO from 300 acres.

Vignamaggio ★★→★★★ Historic, beautiful and very good CHIANTI CLASSICO estate near Greve.

Vigne dal Leon ★★★ Vg producer of COLLI ORIENTALI (FRIULI).

Villa Matilde ★★ Top Campania producer: vg FALERNO and white Falanghina.

Villa Russiz ★★★ Impressive white DOC COLLIO from Gianni Menotti: eg SAUV (look for 'de la Tour'), PINOT BL, TOCAI etc.

Vin Santo or Vinsanto, Vin(o) Santo Term for certain strong sweet wines esp in TUSCANY: usually PASSITO. Can be v fine, esp in Tuscany and TRENTINO.

Vin Santo Toscano Tus w s/sw ★→★★★ Aromatic rich and smooth. Aged in v small barrels called caratelli. Can be as astonishing as expensive, but a good one is v rare and top producers are always short of it. Best from AVIGNONESI, Cacchiano, CAPEZZANA, CONTUCCI, CORZANO & PATERNO, POLIZIANO, SAN GIUSTO A RENTENNANO, SELVAPIANA.

Vino da arrosto 'Wine for roast meat', ie good robust dry red.

Vino Nobile di Montepulciano Tus DOCG r ★★★ **85' 88' 90 91** 93 94 95 (96) Impressive SANGIOVESE red with bouquet and style, rapidly making its name and fortune. RISERVA after 3 years. Best estates include AVIGNONESI, Bindella, BOSCARELLI, La Calonica, Canneto, LE CASALTE, Casella, Fattoria del Cerro, CONTUCCI, Dei, Innocenti, Macchione, Paterno, POLIZIANO, Salcheto, Talosa, Trerose, Valdipiatta and Vecchia Cantina (look for the RISERVA). Vino Nobile is so far very reasonably priced.

Vino novello Italy's equivalent of France's primeurs (as in Beaujolais).

Vino da tavola (vdt) 'Table wine': intended to be the humblest class of Italian wine, with no specific geographical or other claim to fame. See IGT.

Vintage Tunina F-VG w ★★★ A notable blended white from JERMANN estate.

Voerzio, Roberto ★★★ Young BAROLO pace-setter: Brunate is new-style best.

Volpaia, Castello di ★★→★★★ First-class CHIANTI CLASSICO estate at Radda, with elegant, rather light Chianti. VDT red Balifico contains CAB; COLTASSALA is all SANGIOVESE.

Volpe Pasini ★★★ Ambitious COLLIO ORIENTALI estate, esp for good SAUV.

VQPRD Often found on the labels of DOC wines to signify Vini di Qualità Prodotti in Regioni Delimitate.

Where the dreams have no end... ★★★ A memorable VDT CHARD from JERMANN.

Zanella, Maurizio Creator of CA'DEL BOSCO. His name is on his top CAB-MERLOT blend, one of Italy's best.

Zardetto ★★ Vg producer of PROSECCO DI CONEGLIANO-VALDOBBIADENE.

Zerbina, Fattoria ★★★ New leader in Romagna with best ALBANA DOCG to date (a rich PASSITO), good SANGIOVESE and a barrique-aged Sangiovese-CAB VDT called Marzeno di Marzeno.

Zibibbo Si w sw ★★ Fashionable MOSCATO from the island of PANTELLERIA. Good producer: Murana.

Zonin ★→★★ One of Italy's biggest privately owned estates and wineries, based at GAMBELLARA, with DOC VALPOLICELLA etc. Others are at ASTI and in CHIANTI, SAN GIMIGNANO and FRIULI. Also at Barboursville, Virginia (USA).

Germany

Heavier shaded areas are the wine growing regions

The following abbreviations of regional names are used in the text:

Bad	Baden
Frank	Franken
M-M	Mittel-Mosel
M-S-R	Mosel-Saar-Ruwer
Na	Nahe
Rhg	Rheingau
Rhh	Rheinhessen
Pfz	Pfalz
Würt	Württemberg

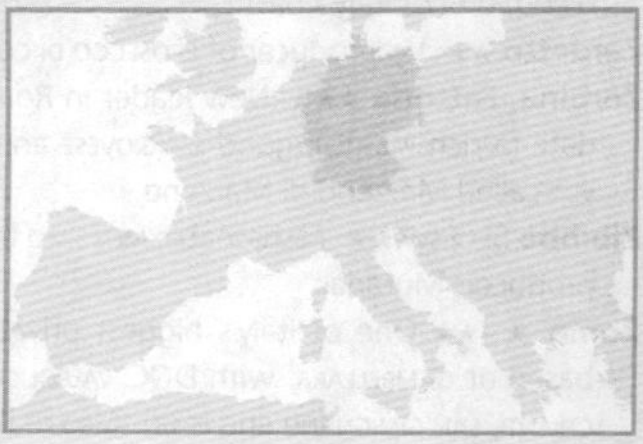

The finest wines of Germany today are precisely the same miracles of tension between sweetness and fruity acidity as they have always been – and most of them, as always, Riesling. What has changed in recent years is the addition to the German repertoire of a range of full-bodied dry wines, including the country's first really good reds, from grapes not specifically associated with Germany – especially the Pinots, and especially from the warmer more southern regions of the Pfalz and Baden-Württemberg.

These fine dry wines are still little seen outside Germany, but they are the cult wines of the '90s. There is a total polarisation between them and the sugar-watery rubbish that still forms the bulk of the export market – especially to Britain.

This is a pivotal time in the politics of German wine. The much-criticized Wine Law of 1971 has come for the first time under serious and sustained challenge from the most responsible producers. The VDP, the association representing the great majority of top-quality growers, has put its weight behind a long-overdue (though still unofficial) classification of the German vineyards. Most of the best (referred to here as 'First Class') are on steep land whose cultivation demands sacrifice. They are now rightly being described as National Cultural Monuments in the same way as abbeys or castles, in an attempt to force a chronically hesitant government to recognise and protect their status. The news in 1997 is that at long last a dialogue is beginning which may lead to law reform. Meanwhile the outrage of allowing their great names to be used for ordinary wines from low-grade grape varieties continues.

The problem is that, officially, German wines are still only classified according to grape ripeness. Most wines (like most French) need sugar added before fermentation to make up for missing sunshine. But unlike in France, German wine from grapes ripe enough not to need extra sugar is made and sold as a separate product: Qualitätswein mit Prädikat, or QmP. Within this top category, natural sugar content is expressed by traditional terms in ascending order of ripeness: Kabinett, Spätlese, Auslese, Beerenauslese, Trockenbeerenauslese.

Qualitätswein bestimmter Anbaugebiete (QbA), the second level, is for wines that needed additional sugar before fermentation. The third level, Tafelwein, like Italian vino da tavola, is free of restraints. Officially it is the lowest grade, but impatience with the outdated law makes it increasingly inviting as a resort for innovative producers who set their own high standards.

Though there is much more detail in the laws, this is the gist of the quality grading. It differs completely from the French system in ignoring geographical difference. In theory all any German vineyard has to do to make the best wine is to grow the ripest grapes – even of inferior grape varieties – which is patent nonsense.

The law distinguishes between degrees of geographical exactness – but in a way that just leads to confusion. In labelling 'quality' wine growers or merchants are given a choice. They can (and generally do) label the relatively small quantities of their best wine with the name of the precise vineyard or Einzellage. Germany has about 2,600 Einzellage names. Obviously only a relative few are famous enough to help sell the wine. Therefore the 1971 law created a second class of vineyard name: the Grosslage. A Grosslage is a group of Einzellagen of supposedly similar character. Because there are fewer Grosslage names, and far more wine from each, they have the advantage of familiarity – a poor substitute for hard-earned fame.

Thirdly, growers or merchants may choose to sell their wine under a regional or Bereich name. To cope with demand for 'Bernkasteler', 'Niersteiner' or 'Johannisberger' these world-famous names were made legal for large districts. 'Bereich Johannisberg' covers the whole of the Rheingau. Bereich on the label means third-rate wine.

Leading growers are now simplifying labels to avoid confusion and clutter. Some use the village name only, or indeed sell top wines under a brand name alone as in Italy. But before German wine can fully recover its rightful place, two things are needed: the banning of inferior grapes from top areas, and official recognition of the vineyard classification which is now well under way. The First Class vineyards are named here and mapped in the 4th edition of *The World Atlas of Wine*. It is after all (in Germany above all) the vineyard and producer that count.

Recent vintages

Mosel-Saar-Ruwer

Mosels (including Saar and Ruwer wines) are so attractive young that, their keeping qualities are not often enough explored, and wines older than about 8 years are unusual. But well-made Riesling wines of Kabinett class gain from at least 5 years in bottle–often much more–Spätlese from 10 to 20, and Auslese and Beerenauslese, anything from 10 to 30 years.

As a rule, in poor years the Saar and Ruwer make sharp lean wines, but in the best years, above all with botrytis, they can surpass the whole world for elegance and thrilling steely 'breed'.

1996 A very variable vintage with fine Spätlese and Auslese from top sites, but only QbA and Tafelwein elsewhere. Many excellent Eisweins.

1995 Excellent vintage, mainly of Spätlese and Auslese of firm structure and long ageing potential.

1994 Another v good vintage, mostly QmP with unexceptional QbA and Kabinett, but many Auslese, BA and TBA. Rich fruit and high acidity. Try to resist: they have a glorious future.

1993 Small excellent vintage: lots of Auslese/botrytis; nr perfect harmony.

1992 A very large crop, threatened by cold and rain in October. Mostly good QbA, but 30% QmP, some exceptional, esp in the Mittelmosel. Have developed quickly and already drink well.

1991 A mixed vintage. Bad frost damage in Saar and Ruwer, many tart QbA wines but also fine Spätlesen. Start to drink.

1990 Superb vintage, though small. Many QmP wines were the finest for 20 years. Try to resist drinking them all too soon.

1989 Large and outstandingly good, with noble rot giving many Auslesen etc. Saar wines best; the Mittelmosel overproduced causing some dilution. Mostly ready to drink.

1988 Excellent vintage. Much ripe QmP, esp in Mittelmosel. For long keeping. Beginning to drink well, but will keep.

1987 Rainy summer but warm Sept/Oct. 90% QbA wines, crisp and lively, to drink soon.

1986 Fair Riesling year despite autumn rain: 13% QmP wines, mostly Kabinett. Fully mature.

1985 A modest summer but beautiful autumn. 40% of harvest was QmP. Riesling vintage from best v'yds, incl Eiswein. Now drinking; will keep.

1983 The best between 76 and 88; 31% Spätlese; Auslesen few but fine. No hurry to drink.

1979 A patchy vintage after bad winter damage. But many excellent Kabinetts and better. Light but well-balanced wines should be drunk up.

1976 Vg small vintage, with some superlative sweet wines and almost no dry. Most wines ready; only the best will keep.

1971 Superb, with perfect balance. At its peak – but no hurry for best wines.

Older fine vintages: 69 64 59 53 49 45.

Rheinhessen, Nahe, Pfalz, Rheingau

Even the best wines can be drunk with pleasure when young, but Kabinett, Spätlese and Auslese Riesling gain enormously in character by keeping for longer. Rheingau wines tend to be longest-lived, improving for 15 years or more, but wines from the Nahe and Pfalz can last as long. Rheinhessen wines usually mature sooner, and dry Franken wines are best at 3–6 years.

1996 An excellent vintage in the Pfalz and some parts of Rheingau with many fine Spätlese, but only good in other regions. Some great Eisweins.

1995 Slightly variable, but some fine Spätlese and Auslese promising to age v well – like the 90s. Weakest in the Pfalz.

1994 Good vintage, mostly QmP, with abundant fruit and firm structure. Need time to develop. Some superb Auslese, BA and TBA.

1993 A small vintage of v good to excellent quality. Plenty of Spätlese and Auslese wines.

1992 Very large vintage, would have been great but for October cold and rain. A third QmP wines of rich stylish quality. Most already drinking well.

1991 A good middling vintage in most regions, though light soils in Pfalz suffered from drought. Some fine wines are emerging. Start to taste.

1990 Small but exceptionally fine. High percentage of QmP will keep well beyond 2000 (try to resist drinking too soon).

1989 Summer storms reduced crop in Rheingau. Vg quality elsewhere, up to Auslese level. Maturing more quickly than expected.

1988 Not quite so outstanding as the Mosel, but comparable with 83. Drinking well.

1987 Good average quality: lively round and fresh. 80% QbA, 15% QmP. Now drinking well.

1986 Well-balanced Rieslings, mostly QbA but some Kabinett and Spätlese. Good botrytis-affected wines in Pfalz. Now drinking well.

1985 Sadly small crops, of variable quality, esp Riesling. Average 65% QmP. Keep the best. Best in the Pfalz.

1983 Vg Rieslings, esp in the Rheingau and central Nahe. Generally about half QbA, but plenty of Spätlesen, now excellent to drink.

1982 A colossal vintage gathered in torrential rain. All 82s should be drunk up.

1976 The richest vintage since 21 in places. Very few dry wines. Generally mature now.

1971 A superlative vintage, now at its peak.

Older fine vintages: 69 67 64 59 53 49 45.

NB On the German vintage notation

Vintage notes after entries in the German section are given in a different form from those elsewhere, to show the style of the vintage as well as its quality. Three styles are indicated:

Bold type (eg 93) indicates classic, super-ripe vintages with a high proportion of natural (QmP) wines, including Spätlese and Auslese.

Normal type (eg 92) indicates 'normal' successful vintages with plenty of good wine but no great preponderance of sweeter wines.

***Italic* type (eg *91*) indicates cool vintages with generally poor ripeness but a fair proportion of reasonably successful wines, tending to be over-acid. Few or no QmP wines, but correspondingly more selection in the QbA category. Such wines sometimes mature more favourably than expected.**

Where no mention is made the vintage is generally not recommended, or most of its wines have passed maturity.

Achkarren Bad w (r) ★★ Village on the KAISERSTUHL, known esp for RULANDER. Best site: Schlossberg. Good wines: DR HEGER and coop.

Adelmann, Graf ★★★ Aristocratic grower with 37 v'yd acres at Kleinbottwar, WURTTEMBERG. Uses the name 'Brussele'. LEMBERGER reds best. Recently wobbly.

Ahr Ahr r ★→★★ **85** *87* **88 89 90** 91 *92* **93** 94 95 **96** Traditional specialized red wine area, south of Bonn. Very light, pale SPATBURGUNDER, esp from Deutzerhof, Kreuzberg, MEYER-NAKEL, NELLES STATE DOMAIN.

Amtliche Prüfungsnummer See Prüfungsnummer.

Anheuser, Paul Well-known NAHE grower (★★) at BAD KREUZNACH.

APNr Abbreviation of AMTLICHE PRUFUNGSNUMMER.

Assmannshausen Rhg r ★→★★★ **76 83 85** *87* **88 89 90** *91 92* **93** 94 **95 96** RHEINGAU village known for its usually pale, light reds, incl AUSLESEN. Top v'yd: Höllenberg. Grosslagen: Steil and Burgweg. Growers incl AUGUST KESSELER, Robert König, VON MUMM, and the STATE DOMAIN.

Auslese Wines from selective harvest of super-ripe grapes, the best affected by 'noble rot' (Edelfäule) and correspondingly unctuous in flavour. Dry Auslesen are too alcoholic for me.

Avelsbach M-S-R (Ruwer) w ★★★ **71 75 76 83** 85 *87* 88 **89 90** *91 92* **93** 94 **95** 96 Village nr TRIER. At (rare) best, lovely delicate wines. Esp BISCHOFLICHE WEINGUTER, Staatliche Weinbaudomäne (see Staatsweingut). Grosslage: Römerlay.

Ayl M-S-R (Saar) w ★★★ **71 75 76 83** 85 *87* 88 **89 90** *91 92* **93** 94 **95** 96 One of the best villages of the SAAR. First-class v'yd: Kupp. Grosslage: SCHARZBERG. Growers incl BISCHOFLICHE WEINGUTER, Lauer, DR WAGNER.

Bacchus Modern, perfumed, even kitsch, grape. Best for KABINETT wines.

Bacharach ★→★★★ District name for southern MITTELRHEIN v'yds just downstream from RHEINGAU. Now part of the new BEREICH 'LORELEY'. Racy RIESLINGS, some v fine. Growers include FRITZ BASTIAN, TONI JOST, Randolph Kauer, Helmut Mades, RATZENBERGER.

Bad Dürkheim Pfz w (r) ★★→★★★ **76 83 85** 86 *87* 88 **89 90** *91* 92 **93** 94 95 **96** Main town of MITTELHAARDT, with the world's biggest barrel (it serves as a tavern) and an ancient September wine festival, the 'Würstmarkt'. Top v'yds: Michelsberg, Spielberg. Grosslagen: Feuerberg, Hochmess, Schenkenböhl. Growers: Kurt Darting, FITZ-RITTER, Karst, Karl Schäfer.

Bad Kreuznach Nahe w ★★→★★★ **75 76** 79 **83 85** 86 *87* 88 **89 90** *91* 92 **93** 94 95 96 Agreeable spa town of many fine vineyards. First-class: Brückes, Kahlenberg and Krötenpfuhl. Grosslage: Kronenberg. Growers include ANHEUSER, Finkenauer, PLETTENBERG.

Baden Huge SW area of scattered v'yds but rapidly growing reputation. Style is substantial, generally dry, relatively low in acid, good for meal-times. Fine Pinots, SPATBURGUNDER, RIES, GEWURZ. Best areas: KAISERSTUHL, ORTENAU.

Badische Bergstrasse/Kraichgau (Bereich) Widespread district of N BADEN. WEISSBURGUNDER and RULANDER make best wines.

Badischer Winzerkeller Germany's (and Europe's) biggest coop, at BREISACH; 25,000 members with 12,000 acres, producing almost half of BADEN'S wine: dependably unambitous.

A German wine selection for 1998

For more than a decade most of Germany's finest wines have been made by small family-owned estates, due mainly to their policy of reducing yields to levels comparable with top French vineyards. The result, with high demand for the best, has been a drought of top wines. During the last couple of years many of these new star producers have substantially increased their vineyard holdings; in years to come there will be much more wine from these talented winemakers. The following are the most prominent:

Robert Weil Kiedrich, Rhg The estate which began the new trend after 1988 takeover by Japanese drinks giant Suntory. Extremely fine, elegant Rieslings incl stupendous Auslese, BA, TBA from 100 acres.

Franz Künstler Hochheim, Rhg When he purchased the famous, but run down Aschrott estate, Künstler more than doubled his vineyard area to 50 acres. Powerful dry Rieslings and luscious Auslese from three of Hochheim's First-class sites: Domdechaney, Hölle and Kirchenstück.

Johannishof Johannisberg, Rhg At the other end of the Rheingau the Eser family have acquired 11 acres of excellent vineyards in Rüdesheim, finally giving them substantial holdings in First-class sites as well as expanding their range of racy, filigree Rieslings.

H Dönnhoff Oberhausen, Na Through a combination of purchasing and swapping vineyards, Helmut Dönnhoff now owns vines in six of the Middle Nahe's First-class vineyard sites. Each gives Rieslings with a different expression of the minerally personality of the region.

Dr Loosen Bernkastel, M-S-R Ernst Loosen caused consternation when he headed a consortium that took over the J L Wolf estate in Wachenheim in the Pfalz. With the first vintage (1996) he has created a distinct 'Mosel-like' style and some of the region's best wines.

Müller-Catoir Neustadt, Pfz Long opposed to any expansion of his estate, Heinrich Catoir recently added 7 acres to his holdings, including a walled vineyard that promises to give wines at least as spectacular as any of the estate's current Riesling prodution.

Badisches Frankenland See Tauberfranken.

Barriques Small new oak casks arrived tentatively in Germany 15 yrs ago. Results are mixed. The oak smell can add substance to the white Pinots, SPATBURGUNDER and LEMBERGER. It usually spoils RIESLING.

Bassermann-Jordan ★★★ 104-acre MITTELHAARDT family estate with many of the best v'yds in DEIDESHEIM, FORST, RUPPERTSBERG etc. 100% RIES. New winemaker Ulrich Mell has put this historic estate back on top with superb 1996 vintage.

Bastian, Weingut Fritz ★★ 12-acre BACHARACH estate. Racy RIESLINGS with MOSEL-like delicacy, best from the First-class Posten v'yd.

Becker, J B ★★→★★★ Dedicated family estate and brokerage house at WALLUF. 30 acres in ELTVILLE, MARTINSTHAL, Walluf. Specialist in dry RIES.

Beerenauslese Lusciously sweet and honeyed wine from harvest of exceptionally ripe individual berries, their sugar and flavour usually concentrated by 'noble rot'. Rare and expensive.

Bensheim See Hessische Bergstrasse.

Bercher ★★★ KAISERSTUHL estate; 40 acres of white and red Pinots at Burkheim. Excellent dry whites and some of Germany's best reds.

> **Warning notice: Bereich**
> District within an Anbaugebiet (region). The word on a label should be treated as a flashing red light. Do not buy. See Introduction and under Bereich names, eg Bernkastel (Bereich).

Bernkastel M-M w ★→★★★★ **71 75 76** 79 **83 85** 86 *87* **88** 89 **90** *91* 92 **93** *94* 95 *96* Top wine town of the MITTELMOSEL; the epitome of RIES. Great First-class v'yd: Doctor, 8 acres (★★★★); First-class v'yds: Graben, Lay. Grosslagen: Badstube (★★★), Kurfürstlay. Top growers incl HERIBERT KERPEN, DR LOOSEN, DR PAULY-BERGWEILER, J J PRUM, Studert-Prüm, THANISCH, WEGELER-DEINHARD.

Bernkastel (Bereich) Wide area of deplorably dim quality but hopefully flowery character. Mostly MULLER-T. Includes all the MITTELMOSEL. Avoid.

Biffar, Josef ★★★ Rising star DEIDESHEIM estate. 40 acres (also WACHENHEIM) of RIES. Intense classic wines.

Bingen Rhh w ★→★★★ **76 83 85** *87* 88 **89 90** *91* 92 **93** 94 95 96 Rhine/NAHE town; fine v'yds: First-class: Scharlachberg. Grosslage: St-Rochuskapelle.

Bingen (Bereich) District name for west RHEINHESSEN.

Bischöfliche Weingüter ★★ Famous M-S-R estate at TRIER, a union of the cathedral properties with 2 other famous charities, the Bischöfliches Priesterseminar and the Bischöfliches Konvikt. 240 acres of top v'yds, esp in SAAR and RUWER. Signs of recovery to high quality after recent disappointments. Ruwer wines currently best (esp EITELSBACH, KASEL).

Blue Nun Famous but fading brand of LIEBFRAUMILCH from SICHEL.

Bocksbeutel Flask-shaped bottle used for FRANKEN wines.

Bodenheim Rhh w ★★ Village nr NIERSTEIN with full earthy wines. Top grower: Kühling-Gillot.

Bodensee (Bereich) Idyllic district of S BADEN, on Lake Constance.

Braun, Weingut Heinrich ★★ 60-acre NIERSTEIN estate. Elegant dry and sweet RIES from First-class v'yds of Nierstein, esp Pettenthal.

Brauneberg M-M w ★★★★ **71 75 76 83 85** 86 87 **88** 89 **90** 91 **92 93** 94 95 96 Top M-S-R village nr BERNKASTEL (750 acres), unbroken tradition for excellent full-flavoured RIES, 'Grand Cru' if anything on the Mosel is. Great First-class v'yd: Juffer-Sonnenuhr. First-class v'yd is Juffer. Grosslage: Kurfürstlay. Growers: Bastgen, FRITZ HAAG, WILLI HAAG, Paulinshof, M F RICHTER.

Breisach Bad Frontier town on Rhine nr KAISERSTUHL. Seat of the largest German coop, the BADISCHER WINZERKELLER.

Breisgau (Bereich) Little-known BADEN district. Good reds and pink WEISSHERBST.

Breuer, Weingut Georg ★★★ Family estate of 36 acres in RUDESHEIM, a CHARTA leader: 6 acres of Berg Schlossberg, also 12.5-acre monopole RAUENTHALER Nonnenberg. Superb quality in recent years, esp full-bodied elegant RIES, and new ideas, incl sparkling Ries-Pinot Bl-Pinot Gr.

Buhl, Reichsrat von ★★★ Historic PFALZ family estate, returning to historic form as of '94. 160 acres (DEIDESHEIM, FORST, RUPPERTSBERG...). Leased by Japanese firm.

Bundesweinprämierung The German State Wine Award, organized by DLG (see below): gives great (Grosse), silver or bronze medallion labels.

Bürgerspital zum Heiligen Geist ★★★ Ancient charitable WURZBURG estate. 275 acres: W'bg, RANDERSACKER etc. Rich dry wines, esp SILVANER, RIES; can be vg.

Bürklin-Wolf, Dr ★★★→★★★★ Famous PFALZ family estate. 222 acres in FORST, DEIDESHEIM, RUPPERTSBERG and WACHENHEIM. Excellent 94s and 95s show the estate is back on top form.

Castell'sches, Fürstlich Domänenamt ★★→★★★ Historic 142-acre princely estate in STEIGERWALD. SILVANER, RIESLANER, also SEKT. Noble dessert wines.

Chardonnay Can now be grown legally throughout Germany but total planted area remains less than 300 acres.

Charta Organization of top RHEINGAU estates making forceful dry RIES to far higher standards than dismally permissive laws require.

Christoffel, J J ★★★ Tiny domain in ERDEN, URZIG. Polished RIES.

Clevner (or Klevner) Synonym in WURTTEMBERG for Blauer Frühburgunder red grape, supposedly a mutation of Pinot N or Italian Chiavenna (early-ripening black Pinot). Confusingly also ORTENAU (BADEN) synonym for TRAMINER.

Crusius ★★→★★★★ 30-acre family estate at TRAISEN, NAHE. Vivid RIES from Bastei, Rotenfels and SCHLOSSBOCKELHEIM. Top wines age v well. Also good SEKT and freshly fruity SPATBURGUNDER dry rosé.

Deidesheim Pfz w (r) ★★→★★★★ **71 76 83 85** 86 *87* **88 89 90** 91 **92** 93 94 *95* **96** Biggest top-quality village of PFALZ (1,000 acres). Richly flavoured lively wines. Also Sekt. First-class v'yds: Grainhübel, Hohenmorgen, Kalkofen, Kieselberg, Langenmorgen, Leinhöhle. Grosslagen: Mariengarten (★★), Hofstück (★). Esp BASSERMANN-JORDAN, BIFFAR, V BUHL, BURKLIN-WOLF, DEINHARD, Kimmich.

Deinhard ★★→★★★ Famous old Koblenz merchants and growers of wines in RHEINGAU, MITTELMOSEL, RUWER and PFALZ (see Wegeler-Deinhard); also vg SEKT (eg Lila). Leaders in new ideas. Heritage range: single-village (DEIDESHEIM, HOCHHEIM, JOHANNISBERG etc) well-made but singularly austere TROCKEN wines.

Deinhard, Dr ★★ Fine 62-acre family estate: some of DEIDESHEIM'S best v'yds.

Deutsche Weinstrasse Tourist road of PFALZ: Bockenheim to SCHWEIGEN.

Deutscher Tafelwein Officially the term for v humble German wines. Now confusingly the flag of convenience for some costly novelties as well (eg BARRIQUE wines). As in Italy, the law will have to change.

Deutsches Weinsiegel A quality seal (ie neck label) for wines which have passed a statutory tasting test. Seals are: yellow for dry, green for medium-dry, red for medium-sweet. Means little; proves nothing.

Diel auf Burg Layen, Schlossgut ★★★ Fashionable 30-acre NAHE estate; known for ageing RULANDER and WEISSBURGUNDER in French BARRIQUES. Also fine traditional RIES. Impressive AUSLESE and EISWEIN.

DLG (Deutsche Landwirtschaftgesellschaft) The German Agricultural Society at Frankfurt. Awards national medals for quality – generously.

Dom German for 'cathedral'. Wines from the famous TRIER cathedral properties have 'Dom' before the v'yd name.

Domäne German for 'domain' or 'estate'. Sometimes used alone to mean the 'State domain' (STAATLICHE WEINBAUDOMANE).

Dönnhoff, Weingut Hermann ★★★ 23-acre NAHE estate with exceptionally fine RIES from NIEDERHAUSEN, Oberhausen etc.

Dornfelder New red grape making deep-coloured everyday wines in the PFALZ.

Durbach Baden w (r) ★★→★★★ **76 83 85** *87* 88 **89 90** *91* 92 **93** 94 95 **96** Village with 775 acres of BADEN'S best v'yds. Top growers: A LAIBLE, H Männle, SCHLOSS STAUFENBERG, WOLFF-METTERNICH. Choose their KLINGELBERGERS (RIES) and CLEVNERS (TRAMINER). Grosslage: Fürsteneck.

To decipher codes, please refer to 'Key to symbols' on front flap of jacket, or to 'How to use this book' on page 6.

Edel Means 'noble'. Edelfäule means 'noble rot': see page 100.

Egon Müller zu Scharzhof ★★★★ Top SAAR estate of 32 acres at WILTINGEN. Its rich and racy SCHARZHOFBERGER RIES in AUSLESEN vintages is among the world's greatest wines; best are given gold capsules. 89s, 90s and 93s are sublime, honeyed, immortal. Le Gallais is a second estate in WILTINGER Braune Kupp.

Eiswein V sweet wine made from frozen grapes with the ice (ie water content) discarded, thus v concentrated in flavour and sugar – of BEERENAUSLESE ripeness or more. Alcohol content can be as low as 5.5%. High acidity gives v long life. Rare and v expensive. S'times made as late as Jan/Feb of following year.

Eitelsbach M-S-R (Ruwer) w ★★→★★★★ **71 75 76 83 85** *87* **88 89 90** *91* 92 **93** 94 **95** 96 RUWER village now part of TRIER, incl superb Great First-class KARTHAUSERHOFBERG vineyard site. Grosslage: Römerlay.

Elbe The wine-river of eastern Germany. See Sachsen.

Elbling Traditional grape widely grown on upper MOSEL. Can be sharp and tasteless; but capable of real freshness and vitality in the best conditions (eg at Nittel or SCHLOSS THORN in the OBERMOSEL).

Eltville Rhg w ★★→★★★ **71 75 76 83** 85 86 87 88 **89 90** *91* 92 **93** 94 **95** 96 Major wine town with cellars of RHEINGAU STATE DOMAIN, FISCHER and VON SIMMERN estates. First-class v'yd: Sonnenberg. Grosslage: Steinmächer.

Enkirch M-M w ★★→★★★ **71 76** 83 **85** *87* **88 89 90** 91 **93** 94 95 96 Little-known MITTELMOSEL village, often overlooked but with lovely light tasty wine. Grosslage: Schwarzlay. Top v'yds: Batterieberg, Zeppwingert.

Erbach Rhg w ★★★→★★★★ **71 76 83** 85 86 *87* 88 **89 90** *91* 92 **93** 94 **95** 96 Top RHG area: powerful perfumed wines, incl superb First-class v'yds Hohenrain, MARCOBRUNN, Siegelsberg, Steinmorgen, Schlossberg. Major estates: SCHLOSS REINHARTSHAUSEN, SCHONBORN. Also BECKER, KNYPHAUSEN, VON SIMMERN etc.

Erben Word meaning 'heirs', often used on old-established estate labels.

Erden M-M w ★★★ **71 75 76 83** *84* **85** 86 *87* **88 89 90** *91* 92 **93** 94 **95** 96 Village between Urzig and Kröv: noble full-flavoured vigorous wine (different in style from nearby BERNKASTEL and WEHLEN but equally long-living). Great First-class v'yds: Prälat, Treppchen. Grosslage: Schwarzlay. Growers incl BISCHOFLICHE WEINGUTER, J J CHRISTOFFEL, Stefan Ehlen, DR LOOSEN, Meulenhoff, Peter Nicolay.

Erstes Gewächs Literally translates as 'first growth'. A new ('94) classification for the top vineyards of the RHEINGAU. Has applied since '92 vintage, but not yet legally recognized.

Erzeugerabfüllung Bottled by producer. Being replaced by 'GUTSABFULLUNG'.

Escherndorf Frank w ★★→★★★ **76** 83 *87* **88** *89* **90** *91* **92 93** 94 *95* 96 Important wine town near WURZBURG. Similar tasty dry wine. Top v'yd: First-class Lump. Grosslage: Kirchberg. Growers incl JULIUSSPITAL, Egon Schäffer, Horst Sauer.

Eser, Weingut August ★★★ 20-acre RHEINGAU estate at OESTRICH. V'yds also in HALLGARTEN, RAUENTHAL (esp Gehrn, Rothenberg), WINKEL. Model wines.

Filzen M-S-R (Saar) w ★★→★★★ **76 83 85** *87* 88 **89 90** *91* 92 **93** 94 **95** 96 Small SAAR village nr WILTINGEN. First-class v'yd: Pulchen. Grower to note: Piedmont.

Fischer, Weingut Dr ★★ 60-acre OCKFEN and WAWERN estate: variable quality wines (83 vg, 90 good).

Fischer Erben, Weingut ★★★ 18-acre RHEINGAU estate at ELTVILLE with high traditional standards. Long-lived classic wines.

Fitz-Ritter ★★ Reliable BAD DURKHEIM estate. 54 acres, some fine RIES.

Forschungsanstalt See Hessische Forschungsanstalt.

Forst Pfz w ★★→★★★★ **71 76 83 85** 86 *87* 88 **89 90** 91 92 **93** 94 95 **96** MITTELHAARDT village with 500 acres of Germany's best v'yds. Ripe, richly fragrant, full-bodied but subtle wines. First-class vineyards: Jesuitengarten, Kirchenstück, Pechstein, Ungeheuer. Grosslagen: Mariengarten, Schnepfenflug. Top growers incl BASSERMANN-JORDAN, DEINHARD, G MOSBACHER, Eugen Müller, Spindler, Werlé.

Germany's quality levels

The official range of qualities in ascending order are as follows:

1 Deutscher Tafelwein: sweetish light wine of no special character. (Unofficially, can be very special.)
2 Landwein: dryish Tafelwein with some regional style.
3 Qualitätswein: dry or sweetish wine with sugar added before fermentation to increase its strength, but tested for quality and with distinct local and grape character.
4 Kabinettwein: dry or dryish natural (unsugared) wine of distinct personality and distinguishing lightness. Can be very fine.
5 Spätlese: stronger, often sweeter than Kabinett. Full-bodied. The trend today is towards drier or even completely dry Spätlese.
6 Auslese: sweeter, sometimes stronger than Spätlese, often with honey-like flavours, intense and long. Occasionally dry and weighty.
7 Beerenauslese: v sweet and usually strong, intense; can be superb.
8 Eiswein: (Beeren- or Trockenbeerenauslese) concentrated, sharpish and very sweet. Can be v fine.
9 Trockenbeerenauslese: intensely sweet and aromatic; alcohol slight. Extraordinary and everlasting.

Franken Franconia Region of excellent distinctive dry wines, esp SILVANER, always bottled in round-bellied flasks (BOCKSBEUTEL). The centre is WURZBURG. Bereich names: MAINDREIECK, STEIGERWALD. Top producers: BURGERSPITAL, CASTELL, FURST, JULIUSSPITAL, WIRSCHING etc.

Freiburg Baden w (r) ★→★★ DYA Wine centre in BREISGAU, N of MARKGRAFLERLAND. Good GUTEDEL.

Freinsheim Pfz w r ★★ Well-known village of MITTELHAARDT with high proportion of RIES. Aromatic spicy wines. Top grower: LINGENFELDER.

Friedrich Wilhelm Gymnasium ★★★ Important 82-acre charitable estate based in TRIER with v'yds in BERNKASTEL, GRAACH, OCKFEN, TRITTENHEIM, ZELTINGEN etc, all M-S-R. 90 91 92 93 should have been better.

Fuhrmann See Pfeffingen.

Gallais Le See Egon Müller.

Geheimrat 'J' Brand-name of good very dry RIES SPATLESE from WEGELER-DEINHARD, OESTRICH, since '83. Epitomizes modern RHEINGAU thinking.

Geisenheim Rhg w ★★→★★★ **71 76** 83 **85** 86 *87* 88 **89 90** *91* 92 **93** 94 95 96 Village famous for Germany's best-known wine school and fine aromatic wines. First-class v'yds are Kläuserweg, Rothenberg. Grosslagen: Burgweg, Erntebringer. Many of the Rheingau's top growers (eg SCHLOSS SCHONBORN) have v'yds in this village.

Gemeinde A commune or parish.

Gewürztraminer (or Traminer) 'Spicy' grape, speciality of Alsace, also giving some impressive wines in Germany, esp in PFALZ, BADEN and WURTTEMBERG.

Remember that vintage information for German wines is given in a different form from the ready/not ready distinction applying to other countries. Read the explanation at the top of page 136.

Gimmeldingen Pfz w ★★ **76** 83 **85** *87* 88 **89 90** *91* **92 93** 94 95 **96** Village just S of MITTELHAARDT. At best, similar wines. Grosslage: Meerspinne. Growers incl: Christmann, MULLER-CATOIR.

Graach M-M w ★★★ **71 75 76 83** *84* **85** 86 *87* **88 89 90** *91* 92 **93** 94 **95** 96 Small village between BERNKASTEL and WEHLEN. First-class v'yds: Domprobst, Himmelreich, Josephshöfer. Grosslage: Münzlay. Many top growers, eg: KESSELSTATT, DR LOOSEN, J J PRUM, WILLI SCHAEFER, SELBACH-OSTER, WEINS-PRUM.

Grans-Fassian ★★ Fine 25-acre MOSEL estate at Leiwen. V'yds there and in PIESPORT and TRITTENHEIM.

Grauburgunder Synonym of RULANDER or Pinot Gris.

Grosser Ring Group of top (VDP) MOSEL-SAAR-RUWER estates, whose annual September auction regularly sets record breaking prices.

Grosslage See Introduction, pages 133–134.

Gunderloch ★★★★ 30-acre NACKENHEIM estate, making some of the finest RIES on the entire Rhine. The undisputed number one in RHEINHESSEN. Recently purchased well known Balbach estate in NIERSTEIN.

Guntersblum Rhh w ★→★★ 83 **85** 88 **89 90** *91* 92 **93** 94 95 *96* Big wine town S of OPPENHEIM. First-class v'yds: Bornpfad, Himmeltal. Grosslagen: Krötenbrunnen, Vogelsgarten. Top grower: RAPPENHOF.

Guntrum, Louis ★★ Large (164-acre) family estate in NIERSTEIN, OPPENHEIM etc. Good SILVANERS and GEWURZTRAMINER as well as RIESLING.

Gutedel German word for the Chasselas grape, used in S BADEN.

Gutsabfüllung Estate-bottled. A new term limited to qualified estates.

Gutsverwaltung Estate administration.

Haag, Weingut Fritz ★★★★ 12-acre top estate in BRAUNEBERG run by Wilhelm Haag, president of GROSSER RING. MOSEL RIES of crystalline purity and racy brilliance for long ageing. Growing reputation.

Haag, Weingut Willi ★★ Tiny 7-acre BRAUNEBERG estate. Full 'old-style' RIES. Some fine AUSLESE.

Haart, Reinhold ★★★ Small estate, the best in PIESPORT, and growing in repute. Refined aromatic wines, capable of long ageing.

Halbtrocken Medium-dry (literally 'semi-dry'). Containing fewer than 18 but more than 9 grams per litre unfermented sugar. Increasingly popular category of wine intended for meal-times, usually better balanced than TROCKEN.

Hallgarten Rhg w ★★→★★★ **71 76 83 85** 86 *87* 88 **89 90** *91* **92 93** 94 **95** *96* Small wine town behind HATTENHEIM. Robust full-bodied wines, seldom seen. Dominated by coops (unusual for RHEINGAU). Weingut Fred Prinz: top estate.

Hattenheim Rhg w ★★→★★★★ **71 75 76 83 85** 87 88 **89 90** 91 **92 93** 94 **95** 96 Superlative 500-acre wine town. First-class v'yds are Engelmannsberg, Mannberg, Pfaffenberg, Nussbrunnen, Wisselbrunnen and most famously STEINBERG (ORTSTEIL). Grosslage: Deutelsberg. MARCOBRUNN lies on ERBACH boundary. Many fine estates incl KNYPHAUSEN, RESS, SCHLOSS SCHONBORN, VON SIMMERN, STATE DOMAIN etc.

Heger, Dr ★★★ Some of BADEN's top red SPATBURGUNDER comes from this 28-acre ACHKARREN estate. Also fine GRAUBURGUNDER. Getting better and better.

Heilbronn Württ w r ★→★★ **88 89 90** *91* 92 **93** 94 95 **96** Wine town with many small growers and a good coop. Best wines are RIES and LEMBERGERS. Seat of DLG competition. Top growers: Amalienhof, Drautz-Able, Heinrich.

Hessen, Prinz von ★★→★★★ Famous 75-acre estate in JOHANNISBERG, KIEDRICH and WINKEL. Improving quality.

Hessische Bergstrasse w ★★→★★★ **76 83 85** *87* **88** 89 **90** *91* **92 93** 94 95 96 Smallest wine region in western Germany (1,000 acres), N of Heidelberg. Pleasant RIES from STATE DOMAIN v'yds at BENSHEIM, Bergstrasser Coop, Heppenheim and Stadt Bensheim.

Hessische Forschungsanstalt für Wein-Obst & Gartenbau Famous wine school and research establishment at GEISENHEIM, RHEINGAU. Good wines incl reds. The name on the label is Forschungsanstalt.

Heyl zu Herrnsheim ★★★ Leading 72-acre NIERSTEIN estate, 60% RIES. An excellent record, recently patchy. Now part-owned by VALCKENBERG.

Hochgewächs A superior level of QBA RIES, esp in MOSEL-SAAR-RUWER.

Hochheim Rhg w ★★→★★★★ **71 75 76** 79 **83** *84* **85** 86 *87* **88 89 90** 91 **92 93** 94 95 **96** 600-acre wine town 15 miles E of main RHEINGAU area, once thought of as best on Rhine. Similar fine wines with an earthy intensity and fragrance of their own. First-class v'yds: Domdechaney, Hölle, Kirchenstück, Königin Viktoria Berg (12-acre monopoly of Hupfeld of OESTRICH, sold only by DEINHARD). Grosslage: Daubhaus. Growers incl ASCHROTT, Hupfeld, FRANZ KUNSTLER, RESS, SCHLOSS SCHONBORN, STAATSWEINGUT, WERNER.

Hock Traditional English term for Rhine wine, derived from HOCHHEIM.

Hoensbroech, Weingut Reichsgraf zu ★★★ Top KRAICHGAU estate. 37 acres. Excellent dry WEISSBURGUNDER, GRAUBURGUNDER and SILVANER wines, eg Michelfelder Himmelberg. Some of BADEN's best dry white wines.

Hohenlohe-Oehringen, Weingut Fürst zu ★★ Noble 47-acre estate in Oehringen and WURTTEMBERG. Substantial dry RIES and powerful reds from SPATBURGUNDER and LEMBERGER grapes.

Hövel, Weingut von ★★★ Very fine SAAR estate at OBERMOSEL (Hütte is 12-acre monopoly) and in SCHARZHOFBERG. Superb wines since '93.

Huxelrebe Modern aromatic grape variety, mainly for dessert wines.

Ihringen Bad r w ★→★★★ **86** 87 88 **89 90** 91 92 **93** 94 95 **96** One of the best villages of the KAISERSTUHL, BADEN. Proud of its SPATBURGUNDER red, WEISSHERBST and GRAUBURGUNDER. Top growers: DR HEGER, Stigler.

Ilbesheim Pfz w ★→★★ 88 **89 90** 91 92 **93** 94 **95 96** Base of vast growers' coop of SUDLICHE WEINSTRASSE 'Deutsches Weintor'. See also Schweigen.

Ingelheim Rhh r w ★★ **88** 89 **90** 91 92 **93** 94 95 96 Town opposite RHEINGAU historically known for its SPATBURGUNDER. First-class v'yds are Horn, Pares, Sonnenberg and Steinacker.

Iphofen Frank w ★★→★★★ **76 79 83 85** *87* **88** *89* 90 *91* 92 **93** *95 96* Village nr WURZBURG. Superb First-class v'yds: Julius-Echter-Berg, Kalb. Grosslage: Burgweg. Growers: JULIUSSPITAL, Ruck, WIRSCHING.

Jahrgang Year – as in 'vintage'.

Johannisberg Rhg w ★★→★★★★ **71 75 76 83 85** 86 *87* 88 **89 90** 91 92 **93** 94 **95** 96 260-acre village with superlative subtle RIES. Top v'yds incl Goldatzel. First-class: Hölle, Klaus, SCHLOSS JOHANNISBERG. Grosslage: Erntebringer. Many good growers. Beware 'Bereich Johannisberg' wines (next entry).

Johannisberg (Bereich) District name for the entire RHEINGAU. Avoid.

Johannishof ★★★ JOHANNISBERG family estate, aka HH Eser. 45 acres. RIESLINGS that justify the great Johannisberg name. Since 96 also RUDESHEIM wines.

Johner, Karl-Heinz ★★★ Tiny BADEN estate at Bischoffingen, in the front line for new-look SPATBURGUNDER and oak-aged WEISSBURGUNDER.

Josephshöfer First-class v'yd at GRAACH, the sole property of VON KESSELSTATT.

Jost, Toni ★★★ Perhaps the top estate of the MITTELRHEIN. 25 acres, mainly RIES, IN BACHARACH and also in the RHEINGAU.

Juliusspital ★★★→★★★★ Ancient WURZBURG religious charity with 374 acres of top FRANKEN V'yds and many top wines. Look for its SILVANERS and RIES.

Kabinett The term for the lightest category of natural, unsugared (QMP) wines. Low in alcohol (RIES averages 7–9%) but capable of sublime finesse. Drink young or with several yrs age.

Kaiserstuhl (Bereich) One of the top BADEN districts, with notably warm climate and volcanic soil. Villages incl ACHKARREN, IHRINGEN. Grosslage: Vulkanfelsen.

GERMANY

Kallstadt Pfz w (r) ★★→★★★ **76 83 85** 86 87 88 **89 90** 91 92 **93** 94 **95 96** Village of N MITTELHAARDT. Its fine rich wines are often underrated. First-class v'yd: Saumagen. Grosslagen: Feuerberg, Kobnert. Growers incl Henninger, KOEHLER-RUPRECHT, Schüster.

Kammerpreismünze See Landespreismünze.

Kanzem M-S-R (Saar) w ★★★ **71 75 76 83 85** *87* **88 89 90** 91 92 **93** 94 **95** 96 Small neighbour of WILTINGEN. First-class v'yd: Altenberg. Grosslage: SCHARZBERG. Growers incl Othegraven, Reverchon. Best is J P Reinert.

Karthäuserhofberg ★★★★ Top RUWER estate of 46 acres at Eitelsbach. Easily recognized by bottles with only a neck-label. Since 1993 back on top form.

Kasel M-S-R (Ruwer) w ★★→★★★ **71 75 76 83 85** 86 *87* **88 89 90** 91 92 **93** 94 **95** 96 Stunning flowery light Römerlay wines. First-class v'yds: Kehrnagel, Nies'chen. Top growers: KARLSMUHLE, VON KESSELSTATT, WEGELER-DEINHARD.

Keller Wine cellar.

Kellerei Winery.

Kerner Modern aromatic grape variety, earlier-ripening than RIES, of fair quality but without Riesling's inbuilt harmony.

Kerpen, Weingut Heribert ★★ Tiny estate in BERNKASTEL, GRAACH, WEHLEN.

Kesseler, Weingut August ★★ 35-acre estate making the best SPATBURGUNDER reds in ASSMANNSHAUSEN. Also good off-dry RIES.

Kesselstatt, von ★★★ The biggest private MOSEL estate, 600 yrs old. Some 150 acres in GRAACH, KASEL, PIESPORT, WILTINGEN etc, plus substantial rented or managed estates, producing aromatic, generously fruity MOSELS. Now belongs to Günther Reh (of Leiwen). Excellent wines made esp since '88.

Kesten M-M w ★→★★★ **71 75 76 83 85** 86 88 89 **90** 91 92 **93** 94 **95 96** Neighbour of BRAUNEBERG. Best wines (from Paulinshofberg v'yd) similar. Grosslage: Kurfürstlay. Top growers: BASTGEN, Paulinshof.

Kiedrich Rhg w ★★→★★★★ **71 76 83 85** 86 87 88 89 **90** 91 **92 93** 94 **95** 96 Neighbour of RAUENTHAL; almost as splendid and high-flavoured. First-class v'yds: Gräfenberg, Wasseros. Grosslage: Heiligenstock. Growers incl FISCHER, KNYPHAUSEN, STATE DOMAIN. R WEIL now top estate.

Klingelberger ORTENAU (BADEN) term for RIESLING, esp at DURBACH.

Kloster Eberbach Glorious 12th-C Cistercian Abbey in HATTENHEIM forest. Monks planted STEINBERG. Now STATE DOMAIN-owned; HQ of German Wine Academy.

Klüsserath M-M w ★★→★★★ **76 83 85 88 89 90** *91* 92 **93** 94 95 *96* Minor MOSEL village, good years are well worth trying. Best vineyard: Brüderschaft. Grosslage: St-Michael. Top growers are FRIEDRICH WILHELM GYMNASIUM and KIRSTEN.

Knyphausen, Weingut Freiherr zu ★★★ Noble 50-acre estate on former Cistercian land (see Kloster Eberbach) in ELTVILLE, ERBACH, HATTENHEIM, KIEDRICH and MARCOBRUNN. Classic RHEINGAU wines, many dry.

Koehler-Ruprecht ★★★→★★★★ Highly rated little (22-acre) estate going from strength to strength; top grower in KALLSTADT. Ultra-traditional winemaking; v long-lived dry RIESLING from K Saumagen is memorable. Since 91 outstanding burgundy-style Pinot N.

Kohl, Helmut Also a small producer of gd dry SEKT at Bauenheim, PFALZ.

Königin Viktoria Berg See Hochheim.

Kraichgau Small BADEN region S of Heidelberg. Top grower: HOENSBROECH.

Kreuznach District name for the entire northern NAHE, now united with SCHLOSSBOCKELHEIM to form BEREICH 'NAHETAL'. See also Bad Kreuznach.

Kröv M-M w ★→★★★ **88 89 90** 91 92 **93** 94 95 *96* Popular tourist resort famous for its Grosslage name: Nacktarsch, or 'bare bottom'. Be very careful.

Künstler, Franz ★★★→★★★★ HOCHHEIM estate recently expanded to 50 acres by purchase of well-known Aschrott estate. Superb dry RIES, esp from first-class H Hölle and Kirchenstück, also excellent AUSLESE.

Laible, Weingut Andreas ★★ 10-acre DURBACH estate. Fine sweet and dry RIES, SCHEUREBE and GEWURZ from First-class Plauelrain v'yd.

Landespreismünze Prizes for quality at state, rather than national, level.

Landwein A category of better quality TAFELWEIN (the grapes must be slightly riper) from 20 designated regions. It must be TROCKEN or HALBTROCKEN. Similar in intention to France's vin de pays but without the buzz.

Lauerburg ★★★ One of the 4 owners of the famous Doctor v'yd, but sadly has sold majority of vine holdings. Wines often excellent and racy.

Leitz, J ★★ Fine little RUDESHEIM family estate for elegant dry RIES. A rising star.

Lemberger Red grape variety imported from Austria – where it is known as Blaufränkisch. Deep-coloured, tannic wines; can be excellent. Or rosé.

Liebfrauenstift 26-acre v'yd in city of Worms; origin of 'LIEBFRAUMILCH'.

Liebfraumilch

Much abused name, accounting for 50% of all German wine exports – to the detriment of Germany's better products. Legally defined as a QBA 'of pleasant character' from RHEINHESSEN, PFALZ, NAHE or RHEINGAU, of a blend with at least 51% RIESLING, SILVANER, KERNER or MULLER-T. Most is mild, semi-sweet wine from Rheinhessen and the Pfalz. Rules now say it must have more than 18 grams per litre unfermented sugar. S'times v cheap and of inferior quality, depending on brand or shipper. Its definition makes a mockery of the legal term 'Quality Wine'.

Lieser M-M w ★★ **71 76 83 85** 86 *87* **88 89 90** *91* 92 **93** 94 **95** 96 Little-known neighbour of BERNKASTEL. Lighter wines. First-class v'yd: Niederberg-Helden. Grosslage: Kurfürstlay. Top grower: Schloss Liesen.

Lingenfelder, Weingut ★★ Small, innovative Grosskarlbach (PFALZ) estate: excellent dry and sweet SCHEUREBE, full-bodied RIES etc.

Loosen, Weingut Dr ★★★★ Dynamic 24-acre St-Johannishof estate in BERNKASTEL, ERDEN, GRAACH, URZIG, WEHLEN. Deep intense RIESLINGS from old vines in great First-class v'yds. Superlative quality since '90.

Lorch Rhg w (r) ★→★★ **71 76 83 85** *87* 88 **89 90** *91* 92 **93** 94 **95** 96 At extreme W of RHEINGAU. Some fine light MITTELRHEIN-like RIESLING. Best grower: von Kanitz.

Loreley (Bereich) New BEREICH name for RHEINBURGENGAU and BACHARACH.

Löwenstein, Fürst ★★★ Top FRANKEN estate. 66 acres. Intense savoury Sylvaners. 45-acre HALLGARTEN estate rented by SCHLOSS VOLLRADS. Mixed quality since '91.

Maindreieck (Bereich) District name for central FRANKEN, incl WURZBURG.

Marcobrunn Historic RHEINGAU v'yd; one of Germany's v best. See Erbach.

Markgräflerland (Bereich) District S of FREIBURG, BADEN. Typical GUTEDEL wine can be delicious refreshment when drunk v young, but best wines are the -BURGUNDERS: WEISS-, GRAU- and SPATBURGUNDER. Also SEKT.

Martinsthal Rhg w ★★→★★★ **71 75 76 83 85** 86 *87* 88 89 **90** *91* 92 **93** 94 95 96 Little-known neighbour of RAUENTHAL. First-class v'yd: Langenberg; also gd: Wildsau. Grosslage: Steinmächer. Growers incl BECKER, Diefenhardt.

Maximin Grünhaus M-S-R (Ruwer) w ★★★★ **71 75 76** 79 **83 85** 86 87 **88 89 90** 91 **92 93** 94 **95** 96 Supreme RUWER estate of 80 acres at MERTESDORF. Wines of firm elegance and great subtlety to mature 20 yrs+.

Mertesdorf See Maximin Grünhaus and Karlsmühle.

Meyer-Näkel, Weingut ★★ 15-acre AHR esate. Fine SPATBURGUNDERS in Dernau and Bad Neuenahr exemplify modern oak-aged German reds.

Mittelhaardt The north-central and best part of the PFALZ, incl DEIDESHEIM, FORST, RUPPERTSBERG, WACHENHEIM, largely planted with RIESLING.

Mittelhaardt-Deutsche Weinstrasse (Bereich) District name for the northern and central parts of the PFALZ.

GERMANY

Mittelmosel The central and best part of the MOSEL, incl BERNKASTEL, PIESPORT, WEHLEN etc. Its top sites are (or should be) entirely RIESLING.

Mittelrhein Northern Rhine area of domestic importance (and great beauty), incl BACHARACH and Boppard. Some attractive steely RIESLING.

Morio-Muskat Stridently aromatic grape variety now on the decline.

Mosbacher, Weingut ★★★ Fine 23-acre estate for some of best dry and sweet RIES of FORST. Three stars on label indicate superior 'Reserve' bottlings.

Mosel The TAFELWEIN name of the area. All quality wines from the Mosel must be labelled MOSEL-SAAR-RUWER. (Moselle is the French – and English – spelling for this beautiful river.)

Mosel-Saar-Ruwer (M-S-R) 31,000-acre QUALITATSWEIN region between TRIER and Koblenz; incl MITTELMOSEL, RUWER and SAAR. The natural home of RIESLING.

Moselland, Winzergenossenschaft Biggest M-S-R coop, at BERNKASTEL, incl Saar-Winzerverein at WILTINGEN. Its 5,200 members produce 25% of M-S-R wines (incl classic method SEKT), but little above average.

Müller zu Scharzhof, Egon See Egon Müller.

Müller-Catoir, Weingut ★★★★ Outstanding 40-acre NEUSTADT estate. Very aromatic powerful wines (RIESLING, SCHEUREBE, RIESLANER, GRAUBURGUNDER and MUSKATELLER). Consistent quality and good value; dry/sweet equally impressive.

Müller-Thurgau Fruity early ripening, usually low-acid grape; commonest in PFALZ, RHEINHESSEN, NAHE, BADEN and FRANKEN; increasingly planted in all areas, incl MOSEL. Should be banned from all top v'yds by law.

Mumm, von ★★ 160-acre estate in JOHANNISBERG, RUDESHEIM etc. Under the same control as SCHLOSS JOHANNISBERG, but v variable quality.

Münster Nahe w ★→★★★ **71 75 76 83 85** 86 87 88 **89 90** 91 92 **93** 94 95 96 Best village of N NAHE, with fine delicate wines. First-class v'yds: Dautenpflänzer, Kapellenberg, Pittersberg. Grosslage: Schlosskapelle. Top growers: Kruger-Rumpf, STATE DOMAIN.

Muskateller Ancient aromatic white grape with crisp acidity. A rarity in the PFALZ, BADEN AND WURTTEMBERG, where it is mostly made dry.

Nackenheim Rhh w ★→★★★★ **76 83 85** 86 87 **88 89 90** 91 **92 93** 94 95 96 Neighbour of NIERSTEIN; both have top Rhine terroir. Best wines (especially First-class Rothenberg v'yd) similar. Grosslagen: Spiegelberg (★★), Gutes Domtal (★). Top grower: GUNDERLOCH.

Nahe Tributary of the Rhine and high-quality wine region. Balanced, fresh, clean but full-bodied, even minerally wines; RIES best. BEREICH: NAHETAL.

Nahetal (Bereich) BEREICH name for amalgamated KREUZNACH and SCHLOSS-BOCKELHEIM districts.

Neckerauer, Weingut Klaus ★★ Interesting, out-of-the-way 40-acre estate at Weissenheim-am-Sand, on sandy N PFALZ soil. Impressive, unpredictable.

Neef M-S-R w ★★ **71 76 83 85** 87 88 **89 90** 91 92 **93** 94 **95** 96 Village of lower MOSEL with one fine v'yd: Frauenberg.

Neipperg, Graf von ★★★ Noble 70-acre estate in Schwaigern, WURTTEMBERG: elegant dry RIES and TRAMINER, and trad-style reds, esp from LEMBERGER.

Neumagen-Dhron M-M w ★★ Neighbour of PIESPORT: fine but sadly neglected.

Neustadt Central town of PFALZ with a famous wine school.

Niederhausen Nahe w ★★→★★★★ **71 75 76 83 85** 86 *87* 88 **89 90** 91 **93** 94 **95** 96 Neighbour of SCHLOSS BOCKELHEIM and NAHE STATE DOMAIN HQ. Graceful powerful wines. First-class v'yds incl Felsensteyer, Hermannsberg, Hermannshöhle. Grosslage: Burgweg. Esp from CRUSIUS, DONNHOFF, Hehner-Kilz, STATE DOMAIN.

To decipher codes, please refer to 'Key to symbols' on front flap of jacket, or to 'How to use this book' on page 6.

Nierstein Rhh w ★→★★★★ **71 75 76 83 85** 86 *87* **88 89 90** 91 **92 93** 94 95 96 Famous but treacherous village name. 1,300 acres incl superb First-class v'yds: Brüdersberg, Glöck, Heiligenbaum, Hipping, Oelberg, Orbel, Pettenthal. Grosslagen: Auflangen, Rehbach, Spiegelberg. Ripe aromatic wines with great 'elegance'. But beware Grosslage Gutes Domtal: a supermarket deception. Growers to choose include GUNDERLOCH, GUNTRUM, HEYL ZU HERRNSHEIM, ST-ANTONY, G A Schneider, Seebrich, Strub, Wehrheim.

Nierstein (Bereich) Large E RHEINHESSEN district of ordinary quality.

Nierstein Winzergenossenschaft The leading NIERSTEIN coop, with above average standards. (Formerly 'Rheinfront'.)

Nobling New white grape: light fresh wine in BADEN, esp MARKGRAFLERLAND.

Norheim Nahe w ★→★★★ **71 76** 79 **83 85** 86 87 88 **89 90 91 92 93** 94 **95** 96 Neighbour of NIEDERHAUSEN. First-class v'yds: Dellchen, Kafels, Kirschheck; Klosterberg comes next. Grosslage: Burgweg. Growers: DONNHOFF, CRUSIUS.

Oberemmel M-S-R (Saar) w ★★→★★★ **71 75 76 83 85** 86 *87* 88 **89 90** *91* 92 **93** 94 **95** 96 Next village to WILTINGEN. V fine wines from First-class v'yd Hütte etc. Grosslage: SCHARZBERG. Esp VON HOVEL, VON KESSELSTADT.

Obermosel (Bereich) District name for the upper MOSEL above TRIER. Generally uninspiring wines from the ELBLING grape, unless v young.

Ockfen M-S-R (Saar) w ★★→★★★ **71 75 76 83 85** 86 *87* **88 89 90** *91* 92 **93** 94 **95** 96 Superb fragrant austere wines. 1st-class v'yd: Bockstein. Grosslage: SCHARZBERG. Growers: DR FISCHER, Jordan & Jordan, WAGNER, ZILLIKEN.

Oechsle Scale for sugar content of grape juice (see page 272).

Oestrich Rhg w ★★→★★★ **71 75 76 83 85** 86 *87* **88 89 90** *91* **92 93** 94 95 96 Big village; variable but some splendid RIES AUSLESE. 1st-class v'yds: Doosberg, Lenchen. Grosslage: Gottesthal. Top growers: AUGUST ESER, WEGELER-DEINHARD.

Offene weine Wine by the glass: the way to order it in wine villages.

Oppenheim Rhh w ★→★★★ **76 83 85** 86 *87* **88 89 90** *91* **92 93** 94 95 96 Town S of NIERSTEIN; spectacular 13th-C church. 1st-class Herrenberg and Sackträger v'yds: top wines. Grosslagen: Guldenmorgen (★), Krötenbrunnen. Growers incl GUNTRUM, C Koch, Kühling-Gillot. None though at full potential.

Ortenau (Bereich) District just S of Baden-Baden. Good KLINGELBERGER (RIES), SPATBURGUNDER and RULANDER. Top village: DURBACH.

Ortsteil Independent part of a community allowed to use its estate v'yd name without the village name, eg SCHLOSS JOHANNISBERG, STEINBERG.

Palatinate English for PFALZ.

Pauly-Bergweiler, Dr ★★★ Fine 27-acre BERNKASTEL estate. V'yds there and in WEHLEN etc. 'Peter Nicolay' wines from URZIG and ERDEN are best.

Perlwein Semi-sparkling wine.

Pfalz 56,000-acre v'yd region S of RHEINHESSEN (see Mittelhaardt and Südliche Weinstrasse). Warm climate: grapes ripen fully. The classics are rich wines, with TROCKEN and HALBTROCKEN increasingly fashionable and well made. Biggest RIES area after M-S-R. Formerly known as 'Rheinpfalz'.

Pfeffingen, Weingut ★★★ Messrs Fuhrmann and Eymael make very good RIES and SCHEUREBE on 26 acres of UNGSTEIN.

Piesport M-M w ★→★★★★ **71 75 76 83 85** 86 *87* **88 89 90** 91 **92 93** 94 **95** 96 Tiny village with famous vine amphitheatre, at best glorious gentle fruity RIES. Great First-class v'yds: Goldtröpfchen and Domherr. Treppchen far inferior. Grosslage: Michelsberg (mainly MULLER-T; avoid). Esp R HAART, Kurt Hain, KESSELSTATT, Reuscher-Haart, Weller-Lehnert.

Plettenberg, von ★★→★★★ 100-acre estate at BAD KREUZNACH. Mixed quality.

Portugieser Second-rate red-wine grape now often used for WEISSHERBST.

Prädikat Special attributes or qualities. See QmP.

Prüfungsnummer The official identifying test-number of a quality wine.

Prüm, J J ★★★★ Superlative and legendary 34-acre MOSEL estate in BERNKASTEL, GRAACH, WEHLEN, ZELTINGEN. Delicate but long-lived wines, esp in WEHLENER SONNENUHR: 81 KABINETT is *still* young.

Qualitätswein bestimmter Anbaugebiete (QbA) The middle quality of German wine, with sugar added before fermentation (as in French 'chaptalisation'), but controlled as to areas, grapes, etc.

Qualitätswein mit Prädikat (QmP) Top category, for all wines ripe enough to be unsugared (KABINETT to TROCKENBEERENAUSLESE). See pages 133 and 141.

Randersacker Frank w ★★→★★★ **76 83** 86 87 **88** 89 **90** 91 92 **93** 94 95 96 Leading village for distinctive dry wine. 1st-class v'yds: Marsberg, Pfülben. Grosslage: Ewig Leben. Growers incl BURGERSPITAL, Martin Göbel, STAATLICHER HOFKELLER, JULIUSSPITAL, Robert Schmitt, Schmitt's Kinder.

Ratzenberger, Jochen ★★ 17-acre estate making racy dry and off-dry RIES in BACHARACH; best from First-class Posten and Steeger St-Jost v'yds.

Rauenthal Rhg w ★★★→★★★★ **71 75 76 83 85** 86 *87* 88 **89 90** *91* **92 93** 94 95 96 Supreme village: spicy complex wine. 1st-class v'yds: Baiken, Gehrn, Nonnenberg, Rothenberg, Wülfen. Grosslage: Steinmächer. Top grower: BREUER. Others incl ESER, S REINHARTSHAUSEN, S SCHONBORN, VON SIMMERN, STATE DOMAIN.

Rebholz ★★★ Top SUDLICHE WEINSTRASSE grower. Many varieties on 25 acres.

Ress, Balthasar ★★→★★★ R'GAU estate (74 good acres), cellars in HATTENHEIM. Also runs SCHLOSS REICHARTSHAUSEN. Variable wines; original artists' labels.

Restsüsse Unfermented grape sugar remaining in (or more often added to) wine to give it sweetness. TROCKEN wines have v little, if any.

Rheinburgengau (Bereich) District name for MITTELRHEIN v'yds around the Rhine gorge. Wines with 'steely' acidity needing time to mature.

Rheinfront, Winzergenossenschaft See Nierstein Winzergenossenschaft.

Rheingau Best v'yd region of Rhine, W of Wiesbaden. 7,000 acres. Classic substantial but subtle RIES. BEREICH name for whole region: JOHANNISBERG.

Rheinhessen Vast region (61,000 acres of v'yds) between Mainz and Worms, bordered by River NAHE, mostly second-rate, but incl top RIESLINGS from NACKENHEIM, NIERSTEIN, OPPENHEIM etc.

Rheinhessen Silvaner (RS) New uniform label for dry wines from SILVANER – designed to give a modern quality image to the region.

Rheinpfalz See Pfalz.

Rhodt SUDLICHE WEINSTRASSE village: esp Rietburg coop; agreeable fruity wines.

Richter, Weingut Max Ferd ★★★ Top 37-acre MITTELMOSEL family estate, based at Mülheim. Fine barrel-aged RIES from: BRAUNEBERG (Juffer-Sonnenuhr), GRAACH, Mülheim (Helenenkloster), WEHLEN (usually models).

Rieslaner Cross between SILVANER and RIES; has made fine AUSLESEN in FRANKEN, where most is grown. Also fine from MULLER-CATOIR.

Riesling The best German grape: fine, fragrant, fruity, long-lived. Only CHARDONNAY can compete as the world's best white grape.

Rosewein Rosé wine made of red grapes fermented without their skins.

Rotwein Red wine.

Rüdesheim Rhg w ★★→★★★★ **71 75 76** 79 *81* 82 **83** 84 **85** 86 87 88 **89 90** 91 **92 93** 94 95 **96** Rhine resort with excellent v'yds; the three best called Rüdesheimer Berg–. Full-bodied wines, fine-flavoured, often remarkable in 'off' years. Grosslage: Burgweg. Most top RHEINGAU estates own some Rüdesheim v'yds. Best growers: G BREUER, JOHANNISHOF, J LEITZ, SCHLOSS SCHONBORN.

Rüdesheimer Rosengarten RUDESHEIM is also the name of a NAHE village near BAD KREUZNACH. Do not be misled by the ubiquitous blend going by this name. It has nothing to do with RHEINGAU Rüdesheim. Avoid.

Ruländer PINOT GRIS: grape giving soft full-bodied wine, alias (as dry wine) GRAUBURGUNDER. Best in BADEN and southern PFALZ.

Ruppertsberg Pfz w ★★→★★★ **83 85** 86 87 88 89 **90** 91 92 **93** 94 *95* **96** Southern village of MITTELHAARDT. First-class v'yds incl Hoheburg, Linsenbusch, Nussbien, Reiterpfad, Spiess. Grosslage: Hofstück. Growers incl BASSERMANN-JORDAN, BIFFAR, VON BUHL, BURKLIN-WOLF, DEINHARD.

Ruwer Tributary of MOSEL nr TRIER. V fine delicate but highly aromatic and well-structured wines. Villages incl EITELSBACH, KASEL, MERTESDORF.

Saale-Unstrut Region in former E Germany, 1,000 acres around confluence of these two rivers at Naumburg, nr Leipzig. Terraced v'yds of WEISSBURGUNDER, SILVANER, GUTEDEL etc and red PORTUGIESER and SPATBURGUNDER have Cistercian origins. Quality leader: Lützkendorf.

Saar Tributary of MOSEL S of RUWER. Brilliant austere 'steely' RIES. Villages incl AYL, OCKFEN, Saarburg, SERRIG, WILTINGEN (SCHARZHOFBERG). Grosslage: SCHARZBERG. Many fine estates.

Saar-Ruwer (Bereich) District covering these 2 regions.

Sachsen Former E-German region (750 acres) in ELBE VALLEY around Dresden and Meissen. MULLER-T dominant, but WEISSBURGUNDER, GRAUBURGUNDER, TRAMINER, RIES give dry wines with more character. Best growers: SCHLOSS PROSCHWITZ, Klaus Siefert, Jan Ulrich, Schloss Wackerbarth, Klaus Zimmerling.

St-Antony, Weingut ★★★ Excellent 50-acre estate. Rich, intense dry and off-dry RIES from First-class v'yds of NIERSTEIN.

St-Ursula Well-known merchants at BINGEN.

Salm, Prinz zu Owner of SCHLOSS WALLHAUSEN in NAHE and Villa Sachsen in RHEINHESSEN. President of VDP.

Salwey, Weingut ★★ Leading BADEN estate at Oberottweil, esp for RIESLING, WEISSBURGUNDER and RULANDER.

Samtrot WURTTEMBERG grape. Makes Germany's closest shot at Beaujolais.

Schaefer, Willi ★★★ The finest grower of GRAACH (but only 5 acres).

Scharzberg Grosslage name of WILTINGEN and neighbours.

Scharzhofberg M-S-R (Saar) w ★★★★ **71 75 76 83 85** 86 *87* **88 89 90** 91 92 **93** 94 **95** 96 Superlative 67-acre SAAR v'yd: austerely beautiful wines, the perfection of RIESLING. Do not confuse with the previous entry. Top estates: EGON MULLER, VON HOVEL, VON KESSELSTATT.

Schaumwein Sparkling wine.

Scheurebe Aromatic grape of high quality (and RIESLING parentage) esp used in PFALZ. Excellent for botrytis wine (BA, TBA).

Schillerwein Light red or rosé QBA; speciality of WURTTEMBERG (only).

Schloss Johannisberg Rhg w ★★★ **76** 79 **83 85** 86 87 **88 89 90** 91 92 93 94 95 96 Famous RHEINGAU estate of 86 acres owned by the Princess Metternich and Oetker family. The original Rhine 'first growth'. Wines incl fine SPATLESE, KABINETT TROCKEN. Unfortunately more could be achieved with this truly great v'yd.

Schloss Proschwitz ★★ Resurrected princely estate at Meissen, leading former E Germany in quality, esp with dry WEISSBURGUNDER.

Schloss Reichartshausen 10-acre HATTENHEIM v'yd run by RESS.

Schloss Reinhartshausen ★★★ Fine 175-acre estate in ERBACH, HATTENHEIM, KIEDRICH, etc. Changed hands in '88. Model RHEINGAU RIESLING. The mansion beside the Rhine is now a luxury hotel.

Schloss Saarstein ★★★ SERRIG estate of 25 acres with consistently fine RIES.

Schloss Salem ★★ 188-acre estate of Margrave of BADEN near L Constance in S Germany. MULLER-T and WEISSHERBST.

Schloss Schönborn ★★★ One of biggest RHEINGAU estates, based at HATTENHEIM. Full-flavoured wines, variable, at best excellent. Also vg SEKT.

For key to grape variety abbreviations, see pages 7–13.

Schloss Staufenberg ★★ 69-acre DURBACH estate. KLINGELBERGER is best wine.
Schloss Thorn Ancient OBERMOSEL estate, remarkable ELBLING, RIES and castle.
Schloss Vollrads Rhg w ★★★ **71 76 83 85** 86 *87* **88 89** 90 *91 92* 93 94 95 96 Great WINKEL estate since 1300. 116 acres. Dry austere RIES; TROCKEN and HALBTROCKEN are specialities; recently unimpressive.
Schloss Wallhausen ★★★ The 25-acre NAHE estate of the PRINZ ZU SALM, one of Germany's oldest. 65% RIES. Vg TROCKEN.
Schlossböckelheim Nahe w ★★→★★★★ **71 75 76** 79 **83 85** 86 87 88 **89 90** 91 92 **93** 94 **95** 96 Village with top NAHE v'yds, including First-class Felsenberg, In den Felsen, Königsfels, Kupfergrube. Firm yet delicate wine. Grosslage: Burgweg. Top growers: CRUSIUS, DONNHOF, STATE DOMAIN.
Schlossböckelheim District name for the whole S NAHE, amalgamated with KREUZNACH to form BEREICH NAHETAL.
Schneider, Weingut Georg Albrecht ★★ Impeccably run 32-acre estate. Classic off-dry and sweet RIES in NIERSTEIN, the best from First-class Hipping.
Schoppenwein Café (or bar) wine: ie wine by the glass.
Schubert, von Owner of MAXIMIN GRUNHAUS.
Schwarzer Adler, Weingut ★★→★★★ Franz Keller and his son make top BADEN GRAU-, WEISS- and SPATBURGUNDER on 35 acres at Oberbergen.
Schweigen Pfz w r ★→★★ **85** 86 *87* 88 **89 90** 91 **92 93** 94 *95* **96** S PFALZ village. Grosslage: Guttenberg. Best growers: Fritz Becker, esp for SPATBURGUNDER, Bernhart.
Sekt German (QBA) sparkling wine, best when label specifies RIES, WEISSBURGUNDER or SPATBURGUNDER. Sekt bA is the same but from specified area.
Selbach-Oster ★★★ 15-acre ZELTINGEN estate among MITTELMOSEL leaders.
Serrig M-S-R (Saar) w ★★→★★★ **71 75 76** 83 **85** 86 87 **88 89 90** 91 **93** 94 **95** 96 Village for 'steely' wines, excellent in sunny yrs. First-class v'yds: Herrenburg, Saarstein, Serriger Schloss, Würzberg. Grosslage: SCHARZBERG. Top growers: SCHLOSS SAARSTEIN, BERT SIMON.
Sichel, Söhne H Famous wine merchants at Alzey, RHEINHESSEN. Owners of BLUE NUN LIEBFRAUMILCH. Now owned by Langguth of TRABEN-TRARBACH.
Silvaner The third most-planted German white grape, usually underrated; best in FRANKEN. Worth looking for in RHEINHESSEN and KAISERSTUHL too.
Simmern, Langwerth von ★★★ Top ELTVILLE family estate. Famous v'yds: Baiken, Mannberg, MARCOBRUNN. Can have some of v best, most elegant R'GAU RIES but poor quality since 93.
Simon, Weingut Bert ★★ One of largest SAAR estates. 80 acres: KASEL, SERRIG.
Sonnenuhr Sundial. Name of several v'yds, esp one at WEHLEN.
Spätburgunder Pinot Noir: the best red wine grape in Germany – esp in BADEN and WURTTEMBERG and, increasingly, PFALZ – generally improving quality, but most still pallid and underflavoured.
Spätlese Late harvest. One better (stronger, sweeter) than KABINETT. Wines to age at least 5 yrs. TROCKEN Spätlesen can be v fine.
Staatlicher Hofkeller ★★★ The Bavarian STATE DOMAIN. 287 acres of finest FRANKEN v'yds with spectacular cellars under the great baroque Residenz at WURZBURG. Quality improving rapidly.
Staatsweingut (or Staatliche Weinbaudomäne) The state wine estates or domains; esp KLOSTER EBERBACH, SCHLOSS-BOCKELHEIM, TRIER.
State Domain See Staatsweingut.
Steigerwald (Bereich) District name for E part of FRANKEN.
Steinberg Rhg w ★★★ **71 75 76** 79 **83 85** 86 **87** 88 89 **90** *91* 92 **93** 94 **95** 96 Famous 79-acre HATTENHEIM walled v'yd, planted by Cistercians 700 yrs ago. Now owned by STATE DOMAIN, ELTVILLE. Some glorious wines; some feeble.
Steinwein Wine from WURZBURG's best v'yd, Stein.

Stuttgart Chief city of WURTTEMBERG, producer of some fine wines (esp RIES).

Südliche Weinstrasse (Bereich) District name for S PFALZ. Quality improved tremendously in last 25 yrs. See Ilbesheim, Schweigen, Siebeldingen.

Tafelwein Table wine. The vin ordinaire of Germany. Frequently blended with other EC wines. But DEUTSCHER TAFELWEIN must come from Germany alone and may be excellent. (See also Landwein.)

Tauberfranken (Bereich) New name for minor Badisches Frankenland BEREICH of N BADEN: FRANKEN-style wines.

Thanisch, Weingut Wwe Dr H ★★ BERNKASTEL estate, incl part of Doctor v'yd.

Traben-Trarbach M-M w ★★ **76 83 85** 86 *87* **88 89 90** *91* 92 **93** 94 **95** 96 Major wine town of 800 acres, 87% of it RIESLING. Top vineyards: Ungsberg, Würzgarten. Grosslage: Schwarzlay. Top grower: MAX FERD RICHTER.

Traisen Nahe w ★★★ **71 75 76** 79 **83 85** 86 *87* **88 89 90** *91* 92 **93** 94 **95 96** Small village incl superlative First-class Bastei and Rotenfels v'yds, making RIES of great concentration and class. Top grower: CRUSIUS.

Traminer See Gewürztraminer.

Trier M-S-R w ★★→★★★ Great wine city of Roman origin, on MOSEL, nr RUWER, now also incl AVELSBACH and EITELSBACH. Grosslage: Römerlay. Big Mosel charitable estates have cellars here among imposing Roman ruins.

Trittenheim M-M w ★★ **71 75 76 83 85** *87* 88 **89 90** *91* 92 **93** 94 95 96 Attractive S MITTELMOSEL light wines. Top v'yds were Altärchen, Apotheke, but now incl second-rate flat land: First-class are Felsenkopf, Leiterchen. Grosslage: Michelsberg (avoid). Growers incl E Clüsserath, GRANS-FASSIAN, Milz.

Trocken

'Dry'. By law trocken on a label means with a maximum of 9 grams per litre unfermented sugar. The new wave in German winemaking upsets the old notion of sweetness balancing acidity and embraces an austerity of flavour that can seem positively Lenten. It is much harder to make dry wines in German conditions, and non-initiates should not expect to fall in love at first sip. To be good, trocken wines need substantial body or alcohol; more than most Riesling Kabinett wines have to offer. Best trocken regions are Pfalz, Baden, Württemberg, Franken. Weissburgunder trocken is more satisfying. Halbtrockens are friendlier. Spätlesen (or QbA) usually make the best trocken wines. Auslese trocken sounds like a contradiction in terms – and often tastes like one. Do not be confused by the apparent link with Trockenbeerenauslesen: they are unrelated.

Trockenbeerenauslese Sweetest, most expensive category of German wine, extremely rare, with concentrated honey flavour. Made from selected shrivelled grapes affected by 'noble rot' (botrytis). TBA for short. See also Edel. Edelbeerenauslese would be a less-confusing name.

Trollinger Common (pale) red grape of WURTTEMBERG; locally v popular.

Ungstein Pfz w ★★→★★★ **71 75 76 83 85** 86 *87* **88 89 90** 91 92 **93** 94 **95 96** MITTELHAARDT village with fine harmonious wines. First-class v'yds: Herrenberg, Spielberg, Weilberg. Top growers: Darting, FITZ-RITTER, PFEFFINGEN, Karl Schäfer. Grosslagen: Honigsäckel, Kobnert.

Urzig M-M w ★★★★ **71 75 76 83 85** 86 87 **88 89 90** 91 **92 93** 94 **95** 96 Village on red sandstone famous for firm, full, spicy wine unlike other MOSELS. First-class v'yd: Würzgarten. Grosslage: Schwarzlay. Growers incl J J CHRISTOFFEL, DR LOOSEN, WEINS-PRUM.

Valckenberg, P J Major merchants and growers at Worms, with Madonna LIEBFRAUMILCH. Also dry RIES. Now part-owner of HEYL ZU HERRNSHEIM.

VDP Verband Deutscher Prädikats und Qualitätsweingüter. The pace-making association of premium growers. Look for their black eagle insignia. President: PRINZ ZU SALM.

Vereinigte Hospitien ★★ 'United Hospices'. Ancient charity at TRIER with large holdings in PIESPORT, SERRIG, TRIER, WILTINGEN etc; but wines recently well below their wonderful potential.

Verwaltung Administration (of property/estate etc).

Wachenheim Pfz w ★★★→★★★★ **71 75 76** 79 **83 85** 86 *87* 88 **89 90** *91* 92 **93** 94 95 **96** 840 acres, including exceptionally fine RIESLING. First-class v'yds are Gerümpel, Goldbächel, Rechbächel etc. Top growers: BURKLIN-WOLF, BIFFAR., WOLF. Grosslagen: Mariengarten, Schenkenböhl, Schnepfenflug.

Wagner, Dr ★★★ Saarburg estate. 20 acres of RIES. Fine wines incl TROCKEN.

Waldrach M-S-R (Ruwer) w ★★ **76 83 85** 88 **89 90** *91* **92 93** 94 **95** 96 Grosslage: Römerlay. Some charming light wines.

Walluf Rhg w ★★★ **75 76** 79 **83 85** *87* **88 89 90** *91* **92 93** 94 95 96 Neighbour of ELTVILLE; formerly Nieder- and Ober-Walluf. Underrated wines. First-class v'yd: Walkenberg. Grosslage: Steinmächer. Growers incl BECKER.

Walporzheim Ahrtal (Bereich) District name for the whole AHR VALLEY.

Wawern M-S-R (Saar) w ★★→★★★ **71 75 76 83** 85 *87* 88 **89 90** 91 **92 93** 94 **95** 96 Small village, fine RIES. First-class v'yd: Herrenberg. Grosslage: SCHARZBERG.

Wegeler-Deinhard ★★★ 136-acre RHEINGAU estate. V'yds: GEISENHEIM, MITTELHEIM, OESTRICH, RUDESHEIM, WINKEL etc. Consistent quality; dry SPATLESE, classic AUSLESE, finest EISWEIN. Also 67 acres in MITTELMOSEL, including major part of BERNKASTELER Doctor, WEHLENER SONNENUHR etc, 46 acres in MITTELHAARDT (DEIDESHEIM, FORST, RUPPERTSBERG). Only the best sites are named on labels. See also GEHEIMRAT 'J'.

Wehlen M-M w ★★★→★★★★ **71 75 76 83 85** 86 *87* **88 89 90** 91 92 **93** 94 **95** 96 Neighbour of BERNKASTEL with equally fine, somewhat richer wine. Great First-class v'yd: SONNENUHR. Grosslage: Münzlay. Top growers: HERIBERT KERPEN, DR LOOSEN, J J PRUM, Studert-Prüm, WEGELER-DEINHARD, WEINS-PRUM.

Weil, Weingut Robert ★★★★ Outstanding 95-acre estate in KIEDRICH; now financed by Suntory of Japan. Superb QmP, EISWEIN; standard wines also vg since '92. Widely considered RHEINGAU'S No 1.

Weinbaugebiet Viticultural region. For TAFELWEIN (eg MOSEL, RHEIN, SAAR).

Weingut Wine estate.

Weinkellerei Wine cellars or winery. See Keller.

Weins-Prüm, Dr ★★→★★★ Classic MITTELMOSEL estate; 12 acres at WEHLEN. WEHLENER SONNENUHR is top wine.

Weinstrasse Wine road. Scenic route through v'yds. Germany has several. The most famous is the Deutsche Weinstrasse in the PFALZ.

Weintor, Deutsches See Schweigen.

Weissburgunder Pinot Blanc. One of the better grapes for TROCKEN and HALBTROCKEN wines: low acidity, high extract. Also much used for SEKT.

Weissherbst Usually pale pink wine of QBA standard or above, from a single variety, even occasionally BEERENAUSLESE, the speciality of BADEN, PFALZ and WURTTEMBERG. Currently fashionable in Germany.

Werner, Domdechant ★★★ Fine family estate on best HOCHHEIM slopes.

Wiltingen M-S-R (Saar) w ★★→★★★★ **71 75 76 83 85** 86 *87* **88 89 90** 91 92 **93** 94 **95** 96 The centre of the SAAR. 790 acres. Beautiful subtle austere wine. Great First-class v'yd is SCHARZHOFBERG (ORTSTEIL); and First-class are Braune Kupp, Hölle. Grosslage (for the whole SAAR): SCHARZBERG. Top growers: EGON MULLER, LE GALLAIS, VON KESSELSTATT etc.

Winkel Rhg w★★★ **71 75 76 83 85** 86 *87* **88 89 90** *91* 92 **93** 94 95 96 Village famous for full fragrant wine, incl SCHLOSS VOLLRADS. First-class vineyards include Hasensprung, Jesuitengarten, Klaus, SCHLOSS VOLLRADS, Schlossberg. Grosslagen: Erntebringer, Honigberg. Growers include DEINHARD, PRINZ VON HESSEN, VON MUMM, BALTHASAR RESS, SCHLOSS SCHONBORN etc.

Winningen M-S-R w★★ Lower MOSEL village nr Koblenz: unusually full RIES for region. Top v'yds: Röttgen, Uhlen. Top grower: Heymann-Löwenstein.

Wintrich M-M w ★★→★★★ **71 75 76 83 85** 86 *87* **88 89 90** 91 **92 93** 94 **95** *96* Neighbour of PIESPORT; similar wines. Top vineyards: Ohligsberg. Grosslage: Kurfürstlay. Good grower: REINHOLD HAART.

Winzergenossenschaft Wine-growers' cooperative, often making sound and reasonably priced wine. Referred to in this text as 'coop'.

Winzerverein The same as the above.

Wirsching, Hans ★★★ Leading estate in IPHOFEN, and indeed FRANKEN. Wines firm, elegant and dry. 100 acres in 1st-class v'yds: Julius-Echter-Berg, Kalb etc.

Wonnegau (Bereich) District name for S RHEINHESSEN.

Wolf ★★ Run down estate in WACHENHEIM recently acquired by consortium headed by Ernst Loosen (see DR LOOSEN) of Bernkastel. From first vintage (1996) PFALZ wines with a Mosel-like delicacy. An estate to watch.

Wolff Metternich ★★→★★★ Noble DURBACH estate: some of BADEN'S best RIES.

Württemberg Vast S area, little known for wine outside Germany. But some vg RIES (esp Neckar Valley). Half is red: LEMBERGER, Trollinger, SAMTROT.

Würzburg Frank ★★→★★★★ **71 76 79 81 83 85** 86 *87* **88 89 90** 91 92 **93** 94 *95 96* Great baroque city on the Main, centre of FRANKEN wine: fine, full-bodied, dry. 1st-class vineyards: Abtsleite, Innere, Leiste, Stein. No Grosslage. See Maindreieck. Growers: BURGERSPITAL, JULIUSSPITAL, STAATLICHER HOFKELLER.

Zell M-S-R w ★→★★★ **76 83 88** 89 **90** *91* 92 **93** 94 **95** 96 The best-known lower MOSEL village, esp for its awful Grosslage: Schwarze Katz ('Black Cat'). RIES on steep slate gives aromatic light wines. Top grower: Albert Kallfelz.

Zell (Bereich) District name for whole lower MOSEL from Zell to Koblenz.

Zeltingen M-M w ★★→★★★★ **71 75 76** 79 **83 85** 86 87 **88 89 90** *91* 92 **93** 94 **95** 96 Top MOSEL village nr WEHLEN. Lively crisp RIES. 1st class v'yd: SONNENUHR. Grosslage: Münzlay. Many estate-owned v'yds, esp PRUM, SELBACH-OSTER.

Zilliken, Forstmeister Geltz ★★★ Former estate of Prussian royal forester at Saarburg and OCKFEN, SAAR. Racy minerally RIESLINGS, incl EISWEIN with excellent ageing potential.

Zwierlein, Freiherr von ★★ 55-acre family estate in GEISENHEIM. 100% RIES.

Luxembourg

Luxembourg has 3,285 acres of v'yds on limestone soils on the Moselle's left bank. High-yielding Elbling and Rivaner (Müller-T) vines dominate, but there are also significant acreages of Ries, Gewürz and (usually best) Auxerrois, Pinot Bl and Pinot Gr. These give light to medium-bodied (10.5–11.5%) dry Alsace-like wines. The Vins Moselle coop makes 70% of the total. Domaine et Tradition estates association, founded in '88, promotes quality from noble varieties. The last seven vintages were all good; 89 90 92 95 outstanding. Best from: Aly Duhr et Fils, M Bastian, Caves Gales, Bernard Massard (surprisingly good Cuvée de l'Ecusson classic method sparkling), Clos Mon Vieux Moulin, Ch de Schengen, Sunnen-Hoffmann.

Spain & Portugal

The following abbreviations are used in the text:

Amp	Ampurdán-Costa Brava
Alen	Alentejo
Bair	Bairrada
Cos del S	Costers del Segre
El B	El Bierzo
Est	Estremadura
La M	La Mancha
Mont-M	Montilla-Moriles
Nav	Navarra
Pen	Penedès
Pri	Priorato
Rib del D	Ribera del Duero
R Ala	Rioja Alavesa
R Alt	Rioja Alta
RB	Rioja Baja
Som	Somontano
Set	Setúbal
U-R	Utiel-Requena
VV	Vinhos Verdes
g	vino generoso
res	reserva

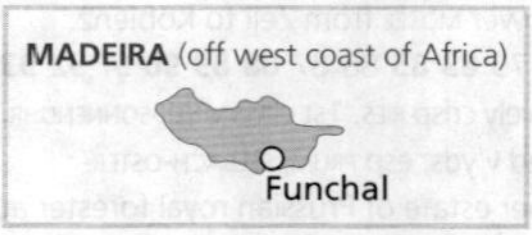

Spain and Portugal joined the EC (and, as far as most of their wine is concerned, the 20th century) 12 years ago. They both made rapid progress; Euro grants allowing large scale re-equipping. There is still much to do, but the continuing state of ferment is increasingly productive, and many splendid new wines are appearing both in the few traditional quality areas and in former bulk-wine regions.

Currently in Spain (apart from sherry country), the north, Rioja, Navarra, Galicia, Rueda, Somontano, Catalonia and Ribera del Duero hold most interest; those in Portugal (apart from the port vineyards and Madeira) are Bairrada, the Douro, Ribatejo, Alentejo, the central coast and the north. In Portugal especially, newly delimited areas have successfully challenged old, traditional appellations such as, for example, Dão.

The following list includes the best and most interesting types and regions of each country, whether legally delimited or not. Geographical references (see map above) are to demarcated regions (DOs and DOCs), autonomies and provinces.

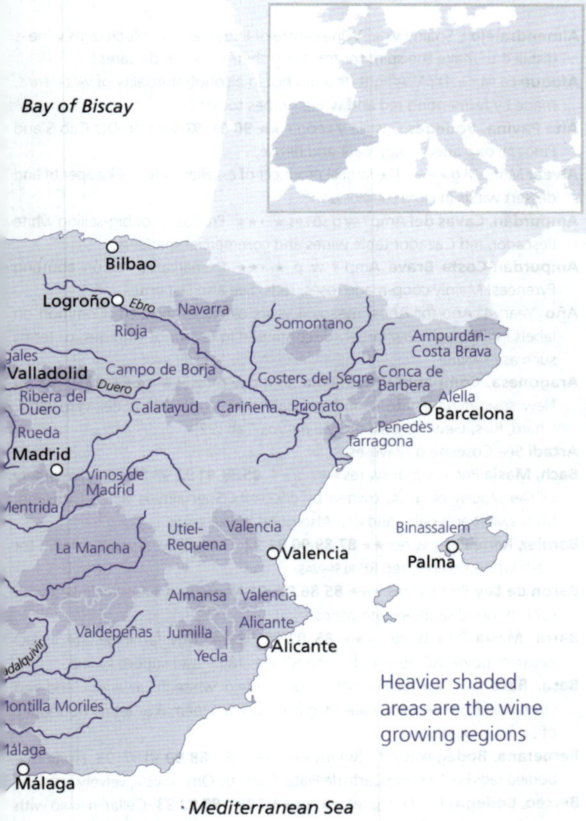

Heavier shaded areas are the wine growing regions

Sherry, port and Madeira, still the greatest glories of Spain and Portugal, have a chapter to themselves on pages 172–179.

Spain

AGE, Bodegas Unidas R Alt r w (p) dr sw res ★→★★ **85 86 87 90 91** 93 Large BODEGA, wide range, recently bought by BODEGAS Y BEBIDAS. Siglo red: reliable; avoid white. Best: Siglo Gran Reserva (**85**) and Azpilicueta Gran Reserva (**82**).

Agramont See Princípe de Viana, Bodegas.

Albariño High-quality aromatic white grape of GALICIA, possibly descended from Alsace Riesling, and its wine. See also Rías Baixas.

Albor See Campo Viejo, Bodegas.

Alella r w (p) dr sw ★★ Small demarcated region just N of Barcelona. Pleasantly fruity wines. (See Marfil, Marqués de Alella, Parxet.)

Alicante r (w) ★ DO. Wines still earthy and overstrong.

Alión Rib del D r ★★★ **91 92** 94 Since discontinuing the 3-yr-old VALBUENA, VEGA SICILIA has acquired second BODEGA to make CRIANZAS with 100% Tempranillo; first fruits impressive. Vigorous and gd short- to mid-term keeping.

Almendralejo E Spain r w ★ Wine centre of Extremadura. Much of its wine is distilled to make the spirit for fortifying sherry. See Lar de Lares.

Aloque La M r★ DYA A light (though not in alcohol) speciality of VALDEPENAS, made by fermenting red and white grapes together.

Alta Pavina, Bodegas Castilla y León r ★★ **90 91 92** Vg non-DO Cab S and Pinot N: oak-aged, spicy, dark and dense.

Alvear Mont-M g★★★ The largest producer of excellent sherry-like aperitif and dessert wines in MONTILLA-MORILES.

Ampurdán, Cavas del Amp r w p sp res ★→★★ Producers of big-selling white Pescador, red Cazador table wines and commercial sparklers.

Ampurdán-Costa Brava Amp r w p ★→★★ Demarcated region abutting Pyrenees. Mainly coop-made rosés, reds. See also last entry.

Año Year: 4° Año (or Años) means 4 years old when bottled. Common on labels in the past, now largely discontinued in favour of vintages, or terms such as CRIANZA.

Aragonesa, Compañía Vitivinícola Som r w p res ★★→★★★ **90 91 92** 94 New SOMONTANO estate. Good varietal wines under Viñas del Vero label: Chard, Ries, Gewürz. Best red Val de Vos Cab (92).

Artadi See Cosechero Alaveses.

Bach, Masía Pen r w p dr sw res★★→★★★ **85 88 91 92** 93 Stately villa-winery nr SAN SADURNI DE NOYA, owned by CODORNIU. Speciality is white Extrísimo, both sweet and oaky, and dry. Also good red RESERVAS.

Barbier, René Pen r w res ★★ **87 89 90 91 92** Owned by FREIXENET, known for fresh white Kraliner, red RB RESERVAS.

Barón de Ley RB r (w) res ★★★ **85 86 87 91** Newish RIOJA BODEGA linked with EL COTO: good single-estate wines.

Barril, Masía Pri r br res ★★★ **85 87 91 93 94** Tiny family estate in DO PRIORATO: powerful fruity reds – the 83 was 18°! – and superb RANCIO.

Basa, Baso r w ★★ Brand name for Verdejo white from RUEDA and red Garnacha from NAVARRA made by gifted young winemaker Telmo Rodriguez of LA GRANJA REMELLURI.

Berberana, Bodegas R Alt r (w) res ★★→★★★ **87 88 90 91 92** 93 Fruity full-bodied reds best: young Carta de Plata, Carta de Oro CRIANZA, velvety RESERVAS.

Berceo, Bodegas R Alt r w p res ★★→★★★ **78 87 89 92** 93 Cellar in HARO with good Gonzalo de Berceo GRAN RESERVA.

Beronia, Bodegas R Alt r w res ★★→★★★ **73 81 82 87 89 93** Small modern BODEGA making reds in traditional oaky style and fresh 'modern' whites. Owned by Gonzalez Byass (see page 174).

Bilbaínas, Bodegas R Alt r w (p) dr sw sp res★★ **82 87 88 89 90 91 92** Large BODEGA in HARO. Wide and usually reliable range incl dark Viña Pomal, lighter Viña Zaco, Vendimia Especial RESERVAS and Royal Carlton CAVA.

Binissalem r w ★★ Best-known MAJORCA DO. See also Franja Roja.

Blanco White.

Bodega Spanish term for (i) a wineshop; (ii) a concern occupied in the making, blending and/or shipping of wine; and (iii) a cellar.

Bodegas y Bebidas Formerly 'Savin'. One of largest Spanish wine companies; wineries all over Spain. Mainly good-quality and value brands. Also controls various prestigious firms, eg CAMPO VIEJO, MARQUES DEL PUERTO.

Bornos, Palacio de Bornos Rueda w sp ★★★ DYA Excellent young whites from Antonio Sanz of Bodegas de Crianza de Castilla la Vieja made from Sauv Bl, Verdejo and blends of Verdejo. Also good sp wines without DO.

Bretón Rioja r res ★★→★★★ **87 89 90 91 95** Respectable Loriñón range and little-seen, expensive, concentrated Dominio de Conté **91** (comparable with CONTINO).

Calatayud (★) Aragón DO (of 4): esp Garnacha. Coop San Isidro holds sway.

Campillo, Bodegas R Ala r (p) res ★★★ **82 85 87 88 89 91** Affiliated with FAUSTINO MARTINEZ, a young BODEGA with good wines.

Campo Viejo, Bodegas R Alt r (w) res ★→★★★ **82 87 88 89 92** 94 Makes the huge-selling Albor wines, a fresh white and Beaujolais Nouveau-style red; 100% Tempranillo Alcorta; and some big fruity red RESERVAS, esp Marqués de Villamagna. See Bobidas y Bebidas.

Can Rafols dels Caus Pen r w ★★ **87 88 89 90** Young small PENEDES BODEGA: own-estate fruity Cab, pleasant Chard-Xarel-lo-Chenin; good Gran Caus Cab-Merlot (**90**) and less-expensive Petit Caus range.

Rioja's characteristic style

To the Spanish palate the taste of luxury in wine is essentially the taste of (American) oak. Oak contains vanillin: hence the characteristic vanilla flavour of all traditional Spanish table wines of high quality – exemplified by the reservas of Rioja (red and white). Fashion swung (perhaps too far) against the oaky flavour of old Rioja whites but the pendulum is swinging back, although to subtler oak flavours than in the old days.

Canary Islas r w p g ★→★★ Until recently there were few wines of any quality other than the dessert Malvasías from Bodegas El Grifo and Bodegas Mozaga on Lanzarote. No fewer than 8 DOs have now been created and modernised bodegas, esp on TENERIFE are making improved wines – if somewhat expensive for what they are.

Caralt, Cavas Conde de Pen r w sp res ★★ **86 88 87 90 91** CAVA wines from outpost of FREIXENET, esp good vigorous Brut NV; also pleasant still wines.

Cariñena r (w p) ★ Coop-dominated DO: large-scale supplier of strong everyday wine. Being invigorated (and wines lightened) by new technology.

Casa de la Viña Valdepeñas r (w p) ★★ **88 90** 94 BODEGAS Y BEBIDAS-owned estate, since '80s: sound range of fruity 'Cencibel' wines. Drink young.

Casar de Valdaiga El B r w ★★ Fruity red from Pérez Carames, N of LEON.

Castell de Remei Cos de S r w p ★★→★★★ **88 89 90** 91 **93** Historic v'yds/winery revived, re-equipped, replanted since '83. Good Cab-Tempranillo, Merlot.

Castellblanch Pen w sp ★★ PENEDES CAVA firm, owned by FREIXENET. Look for Brut Zero (**93**) and Gran Castell GRAN RESERVAS (**90**).

Castilla-León r p w ★→★★ **88 91 92 94** N region to watch: fruity dry refreshing wines, esp from Vinos de León (aka VILE): eg young Coyanza, more mature Palacio de Guzmán (92), full-blooded Don Suero RESERVA (**91**).

Castillo de Monjardín Nav r w ★★→★★★ 93 95 Newish winery making excellent fragrant oaky Chard (95) and good but less-impressive reds.

Castillo Ygay R Alt r w ★★★★ (r) **25 34 42 52 59 64 68 70 75 78 82 85 87** (Current white vintage is **85**) See Marqués de Murrieta.

Cava Official term for any classic method Spanish sparkling wine, and the DO covering the areas up and down Spain where it is made.

Cenalsa See Príncipe de Viana, Bodegas.

Cenicero Wine township in RIOJA ALTA of Roman origin.

Centro Españolas, Bodegas La M r w p ★★ **92 93** 95 Large modern BODEGA best known for creditable red Allozo made from 100% Tempranillo.

Cepa Wine or grape variety.

Cervera, Lagar de Rías Baixas w ★★★ DYA Makers of one of best ALBARINOS: flowery and intensely fruity with subdued bubbles and a long finish.

NB Vintages in colour are those you should choose first for drinking in 1998.

Chacolí País Vasco w (r) ★ DYA Alarmingly sharp, often fizzy wine from the Basque coast, now possessing its own DO, which applies to all 141 acres! It contains only 9–11% alcohol. Best producer: Txomín Etxaníz.

Chivite, Bodegas Julián Nav r w (p) dr sw res ★★→★★★ **85 87** 88 89 **90 92 94** Biggest NAVARRA BODEGA. Now some of Spain's top reds; flowery well-balanced white esp Chivite Colección 126 (**94**) and vg **95** rosé. See Gran Feudo.

Cigales r p ★→★★ Recently demarcated region north of Valladolid, esp for light reds (traditionally known as CLARETES).

Clarete Traditional term, now banned by EC, for light red wine (or dark rosé).

Codorníu Pen w sp ★★→★★★ One of the two largest firms in SAN SADURNI DE NOYA making gd CAVA: v high tech, 10M bottles ageing in cellars. Mature Non Plus Ultra, fresh Anna de Codorníu or premium Jaume de Codorníu RESERVA.

Compañía Vinícola del Norte de España (CVNE) R Alt r w (p) dr sw res ★★→★★★ **87 88 89 90 91 92** 93 Top RIOJA BODEGA. Monopole (93) is one of Spain's the best oaky whites. Recent vintages of the red CRIANZA have not always been up to old high standards. Excellent red Imperial and Viña Real RESERVAS. CVNE is pronounced 'coonay'. See also Contino.

Con Class, Bodegas Rueda w ★★→★★★ DYA Despite BODEGA's name: exciting Verdejo/Viura and Sauv Bl, esp RUEDA Superior (95).

Conca de Barberá Pen w (r p) Catalan DO region growing Parellada grapes for making CAVA. Its best wine is TORRES MILMANDA Chard. See also SANTARA.

Condado de Haza Rib del D r ★★★ 94 Alejandro Fernandez's new BODEGA. Pure Tinto Fino aged in oak. Similar to PESQUERA: first vintage is a winner.

Condado de Huelva DO See Huelva.

Consejo Regulador Official organization for the control, promotion and defence of a DENOMINACION DE ORIGEN.

Contino R Ala r res ★★★ **85 86 87 88 89 91** 94 Very fine single-v'yd red made by a subsidiary of COMPANIA VINICOLA DEL NORTE DE ESPANA.

Corral, Bodegas R Alt r w p ★★★ **87 90 91** Don Jacobo wines from BODEGA by the Pilgrim Way to Santiago; marked recent improvement.

Cosecha Crop or vintage.

Cosecheros Alaveses R Ala r ★★→★★★ **90 91 92 94** 95 Up-and-coming RIOJA coop, esp for good young unoaked red Artadi and RESERVA Viña el Pisón.

Costers del Segre Cos del S r w p sp Small demarcated area around the city of Lleida (Lérida) and famous for the v'yds of RAIMAT.

Covides Pen r w p sp res ★★→★★★ **89 92** 94 Large former coop making good Duc de Foix w and Cab S, Cab S-Tempranillo; also first-rate Duc de Foix CAVA.

Covisa See Aragonesa, Compañia Vitivinicola.

Criado y embotellado por... Grown and bottled by...

Crianza Literally 'nursing'; the ageing of wine. New or unaged wine is 'sin crianza' or 'joven' (young). Reds labelled 'crianza' must be at least 2 yrs old (with 1yr in oak, in some areas 6 months), and must not be released before the third yr.

Cumbrero See Montecillo, Bodegas.

De Muller Tarragona br (r w) ★★→★★★ Venerable TARRAGONA firm specializing in altar wine, superb sumptuous v old SOLERA-aged dessert wines. Incl Priorato DULCE, PAXARETE. Also r and w Solimar and Mas de Vells.

Denominación de Origen (DO) Official wine region (see page 154).

Denominación de Origen Calificada (DOCa) Classification for wines of the highest quality; so far only RIOJA benefits (since '91).

Díaz e Hijos, Jesús Madrid r w p res ★★ **86 91 92 93** 94 The reds from this small BODEGA near Madrid, though variable, win many prizes.

Domecq R Ala r (w) res ★★→★★★ **85 87 89 90** 92 RIOJA outpost of sherry firm. Inexpensive Viña Eguía and excellent Marqués de Arienzo CRIANZAS and RESERVAS, fragrant and medium bodied.

Don Darias/Don Hugo Alto Ebro r w ★ Huge-selling, modestly priced wines, v like RIOJA, from undemarcated Bodegas Vitorianas. Sound red, white.

Dulce Sweet.

El Bierzo DO since '90, N of León. See Casar de Valdaiga.

El Coto, Bodegas R Ala r (w) res ★★ **85 86 90 91** 92 93 BODEGA best known for light, soft, red El Coto and Coto de Imaz.

Elaborado y añejado por... Made and aged by...

Enate Somontano DO r w ★★→★★★ **92 93** 94 Good wines from SOMONTANO in the north: light, clean, fruity incl Chard (94), Chard-Macabeo (95) and Cab S blends (the CRIANZA is full and juicy). Avoid the Gewürz.

Espumoso Sparkling (but see Cava).

EVENA Nav Gov't research station revolutionizing NAVARRA. Run by J OCHOA.

Fariña, Bodegas Toro r w res ★★ **87 89 90 91** 92 94 Rising star of new DO TORO: good spicy reds. Gran Colegiata is cask-aged; Colegiata not. Good red Primer bursting with fruit.

Faustino Martínez R Ala r w (p) res ★★→★★★ **86 88 89 90 91** Bodega with good reds. GRAN RESERVA is Faustino I. Do not be put off by the repellent fake-antique bottles.

Fillaboa, Granxa Rías Baixas w ★★★ DYA New small firm making delicately fruity ALBARINO.

Franco-Españolas, Bodegas R Alt r w dr sw res ★→★★ **91** 93 Old-est'd RIOJA BODEGA now part of group controlled by Marcos Eguizabal. Bordón is fruity red. Semi-sweet white Diamante is a Spanish favourite.

Franja Roja Majorca r res ★★ **87 89 91** 92 93 Best-known MAJORCA BODEGA at Binissalem making somewhat old-fashioned José L Ferrer wines.

Freixenet Cavas Pen w sp ★★→★★★ Huge CAVA firm, rivalling CODORNIU in size. Range of good sparklers, notably bargain Cordón Negro in black bottles, Brut Nature (91), Reserva Real and Premium Cuvée DS (89). Also owns Gloria Ferrer in California, Champagne Henri Abelé (Reims) and a sparkling wine plant in Mexico. Paul Cheneau is low-price brand.

A Spanish choice for 1998
Reserva Limousin '93 Rueda
Fillaboa '95 Albariño
Guitán Godello '95 Valdeorras
Chivite Colección 125 Tinto '93 Navarra
Scala dei Tinto Novell '94 Priorato
Tinto Pesquera '90 Ribera del Duero
Alión '92 Ribera del Duero
Gran Coronas Mas de la Plana '82 Torres
Sibarita sherry from Pedro Domecq

Galicia Rainy NW Spain: esp for fresh aromatic, not cheap whites, eg ALBARINO.

Generoso (g) Aperitif or dessert wine rich in alcohol.

González y Dubosc, Cavas Pen w sp ★★ A branch of the sherry giant GONZALEZ BYASS. Pleasant sparkling wines exported as 'Jean Perico'.

Gran Feudo Nav w res ★★→★★★ **88 89 90 92** 94 Brand name of fragrant white, refreshing rosé, soft plummy red; the best-known wines from CHIVITE.

Gran Reserva See Reserva.

Gran Vas Pressurized tanks (French cuves closes) for making cheap sparkling wines; also used to describe this type of wine.

Grandes Bodegas Rib del D r ★→★★ **94 95** 96 Recently reorganized and with its own extensive v'yds, this BODEGA (in a region notorious for high prices) makes affordable Marqués de Velilla quality wines. Buy nothing before '94.

Guelbenzu, Bodegas Nav r res ★★→★★★ **89 90** 92 93 **94** Family estate making conc full-bodied reds. Watch for new 95 Jardin from 40-yr-old Garnacha and 89 Evo Gran Reserva to keep.

Guitán Godello Valdeorras w ★★★→★★★★ **95** Made by Bodegas Tapada, these splendidly fruity fragrant and complex 100% Godello wines, rated among top whites in Spain, typify renaissance of native grapes in Galicia. The barrel-fermented type has the slight edge.

Gutiérrez de la Vega Alicante r w ★★ Eccentric grower in Alicante DO. Rare expensive wines, rarely leaving Spain; sold as 'Casta Diva'. Moscatel 'Cosecha Miel' (**95**) is huge sweet and apricotty.

Haro Wine centre of the RIOJA ALTA, a small but stylish old city.

Hill, Cavas Pen w r sp res ★★→★★★ **88 89** 91 93 95 Old PENEDES firm: fresh dry white Blanc Cru, good Gran Civet, Gran Toc reds, first-rate young Masía Hill Tempranillo and delicate RESERVA Oro Brut CAVA.

Huelva Condado de Huelva (DO) r w br ★→★★ W of Cádiz. White table wines and sherry-like GENEROSOS; formerly imp't source of 'Jerez' for blending.

Jean Perico See González y Dubosc.

Joven (vino) Young, unoaked wine.

Jumilla r (w p) ★→★★ DO in mountains N of Murcia. Its overstrong (up to 18%) wines are being lightened by earlier picking and better winemaking, esp by French-owned Bodegas VITIVINO (eg Altos de Pío).

Juvé y Camps Pen w sp ★★★ Family firm. Top quality CAVA, from free-run juice only, esp Reserva de la Familia (92) and Gran Juvé y Camps (91).

Laguardia Picturesque walled town at the centre of the RIOJA ALAVESA.

Lan, Bodegas R Alt r (p w) res ★★ **87 88 90 92 93** 95 Huge modern BODEGA: red Lanciano and Lander, white Lan Blanco. Recent vintages disappointing.

Lar de Lares SW r res ★★ **84 87 89 91** 95 Meaty GRAN RESERVA from Bodegas Inviosa, in remote Extremadura (in SW). Quality of younger Lar de Barros has declined and the Lar de Oro Cab is disappointing.

León, Jean Pen r w res ★★★ 82 85 **86** 87 **88 89 90** Small firm; TORRES-owned since '95. Good oaky Chard (**93**), deep full-bodied Cab that repays ageing.

Logroño First town of RIOJA region. HARO has more charm (and BODEGAS).

López de Heredia R Alt r w (p) dr sw res ★★→★★★ **76 78 86** 87 **88 89** 90 92 Old-est'd HARO BODEGA: exceptionally long-lasting, v traditional wines. Patchy since '85. Viña Tondonia (r and w): delicate and fine; Viña Bosconia fine, beefy.

López Hermanos Málaga ★★ Large BODEGA for commercial MALAGA wines, incl popular Málaga Virgen and Moscatel Gloria.

Los Llanos Valdepeñas r (p w) res ★★ **84 87 90 92** 94 One of the growing number of VALDEPENAS BODEGAS to age wine in oak. Markets a RESERVA, GRAN RESERVA and premium Pata Negra Gran Reserva (**83**) of 100% Cencibel (Tempranillo). Also clean fruity white, Armonioso.

Málaga br sw ★★→★★★ Demarcated region around city of Málaga, much depleted by the 1996 closure of its best BODEGA, Hermanos Scholtz. At their best Málaga dessert wines can resemble tawny port.

Majorca FRANCA ROJA, Herens de Ribas, Miguel Oliver and Jaume Mesquida make island's only wines of interest (eg Chard) – otherwise, drink ROSADOS or Catalan.

Mancha, La La M r w ★→★★ Vast demarcated region N and NE of VALDEPENAS. Mainly white wines, the reds lacking the liveliness of the best Valdepeñas but showing signs of improvement. To watch.

Marfíl Alella w (p) ★★ Brand of Alella Vinícola (oldest-est'd producer in ALELLA). Means 'ivory'. Now for lively, rather pricey, new-style dry whites.

For key to grape variety abbreviations, see pages 7–13.

Marqués de Alella Alella w (sp) ★★→★★★ **94 95** (DYA) Light and fragrant white ALELLA wines from PARXET, some from Chardonnay (including barrel-fermented 'Allier'), made by modern methods. Also CAVA.

Marqués de Cáceres, Bodegas R Alt r p w res ★★→★★★ **82 85 86 87 89 91 92** Good RIOJAS made by modern French methods from CENICERO (R Alt) grapes; also surprisingly light, fragrant white (DYA) and sweet Satinela.

Marqués de Griñón La M r w ★★★ **87 88 92** Enterprising nobleman making v fine Cab and a delicious new (93) 'Shiraz' nr Toledo, S of Madrid, a region not known for wine. Fruity wines to drink fairly young. Also good RIOJAS (**89 90 91 92 94**) and Durius, a red from RIB DEL DUERO area. Owned by BODEGAS BERBERANA.

Marqués de Monistrol, Bodegas Pen p r sp dr sw res ★★→★★★ **85 89** 91 92 Old BODEGA now owned by BERBERANA. Reliable CAVAS. Fresh Merlot (**91**).

Marqués de Murrieta R Alt r p w res ★★★→★★★★ **34 42 52 59 62 64 68 70 78 83 85 89 90 91 92** Historic, much-respected BODEGA near LOGRONO, formerly for some of best RIOJAS. Also famous for red CASTILLO YGAY, old-style oaky white and wonderful old-style RESERVA ROSADO. Except Rosado, recent quality variable; but currently back on form with deep brandy-scented 89.

Marqués del Puerto R Alt r (p w) res ★★→★★★ **85 87 88 89** 93 Small firm, was Bodegas López Agos, now owned by BODEGAS Y BEBIDAS. Reliable.

Marqués de Riscal R Ala r (p w) res ★★★ **81 86 87 88 89 90 91 92** Best-known BODEGA of RIOJA ALAVESA. Its red wines are relatively light and dry. Old vintages are v fine, some more recent ones variable; currently are right back on form. Baron de Chirel, 50% Cab S (**91**) is magnificent. Whites from RUEDA, incl a vg Sauv and oak-aged RESERVA Limousin (**93**).

Martínez-Bujanda R Ala r p w res ★★★ **87 89 90 91 92** 93 95 Refounded ('85) family-run RIOJA BODEGA, remarkably equipped. Excellent wines, incl fruity SIN CRIANZA, irresistible ROSADO, noble Valdemar RESERVAS and making waves with a new (**89 90**) 100% Garnacha.

Mascaró, Cavas Pen r p w sp ★★→★★★ **88 89 90 92** Top brandy maker, good sparkling, fresh lemony dry white Viña Franca, excellent (**88**) Anima Cab S.

Mauro, Bodegas nr Valladolid r ★★→★★★ **87 89 90 91 92 93 94** Young BODEGA in Tudela del Duero with vg round fruity Tinto del País (Tempranillo) red. Not DO as some of the fruit is from outside RIBERA DEL DUERO.

Méntrida La M r w ★ DO west of Madrid, source of everyday red wine.

Milmanda ★★★ See Conca de Barberá, Torres.

Monopole See Compañía Vinícola del Norte de España (CVNE).

Montecillo, Bodegas R Alt r w (p) res ★★ **86 91** 95 RIOJA BODEGA owned by OSBORNE. Old GRAN RESERVAS (eg **73**) are magnificent. Now reds are appealing young but recent vintages fragile.

Montecristo, Bodegas Mont-M ★★ Well-known brand of MONTILLA-MORILES.

Monterrey Gal r ★ Region nr N border of Portugal; strong VERIN-like wines.

Montilla-Moriles Mont-M g ★★→★★★ DO nr Córdoba. Its crisp sherry-like FINO and AMONTILLADO contain 14–17.5% natural alcohol and remain unfortified. At best, singularly toothsome aperitifs.

Muga, Bodegas R Alt r (w sp) res ★★★ **81 85 89 90** Small family firm in HARO, known for some of RIOJA's best strictly trad reds. Wines are light but highly aromatic, with long complex finish. Best is Prado Enea (81 outstanding, but 86 87 88 far below par). Whites and CAVA less good.

Navajas, Bodegas R Alt r w res ★★→★★★ **85 86 87 89 90 91 92 94** Small firm: bargain reds, CRIANZAS, RESERVAS, fruity and full-bodied. Also excellent oak-aged white Viura and cherry/vanilla-ish CRIANZA ROSADO.

Navarra Nav r p (w) ★★→★★★ Demarcated region; rosés and sturdy reds. Stylish Tempranillo and Cab reds, some RESERVAS up to RIOJA standards. See Chivite, Guelbenzu, Palacio de la Vega, Ochoa, Princípe de Viana.

Nuestro Padre Jésus del Perdón, Coop de La M r w ★→★★ **87 89 92 94** Bargain fresh white Lazarillo and more-than-drinkable Yuntero; 100% Cencibel (alias Tempranillo) aged in oak.

Ochoa Nav r p w res ★★→★★★ **88 89 90 92 93** Small family BODEGA now with an excellent Moscatel, but better known for well-made red and rosés, incl 100% Tempranillo. Outstanding early vintages.

Olarra, Bodegas R Alt r (w p) res ★★ Vast modern BODEGA in LOGRONO, one of the showpieces of RIOJA. Interesting 5–6 yrs ago, esp for silky, well-balanced Cerro Añón reds, but quality now disappointing.

Pago de Carraovejas Rib del D r res ★★→★★★ **91 92 94** 95 New estate: some of the region's most stylish, densely fruity TINTO Fino Cabernet.

Palacio, Bodegas R Ala r p w res ★★★ **85 87 89 90 91 93** 94 Since this old family firm parted company with Seagram in '87 its wines have regained much of former reputation. Esp Glorioso RESERVA and Cosme Palacio (**91**).

Palacio de Fefiñanes Rías Baixas w res ★★★ Famous for atypical ALBARINO. No bubbles and oak-aged 3–5 yrs.

Palacio de la Vega Nav r p w res ★★ **91 92** 93 94 New BODEGA with juicy Tempranillo JOVEN (like primeur) and much promise.

Parxet Alella w p sp ★★→★★★ Excellent fresh, fruity, exuberantly fizzy CAVA (only one from ALELLA): esp Brut Nature. Also elegant white Alella, 'MARQUES DE ALELLA'.

Paternina, Bodegas R Alt r w (p) dr sw res ★→★★ Known for its standard red brand Banda Azul. Conde de los Andes label was fine, but the much lauded 78 is strictly for fans of oak/volatile acidity, and recent vintages, as of their other RIOJAS, are disappointing. Most consistent is Banda Dorada white (DYA).

Paxarete Traditional intensely sweet dark-brown almost chocolatey speciality of TARRAGONA. Not to be missed. See De Muller.

Pazo Ribeiro r p w ★★ DYA Brand name of the RIBEIRO coop, whose wines are akin to VINHOS VERDES. Rasping red is local favourite. Pleasant slightly fizzy Pazo whites are safer; Viña Costeira has quality.

Pazo de Barrantes Rías Baixas w ★★★ **95** DYA New ALBARINO from RIAS BAIXAS, from an estate owned by the late Conde de Creixels of MURRIETA. Delicate, exotic and of impeccable quality, 95 the best vintage yet.

Penedès Pen r w sp ★→★★★ Demarcated region including Vilafranca del Penedès, SAN SADURNI DE NOYA and SITGES (but not CAVA). See also Torres.

Perelada Amp w (r p) sp ★★ In the demarcated region of AMPURDAN on the Costa Brava. Best known for sparkling, both CAVA and GRAN VAS.

Pérez Pascuas Hermanos Rib del D r (p) res ★★★ **88 89 90 91 92** 94 Immaculate tiny family BODEGA in RIBERA DEL DUERO. In Spain its fruity and complex red Viña Pedrosa is rated one of the country's best.

Pesquera Rib del D r ★★★ **87 88 89 90 91 92** 94 Small quantities of RIBERA DEL DUERO from Alejandro Fernández. Robert Parker has rated it level with B'x Grands Crus. Janus (**86**) is special (even more expensive) bottling. See also Condado de Haza.

Piedmonte S Coop, Bodegas Nav ★★→★★★ **93 94** Up-and-coming coop making first-rate Oligitum Cab S-Tempranillo and Merlot.

Piqueras, Bodegas La M r ★★→★★★ **83 85 86 88 89 90 91** Small family BODEGA. Some of LA MANCHA'S best reds: Castillo de Almansa CRIANZA, Marius GRAN RESERVA.

Pirineos, Bodega Som w p r ★★→★★★ **90 91 93** 95 Former coop and pioneer winemaker in SOMONTANO. Best are the Montesierra range and oak-aged Señorio de Lazán RESERVA.

Príncipe de Viana, Bodegas Nav r w ★★ **90 91 92 93** 94 95 Large firm (formerly 'Cenalsa'), blending and maturing coop wines and shipping a range from NAVARRA, incl flowery new-style white and fruity red, Agramont.

Priorato Pri br r ★★★ **87 88 89 91 92 93 94** 95 DO enclave of TARRAGONA, known for alcoholic RANCIO, and splendidly full-bodied, almost black reds, often used for blending, but at their brambly best one of Spain's triumphs. Lighter blend is good carafe wine. See Barril, De Muller, Scala Dei. Small boutique BODEGAS such as Clos Martinet, L'Ermita and Clos de l'Obac are now ranked among Spain's stars.

Protos, Bodegas Rib del D r w res ★★→★★★ **86 87 89** 91 92 94 95 Formerly Peñafiel's coop and the region's second oldest BODEGA. Originally privatized ('91) as 'Bodegas Ribera del Duero'. Much improved by new oenologist.

Raimat Cos del S r w p sp ★★→★★★ (Cab) **85 86** 87 **88 89** 90 91 **92** Clean, structured wines from new DO nr Lérida, planted by CODORNIU with Cab, Chard, other foreign vines. Good 100% Chard CAVA.

Rancio Maderized (brown) white wine of nutty flavour.

Raventós i Blanc Barcelona w sp ★★→★★★ **91** Excellent CAVA aimed at top of market, also fresh El Preludi white (94).

Remelluri, La Granja R Ala r res ★★★ **85 87 88** 89 90 91 92 Small estate (since '70), making vg traditional red RIOJAS and improving all the time.

Reserva (res) Good quality wine matured for long periods. Red reservas must spend at least 1 year in cask and 2 in bottle; gran reservas 2 in cask and 3 in bottle. Thereafter many continue to mature for years.

Rías Baixas w ★★→★★★ NW DO embracing subzones Val do Salnés, O Rosal and Condado de Tea, now for some of the best (and priciest) cold-fermented Spanish whites, mainly from ALBARINO grapes.

Ribeiro r w (p) ★→★★ Demarcated region on N border of Portugal: wines similar in style to Portuguese VINHOS VERDES – and others.

Ribera del Duero Rib del D **89 90 91 94** Fashionable fast-expanding DO east of Valladolid, now revealed as excellent for TINTO Fino (Tempranillo) reds. Vintages are somewhat variable and prices are high. See Pérez Pascuas, Pesquera, Torremilanos, Vega Sicilia. Also Mauro.

Ribera del Duero, Bodegas See Bodegas Protos.

Rioja r p w sp **64 70 75 78 81 82 85 89 91 92** 94 95 N upland region along River Ebro for many of Spain's best red table wines in some 60 BODEGAS DE EXPORTACION. Tempranillo predominates. Other grapes and/or oak included depending on fashion and vintage. Subdivided into 3 areas:

Rioja Alavesa N of the R Ebro, produces fine red wines, mostly light in body and colour but particularly aromatic.

Rioja Alta S of the R Ebro and W of LOGRONO, grows most of the finest, best-balanced red and white wines; also some rosé.

Rioja Baja Stretching E from LOGRONO, makes coarser red wines, high in alcohol and often used for blending.

Important note:

An extended range of vintages is printed for a number of Rioja bodegas. But remember that the quality of the older reservas and gran reservas is dependent on proper cellarage. Old wines kept for any period in the racks of a warm restaurant soon deteriorate. Riojas do not now last as long as their oakier predecessors – some of the 85s and 89s are already drying out – but depending upon the bodega, an older vintage from the '60s or early '70s may well be memorable. Currently 91 92 94 are the safest choices.

Spain entries also cross-refer to Sherry, Port & Madeira, pages 172–179.

SPAIN

La Rioja Alta, Bodegas R Alt r w (p) dr (sw) res ★★★ **82 84 85 87 88 89 91** Excellent RIOJAS, esp red CRIANZA Viña Alberdi, velvety Ardanza RES, lighter Araña Reserva, splendid Reserva 904 and marvellous RESERVA 890 (85) – but drink it soonish; these wines are not lasting as long as they used to.

Rioja Santiago R Alt r (p w dr sw) res ★→★★ **87 89 90 91 94** 95 BODEGA at HARO. Its top reds, Condal and Gran Enológica, are respectable.

Riojanas, Bodegas R Alt r (w p) res ★★→★★★ **64 73 75 81 85 88 91 92** 93 Old BODEGA for trad Viña Albina and big mellow Monte Real RESERVAS (**88**).

Rosado Rosé.

Rovellats Pen w p sp ★★→★★★ **92** Small family firm making only good (and expensive) CAVAS, stocked in some of Spain's best restaurants.

Rueda br w ★→★★ Small historic DO west of Valladolid. Traditional FLOR-growing, sherry-like wines up to 17% alcohol, now for fresh whites, esp MARQUES DE RISCAL. Its secret weapon is the Verdejo grape.

Ruíz, Santiago Rías Baixas w ★★★ DYA Small prestigious RIAS BAIXAS company, now owned by BODEGAS LAN: fresh lemony ALBARINO, aged on lees, is one of best.

Salceda, Viña R Ala r res ★★→★★★ **87 89 91 92** Fruity light balanced reds.

San Sadurní de Noya Pen w sp ★★→★★★ Town S of Barcelona, hollow with CAVA cellars. Standards can be v high, though the flavour (of Parellada and other grapes) is quite different from that of champagne.

San Valero, Bodega Cooperativa Cariñena r p w res ★→★★ **87 90 91** 95 Large CARINENA coop; some modern wines. Good red CRIANZA Monte Ducay, fresh ROSADO with slight spritz, and (value) young unoaked Don Mendo.

Sangre de Toro Brand name for a rich-flavoured red from TORRES.

Sangría Cold red wine cup traditionally made with citrus fruit, fizzy lemonade, ice and brandy. But too often repulsive commercial fizz.

Sanlúcar de Barrameda Centre of the Manzanilla district (see Sherry).

Santara Conc de Barberà w r ★→★★ DYA Brand name for big-selling and v drinkable Chard, Cab S and Cab S-Merlot made for Concavinos by flying winemaker Hugh Ryman.

Sarría, Bodega de Nav r (p w) res ★★→★★★ **85 86 90 91** Quality remains high, though Duarte family's departure and death of oenologist Francisco Morriones dimmed the lustre of this model estate's international reputation.

Scala Dei, Cellers de Pri r w p res ★★→★★★ **87 88 91 92 94** 95 96 One of few BODEGAS in PRIORATO. Full Cartoixa RESERVAS and lighter Negre. New: breathtaking black old-style 14% Bru de Vins (94) and savoury barrel-fermented Garnacha Blanca Blanc Prior (**95**).

Schenk, Bodegas Valencia r w p ★★ **88 92** 94 Decent Estrella Moscatel and good Monastrell/Garnacha labelled as Cavas Murviedro and Los Monteros.

Seco Dry.

Segura Viudas, Cavas Pen w sp ★★→★★★ CAVA from SAN SADURNI (FREIXENET-owned). Buy the Brut Vintage, Aria or RESERVA Heredad.

Serra, Jaume Pen r p w res ★★ Good dry pétillant Albatros and Cab S rosés (DYA) as well as easy-drinking 'Cristalino' CAVA. Other wines to be avoided.

Solís, Felix Valdepeñas r ★★ Large BODEGA in VALDEPENAS making sturdy oak-aged reds, Viña Albali, RESERVAS (**87 89**) and fresh white.

Somontano Som Pyrenees foothills DO. Best-known BODEGAS: old French-est'd Lalanne (esp Viña San Marcos red: Moristel-Tempranillo-Cab S; white Macabeo, Chard), BODEGA PIRINEOS, new COVISA (Viñas del Vero). Also Viñedos y Crianzas del Alto Aragón (excellent ENATE range).

Tarragona r w br dr sw ★→★★★ (i) Table wines from demarcated region (DO); of little note. (ii) Dessert wines from the firm of DE MULLER.

Tenerife r w ★→★★ DYA Now 4 DOs making sometimes more than drinkable young wines. Best bodegas: Flores, Monje and Insulares (Viña Norte label).

Tinto Red.

Toro r ★→★★ DO 150 miles NW of Madrid. Formerly for over-powerful (up to 16%) reds, now often tasty and balanced. See Bodegas Fariña.

Torremilanos Rib del D r res ★→★★★ **86 87 89 91 92** 94 Label of Bodegas López Peñalba, a fast-expanding family firm nr Aranda de Duero. Tinto Fino (Tempranillo) is smoother, more RIOJA-like than most.

Torres, Miguel Pen r w p dr s/sw res ★★→★★★★ **87 88 89 90 92 93 94** World-famous family company for many of the best PENEDES wines; a flagship for all Spain. Wines are flowery white Viña Sol, Green Label Fransola Sauv (**94**) and Gran Viña Sol, Parellada, MILMANDA oak-fermented Chard (**94**), semi-dry aromatic Esmeralda, Waltraud Ries (**95**), red Tres Torres, Gran Sangre de Toro, vg Gran Coronas (Cabernet Sauvignon) RESERVAS (**88**), fresh soft Las Torres Merlot and Santa Digna Pinot. Mas Borrás (**91**) is 100% Pinot N. Also in Chile and California.

Utiel-Requena U-R r p (w) Demarcated region W of Valencia. Sturdy reds and thick hyper-tannic wines for blending; also light fragrant rosé.

Valbuena Rib del D r ★★★ **84 85 86 88 89 90 91** Made with the same grapes as VEGA SICILIA but sold when 5 yrs old. Best at about 10 yrs. Some prefer it to its elder brother. 88 is outstanding. But see Alión.

Valdeorras Gal r w ★→★★★ DO E of Orense. Fresh dry wines; at best Godellos are now rated among top white wines in Spain. See Guitián Godello.

Valdepeñas La M r (w) ★→★★ Demarcated region nr Andalucían border. Mainly red wines, high in alcohol but surprisingly soft in flavour. Best wines (eg LOS LLANOS, FELIX SOLIS and CASA DE LA VINA) now oak-matured.

Valduero, Bodega Rib del D r **86** 89 **91** 92 94 Newish BODEGA: vg, value RESERVAS.

Valencia r w ★ Demarcated region exporting vast quantities of clean and drinkable table wine; also refreshing whites, esp Moscatel.

Vega Sicilia Rib del D r res ★★★★ **41 48 53 59 60 61 62 64 66 67 69 70 72 73 74 75** 76 **79 80 82 83 85** Top Spanish wine: full fruity piquant rare and fascinating. Up to 16% alcohol; best at 12 to 15 years from date of vintage. Reserva Especial is a blend, chiefly of 62 and 79(!). See also Valbuena, Alión. Now investing in Tokaji, Hungary.

Vendimia Vintage.

Verín Gal r ★ Town near N border of Portugal. Its wines are the strongest from GALICIA, without a bubble, and with up to 14% alcohol.

Viña Literally, a vineyard. But wines such as Tondonia (LOPEZ DE HEREDIA) are not necessarily made with grapes from only the v'yd named.

Viña Pedrosa See Pérez Pascuas.

Viña Toña Pen w ★★→★★★ DYA Clean fresh fruity whites of Xarel-lo (100%), unoaked Chard, Parellada and Macabeo, from small Celler R Balada. Justifiably high reputation.

Viñas del Vero Som w p r res ★★→★★★ See ARAGONESA COMPANIA VITIVINICOLA.

Vinícola de Castilla La M r p w ★★ **84 86 92** 93 **94** 95 One of largest LA MANCHA firms. Red and white Castillo de Alhambra are palatable. Top are Cab, Cencibel (Tempranillo), Señorío de Guadianeja (**84 86**) GRAN RESERVAS.

Vinícola Navarra Nav r p w res ★★ **89 90 91** 94 Old-est'd firm, now part of BODEGAS Y BEBIDAS, but still thoroughly traditional. Best wines Las Campañas (**91**) and Viña del Recuerdo (93).

Vinival, Bodegas Valencia r p w ★ Huge Valencian consortium marketing the most widely drunk wine in the region, Torres de Quart (rosé best).

Vino común/corriente Ordinary wine.

Yecla r w ★ DO north of Murcia. Decent red from Bodegas Castaño.

Yllera Rib del D r ★★ **90 91** 92 Good-value RIBERA DEL DUERO red from now privatized Los Curros coop (but bottled in RUEDA so not DO).

SPAIN

Portugal

Abrigada, Quinta da Alenquer r w res ★★ **90 92** Family estate: characterful light whites, cherry-like Castelão Francês (PERIQUITA). Best: oaked GARRAFEIRAS.

Adega A cellar or winery.

Alenquer r w Aromatic reds, whites from IPR just N of Lisbon. Good estate wines from QUINTAS DE ABRIGADA and PANCAS.

Alentejo r (w) ★→★★★ 92 93 94 95 96 Vast tract of SE Portugal with only sparse v'yds, over the R Tagus from Lisbon, but rapidly emerging potential for excellent wine. To date the great bulk has been coop-made. Estate wines from CARTUXA, HERDADE DE MOUCHAO, JOSE DE SOUSA, QUINTA DO CARMO (now part Rothschild-owned) and ESPORAO have potency and style. Best coops are at BORBA, REDONDO and REGUENGOS. Growing excitement here. Now classified as a VINHO REGIONAL subdivided into 5 DOCs: BORBA, REDONDO, REGUENGOS, PORTALEGRE, VIDIGUEIRA; and 3 IPRS: Granja-Amareleja, Moura, EVORA.

Algarve r w ★ Wines of the holiday area are covered by DOCs Lagos, Tavira, Lagoa and Portimão. Nothing to write home about.

Aliança, Caves Bair r w sp res ★★→★★★ Large BAIRRADA-based firm making classic method sparkling. Reds and whites incl good Bairrada wines and mature DAOS. Aliança Tinta Velha is a best-selling red in Portugal.

Almeirim Ribatejo r w ★ Large new IPR east of ALENQUER. Its coop makes the admirably fruity, extremely inexpensive Lezíria.

Alta Mesa See Estremadura.

Arinto White grape best from central and S Portugal where it retains acidity and produces fragrant crisp dry white wines.

Arrábida Terras do Sado r w IPR. Reds mostly from CASTELAO FRANCES (or PERIQUITA) some Cab S and Chard allowed.

Arruda, Adega Cooperativa de Est r res ★ **94 95** Vinho Tinto Arruda is a best buy, but avoid the reserva. (Arruda is now an IPR.)

Aveleda, Quinta da VV w ★★ DYA Reliable VINHO VERDES made on the Aveleda estate of the Guedes family. Sold dry in Portugal but slightly sw for export.

Azevedo, Quinta do VV w ★★ DYA Superior VINHO VERDE from SOGRAPE. 100% LOUREIRO grapes.

Bacalhoa, Quinta da Set r res ★★★ 91 92 93 **94** American-owned estate nr SETUBAL. Its fruity mid-weight Cab is made by J P VINHOS.

Bairrada Bair r w sp ★→★★★ 85 86 87 88 89 90 **91 92** 94 95 DOC for excellent red GARRAFEIRAS. Also good classic method sparkling. Now an export hit.

Barca Velha Douro r res ★★★★ 78 81 82 83 85 Perhaps Portugal's best red, made in v limited quantities in the high DOURO by the port firm of FERREIRA (now owned by SOGRAPE). Powerful resonant wine with deep bouquet, but being challenged by younger rivals (see Redoma).

Beiras VINHO REGIONAL including DAO, BAIRRADA and granite mt ranges of central Portugal. IPRS: CASTELO Rodrigo, COVA DE BEIRA, LAFOES, PINHEL.

Borba Alen r ★→★★ Small DOC nr EVORA; some of the best ALENTEJO wine.

Borba, Adega Cooperativa de Alen r (w) res ★→★★ 91 **92 93** 94 Leading ALENTEJO coop modernized with stainless steel and oak by EC funding. Big fruity vinho do ano red and vg reserva.

Borges & Irmão Merchants of port and table wines at Vila Nova de Gaia, incl GATAO and (better) Gamba VINHOS VERDES, sparkling Fita Azul.

Branco White.

Brejoeira, Palacio de VV w (r) ★★★ Outstanding estate-made VINHO VERDE from MONCAO: astonishing fragrance and full flavour. 100% Alvarinho grapes.

Bright Brothers (r) 92 93 **94 95** The gifted Australian Peter Bright, formerly with J P VINHOS, has teamed up with his brother to make several attractive RIBATEJO wines and DOURO reds.

Buçaco Beiras r w (p) res ★★★★ (r) **51 53 57 58 60 63 67 70 72 75 77 78 82 85 92** (w) **56 65 66 70 72 75 78** 82 **84 85 86 91** Legendary speciality of the Palace Hotel at Buçaco nr Coimbra, not seen elsewhere. At best incredible quality, worth the journey. So are the palace and park.

A Choice for 1998 from Portugal

Douro: Barca Velha 85, Quinta da Gaivosa (red) 95, Quinta da Crasto Touriga Nacional 95, Niepoort Redoma red 91

Alentejo: Esporão red 94, Sogrape Vinha do Monte 94, José da Sousa Garrafeira 91

Bairrada: Luis Pato Quinta do Ribeirinho Pe Franco 95

Beiras: Quinta da Foz do Arouce red 89

Dão: Quinta dos Roques Reserva 92, Caves São João Porta dos Cavaleiros Reserva (cork label)

Terras do Sado: Periquita Classico 92

Moscatel de Setúbal: JM de Fonseca 91

Bucelas Est w ★★★ Tiny demarcated region N of Lisbon in the hands of 3 producers. Quinta da Romeira make attractive wines from the ARINTO grape.

Camarate, Quinta de Est r ★★ **89 90** Notable red from JOSE MARIA DA FONSECA, S of Lisbon, incl detectable proportion of Cab S.

Carcavelos Est br sw ★★★ Normally NV. Minute DOC W of Lisbon. Rare sweet aperitif or dessert wines average 19% alcohol and resemble honeyed MADEIRA. The only producer is now Quinta dos Pesos, Caparide.

Carmo, Quinta do Alen r w res ★★★ **86 87 88 89 92 93** Beautiful small ALENTEJO ADEGA, partly bought '92 by Rothschilds (Lafite). 125 acres, plus cork forests. Fresh white, red better. 2nd wine: Dom Martinho (**90**).

Cartaxo Ribatejo r w ★ District in RIBATEJO N of Lisbon, now an IPR area making everyday wines popular in the capital.

Cartuxa, Herdade de Alen r w ★ **89 90 91** 94 Vast estate nr EVORA with nearly 500 v'yd acres. Big ripe flavoured reds esp Pera Manca, one of the Alentejo's best (and most expensive) reds; soft creamy whites.

Carvalho, Ribeiro & Ferreira N Lisbon r w res ★★→★★★ Have now ceased trading but SERRADAYRES and good GARRAFEIRAS from the RIBATEJO are still seen.

Casa de Sezim VV w ★ DYA Estate-bottled VINHO VERDE from a member of the association of private producers, APEVV.

Casal Branco, Quinta de Ribatejo r ★ Big concern making good reds: Falua (DYA) and Falcoaria (92).

Casal García VV w ★★ DYA Big-selling VINHO VERDE, made at AVELEDA.

Casal Mendes VV w ★★ DYA The VINHO VERDE from CAVES ALIANCA.

Casaleiro Trademark of Caves Dom Teodosio-João T Barbosa, who make a variety of standard wines: DAO, VINHO VERDE etc.

Castelão Francês Red grape widely planted throughout S Portugal. Good firm-flavoured reds, often blended with Cab S. Aka PERIQUITA.

Castelo Rodrigo Beiras r w IPR reds resembling lighter style of DAO.

Cepa Velha VV w (r) ★★★ Brand name of Vinhos de Monção. Their Alvarinho is one of the best VINHOS VERDES.

Chaves Trás-os-Montes r w IPR. Sharp pale fizzy reds from granite soils. Rounder ones from schist.

Colares r ★★ Small DOC on the sandy coast W of Lisbon. Its antique-style dark-red wines, rigid with tannin, are from ungrafted vines. They need ageing, but TOTB (the older the better) no longer. See Paulo da Silva.

Portugal entries also cross-refer to Sherry, Port & Madeira, pages 172–179.

Consumo (vinho) Ordinary wine.

Coruche Ribatejo r w Large IPR of Sorraia River basin NE of Lisbon.

Côtto, Quinta do Douro r w res ★★★ **85 90 94** Pioneer table wines from port country; vg red Grande Escolha and also Q do Côtto are dense fruity tannic wines for long keeping. Also port.

Cova da Beira Beiras r w Largest of the IPRS nr Spanish border. Light reds best.

Crasto, Quinta do Douro r dr sw (★) **94 95 96** Top estate nr Pinhão for port and excellent oak-aged reds.

Dão r w res ★★ **85 90 91 92** 94 DOC region round town of Viseu. Produces some of Portugal's best-known but often dull table wines: solid reds of some subtlety with age; substantial dry whites. Most sold under brand names. But see Roques, Maias, Saes, Fonte do Ouro, Terras Altas, Porta dos Cavalheiros, Grao Vasco, Duque de Viseu etc.

DOC (Denominacâo de Origem Controlada) Official wine region. There are 18 in Portugal, including BAIRRADA, COLARES, DAO, DOURO, SETUBAL, VINHO VERDE; and new in '95: BORBA, PORTALEGRE, REDONDO, REGUENGOS, VIDIGUEIRA in the ALENTEJO. See also IPR, Vinhos Regionals.

Doce (vinho) Sweet (wine).

Douro r w **82 83 84 85 86 87 88 89 90 91 92 94 95** Northern river whose valley produces port and some of Portugal's most exciting new table wines. See Barca Velha, Quinta do Côtto, Redoma, etc. Watch this space.

Duque de Viseu Dão r **90 91 92 94** High quality red DAO from SOGRAPE.

Esporão, Herdade do Alen w r ★★→★★★ **89 90 91 92 93** 94 Owners Finagra spent US $10 million on space-age winery surrounded by 900 new v'yd acres. Wines are made (since '92) by Australian David Baverstock: light fresh Roupeiro white, fruity young red Alandra, superior (**91 92**) Cab S – Esporão, with a touch of Cab S, is one of ALENTEJO's best reds. Also incl Monte Velho gently oaked reds and fruity whites.

Espumante Sparkling.

Esteva Douro r ★ **92 94 95** V drinkable DOURO red from port firm FERREIRA.

Estremadura VINHO REGIONAL on Portugal's W coast, s'times called 'Oeste'. Large coops. Alta Mesa from São Marmade de Ventosa coop is good. IPRS: ALENQUER, ARRUDA, Encostas d'Aire, Obidos, TORRES VEDRES.

Evelita Douro r ★★ Reliable middle-weight red made near Vila Real by REAL COMPANHIA VINICOLA DO NORTE DE PORTUGAL.

Evora Alen r w Large new IPR south of Lisbon.

Fernão Pires White grape making ripe-flavoured slightly spicy whites in RIBATEJO. (Known as Maria Gomes in BAIRRADA.)

Ferreirinha Douro r res ★★★ **80 84 86 90** Reserva Especial. Second wine to BARCA VELHA, made in less than ideal vintages.

Fonseca, José Maria da Est r w dr sw sp res ★★ Venerable firm in Azeitão nr Lisbon with one of the longest and best ranges in Portugal, incl dry white PASMADOS, PORTALEGRE and QUINTA DE CAMARATE; red PERIQUITA, PASMADOS, TERRAS ALTAS, DAO, several GARRAFEIRAS; and famous dessert SETUBAL. Fonseca also owns JOSE DE SOUSA and makes the wines for CASA DA INSUA. LANCERS rosé is less distinguished, but Lancers Brut is a surprisingly drinkable sparkling wine made by a continuous process of Russian invention.

Fonte do Ouro Dão r ★ **92** Good balanced red from well-run single estate.

Foz do Arouce, Quinta da Beiras r ★★ **90 91** Big cask-aged red from heart of BEIRAS.

Franqueira, Quinta da VV w ★ Typically dry, fragrant VINHO VERDE made by Englishman Piers Gallie.

Fuiza Bright Ribatejo r w ★ **94 95 96** Joint venture with Peter Bright (BRIGHT BROS). Good Chard, Sauv, Merlot and Cab S.

Gaivosa, Quinta de Douro r ★ 92 94 **95** Important estate near Regua. Deep concentrated cask-aged reds from port grapes. Quinta do Vale da Raposa (95) is lighter fruity red from same producer.

Garrafeira Label term: merchant's 'private reserve', aged for minimum of 2 years in cask and 1 in bottle, but often much longer. Usually their best, though traditionally often of indeterminate origin. Now has to show origin on label.

Gatão VV w ★ DYA Standard BORGES & IRMAO VINHO V; fragrant but sweetened.

Gazela VV w ★★ DYA Reliable VINHO VERDE made at Barcelos by SOGRAPE since the AVELEDA estate went to a different branch of the Guedes family.

Generoso Aperitif or dessert wine rich in alcohol.

Grão Vasco Dão r w res ★★ **91 92 94** One of the best and largest brands of DAO, from a new high-tech ADEGA at Viseu. Fine red GARRAFEIRA (91); fresh young white (DYA). Owned by SOGRAPE.

IPR Indicacões de Proveniência Regulamentada. See below.

Thirty-one new Portuguese wine regions came into play in 1990; there are now 47. These 'IPRs' (Indicacões de Proveniência Regulamentada) are on a six-year probation for DOC status. In EC terminology they are VQPRDs. Those which really perform are included in this edition. 1992 saw nine new broader 'Vinhos Regionais' introduced: Alentejo, Algarve, Beiras, Estremadura, Ribatejo, Rios do Minho, Terras Durienses, Terras do Sado, Trás os Montes.

José de Sousa Alen r res ★★ 90 91 **92 93 94** (was Rosado Fernandes) Small firm recently acquired by JOSE MARIA DA FONSECA, making the most sophisticated of the full-bodied wines from the ALENTEJO (although now slightly lighter in style), fermenting them in earthenware amphoras and ageing them in oak.

J P Vinhos Set r w sp res ★★ One of best-equipped and best-run wineries. Delicious João Pires Branco (Moscato), Catarina (with Chard), dry red and white Santa Marta, red Santo Amaro made by macération carbonique, Meia Pipa TINTO DE ANFORA, QUINTA DA BACALHOA, dessert SETUBAL, classic sparkling J P Vinhos Bruto and Cova da Ursa oak-fermented Chard.

Lafões Beiras r w IPR between DAO and VINHO VERDE.

Lagosta VV w DYA VINHO VERDE white from the REAL COMPANHIA VINICOLA DO NORTE DE PORTUGAL.

Lancers Est p w sp ★ Sweet carbonated rosé and sparkling white extensively shipped to the US by JM DA FONSECA.

Lagoalva de Cima, Quinta da r w ★ 91 92 RIBATEJO estate of 125 aces. Second label: Monte da Casta.

Lezíria See Almeirim.

Loureiro Best VINHO VERDE grape variety: crisp fragrant white wines.

Madeira br dr sw ★★→★★★★ Portugal's Atlantic island making famous fortified dessert and aperitif wines. See pages 172–179.

Maduro (vinho) A mature table wine – as opposed to a VINHO VERDE.

Maias, Quinta das Dão ★★ 90 91 92 **94** New wave quinta: solid reds to age.

Mateus Rosé Bair p (w) ★ World's biggest-selling medium-sweet carbonated rosé, from SOGRAPE at Vila Real and Anadia in BAIRRADA.

Monção N subregion of VINHO VERDE on River Minho: best wines from the Alvarinho grape. See Palacio de Brejoeira.

Morgadio de Torre VV w ★★ DYA Top vv from SOGRAPE. Largely Alvarinho.

Mouchão, Herdade de Alen r res ★★★ **74 82** 89 90 91 92 Perhaps top ALENTEJO estate, ruined in '74 revolution; since replanted and fully recovered.

NB Vintages in colour are those you should choose first for drinking in 1998.

Palmela Terras do Sado r w Sandy soil IPR. Reds esp long-lived.

Pancas, Quinta das Est r w res ★★ **91 92 94 95** Red and white Cab S and Chard from estate with NAPA connections nr ALENQUER (NW of Lisbon). 80% Cab has been much praised, but is somewhat heavy and closed. Quinta Dom Carlos is vg white made here from ARINTO grapes.

Pasmados V tasty JOSE MARIA DA FONSECA red from SETUBAL peninsula (**90 91**).

Pato, Luis Bair r sp ★★→★★★ **85 89 90 91 92 94** 95' Some of top estate-grown BAIRRADA incl tremendous red QUINTA DE RIBEIRINHO and João Pato. '95 reds notable esp Quinta do Ribeirinho Pé Franco. Also classic method sparkling.

Paulo da Silva, Antonio Bernardino Colares r (w) res ★★→★★★ **84 85 87 88** His COLARES Chitas is one of the v few of these classics still made.

Pedralvites, Quinta de Bair w ★→★★ DYA **95 96** Pleasant BAIRRADA white with apple and apricot flavours from the Maria Gomes grape, by SOGRAPE.

Periquita Est r ★★ **90 91 94** Enjoyable robust reds, made by JOSE MARIA DA FONSECA at Azeitão S of Lisbon. Periquita is an alias of CASTELAO FRANCES, a grape much grown in the RIBATEJO.

Pinhel Beiras w (r) sp ★ IPR region E of DAO: similar white, mostly sparkling.

Pires, Vinhos João See J P Vinhos.

Planalto Douro w ★★ DYA **95 96** Good white wine from SOGRAPE.

Planalto Mirandês Trás-os-Montes r w Large IPR NE of DOURO. Port grapes in reds. Verdelho in whites.

Ponte de Lima, Cooperativa de VV r w ★★ Maker of one of the best bone-dry red VINHOS VERDES, and first-rate dry and fruity white.

Porta dos Cavalheiros Dão ★★ **85 88 89 90 91 92** One of the best red DAOS, matured by CAVES SAO JOAO in BAIRRADA.

Portalegre Alen r w New DOC on Spanish border. Strong fragrant reds with potential to age. Alcoholic whites.

Quinta Estate.

Ramada Est r w ★ **95** Modestly-priced red from the São Mamede de Ventosa coop: fruity and v drinkable.

Ramos-Pinto, Adriano Douro r ★★ **91 92 94 95** Rich red Duas Quintas from go-ahead port house.

Raposeira Douro w sp ★★ Well-known fizz made by the classic method at Lamego. Ask for the Bruto. An outpost of Seagram.

Real Companhia Vinícola do Norte de Portugal Giant of the port trade (see page 177); also produces EVELITA, LAGOSTA etc.

Redoma ★★★ Amazing mouthfilling red from port-shippers NIEPOORT (**91**). Also good white.

Redondo Alen r w Nr Spanish border. One of Portugal's best large coops. Newly granted DOC status.

Reguengos Alen r (w) res ★→★★ Important DOC nr Spanish border. Incl JOSE DE SOUSA and ESPORAO estates, plus large coop for good reds.

Ribatejo r w **90 91 92 94 95** VINHO REGIONAL on R Tagus north of Lisbon. Good GARRAFEIRAS and younger wines from ALMEIRIM coop, FUIZA BRIGHT and BRIGHT BROS. IPRS: ALMEIRIM, CARTAXO, Chamusca, Coruche, Santarém, Tomar.

Ribeirinho, Quinta do Bair r sp ★★→★★★ **85 92 95** Vg tannic, concentrated reds from LUIS PATO. Limited-edition Vinhos Velhas (94): magnificent.

Rios do Minho VINHO REGIONAL covering NW – similar area to VINHO VERDE.

Roques, Quinta dos Dão r ★ **92 94** Promising estate for big solid oaked reds.

Rosa, Quinta de la Douro r ★★ **92 94 95** Firm oak-aged red from old port v'yds and young peppery Quinta das Lamelas, from Australian winemaker David Baverstock.

A general rule for Portugal: choose youngest vintages of whites, oldest of red.

Rosado Rosé.

Rosado Fernandes See José de Sousa.

Saes, Quinta de Dão r w ★★ 91 92 94 Small mountain v'yd making refined wines. Quinta de Pellada also making gd wines under same ownership.

Saima, Casa de Bair r w ★★ 85 87 90 91 **94** Promising estate: firm reds (from Baga grapes).

São Domingos, Comp dos Vinhos de Est r ★ **95** Reds (Espiga, Palha-Canas), from estate managed by José Neiva, maker of ALTA MESA.

São João, Caves Bair r w sp res ★★→★★★ 83 85 90 **91 92** One of region's top firms, known for fruity and full red BAIRRADA: Frei Joao and PORTA DOS CAVALHEIROS DAOS. Also fizz.

Seco Dry.

Serradayres Ribatejo r (w) res ★ 92 94 Blended RIBATEJO table wines from CARVALHO, Ribeiro & Ferreira. Recently much improved.

Entre Serras r w ★ 92 94 Property in BEIRAS making sound barrel-fermented Chard (DYA) and soft light reds.

Setúbal Set br (r w) sw (dr) ★★★ Tiny demarcated region S of the River Tagus, where FONSECA make a highly aromatic Muscat-based dessert wine usually sold at 6 and 20 yrs old.

Sogrape Sociedad Comercial dos Vinhos de Mesa de Portugal. Largest wine concern in the country, making VINHOS VERDES, DAO, BAIRRADA, ALENTEJO, MATEUS ROSE, Vila Real red etc, and now owners of FERREIRA and OFFLEY port.

Tamariz, Quinta do VV w ★ Fragrant VINHO VERDE from Loureiro grapes only.

Terra Franca Bair r res ★ 90 91 92 **94** Sound red BAIRRADA from SOGRAPE, available also as a GARRAFEIRA (85 89).

Terras Altas Dão r w res ★ 91 92 94 Reliable DAO from FONSECA.

Terras do Sado VINHO REGIONAL covering sandy plains around Sado estuary. IPRS: ARRABIDA and PALMELA.

Tinta Roriz Major port grape (red) making good DOURO table wines and increasingly planted elsewhere for similarly full-bodied reds. This Portuguese variant of Tempranillo is also known in ALENTEJO as Aragonez.

Tinto Red.

Tinto da Anfora Est r ★★ 89 90 91 **92** Deservedly popular juicy and fruity red from J P VINHOS.

Torres Vedras Est r w IPR area N of Lisbon famous for Wellington's 'lines'. Major supplier of bulk wine; one of biggest coops in Portugal.

Touriga Nacional Top red grape used for port and DOURO table wines; now increasingly elsewhere, esp DAO, ALENTEJO, ESTREMADURA.

Trás-os-Montes VINHO REGIONAL covering mountains of NE Portugal. Light reds and rosés. IPRs: CHAVES, PLANALTO-MIRANDES, Valpacos.

Trincadeira Vg red grape in ALENTEJO for spicy single-varietal wines.

Velhas, Caves Bucelas r w res ★ Until very recently the only maker of BUCELAS; also good DAO and (**80**) Romeira GARRAFEIRAS.

Verde Green (see Vinhos Verdes).

Vidigueira Alen w r ★ DOC for traditionally-made unmatured whites from volcanic soils and some plummy reds.

Vinho Regional Larger provincial wine region, with same status as French vin de pays: they are: ALGARVE, ALENTEJO, BEIRAS, ESTREMADURA, RIBATEJO, RIOS DO MINHO, TRAS OS MONTES, TERRAS DO SADO. See also DOC, IPR.

Vinhos Verdes VV w ★→★★★ r ★ DOC between R Douro and N frontier with Spain, for 'green wines' (which may be white or red): made from grapes with high acidity and (originally) undergoing a special secondary fermentation to leave them with a slight sparkle. Today the fizz is usually just added CO_2. Ready for drinking in spring after harvest.

PORTUGAL

Sherry, Port & Madeira

Sherry, port and Madeira are the world's great classic fortified wines: reinforced with alcohol up to between 15 percent (for a light sherry) and 22 (for vintage port). No others have ever supplanted them for quality or value – despite many attempts.

1997 saw a significant upturn in port exports and sales, most dramatically in the US, while for sherry, 1996 was a historic year. At last its name was legally recognized as belonging to Spain alone. The Cape, Cyprus and other imitators of this great wine are now having to find other names.

The map on pages 154–55 locates the port (Douro) and sherry (Jerez) districts. Madeira is an island 400 miles out in the Atlantic off the coast of Morocco, a port of call for west-bound sailing ships: hence its historical market in North America.

Shippers (that is producers, blenders and bottlers) are still far more important than growers in these industries. This section lists both types of wines and shippers' names with the names and vintages (if any) of their best wines.

Abad, Tomás Small sherry BODEGA owned by LUSTAU. Vg light FINO.

Almacenista Individual matured but unblended sherry; usually dark dry wines for connoisseurs. Often superb quality and value. See Lustau.

Amontillado A FINO aged in cask beyond its normal span to become darker, more powerful and pungent. The best are natural dry wines.

Amoroso Type of sweet sherry, v similar to a sweet OLOROSO.

Barbadillo, Antonio Much the largest SANLUCAR firm, with a range of 50-odd MANZANILLAS and sherries mostly excellent of their type, including Sanlúcar FINO, superb SOLERA manzanilla PASADA, Fino de Balbaina, austere Princípe dry AMONTILLADO. Also young Castillo de San Diego table wines.

Barbeito One of the last independent MADEIRA shipping firms, now Japanese controlled. Wines incl rare vintages, eg MALMSEY 1901 and the latest, BUAL 1960.

Barros Almeida Large family-owned port house with several brands (incl Feist, Feuerheerd, KOPKE): excellent 20-yr-old TAWNY and many COLHEITAS.

Barros e Sousa Tiny family-owned Madeira producer with old lodges in centre of Funchal. Extremely fine but now rare vintages, plus gd 10 yr old wines.

Blandy One of two top names used by MADEIRA WINE CO. Duke of Clarence Rich Madeira is their most famous wine. 10-year-old reserves (VERDELHO, BUAL, MALMSEY) are good. Many glorious old vintages can be seen, though mostly nowadays at auctions.

Blázquez Sherry BODEGA at PUERTO DE SANTA MARIA owned by DOMECQ. Outstanding FINO, Carta Blanca, v old SOLERA OLOROSO Extra, and Carta Oro AMONTILLADO al natural (unsweetened).

Bobadilla Large JEREZ BODEGA, recently bought by OSBORNE and best known for v dry Victoria FINO and Bobadilla 103 brandy, esp among Spanish connoisseurs.

Borges, H M Independent MADEIRA shipper of old repute.

Brown sherry British term for a style of budget dark sweet sherry.

Bual One of the best grapes of MADEIRA, making a soft smoky sweet wine, usually lighter and not as rich as MALMSEY. (See panel on page 179.)

Burdon English-founded sherry BODEGA owned by CABALLERO. Puerto FINO, Don Luis AMONTILLADO and raisiny Heavenly Cream are top lines.

Burmester Old, small, family port house with fine soft sweet 20-yr-old TAWNY; also vg range of COLHEITAS. Vintages: 48 55 58 60 63 70 77 80 84 85 89 91 94.

Caballero Important sherry shipper at PUERTO DE SANTA MARIA, best known for Pavón FINO, Mayoral Cream OLOROSO, excellent BURDON sherries and PONCHE orange liqueur. Also owners of LUSTAU.

Cálem Old family-run Portuguese house; had fine reputation, but recent vintages not as gd. Owns Quinta da Foz (82 84 86 87 88 89 90 92). Vintages: **50 55' 58 60 63' 66 70 75 77'** 80 83 **85** 91 94.Reliable light TAWNY; gd range of COLHEITAS: **48 50 52 57 60 62 65 78 84** 86.

Churchill The only recently founded port shipper, already highly respected for excellent vintages 82 and 85, also 91 94. Vg traditional LBV. Quinta da Agua Alta is Churchill's single-QUINTA port: 83 87 90 92.

Cockburn British-owned (Allied-DOMECQ) port shipper with a range of gd wines incl the v popular fruity Special Reserve. Fine VINTAGE PORT from high v'yds can look deceptively light when young, but has great lasting power. Vintages: **55 60 63' 67 70' 75** 83 **85** 91 94. Note: for many shippers, 85 generally not as gd as first thought.

Colheita Vintage-dated port of a single yr, but aged at least 7 winters in wood: in effect a vintage TAWNY. The bottling date is also shown on the label. Excellent examples come from KOPKE, CALEM, NIEPOORT and Krohn.

Cossart Gordon At one time the leading firm of MADEIRA shippers, founded 1745, with BLANDY now one of the two top-quality labels of the MADEIRA WINE CO. Wines slightly less rich than Blandy's. Best-known for Good Company Finest Medium Rich but also producing 5-yr-old reserves, old vintages (latest 74) and SOLERAS (esp BUAL 1845).

A choice of port and Madeira for 1998

White: **Churchill's Dry White**
Premium Ruby: **Warre's Warrior**
LBV: **Ferreira's Traditional 1991**
Tawny: **Niepoort 20 Year Old**
Vintage: **Fonseca 1966, Fonseca Guimaraens 1976**
Madeira: **Henriques and Henriques 10 Year Old Verdelho, d'Oliveira 10 Year Old (Sweet), d'Oliveira 1968 Bual**

Crasto, Quinta do Well-situated estate producing reasonable ports, esp lbv. Vintages (85 87 91) are early maturing.

Cream Sherry A style of amber sweet sherry made by sweetening a blend of well-aged OLOROSOS. It originated in Bristol, England.

Croft One of the oldest firms shipping VINTAGE PORT: since 1678; now owned by Grand Met Co. Well-balanced vintage wines tend to mature early (since 66). Vintages: **55 60 63' 66 67 70' 75 77' 82 85** 91 94; and lighter vintage wines under name of their Quinta da Roeda in several other years (**78 80 83** 87). Distinction is their most popular blend. MORGAN is a small separate company (see also Delaforce). Also in sherry business with Croft Original (PALE CREAM) and Particular (med), Delicado (FINO, also med), and gd PALO CORTADO.

Crusted Term for vintage-style port, usually blended from several vintages not one. Bottled young, then aged so it forms a 'crust'. Needs decanting. Specifically for UK market – not recognized in Portugal.

Cruz Huge brand and market leader in France. (The French take 40% of all port exports.) Standard TAWNY in French style – not brilliant quality. Owned by French co La Martiniquaise.

Delaforce Port shipper owned by CROFT, best known in Germany. His Eminence's Choice is a v pleasant TAWNY; VINTAGE CHARACTER is also good. Vintage wines are v fine, among the lighter kind: **55 58 60 63' 66' 70 74 75 77' 82 85** 94; Quinta da Côrte in **78** 80 84 87 91.

Delgado, Zuleta Old-established SANLUCAR firm best known for marvellous La Goya MANZANILLA PASADA.

Diez-Merito SA Sherry house famous for FINO Imperial and Victoria Regina OLOROSO. Bought by Rumasa and incorporated into BODEGAS INTERNACIONALES. Control passed to Marcos Eguizabal (of PATERNINA in RIOJA). Now apparently exists as little more than a name. Its excellent DON ZOILO sherry has been sold to the MEDINA group, and Gran Duque de Alba brandy to WILLIAMS & HUMBERT.

Domecq Giant family-run sherry BODEGA at JEREZ, recently merged with Allied-Lyons as Allied-Domecq, famous also for Fundador and other brandies. Double Century Original OLOROSO, its biggest brand, now replaced by Pedro Cream Sherry; La Ina is excellent FINO. Other famous wines incl Celebration CREAM, Botaina (old AMONTILLADO) and magnificent Rio Viejo (v dry amontillado) and Sibarita (PALO CORTADO). Recently: a range of wonderful old SOLERA sherries (Sibarita, Amontillado 51-1a and Venerable Oloroso). Also in RIOJA and Mexico.

> **Top-quality sherry is now the best-value wine in the world. Supreme old dry wines cost less than Another Chardonnay.**

Don Zoilo Luxury sherries, including velvety FINO, recently sold by BODEGAS INTERNACIONALES to the MEDINA group (Luis Paez).

Dow Old port name, well-known for relatively dry but splendid vintage wines, said to have a faint 'cedarwood' character. Also vg VINTAGE CHARACTER and Boardroom, a 15-year-old TAWNY. Quinta do Bomfim is single-QUINTA port (**78 79 82 84** 86 87 88 89 90 92). Vintages: **55 60 63' 66' 70' 72 75** 77' 80 83 85' 91 94. Dow, GOULD CAMPBELL, GRAHAM, QUARLES HARRIS, SMITH WOODHOUSE, WARRE all belong to the Symington family.

Duff Gordon Sherry shippers best known for El Cid AMONTILLADO. Also good FINO Feria and Nina Medium OLOROSO. Owned by OSBORNE.

Eira Velha, Quinta da Small port estate with old-style vintage wines shipped by MARTINEZ. Vintages: 78 82 87 92 94.

Ferreira One of the biggest Portuguese-owned port growers and shippers (since 1751). Largest selling brand in P. Well-known for old TAWNIES and juicily sweet, relatively light vintages: **60 63' 66 70' 75 77' 78** 80 82 85' 87 91 94. Also Dona Antónia Personal Reserve, splendidly rich tawny Duque de Bragança and single-QUINTA wines Quinta do Seixo (83) and Q do Leda (90).

Fino Term for lightest, finest sherries, completely dry, v pale, delicate but pungent. Fino should always be drunk cool and fresh: it deteriorates rapidly once opened. TIO PEPE is the classic. Use half bottles if possible.

Flor A floating yeast peculiar to FINO sherry and certain other wines that oxidize slowly and tastily under its influence.

Fonseca Guimaraens British-owned port shipper with a stellar reputation; connected with TAYLOR'S. Robust deeply coloured vintage wine, among the v best. Vintages: Fonseca **60 63' 66' 70' 75 77' 80 83** 85' 92 94; Fonseca Guimaraens **76 78 82 84** 86 87 88 91 94. Quinta do Panascal **78** is a single-QUINTA wine. Also delicious VINTAGE CHARACTER Bin 27.

Forrester Port shipper and owner of the famous Quinta da Boa Vista, now owned by SOGRAPE. The vintage wines tend to be round 'fat' and sweet, good for relatively early drinking. Baron de Forrester is vg TAWNY. Vintages: (Offley Forrester) **55 60 62' 63' 66 67 70' 72 75 77' 80 82** 83 85' 87 89 94.

Garvey Famous old sherry shipper at JEREZ, now owned by José María Ruiz Mateos. The finest wines are deep-flavoured FINO San Patricio, Tio Guillermo Dry AMONTILLADO and Ochavico Dry OLOROSO. San Angelo Medium amontillado is the most popular. Also Bicentenary PALE CREAM.

González Byass Enormous family-run firm shipping the world's most famous and one of v best FINO sherries: TIO PEPE. Brands include La Concha medium AMONTILLADO, Elegante dry fino and new El Rocío MANZANILLA Fina, San Domingo PALE CREAM, Nectar CREAM and Alfonso Dry OLOROSO. Amontillado del Duque is on a higher plane, as are Matusalem and Apostoles: respectively sweet and dry old olorosos of rare quality. Also makers of top-selling Soberano and exquisite Lepanto brandies. Now linked with Grand Metropolitan.

Gould Campbell See Smith Woodhouse.

Graham Port shipper famous for some of the richest, sweetest and best of VINTAGE PORTS, largely from its own Quinta dos Malvedos (**52 57 58 61 65 68 76 78 79 80 82 84** 86 87 88 90 92). Also excellent brands, incl Six Grapes RUBY, LBV, and 10- and 20-yr-old TAWNIES. Vintages: **55' 60 63' 66' 70' 75** 77' 80 83 85' 91 94.

Guita, La Famous old SANLUCAR BODEGA noteworthy for its particularly fine MANZANILLA PASADA.

Hartley & Gibson See Valdespino.

Harvey's Important pillar of the Allied-DOMECQ empire, along with TERRY. World-famous Bristol shippers of Bristol Cream and Bristol Milk (sweet), Club AMONTILLADO and Bristol Dry (medium), Luncheon Dry and Bristol FINO (not v dry). More to the point is its very good '1796' range of high quality sherries comprising Fine Old Amontillado, PALO CORTADO and Rich Old OLOROSO. Harvey's also controls COCKBURN and has been a MADEIRA shipper since 1796 (vg range).

> **Sherry: which to choose**
> **The sherry industry has been so badly depleted in recent years that a list of truly excellent wines still being made is needed to keep it in focus. They include:** Barbadillo manzanillas; Blázquez Carta Blanca fino; Domecq La Ina fino, Rio Viejo oloroso, Sibarita palo cortado; González Byass Tio Pepe fino, Amontillado del Duque, Matusalem and Apostoles dry and sweet olorosos; Hildago La Gitana manzanilla fino; Lustau Almacenista range; Osborne Fino Quinta and 'Rare' range (esp Alonso del Sabio); Páez Don Zoilo fino; Sandeman Don fino, Royal Corregidor sweet oloroso; de Soto Soto fino; Valdespino Inocente fino, Don Tomás amontillado; Williams & Humbert Pando fino and palo cortado.

Henriques & Henriques The biggest independent MADEIRA shipper at Câmara de Lobos, now with the largest, most modern cellars on the island: wide range of well-structured, rich, toothsome wines – the 10 year-olds are gold and platinum medal winners. Also a good extra-dry aperitif, Monte Seco, and v fine old reserves and vintages.

Hildalgo, Vinícola Old family firm based in SANLUCAR DE BARRAMEDA, best known for high-quality sherries: pale MANZANILLA La Gitana, fine OLOROSO Seco and Jerez CORTADO.

Internacionales, Bodegas Once the pride of the now-defunct Rumasa and with such famous houses as BERTOLA, VARELA and DIEZ-MERITO, the company was taken over by the entrepreneur Marcos Eguizabal. See MEDINA.

Jerez de la Frontera Centre of the sherry industry, between Cádiz and Seville in southern Spain. The word 'sherry' is a corruption of the name, pronounced in Spanish 'hereth'. In French, Xérès.

Sherry, Port & Madeira entries also cross-refer to Spain and Portugal sections, respectively pages 154–165 and 166–171.

SHERRY, PORT & MADEIRA

Kopke The oldest port house, founded by a German in 1638. Now belongs to BARROS ALMEIDA. Fair-quality vintage wines (**55 58 60 63 65 66 67 70 74 75 77 78 79 80 82** 83 85 87 89 91 94) and excellent COLHEITAS.

Late-bottled vintage (LBV) Port from a single vintage kept in wood for twice as long as VINTAGE PORT (about 5 years), therefore lighter when bottled and ages more quickly. Traditional late-bottled vintage 'throws a crust' like Vintage P (WARRE, SMITH WOODHOUSE, NIEPOORT, CHURCHILL, FERREIRA LBVs all qualify).

Leacock One of the oldest MADEIRA shippers, now a label of the MADEIRA WINE company. Basic St-John range is v fair; 10-yr-old Special Reserve MALMSEY and 15-yr-old BUAL are excellent.

Lustau One of the largest family-run sherry BODEGAS in JEREZ (now controlled by CABALLERO), making many wines for other shippers, but with a vg Dry Lustau range (esp FINO and OLOROSO) and Jerez Lustau PALO CORTADO. Pioneer shipper of excellent ALMACENISTA and 'landed age' wines; AMONTILLADOS and olorosos aged in elegant bottles before shipping. See also Abad.

Macharnudo One of the best parts of the sherry v'yds, N of JEREZ, famous for wines of the highest quality, both FINO and OLOROSO.

Madeira Wine Company Formed in 1913 by two firms as the Madeira Wine Association, subsequently to include all the British MADEIRA firms (26 in total) amalgamated to survive hard times. Remarkably, three generations later the wines, though cellared together, preserve their house styles. BLANDY and COSSART GORDON: top labels. Now controlled by the Symington group (see Dow).

Malmsey The sweetest and richest form of MADEIRA; dark amber, rich and honeyed yet with Madeira's unique sharp tang. Word is English corruption of 'Malvasia' qv. See panel on page 179.

Manzanilla Sherry, normally FINO, which has acquired a peculiar bracing salty character from being aged in BODEGAS at SANLUCAR DE BARRAMEDA, on the Guadalquivir estuary nr JEREZ.

Manzanilla Pasada A mature MANZANILLA, half-way to an AMONTILLADO-style wine. At its best (eg LA GUITA) one of the most appetizing of all sherries.

Marqués del Real Tesoro Old sherry firm, famous for its MANZANILLA and AMONTILLADO, bought by the enterprising José Estévez. Shrugging off the current slump in sales he has built a spanking new BODEGA – the first in years. Tío Mateo, for which the SOLERA was acquired from the now defunct Palomino & Vergara via HARVEY'S, is a vg FINO.

Martinez Gassiot Port firm, subsidiary of COCKBURN, known esp for excellent rich and pungent Directors 20-yr-old TAWNY, CRUSTED and LBV. Vintages: **55 60 63 67 70 75 82** 85 87 91 94.

Medina, José Originally a SANLUCAR family BODEGA, now a major exporter, especially to the Low Countries. By taking over the buildings and huge sherry stocks of the former BODEGAS INTERNACIONALES and by the more recent acquisition of WILLIAMS & HUMBERT, the Medina group, which also embraces Pérez Megia and Luis Paez, has probably become the biggest sherry grower and shipper, with some 25% of total volume.

Miles Formerly Rutherford & Miles. MADEIRA shipper famed for Old Trinity House Medium Rich etc. Latest vintage 73 VERDELHO. Now a MADEIRA WINE CO label.

Niepoort Small (Dutch) family-run port house with long record of fine vintages (**42 45 55 60 63 66 70 75 77 78** 80 **82** 83 87 91 92 94) and exceptional COLHEITAS. Also excellent SINGLE QUINTA port, Quinta do Passadouro (91 92 94).

Noval, Quinta do Historic port house now French (AXA) owned. Intensely fruity structured and elegant VINTAGE PORT; a few ungrafted vines still at the QUINTA make a small quantity of Nacional – extraordinarily dark, full, velvety, slow-maturing wine. Also vg 20-yr-old TAWNY. Vintages: **55' 58 60 63 66' 67 70' 75 78 82** 85' 87 91 94.

Offley Forrester See Forrester.

Oloroso Style of sherry, heavier and less brilliant than FINO when young, but maturing to greater richness and pungency. Naturally dry, but frequently sweetened for sale.

Passing the port

Vintage port is almost as much a ritual as a drink. It always needs to be decanted with great care (since the method of making it leaves a heavy deposit in the bottle). All except very old ports can safely be decanted the day before drinking. A week may not be too long. At table the decanter is traditionally passed from guest to guest clockwise. Vintage port can be immensely long-lived. Particularly good vintages older than those mentioned in the text include 1904 08 11 20 27 34 35 45 50. Bottles over 25 years old usually have very fragile corks. The answer is to cut the bottle neck with red-hot 'port tongs' – a great party trick.

Osborne Enormous Spanish firm with well-known brandies but also good sherries including Fino Quinta, Coquinero dry AMONTILLADO, 10 RF (or Reserva Familiale) Medium OLOROSO. NB: a range of v fine 'Rare' sherries, top quality with numbered bottles. See also Duff Gordon.

Pale Cream Popular style of pale sherry made by sweetening FINO, pioneered by CROFT'S Original.

Palo Cortado A style of sherry close to OLOROSO but with some of the character of an AMONTILLADO. Dry but rich and soft. Worth looking for.

Pasada Style of FINO or MANZANILLA which is close to AMONTILLADO: a stronger drier wine without FLOR character.

Pereira d'Oliveira Vinhos Family-owned MADEIRA co est'd 1850. V good basic range as well as 5 and 10 yr olds; fine old reserve VERDELHO 1890, BUAL 1908 and Malvasia 1895.

Pinhão Small town at the heart of port country, in the upper DOURO.

Poças Junior Family port firm specializing in TAWNIES and COLHEITAS.

Ponche An aromatic digestif made with old sherry and brandy, flavoured with herbs and presented in eye-catching silvered bottles. See Caballero, de Soto.

Puerto de Santa María Second city and former port of the sherry area, with important BODEGAS.

PX Short for Pedro Ximénez, grape part sun-dried: used in JEREZ for sweetening.

Quarles Harris One of the oldest port houses, since 1680, now owned by the Symingtons (see Dow). Small quantities of LBV, mellow and well-balanced. Vintages: **60 63' 66' 70' 75** 77' 80 83 85' 91 94.

Quinta Portuguese for 'estate'. Also traditionally used to denote VINTAGE PORTS which are usually (legislation says 100%) from estate's v'yds, made in good but not exceptional vintages. Now several excellent QUINTAS produce wines from top vintages in their own right, esp VESUVIO, LA ROSA and Passadouro.

Rainwater A fairly light, medium dry blend of MADEIRA – traditional in US.

Ramos-Pinto Dynamic small port house specializing in single-QUINTA TAWNIES of style and elegance; now owned by champagne house Louis Roederer.

Real Companhia Vinícola do Norte de Portugal Aka Royal Oporto Wine Co and Real Companhia Velha; large port house, with a long political history. Many brands and several QUINTAS, incl Quinta dos Carvalhas which makes TAWNIES and COLHEITAS. Vintage wines generally dismal.

Rebello Valente Name used for the VINTAGE PORT of ROBERTSON. Light but elegant and well-balanced, maturing rather early. Vintages: **55' 60 63' 66' 67 70' 72 75 77' 80** 83 85' 94.

SHERRY, PORT & MADEIRA

Robertson Subsidiary of SANDEMAN, shipping (almost only to Holland) REBELLO VALENTE VINTAGE, LBV, Robertson's Privateer Reserve, Game Bird TAWNY, 10-yr-old Pyramid and 20-yr-old Imperial. Vintages: **63' 66' 67 70' 72 75 77' 80** 83 85' 94.

Rosa, Quinta de la Fine single-QUINTA port from the Bergqvist family at PINHAO. Recent return to traditional methods and stone lagares. Look for 85 88 90 91 92 94 vintages.

Rozes Port shippers controlled by Moët-Hennessy. RUBY V popular in France; also TAWNY. Vintages: **63 67 77' 78** 83 85 87 91 94.

Ruby Youngest (and cheapest) port style: simple, sweet and red. The best are vigorous, full of flavour; others can be merely strong and rather thin.

Sanchez Romate Family firm in JEREZ since 1781. Best known in Spanish-speaking world, esp for brandy Cardenal Mendoza. Good sherry: FINO Cristal, OLOROSO Don Antonio, AMONTILLADO NPU ('Non Plus Ultra').

Sandeman A giant of the port trade and a major figure in the sherry one, owned by Seagram. Founder's Reserve is their well-known VINTAGE CHARACTER; TAWNIES are much better. Partners' RUBY is new (94). Vintage wines are at least adequate – some of the old vintages were superlative (**55' 57 58 60' 62' 63' 65 66 67 68 70' 72 75 77 80 82**). Of the sherries, Medium Dry AMONTILLADO is top-seller, Don FINO is vg; also two excellent CREAM SHERRIES: Armada, and rare de luxe Royal Corregidor. Also shippers of MADEIRA since 1790 (elegant RAINWATER, fine Rich).

Sanlúcar de Barrameda Seaside sherry town (see Manzanilla).

Sercial MADEIRA grape for driest of the island's wines – a supreme aperitif. (See panel on the next page.)

Silva Vinhos New Madeira producer (founded '90) with modern lodges at Estreito de Camara de Lobos. Gd basic wines from Tinta Negra Mole grapes.

Smith Woodhouse Port firm founded in 1784, now owned by the Symington family (see Dow). Gould Campbell is a subsidiary. Relatively light and easy wines incl Old Lodge TAWNY, Lodge Reserve VINTAGE CHARACTER (widely sold in USA). Vintages (v fine): **60 63' 66' 70' 75** 77' 80 83 85' 91 92 94. Gould Campbell Vintages: **60 63 66 70 75** 77 80 83 85 91 94.

Solera System used in making both sherry and (in modified form) MADEIRA, also some port. It consists of topping up progressively more mature barrels with slightly younger wine of the same sort, the object being to attain continuity in the final wine. Most sherries when sold are blends of several solera wines.

Soto, José de Best known for inventing PONCHE, this family firm, which now belongs to the former owner of RUMASA, José María Ruiz Mateos, also makes a range of good sherries, esp the delicate FINO.

Tawny Style of port aged for many yrs in wood (VINTAGE PORT is aged in bottle) until tawny in colour. Many of the best are 20 yrs old. Low-price tawnies are blends of red and white ports. Taste the difference.

Taylor, Fladgate & Yeatman (Taylor's) Often considered the best of the port shippers, esp for full rich long-lived VINTAGE wine and TAWNIES of stated age (40-yr-old, 20-yr-old etc). Their VARGELLAS estate is said to give Taylor's its distinctive scent of violets. Vintages: **55' 60' 63' 66' 70' 75** 77' 80 83' 85' 92' 94. QUINTA DE VARGELLAS is shipped unblended in certain (lesser) years (**67 72 74** 76 78 82 84 86 87 88 91). Also now Terra Feita single-QUINTA wine (82 86 87 88 91). Their LBV is also better than most.

Terry, Fernando A de Magnificent BODEGAS at PUERTO DE SANTA MARIA, now part of Allied-Domecq. Makers of Maruja MANZANILLA and a range of popular brandies. The blending and bottling of all HARVEY's sherries is carried out at the vast modern El Pino plant.

Tío Pepe The most famous of FINO sherries (see González Byass).

Valdespino Famous family BODEGA at JEREZ, owner of the Inocente vineyard and making the excellent aged FINO of that name. Tío Diego is its dry AMONTILLADO, Solera 1842 an OLOROSO, Don Tomás its best amontillado. Matador is the name of Valdespino's popular range. In the US, where their sherries rank No 3 in sales volume, they are still sold as 'Hartley & Gibson'.

Vargellas, Quinta de Hub of the TAYLOR's empire, giving its very finest ports. The label for in-between vintages. See Taylor Fladgate & Yeatman.

Since 1993, Madeiras labelled Sercial, Verdelho, Bual or Malmsey must be at least 85% from that grape variety. The majority, made using the chameleon Tinta Negra Mole grape, which easily imitates each of these grape styles, may only be called Seco (Dry), Meio Seco (Medium Dry), Meio Doce (Medium Rich) or Doce (Rich) respectively. Meanwhile replanting is building up supplies of the (rare) classic varieties.

Verdelho MADEIRA grape for fairly dry but soft wine without the piquancy of SERCIAL. A pleasant aperitif and a good all-purpose wine. Some glorious old vintage wines. (See panel on next page.)

Vesuvio, Quinta de Enormous 19th-C FERREIRA estate in the high DOURO. Bought '89 by Symington family. 130 acres planted. Esp 89 90 91 92 94.

Vintage Character Somewhat misleading term used for a good quality, full and meaty port like a premium RUBY. Lacks the splendid 'nose' of VINTAGE PORT.

Vintage Port The best port of exceptional vintages is bottled after only 2 yrs in wood and matures very slowly for up to 20 or more in bottle. Always leaves a heavy deposit and therefore needs decanting.

Warre The oldest of all British port shippers (since 1670), owned by the Symington family (see Dow) since 1905. Fine elegant long-maturing vintage wines, a good TAWNY (Nimrod), VINTAGE CHARACTER (Warrior), and excellent LBV. Single-v'yd Quinta da Cavadinha is a new departure (**78 79** 82 84 86 87 88 89 90 92). Vintages: **55' 58 60 63' 66' 70 75** 77' 80 83 85' 91 94.

White Port Port made of white grapes, golden in colour. Formerly made sweet, now more often dry: a fair aperitif but a heavy one.

Williams & Humbert Famous first-class sherry BODEGA, now owned by the MEDINA group. Dry Sack (medium AMONTILLADO) is its best-seller; Pando an excellent FINO; Canasta CREAM and Walnut BROWN are good in their class; Dos Cortados is its famous dry old OLOROSO. Also the famous Gran Duque de Alba brandy acquired from DIEZ-MERITO.

Wisdom & Warter Not a magic formula for free wine, but an old BODEGA (controlled by GONZALEZ BYASS) with good sherries, especially AMONTILLADO Tizón and v rare SOLERA. Also FINO Olivar.

Switzerland

Heavier shaded areas are the wine growing regions

Switzerland is handicapped by high prices and the fact that her top wines come from tiny estates – hence all are drunk locally. Yet almost all Swiss wines (especially whites) are enjoyable and satisfying – if dear. Switzerland has some of the world's most intensive wine production; costs are high and nothing less is viable. All the most important vineyards (28,000 out of 37,000 acres) are in French-speaking areas: along the south-facing slopes of the upper Rhône Valley (Valais) and Lake Geneva (Vaud). Wines from German- and Italian-speaking zones are mostly drunk locally. Wines are known by place, grape names and legally controlled type names and are usually drunk young. 1988 saw the establishment of a Swiss cantonal and federal appellation system which is still being implemented.

Aargau Wine-growing canton in E Switz (963 acres). Best for fragrant RIES-SYLVANER and rich BLAUBURGUNDER.

Aigle Vaud r w ★★→★★★ Well-known for elegant whites and supple reds.

Aligoté White Burgundy variety doing well in the VALAIS and GENEVA.

Amigne Trad VALAIS white grape, esp of VETROZ. Full-bodied tasty, often sweet.

Ardon Valais r w ★★→★★★ Wine commune between SION and MARTIGNY.

Arvine Old VALAIS white grape (also 'Petite Arvine'): dry and sweet, elegant long-lasting wines with characteristic salty finish. Best in SIERRE, SION.

Auvernier NE r p w ★★→★★★ Old wine village on Lake NEUCHATEL and biggest wine-growing commune of the canton.

Basel Second-largest Swiss town and canton with many vines: divided into Basel-Stadt and Baselland. Best wines: RIES-SYLVANER, BLAUBURGUNDER, CHASSELAS.

Beerliwein Originally wine of destemmed BLAUBURG'R (E). Today name for wine fermented on skins traditionally rather than SUSSDRUCK.

Bern Swiss capital and canton of same name. V'yds in W (BIELERSEE: CHASSELAS, PINOT, SPECIALITIES) and E (Thunersee: BLAUBURGUNDER, RIES-SYLVANER); 632 acres. Prized by Germanic Swiss.

Bex Vaud r w ★★ CHABLAIS appellation, esp for red wines.

Bielersee r p w ★→★★ Wine region on N shore of the Bielersee (dry light CHASSELAS, PINOT N) and at the foot of Jolimont (SPECIALITIES).

Blauburgunder German-Swiss name for PINOT N. (Aka Clevner.)

Bonvillars Vaud r p w ★→★★ Characterful red AC of upper end of L Neuchâtel.

Bündner Herrschaft Grisons r p w ★★→★★★ Best German-Swiss region incl top villages: Fläsch, Jenins, Maienfeld, Malans. Serious BLAUB'R ripens esp well due to warm Föhn wind, cask-aged vg. Also CHARD, SPECIALITIES.

Recent vintages

1996 Similar to 1995: rainy September followed by sunny October led to good quality fruit.

1995 Variable year: humid June, hot dry July, wet September; very sunny harvest led to very good wines.

1994 Summer close to perfect; but rainy harvest.

1993 Classic year: wines better than expected.

Calamin Vaud w ★★→★★★ LAVAUX v'yds next to DEZALEY: lush fragrant whites.

Chablais Vaud r w ★★→★★★ Wine region on right bank of Rhône and upper end of L Geneva, incl VILLAGES: AIGLE, BEX, Ollon, VILLENEUVE, YVORNE. Robust full-bodied reds and whites

Chamoson Valais r w ★★→★★★ Largest VALAIS wine commune, esp for SYLVANER.

Chardonnay Long-est'd in French Switzerland, now also in other parts of the country.

Chasselas (Gutedel) Top white grape of French cantons: neutral in flavour, so takes on local character: elegant (GENEVA), refined and full (VAUD), potent and racy (VALAIS), pleasantly pétillant (lakes Bienne, Neuchâtel, Murtensee). In east only in BASEL.

Completer Native white grape, only used in GRISONS making aromatic generous wines that keep well. ('Complet' was a monk's final daily prayer, or 'nightcap'.)

Cornalin Local VALAIS speciality; dark spicy v strong red. Best: SALGESCH, SIERRE.

Cortaillod Neuchâtel r (w) ★★ Small village S of Lake N: esp PINOT N, OEIL DE P.

Côte, La Vaud r p w ★→★★★ Largest VAUD wine area between Lausanne and Geneva (N shore of Lake). Whites with elegant finesse; fruity harmonious reds. Esp from MONT-SUR-ROLLE, Vinzel, Luins, Féchy, Morges etc.

Côtes de l'Orbe Vaud r p w ★→★★ N VAUD appellation between Lake Neuchâtel and Lake Geneva esp for light fruity reds .

Dézaley Vaud w (r) ★★★ Celebrated LAVAUX v'yd on slopes above L Geneva, once tended by Cistercian monks. Unusually potent CHASSELAS, develops esp after ageing. Red Dézaley is a GAMAY-PINOT N-MERLOT-SYRAH rarity.

Dôle Valais r ★★→★★★ Appellation for PINOT N, can also be blend of PINOT, GAMAY and other varieties (at least 51% PN): full, supple, often vg. Lightly pink Dôle Blanche is pressed immediately after harvest. Eg from MARTIGNY, SIERRE, SION, VETROZ etc.

Epesses Vaud w (r) ★★→★★★ LAVAUX appellation: supple full-bodied whites.

Ermitage Alias the Marsanne grape; a VALAIS SPECIALITY. Concentrated full-bodied dry white, s'times with residual sugar. Esp from FULLY, SION.

Féchy Vaud ★★→★★★ Famous appellation of LA COTE, esp elegant whites.

Federweisser German-Swiss name for white wine from BLAUBURGUNDER.

Fendant Valais w ★→★★★ VALAIS appellation for CHASSELAS. Wide range of wines. Better ones now use village names only (FULLY, SION etc).

Flétri/Mi-flétri Late-harvested grapes from which sweet and slightly sweet wine (respectively) is made; SPECIALITY in VALAIS.

Fribourg Smallest French-Swiss wine canton (279 acres, nr Jura). Esp for CHASSELAS, PINOT N, GAMAY, SPECIALITES from VULLY, L Murten, S Lake Neuchâtel.

Fully Valais r w ★★→★★★ Village nr MARTIGNY: excellent ERMITAGE and GAMAY.

Gamay Red Beaujolais grape; abounds in French cantons but is forbidden in German. Fairly thin wine used mostly for blends. (See Salvagnin, Dôle).

Geneva Capital, and French-Swiss wine canton; the third largest (3,362 acres). Key areas: MANDEMENT, Entre Arve et Rhône, Entre Arve et Lac. Mostly CHASSELAS, GAMAY. Also lately CHARD, Cab, PINOT and good ALIGOTE.

Gewürztraminer Grown in Switzerland as a SPECIALITY variety.

Glacier, Vin du (Gletscherwein) Fabled oxidized wooded white from rare Rèze grape of Val d'Anniviers; offered by the thimbleful to visiting dignitaries.

Goron Valais r ★ AC for pleasant reds and DOLE that fails to make the grade.

Grand Cru Quality designation. Implication differs by canton: in VALAIS, GENEVA and VAUD used where set requirements fulfilled.

Grisons (Graubünden) Mountain canton, mainly in German Switz (BUNDNER HERRSCHAFT, Churer Rheintal; esp BLAUBURGUNDER) and partly S of Alps (Misox, esp MERLOT). 921 acres, primarily for red, also RIES-SYLVANER and SPECIALITIES.

Heida (Païen) Old VALAIS white grape (Jura's Savagnin) for country wine of upper Valais (Visperterminen v'yds 1,000 m+). Successful in lower Valais too.

Humagne Strong native white grape (VALAIS SPECIALITY). Humagne Rouge (unrelated, from Aosta Valley) also. Esp from CHAMOSON, LEYTRON.

Landwein (Vin de pays) Trad light easy white and esp red BLAUB'R from east.

Lausanne Capital of VAUD. No longer with v'yds in town area, but long-time owner of classics: Abbaye de Mont, Château Rochefort (LA COTE); Clos des Moines, Clos des Abbayes, Dom de Burignon (LAVAUX). Pricey.

Lavaux Vaud w (r) ★→★★★ Scenic region on N shore of L Geneva between Montreux and Lausanne. Delicate refined whites, good reds. Best: CALAMIN, Chardonne, DEZALEY, EPESSES, Lutry, ST-SAPHORIN, VEVEY-MONTREUX and Villette.

Leytron Valais r w ★★→★★★ Commune nr SION/MARTIGNY, esp Le Grand Brûlé.

Mandement r w ★→★★ Geneva wine area incl Satigny, the largest wine commune of Switzerland. Wines of local interest only.

Martigny Valais r w ★★ Lower VALAIS commune esp for HUMAGNE ROUGE.

Merlot Grown in Italian Switzerland (TICINO) since 1907 (after phylloxera destroyed local varieties): aromatic, soft. Also used with Cab.

Mont d'Or, Domaine du Valais w s/sw sw ★★→★★★ Well-sited property nr SION: rich concentrated demi-sec and sweet wines, notable SYLVANER.

Mont-sur-Rolle Vaud w (r) ★★ Important appellation within LA COTE.

Morges Vaud r p w ★→★★ Largest LA COTE/VAUD AOC: CHASSELAS, fruity reds.

Neuchâtel City and canton. V'yds (1,530 acres) from L Neuchâtel to BIELERSEE. Mainly CHASSELAS: fragrant lively (sur lie, sp). Also (increasingly) good PINOT N (esp OEIL DE PERDRIX), PINOT GR, CHARD.

Nostrano Word meaning 'ours', applied to red wine of TICINO, made from native and Italian grapes (Bondola, Freisa, Bonarda etc).

For key to grape variety abbreviations, see pages 7–13.

Oeil de Perdrix Pale PINOT rosé. Esp (originally) NEUCHATEL'S; also VALAIS, VAUD.

Pinot Blanc (Weissburgunder) Newly introduced grape variety producing full-bodied elegant wines.

Pinot Gris (Malvoisie) Widely planted white grape for dry and residually sweet wines. Makes v fine late-gathered wines in VALAIS (called Malvoisie).

Pinot Noir (Blauburgunder) Top red grape. Esp: BUNDNER H, NEUCHATEL, VALAIS.

Rauschling Old white ZURICH grape; esp for discreet fruit, elegant acidity.

Riesling (Petit Rhin) Mainly in the VALAIS. Excellent botrytis wines.

Riesling-Sylvaner Swiss for Müller-THURGAU (top white of E; a SPECIALITY in W). Typically elegant wines with nutmeg aroma and some acidity.

St-Gallen E wine canton nr L Constance (540 acres). Esp for BLAUBURG'R (full-bodied), RIES-SYLVANER, SPECIALITIES. Incl Rhine Valley, Oberland, upper L Zürich.

St-Leonard Valais r w ★★→★★★ Wine commune between SIERRE and SION.

St-Saphorin Vaud w (r) ★★→★★★ Famous appellation of LAVAUX producing fine light whites.

Salvagnin Vaud r ★→★★ GAMAY and/or PINOT N appellation. (See also Dôle.)

Schaffhausen German-Swiss canton and wine town on River Rhine. Esp BLAUBURGUNDER; also some RIESLING-SYLVANER and SPECIALITIES.

Schafis Bern r p w ★→★★ Top BIELERSEE village and name for wines of its N shore.

Schenk Europe-wide wine giant, founded and based in Rolle (VAUD). Owns firms in Burgundy, Bordeaux, Germany, Italy, Spain.

Sierre Valais r w ★★→★★★ Sunny resort and famous wine town. Known for Fendant, PINOT N, ERMITAGE, Malvoisie. Vg DOLE.

Sion Valais r w ★★→★★★ Capital/wine centre of VALAIS. Esp Fendant de Sion.

Sylvaner (Johannisberg, Gros Rhin) White grape esp in warm VALAIS v'yds. Heady, spicy: some with residual sweetness.

Spezialitäten (Spécialités/Specialities) Wines of unusual grapes: vanishing local Gwäss, Elbling, Bondola, etc, resurgent Arvine and Amigne, or modish Chenin Bl, Sauv, Cab (first grown experimentally). Eg VALAIS: 43 of its 47 varieties are considered 'specialities'.

Süssdruck Dry rosé/bright red wine: grapes pressed before fermentation.

Thurgau German-Swiss canton beside Bodensee (632 acres). Wines from the valley of Thur: Weinfelden, Seebach, Nussbaum and Rhine. S shore of the Untersee. Esp BLAUBURGUNDER, also good RIES-SYLVANER (ie Müller-Thurgau: Dr Müller was born in the region).

Ticino Italian-speaking S Switzerland (with Misox), growing mainly MERLOT (good from mountainous Sopraceneri region) and SPECIALITIES. Trying out Cab (cask-matured Bordeaux style), Sauv, Sém, Chard, Merlot rosé.

Valais (Wallis) Rhône Valley from German-speaking upper-V to French lower-V. Largest and most varied wine canton in French Switz (13,162 acres). Near-perfect climatic conditions. Wide range: 47 grape varieties including FENDANT, SYLVANER, GAMAY, PINOT N, plus many SPECIALITES. Esp white.

Vaud (Waadt) Region of L Geneva and the Rhône. French Switzerland's 2nd largest wine canton (9,500 acres) incl CHABLAIS, LA COTE, LAVAUX and Bonvillars, Côtes de l'Orbe, VULLY. CHASSELAS stronghold. Also GAMAY, PINOT N etc.

Vétroz Valais w r ★★→★★★ Top village nr SION, esp famous for AMIGNE.

Vevey-Montreux Vaud r w ★★ Up-and-coming appellation of LAVAUX. Famous wine festival held about every 30 years; next in 1999.

Villeneuve Vaud w (r) ★★→★★★ Nr L Geneva: powerful yet refined whites.

Vispertal Valais w (r) ★→★★ Upper VALAIS v'yds esp for SPECIALITIES.

Vully Vaud w (r) ★→★★ Refreshing white from L Murten/FRIBOURG area.

Yvorne Vaud w (r) ★★★ Top CHABLAIS appellation for strong fragrant wines.

Zürich Capital of largest German-speaking wine canton (same name). Mostly BLAUBURGUNDER; also PINOT GRIS, GEWURZ, and esp RIES-SYLVANER and RAUSCHLING.

Austria

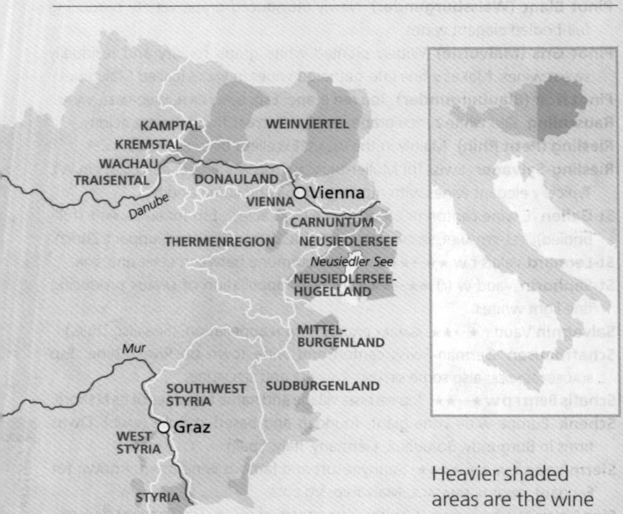

Heavier shaded areas are the wine growing regions

In ten stirring years Austria has emerged as a vigorous, innovative producer of dry white and dessert wines up to the very finest quality. Her red wines (20 percent of vineyards) are starting to make an international reputation too. New laws, passed in 1985 and revised for the 1993 vintage, include curbs on yields (Germany: please copy) and impose higher levels of ripeness for each category than their German counterparts. Many regional names, introduced under the 1985 law, are still unfamiliar outside Austria. This is a country to explore.

Ausbruch PRADIKAT wine (v sweet) between Beerenauslese and Trockenbeerenauslese in quality. Traditionally produced in RUST.

Ausg'steckt ('hung up') HEURIGEN are not open all year. To show potential visitors wine is being served, a green bush is hung up above the door.

Bergwein Legal designation for wines made from grapes grown on slopes with an incline of over 26%.

Blauburger Austrian red grape variety. A cross between BLAUER PORTUGIESER and BLAUFRANKISCH. Dark-coloured but light-bodied; simple wines.

Blauer Burgunder (Pinot Noir) A rarity. Vintages fluctuate greatly. Best in BURGENLAND, KAMPTAL, THERMENREGION (from growers Achs, BRUNDLMAYER, STIEGELMAR UMATHUM and WIENINGER).

Blauer Portugieser Light, fruity wines to drink slightly chilled when young. Mostly made for local consumption. Top producers: Fischer, Lust.

Blauer Wildbacher Red grape used to make SCHILCHER wines.

Blauer Zweigelt BLAUFRANKISCH-ST-LAURENT cross: high yields and rich colour. Top producers (especially Heinrich, Pitnauer, Pöckl, UMATHUM) are making it a reputation.

Blaufränkisch (Lemberger in Germany, Kékfrankos in Hungary) Austria's most widely planted red grape variety, especially in MITTELBURGENLAND: wines with good body, peppery acidity and a fruity taste of cherries. Often blended with CAB S. Best from GESELLMANN, Iby, IGLER, Krutzler, Nittnaus, TRIEBAUMER and WENINGER.

Bouvier Indigenous grape, producing light wines with low acidity but plenty of aroma, esp good for Beeren- and Trockenbeerenauslese.

Bründlmayer, Willi r w sp ★★→★★★★ **90 92 93 94 95** Leading LANGENLOIS-KAMPTAL estate. Vg wines: both local (RIES, GRUNER V) and international (CHARD, red) styles. Also Austria's best Sekt.

Recent vintages

1996 Small crop of variable quality. Generally light and fresh wines for drinking young, but more serious wines from top sites.

1995 Rain threatened to ruin the harvest, but late pickers and dessert winemakers hit the jackpot.

1994 Unusually hot summer and fine autumn resulted in v ripe grapes. An excellent vintage.

1993 Frost damage caused a smaller-than-average yield which produced excellent wines.

1992 Extremely hot summer may have led to acidity problems in some areas. Very good wines from the Wachau, Kamptal-Donauland and Styria. Good red wine year (esp Burgenland).

1990 One of the best vintages of the last 50 yrs.

Burgenland Province and wine area (40,000 acres) in E next to Hungarian border. Warm climate. Ideal conditions, esp for botrytis wines near NEUSIEDLERSEE, also reds. Four wine regions: MITTELBURGENLAND, NEUSIEDLER SEE, NEUSIEDLERSEE-HUGELLAND and SUDBURGENLAND.

Buschenschank The same as HEURIGE; often a country cousin.

Cabernet Sauvignon Increasingly cultivated in Austria; used esp in blends.

Carnuntum r w Wine region since '94, E of Vienna, bordered by the Danube to the north. Best producers: Glatzer, Pitnauer.

Chardonnay Increasingly grown, mainly barrique-aged. Also trad in STYRIA as 'MORILLON' (unoaked): strong fruit taste, lively acidity. Esp BRUNDLMAYER, Loimer, MALAT, POLZ, SATTLER, STIEGELMAR, TEMENT, Topf, Velich, WIENINGER.

Deutschkreutz r (w) MITTELBURGENLAND red wine area, esp for BLAUFRANKISCH.

Donauland (Danube) w (r) Wine region since '94, just W of Vienna. Includes KLOSTERNEUBURG south of Danube and Wagram north of the river. Mainly whites, esp GRUNER VELTLINER. Best producers include: Chorherren Klosterneuburg, Leth, Wimmer-Cerny, R Zimmermann.

Dürnstein w Wine centre of the WACHAU with famous ruined castle. Mainly GRUNER V, RIES. Top growers: FREIE WEINGARTNER WACHAU, KNOLL, PICHLER, Schmidl.

Eisenstadt r w dr sw Capital of BURGENLAND and historic seat of Esterházy family. Major producer: Esterházy.

Falkenstein w Wine centre in the eastern Weinviertel nr Czech border. Good GRUNER VELTLINER. Best producers: Jauk, Luckner, SALOMON-UNDHOF.

Federspiel Medium quality level of the VINEA WACHAU categories, roughly corresponding to Kabinett. Fruity, elegant wines.

Feiler-Artinger r w sw ★★★→★★★★ **90 91 92 93 94 95 96** Outstanding RUST estate. Top AUSBRUCH dessert wines since 93. Also good dry whites and reds.

Freie Weingärtner Wachau w (r) ★★→★★★ **91 92 93 94 95 96** Important and vg growers' cooperative in DURNSTEIN. Excellent GRUNER VELTLINER, RIES.

Gamlitz w Town in southern STYRIA. Growers incl Lackner-Tinnacher, SATTLER.

Gemischter Satz A blend of grapes (mostly white) grown, harvested and vinified together. Traditional wine, still served in HEURIGEN.

Gesellmann, Engelbert r (w) ★★→★★★ **90 92 93 94 95 96** Estate in DEUTSCH-KREUTZ. Vg red and white: both traditional and international styles.

Gols r w dr sw Largest BURGENLAND wine commune (N shore of NEUSIEDLER SEE). Best producers: Beck, HEINRICH, Leitner, Nittnaus, Renner, STIEGELMAR.

Grüner Veltliner Austria's national white grape (over a third of total v'yd area). Fruity, racy, lively young wines. Distinguished age-worthy Spätlesen. Best producers: BRUNDLMAYER, FREIE WEING'R WACHAU, HIRTZBERGER, Högel, KNOLL, MANTLER, Nigl, NIKOLAIHOF, Pfaffl, F X PICHLER, PRAGER, Schmelz, Walzer.

G'spritzer Popular refreshing summer drink, usually white wine-based; made sparkling by adding soda or mineral water. Esp in HEURIGEN.

Gumpoldskirchen w r dr sw Resort village S of Vienna, famous for HEURIGEN. Centre of THERMENREGION. Distinctive, tasty wines from ZIERFANDLER and ROTGIPFLER grapes. Best producers: Biegler, Schellmann.

Heinrich Gernot r w dr sw ★★→★★★ **90 91 92 93 94** 95 **96** Young modern estate in GOLS with Pannobile and (esp) red Gabarinza labels.

Heurige Wine of the most recent harvest, called 'new wine' for one yr, then classified as 'old'. Heurigen are wine houses where growers-cum-patrons serve wine by glass/bottle with simple local food – an institution, esp in VIENNA.

Hirtzberger, Franz w ★★★★ **90 91 92 93 94 95 96** Leading producer with 22 acres at SPITZ AN DER DONAU, WACHAU. Esp RIES and GRUNER VELTLINER.

Horitschon MITTELBURGENLAND region for reds. Best: Anton Iby, WIENINGER.

Igler, Hans r ★★→★★★ **90 92 93 94 95 96** DEUTSCHKREUTZ estate; pioneer reds.

Illmitz w (r) dr sw SEEWINKEL region famous for Beeren- and Trockenbeerenauslese. Best from KRACHER, Haider, Alois and Helmut Lang, Opitz.

Jamek, Josef w ★★ **91 92 93 94 95 96** Well-known estate and restaurant at Joching in the WACHAU. Pioneer of dry whites since the '50s.

Jurtschitsch/Sonnhof w (r) dr (sw) ★→★★★ **92 93 94 95 96** Domaine run by three brothers: vg whites (RIES, GRUNER VELTLINER, CHARD).

Kamptal r w Wine region since '94, along R Kamp N of Wachau. Top v'yds: LANGENLOIS, STRASS, Zöbing. Best growers: BRUNDLMAYER, Dolle, Ehn, Schloss Gobelsburg, Hiedler, Hirsch, JURTSCHITSCH, Loimer, METTERNICH-SANDOR, Topf.

Kattus ★→★★ Producer of traditional Sekt in VIENNA.

Kellergassen Picturesque alleyways lined with wine presses and cellars, devoted exclusively to the production, storage and consumption of wine, situated outside the town, typical of the WEINVIERTEL region.

Klöch w W STYRIA wine town famous for Traminer. Best from Stürgkh.

Kloster Und Winetasting centre in a restored Capuchin monastery nr KREMS, run by ERICH SALOMON.

Klosterneuburg r w Main wine town of DONAULAND. Rich in tradition with a famous Benedictine monastery and a wine college founded in 1860. Best producers: Chorherren Klosterneuburg, Zimmermann.

KMW Abbreviation for 'Klosterneuburger Mostwaage' (must level), the unit used in Austria to measure the sugar content in grape juice.

Knoll, Emmerich w ★★★★ **91 92 93 94 95 96** V traditional, highly regarded estate in Loiben, WACHAU, producing showpiece GRUNER VELTLINER and RIESLING.

Kollwentz-Römerhof w r dr (sw) ★★→★★★ **90 92 93 94 95 96** Innovative wine producer in Grosshöflein nr EISENSTADT: Sauv Bl, Eiswein and reds.

Kracher, Alois w (r) dr (sw) ★★★→★★★★ **81 89 90 92 93 94 95 96** 1st class small ILLMITZ producer; speciality: PRADIKATS (dessert wines), some barrique-aged, others not.

Krems w (r) dr (sw) Ancient town, W of VIENNA. Capital of KREMSTAL. Best from Forstreiter, SALOMON, Weingut Stadt Krems, Walzer.

Kremstal w (r) Wine region since '94 esp for GRUNER V and RIES. Top growers: MALAT, MANTLER, Nigl, SALOMON, Wiegut Stadt Krems.

Langenlois r w ★★→★★★ Wine town and region in KAMPTAL with 5,000 acres. Best producers: BRUNDLMAYER, Ehn, Hiedler, JURTSCHITSCH, Loimer.

Lenz Moser ★★→★★★ Major producer nr KREMS, now in 5th generation. Lenz Moser III invented a high-vine system. Also incl wines from Schlossweingut Malteser Ritterorden (wine estate of the Knights of Malta) in Mailberg, WEINVIERTEL and Klosterkeller Siegendorf in BURGENLAND.

Loiben w In lower, wider part of Danube Valley (WACHAU). Ideal conditions for RIES and GRUNER VELTLINER. Top: Alzinger, FREIE WEINGARTNER, KNOLL, F X PICHLER.

Malat, Gerald w r sp ★★→★★★ **90 91 92 93 94 95 96** Modern producer in Furth, S of KREMS: vg trad and 'international' wines. Good classic sparkling.

Mantler, Josef w ★★→★★★ **86 90 92 93 95 96** Leading trad estate in Gedersdorf nr KREMS. Vg RIES, GRUNER VELTLINER, CHARD, and rare Roter Veltliner (synonym for Malvasia grape, white wine).

Mayer, Franz w With 60 acres, the largest producer in VIENNA. Traditional jug wines (at picturesque HEURIGE Beethovenhaus – yes, he drank here), plus in contrast, excellent 'older-vintage' (20–30 yrs) RIESLING.

Messwein Mass wine: must have ecclesiastical approval and natural must.

Metternich-Sándor, Schlossweingüter w (r) ★→★★ Large wine estate in STRASS; 173 acres of vineyard jointly run with Adelsgütern Starhemberg, Abensberg-Traun and Khevenhüller-Metsch estates.

Mittelburgenland r (w) dr (sw) Wine region on Hungarian border protected by three hill ranges. Makes large quantities of appellation-controlled red (esp BLAUFRANKISCH). Producers: GESELLMANN, Iby, IGLER, WIENINGER.

Mörbisch r w dr sw Region on W shore of NEUSIEDLER SEE. Schindler is good.

Morillon Name given in STYRIA to CHARDONNAY.

Müller-Thurgau See Riesling-Sylvaner.

Muskat-Ottonel Grape for fragrant, often dry whites, interesting PRADIKATS.

Muskateller Rare aromatic grape, popular again. Best from STYRIA and WACHAU. Top growers: Gross, HIRTZBERGER, Lackner-Tinnacher, F X PICHLER, POLZ, SATTLER.

Neuburger Indigenous white grape: nutty flavour; mainly in the WACHAU (elegant, flowery), in the THERMENREGION (mellow, well-developed) and in N BURGENLAND (strong, full). Best from FREIE WEINGARTNER, HIRTZBERGER.

Neusiedler See V shallow (max 1.5m deep) BURGENLAND lake on Hungarian border. Warm temperatures, autumn mists encourage botrytis. Gives name to wine regions of NEUSIEDLERSEE-HUGELLAND and NEUSIEDLERSEE.

Neusiedlersee r w dr sw Region N and E of NEUSIEDLER SEE. Best growers: Beck, HEINRICH, KRACHER, Nittnaus, Opitz, Pöckl, UMATHUM, Velich.

Neusiedlersee-Hügelland r w dr sw Wine region W of NEUSIEDLER SEE based around OGGAU, RUST and MORBISCH on the lake shores, and EISENSTADT in the foothills of the Leitha Mts. Best producers: FEILER-ARTINGER, KOLLWENTZ, Mad, Prieler, Schröck, ERNST TRIEBAUMER, Wenzel.

Niederösterreich (Lower Austria) With 58% of Austria's v'yds: CARNUNTUM, DONAULAND, KAMPTAL, KREMSTAL, THERMENREGION, WACHAU, WEINVIERTEL.

Nigl w **91 92 93 94 95 96** Top grower of KREMSTAL making sophisticated dry RIESLING and GRUNER VELTLINER.

Nikolaihof w ★★★ **90 91 92 93 94 95 96** Famous Mautern building and WACHAU estate: top RIES, GRUNER V.

Nussdorf VIENNA district famous for HEURIGEN and vg Ried Nussberg.

Oggau Wine region on the W shore of NEUSIEDLER SEE.

Pichler, Franz Xavier w ★★★★ **90 91 92 93 94 95 96** Top WACHAU producer with v intense rich RIES, GRUNER VELTLINER (esp Kellerberg) and MUSKATELLER of great breed. Widely recognized as Austria's No 1 grower.

AUSTRIA

Polz, Erich and Walter w ★★★ **91 92 93 94 95 96** S STYRIAN (Weinstrasse) growers: top Hochgrassnitzberg label: Sauv, CHARD.

Prädikatswein Quality graded wines from Spätlese upwards (Spätlese, Auslese, Eiswein, Strohwein, Beerenauslese, AUSBRUCH and Trockenbeerenauslese). In Austria these are invariably dessert wines. See Germany, page 141.

Prager, Franz w ★★★★ **90 91 92 93 94 95 96** Together with JOSEF JAMEK, pioneer of top-quality WACHAU dry white. His son-in-law Anton Bodenstein is now developing new varieties and great PRADIKAT wines.

Renomierte Weingüter Burgenland Wine estates association founded in '95 by 9 top producers in the state of BURGENLAND to promote region's top wines. Members incl KRACHER, TRIEBAUMER, UMATHUM.

Retz r w Important region in W WEINVIERTEL. Esp Weinbauschule Retz.

Ried Single v'yd: when named on the label it is usually a good one.

Riesling On its own always means German RIES. WELSCHRIES (unrelated) is labelled as such. Top growers: BRUNDLMAYER, FREIE W WACHAU, HIRTZBERGER, Högl, KNOLL, NIGL, NIKOLAIHOF, F X PICHLER, PRAGER, SALOMON-UNDOF.

Riesling-Sylvaner Name used for Müller-T, which accounts for about 10% of Austria's grapes. Best producers: HIRTZBERGER, JURTSCHITSCH.

Rotgipfler Fragrant indigenous grape of THERMENREGION. With ZIERFANDLER makes lively, interesting wine. Esp Biegler, Schellmann, Stadelmann.

Rust w r dr sw BURGENLAND region, famous since 17th C for super-sweet AUSBRUCH; now also for red and dry white. Esp from FEILER-ARTINGER, Schandl, Heidi Schröck, ERNST TRIEBAUMER, Paul Triebaumer, Wenzel. The Cercle Ruster Ausbruch is a group of a dozen producers set on reestablishing the preeminence of their powerful Sauternes-like dessert wines, from a wide range of grapes. Standards are already very high.

St-Laurent Traditional red wine grape, potentially vg, with cherry aroma, believed to be related to Pinot N. Esp from Fischer, Mad, STIEGELMAR, UMATHUM.

Salomon-Undhof w ★★★ Vg producer of RIES, WEISSBURGUNDER, Traminer in KREMS. Erich Salomon also owns/runs KLOSTER UND winetasting centre.

Sattler, Willi w ★★→★★★ **90 92 93 94 95 96** Top S STYRIA grower. Esp for Sauvignon, MORILLON.

Schilcher Rosé wine from indigenous BLAUER WILDBACHER grapes (sharp, dry: high acidity). Speciality of W STYRIA. Vg: Klug, Lukas, Reiterer, Strohmeier.

Schlumberger Largest sparkling winemaker in Austria (VIENNA); wine is bottle-fermented by unique 'Méthode Schlumberger'. Delicate fruity.

Seewinkel ('Lake corner'.) Name given to the southern part of NEUSIEDLERSEE incl Apetlon, ILLMITZ and Podersdorf. Ideal conditions for botrytis.

Servus w BURGENLAND everyday light and mild white wine brand.

Smaragd Highest-quality category of VINEA WACHAU, similar to dry Spätlese.

Spätrot-Rotgipfler Typical THERMENREGION (Spätrot and ROTGIPFLER) wine.

Spitz an der Donau w W WACHAU region: vg individual microclimate: esp from Singerriedel v'yd. Top growers are: HIRTZBERGER, FREIE WEINGARTEN, Högl, Lagler.

Steinfeder VINEA WACHAU quality category for very light fragrant dry wines.

Stiegelmar, Georg w r dr sw ★→★★★ **90 91 92 93 94 95 96** GOLS grower: consistent for CHARD, Sauv Bl, red wine and unusual specialities.

Strass w (r) Wine centre in the KAMPTAL region for good Qualität white wines. Best producers: Dolle, METTERNICH-SANDOR, Topf.

Styria (Steiermark) The southernmost wine region of Austria bordering Slovenia. Its Qualitätswein are gaining real prestige. Incl SUDSTEIERMARK, SUD-OSTSTEIERMARK and WESTSTEIERMARK (S, SW and W Styria).

To decipher codes, please refer to 'Key to symbols' on front flap of jacket, or to 'How to use this book' on page 6.

Süd-Oststeiermark (SW Styria) w (r) STYRIAN region with islands of v'yds. Best producers: Neumeister, Winkler-Hermaden.

Südburgenland r w Small S BURGENLAND wine region: good red wines. Best producers: Krutzler, Wachter, Wiesler.

Südsteiermark (S Styria) w Best wine region of STYRIA: makes v popular whites (MORILLON, MUSKATELLER, WELSCHRIESLING and Sauv Bl). Top producers: Gross, Lackner-Tinnacher, Muster, POLZ, SATTLER, TEMENT, Wohlmuth.

Tement, Manfred w ★★★→★★★★ **90 92 93 94 95 96** Vg and renowned estate on S STYRIA Weinstrasse for beautifully made traditional ('Steirisch Klassik') and international whites.

Thermenregion r w dr sw Wine/hot-springs region, S of VIENNA. Indigenous grapes (eg ZIERFANDLER, ROTGIPFLER) and gd reds. Main centres: Baden, GUMPOLDSKIRCHEN Tattendorf, Traiskirchen. Top producers: Alphart, Biegler, Fischer, Reinisch, Schafler, Schellmann, Stadelmann.

Traditionsweingüter Association of wine estates in KAMPTAL and KREMSTAL, committed to qualty and v'yd classification. Members include BRUNDLMAYER, Loimer, G MALAT, Nigl, SALOMON-UNDHOF.

Traisental New region: 1,750 acres just south of Krems on Danube. Mostly dry whites in style similar to WACHAU. Top producer: Neumayer.

Triebaumer, Ernst r (w) dr sw ★★★ **90 91 92 93 94 95 96** One of the best red wine producers in Austria (RUST). Top wines: BLAUFRANKISCH (top label: Mariental) and CAB-Merlot.

Umathum, Josef w r dr sw ★★→★★★ **90 91 92 94 95 96** Distinguished NEUSIEDLERSEE producer for vg reds; whites also from BLAUER BURGUNDER grapes.

Velich w sw BURGENLAND The brothers Velich make burgundian-style 'Tiglat' CHARDONNAY and since '95 some of top PRADIKATS in the SEEWINKEL.

Vienna w (r) ('Wien' in German and on labels.) The Austrian capital is a wine region in its own right (1,500 v'yd acres in suburbs). Simple lively increasingly well-made wines, served in HEURIGEN: esp Bernretter, MAYER, Schilling, WIENINGER.

Vinea Wachau WACHAU appellation started by winemakers in '83 with three categories of dry wine: STEINFEDER, FEDERSPIEL and SMARAGD.

Wachau w Danube wine region W of KREMS: some of Austria's best wines, incl RIES, GRUNER V. Top producers: Alzinger, FREIE WEINGARTNER, HIRTZBERGER, Högl, JAMEK, KNOLL, NIKOLAIHOF, F X PICHLER, PRAGER.

Wagram r w Large wine region with loess terraces in DONAULAND. Best producers: Leth, Wimmer-Cerny.

Weinviertel 'Wine Quarter' w (r) Largest Austrian wine region, between the Danube and the Czech border. Mostly light refreshing whites esp from Falkenstein, Poysdorf, RETZ. Best producers: Hardegg, Jauk, Luckner, Lust, Malteser Ritterorden, Pfaffl, Taubenschuss, Zull.

Weissburgunder (Pinot Bl) Ubiquitous: good dry wines and PRADIKATS. Esp Beck, Fischer, Gross, HEINRICH, HIRTZBERGER, Jement, POLZ, TEMENT.

Welschriesling White grape, not related to RIESLING, grown in all wine regions: light, fragrant, young-drinking dry wines and good PRADIKATS.

Weststeiermark (West Styria) p Small Austrian wine region specializing in SCHILCHER. Esp from Klug, Lukas, Reiterer, Strohmeier.

Wien See Vienna.

Wieninger, Fritz w r ★★→★★★ **90 91 92 93 94 95 96** Vg VIENNA-Stammersdorf grower: HEURIGE, CHARD, BLAUER BURGUNDER reds and esp good GRUNER VELTLINER and RIES.

Winzer Krems Wine growers' cooperative in KREMS: dependable solid whites.

Zierfandler (Spätrot) White grape variety grown almost exclusively in the THERMENREGION. With the ROTGIPFLER produces robust lively wines which age well. Best producers: Biegler, Schellmann, Stadlmann.

AUSTRIA

Central & Southeast Europe

Heavier shaded areas are the wine growing regions

To say that parts of the region covered by this map are somewhat provisional these days is an understatement. But new regional autonomies and new statehoods are closely followed by higher aspirations in winemaking and new international interest and/or investment.

In several much-publicized cases this takes the form of international 'flying winemakers' pitching their tents at vintage-time, usually to make wines acceptable to Western supermarkets from predictable grape varieties. But the change of style this brings has its effect on indigenous winemaking, too; often with happy results, making fresher and fruiter wines of intriguingly different flavours.

So far, Hungary and Bulgaria, and perhaps Moldova, as well as Czechoslovakia, have taken the lead in what has become an area to follow with fascination. The potential of other ex-Communist states is still on hold.

In this section, references are arranged country by country, each shown on the map on this page. Labelling in all the countries involved, except Greece and Cyprus, is broadly based on the international pattern of place name and grape variety. Main grape varieties are therefore included alongside areas, producers and other terms in the alphabetical listings.

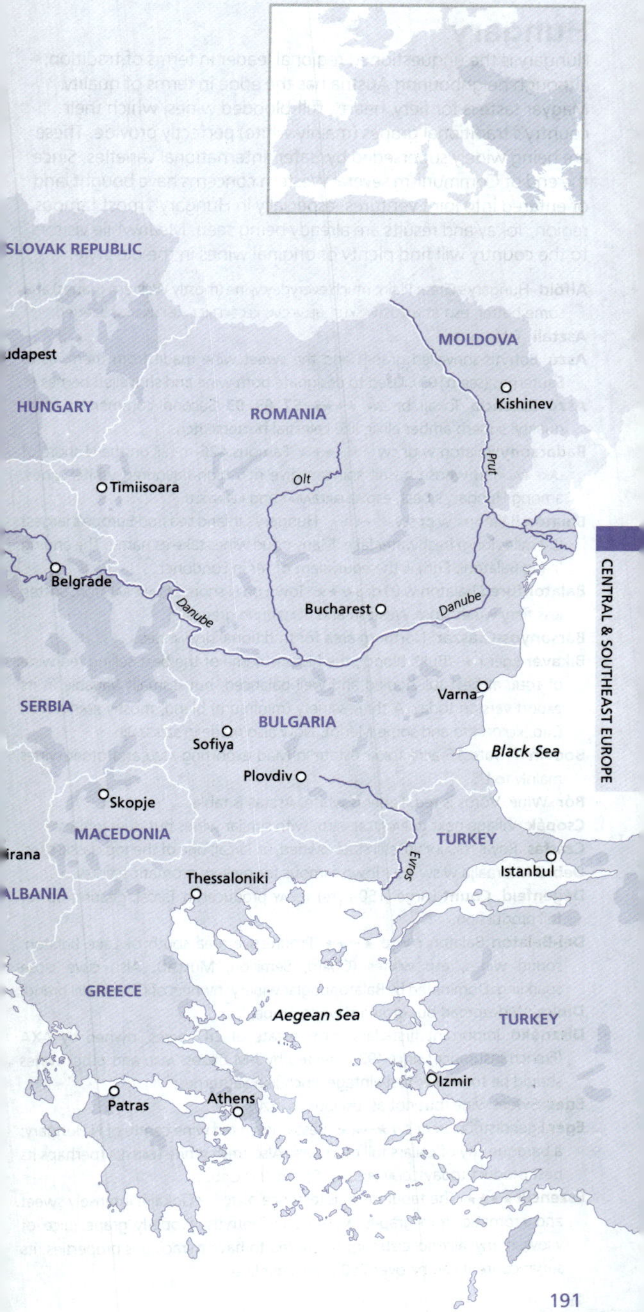
SLOVAK REPUBLIC
udapest
HUNGARY
ROMANIA
MOLDOVA
Kishinev
Prut
Olt
Timiisoara
Belgrade
Danube
Bucharest
Danube
Varna
SERBIA
BULGARIA
Sofiya
Black Sea
Plovdiv
Skopje
MACEDONIA
TURKEY
irana
Evros
Istanbul
Thessaloniki
ALBANIA
GREECE
Aegean Sea
TURKEY
Izmir
Patras
Athens

Hungary

Hungary is the unquestioned regional leader in terms of tradition, although neighbouring Austria has the edge in terms of quality. Magyar taste is for fiery, hearty, full-blooded wines, which their country's traditional grapes (mainly white) perfectly provide. These are being widely superseded by 'safer' international varieties. Since the end of Communism several Western concerns have bought land or entered into joint ventures, especially in Hungary's most famous region, Tokay and results are already being seen. Meanwhile visitors to the country will find plenty of original wines in the old style.

Alföld Hungary's Great Plain: much everyday wine (mostly Western grapes) and some better, esp at HAJOS-VASKUT, HELVECIA, KECSKEMET, KISKUNSAG, Szeged.

Asztali Table wine.

Aszú Botrytis-shrivelled grapes and the sweet wine made from them, as in Sauternes (see p100). Used to designate both wine and shrivelled berries.

Aszú Eszencia Tokaji br sw ★★★★ **57 63 93** Second commercial TOKAY quality: superb amber elixir, like celestial butterscotch.

Badacsony Balaton w dr sw ★★→★★★ Famous 426-m hill on the N shore of LAKE BALATON whose basalt soil can give rich high-flavoured white wines, among Hungary's best, esp SZURKEBARAT and KEKNYELU.

Balaton Balaton r w dr sw ★→★★★ Hungary's inland sea and Europe's largest (50 miles long) freshwater lake. Many good wines take its name. The ending 'i' (eg Balatoni, Egri) is the equivalent of -er in Londoner.

Balatonfüred Balaton w (r) dr sw ★★ Town on N shore of LAKE BALATON. Softer, less fiery wines from Western and OLASRIZLING grapes.

Bársonyos-Csàszàr Northern area for traditional dry whites.

Bikavér Eger r ★ 'Bull's Blood', the historic name of the best-selling red wine of EGER: at best full-bodied and well-balanced, but dismally variable in its export version today. A three-variety (minimum) blend, mostly KEKFRANKOS, Cab, KEKOPORTO and some Merlot. Now also made in SZEKSZARD.

Bodvin Private 16-acre TOKAY estate in Mád exporting ASZU and other wines mainly to US.

Bór Wine. Vörös is red, Fehér is white, Asztali is table.

Csopák Village next to BALATONFURED, with similar wines but drier whites.

Czárfás Royal TOKAJI v'yd, still state-owned, at Tarcal; one of the top classic sites.

Debrö Mátraalja w sw ★★ Town famous for mellow aromatic HARSLEVELU.

Dégenfeld, Count Large (150-acre) TOKAY producer in Tarcal, gearing up for full production.

Dél-Balaton Balaton r w p ★→★★ Progressive area south of Lake Balaton: sound wines, esp whites (Chard, Sémillon, Muscat). Also cuve close sparkling. Dominated by Balatonboglár winery: owners of Chapel Hill brand.

Dinka Widespread but ordinary white grape.

Disznókö Important first-class TOKAY estate of 247 acres, owned by AXA (French insurance) since '92, directed by J-M Cazes. ASZU and other wines should be top-class; first vintage v rich like Sauternes.

Edes Sweet wine (but not as luscious as ASZU).

Eger Eger district r w dr sw ★→★★ Best-known red wine centre of N Hungary; a baroque city of cellars full of BIKAVER. Also fresh white LEANYKA (perhaps its best product today), OLASZRIZLING, Chard and Cab.

Eszencia ★★★★ The fabulous quintessence of TOKAY (Tokaji): intensely sweet and aromatic from grapes wizened by botrytis. Properly grape juice of v low, if any, alcoholic strength, reputed to have miraculous properties: its sugar content can be over 750 grams per litre.

Etyek Nr Budapest. Source of modern standard wines, esp Chard, Sauv Bl.

Ezerjó ('Thousand blessings') Widespread variety but at MOR makes one of Hungary's best dry white wines; potentially distinguished, fragrant and fine.

Felsöbabad Regional cellar S of Budapest with authentic (but in Hungary unauthorized) fragrant Pinot N.

François President French founded (1882) sparkling wine producer at Budafok, nr Budapest. Vintage wine: President.

Furmint The classic grape of TOKAY (Tokaji), with great flavour and fire, also grown for table wine at LAKE BALATON and in SOMLO.

Hajós Alföld r ★ Village in S Hungary known for good lively Cab S wines of medium body and ageing potential.

Hárslevelü 'Linden-leaved' grape used at DEBRO and as second main grape of TOKAY (cf Sém/Sauv in Sauternes). Gentle mellow wine: aromatic and full.

Helvécia (Kecskemét) Historic ALFOLD cellars. V'yds ungrafted: phylloxera bugs cannot negotiate sandy soil. Whites and rosés modernist; reds traditional.

Hétszölö Noble first-growth 116-acre estate at TOKAJI bought by Grands Millésimes de France and Suntory. Second label: Dessewffy.

Hungarovin Traders/producers with huge cellars at Budafok nr Budapest: mainly 'Western varietals', also cuve close, transfer and classic sparkling. Now owned by German Sekt specialist, Henkell.

Izsák Major sparkling wine producer; the majority by cuve close.

Kadarka Red grape for vast quantities of everyday wine in S, but can produce ample flavour and interesting maturity (eg esp at SZEKSZARD and VILLANY).

Kecskemét Major town of the ALFOLD. Much everyday wine, some better.

Kékfrankos Hungarian for Blaufränkisch; reputedly related to Gamay. Good light or full-bodied reds, esp at SOPRON. Used in BIKAVER at EGER.

Kéknyelü ('Blue stalk') High-flavoured, low-yielding white grape making the best and 'stiffest' wine of MT BADACSONY. It should be fiery and spicy stuff.

Kékoporto 'Kék' means blue, so this grape could be the German Portugieser. Makes concentrated oakable red; esp from VILLANY, s'times in BIKAVER.

Kisburgundi Kék German Spätburgunder: Pinot Noir.

Kiskunság Largest region in Great Plain. Gd KADARKA esp from Kiskunhalas.

Különleges Minöség Special quality: highest official grading.

Lauder-Lang Partnership of famous international Hungarians to make TOKAY at Mád. Also v'yds at EGER and the famous Gundel's restaurant in Budapest.

Leányka or Király ('Little girl') Old Hungarian white grape also grown in Transylvania. Makes admirable aromatic faintly Muscat dry wine in many areas. Király ('Royal') Leányka is supposedly superior.

Mátraalja w (r) ★★ Wine district in the foothills of the Mátra range in N Hungary, around town of Gyöngyös (site of huge modernised winery) incl DEBRO, NAGYREDE. Promising dry white SZURKEBARAT, Chardonnay, MUSKOTALY and Sauvignon Blanc wines. Recent French and Australian investment.

Mecsekalja S Hungary district, known for good whites of PECS esp sparkling.

Médoc Noir The Merlot grape.

Megyer, Château Joint venture estate between TOKAY TRADING HOUSE and French investors Saros-Patak. See also Ch Pajzos.

Meézesfehér Widely planted 'white honey' grape; sweet, soft wine esp from EGER and MATRAALJIA.

Minöségi Bor Quality wine. Hungary's appellation contrôlée.

Mór N Hungary w ★★→★★★ Region long-famous for fresh dry EZERJO. Now also Riesling and Sauvignon. Wines now mostly exported.

Muskotály The yellow Muscat. Makes light, though long-lived, wine in Tokaji and EGER. A little goes into the TOKAY blend (cf Muscadelle in Sauternes). V occasionally makes an ASZU wine solo.

HUNGARY

Nagyburgundi Literally 'great burgundy': indigenous grape, not Pinot N as sometimes thought. Sound solid wine esp around VILLANY and SZEKSZARD.

Olaszrizling Hungarian name for the Italian Riesling or Welschriesling.

Oportó Red grape increasingly used for soft jammy wines to drink young.

Oremus Ancient TOKAJI v'yd of founding Rakóczi family at Sárospatak, being reconstituted by owners of Spain's Vega Sicilia.

Pajzos, Château TOKAY estate and part of TOKAY TRADING HOUSE/Sárospatak joint venture. See also Ch Megyer.

Pécs Mecsek w (r) ★→★★ Major southern wine city. Esp for sparkling wines OLASZRIZLING and Pinot Bl etc.

Pezsgö Sparkling wine, made mostly by the transfer method, can often be very palatable.

Pinot Noir Normally means NAGYBURGUNDI. But see Felsöbabad.

Puttonyos Measure of sweetnes in TOKAJI ASZU. A 'putt' is a 20–25 kilo measure, traditionally a hod of Aszù grapes. The number of 'putts' per barrel (136 litres) of dry base wine determines the final richness of the wine, from 3 putts to 7. 3 is equal to 60 grams of sugar per litre, 4: 90, 5: 120, 6: 150. ASZU ESZENCIA must have 180. See Eszencia for the really sticky stuff.

Royal Tokaji Wine Co Early Anglo-Danish-Hungarian joint venture at Mád (TOKAJI). 150 acres, mainly first or second growth. First wine (90) a revelation: 91 and (esp) 93 are making waves.

Siklós Southern district, with mainly small producers, known for its white wines: esp HARSLEVELU, also Chard, TRAMINI, OLASZRIZLING.

Somléo N Hungary w ★★ Isolated small v'yd district N of BALATON: white wines (formerly of high repute) from FURMINT and ancient Juhfark grapes.

Sopron W Hungary r ★★ Historic enclave S of Neusiedlersee (see Austria): light KEKFRANKOS, Austrian-style sweet wines, but now mostly for Cab etc.

Szamorodni Word meaning 'as it comes'; used to describe TOKAY without the addition of ASZU grapes. Can be dry or (fairly) sweet, depending upon proportion of Aszú grapes naturally present. Sold as an aperitif.

Száraz Dry, esp of TOKAJI SZAMARODNI.

Szekszárd r ★★ District in south-central part of Hungary; some of country's top reds from Cab and Merlot. Also KADARKA red wine which needs age (say 3–4 yrs); can also be botrytised ('Nemes Kadar'). Good organic wines, BIKAVER and good Chard and OLASZRIZLING too.

Szepsy Istvan Family TOKAY estate in Mád and Tarcal with highest standards: wines v rare. The Szepsy family 'invented' Tokay in 1630.

Szürkebarát Literally means 'grey friar': Pinot Gr, which makes rich (not necessarily sweet) wine in the BADACSONY v'yds and elsewhere.

Tokay (Tokaji) Tokaji w dr sw ★★→★★★★ The ASZU is Hungary's famous liquorous sweet wine (since circa 1660), comparable to a highly aromatic and delicate Sauternes, from hills in the NE close to the Russian (Belarus) border. The appellation covers 13,500 acres. See Aszú, Eszencia, Furmint, Puttonyos, Szamorodni. Also dry table wine of character.

Tokay Trading House The state-owned TOKAY co, with 180 acres of the magnificent Czárfás v'yd. Sales 60% in Hungary.

Tramini Gewürztraminer, esp in SIKLOS.

Villány r p (w) ★★ Southernmost town of Hungary and well-known centre of red wine production. Villányi Burgundi: largely KEKFRANKOS can be good. Cabs S and F and Pinot N are v promising. See also Nagyburgundi.

Villány-Siklós Wine region named after the two towns.

Zweigelt Indigenous (S) red grape: deep-coloured spicy flavoursome wine.

Bulgaria

Since 1978 Bulgaria has come from nowhere to be the world's sixth-largest exporter of bottled wines, trading up to 85 percent of production. Enormous new vineyards and wineries have overwhelmed an old, if embattled, wine tradition. The formerly state-run and state-subsidized wineries learned almost everything from the New World and offer Cabernet, Chardonnay and other varieties at bargain prices. Controlled appellation ('Controliran') wines, introduced in 1985, have been joined by oak-flavoured 'Reserve' bottlings, simpler wines of Declared Geographical Origin and Country Wines. Bulgaria's main wine regions are the northern Danube Valley, the eastern Black Sea region, southwest Struma Valley, southern Maritsa River and Stara Planina.

The recent drop in sales to Russia has led to a new emphasis on quality, somewhat higher prices and a ban on planting outside the 27 Controliran regions. There are 320,000 acres of vines in all.

In 1990 the organizing monopoly, Vinprom, was disbanded to give wineries autonomy (30 at first; then increasingly more, along with privatization). A brisk air of competition provokes even greater efforts.

Assenovgrad Main MAVRUD-producing cellar on the outskirts of PLOVDIV – stainless steel being introduced. Mavrud and CAB can last well.

Boyar, Domaine Bulgaria's first independent wine merchant for almost 50 yrs: based in Sofia, set up '91, now marketing in the UK.

Burgas Black Sea resort and source of rosé (the speciality), easy whites (incl a MUSCAT blend) and increasingly reds too.

Cabernet Sauvignon Highly successful (with four times California's acreage). Dark vigorous fruity wine, v drinkable young; top qualities good with age.

Chardonnay Rather less successful (than CABERNET). Many wines appear to be blends with less exalted varieties. V dry but full-flavoured wine, can improve with a yr in bottle. Some recent oaky examples are promising.

Controliran Top-quality wines (single grape variety) of AC-style status. The system was begun in '78: 27 regions were est'd by late '80s.

Country Wines Regional wines (cf French Vins de Pays), often 2-variety blends.

Damianitza MELNIK winery with good Stambolovo MERLOT and Melnik CAB.

Danube Cool northern region, mostly for reds: incl SUHINDOL and SVISHTOV.

Dimiat The common native white grape, grown in the E towards the coast. Agreeable dry white without memorable character.

Euxinograd (Château) Ageing cellar on the coast, in a once-royal palace.

Gamza Good red grape, the Kadarka of Hungary. Aged wines, esp from LOVICO SUHINDOL, can be delicious.

Harsovo Southwest region, esp for MELNIK.

Haskovo S region, principal source of MERLOT for export. Incl ASSENOVGRAD, ORIACHOVITSA, PLOVDIV, STAMBOLOVO, SLIVEN and other areas.

Iskra Sparkling wine, normally sweet but fair quality. Red, white or rosé.

Kadarka Widespread (Albanian) red grape; spicy in good yrs (see Hungary).

Karlovo Town famous for its 'Valley of Roses' and MUSCAT.

Khan Krum Company near VARNA: modern whites, esp oaked CHARD, lighter Chard and SAUV.

Korten Subregion of SLIVEN. Korten CAB is more tannic than most.

Lovico Suhindol Neighbour of PAVLIKENI, site of Bulgaria's first coop (1909). Good GAMZA (CONTROLIRAN), CAB, MERLOT, PAMID, blends. First to declare independence after collapse of state monopoly ('90). Privatized '92. Now B's most important winery/coop, giving guidance to contributing v'yds.

Mavrud Grape variety and darkly plummy red from S Bulgaria, esp ASSENOVGRAD. Can mature 20 yrs. Considered the country's best.

Melnik City of SW and highly prized grape. Dense red; locals say it can be carried in a handkerchief. Needs at least 5 yrs; lasts 15. Also ripe age-worthy CAB.

Merlot Soft red grape variety grown mainly in HASKOVO in the south.

Misket Indigenous Bulgarian grape: mildly aromatic wines; white and red Misket often used to fatten up white blends.

Muscat Ottonel Normal Muscat grape, grown in E for mid-sweet fruity white.

Novi Pazar Controlled appellation CHARD winery nr VARNA with finer wines.

Novo Selo Controliran red GAMZA from the north.

Oriachovitza Major S area for Controliran CAB-MERLOT. Rich savoury red best at 4–5 yrs. Recent RESERVE Cab releases have been good.

Pamid The light soft everyday red of the southwest and northwest.

Pavlikeni Northern wine town with a prestigious estate specializing in GAMZA and CAB of high quality. Also light COUNTRY WINE MERLOT and Gamza blend.

Peruschitza PLOVDIV'S winery, nr ASSENOVGRAD, esp for reds.

Petrich Warm SW area for soft fragrant MELNIK, also blended with CAB.

Pleven N cellar for PAMID, GAMZA, CAB. Also Bulgaria's wine research station.

Plovdiv Southern HASKOVO wine town and region, source of good CAB and MAVRUD. Winemaking mostly at ASSENOVGRAD.

Preslav Bulgaria's largest white wine cellar, in NE region. Esp for SAUV BL and RESERVE CHARD. Also makes rather good brandy.

Provadya Another centre for good white wines, esp dry CHARD.

Reserve Used on labels of selected and oak-aged wines. Usually with 2–4 yrs in oak vats (often American); may or may not be CONTROLIRAN.

Riesling In Bulgaria normally refers to Italian Riesling (Welschriesling). Some Rhine Riesling is grown: now made into Germanic-style white.

Rkatziteli One of Russia's favourite white grapes for strong sweet wine. Produces bulk dry or medium whites in NE Bulgaria.

Russe NE wine town on Danube. Fresh high-tech whites: Welschries-MISKET, med-dry Welschries, CHARD, MUSCAT, gd Aligoté. Also reds, esp YANTRA V CAB.

Sakar SE wine area for CONTROLIRAN MERLOT, some of Bulgaria's best.

Sauvignon Blanc Grown in E Bulgaria, recently released for export.

Schumen Eastern region, especially for whites.

Sliven Big producing S region, esp for CAB. Also MERLOT and Pinot N (Merlot is blended with Pinot in a COUNTRY WINE), Silvaner, MISKET and CHARD.

Sofia The country's capital with large pace-setting winery, but no v'yds.

Sonnenkuste Brand of medium-sweet white sold in Germany.

Stambolovo Wine area esp for CONTROLIRAN MERLOT from HASKOVO.

Stara Planina Balkan mountain region of central Bulgaria, incl KARLOVO.

Stara Zagora S region of ORIACHOVITSA: CAB and MERLOT to RESERVE quality.

Suhindol N Red CONTROLIRAN from between DANUBE and Balkan Mountains.

Sungarlare E town giving its name to a dry CONTROLIRAN MISKET; also CHARD.

Svishtov CONTROLIRAN CAB-producing winery by the Danube in the north. A front-runner in Bulgaria's controlled appellation wines.

Tamianka Sweet white wine of eponymous aromatic grape. (Aka Tamiîoasa.)

Targovishte Independent cellar nr SCHUMEN. Esp medium and sweet whites.

Tirnovo Strong sweet dessert red wine.

Varna Major coastal (Black Sea) appellation for CHARD (buttery or unoaked, Ch Euxinograd promising), SAUV. Also Aligoté, Ugni Bl (s'times blended).

Yantra Valley DANUBE region, CONTROLIRAN for CABERNET SAUVIGNON since '87.

For key to grape variety abbreviations, see pages 7–13.

The Former Yugoslav States

Before its disintegration in 1991 Yugoslavia was well-established as a supplier of wines of international calibre, if not generally of exciting quality. Now all newly formed states are again working on export. Current political disarray and competition from other East European countries makes commercial contacts difficult (except in Slovenia, whose 'Riesling' was the pioneer export, since followed by Cabernet, Pinot Blanc, Traminer and others). All regions, except the central Bosnian highlands, make wine, almost entirely in giant cooperatives, although many small private producers are emerging with the '90s. The Dalmatian (Croatian) coast and Macedonia have good indigenous wines whose roots go deep into the ancient world.

Slovenia

Barbara Vg sparkling from Janez Istenic and family.

Bela Krajina SAVA area, esp 'Ledeno LASKI RIZLING' (late-harvest frozen grapes).

Beli Pinot The Pinot Bl, a popular grape variety. Belo is white.

Bizeljsko-Sremic In SAVA district. Full-flavoured local variety reds and LASKI R.

Brda Slovene upper part of Collio DOC (Italy). Many estates on both sides.

Crno vino Red (literally 'black') wine.

Curin-Prapotnik Pioneer Slovenian white wine trader.

Cvicek Traditional pale red or dark rosé of the SAVA VALLEY. ('Schilcher' in Austria.)

Dolenjska SAVA region: CVICEK, LASKI RIZLING and Modra Frankinja (dry red).

Drava Valley (Podravski) Slovene wine region. Mainly whites from aromatic (WELSCHRIES, Muscat Ottonel) to flamboyant (RIES and SAUV); also Eisweins and Beerenauslesen as in neighbouring Austria.

Drustvo Vinogradnikov BRDA assoc of 45 growers/winemakers (with SAVA, DRAVA and Morava equivalents).

Gorna Radgona Winery for sparkling, late-harvest sweet and Eiswein. Many grape varieties used, mostly in blends.

Grasevina Slovenian for Italian RIES. The normal 'Riesling' of the region.

Hlupic Jurij Producer of fine whites from around Haloze.

Jeruzalem Slovenia's most famous v'yd, at LJUTOMER. Its best wines are late-picked RAJNSKI RIZLING and LASKI RIZLING. Also makes tank fermented sparklers.

Kakovostno Vino Quality wine (one step down from VRHUNSKO).

Kontrolirano poreklo Appellation. Wine must be 80% from that region.

Koper Hottest area of LITTORAL between Trieste and Piran. Full rich MERLOTS.

Kmetijska Zadruga Wine farmers' cooperative.

Kraski Means grown on the coastal limestone or Karst. A region famous for REFOSCO wines eg Kraski Teran and oak-aged Teranton.

Laski Rizling Yet another name for Italian RIES. Best-known Slovene wine, not best quality. Top export brand: 'Cloburg' from Podravski (DRAVA) region.

Littoral (Primorski) Coastal region bordering Italy (Collio) and the Med. Esp good reds: Cab, Merlot (aged in Slovene oak), Barbera and REFOSCO.

Ljutomer (or Lutomer)-Ormoz Slovenia's best-known, probably best white wine district, in NE (DRAVA); esp LASKI RIZLING, at its best rich and satisfying. Ormoz winery also has sparkling and late-harvest wines.

Malvazija Ancient Greek white grape for luscious (now also lively fresh) wine.

Maribor Important centre in NE (DRAVA). White wines, mainly from VINAG, incl LASKI RIZLING, RIES, SAUV, Pinot Bl and Traminer.

Merlot Reasonable in Slovenia. Comparable with neighbouring NE Italian.

Metlika BELA KRAJINA wine centre with warm Kolpa River v'yds.

Namizno Vino Table wine.

Pozna Trgatev Late harvest.

Ptuj Historic wine town with trad-based coop: wines clean, mostly white.

Radgona-Kapela DRAVA district next to Austrian border, esp late-harvest wines, eg RADGONSKA RANINA, also classic method sparkling.

Radgonska Ranina Ranina is Austria's Bouvier grape. Radgonska is nr MARIBOR. The wine is sweet. Trade name is Tigrovo Mljeko (Tiger's Milk).

Refosk Vg Italian red ('Refosco') grape in E and in ISTRIA (Croatia) as TERAN.

Renski Rizling Rhine RIES: rare here, but a little in LJUTOMER-ORMOZ.

Riesling Formerly meant Italian Ries. Now legally limited to real Rhine Riesling.

Sauvignon Blanc Vg with the resources to make it well; otherwise horrid.

Sava Valley Central Slovenia: light dry reds, eg CVICEK. Northern bank is for whites, eg LASKI RIZLING, Silvaner and recent Chard and SAUV BL.

Sipon Name for Furmint of Hungary – locally prized, p'haps has a future.

Slamnak A late-harvest LJUTOMER estate RIES.

Slovenijavino Slovenia's largest exporter. Wines (esp WELSCHRIES) bought in and blended with care for Slovin, Ashewood and Avia brands.

Tigrovo Mljeko See Radgonska Ranina.

Tokaj The Pinot Gr, making rather heavy white wine.

Vinag Huge production cellars at MARIBOR. Top wine: Cloburg LASKI RIZLING.

Vinakras Sezana v'yds for deep purple fresh-tasting TERAN.

Vipava LITTORAL region with tradition of export to Austria and Germany: good Cab, MERLOT, Barbera, Chard. Vipava winery is the most modern.

Vrhunsko Vino Top-quality wine.

Croatia

Babi Standard red of DALMATIA, ages better than ordinary PLAVAC.

Badel Top négociant of Croatian wines.

Banat Region partly in Romania: up-to-date wineries making adequate RIES.

Baranjske Planote SLAVONIA area for RIES and BIJELI BURGUNDAC.

Benkovac Town and wine cellar: wines look good as it emerges from war.

Bogdanusa Local white grape of the DALMATIAN islands, esp Hvar and Brac. Pleasant, refreshing faintly fragrant wine.

Bolski Plavac Top-quality vigorous red from Bol on the island of Brac.

Burgundac Bijeli Chard, grown in SLAVONIA.

Dalmacijavino Coop at Split: full range of DALMATIAN coastal/island wines.

Dalmatia The coast of Croatia, from Rijeka to Dubrovnik. Has a remarkable variety of characterful wines, most of them potent.

Dingac Heavy sweetish PLAVAC red, speciality of steep mid-DALMATIAN coast.

Faros Substantial age-worthy PLAVAC red from the island of Hvar.

Grasevina Local name for ubiquitous LASKI RIZLING. Best from Kutjevo.

Grk White grape, speciality of the island of Korcula, giving strong, even sherry-like wine, and also a lighter pale one.

Istravino Rijeka Oldest wine négociant of Croatia.

Istria Peninsula in the N Adriatic, Porec its centre: a variety of pleasant wines, Merlot as good as any. V dry TERAN is perfect with local truffles.

Kontinentalna Hrvatska Inland Croatia. Mostly for whites (GRASEVINA).

Marastina Strong herbal dry DALMATIAN white, best from Lastovo.

Opol Pleasant light pale PLAVAC red from Split and Sibenik in DALMATIA.

Plavac Mali DALMATIA red grape; wine of body, strength, ageability. Current thinking has it as Zinfandel. See Dingac, Opol, Postup. Also white, Plavac Beli.

Plenkovic Tough new private grower: good Zlatan PLAVAC reds from Hvar Island.

Polu Semi... Polu-slatko is semi-sweet, polu-suho is semi-dry.

Portugizac Austria's Blauer Portugieser: plain red wine.

Posip Pleasant white of the DALMATIAN islands, notably Korcula.

Postup Soft heavy DALMATIAN red of Peljesac peninsula. Highly esteemed.
Prosek Dessert wine from ISTRIA and DALMATIA: 15% (can be almost port-like).
Slavonija N Croatia, on Hungarian border between Slovenia and Serbia. Big producer. Standard wines, esp white, incl most of former 'Yugoslav RIES'. Well-known for its oak forests.
Stolno vino Table wine.
Teran Stout dark red of ISTRIA. See Refosk (Slovenia).
Vrhunsko Vino New origin-based designation for quality wines.
Vugava Rare white variety of Vis in DALMATIA. Linked (at least in legend) with Viognier of the Rhône Valley.

Bosnia and Herzegovina

Blatina Ancient MOSTAR red grape and wine from pebbled W bank of Neretva.
Kameno Vino White wine of unique irrigated desert v'yd in Neretva Valley.
Mostar Means 'old bridge'. Was Herzegovina's Islamic-looking wine centre, but cellars destroyed during the civil war. Ljubuski and Citluk are rebuilding. Potentially admirable ZILAVKA white and BLATINA red.
Samotok Light red (rosé/'ruzica') wine from run-off juice (and no pressing).
Zilavka White grape of MOSTAR, making wines rather neutral when exported, but can be dry pungent and memorably fruity with a faint flavour of apricots.

Serbia

Amselfelder Reds from KOSOVO POLJE (once top cellars). Disagreeably sweet.
Bijelo (Beli) White.
Burgundac Crni Local widely planted equiv of Pinot N – like German version.
Cabernet Sauvignon Now introduced in many places with usually pleasant, occasionally exciting results. See Kosovo.
Crno Black, ie red wine.
Fruska Gora Hills in VOJVODINA, on the Danube NW of Belgrade, with modern v'yds and a wide range of wines incl Traminer and Sauv Bl.
Game Pronounced 'Gamay'. Pleasant red wines from KOSOVO.
Kameno Vino White from unique (irrigated) v'yd at Medugorje-Caplina in Neretva Valley.
Kosovo (or Kosmet) Region in the S between SERBIA and MACEDONIA. Source of AMSELFELDER and some lively Cab. Kos means blackbird.
Kosovo Polje Pinot N-covered Mediterranean-warm polder surrounded by mts. Was base for German AMSELFELDER; post-war sees more Spanish interest.
Leskovac Region in Serbia for good whites, eg Sauv Bl.
Kratosija Much-praised local red grape for good-quality, drinkable wines.
Montenegro Small southwest region known for VRANAC red wines.
Muscat-Ottonel The E European Muscat, grown in VOJVODINA.
Oplenac Cab-producing region in Serbia.
Plovdina Native dark-skinned red grape of Macedonia grown here too.
Prokupac Native sturdy red grape and wine. Best from ZUPA.
Ruzica Rosé. Usually from PROKUPAC. Darker than most, and better.
Smederevka Major white grape of Serbia and Kosovo. Fresh dry wines.
Stono Vino Table wine.
Suvarak Late-harvested dessert wine (15%) from PROKUPAC grapes.
Velika Morava Area of Serbia famous for Laski Riesling.
Vojvodina Big plain (also Hungary, Romania). Sandy soil vg esp for white vines.
Zupa Central Serbia. Serbia's oldest and most famous vineyard district giving its name to above-average red and rosé (dark and light red) wines from PROKUPAC, PLOVDINA grapes: respectively Zupsko CRNO, Z RUZICA.

Montenegro

13 July State-controlled coop (mainly, but not just grapes) with high-tech Italian equipment, outside PODGORICA. VRANAC is high quality.

Cemovsko Polje Vast pebbled semi-desert plain; esp VRANAC. Awaits discovery.

Crmnica Lake-side/coastal v'yds esp for Kadarka grape (see Macedonia).

Crna Gora Black Mountains.

Duklja Late-picked semi-sweet version of VRANAC.

Krstac Montenegro's top white grape and wine; esp from CRMNICA.

Merlot Since '80: good wood-aged results.

Podgorica Ancient name reintroduced for capital Titograd.

Vranac Local vigorous and abundant red grape and wine. Value.

Macedonia

Belan White Grenache. Makes neutral Gemischt wine.

Crna Reka River with many artificial lakes for irrigation.

Crveno suvo vino Red dry wine.

Kadarka Major red grape of Hungary; here closer to its origins around L Ohrid.

Kratosija Locally favoured red grape; sound wines.

Plovdina Native (S) grape for mild red, white; esp blended with tastier PROKUPAC.

Prokupac Serbian and Macedonian top red grape. Makes dark rosé (RUZICA) and full red of character, esp at ZUPA. PLOVDINA often added for smoothness.

Rkatsiteli Russian (white) grape making a home close to the Bulgarian border.

Temjanika Grape for spicy semi-sweet whites. (Tamianka in Bulgaria.)

Teran Transferred from ISTRIA, but Macedonia's version is less stylish.

Tikves Much favoured hilly v'yd region (20,000 acres). Esp for pleasant dark red Kratosija; fresh dry Smederevka (see Serbia) – locally mixed with soda.

Traminac The Traminer. Also grown in Vojvodina and Slovenia.

Vardar Valley Brings the benefits of the Aegean Sea to inland v'yds (just as the Rhône Valley channels Mediterranean warmth into France).

Vranec Local name for Vranac of Montenegro (qv).

Vrvno Vino Controlled origin designation for quality wines.

Former Czechoslovakia

The country was re-established in January '93 as the Czech (Moravia and Bohemia) and Slovak republics. While there was little or no tradition of exporting from this mainly white wine region, good wines have emerged since 1989. Labels will say whether they are blended or from single grape varieties. All are worth trying for value. Privatization and foreign investment bode well for the future.

Moravia Favourite wines in Prague: variety and value. V'yds situated along Danube tributaries. Many wines from Austrian border: similar grapes, Grüner Veltliner, Müller-T, Sauv, Traminer, St-Laurent, Pinot N, Blauer Portugieser, Frankovka etc; and similar wines, eg from **Mikulov** (white, red, dry, sweet classic-method sparkling; especially popular Valtice Cellars, est'd 1430, and traditional Vino Mikulov), **Satov** (modern, mostly white – incl Sauv, Grüner Veltliner, Müller-Thurgau – grapes from local farms and coops) and **Znojmo** (long-est'd, ideal limestone soil; local white grapes, Grüner-V, Müller-T, Sauv, 'Tramín' and sweetish prize-winning 'Rynsky Ryzlink' (82) from Znovín). Other regions: Jaroslavice (oak-aged reds), Prímetice (full aromatic whites), Blatnice, Hustopece, sunny Pálava, Saldorf (esp Sauv, 'Rynsky' Ries) and Velké Pavlovice (good Ruländer, Traminer, St-Laurent and award-winning Cab 92, still expanding). Moravia also has sparkling.

Bohemia Winemaking since 9th C. Same latitude and similar wines to eastern Germany. Best: N of Prague, in Elbe Valley, and (best-known) nr Melník (King Karel IV bought in Burgundian vines in 15th C; today Ries, Ruländer and Traminer predominate). 'Bohemia Sekt' is growing, eg increasingly popular from Stary Plzenec: tank-fermented (mostly), some oak used, with grapes from SLOVAKIA and MORAVIA too; French advice. Also some interesting Pinot N. Top wineries: **Lobkowitz** (at Melnik), **Roudnice, Litomerice, Karlstein**.

Slovakia Warmest climatic conditions and most of former Czechoslovakia's wine. Best in eastern v'yds neighbouring Hungary's Tokay region. Slovakia uses Hungarian varieties, international varieties (Ries, Gewürz, Pinot Bl, Sauv Bl and Cab S) and makes a little Tokay too. Key districts: Malo-Karpatská Oblast (largest region, in foothills of the Little Carpathians, incl Ruländer, Ries, Traminer, Limberger etc), Malá Trna, Nové Mesto, Skalice (small area, mainly reds), and (in Tatra foothills) Bratislava, Pezinok, Modra.

Romania

Romania has a long winemaking tradition but potential for quality was wasted during decades of supplying the Soviet Union with cheap, sweet wine. The political situation has sadly allowed little progress. Quantity is still the goal (with considerable domestic consumption) despite there being some superbly sited vineyards. But with modern, cleaner winemaking, earlier bottling and increasing exports, Romania's wine industry could ultimately rival that of Bulgaria.

Aiud TIRNAVE region with wine school, quality and a 'flor sherry'-style wine.

Alba Iulia Town in warm TIRNAVE area of TRANSYLVANIA, known for off-dry white (Italian RIES, FETEASCA, MUSKAT-OTTONEL), bottle-fermented sparkling.

Aligoté The junior white burgundy grape makes pleasantly fresh white.

Băbească Traditional red grape of the FOCSANI area: agreeably sharp wine tasting slightly of cloves. (Means 'grandmother grape'.)

Banat Plain on border with Serbia. Workaday Italian RIES, SAUV BL, MUSKAT-OTTONEL; light red CADARCA, CABERNET and Merlot.

Baratca Gentle slopes around PAULIS for good Merlot and Cabernet.

Burgund Mare 'Big Burgundian'. A clone of Pinot N, not the real thing.

Buzav Hills Good red wines (CABERNET, Merlot, BURGUND M) from continuation of DEALUL MARE region.

Cabernet Sauvignon Increasingly grown, esp at DEALUL MARE, to make dark intense wines, though sometimes too sweet for Western palates.

Cadarca Romanian spelling of the Hungarian Kadarka.

Chardonnay Used at MURFATLAR to make sweet dessert wine. Dry and oak-aged styles.

Cotesti Warmer part of the FOCSANI area making deep-coloured reds of PINOT N, Merlot etc, and dry whites claimed to resemble Alsace wines.

Cotnari Region at Moldavia's N v'yd limit; good botrytis. Famous (rarely seen) historical wine: light dessert white from local GRASA, FETEASCA ALBA, TAMAIIOASA, rather like v delicate Tokay, gold with tints of green.

Crisana Western region including historical Miniş area (since 15th-C: reds, especially CADARCA, and crisp white Mustoasa), Silvania (esp FETEASCA), Diosig, Valea lui Mihai.

Dealul Mare Important up-to-date well-sited v'yd area in southeast Carpathian foothills. Red wines from FETEASCA NEAGRA, CAB, Merlot, PINOT N (most potential) etc. Whites from TAMIIOASA etc. Look out for Dionis label (fine reds).

ROMANIA

Dobrudja Sunny dry Black Sea region. Incl MURFATLAR. Quality is good.

Drăgăşani Region on River Olt south of the Carpathian Mountains, since Roman times. Both traditional and 'modern' grapes (esp Sauv). Good MUSKAT-OTTONEL, reds (CAB).

Fetească Romanian white grape with spicy, faintly Muscat aroma. Two types: F Albă (same as Hungary's Leányka, considered more ordinary, but base for sparkling wine and sweet COTNARI) and F Regala (F Albă x Furmint cross, good acidity and good for sparkling).

Fetească Neagră Red Feteasca. Light wines, made coarse by clumsiness, good when aged (blackcurranty and deep red).

Focsani Important MOLDAVIA region incl COTESTI, NICORESTI and ODOBESTI.

Grasă A form of the Hungarian Furmint grape grown in Romania and used in, among other wines, COTNARI. Prone to botrytis. Grasa means 'fat'.

Iaşi Region for fresh acidic whites (F ALBA, also Welschries, ALIGOTE, spumante-style MUSKAT O): Bucium, Copu, Tomesti. Reds: Merlot, CAB; top BABEASCA.

Istria-Babadag Newish wine region N of MURFATLAR (CAB S, Merlot, F ALBA etc).

Jidvei Winery in the cool Carpathians (TIRNAVE) among Romania's N-most v'yds. Good whites: FETEASCA, Furmint, RIES, SAUV BL.

Lechinta Transylvanian wine area. Wines noted for bouquet (local grapes).

Moldavia NE province. Largest Romanian wine area with 12 subregions incl IASI, FOCSANI, PANCIU. Temperate, with good v'yd potential.

Murfatlar V'yds nr Black Sea, 2nd-best botrytis conditions (see Cotnari): esp sweet CHARD, late-harvest CAB. Now also full dry wines and sparkling.

Muskat Ottonel The E European Muscat, a speciality of Romania, esp in cool climate TRANSYLVANIA and dry wines in MOLDAVIA.

Nicoreşti Eastern area of FOCSANI, best known for its red BABEASCA.

Odobeşti The central part of FOCSANI; white wines of FETEASCA, RIES etc.

Oltenia Wine regions including DRAGASANI. Sometimes also a brand name.

Panciu Cool MOLDAVIA region N of ODOBESTI. Good still and sparkling white.

Paulis Small estate cellar in town of same name. Barrique-aged Merlot is one of its treasures.

Perla The speciality of TIRNAVE: a pleasant blended semi-sweet white of Italian RIES, FETEASCA and MUSKAT-OTTONEL.

Pinot Noir Grown in the south: can surprise with taste and character.

Piteşti Principal town of the Arges region S of Carpathians. Trad whites.

Premiat Reliable range of higher-quality wines for export.

Riesling Actually Italian Riesling. V widely planted. No exceptional wines.

Sadova Town in the SEGARCEA area exporting a sweetish rosé.

Sauvignon Blanc Romania's tastiest white, esp blended with FETEASCA.

Segarcea Southern wine area near the Danube. Rather sweet CAB.

Tamîîoasa Traditional white grape known as 'frankincense' for its exotic scent and flavour. Pungent sweet wines often affected by botrytis.

Tîrnave Important Transylvanian wine region (Romania's coolest), known for its PERLA and much FETEASCA R. Well-situated for dry and aromatic wines (esp Pinot Gr, Gewürz), eg JIDVEI'S. Also bottle-fermented sparkling. Germanic-style.

Trakia Export brand. Better judged for Western palates than most.

Transylvania See Alba Iulia, Lechinta, Tîrnave.

Valea Călugărească 'Valley of the Monks', part of DEALUL MARE with go-ahead research station. Currently proposing new AC-style rules. CAB (esp Special Reserve 85), Merlot, PINOT are admirable, as are Italian RIES, Pinot Gr.

Vin de Mesa Most basic wine classification – for local drinking only.

VS and VSO Higher quality wines; VSO requires specified grapes and region.

VSOC Top-range wines: CMD is late harvest, CMI late harvest with noble rot, CIB is from selected nobly rotten grapes (like Beerenauslese).

Greece

Since Greece's entry into the EC in 1981, its antique wine industry has started moving into higher gear. Some is still fairly primitive, but a new system of appellations is in place and the past decade has seen much investment in equipment and expertise. Modern, well-made, but still authentically Greek wines are well worth tasting.

Achaia-Clauss Well-known wine merchant with cellars at PATRAS, in north PELOPONNESE. Makers of DEMESTICA etc.

Agiorgitiko Widely planted red-wine grape in the NEMEA region.

Agioritikos (Appellation) Good medium white and rosé from Agios Oros or Mt Athos, Halkidiki's monastic peninsula. Source of Cab etc for TSANTALI.

Amintaion Light red or rosé, often pétillant, from MACEDONIA.

Ankiralos Fresh white from the Aegean-facing v'yds of Thessaly.

Attica Region round Athens, the chief source of RETSINA.

Autocratorikos New semi-sparkling medium-dry white from TSANTALI.

Botrys Old-established Athenian wine and spirits company.

Boutari Merchants and makers with high standards in MACEDONIAN and other wines, esp NAOUSSA and SANTORINI. Grande Réserve is excellent (90).

Caïr Label of the RHODES coop. Makes Greece's only classic sparkling wine.

Calliga Modern winery with 800 acres on CEPHALONIA. ROBOLA white and Monte Nero reds from indigenous grapes are adequately made.

Cambas, Andrew Important wine-growers and merchants in ATTICA.

Carras, John Estate at Sithonia, Halkidiki. Interesting COTES DE MELITON wines. Ch Carras: claret-style oak-aged red (**75 79 81 83 84 85 87 90**) able to age 20 yrs. Also non-appellation, eg Ambelos.

Cava Legal term for blended aged red and white. Eg, Cava Boutari (NAOUSSA-NEMEA blend) and Cava Tstantalis (NAOUSSA-Cab).

Cephalonia (Kephalonia) Ionian island: good white ROBOLA, red Thymiatiko.

Château Lazaridis Family estate NE of Salonika for fine red, white and rosé.

Corfu Adriatic island with wines scarcely worthy of it. Ropa is traditional red.

Côtes de Meliton Appellation (since '81) of CARRAS estate: red (esp Cab and Limnio) and white (again, Greek and French grapes), incl Ch Carras.

Crete Island with potential for excellent wine but current phylloxera problems. Best now from BOUTARI, Kourtaki and indigenous grapes.

Danielis One of the best brands of dry red wine, from ACHAIA-CLAUSS.

Demestica A reliable brand of dry red and white from ACHAIA-CLAUSS.

Emery Maker of good CAVA Emery red and vg Villare white on RHODES.

Epirus Central Greek region with high-altitude vines (1,200 metres): 'Katoyi' Cab is celebrated expensive, 'Zitsa' is dry, demi-sec and sparkling white.

Gentilini Up-market white from CEPHALONIA; a ROBOLA blend, soft and very appealing. Now also a v promising oak-aged version. To follow.

Gerovassiliou Small, high quality estate nr Salonika owned by Bordeaux-trained E Gerovassiliou: also winemaker at CH CARRAS.

Goumenissa (Appellation) Oaked red from W MACEDONIA. Esp BOUTARI, Aïdarini.

Hatzimichali Small Atalanti estate. Greek-grape whites; reds incl Cab, Merlot.

Ilios Very drinkable standard RHODES wine from CAIR.

Kokkineli The rosé version of RETSINA: like the white. Drink cold.

Kosta Lazaridis, Domaine Not to be confused with CHATEAU LAZARIDIS, but also for quality red, white, rosé from local and international grapes.

Kouros Highly rated white from KOURTAKIS of ATTICA; also red from NEMEA.

Kourtakis, D Athenian merchant with mild RETSINA and good dark NEMEA.

Kretikos White wine made by BOUTARI from CRETAN varieties.

Lemnos (Appellation) Aegean island: sweet golden Muscat RETSINA, KOKKINELI.

GREECE

Lindos Higher-quality RHODES wine (from Lindos or not). Acceptable, no more.
Macedonia Quality wine region in the north, for XYNOMAVRO, esp NAOUSSA.
Malvasia White grape said to be from Monemvasia (south PELOPONNESE).
Mantinia (Appellation) Fresh aromatic widely made PELOPONNESE white.
Mavro Black – the word for dark (often sweet) red wine.
Mavrodaphne (Appellation) 'Black laurel'. Dark, sweet, port/recioto-like conc red; fortified to 15–22%. Speciality of PATRAS, N PELOPONNESE. To age.
Mavroudi Red wine of Delphi and N shore of Gulf of Corinth: dark, plummy.
Mercouri PELOPONNESE family estate. V fine Refosco (locally called Mercouri) red.
Metsovo Town in Epirus (north) producing Cab blend called Katoi.
Minos Popular CRETAN brand; the Castello red is best.
Moscophilero Lightly spicy grape that makes MANTINIA.
Naoussa (Appellation) Above-average strong dry XYNOMAVRO red from MACEDONIA in the north, esp from BOUTARI, the coop and TSANTALI.
Nemea (Appellation) Town in E PELOPONNESE famous for its lion (a victim of Hercules), fittingly forceful MAVRO, AGIORGITIKO grapes (unique spicy red).
Oenoforos PELOPONNESE estate for top white Asprolithi from local Roditis grape.
Patras (Appellation) White wine (eg plentiful dry Rhoditis and rarer Muscats) and wine town on the Gulf of Corinth. Home of MAVRODAPHNE.
Pegasus, Château NAOUSSA estate for superior red (esp **81 86** 88).
Peloponnese Southern land mass of mainland Greece, with half of the country's v'yds, incl NEMEA and PATRAS; vines mostly used for currants.
Rapsani Interesting oaked red from Mt Ossa. Rasping until rescued by TSANTALI.
Retsina ATTICA speciality white: with Aleppo pine resin added, tasting of turps; oddly appropriate with Greek food. Modern retsina: often too mild.
Rhodes Easternmost Greek island. Chevalier de Rhodes is a pleasant red from CAIR. Makes Greece's best sparkling. See also Caïr, Emery, Ilios.
Robola (Appellation) Dry CEPHALONIA white: pleasant, soft, quite characterful.
Samos (Appellation) Island nr Turkey with ancient reputation for sweet pale golden Muscat and Malvasia. Esp (fortified) Anthemis, (sun-dried) Nectar.
Santorini Dramatic volcanic island N of CRETE: sweet Visanto (sun-dried grapes, once Orthodox church communion wine), v dry white. Potential.
Semeli, Château Estate nr Athens making good white and red, incl Cab S.
Skouras Highly innovative, exciting wines. Esp Megas Oenos. PELOPONNESE.
Strofilia Brand of 'boutique' winery at Anavissos. Good whites; reds incl Cab.
Tsantali Producers at Agios Pavlos with wide range of country and appellation wines, incl MACEDONIAN and wine from the monks of Mt Athos, NEMEA, NAOUSSA, RAPSANI and Muscat from SAMOS and LIMNOS. CAVA is a blend.
Vaeni Good red from NAOUSSA producers' coop.
Xynomavro The tastiest of many indigenous Greek red grapes – though its name means acidic-black. Basis for NAOUSSA and other northern wines.
Zitsa Mountainous N Epirius appellation. Delicate Debina white, still or fizzy.

Cyprus

Cyprus exports most of its production, generally strong red wines of reasonable quality and low-price Cyprus 'sherry' (a term banned in the EU since 1995), though treacly old Commandaria is the island's finest product. As with Bulgaria, the fall of the USSR as a major wine market had grave results. Cyprus is now forced to compete against high European standards. Until recently, only two local grapes were grown; now another 12 have emerged. International favourites are inevitably being planted, but many growers still believe in the individuality of their own varieties. Cyprus has never had phylloxera.

Afames Village at the foot of Mt Olympus, giving its name to dry tangy red (MAVRO) wine from SODAP.

Alkion A smooth light dry KEO white (XYNISTERI grapes from Akamas, Paphos). Grapes harvested just before ripeness.

Aphrodite Consistent medium-dry XYNISTERI white from KEO.

Arsinoë Dry white wine from SODAP, named after an unfortunate female whom the last entry turned to stone.

Bellapais Fizzy medium-sweet white from KEO, named after the famous abbey nr Kyrenia. Essential refreshment for holiday-makers.

Commandaria Good-quality brown dessert wine since ancient times in hills N of LIMASSOL. Delimited area comprises 14 specified villages; named after a crusading order of knights. Made by solera maturation of sun-dried XYNISTERI and MAVRO grapes. Best (as old as 100 yrs) is superb, of incredible sweetness, fragrance, concentration. Unfortunately, most is just standard Communion wine.

Domaine d'Ahera Modern-style lighter estate red from KEO. (From Grenache – recent on the island – and local Lefkas grapes.)

Emva Brand name of well-made fino, medium and cream SHERRIES.

ETKO See Haggipavlu.

Haggipavlu Wine merchant at LIMASSOL since 1844. Trades as ETKO. Known for Emva range, but also produces quality table wines in tiny quantities.

Heritage A KEO rich dry red from rare indigenous Pambakina grape; matured in new oak.

KEO The biggest and most go-ahead firm at LIMASSOL. Standard KEO Dry White and Dry Red are vg value. See also Othello, Heritage and Aphrodite.

Khalokhorio Principal COMMANDARIA village, growing only XYNISTERI.

Kokkineli Rosé: the name is related to 'cochineal'.

Kolossi Crusaders' castle nr Limassol; gives name to table wines from SODAP.

Laona The largest of the small independent regional wineries at Arsos, now owned by KEO. Good range incl an oak-aged red and a fruity dry white.

Limassol 'The Bordeaux of Cyprus'. Southern wine port (and its region): location for all four main Cyprus wineries.

Loel Major producer. Range includes red 'Hermes', Commandaria 'Alasia' and some of island's best brandies.

Mavro The black grape of Cyprus (and Greece) and its dark wine.

Monte Roya Modern regional winery at Chryssoroyiatissa Monastery.

Muscat All major firms produce pleasant low-price (15% alcohol) Muscats.

Opthalmo Black grape (red/rosé): lighter, sharper than MAVRO. Not native.

Othello A good standard dry red wine (made with MAVRO and OPTHALMO grapes from the PITSILIA region). Solid and satisfying version from KEO. Best drunk at 3–4 years.

Palomino Soft dry white made of this (sherry) grape by LOEL and SODAP. V drinkable ice-cold. Imported to make Cyprus SHERRY.

Pitsilia Region south of Mount Olympus for some of the best white and COMMANDARIA wines.

Rosella Light dry fragrant rosé from KEO. OPTHALMO from PITSILIA.

St-Panteleimon Brand of medium-sweet white from KEO.

Semeli Good traditional red from HAGGIPAVLU. Best at 3–4 years old.

Sherry Sherry-style wine is an island staple. The best is dry. Since 1995 the term has been forbitten for wines on sale in the European Community.

SODAP Major wine coop at LIMASSOL. Top wine: red AFAMES.

Thisbe Fruity medium-dry light KEO wine (of XYNISTERI grapes from LIMASSOL).

Xynisteri The native aromatic white grape of Cyprus.

Asia & North Africa

Algeria As a combined result of Islam and the EC, once massive v'yds have dwindled in the last decade from 860,000 acres to about 100,000; many vines are 40+ yrs old and won't be replaced. Red, white and esp rosé wines of some quality and power are still made in coastal hills of Tlemcen, Mascara (good red and white), Haut-Dahra (strong red, rosé), Zaccar, Tessala, Médéa and Aïn-Bessem (Bouira esp good). Sidi Brahim is a drinkable red brand. These had VDQS status in French colonial days. Wine is still the third-largest export. Algeria is also a cork producer.

China Germans and Russians started making wine on Shantung (now 'Shandong') peninsula in the late 1800s. Since 1980 a modern industry, initiated by Rémy-Martin, has made adequate white Dynasty and Tsingtao wines (latitude: same as S France). New plantings of better varieties in Shandong and Tianjin (further north) promise more interest. Basic table wines are made of the local Dragon Eye and Muscat Hamburg grapes (esp in Tianjin). In Qingdao (China's only maritime climate) Huadong Winery (Allied-Lyons owned) has made very palatable Welschries and Chard and is experimenting with Cab S, Syrah and Gewürz. Dragon Seal Wines (nr Peking) have Dragon Eye grapes, recent Chard (with oak), and more planned. Other foreign investors and innovators are Seagram (Summer Palace), Pernod-Ricard (Beijing Friendship Winery). In '92 Rémy Martin launched 'Imperial Court', China's first classic method sparkling, nr Shanghai. Chinese wines have now received medals in international competitions. Expect surprise developments.

India In 1985 a Franco-Indian firm launched a Chard-based sparkling wine, Omar Khayyám, made at Náráyangoan, nr Poona, SE of Bombay. It sets an astonishing standard. Plans are to export up to 2M bottles and to add still Chard and Cab. Sweeter Marquise de Pompadour followed, also slightly drier Princess Jaulke, with advice from Charbaut of Champagne – still improving. Now nr Bangalore there is Cab, from Grover V'yds in Dodballapur Hills.

Japan Japan has a small wine industry, mostly in Yamanashi Prefecture, W of Tokyo, but extending as far as cool Hokkaidò (N island). Most wine is blended with imports from S America, Eastern Europe, etc. But premium Sémillon, Chardonnay, Cabernet and local white Kôshû, are the new surprises. Top producers are Manns, Sanraku (Mercian label) and Suntory. Château Mercian and Suntory lead with quality Chard, Cabernet etc.

The most interesting (and expensive) are Suntory's Ch Lion red B'x-blend and vg botrytis Sém; Ch Mercian's Kikyogahara Merlot, and esp Jyonohira Cab of extraordinary denseness and quality. Manns not only has Chard, Cab (French oaked) but emphasizes local varieties (Kôshû, Zenkôji – China's Dragon Eye) and local Euro crosses (adapted to Japan's rainy climate) too. 2nd-rank are Sapporo (Polaire label), Kyowa Hakko Kogyo (Ste-Neige), Marufuji (big-selling Rubaiyat), Shirayuri Winery (L'Orient label), Maruki and Ch Lumière.

Regrettably, labelling laws have been so lax that misrepresentation of imported wines as 'Japanese' has been rule rather than exception. Law now stipulates that if imported wine in bottle is above 50% it must be indicated on label (larger figure printed before smaller). But local wines are now attracting interest, and Katsunuma district is capitalizing by introducing Certificate of Origin labels. All the signs are that wine has a big future in Japan.

For key to grape variety abbreviations, see pages 7–13.

Lebanon The small Lebanese industry (7, 500 acres), based in Ksara in Beka'a Valley NE of Beirut, makes wines of vigour and quality. Two wineries of note. Ch Musar (★★★), the heroic survivor of yrs of civil war, for splendid claret-like matured reds, mainly Cab; a full-blooded oaked white, from indigenous Obaideh grapes (like Chard), surprisingly capable of ageing 10–15 yrs; and a lighter red wine, 'Tradition': 75% Cinsaut, 25% Cab S. Ch Kefraya makes: 'Rouge de K' Cinsaut-Carignan, 'Château Kefraya' is fragrant and from best yrs only; there is rosé and white too; all early-drinking.

Morocco Morocco makes North Africa's best wine (85% red, from Cinsaut, Grenache, Carignan), from v'yds along Atlantic coast (Rabat to Casablanca, light, hopefully fruity with speciality white – 'Gris' – from red grapes) and around Meknès and Fèz (solid full-bodied, best-known). Also further east around Berkane and Angad (tangy, earthy) and in the Gharb and Doukkalas regions. But in 10 years v'yds have declined from 190,000 to 35,000 acres. Main producers are Dom de Sahari (nr Meknès, French investment, a new winery in '93, Cab S and Merlot vines, along with local grapes), Celliers de Meknès (state-owned coop: recent investment resulting in clean, modern-tasting wines), Chaudsoleil, and Sincomar. Chantebled, Tarik and Toulal are drinkable reds. Vin Gris (10% of production), esp de Boulaoune, is the best bet for hot-day refreshment. Cork production is also important.

Tunisia Tunisia now has 37,000 v'yd acres (there were 120,000 10 yrs ago). Traditionally her speciality was sweet Muscat (more recently: dry Muscat de Kelibia), but most wines are reasonable reds and light rosés from Cap Bon, Carthage, Mornag, Tébourba and Tunis. Trying to improve quality. Best producers Ch Thibar, Mornag and Royal Tardi.

Turkey Most of Turkey's 1.5 million acres of v'yds produce table grapes; only 3% are for wine. Wines from Thrace, Anatolia and the Aegean are very drinkable. Indigenous varieties (there are over 1,000: 60 are commercial) such as Emir, Narince (for white) and Bogazkere, Oküzgözü (for red) are used along with Ries, Sém, Pinot N, Grenache, Carignan and Gamay. Trakya (Thrace) white (light Sém) and Buzbag (E Anatolian) red are the well-known standards of Tekel, the state producer (with 21 state wineries). Diren, Doluca, Karmen, Kavaklidere and Taskobirlik are private firms of fair quality. Doluca's Villa Neva red from Thrace is well made, as is Villa Doluca. Kavaklidere makes good light Primeurs (white 'Cankaya' and red 'Yakut') from local grapes. But Buzbag remains Turkey's most original and striking wine.

The old Russian Empire

Some 2.2 million acres of vineyards make the 16 republics of the former USSR collectively the world's fourth-biggest wine producer. Russia is the largest of the 12 producing wine, followed by Moldova, the Ukraine (including top Crimea region) and Georgia. Russians have a sweet tooth for table, dessert and sparkling wines.

Russia Makes fair Riesling (Anapa, Arbau, Beshtau) and sw sparkling Tsimlanskoye 'Champanski. Abrau Durso, a great speciality, is classic sparkling (since 1870) from Pinot, Chard and Cab F (similar climate to Champagne). Also Chard, Sauv, Welschriesling (heavy, often oxidized), processed in state wineries nr Moscow, St-Petersburg etc. Best are Don Valley v'yds (Black Sea Coast of the Caucasus), for Ries, Aligoté, Cab.

Moldova The most temperate climate (as in N France) and now most modern outlook, Moldova has high potential: esp whites from centre, reds from S, red and fortified nr Black Sea (W), making more wine than Australia. Grapes incl Cab, Pinot N, Merlot, Saperavi (fruity), Ries, Chard, Pinot Gr, Aligoté, Rkatsiteli. Former Moscow bottling was disastrous. A startling glimpse of potential was given in '92 by release of 63 Negru de Purkar. Purkar may be top winery but also good are Krikova: esp Kodru 'Claret' blend, Krasny Reserve Pinot-Merlot-Malbec, sp. Romanesti winery (since '82) has French varieties; Yavloveni, fino- and oloroso-style 'flor sherries'. Good old-vine Cab from Tarakliya. Western and antipodean (Penfolds since '93) investment at Hincesti enables local clean bottling, better winemaking, future improvements and produces (to date) Moldova's most modern-tasting wines: Ryman's Chard is vg. Half v'yds still state farmed: progress (and privatization) not smooth, but worth following. Appellation system in pipeline.

Crimea (Ukraine) Crimea produces first-class dessert wines, revealed in '90 by the sale of old wines from the Tsar's Crimean cellars at Massandra, nr Yalta (top-quality Muscats, port-, Madeira-like wines). Alupka Palace fortified (European grapes, since 1820s), adequate classic sp from Novi Svet and Grand Duchess (from Odessa Winery founded 1896 by H Roederer). Reds have potential (eg Alushta from Massandra). All still made under state monopoly. Ukraine also has Aligoté and Artemosk sp (Romanian grapes). To follow.

Georgia Uses antique methods for tannic wines for local drinking, newer techniques for exports (Mukuzani, Tsinandali); Georgians are reluctant to modernize. Kakhetià (E): famed for big red, acceptable white. Imeretia (W): milder, highly original, oddly-fermented wines. Kartli: central area. Cheap, drinkable sp attracts investment from champagne and cava companies. As equipment, techniques and attiudes evolve, Georgia could be an export hit.

Israel

Since being re-established in the 1880s by Edmond de Rothschild, the Israeli wine industry has been primarily of kosher interest until the recent introduction of Cab, Merlot, Sauv, Chard. Traditionally vines were planted in coastal Samson and Shomron but new cooler Golan Heights vineyards (1,200-metre altitude) have resulted in great improvements. More than two-thirds of production is white.

Barkan Large winery: good Sauv Bl and Emerald Ries.

Baron Small family grower. Good dry Muscat, Sauv Bl and soft, fruity Cab S.

Binyamina (Formerly Eliaz) Medium-sized winery with light-style wines.

Carmel Coop, est 1882, with Israel's largest wineries. Top wines: Estate Merlot, Private Collection Cab S, Chard. 'Selected Vineyards' range: gd value.

Galil/Galilee Region incl Golan Heights (Israel's top v'yd area).

Gamla Soft fruity Cab S, oaky Chard and grassy Sauv Bl. Full Cab S, delicately oaked Chard and grassy Sauv Bl from Golan Heights Winery (See Yarden.).

Samson Central coastal plain wine region (SE of Tel Aviv to W of Jerusalem).

Segal Family winery (aka Askalon). Raisiny Cab S-Carignan under Ben Ami label. New joint venture with Wente Bros (see California).

Shomron Wine region in valleys around Zichron-Yaacov, nr Haifa.

Yarden Young ('83) Golan Heights winery; California influence. Full oaky Cab, complex Merlot, barrel-fermented Chard, crisp Sauv Bl; gd classic method sp.

England & Wales

Well over two million bottles a year are now being made here from over 400 vineyards, amounting in total to some 2,000 acres. Almost all are white and are developing a new and distinctive crisp English style, many from new German varieties designed to ripen well in cool weather. Acidity is often high, which means that good examples have a built-in ability (and need) to age. Four years is a good age for many, and up to eight for some. Experiments with both oak-ageing and bottle-fermented sparkling are succeeding; especially the latter. The English Vineyards Association seal is worn by tested wines (the EVA has now become the United Kingdom Vineyards Association). Since 1991 non-hybrid English wines may be labelled as 'Quality Wine', taking them into the European Community quality bracket for the first time – although the English criteria are higher than those of the EC. But as the (excellent) hybrid Seyval Blanc is so important here, few growers apply. NB: Beware 'British Wine', which is neither British nor indeed wine, and has nothing to do with the following.

Adgestone nr Sandown (Isle of Wight) Prize-winning 8.5-acre v'yd on chalky hill site. Est'd '68. Wines with good structure and longevity.

Astley Stourport-on-Severn (Hereford and Worcester) 5 acres; some fair wines. Madeleine Angevine and Kerner are prize-winning.

Barkham Manor E Sussex 34 acres since '85. Wide range. Modern winery.

Barnshole nr Canterbury (Kent) New v'yd of interest; Schönburg good.

Battle Wine Estate Battle, (E Sussex) 50 acres now with own winery and New Zealand-trained winemaker. Wines improving and starting to win medals.

Bearsted Maidstone (Kent) 4 acres planted '86. Improving, esp Bacchus.

Beaulieu Abbey Brockenhurst (Hampshire) 4.6-acre v'yd, established '58 by Gore-Browne family on old monastic site. Good rosé and sparkling wine.

Biddenden nr Tenterden (Kent) 18-acre v'yd planted '69: wide range includes Ortega and Dornfelder. Good cider too.

Bookers Bolney (W Sussex) 5 acres of Müller-T; other varieties planted '92.

Bothy Abingdon (Oxfordshire) 3 acre. Carefully made wines: reasonable quality.

Boze Down Whitchurch-on-Thames (Oxfordshire) 4.5 acres. Wide range. of high-quality wines esp reds.

Breaky Bottom Lewes (E Sussex) 5.5-acre v'yd. Semi-cult following. Good dry wines, esp award-winning Seyval (**89 90**), Müller-T. Sparkling: v good.

Brecon Court Usk (Monmouthshire) 8 acres recently planted. Worth watching.

Bruisyard Saxmundham (Suffolk) 10 acres Müller-T: oaked, sparkling. Since '74.

Cane End Reading (Berkshire) 12 acres; mixed vines. Good sweet late-harvest Bacchus in '90. Interesting style.

Carr Taylor Vineyards Hastings (E Sussex) 35 acres, est'd '73. Pioneer of UK classic method sparkling wine: Kerner-Reichensteiner (vintage, NV), Pinot N rosé. Some lively, intense, balanced wines.

Carters Colchester (Essex) Young v'yd making a mark. Interesting varietals.

Challenden Sandhurst (Kent) Newish tiny v'yd: Huxelrebe and Faberebe. Fruity wines and good sparkling.

Chapel Down Winery Tenterden (Kent) New winery venture, blending from bought-in grapes, esp classic-method sparkling. Barrel-fermented 'Epoch I' red is good, as are 'sur lie' still and sparkling.

Chiddingstone Edenbridge (Kent) 66-acre v'yd with stress on dry French-style wines, esp good Pinot Bl de Noir. Some barrique-ageing.

Chilford Hundred Linton (Cambridgeshire) 18 acres: fairly dry wines since '74.

Chiltern Valley Henley-on-Thames (Oxfordshire) 3 acres of own v'yds high up on chalk, plus neighbouring growers': incl prize-winning unusual oak-aged sweet late-harvest Noble Bacchus, Old Luxters Dry Reserve.

Danebury Stockbrige (Hants) 5 acres: Auxerrois and Bacchus. Interesting wines.

Davenport Rotherfield (E Sussex) Vines here and in Kent. Young winery: serious wines. Australian-trained winemaker.

Denbies Dorking (Surrey) 250-acre v'yd (England's biggest); first harvest '89. Impressive winery: worth the trip, improving wines, esp '92 dessert Botrytis.

Eglantine Loughborough (Leicestershire) 3.3 acre v'yd with many varieties.

Elmham Park East Dereham (Norfolk) 4.5-acre v'yd, est '66. Light flowery wines (with ageing potential), Madeleine Angevine esp good. Also apple wine.

Frithsden Hemel Hempstead (Hertfordshire) 2.8-acre v'yd: mainly Müller-T.

Gifford's Hall Bury St-Edmunds (Suffolk) 12 acre-v'yd for interesting wines (incl oak-aged) and visitor facilities.

Gildridge Lewes (E Sussex) About 2 acres of mixed varieties. Wines improving.

Halfpenny Green W Midlands 28 v'yd-acres; esp good Madeleine Angevine.

Hambledon nr Petersfield (Hampshire) The first modern English v'yd, planted in '51 on a chalk slope with advice from Champagne.

Harden Farm Penshurst (Kent) 18 acres. Member of Winegrowers coop.

Harling Norwich (Norfolk) 6.7 acres Müller-T and Bacchus under new ownership. Wines made at Shawsgate.

Headcorn Maidstone (Kent) 5-acre medal-winning v'yd: Seyval Bl etc.

Hidden Spring Horam (E Sussex) 9 acres. Esp oaked Dry Reserve, Dark Fields red.

Horton Estate Wimborne (Dorset) 9 acres. Bacchus, Reichenstein and selection of reds. Wines showing promise.

Kent's Green Taynton (Gloucestershire) Tiny v'yd of Müller-T and Huxelrebe. Award-winning wines produced at Three Choirs.

La Mare Jersey (Channel Islands) Only (but long-est'd) CI v'yd. Fair wines.

Lamberhurst (Kent) One of the best: est'd '72; now with 25 acres. Consistent range of award winners (83 85 90), reds, sparkling, oak-aged. Medium-dry 91 Bacchus esp good. Winemaker for many other growers.

Leeds Castle Maidstone (Kent) Long-est'd 2.7 acres of vines. Wines sold only at castle outlets. Made at Lamberhurst.

Lillibrook Manor Maidenhead (Berkshire) 1 acre of Müller-T, Schönberger and Bacchus. Improving wines.

Llanerch S Glamorgan (Wales) 5.5 acres est'd '86. Wines sold under Cariad label. Individual style developing, worth its awards. Good rosé.

Meon Valley Southampton (Hampshire) 25 acres: variable, reds interesting.

Milton Keynes Milton Keynes (Bucks) New 4-acre v'yd starting to produce fine wines. To watch.

Moorlynch Bridgewater (Somerset) 16 acres of an idyllic farm. Good wines esp Estate Dry and sparkling.

New Hall nr Maldon (Essex) 90+ acres of mixed farm planted with Huxelrebe, Müller-T and Pinot N etc. Some vinified elsewhere.

Northbrook Springs Bishops Waltham (Hampshire) 13 acres of young vines and improving wines. Gold medal in English Wine of Year competition '95.

Nutbourne Manor nr Pulborough (W Sussex) 18.5 acres: elegant and tasty Schönburger and Bacchus.

Nyetimber West Chiltington (W Sussex) 42-acre v'yd of Chard, Pinot N, Pinot Meunier specializing in bottle-fermented sparkling. First vintage 95. Looks v promising.

Painshill Cobham (Surrey) 1.8 acres planted on original 1742 v'yd site. Deeply sloping and overlooking a large lake: should produce good wines.

Partridge Blandford (Dorset) 5 acres. Good Bacchus.

Paunton Court Bishop's Frome (Worcestershire) 3.75-acre young v'yd. Wine made at Three Choirs.

Penshurst Tunbridge Wells (Kent) 12 acres since '72, incl good Seyval Bl and Müller-T. Fine modern winery.

Pilton Manor Shepton Mallet (Somerset) Hillside v'yd (est'd '66), now only 4 acres. Wines regaining form, esp Westholme Late Harvest.

Ridge View Ditchling Common (E Sussex) New 16-acre v'yd specializing in sparkling wine. Chard, Pinot N and Pinot Meunier only. One to watch.

Rock Lodge nr Haywards Heath (Sussex) 6.2-acre v'yd since '65. Fumé (oak-aged Ortega-Müller-T blend) and Impresario sparkling recommended.

Rosemary Ryde (Isle of Wight) One of largest vineyards on I of W. Wines yet to make much impression, but should be watched.

Rowenden Rolvenden (Kent) 2 acres. Good Huxelrebe and Reichensteiner.

St Anne's Newent (Gloucestershire) Small v'yd (2.3 acres) making 'low-tech' wines traditionally.

St Augustine's Aust (Gloucestershire) Wines made at Three Choirs.

St George's Waldron, Heathfield (E Sussex) Well-known as tourist attraction. Currently up for sale due to owners' retirement.

St Sampson Golant (Cornwall) 4 acres; some of the county's better wines.

Sandhurst Cranbrook (Kent) Mixed farm with 16 acres of vines. Improving wines, esp 91 Seyval, 92 Bacchus (both oak-aged). Sparkling Pinot N-Seyval.

Scott's Hall Ashford (Kent) Boutique v'yd: oak-aged white, sparkling rosé.

Seddlescombe Organic Robertsbridge (E Sussex) The UK's main organic v'yd. 15 acres for range of wines with quite a following.

Sharpham Totnes (Devon) 5 acres. Now own winery: getting interesting.

Shawsgate Framlingham (Suffolk) 17 acres: good Seyval-Müller-T. Wins awards.

Standen East Grinstead (W Sussex) Young 2.2-acre v'yd: good promise.

Staple St James nr Canterbury (Kent) 7 acres planted '74. Excellent quality. Müller-T and Huxelrebe especially interesting.

Sugar Loaf Abergavenny (Wales) 5 acres. Wines made at Three Choirs.

Tenterden Tenterden (Kent) 15 acres, planted '79. Wines very dry to sweet, Müller-T, oak-aged Seyval (vg 81, 91 Trophy winner), rosé, sparkling.

Thames Valley Twyford (Berkshire) 25-acre v'yd: all styles of wine. Serious oak-matured white, red; classic-method sparkling; also late-harvest sweet.

Thorncroft Leatherhead (Surrey) 8 acres making interesting late-harvest botrytis wine from Ortega. Also makes range of elderflower products.

Three Choirs Newent (Gloucestershire) 64 acres, est'd '74. Müller-Thurgau, Seyval Bl, Schönburger, Reichensteiner, and esp Bacchus Dry, Huxelrebe. Recent new £1-million winery. English 'Nouveau' is popular.

Tiltridge Upton-upon-Severn (Worcestershire) Small 1-acre v'yd with good local following.

Titchfield Titchfield (Hampshire) Young 2-acre v'yd starting to make fair wines.

Wellow Romsey (Hampshire) 45-acre v'yd with checkered financial history, now starting to reorganise itself. One to watch.

Wickham Shedfield (Hampshire) 12-acre v'yd (since '84): starting to show some style. Vintage Selection is worth trying.

Wooldings Whitchurch (Hampshire) Young 8-acre v'yd. Vg Schönburger.

Wootton Shepton Mallet (Somerset) Now reduced to 1.8 acres due to partial retirement of owner. Still making good Schönburger.

Wroxeter Roman Shrewsbury (Shropshire) Young ('91) 6-acre v'yd planned on site of Roman town (but no v'yd). One to watch.

Wyken Bury-St-Edmunds (Suffolk) Range starting to look good, esp dry Bacchus white and full dark red. Good restaurant too.

North America

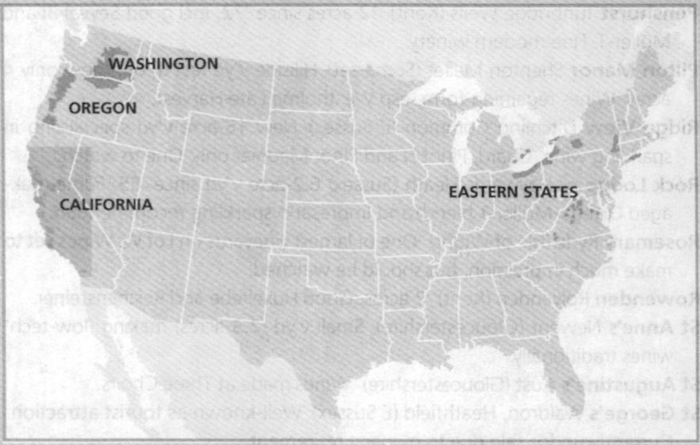

California

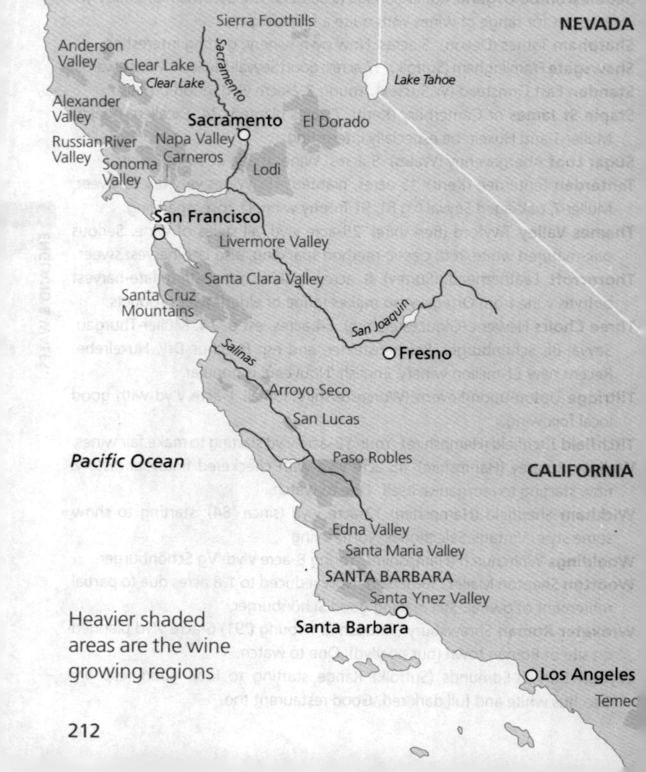

Heavier shaded areas are the wine growing regions

The wine boom carried California to dizzy heights in the 1970s and 1980s. The 1990s have seen retrenchment – and a very expensive plague of phylloxera which will cause the replanting of many of the vineyards of the west. In the long run the effect of this enforced slow-down will be beneficial: more of the right grapes in the right places for growers willing to turn away from the immediate financial rewards of Chardonnay and Merlot.

At the same time America's old puritanical streak allied to the country's not-so-latent hypochondria were retreating in the face of growing evidence that drinking mealtime wine at the very least does no harm, and may well confer some benefits of health. And so a new expansion of wineries took firm hold by 1995, in spite of diminished vineyard area.

This edition records some 280 of the 700-odd wineries now operating. Brevity is not dismissive; it is intended to be practical. Vintages given reflect the probable maturity of wines kept in, say, reasonable restaurant conditions. Some considerably older bottles kept in ideal cellars will still be excellent. Chardonnays can sometimes mature for ten years with ease, Cabernets for 20. But this is the exception, not the rule.

Appellation areas (AVAs) are now an important fact of life. They are being registered thick and fast: the current total is nearing 100, with 11 in Napa alone. But it is still much too soon to use them as a general guide to style. Listed below are the regions usually referred to. Grapes and makers' names, though, remain the key.

Principal vineyard areas

Central Coast

A long sweep of coast with scattered though increasing wine activity, from San Francisco Bay south to Santa Barbara.

Carmel Valley Tiny coastal area; sometimes impressive Cab and Chard.

Livermore Valley E of San Francisco Bay long famous for white wines (esp Sauv Bl). Though area largely built over, v'yds and wineries: surprisingly resilient.

Monterey See Salinas Valley.

Salinas Valley/Monterey The Salinas Valley runs SE inland from Monterey. After frenzied expansion in the '70s interest shifted sharply south to warmer zones. Currently refining its internal divisions: Arroyo Seco AVA (esp Chard and Ries), Santa Lucia Highlands AVA (Chard, has hopes for Pinot N), San Lucas AVA (steady commercial wines).

San Luis Obispo Biggest, warmest district is Paso Robles (6,000 acres of esp Zin, Cab S); finest is Edna Valley (1,000 acres, esp Chard); newest is Arroyo Grande (500 acres, esp Pinot N and sparkling).

Santa Barbara Santa Maria Valley is dominant, esp for vg Chardonnay and distinctive Pinot N. The smaller Santa Ynez Valley also has cool foggy conditions: good for Burgundian varieties at seaward end, B'x or Rhône varieties in warmer inland areas.

Santa Cruz Mts Wineries (though few v'yds) are scattered round the Santa Cruz Mts S of San Francisco Bay, from Woodside down to Gilroy.

South Coast

Temecula (Rancho California) Small area in S California, 25 miles inland, halfway between San Diego and Riverside. Mainly whites.

NORTH AMERICA

North Coast

Encompasses Lake, Mendocino, Napa and Sonoma counties, all north of San Francisco.

Carneros, Los Important cool region N of San Francisco Bay, shared between NAPA and SONOMA counties. Esp for Chard and Pinot N.

Lake Clear Lake AVA: warm climate, most impressive for Sauv Bl, good for Cab S. Small Guenoc Valley AVA similar.

Mendocino North of SONOMA. A varied climate, coolest in Anderson Valley nr the coast, warm inland around Ukiah (Zin, Barbera).

Napa The Napa Valley, N of San Francisco Bay. The oldest and most-honoured of California wine valleys busily fragmenting itself: Stag's Leap AVA (Cab), CARNEROS AVA (shared with SONOMA, good Chard, Pinot N and sparkling), Mt Veeder AVA (Cab), Howell Mountain AVA (Cab, Zinfandel, Chard), Atlas Peak AVA (Sangiovese) and new AVAs on the valley floor, Rutherford, Oakville and St-Helena.

Sonoma County N of San Francisco Bay, between rival NAPA and the sea. California's most divided wine area. Has a dozen AVAs in two separate drainage basins: (1) tipped to SF Bay: Sonoma Valley AVA ('Valley of the Moon', versatile, includes Sonoma Mountain and part of CARNEROS, see Napa); (2) orientated to ocean: Russian River drainage: includes warmer inland valleys Alexander (Cab, Italian varieties), Dry Creek (Zin, Rhône varieties), Knights – and cooler seaward AVAs of Russian River Valley (Chalk Hill, Sonoma-Green Valley, all for Pinot N, Chard, sparkling).

The Interior

Amador County E of Sacramento. Vg Zinfandel, esp Shenandoah Valley AVA.

Lodi Town and district at the N end of the SAN JOAQUIN VALLEY, its hot climate modified by a westerly air-stream.

San Joaquin Valley The great central valley of California, fertile and hot, the source of most of the jug and dessert wines in the state. (Incl LODI AVA and the Clarksburg AVA on the Sacramento River delta.)

Sierra Foothills Encompasses AMADOR (Shenandoah Valley, Fiddletown AVAs), El Dorado (AVA of the same name), Calaveras counties, among others. Zin is universal grape; Rhône and Italian varieties seen more and more.

Recent vintages

California's climate is far from being as consistent as its 'land of sunshine' reputation. Although, on the whole, grapes ripen regularly, they are subject to spring frosts in many areas, sometimes a wet harvest-time and (too often) drought.

Wines from the San Joaquin Valley tend to be most consistent year by year. The vintage date on these, where there is one, is more important for telling the age of the wine than its character.

Vineyards in the Central Coast region are widely scattered; there is little pattern. The Napa and Sonoma valleys are the areas where comment can usefully be made on the last dozen or more vintages of the most popular varietal wines: Cabernet Sauvignon and Chardonnay.

Chardonnay

NB These ageing assessments are based on well-balanced wines with fruit flavours dominant. Very rich and oaky examples tend to be v short-lived: 2 yrs at most. Marker wines for good ageing qualities incl Acacia, Bouchaine, Clos du Bois-Calcaire, Dehlinger, Freemark Abbey, Navarro, Silverado, Trefethen.

1996 Smaller crop than '95, but young wines attractive; vintage could turn out to be above-average.
1995 Small crop, benign harvest. Still pleasing in youth. The usual candidates may age.
1994 The buttery-toasty models are fading, but wines made to age begin to live up to early promise. Best since '91.
1993 Time to drink up all but the most reliable agers.
1992 Soft early, most have already started to fade.
1991 Excellent year for keeping known agers. Rest on downslope.
1990 Serviceable vintage. Should be drunk up by now.
1989 Late rains caught – and spoiled – many. But best agers among rain-beaters still splendid.
1988 Forget them.
1987 Only Trefethen and Freemark Abbey remain in anything more than passable form.
1986 Forget them.
1985 Should have been drunk by now.

Cabernet Sauvignon

NB As with Chardonnays, over-rich and over-oaky wines usually collapse quickly. The markers for the assessments below are not Reserves, but fine standard Cabernets from eg Caymus, Clos du Val, Freemark Abbey, Hafner, Jordan, Laurel Glen, Louis M Martini (Monte Rosso), Pine Ridge, Silverado.

1996 Tiny crop, intense flavours. Somehow foreshadows great early charm; durability still in question.
1995 Tiny crop, intense flavours, soft textures. Seem to be evolving quickly.
1994 In barrel looked best since '91. Pleasing early, possibly durable.
1993 A bit stolid; plain, lacking focus.
1992 Beginning to look desolately like the '88s.
1991 After latest harvest ever, leanest, raciest, best focussed wines in years. Still slightly reticent.
1990 Picture-perfect California vintage: ripe, enveloping, still showing more fruit than maturity.
1989 Dark, flavoursome, but early promise of age-worthiness fading, even in the best. Drink up.
1988 Bland, lacking focus and structure.
1987 Evolving as perhaps the best of the decade overall.
1986 Quickly approachable vintage. Baby fat is now fleshy.
1985 Still so hard they may not come round before the flavours die. Some already in that pickle.
1984 Showy early. Drink up now except only proven agers.
1983 Most have faded badly.
1982 Long written off, yet many Napas now wonderfully harmonious, complex. However, even best v fragile. Hurry.
1981 Best at peak, most slightly past.
1980 High reputation but merely good and solid. Over-tannic. Should drink up.
1979 Apparently lightish, but the best kept going sturdily. Drink up.
1978 Wonderful early; most faded now. Drink up.
1977 Attractive wines now mainly crumbling. Drink up.
1976 Drought made v concentrated wines. Good ones are v ripe and potent now. Drink up.
1975 Delicate, charming; mature. Still in good form and able to wait.
1974 Blockbuster wines: some flopped, the best are ripe and ready. Drink up.

California wineries

Acacia Napa ★★★ (Chard) **89 91 92 93 94** 95 (Pinot N) **87 88 89 90 91 92** 93 **94** 95 Long-time specialist in durable, deep CARNEROS Chard and Pinot; on a quality run with both. Former single-v'yd wines now blended into extra-oaky Reserves due to depredations of phylloxera.

Adelaida Cellars San Luis Obispo ★★ Supple Cab, vigorous Zin the mainstays, now joined by Sangiovese and Rhône varieties.

Alderbrook Sonoma ★★ New owner, new winemaker in '94; expanding volume and softening style of Chard, Sauv. Zin and other reds newly added.

Alexander Valley Vineyards Sonoma ★★ Cab S mostly likely of 6 wines to live up to promise of fine v'yd. Whites quirky at best.

Almaden San Joaquin ★ Famous pioneer name, now a CANANDAIGUA-owned everyday brand, operated from Madera. 1 million+ cases.

S Anderson Vineyard Napa ★★★ (Cab) **89 90** 91 94 **95** (Brut) **90 91** 92 93 Classic sparkling. Cab (from neighbour in Stag's Leap) is stunning. Chard improving as new CARNEROS v'yd kicks in.

Arrowood Sonoma ★★→★★★ (Chard) **95** 96 (Cab) **85 87 90 91** 92 94 95 96 Long-time CHATEAU ST JEAN winemaker Dick A on peak form with supple, age-worthy Cab S. Chard (esp Res) for oak-lovers.

Araujo Napa ★ Eisele v'yd, now estate: dark, brooding Cab S.

Artisans and Estates Diverse specialist winery group collected by KENDALL-JACKSON: incl CAMBRIA, Camelot, LA CREMA, Edmeades, Hartford Court, R PEPI, J Stonestreet.

Atlas Peak Napa ★★ From Antinori-owned v'yds in E hills, Allied-Hiram Walker-owned winery makes ever-improving Sangiovese and Sangiovese-Cab 'Consenso'.

Au Bon Climat Sta Barbara ★★★ (Chard) **91 92 93 94** 95 96 (Pinot N) **90 91 92 93** 94 **95** Jim Clendenen listens to his private drummer: ultra-toasty Chard, flavourful Pinot N, light-hearted Pinot Bl. Italian varietals under Podere dellos Olivos label. Also for QUPE and VITA NOVA (Santa Maria Valley) wines.

Barnett Napa ★ Tiny producer. Intriguing Cab from estate high on Spring Mtn.

Beaucanon Napa ★★ Bordeaux owners Lebègue turning out consistently supple stylish Cab S, Merlot and improving Chard from own 250 acres. LaCrosse is second label.

Beaulieu Vineyard Napa ★★ (Cab) **36 45 49 58 65 80 90 92** 94 95 Long-time growers and makers of famous age-worthy Georges Delatour Private Reserve Cab. Best value: lean oak-free Sauv and polished CARNEROS Chard. HEUBLEIN-owned.

Belvedere Sonoma ★★ William Hambrecht uses mostly his own grapes for Alexander Valley Cab S, Dry Creek Valley Zin, Russian River Chard.

Benziger Family Winery Sonoma ★★ Called Benziger of Glen Ellen until Proprietors Reserve sold to HEUBLEIN. Now all SONOMA grapes and dotty for oak in everything in a wide range.

Beringer Napa ★★→★★★ (Chard) **95 96** (Cab S) **80 81 84 87** 90 91 92 95 96 Century-old winery restored to front rank. Well-defined Cabs (NV Private Reserve, Knights Valley) far outshine fat, ultra-oaky Chardonnays; Zin more than just worthy. Also own CHATEAU SOUVERAIN, MERIDIAN, NAPA RIDGE, (as of '96) CH ST JEAN and (as of '96) STAG'S LEAP WINERY.

Boeger El Dorado ★★ Mostly estate wines. Attractive Merlot, Barbera, Zin – all less bold than many neighbours.

Bonny Doon Livermore ★★★ Literary, adventurous Rhône-pioneer makes fascinating Le Sophiste (white), red Cigare Volant and Old Telegram; Vin Gris de Cigare is also delicious. Newer Italian varieties are now claiming equal attention.

Bouchaine Carneros ★★★ (Chard) **89 90 91 92 93 94** 95 96 (Pinot) **91 92** 93 94 95 96 Long somnolent, recently inspired or close to it. Chard and Pinot N both in upper ranks of region. Renovated cellars may have helped.

Brander Vineyard Sta Barbara ★★ Long-time regional of Sta Ynez Valley looking more to power, less to finesse in recent vintages of Sauv and Meritage-type Bouchet.

Bronco Wine Company San Joaquin ★→★★ Umbrella label for varietal wines: LAURIER (cream of crop), Forest Glen, Grand Cru, Hacienda, Napa Creek, RUTHERFORD VINTNERS. C C Vineyard and J F J Bronco are labels for penny-saver generic wines.

In 1970, California Chardonnay plantings produced roughly 370,000 cases of wine. In 1996, the potential was approximately 20,088,000 cases.

Bruce, David Sta Cruz Mts ★★★ (Pinot) **87 89 90 91** 92 93 94 95 Long-time source of eccentric bruiser (now moderated) Chard. Pinot N (from own and SONOMA vines) is forte.

Buehler Napa ★★ (Chard) **92 93** 95 (Cab S) **89 90 91** 92 95 In E hills: has settled in as source of vg modest-priced NAPA Cab S , Zin and Russian River Valley Chard.

Buena Vista Carneros ★★ (Chard) **91 94** 95 96 (Cab S) **81 82 87 90 92** 93 94 95 96 Back on form after two stumbling yrs with delicious taste-the-grapes CARNEROS Chard, Merlot and (well-kept secret) intense, ageless Cab S from 1,100-acre property in the AVA. Also fine Lake County Sauv.

Burgess Cellars Napa ★★ (Zin) **90 91** 94 95 96 Emphasis on dark weighty well-oaked reds; Cab rather plain-faced, Zin more compelling.

BV Abbreviation of BEAULIEU VINEYARD used on its labels.

Bynum, Davis Sonoma ★★ (Chard) **93 94 95** 96 (Pinot N) **91 92 93** 94 95 96 Steady for years. Now turning to single-v'yd wines and gaining added depth: especially Russian River Valley Chard, Pinot N, vg Sauv Bl and Gewürz.

Byron Vineyards Sta Barbara ★★★ (Chard) **91 92 93** 95 96 (Pinot) **84 88 89 90 91 93** 94 95 96 Prospering under R MONDAVI-ownership; estate Pinot N leads with Chard not far behind.

Cain Cellars Napa ★★★ (Cain Five) **85 86 87 90'** 91 92 94 Focal point is increasingly stylish supple Cain Five, blended from Cab varieties grown in estate v'yd on Spring Mt. Cain Cuvée is declassified C Five that s'times rivals it; white is (also fine) MONTEREY Sauv Musqué.

Cafaro Napa ★★ Winemaker label for sturdy-to-stolid Cab and Merlot.

Cakebread Napa ★★★ (Chard) **95** 96 (Cab S) **81 85 86 87 90 91** 92 94 95 Bold well-oaked style rules in Sauv, Chard and Cab.

Calera San Benito ★★★ (Chard) **95** 96 (Pinot) **82 85 87 91** 92 94 95 96 Dry sunny chalky hills nr Chalone lead to booming Rhône-weight estate Pinot Ns named after individual v'yd blocks (Reed, Selleck, Jensen). Also for perfumiest Viognier.

Callaway Temecula ★★ (Chard) **85 90 91 92 94 95** 96 Oak-free, lees-aged Chard is a triumph from this warm dry region; Fumé Blanc also good.

Cambria Sta Barbara ★★ Part of KENDALL-JACKSON'S ARTISANS AND ESTATES group. Watch for Chard and enticing Pinot N.

Canandaigua Huge NY firm with major role in California; now No 2 to GALLO and growing. Today includes INGLENOOK, DUNNEWOOD, Paul Masson, COOKS.

NB Vintages in colour are those you should choose first for drinking in 1998.

Carmenet Sonoma ★★→★★★ (Cab S blend) **87 90** 91**92** 94 95 CHALONE-owned mountain v'yd and winery above SONOMA town: classy plummy Cab-based blends (Dynamite, Moon Mountain, Vin de Garde etc). Also MONTEREY Sauv blend and CARNEROS Chard.

Carneros Creek Carneros ★★→★★★ (Chard) **95** 96 (Pinot N) **85 87 90** 91**92** **93** 94 95 96 Resolute explorer of climates and clones in CARNEROS focussing predominantly on Pinot N. Well-oaked Reserve, lightheartedly fruity Fleur and split-the-difference estate bottlings. Also deftly oaked Chard. 25,000 cases.

Castoro San Luis Obispo ★★ Paso Robles estate, as substantial as its wines (Cab S and Zin).

Caymus Napa ★★★→★★★★ (Cab S) **74 75 78 79 81** 85**87 90** 91 92 94 95 Dark firm textbook American-oaked Cab 'Special Selection' is the celebrated core; slightly lighter regular bottling not far behind. Developing v'yds in MONTEREY, SONOMA for other varieties.

Cedar Mountain Livermore ★★ One of most ambitous in new wave of estate wineries: Cab and Chard.

Chalk Hill Sonoma ★★ From large estate nr Windsor, me-too Chard, similarly oaky Sauv. Still groping for a style for Cab. New winemaker in '96.

Chalone Monterey ★★★ (Chard) **89 90 91** 92 **93** 94 95 96 Unique hilltop estate high in Gavilan Mts; source of smoky woody flinty Chard and dark tannic Pinot N, both slow-to-open burgundy-imitations (Pinot N can go 15 yrs). Also Pinot Bl and Chenin styled after Chard. 25,000 cases. Also owns ACACIA, CARMENET, EDNA VALLEY VINEYARD, Gavilan and Canoe Ridge (Washington). Has links with (Lafite) Rothschilds.

Chappellet Napa ★★★ (Cab S) **75 76 78 82 84** 86 87 90 91' 92 94 Beautiful amphitheatrical hill v'yd. Cab S has been lean racy to age. Chard and Chenin Bl too. In rough patch just now.

Château Montelena Napa ★★★ (Chard) **92 93** 95 95 96 Understated age-worthy Chard and recently modified (91 92) but still tannic potent Calistoga-estate Cab to age for ever.

Château Potelle Napa ★★ French-owned new producer of balanced quietly impressive Chard (with toasty Reserve version). Also Cab S and luxury-priced Mt Veeder Zin.

Château St Jean Sonoma ★★→★★★ (Chard) **90 91 92 93** 94 95 Known for intense, richly textured, individual-v'yd Chards (Robert Young, Belle Terre, McCrea), Fumé Bl (Petite Etoile), and sweet botrytised Ries and Traminers (Robert Young, Belle Terre). Reds gaining in volume. Bought from Suntory in '96 by BERINGER owners.

Château Souverain Sonoma ★★ (Cab S) **85 87** 90 **91** 94 95 96 Reliable Chard, Alexander Valley Cab S and Dry Creek Zin, all lately with lots of oak. 150,000 cases. Same owner as BERINGER.

Château Woltner Napa ★★→★★★ Howell Mountain estate Chards (incl expensive 'Frederique') from ex-owners of Ch La Mission Haut Brion. Tasty young but have yet to find the secret of long life.

Chimney Rock Napa ★★ (Cab S) **87** 90 91 92 94 95 Supple mannerly Cab and Sauv from Stag's Leap district. Chard, newly CARNEROS, on upswing.

The Christian Brothers Madera (San Joaquin Valley) ★ One-time NAPA VALLEY institution, now shrunk to brandy-only label for HEUBLEIN.

Christopher Creek Sonoma ★★ Expat Briton pouring heart and soul into Syrah and Petite Sirah in small lots from the Russian River Valley.

Cline Cellars Carneros ★★ Originally Contra Costa (imp't v'yds still there), now in SONOMA/CARNEROS and still dedicated mostly to husky Rhône Rangers (blends and varietals), eg Côtes d'Oakley, Mourvèdre.

Clos du Bois Sonoma ★★→★★★ (Chard) 94 95 96 (Cab) **87** 90 91 92 94 95 96 Sizeable (400,000-case) Allied-Hiram Walker firm at Healdsburg. Winemaker Margaret Davenport hitting impressive stride with Cab S, Cab blends, Chard, Sauv. Top are single-v'yd incl Cab 'Briarcrest', Chard 'Calcaire'.

Clos Pegase Napa ★★★ (Chard) **92** 93 94 95 96 (Cab S) 85 **86** 87 90 91 94 95 Post-modernist winery-cum-museum (or vice versa) improving on already good reputation esp with CARNEROS Chard and Calistoga Cabs.

Clos du Val Napa ★★★ (Chard) **90 91 92** 93 **94 95** 96 (Cab) 72 **74** 75 77 **80** 81 **82** 83 85 86 87 90 91 94 95 96 French-run. Cab S, Cab-based Reserve from Stag's Leap district perhaps NAPA's best agers of all, yet accessible early. Merlot also sure-footed. Understated silky CARNEROS Chard is best white. 55,000 cases.

Codorníu Carneros ★★★ California arm of great Catalan cava co is competing well with local Champenois. New ('97) winemaker now making substantial quantities of still Pinot N and Chard too.

Cohn, B R Sonoma ★★→★★★ Widely praised SONOMA estate Cab S: oaky young, oaky old and oaky in between.

Concannon Livermore ★★ WENTE VINEYARDS now owns this historically famous source of Sauv. Starting to specialize in Rhône varieties.

Conn Creek Napa ★★ Best known for supple, almost juicy Cab: as of '93 concentrating on this and 'Anthology' blend. Owned by Château Ste Michelle (see Washington).

Cooks Penny-saving 'Cooks Champagne' and others from San Joaquin; belongs to CANANDAIGUA.

Corbett Canyon San Luis Obispo ★→★★ (Pinot N Res) **89 90 91 92 93** 95 96 Large (500,000 cases) Central Coast producer with s'times memorable Reserve Pinot N. Mostly is abundant source of modest Coastal Classic varietals.

Corison Napa ★★→★★★ (Cab) 87 **90** 91 92 94 95 Long-time winemaker at CHAPPELLET on her own making supple flavoursome Cab promising to age well.

Cosentino Napa ★★ (Pinot N) 93 **94** 95 96 Irrepressible winemaker-owner always full-tilt. Results s'times odd, sometimes brilliant, never dull. CARNEROS Pinot Ns are to seek first.

Crichton Hall Napa ★★ Ambitious estate-launched Chard label; now also CARNEROS Merlot, Pinot.

Cronin Sta Cruz Mtns ★★ Lilliputian cult producer of Brobdignagian buttered toast Chards from varied sources.

Culbertson Temecula ★★ Specialist in classic sparkling: labelled Thornton.

Curtis Sta Barbara ★★ (Chard) **92 93 94** 95 96 Renamed from Carey Cellars in '96. Impressive since acquisition by FIRESTONE for esp tropical Chard, also Sauv and Merlot of the capsicum persuasion.

Cuvaison Napa ★★★ (Chard) 92 93 **94** 95 96 (Merlot) **85 86** 87 **90** 91 **92** 94 95 96 Lean crisp CARNEROS Chard is steadily top rank. Dark ripe Merlot and up-valley Cab following suit. Recent CARNEROS Pinot begins to shine.

Dalla Valle Napa ★★→★★★ Larger-than-life founder Gustave DV died in '95; his widow continues with epically scaled estate Cab, Cab-based 'Maya'.

Dehlinger Sonoma ★★★ (Pinot) **87 89** 90' 91 **92 93** 94 95 96 Focus ever stronger on estate Russian River Valley Pinot Noirs, and rightly. Chard good too. Family-owned.

DeLoach Vineyards Sonoma ★★★ (Chard) **92 93** 94 95 96 (Zin) **81 87 90** 91 **92 93 95** Fruit-rich Chard still the mainstay of reliable 80,000-case Russian River Valley winery. Pinot N ever better, and gargantuan single-v'yd Zins (Papera, Pelletti) finding an audience.

de Lorimier Sonoma ★★ Alexander Valley estate winery: worthy Sauv-Sém and Cab family blends; also Chard.

Diamond Creek Napa ★★★★ (Cab S) **76 77 78 79 80 81 82 83 84 85 86 87 88 89** 90 91 92 93 94 95 96 Austere, stunningly high-priced cult Cabs from hilly v'yd nr Calistoga go by names of v'yd blocks, eg Gravelly Meadow, Volcanic Hill. 3,000 cases.

Domaine Carneros Carneros (★★★) Showy US outpost of Taittinger in CARNEROS echoes austere style of its parent in Champagne. Recent Blanc de Blancs leads the way. 25,000+ cases.

Domaine Chandon Napa ★★→★★★ Maturing v'yds, maturing style, broadening range taking Moët & Chandon's California arm to new heights. Look esp for NV Reserve, Brut Rosé. 350,000 cases.

Domaine Napa Napa Sadly, now defunct.

Domaine Saint-Gregory Mendocino ★ Companion label to MONTE VOLPE, for wines from French grapes.

Dominus Napa ★★★★ **83 84 85 86 87 88 89** 90 **91** 95 Christian Moueix of Pomerol is now sole owner of v fine v'yd. Massively tannic Cab-based blend up to 88, now looks amazingly like fine B'x (tannins softer in 90 91). Dave Ramey is new winemaker.

Dry Creek Vineyard Sonoma ★★ Unimpeachable source of dry tasty whites, esp Chard and Fumé Blanc, but also Chenin Bl. Cab S and Zinfandel rather underrated. 110,000 cases.

Duckhorn Vineyards Napa ★★★ (Merlot) **85 86 87 90'** 91 92 93 94 95 Known for dark, tannic, almost plummy-ripe single-v'yd Merlot (Three Palms, Vine Hill). Now also Cab-based blend 'Howell Mountain'. Also vg Sauv. 18,000 cases.

Dunn Vineyards Napa ★★★ (Cab) **87** 89 **90** 91 92 93 94 95 Owner-winemaker Randall Dunn makes dark tannic austere Cab from Howell Mt, slightly milder from valley floor. 4,000 cases.

Dunnewood Mendocino ★→★★ Canandaigua-owned producer of reliably good value North Coast varietals.

Durney Vineyard Monterey ★★→★★★ (Cab) **83** 95 96 New owners reviving estate after death of eponymous founder. Esp dark robust Carmel Valley Cab, rich Chard. Cachagua line is ★★.

Eberle Winery San Luis Obispo ★★ Burly ex-footballer makes Cab and Zin in his own image. Also look for their polar opposite: Muscat Canelli.

Edna Valley Vineyard San Luis Obispo ★★ (Chard) 93 **94 95** 96 Decidedly toasty Chard from a joint venture of local grower and CHALONE. Pinot N best drunk soon after vintage. 48,000 cases.

Estancia MONTEREY white (good-value Chard, Sauv) and Alexander Valley red (Cab and Sangiovese) made at FRANCISCAN.

Etude Napa ★★★ (Pinot N) **87 89 90 91 92 93** 94 95 96 Winemaker-owned cellar of respected consultant Tony Soter. Burnished CARNEROS Pinot (**87** 89 90 91 95). Polished NAPA Cab, plus experiments eg Pinots Gris and Meunier.

Far Niente Napa ★★★ (Chard) **94** 95 96 (Cab S) **91 92** 94 95 96 Opulence appears to be the goal in both Cab S and Chard from luxury mid-NAPA estate.

Farrell, Gary Sonoma ★★→★★★ (Pinot) **89 90 92 93 94 95** 96 Winemaker's label for brilliant well-oaked toasty Russian River Pinots; also Chard, berryish Zin.

Ferrari-Carano Sonoma ★★→★★★ (Chard) **95** 96 (Cab) **87 90 92** 94 95 96 Shifting styles make wines hard to track: showcase winery drawing on SONOMA v'yds for toasty Chard, sturdy Cab S, intriguing Sangiovese.

Fetzer Mendocino ★★ Consistently good value from least expensive (Sun Dial, Valley Oaks) to expensive (Reserve) ranges. 3M cases. From organic v'yds.

Ficklin San Joaquin ★★ First in California to use Douro grapes. Since 1948, Tinta California's best 'port'. Sometimes vintages.

Field Stone Sonoma ★★ Flavourful estate-grown Alexander Valley Cab S too often overlooked. Old-vine Petite Sirah can be impressive.

Firestone Sta Barbara ★★→★★★ (Chard) **94 95** 96 (Merlot) **90 91 92** 94 95 96 Fine Chard overshadows but does not outshine delicious Ries. Merlot good; Cab one of region's best. Owns CURTIS.

Fisher Sonoma ★★ Hill-top SONOMA grapes for often fine Chard; NAPA grapes dominate steady Cab. 10,000 cases.

California wines to try in 1998

Mumm Napa Valley DVX
Roederer Estate Mendocino, L'Ermitage (luxury cuvée)
Bouchaine Carneros Chardonnay
Gary Farrell Russian River Valley Pinot Noir
Freemark Abbey Napa Valley Cabernet Sauvignon, Sycamore Vineyard
Lane Tanner Santa Maria Valley Pinot Noir, Sierra Madre Plateau
Seghesio Sonoma County Zinfandel
Shafer Vineyards Napa Valley Cabernet Sauvignon, Hillside Selection

Flora Springs Wine Co Napa ★★→★★★ (Chard) 95 96 (Trilogy) **85 86 87 90 91 92** 94 95 96 Old stone cellar. Fine Sauvignon Soliloquy parallels oak-fermented Chard, flavoursome Reserve Cab and luxury Cab blend Trilogy. Sangiovese to be watched. 18,000 cases.

Fogarty, Thomas Sta Cruz Mts ★★ Fine Gewürz from VENTANA sets the pace; whole line is well-made.

Folie à Deux Napa ★ Veteran winemaker Dr Richard Peterson heads the revival of a small winery once known for fine Chard.

Foppiano Sonoma ★★ Long-est'd wine family turning out fine reds, esp Petite Sirah. Fox Mountain: label for Chard, Sauv; second label: Riverside.

Forman Napa ★★★ The winemaker who brought STERLING its first fame in the '60s now makes excellent Cab and Chard on his own. 15,000 cases.

Foxen Sta Barbara ★★★ (Pinot N) **89 90 91 92 93 94** 95 96 Tiny winery nestled between the Santa Ynez and Santa Maria valleys. Always bold, frequently brilliant Pinot N.

Franciscan Vineyard Napa ★★ (Cab) **85 87 89 90 91 92** 94 95 96 Big v'yd at Oakville: increasingly stylish Chard, Cab, Zin. Sister labels: MOUNT VEEDER, ESTANCIA, Pinnacles (MONTEREY).

Franzia San Joaquin ★ Penny-saver wines (eg Franzia label); varietals under many labels. All say 'Made and bottled in Ripon'. 5M cases.

Freemark Abbey Napa ★★★ (Chard) **89 90 91 92 93 94** 95 96 (Cab S) **67 69 72 74 75 80 81 82 83 85 87 91** 92 94 95 96 Underrated today, but consistent for inexhaustible stylish Cabernet Sauvignons (esp single-v'yd Sycamore and Bosché) of great depth. Vg deliciously true-to-variety Chardonnay. Also late-harvest Riesling Edelwein, infrequent but always among California's finest.

Fritz, J Sonoma ★★ With '95s new winemaker abruptly changed style from fruit-first and racy to oaky and fat, esp in whites.

Frog's Leap Napa ★★→★★★ (Cab S) **82 87 90 91 92** 94 95 96 Small winery, charming as its name (and T-shirts) and organic to boot. Lean racy Sauv, Zin, Cab, Merlot usually understated; toasty Chard quite the reverse.

Gainey Vineyard, The Sta Barbara ★★ Steadily attractive Chard, Sauv, Cab and esp Pinot N. 12,000 cases.

To decipher codes, please refer to 'Key to symbols' on front flap of jacket, or to 'How to use this book' on page 6.

Gallo, E & J San Joaquin ★→★★★ (Chard) 95 96 (Cab S) **90 91** 92 93 94 95 Having mastered the world of commodity wines (Hearty 'Burgundy', Pink Chablis etc) this 40M-case family firm (the world's biggest) is turning ever-sharper focus on SONOMA holdings for single-v'yd wines and specialities. Top estate Cab, Zin are excellent; Chard closing the gap.

Gan Eden Sonoma ★★ Kosher producer of traditional single-grape wines has won substantial praise for Chards.

Geyser Peak Sonoma ★★ Since brief marriage with Penfolds of Australia, extensive v'yds of Henry Trione in Alexander and Russian River valleys (lovely grapes) make Penfolds-style wine. Well-oaked Chard, Cab now joined by Shiraz, all mostly from winery-owned v'yds. Also: superb new-mown Sauv. Second label: Canyon Road.

Glen Ellen Proprietor's Reserve HEUBLEIN widely sourced penny-saver varietal brand purchased '94 from BENZIGER.

Gloria Ferrer Carneros ★★ Substantial classic-sparkling winery of Spain's Freixenet has scored well, esp for Cuvée Royale and Cuvée Carneros. Smoky, silky CARNEROS Pinot N commands attention.

Green and Red Napa ★★ Tiny winery. Vigorous Tuscan-tasting Zin and rustic Chard worth a hunt.

Greenwood Ridge Mendocino ★★ (Pinot) 91 **93** 95 96 Est'd specialist in racy Anderson Valley Ries more recently appreciable for melony Sauv, herby Merlot. Pinot N begins to convince, too. 4,000 cases.

Grgich Hills Cellars Napa ★★★ (Chard) **91** 93 94 95 96 (Cab S) **80 81 83 84 85 86 87** 89 90 91 95 Winemaker Grgich and grower Hills join forces on a stern deftly-oaked Chard, impressively long-ageing rich Cab, Sauv Bl, and – too little noticed – Spätlese-sweet Ries. Also plummy thick SONOMA Zin. 40,000 cases.

Groth Vineyards Napa ★★→★★★ (Cab S) **82 85 86 87 88** 90 91 92 95 Estate at Oakville challenges leaders among NAPA Cab and Sauv Bl. Also vg Chard.

Guenoc Vineyards Lake County ★★ Ambitious winery/v'yd venture just N of NAPA county line. Property once Lillie Langtry's challenge to Bordeaux. Now best known for surprisingly fine Chard. Also vg Cab, Zin.

Guild Long-time cooperative and its many labels, esp COOKS, DUNNEWOOD, bought by and absorbed into CANANDAIGUA.

Gundlach-Bundschu Sonoma ★★→★★★ (Chard) **93** 94 95 96 (Cab) **85 90** 91 **92** 94 95 96 Pioneer name solidly revived by fifth generation. Versatile Rhinefarm v'yd signals memorably individual Gewürz, Merlot, Zin, Pinot N. 50,000 cases.

Hafner Sonoma ★★ (Cab S) **87 89 91 92** 94 95 Semi-secretive Alexander V winery for flavourful ageable Cab. Also agreeable Chard. 8,000 cases.

Hagafen Napa ★★ First and perhaps still finest of the serious kosher producers. Esp Chard and Johannisberg Ries. 6,000 cases.

Handley Cellars Mendocino ★★ (Chard) **89 90 91** 92 93 94 95 Winemaker-owned producer of excellent Anderson Valley classic sparklers. Also still Pinot N (91 92) and Gewürz, and, from family v'yd in Dry Creek Valley, superior Chard and Sauv.

Hanna Winery Sonoma ★★ 600 acres of Russian River and Alexander valleys with sound middle-of-the-road Chard, Cab, Sauv. New winemaker in '96.

Hanzell Sonoma ★★★ (Chard) **91 94** 95 96 (Pinot N) **93** 94 95 96 The late founder revolutionized California Chards, Pinot Ns with new oak in late '50s. Three owners later Hanzell remains a throwback source of original ripe full-flavoured wines from SONOMA estate v'yd.

Haywood Vineyard Sonoma ★★ BUENA VISTA-owned SONOMA vineyards esp good for Chard, Zin. Vintner Select line for bought-in wine.

Heitz Napa ★★★→★★★★ (Cab)74 **78 79 80 84**87 91 92 94 95 96 Individualist winemaker set lofty standards for his peers in '60s and '70s with dark deep emphatic Cabs, esp Martha's Vineyard. Newer Trailside Vineyard in similar league. Bella Oaks one step back. Whites can be eccentric but dry Grignolino Rosé brilliant. 40,000 cases.

The vigorous strain of phylloxera that is forcing Napa and Somona to replant about half of their 60,000 acres of vineyard on new rootstocks is being combated: Napa is expected to pass its planting halfway mark in 1997, Sonoma about two years later.

Hess Collection, The Napa★★→★★★ (Chard) **94** 95 96 (Cab S) **87**91 92 93 94 95 A Swiss art collector's winery-cum-museum in former Mont La Salle winery of CHRISTIAN BROTHERS. Steady Cab, Chard on Mount Veeder. Non-Napa Hess Selection label is vg value. 40,000 cases.

Heublein Vast drinks firm with ambivalent interest in wine. (See Beaulieu, Christian Bros, Glen Ellen Proprietor's Reserve, M G Vallejo).

Hidden Cellars Mendocino ★★ Ukiah producer of Sauv Bl, Zin often from single v'yds.

Hill Winery, William Napa ★★ (Cab S) **85 87 91** 92 93 94 95 96 Since '94 a Wine Alliance stable-mate to ATLAS PEAK, CLOS DU BOIS. Good Chard, Cab, but Sauv, Merlot have shown greater promise. Jill Davis, ex-BUENA VISTA, the new winemaker.

Hill & Thoma Partnership Diverse, mostly emerging holdings. Carneros Bighorn (Chard, Pinot N), Domaine Clos du Fontaine (NAPA Cab), Parducci: recently acquired historic Mendocino winery with heretofore long list. And, in Oregon, Van Duzer (Chard, Pinot N).

Hop Kiln Sonoma ★★ Source of sometimes startlingly fine 'Valdiguie' (aka Napa Gamay). Russian River Gewürz is full-flavoured and large-scale.

Husch Vineyards Mendocino★★ Reliable Ukiah Chard, Sauv, Cab; sometimes outstanding Pinot N and Gewürz from Anderson Valley. 15,000 cases.

Inglenook Napa ★★→★★★ (Cab) **55 56 62 68 78 81 87** History-rich NAPA name (but not property) purchased by CANANDAIGUA. Inglenook Navalle label active, Napa not at present. V'yd and splendid old cellars now part of NIEBAUM-COPPOLA.

Iron Horse Vineyards Sonoma★★★ (Chard)94 95 96 (Brut) **90** 91 92 93 Substantial Russian River property increasingly focussed on classic ageworthy sparklings that hover between finesse and boldness, but continues with Chard and Pinot from same estate v'yd, plus Cab and Sauv from affiliated Alexander V vines.

Jade Mountain Napa (★★) Sharing winery with WHITE ROCK and pursuing lofty goals using Rhône varieties, esp Syrah.

Jekel Vineyards Monterey ★★ (Chard) **91 92 93**95 96 Jekel's ripe juicy Ries is most successful wine from SALINAS v'yds. Also good Chard, intensely regional (capsicum-flavoured) Cab. 60,000 cases.

Jepson Vineyards Mendocino ★★ Sound steady Chard, Sauv Bl and classic sparkling from estate in Ukiah area. Also pot-still brandy.

Jordan Sonoma ★★★ (Chard) **94**95 96 (Cab S) **82 84 85 87 90 91** 93 94 95 96 Extravagant Alexander Valley estate models its Cab on supplest Bordeaux. And it lasts. (Chard is less successful.) Separate classic sparkling called simply 'J' is deft, soft, luxurious (**89 90 91**). 75,000 cases.

Karly Amador ★★ Among more ambitious sources of SIERRA FOOTHILLS Zin.

Keenan Winery, Robert Napa ★★ Winery on Spring Mountain: supple, restrained Cab, Merlot under new winemaker Nils Venge; also Chard.

CALIFORNIA

Kendall-Jackson Lake County ★★→★★★ Staggeringly successful with style aimed at widest market: esp broadly sourced off-dry toasty Chard. Even more noteworthy for the development of a diversity of wineries under the umbrella of 'ARTISANS AND ESTATES'.

Kenwood Vineyards Sonoma ★★→★★★ (Chard) **90 91 92** 93 95 (Cab S) **87 88 89** 90 **91** 95 Substantial producer of reliable Chard and Cab S (incl single-v'yd Jack London). Esp worth seeking for stellar v'yd-first Sauv, single-v'yd Zin (Nuns Canyon, Mazzoni).

Kistler Vineyards Sonoma ★★★ (Chard) **93 94 95** 96 Chards much in smoky buttery style (esp single v'yd). Pinot N and Cab more recent.

Konocti Cellars Lake County ★★ Excellent value Sauv, good Chard, but most intriguing is refreshing Cab Franc.

Korbel Sonoma ★★ Long-est'd classic-sparkling specialist with widely placed emphasis on fruit flavours. Lots of fizz; Natural, Brut, Blanc de Blancs are best.

Krug, Charles Napa ★★ (Chard) **94** 95 96 (Cab S) **80 84 85 91** 92 93 94 95 96 Historically important winery with generally sound wines. Cabs at head of list, CARNEROS Chards, Pinot Ns not far behind. CK-Mondavi is jug brand.

Kunde Estate Sonoma ★★→★★★ (Chard) **95** 96 Long-time large growers emerging as winemaking force with buttery Chard, flavourful Sauv (lightly touched with Viognier). Cab, Cab Reserve, Merlot, Zin still finding a footing.

La Crema Sonoma ★★ (Chard) **94** 95 96 (Pinot N) **90 91 93** 94 95 96 Part of K-J's ARTISANS AND ESTATES group, turning ever-more to Russian River Valley AVA as a source for Chard and Pinot N wines of vg and improving quality.

La Jota Napa ★★ Pricey Cab S from small estate on Howell Mountain.

Lakespring Napa ★★ Label of one-time NAPA winery bought '95 by Frederick Wildman (same owner as MARK WEST); wines being custom-made by assoc v'yd group.

Lambert Bridge Sonoma ★★ New owners have resurrected briefly defunct cellar with Dry Creek Valley v'yd: fine track record for Chard, Cab S.

Landmark Sonoma ★★ (Chard) **95** 96 Long-time Chard specialist moving from crisp and fresh to me-too toasty-buttery.

Laurel Glen Sonoma ★★★ (Cab S) **82 85 86 89 90 91** 92 93 95 96 Big-scale firm, distinctly regional Cab from steep hilly v'yd in Sonoma Mountain sub-AVA. Counterpoint is good-value second label. 5,000 cases.

Laurier Sonoma ★★ (Chard) **94 95** 96 Crown-jewel label of BRONCO WINE CO. Currently aiming high with Chard. Pinot N began with 93.

Lava Cap El Dorado ★★ Where bold styles rule, these are understated, intriguing. Zins, Cabs and others.

Lazy Creek Mendocino ★★ 'Retirement hobby' of a long-time restaurant waiter yields serious Anderson Valley Gewürz and Chard. Also Pinot N.

Leeward Winery Ventura ★★ (Chard) **95** 96 Ultra-toasty Central Coast Chards are the mainstay. 18,000 cases.

Liberty School San Luis Obispo ★→★★ Ex-second label of CAMUS bought in '96 by its primary supplier of Cab S and moved to his v'yd at Paso Robles.

Liparita Napa ★★ Erstwhile estate now making Chard, Cab, Merlot in leased space from bought-in Howell Mt grapes. Merry Edwards consults. Winery to come.

Lockwood Monterey ★★ Huge v'yd in S SALINAS VALLEY supplying show-case winery. Terroir is foremost throughout range.

Lohr, J Central Coast ★→★★ Large wide-reaching firm at peak with Paso Robles Cab S 'Seven Oaks'. Mainstream line subtitled Cypress.

Long Vineyards Napa ★★★ (Chard) **95** 96 (Cab) **80 81 82 83 84 85 86 87 90** 91 92 94 95 96 Tiny neighbour of CHAPPELLET: lush Chard, flavourful Cab, luxury prices.

Lyeth Vineyard Sonoma ★★ Former winery/estate, now a négociant label for Burgundian J C Boisset's California arm. Good red, excellent white MERITAGE types. Also Chard. Christophe is second label. Boisset also own WHEELER.

Lytton Springs Sonoma ★★ Bought and then closed down by RIDGE; its grapes go into proprietorial Ridge Lytton Springs.

MacRostie Carneros ★★ Chards, the flagship, are less buttery (95) than formerly. Also Pinot N, Merlot.

Madrona El Dorado ★★ Loftiest v'yds in SIERRA FOOTHILLS, good for steady Chards (among others). 10,000 cases.

Maison Deutz San Luis Obispo ★★→★★★ California arm of Champagne Deutz (qv) shows a firm sense of style: grapes from Arroyo Grande AVA. Now also still wines (Pinot N, Chard) under Carpe Diem label.

Mark West Vineyards Sonoma ★★ V satisfactory Gewürztraminer, sturdy-to-rustic Chard, Pinot and Bl de Noirs sparkling. Now owned by Associated Vintners Group.

Markham Napa ★★ (Cab S) **87 90 91 92** 93 94 95 96 Recently good to excellent, esp Merlot and Cab S grown in own v'yds. ('Laurent' label discontinued.)

Martin Bros San Luis Obispo ★★ Entirely dedicated to Italian varieties (Nebbiolo, Sangiovese), or styles ('Vin Santo', chestnut-aged Chard). Bros recently split.

Martini, Louis M Napa ★★→★★★ (Cab S) **52 55 59 64 68 70 74 78 79 80 83 85 87 90 91** 92 93 94 95 96 Historic family-owned winery with high standards, esp single v'yd Cab (Monte Rosso), Merlot (Los Vinedos del Rio) and reserve Cab. Zins s'times surpassing.

Masson Vineyards Monterey ★→★★ This is the 'Fighting varietal' spoke in CANANDAIGUA'S growing wheel of California wineries and labels. Taylor California Cellars is lower-priced companion label.

Matanzas Creek Sonoma ★★★ (Chard) **94** 95 96 (Merlot) **91 92 93** 94 95 96 Fine ripe toasty-oaky Chard, Sauv, and renowned ultra-fleshy Merlot. Once-clear style drifting just a bit of late.

Maurice Car'rie Temecula ★★ Setting standards for its region with reliable, approachable Chard, Sauv and others.

Mayacamas Napa ★★★ (Chard) **91 94** 95 96 (Cab S) **69 73 78 81 85 87 90 91** 94 95 96 Vg small v'yd with rich Chard and firm (but no longer steel-hard) Cab. Some Sauv, Pinot. 5,000 cases.

Mazzocco Sonoma ★★ Good and improving Chard, Cab from Alexander and Dry Creek valley estate v'yds.

McDowell Valley Vineyards Mendocino ★★ Grower-label for family with hearts set on Rhône varieties, esp ancient-vine Syrah and Grenache.

Meridian San Luis Obispo ★★ Fast-growing sibling to BERINGER making mark with single-vineyard Edna Valley Chard, Paso Robles Syrah. Also Sta Barbara Chard, Pinot N, Paso Robles Cab S. 300,000 cases.

Meritage Trademarked name for reds or whites using Bordeaux grape varieties. Aiming for 'varietal' status and gaining ground.

Merryvale Napa ★★ Sauv-Sém white MERITAGE is best. Middle-of-the-road are Chard, Cab S and red Meritage.

Michael, Peter Sonoma ★★→★★★ Partly Knights Valley estate-v'yd, partly bought-in Howell Mt: larger-than-life, Frenchified Chard, Merlot, Cab.

Michel-Schlumberger Sonoma ★★ Dry Creek Valley winery with rein-vigorating Alsace input; esp evident with newly subtle Cab S.

Mill Creek Sonoma ★★ Oft-overlooked reliable producer of Dry Creek Valley Cab, Merlot, Chard, Sauv.

For key to grape variety abbreviations, see pages 7–13.

Mirassou Central Coast ★★ Fifth-generation grower and pioneer in Monterey (SALINAS) gets highest marks for Pinot Bl classic sp. Chard, Pinot worth a look.

Mondavi, Robert Napa ★★→★★★★ (Chard) **94** 95 96 (Cab) **71 73 74 75 79 81 82 84** 85 87 **89 90** 91 92 93 94 95 96 Winery with brilliant quarter-century record of innovation in styles, equipment, technique. Famous successes: Sauv ('Fumé Bl'), Cab, Chard, even Pinot N. 'Reserves' are marvels, regularly among California's best. New are expensive district wines eg CARNEROS Pinot N, Oakville Cab S, Stag's Leap Sauv. Mid-price is Coastal line (vg début Sauv). Less pricey California appellation varietals: Mondavi-Woodbridge. 500,000 cases. See also Opus One.

Mont St John Carneros ★★ Old NAPA wine family makes good value Pinot N, Chard from own v'yd; buys in for solid Cab.

A personal selection of California Merlot to try in 1998
Buena Vista Carneros, Estate
Clos du Val Stag's Leap District Napa Valley
Gary Farrell Sonoma County, Ladi's Vineyard
Greenwood Ridge Anderson Valley, Estate
Louis M Martini Russian River Valley, Los Vinedos del Rio

Monte Volpe Mendocino ★★ Greg Graziano looks to his heritage and wins with brisk Pinot Bianco, tart Barbera, juicy Sangiovese. French varieties separately labelled as DOM ST-GREGORY.

Monterey Peninsula Monterey ★★ Now part of group owning QUAIL RIDGE in NAPA; making same bold MONTEREY, Amador wines as before.

Monterey Vineyard, The Monterey ★★ Seagram-owned label for good-value Salinas Valley Chard, Pinot N, Cab. Classic and more costly Limited Release.

Monteviña Amador ★★ Owned by SUTTER HOME. Turning more to Italian varieties (30 trial plantings) but hearty SIERRA Zin still the foundation stone.

Monticello Cellars Napa ★★ (Cab S) **85 87 91** 92 93 94 95 96 Basic line under Monticello label, reserves under Corley. Both incl Chard, Cab S. Reserve Pinot is the most intriguing.

Morgan Monterey ★★→★★★ (Pinot) **92 93 94** 95 96 Winemaker-owner. Basic Pinot N blends MONTEREY, CARNEROS but deep earthy possibly age-worthy Reserve is all Monterey now. Also toasty Chard, herby SONOMA Sauv.

Mount Eden Vineyards Sta Cruz Mts ★★ (Chard) **92 93** 94 95 96 Big expensive Chard from old Martin Ray v'yds; gentler MONTEREY version. Also Pinot N, Cab.

Mount Veeder Napa ★★ Once steel-hard Mt Veeder Cab now merely austere, as is more recent red MERITAGE. FRANCISCAN-owned.

Mumm Napa Valley Napa ★★★ G H Mumm-Seagram joint venture out of the box fast. Still-expanding range includes cheery Blanc de Noir, distinctive single-v'yd Winery Lake and opulent luxury DVX.

Murphy-Goode Sonoma ★★ Large Alexander V estate. Whole range lavishly oaked, esp reserves. Pinot Bl, Sauv Merlot to explore.

Nalle Sonoma ★★→★★★ (Zin) 88 **89** 90 91 **93** 94 95 96 Winemaker-owned Dry Creek cellar getting to the very heart of Zin: wonderfully berryish young; that and more with age. 2,500 cases.

Napa Ridge Sonoma(!) ★ BERINGER affiliate ensconced in old Italian Swiss colony winery, churning out solid, attractive, broadly-sourced Chard, Cab, others.

Navarro Vineyards Mendocino ★★→★★★ (Chard) **89 90 91 92 93** 94 95 96 From Anderson Valley, splendidly age-worthy Chard, perhaps the grandest Gewürz in state. Even more special: late-harvest Ries, Gewürz. Pinot N not to be ignored. Only self-deprecating prices keep this from being cult favourite of big-shot collectors.

Newton Vineyards Napa ★★→★★★ (Chard) **95** 96 (Cab S) **87 91 92** 94 95 96 Luxurious estate growing more so; formerly ponderous style now reined back to the merely opulent for Chard, Cab, Merlot.

Niebaum-Coppola Estate Napa ★★★ Movie-man Coppola's luxuriously wayward hobby much invigorated since acquisition of INGLENOOK winery and 220-acre v'yd (but not name). Flagship wine (Cab-based) Rubicon beginning to take form; more accessible Coppola Family varietals quicker to show upturn.

Opus One Napa ★★★★ (Cab S) **85 87 90 91 92** 93 94 95 96 Joint venture of R MONDAVI and Baronne Philippine de Rothschild. Spectacular new winery opened '92. Wines are showpieces too. 10,000 cases.

Parducci Mendocino ★★ Long-est'd Ukiah v'yds and winery purchased in '96 by HILL & THOMA. New direction remains to be seen.

Pecota, Robert Napa ★★ Drink-young Cab, Sauv, Chard, Gamay.

Pedroncelli Sonoma ★★ (Cab S) **85 89 90 91 92** 94 95 96 Old-hand in Dry Creek turns out honest, fairly priced Cab, Zin. Chard and Sauv often show a turn of speed.

Pepi, Robert Napa ★★ Since '95 purchase by K-J for ARTISANS AND ESTATES focus has turned to Sauv and Sangiovese wines but NAPA abandoned as sole source in favour of broader reach.

Phelps, Joseph Napa ★★★ (Chard) **94** 95 96 (Cab S) **75 81 82 85 87 90 91** 92 94 95 96 Deluxe winery and beautiful vineyard: impeccable standards. Vg Chard, Cab S (esp Backus) and Cabernet-based Insignia. Splendid late-harvest Ries and Sémillon. Also look for promising Rhône series under Vin du Mistral label.

Philips, R H Yolo, Sacramento Valley ★→★★ Pioneer in Dunnigan Hills NW of Sacramento trying everything on huge property, succeeding best with Syrah, Viognier and pretty good Chard.

Pine Ridge Napa ★★→★★★ (Chard) **93 94 95** 96 (Cab S) **82 85 87 90 91 92** 94 95 96 At growing winery in Stag's Leap district, gentlemanly Cabs are best (Stag's Leap, Rutherford etc), Merlot not bad either. Dry oak-aged Chenin 'Petite Vigne' is intriguing and there is Chard too, of course.

Piper Sonoma Sonoma ★★ Owning Piper-Heidsieck sold to JORDAN IN '97 but will continue to produce wines there under lease arrangement. Russian River AVA will be the source.

Preston Sonoma ★★ One of California's pioneer 'terroiristes' concentrating on wines best suited to his Dry Creek v'yds: esp top Sauv and Zin, with promising Barbera, Syrah and Marsanne experiments.

Quady Winery San Joaquin ★★ Imaginative Madera Muscat dessert wines, including celebrated orangey 'Essencia', dark 'Elysium' and Moscato d'Asti-like 'Electra'. 'Starboard' is a play on port; a better name than wine.

Quartet See Roederer Estate.

Quail Ridge Napa ★★ Third owner has installed winery at Rutherford (ex-DOMAINE NAPA); still worthy toasty Chard, rich Sauv. Also Cab, Merlot.

Quivira Sonoma ★★ Sauv, Zin, others, from Dry Creek Valley estate. More enamoured of oak than v'yd in recent vintages.

Qupé Sta Barbara ★★→★★★ Never-a-dull-moment cellar-mate of AU BON CLIMAT. Marsanne, Pinot Bl, Syrah are all well worth trying.

Rafanelli, A Sonoma ★★ (Cab) **84 87 90 91** 92 94 95 96 (Zin) **90 91 93** 94 95 96 Hearty, fetchingly rustic Dry Creek Zin; Cab of striking intensity.

Rancho Sisquoc Sta Barbara ★★ Long-time friends-and-family winery edging onto larger stage with toasty Chard, lean Ries from sizeable estate.

Ravenswood Sonoma ★★★ Major critical success for (or despite) great bruiser single-v'yd Zins of skull-rattling power.

Raymond Vineyards and Cellar Napa ★★ (Chard) **94 95** 96 (Cab S) **82 84 85 87 90 91** 92 94 95 96 Old NAPA wine family now with Japanese partners. 'Generations' signifies well-oaked top-of-the-line Chard, Cab. Amberhill is consistent good value commodity second label.

Renwood Amador ★ Old Santino winery. Ambitious new player in SIERRA FOOTHILLS Zin game. Several single-v'yd bottlings.

Ridge Sta Cruz Mts ★★★★ (Cab S) **83 85 86 87 89 90 91 92** 93 94 95 96 Winery of highest repute among connoisseurs. Drawing from NAPA (York Creek) and its own mountain v'yd (Monte Bello) for concentrated Cabs, worthy of long maturing in bottle but needing less than formerly (MB 90 91 more approachable than 80). But power remains in SONOMA (Lytton Springs) and San Luis Obispo (Dusi) Zinfandels and other red wines. Also v pleasant Chardonnays from Santa Cruz.

Rochioli, J Sonoma ★★★ (Pinot N) **91 92** 93 **94** 95 96 Long-time Russian River grower making vg Pinot N, Sauv from own vines, long-celebrated under other labels.

Count on typical Napa Valley and other North Coast Cabernet Sauvignons to last eight years in good form. Do not expect any but famously durable ones to stay at their peak beyond 15.

Roederer Estate Mendocino ★★★ Anderson Valley branch of champagne house (est '88). Resonant Roederer style apparent esp in luxury cuvée l'Ermitage. Still stuns the Champenois. 25,000 cases, poised to triple. Sold as 'Quartet' in Europe.

Rombauer Vineyards Napa ★★ Well-oaked Chard, dark Cab S (esp reserve-style 'Meilleur du Chai'). Now also owner of the revived Hanns Kornell sparkling wine cellars and NAPA cellars.

Roudon-Smith Sta Cruz Mts ★★ Chard, Cab. 10,000 cases.

Round Hill Napa ★★ Only Cab, Chard, Merlot but in 3 price ranges under 2 labels: inexpensive California, top-of-the-line Reserve Round Hills plus intermediated NAPA line under RUTHERFORD RANCH.

Rutherford Hill Napa ★★ Aims to dominate NAPA Merlot market but finer Chard XVS and Cab XVS (the reserves) rather undercut the plan. Acquired in late '96 by Paterno Imports of Chicago, which plans to continue emphasis on Merlot and reinvigorate Cab.

Rutherford Ranch Intermediate ROUND HILL wine (see above). Value.

Rutherford Vintners Napa ★★ One-time NAPA winery, now BRONCO label.

St Clement Napa ★★→★★★ (Chard) **95** 96 (Cab) **85 87 90 91 92** 94 95 96 Firm CARNEROS Chard, NAPA Cab, Merlot. Age-able Pope Valley Sauv the star. Japanese-owned.

St Francis Sonoma ★★ (Chard) **94 95** 96 (Cab S) **87 90 91 92** 94 95 96 Firm v tasty SONOMA VALLEY estate Chard. Steady Merlot. Also Cab.

St Supéry Napa ★★ French-owned; supplied by 500-acre v'yd in Pope Valley. Easy Sauv Bl, accessible Cab, Merlot. Also Chard. 50,000 cases.

Saintsbury Carneros ★★★ (Chard) **81 91 93 94** 95 96 (Pinot N) **89 90 91 92 93 94** 95 96 Contends as AVA's finest and longest-lived Pinot N. Lighter Pinot Garnet and oaky Chard also vg. 45,000 cases.

Sanford Sta Barbara ★★★ (Pinot N) **84 86 87 89 92** 94 95 96 Specialist in intense, firmly tannic, age-worthy Pinot Noir (esp Barrel Select). Also exceptionally bold Chard; firmly regional long-lived Sauv Bl. 40,000 cases.

Santa Barbara Winery Sta Barbara ★★ (Chard) **93 94** 95 96 (Pinot) **90 91 94** 95 96 Former jug-wine producer, now among regional leaders, esp for Reserve Chard. Also Pinot N, Cab. 28,000 cases.

Santa Cruz Mountain V'yd Sta Cruz Mts ★★ Huge, tannic, heady Pinot N and subtler Rhône-variety reds. 2,500 cases.

Sausal Sonoma ★★ Steady large-scale Alexander Valley estate esp notable for its Zin and Cabs.

Scharffenberger Mendocino ★★ First to try MENDOCINO for serious classic sparkling. Now Clicquot-owned and doing well. 25,000 cases.

Schramsberg Napa ★★★★ Dedicated specialist: California's best sparkling. Historic caves. Reserve splendid; Bl de Noir outstanding, deserves 2–10 yrs. Luxury cuvée J Schram is America's Krug.

Schug Cellars Carneros ★★ (Chard) **93 94** 95 96 (Pinot N) **89 90 91 94** 95 96 German-born and trained owner-winemaker developing refined Chard and Pinot N from CARNEROS after relocating from NAPA in '91. 10,000 cases.

Sebastiani Sonoma ★→★★ Substantial old family firm working low end of market (August Sebastiani Country, Vendange, Talus) but able to compete above this price level, esp with Sonoma Creek. 4 million cases.

Seghesio Sonoma ★★ (Zin) **89 90 91 92 93** 94 95 96 Able family of long-time growers turning away from Cab, Chard wars to focus on wines they grow best: exceptional Zins, Alexander Valley Sangiovese 'Vitigno Toscano', value Russian River Pinot N.

Sequoia Grove Napa ★★ NAPA Cabs (Napa, Estate): dark and firm. Same, alas, can be said of Chards.

Shadow Creek DOMAINE CHANDON label for non-NAPA/CARNEROS classic sparkling.

Shafer Vineyards Napa ★★★ (Chard) **95** 96 (Cab S) **87 90 91 92** 94 95 With '95, oak completely overshadows grape in single-v'yd Red Shoulder Ranch Chard (CARNEROS), and begins to do in Cab (Stag's Leap).

Sierra Vista El Dorado ★★ Steady SIERRA FOOTHILLS Chard, Cab, Zin, Syrah.

Silver Oak Napa/Sonoma ★★★ Separate wineries in NAPA and Alexander Valleys make Cab S only, both with same intense American oak note. They sell out on release.

Silverado Vineyards Napa ★★→★★★ (Chard) **90 93** 95 96 (Cab S) **85 87 90 91 92 93** 95 96 Showy hilltop Stag's Leap district winery. Cab, Chard, Sauv and newer Sangiovese all consistently refined.

Simi Sonoma ★★★ (Chard) **85 91 93 94** 95 96 (Cab) **74 81 85 87 90 91 92** 94 95 96 Restored historic winery has flowered under dedicated direction of Zelma Long. Long-lived Cab. Chard, Sauv and new Sauv-Sém Sendal. Reserves, like most, try too hard. Seductive Cab rosé for picnics.

Sinskey Vineyards, Robert Napa ★★ Winery in Stag's Leap, v'yds in CARNEROS for boldly oaked, firm Chard, red MERITAGE, Pinot N.

Smith & Hook Monterey ★★ (Cab S) **86 88 90 91** 92 95 Specialist in dark age-worthy SALINAS VALLEY Cabs. Regional flavour so herbaceous you can taste dill (fades with time).

Smith-Madrone Napa ★★ Chard from Spring Mt estate has had ups and downs; now up (**91 92 93**). Ries admirably supports an almost-lost NAPA tradition. Don't miss it.

Sonoma-Cutrer Vineyards Sonoma ★★★ (Chard) **87 94** 95 96 Ultimate specialist in Chard esp single v'yd. Les Pierres is No 1 ager; Russian River Ranches is quickest to evolve. Exploring Pinot N. In rough patch just now.

Spottswoode Napa ★★★→★★★★ (Cab S) **86 87 91** 94 95 96 Firm resonant luxury Cab from small estate v'yd in St Helena town. Also supple polished Sauv. 3,500 cases.

Stag's Leap Wine Cellars Napa ★★★★ (Chard) **91 92 93** 95 (Cab S) **75 77 78 83 84 86 87** 89 90 **91** 92 95 Celebrated v'yd for silky, seductive Cabs (SLV, Fay, top-of-line Cask 23), Merlots; non-estate vg; also Chard, Sauv, Ries. 50,000 cases.

CALIFORNIA

Stag's Leap Winery Napa ★★ Neighbour to STAG'S LEAP WINE CELLARS is known for muscular Petite Syrah. Owners of BERINGER bought the 25,000-case winery and most of its v'yd in '97.

Staglin Napa (★★★) (Cab S) **90 91 92 93** 95 From small Rutherford v'yd designed by the late André Tchelistcheff, consistently superior, startlingly silky Cabs. 1,000 cases made annually.

Steele Wines Lake (★★→★★★) Long-time K-J winemaker patrols whole coast for sources of big, boldly oaked Chard, Pinot N, Cab, Zin. Pricey.

Stemmler, Robert Sonoma ★★ Soft easy Pinot N made at BUENA VISTA by RS.

Sterling Napa ★★→★★★ Scenic Seagram-owned winery with extensive v'yds and inexplicable ups and downs. Tart Sauv and firm basic bottling of Cab most reliably attractive.

Stony Hill Napa ★★★ (Chard) **91 92 93** 94 95 96 Hilly v'yd and winery for many of California's v best whites over past 30 yrs. Founder Fred McCrea died in '77, widow Eleanor in '91; son Peter carries on powerful tradition. Chard (both estate and non-estate SHV) is less steely, more fleshy than before. Oak-tinged Riesling and Gewürz are understated but age-worthy.

Storybook Mountain Napa ★★ NAPA's only dedicated Zin specialist with a heartily oaked model from Calistoga v'yds.

Strong Vineyard, Rodney Sonoma ★★ (Chard) **93 94 95** 96 (Cab) **87 90 91 92** 93 94 95 96 Formerly Sonoma V'yds; produces good basic bottlings, better single-v'yd ones (Alexander's Crown Cab, Chalk Hill Chard, Charlotte's Home Sauv, River East Pinot N).

Sutter Home Napa ★★ Best known for sweet white Zin; most admired for sometimes heady Amador Zin. Has soared from 25,000 to 7.5M cases since the mid-'70s.

Swan, Joseph Sonoma ★★ (Zin) **77 78 79 80 81 82 83 84 85 86 87** 90 91 92 95 Ultra-bold Zins, Pinots of late Joe Swan, now directed by his son-in-law.

Swanson Napa ★★→★★★ Beginnng to emerge from over-oaked phase. Estimable age-worthy Chards lead list; Cab and Merlot are worth note. Sangiovese and Syrah gaining.

Taft Street Sonoma ★★ After muddling along, has hit an impressive stride with esp good-value Russian River Chards, Merlots. 18,000 cases.

Talbott, R Monterey Wealthy owner doing well with big toasty Chards from Santa Lucia Highlands AVA, Carmel Valley.

Tanner, Lane Santa Barbara ★★★ (Pinot N) **90** 91 **93** 94 **95** 96 Owner-winemaker with often superb single-v'yd Pinot Noirs (Bien Nacido, Sierra Madre Plateau). Drink immediately or keep.

Torres Estate, Marimar Sonoma ★★★ Sister of Catalan hero makes ultra-buttery Chard, lovely Pinot from Russian River Valley estate.

Trefethen Napa ★★★ (Chard) **81 83 84 85 86 87 90 91 92 93** 94 95 96 (Cab) **74 75 79 80 84 85 87 89 90 91 92** 94 95 96 Respected family winery. Vg dry Ries, tense Chard for ageing (late-released Library wines show how well). Cab shows increasing depths. Low-priced wines subtitled 'Eshcol'.

Truchard Carneros ★★→★★★ From warmer, inner-end of CARNEROS comes one of the flavoury, firmly built Merlots that give the AVA identity. Also Chard, Cab.

Tudal Napa ★★ (Cab S) **80 84 86 87 89 90 91** 92 93 94 95 96 Tiny estate winery N of St Helena; steady source of dark firm ageable Cabs.

Turley Napa ★ Former partner in FROG'S LEAP, now focussed on Rhône varieties. Style leans heavily on oak.

Tulocay Napa ★★ (Pinot N) **85 89 90 91 92** 94 95 Tiny winery at Napa City. Pinot esp can be v accomplished. Cab is also worth attention.

Turnbull Wine Cellars Napa ★★ (Cab) **85 87 90 91** 92 93 94 95 96 Rich full minty Cab from estate facing ROBERT MONDAVI winery.

Ventana Monterey ★★ '78 winery, showcase for owner's v'yds: watch for Chard and esp Sauv from Musqué clone.

Viader Napa ★★ 90 **91** 95 Argentine Delia Viader fled to California to do her own thing: dark Cab-based blend from estate in hills above St Helena.

Viansa Carneros ★★ Sam SEBASTIANI'S reliable label for Italianate varietals: Nebbiolo, Sangiovese; also Sangio-Cab ('Thalia') from SONOMA, NAPA.

Vichon Winery Originally located in NAPA, but moved lock, stock and barrel to Languedoc by owner R MONDAVI with the '95 vintage. Still for modest-priced varietals.

Villa Mount Eden Napa ★★ Owned by Washington's Ch Ste Michelle, which has it doing two jobs: 'Grand Reserve' wines from carefully chosen v'yds the length and breadth of state (NAPA Cab, Sta Barbara Pinot N top the list), 'Cellar Select' line useful for modest priced varietals.

Vine Cliff Napa (★★★) New well-heeled family winery in E hills above Oakville. V ambitious with estate Chard, Cab S. Shows promise.

Vita Nova Sta Barbara ★★ Label from stable of AU BON CLIMAT. To watch esp for regionally distinctive Bordelais red blend.

Wente Vineyards Livermore and Monterey ★★ Historic specialist in whites, esp LIVERMORE Sauv and Sém. MONTEREY sweet Ries can be exceptional. A little classic sparkling. Also owns CONCANNON. 300,000 cases.

Whaler Mendocino ★★ Family-owned estate winery producing deep dark Zin from E hills of Ukiah Valley.

Wheeler Sonoma ★★ Was William Wheeler until bought by J C Boisset (see France). Steady source of middle-of-the-road Chard, Cab.

White Rock Napa ★★★ French owner placing faith in impressive vineyard-foremost Cab-based red, full of finesse, called simply 'Claret'. Also Chard.

White Oak Sonoma ★★ (Zin) **87 88** 90 91 95 Vibrant Zin dominates; fruit-rich ALEXANDER VALLEY Chard and Sauv underrated.

Whitehall Lane Napa ★★ Recently bought from Japanese owners by San Francisco family. Heady and boldly oaked obligatory Chard, Cab.

Wild Horse Winery San Luis Obispo ★★→★★★ (Pinot) **86 87 89 90 91** 92 94 95 96 Owner-winemaker has a particular gift for Pinot N (mostly San Louis Obispo and Sta Barbara grapes). Also worthy Chard, Merlot.

Williams Selyem Sonoma ★★★★ (Pinot) **90 91 92 93 94** 95 96 Intense smoky Russian River Pinot esp Rochioli and Allen v'yds. Now reaching to SONOMA COAST, MENDOCINO too. Followers get in line to pay high prices for emphatic individuality.

Zaca Mesa Sta Barbara ★★ Turning away from Chard and Pinot to concentrate on Rhône varieties (especially Marsanne and Syrah) and blends (Cuvée Z) grown on estate.

ZD Napa ★★→★★★ (Pinot) **90 92 93** 95 96 Lusty Chard tattooed by American oak is ZD signature wine. Pinot N is often finer. 18,000 cases.

NB Vintages in colour are those you should choose first for drinking in 1998

The Pacific Northwest

America's main quality challenge to California lies in Oregon and Washington, on the same latitudes of the Pacific Coast as France is on the Atlantic. As in California, the modern wine industry started in the 1960s. Each of the northwestern states (Oregon, Washington, Idaho) has developed a distinct identity. The small production of Canada's British Columbia fits in here too.

Oregon's vines (6,050 acres) lie mainly in the cool temperate Willamette and warmer Umpqua valleys between the Coast and Cascade ranges, in sea-tempered climates giving delicate flavours.

Washington's vineyards (11,300 acres) are mostly east of the Cascades in a dry, severe climate scarcely curbed by the Yakima and Columbia rivers. Idaho's are east of Oregon along the Snake River. Both regions have hot days and cool nights which preserve acidity and intensify flavours.

An apparent shift in weather patterns has resulted in two back-to-back vintages of the cool-and-wet persuasion. In 1995, the rain hit Oregon in early October, breaking a run of fine vintages dating from 1988. Washington was similarly affected.

In January, 1996, an Arctic cold front hit the Northwest. In eastern Washington, conditions were so bad that many vineyards were killed off. Grapes for the 1997 harvest, though high in quality were short in supply. Western Oregon vineyards were unaffected by the freeze. However, fall rains played havoc with vintners' nerves. For all the worrying, quality was surprisingly high. Although 1997 Oregon wines are a bit lower in alcohol, they show bright, fully developed flavours.

Oregon

Acme Wineworks (John Thomas) Yamhill County ★★ **92 93** 94 95 Consistent, good-value Pinot N from small producer; excellent Pinot also under John Thomas label. Very limited supply.

Adelsheim Vineyard Willamette ★★★ (Chard) **93 94** 95 (Merlot) **92** 93 94 (Pinot) **90 91 92 93** 94 95 Nicely oaked Pinot Noir, Chard best early. Pinots Gris and Blanc are clean, bracing.

Amity Willamette ★★ (w) **91 92 93 94** 95 Excellent Gewürz and Riesling. Pinot Bl since '94.

Archery Summit Yamhill Country ★★★ Flashy new operation of NAPA owner Gary Andrus. Impressive Pinot N and 'Vireton' (Pinot Gr blend).

Beaux Frères Yamhille County ★★★ **91 92 93** 94 95 Excellent Pinot N made in the big, extracted, new oak style. Part-owned by wine critic Robert Parker.

Benton-Lane Willamette ★★ Exciting newcomer, California owned, focussing on Pinot N. Currently v limited production.

Bethel Heights Willamette ★★★ (Pinot N) **90 91 92 93** 94 95 Deftly made Pinot N ('Early Release', Vintage and Selected) from estate nr Salem. Chard vg since '93, new, notable Pinot Bl.

Cameron Yamhill County (Pinot) ★★ **92 93** 94 95 Eclectic producer of Pinot N, Chard: some great, others conversation pieces. Vg Pinot Bl.

Chehalem Yamhill County ★★★ (Pinot N) **90 91 92 93 94** 95 Premium estate winery, established since '90. Top quality Pinot N, Chard, Pinot Gr. Reserve Pinot N '94: collaboration between the winemaker and Burgundian winemaker Patrice Rion.

Cristom N Willamette ★★★ ♯ (Pinot N) 92' **93 94** 95 Delicious Pinot N and buttery smooth Chard.

Domaine Drouhin Willamette ★★★★ 88 89 90 **91 92' 93** 94 95 Superb estate-grown Pinot N from one of the first families of Burgundy.

Domaine Serene Willamette ★★ Big meaty Pinot N from former PANTHER CREEK winemaker. Very small production.

Elk Cove Vineyards Willamette ★★ Fairly consistent producer of a range of wines featuring Pinot N, Pinot Gr, Chard, Riesling. Some excellent dessert wines. Look for vineyard-designated 'La Bohème'.

Eola Hills Nr Salem (Willamette) ★★ Consistently good quality and value, esp Pinot N, Chard and Ries.

Erath Vineyards Willamette ★★★ (Pinot) **91 92** 93 94 Excellent Chard and Pinot Gr, Gewürz and Pinot Bl. Top-tier Pinots and whites are among Oregon's finest, others: gd value. Especially lovely are some of the old Pinots, 76 80 82.

Evesham Wood Nr Salem Willamette ★★★ Small family winery has arrived with fine Pinot N (**91 92** 93 94 95), Pinot Gr and dry Gewürz.

Eyrie Vineyards, The Willamette ★★ Pioneer ('65) winery with Burgundian convictions. Older vintages of Pinot N are treasures (75 76 **80** 83 **85** 86); Chards and Pinot Gr: rich yet crisp and age beautifully.

Firesteed Willamette ★★ Light, no-oak Pinot N. Delicious, early-drinking and v good value.

Flynn Vineyards Willamette ★ Tasty, reasonably priced sparkling wine.

Foris Vineyards Rogue Valley ★★ Range of wines (Pinot N, Chard etc) from warmer southern Oregon. Merlot and Gewürz are esp good.

Henry Estate Umpqua Valley ★ Distinctive Pinot (American oak), good Gewürz.

Hinman Vineyards/Silvan Ridge S Willamette ★→★★ Wide range of varietals; good value.

Ken Wright Cellars Yamhill County ★★★ 93 94 95 Big, ripe Pinot N that has a cult following. Also vg Chard and Melon de Bourgogne.

King Estate S Willamette ★★ 92 93 **94** 95 Huge beautiful new estate. Vg Pinot Gr; Chard and Pinot N improving.

Lange Winery Yamhill County ★★ Small family winery; look for reserve Pinot N and Pinot Gr.

Laurel Ridge Winery Willamette★★ Reliable classic-method sp and Sauv Bl.

Montinore Vineyards Willamette ★★ Ambitious winery with huge 465-acre v'yds in Washington County. Quality suffered in 95 and 96 vintages.

Nicolas Rolin Portland (Willamette) ★★ V small producer of consistent Pinot N.

Oak Knoll Willamette ★★ Started with fruit wines; now one of Oregon's larger Pinot N producers.

Panther Creek Willamette ★★ (Pinot N) 89 90 **91 92 93** 94 95 Vg Pinot N and Melon de Bourgogne. Same winemaker as ST-INNOCENT.

Ponzi Vineyards Willamette Valley ★★ (Pinot N) **89 90 91 92** 93 94 95 Small winery almost in Portland, well-known for Ries, Pinot Gr, Chard, Pinot N. Experimenting with Arneis. Some inconsistency in last two vintages.

Rex Hill Willamette ★★★ (Pinot N) 88 89 90 **91 92'** 93 94 95 Excellent Pinot N, Pinot Gr and Chard from several N Willamette vineyards. Reserves are among Oregon's best; Kings Ridge label is great value.

St-Innocent Willamette ★★ Gaining reputation for delicious, forward Pinot N; pleasant Chard.

Shafer Vineyard Cellars Willamette ★ Small producer. Frequently good Pinot N, Chard.

For key to grape variety abbreviations, see pages 7–13.

THE PACIFIC NORTHWEST

Sokol Blosser Willamette ★★★ (Pinot N) **90 91 92' 93 94** 95 Consistently good, easy-to-drink Pinot N and Chard; Redland (reserve) Pinot N and Chard are excellent. Often vg Riesling.

Torii Mor Yamhill County ★★ New (since 1993), tiny and promising, with established Pinot N vineyard (planted 1977) in Dundee Hills.

Tualatin Vineyards Willamette ★★ (Pinot) **93 94** 95 (Chard) **92 93 94** 95 Pioneer estate winery, vg Chard, Pinot N vg, also good Ries and Gewürz. Winery sold early in '97 to Willamette Valley Vineyards.

Tyee S Willamette ★★→★★★ Small, family owned and run winery is especially good with dry Gewürz, Ries and Pinot Bl. Pinot N improving.

Valley View Vineyards Rogue Valley ★★ Family owned estate saw leap in quality with '90 vintage. Cabernet (**90 91 92** 93 94), Merlot, Chard (**92 93 94** 95) and Sauvignon Bl are vg, sometimes exciting.

Van Duzer Willamette ★★ Owned by William Hill (see California). Vg Ries, Chard and Pinot N.

Willakenzie Estate Yamhill County ★★ Released first wines in 1996; delicious Pinot Gr, Pinot Bl, Chard and Pinot N. Well-financed, state-of-the-art facility; French winemaker.

Willamette Valley Vineyards Willamette ★★ Pubescent winery nr Salem. Moderate- to high-quality Chard, Ries, Pinot N. Founders' Reserve wines best.

Yamhill Valley Vineyards Willamette ★ Improving estate near college town of McMinnville focussing on Pinot Gr, Chard and Pinot N.

Washington & Idaho

Andrew Will Puget Sound (Washington) ★★★ New small winery. Exceptional Cab S, Merlot and barrel-fermented Chenin Bl from E Washington grapes.

Arbor Crest Spokane (Washington) ★★ Est'd mid-size winery makes dependable Chard, Sauv Bl, Merlot and late-harvest Ries.

Barnard Griffin Pasco, Columbia Valley (Washington) ★★★ Small producer: well-made Merlot, Chard (esp barrel-fermented) and Sauv Bl. Very consistent.

Canoe Ridge Walla Walla (Columbia Valley) ★★★ New winery owned by Chalone Group (California). Impressive **93 94 95** Chard and Merlot.

Caterina Spokane ★ Improving Cab, Merlot, Chard and Sauv Bl from Columbia Valley grapes.

Château Ste-Michelle Woodinville (Washington) ★★★ Ubiquitous regional giant is Washington's largest winery; also owns COLUMBIA CREST and SNOQUALMIE. Major E Washington v'yd holdings, first-rate equipment and skilled winemakers keep Chard (**92 93 94** 95) Sém, Sauv Bl, Ries, Cab (**83 85 86 87 88 89 90 91 92** 93 94) and Merlot in front ranks. Vineyard-designated Cab and Chard are exceptionally fine (for those who like the taste of new French oak early on) and ageworthy.

Chinook Wines Yakima Valley (Washington) ★★★ Owner-winemakers Kay Simon and Clay Mackey purchase local grapes for sturdy Chard, Sauv and Merlot.

Columbia Crest Columbia Valley ★★★ Separately run CHATEAU STE-MICHELLE label for delicious well-made accessible wines priced one cut lower – most of them from big River Run v'yd. Reserve line is best Cab (**88 90 91 92 93** 94 95), Merlot and Chard are best. Value.

Columbia Winery Woodinville ★★★→★★★★ (Cab) **79 83 85 87 88 89 90 91** 92 93 94 Pioneer ('62, as Associated Vintners): still a leader. Balanced stylish understated single-v'yd wines, esp Merlot (Milestone), Cabernets (Otis, Red Willow, Sagemoor), Syrah (Red Willow). Oak-fermented Woodburne Chard, vg fruity long-lived Sém, Gewürz and late-harvest Ries. Reds consistently among finest.

Covey Run Yakima Valley ★★ (Chard) 92 93 **94** 95 Mostly estate. Intriguing Aligoté; intense heady Merlot, Cab. Purchased by Associated Vintners (See Columbia Winery) in '96.

DeLille Cellars/Chaleur Estate Woodinville ★★★ Exciting new winery for vg red 'Bordelais' blends: Chaleur Estate **92 93** 94 95 (needs 5 yrs age), 'D2' (more forward, affordable). Expert winemaking and access to some of best vineyards in E Washington. Made first white (Sauv-Sém blend) in 95.

Gordon Brothers Columbia Valley ★★ Tiny cellar for consistent Chard (Reserve 91), Merlot and Cab.

Hedges Cellars Yakima Valley ★★★ Made its name exporting its wines to Europe and Scandinavian countries. Now boasts fine v'yd (Red Mountain), château-style winery, delicious Cab, Merlot, Sauv Bl.

Hogue Cellars, The Yakima Valley ★★★ (Cab) 87 88 89 **90 91 92 93** 94 Leader in region, known for excellent wines esp Ries, Chard, Merlot, Cab. Produces quintessential Washington Sauv Bl.

Kiona Vineyards Yakima Valley ★★ Good v'yd for substantial Cabs and (Austrian) Lemberger; fruity Chard and Ries. Also v fine late-harvest Ries and Gewürz.

Latah Creek Spokane ★ Small cellar best known for Chard, Chenin Bl. Can be erratic with reds.

> **A choice of Pacific Northwest wines for 1998**
> **Leonetti** Cabernet Sauvignon (Washington)
> **The Hogue Cellars** Sauvignon Blanc (Washington)
> **Domaine Drouhin** Pinot Noir (Oregon)
> **Chateau Ste Michelle** Chardonnay Cold Creek (Washington)
> **Tyee Wine Cellars** Gewürztraminer (Oregon)
> **Chehalem** Pinot Gris Reserve (Oregon)
> **Columbia** Cabernet Sauvignon Red Willow Vineyard (Washington)

Leonetti Walla Walla ★★★★ (r) 83 **85 86 88 91 92 93** 94 95 The top Washington estate. Harmonious individualistic Cab, fine big-boned, yet succulent Merlot: bold, ageworthy.

Matthews Cellars W Washington Small new winery for promising blended whites and delicious Merlot.

McCrea Puget Sound ★★ Small winery for delicious Chard and Grenache. Experiments with Rhône blends are in progress.

Paul Thomas Yakima Valley ★★ Forward and sensibly priced Chard, Sauv Bl, Chenin, Cab, Merlot. (Also excellent fruit wines made in dry table wine style.)

Preston Wine Cellars Columbia Valley ★ Wide range. Some eccentric, some conventional/sound. Occasionally wonderful Cab, Merlot.

Quilceda Creek Vintners Puget Sound ★★★★ (Cab) 85 87 **88 89 90 91 92 93** 94 95 Expertly crafted ripe well-oaked Cab S from Columbia Valley grapes is the speciality.

Rose Creek Vineyards S Idaho ★★ Small family winery; good esp for Chard.

Ste Chapelle Caldwell ★★ Pleasant, forward Chard, Ries, Cab, Merlot from local and E Washington v'yds. Attractive sparkling wine: good value.

Silver Lake Woodinville ★★ Cab, Merlot, Chard and Sauv show consistency. New sparkling wine facility under construction.

Snoqualmie Puget Sound ★★ Consistent quality. Whites best.

Stewart Vineyards Yakima Valley ★★ Estate v'yds well-suited to Chard and Ries. Promising Cab.

Thurston Wolfe Yakima Valley ★★★ Tiny eclectic winery: excellent Lemberger (red), late-harvest Sauv, Black Muscat, Cabernet 'Port'.

Washington Hills Cellars/Apex Yakima Valley ★★ Solid line includes Sém, Fumé, Cab, Chard, Merlot and late-harvest Ries, Gewürz. Apex label is a rung up in quality.

Waterbrook Walla Walla ★★★ (r) 89 90 **91 92** 93 94 Stylish, distinctive Chard, Sauv, Cab, Merlot from a winery that has hit its stride.

Woodward Canyon Walla Walla ★★★ (r) **83 85 87 88 89 90** 91 92 93 94 Small top-notch cellar: well-oaked ultra-bold Cab, buttery Chard. Also Charbonneau blends (Merlot-Cab, Sauv-Sém).

British Columbia

A small but locally significant wine industry has developed since the '70s in Canada's Okanagan Valley, 150 miles east of Vancouver, in climatic conditions not very different from eastern Washington.

Blue Mountain ★★ **95** Sm property. Vg Pinot Gris, v fair Pinot N and sparkling.

Gray Monk ★★ **92 94** Good Okanagan Auxerrois, Gewürz and Pinot Blanc.

Lang Vineyards 94 Juicy Pinot Meunier.

Mission Hill ★→★★★ **93 94 95** Caused a gold medal stir in '94. Esp for Reserve Chard, Pinot Blanc.

Quails' Gate ★★ **94 95** Producing Chard, Chenin Bl, Pinot N, Ries Ice Wine.

Sumac Ridge ★★ **94 95** Gewürz and Pinot Bl from improving property.

East of the Rockies & Ontario

Producers in New York (there are now 108 in 6 AVAs) and other eastern states, as well as Ohio (44 in 4 AVAs) and Ontario (35), traditionally made wine from hardy native grapes, varieties of 'Vitis labrusca' whose wine has strong 'foxy' flavour, off-putting to non-initiates. To escape the labrusca flavour, growers then turned to more nuanced French-American hybrids. Today consumer taste plus cellar and vineyard technology have largely bypassed these, although Seyval Blanc and Vidal keep their fans. Chardonnay, Riesling, Cabernet Sauvignon and Merlot are now firmly established. Pinot Noir and Cabernet Franc are emerging with some notable results. Success is mixed, but progress, from Virginia to Ontario, is accelerating, particularly on Long Island.

Northeastern grape varieties

Aurora (Aurore) One of the best white French-American hybrids; the most widely planted in New York. Good for sparkling.

Baco Noir One of the better red French-American hybrids: high acidity but clean dark wine which usually needs ageing.

Catawba Old native American grape, perhaps the second most widely grown. Pale red and 'foxy' flavoured. Appears in crowd-pleasing dry, off-dry and sweet wines, still and sparkling.

Cayuga White Hybrid created at Cornell Uni. Delicate fruity off-dry wine.

Chambourcin Red hybrid of French origin: under-appreciated Loire-like reds and agreeable rosé.

Chelois Red hybrid. Dry medium-bodied burgundy-style wine.

Concord Labrusca variety, by far the most widely planted grape in New York. Heavy 'foxy' sweet one-dimensional red wines, but mostly grape juice and jelly. Long a staple of kosher wines.

De Chaunac Red wine hybrid found in New York and Canada. Avoid.

Maréchal Foch Workmanlike red French hybrid. Depending on vinification yields boldly flavoured or nouveau-style wines.

Niagara Quintessential labrusca greenish-white grape, s'times called 'white Concord': lovely aromatic sweet wine; wants to be gobbled right from vine.

Ravat (Vignoles) French-American white hybrid of intense flavour and high acidity, often made in yummy prize-winning 'late harvest' style.

Seyval Popular French-American hybrid that can produce stylish dry whites.

Vidal Mainstay French-American hybrid grape for full-bodied personable dry white wines.

Wineries and vineyards

Allegro ★★ **91 92 94** 95 **96** Est Pennsylvania maker of noteworthy Chard, Cab.

Bedell ★★★ 93 94 95 96 LONG ISLAND winery known for excellent Merlot and Cabernet Sauvignon.

Biltmore Estate ★★ **93 94 95** 96 North Carolina winery on 8,500-acres with 253-room mansion, America's largest. Chard and sparkling.

Canandaigua Wine Co ★→★★ FINGER LAKES winery with many California properties. Major producer (second largest in the US, behind Gallo) of labrusca, and table and sparkling wines. Owns Manischewitz, the best-selling kosher sweet wine. See California.

Cave Spring ★★★ 95 96 Ontario boutique: sophisticated Chard and Ries.

Chaddsford ★★ **93 94** 95 **96** Pennsylvania producer since '82: esp for burgundy-style Chard.

Chamard ★★ **93** 94 95 96 Connecticut's best winery, owned by Tiffany's chairman. Top Chard. AVA is Southeastern New England.

Château des Charmes ★★→★★★ **91 93** 94 95 **96** Show-place château-style Ontario winery (opened '94). Fine Chard, Aligoté, Cab, sparkling.

Clinton Vineyards ★★ **92 93 95 96** Hudson River winery known for clean dry SEYVAL BL and spirited Seyval sparkling.

Debonné Vineyards ★★ **93** 94 **95 96** Popular Ohio estate (in Lake Erie AVA): hybrids, eg CHAMBOURCIN and VIDAL; and vinifera, eg Chard, Ries.

Finger Lakes Beautiful historic upstate New York cool-climate v'yd region, source of most of the state's wines. Also the seat of New York State's 'vinifera revolution'. Top wineries: Lamoreaux Landing, FOX RUN, GLENORA, STANDING STONE. To watch.

Firelands ★★ **91 93 95 96** Ohio estate on Isle St George in LAKE ERIE AVA, growing Chard and Cab.

Fox Run ★★ **93 95 96** New owner, new winemaking facility and new winemaker have resulted in some of FINGER LAKES best Chard, Ries and Merlot and sparkling wines.

Frank, Dr Konstantin (Vinifera Wine Cellars) ★★ **93** 94 95 96 Small, influential winery. The late Dr F was a pioneer in growing European vines in the FINGER LAKES. Vg Chateau Frank sparkling.

Glenora Wine Cellars ★★ **91 93 94** 95 96 FINGER LAKES producer of good sparkling wine, Chard and Ries.

Gristina ★★ **93 94** 95 96 Promising young winery on LONG ISLAND'S N FORK AVA with Chard, Cab and Pinot N.

Hamptons (Aka South Fork) LONG ISLAND AVA. The top winery is moneyed SagPond. Duck Walk is up and coming.

Hargrave Vineyard ★★★ **93 94** 95 96 LONG ISLAND's pioneering winery, v'yds since '72 on NORTH FORK. Good Chard, Cab S and Cab F.

Henry of Pelham ★★★ **94** 95 96 Elegant Ontario Chard and Ries; distinctive BACO NOIRE.

Hillebrand Estates ★→★★ **94** 95 96 Aggressive Ontario producer attracting attention with Chard and Bordeaux-style red blend.

Hudson River Region America's oldest winegrowing district (21 producers) and New York's very first AVA. Straddles the river, two hours' drive N of Manhattan.

Inniskillin ★★★ **93 94** 95 96 Outstanding (VINCOR-owned) producer that spear-headed birth of modern Ontario wine industry. Skilful burgundy-style Chard and Pinot N. Vg Ries, VIDAL ice wine, Pinot Gris and Auxerrois.

Knapp ★(★) **93 94 95** 96 Versatile FINGER LAKES winery. Tasty Bordeaux-style blend, Cab, Ries, Bl de Bls sparkling.

Lake Erie The biggest grape-growing district in the eastern US; 25,000 acres along the shore of Lake Erie, incl portions of New York, Pennsylvania and OHIO. 90% is CONCORD, most heavily in New York's Chautauqua County. Also the name of a tristate AVA: NY's sector has 7 wineries, Pennsylvania's 5 and Ohio's 22.

Lakeridge ★★ Popular Florida winery nr Disneyland. Esp for Muscadine. Spumante-like sparkling from local Carlos grapes flies off the shelf. Rarely uses vintage dates.

Lakeview ★★ ONTARIO producer acquiring name for full-flavoured reds.

Lamoreaux Landing ★★→★★★ **94** 95 96 Young, stylish, talented FINGER LAKES house: promising Chard and Ries from striking Greek-revival winery.

Lenz ★★★ 93 **94** 95 96 Classy winery of NORTH FORK AVA. Fine austere Chard in the Chablis mode, also Gewürz, Merlot and sparkling wine.

Long Island Most exciting new wine region E of Rockies and a hothouse of experimentation. Currently 1,300 acres all vinifera (47% Chard) and 2 AVAs (NORTH FORK and HAMPTONS). Most of its 17 wineries are on the North Fork. Best varieties: Chard, Cab, Merlot. A long growing season; relatively little frost.

Michigan Potentially America's finest cool-climate Ries area; 18 commercial wineries. Best incl: St-Julien Wine Co, Ch Grand Traverse, Tabor Hill, Good Harbour. Watch Fenn Valley, Bowers Harbor (for sparkling version).

Millbrook ★★★ **91 93 95** 96 Top HUDSON RIVER REGION winery. Money-no-object viticulture and savvy marketing has lifted spiffy, whitewashed Millbrook in big old barn into New York's firmament. Burgundian Chards; splendid, Cab F can be delicious.

North Fork LONG ISLAND AVA (of 2). Top wineries: BEDELL, GRISTINA, HARGRAVE, LENZ, PALMER, PAUMANOK, PELLEGRINI, PINDAR. 2½ hrs' drive from Manhattan.

Ohio 5 AVAs notably LAKE EYRIE and Ohio Valley

Ontario Main E Canada wine region, on Niagara Peninsula: 35 producers. Heavy investment and glimmerings of great future. Ries, Chard, even Pinot N, show incipient longevity. Ice wine is flagship.

Palmer ★★★ **93 94** 95 **96** Superior LONG ISLAND (N FORK) producer and byword in Darwinian metropolitan market. High profile due to perpetual-motion marketing; fast growth. Flavourful Chard, Sauv and Chinon-like Cab F.

Paumanok ★★ 93 **94 95 96** Rising LONG ISLAND (N FORK) winery, with promising Cab, Merlot, Ries, and savoury late-harvest Sauv Bl.

Pellegrini ★★★ **93 94** 95 LONG ISLAND'S most enchantingly designed winery (on N FORK), opened '93. Opulent Merlot, stylish Chard, B'x-like Cab. Inspired winemaking. Exceptionally flavourful wines.

Pindar Vineyards ★★→★★★ 93 94 95 **96** Huge 287-acre mini-Gallo winery of N FORK, LONG ISLAND. Wide range of toothsome blends and popular varietals, incl Chard, Merlot, and esp gd Bordeaux-type red blend, Mythology.

Sakonnet ★★ **94** 95 **96** Largest New England winery, based in Little Compton, Rhode Island (SE New Eng AVA). Its regional reputation, resting on Chard, VIDAL and dry Gewürz, has blossomed since '85.

Standing Stone ★★ **93 94 95** One of newest and most promising FINGER LAKES wineries with v good Ries, Gewürtz and Cab Franc.

Tomasello ★★ **93 94 95 96** Progressive New Jersey winery. Good Blanc de Noirs sparkling and CHAMBOURCIN. Promising Cab S.

Unionville Vineyards ★★→★★★ **93 95 96** New Jersey's best winery, est '91. Lovely Ries, French-American hybrids elevated to nr-vinifera status.

Vincor International ★→★★ Canada's biggest winery (formerly Brights-Cartier), in Ontario, BC, Quebec, New Brunswick. Mass-market and premium wines; varietals, blends, Canadian and imported grapes. Owns INNISKILLIN. Also Jackson-Triggs and Sawmill Creek labels.

Vineland Estates ★★ **92 93 94 95 96** Good Ontario producer whose VIDAL and Ries ice wines are much admired. Dry and semi-dry Ries are equally admirable.

The Vintners Quality Alliance Canada's voluntary appellation body, started in Ontario but now includes British Columbia. Its self-policing of standards has rapidly raised respect and awareness of Canadian wines to high levels.

Wagner Vineyards ★★ **93 95 96** Famous FINGER LAKES winery. Barrel-fermented Chard, dry and sweet Ries and ice wine. Charming to visit.

Westport Rivers ★★ **93 94 95 96** Massachusetts house est'd '89. Good Chard and fledgling sparkling. (Southeastern New England AVA.)

Wiemer, Hermann J ★★→★★★ **93 94 95 96** Creative German-born FINGER LAKES winemaker. Interesting Ries incl vg sparkling and 'late harvest'.

94 Wollersheim ★★ Wisconsin winery specializing in variations of Maréchal Foch. 'Prairie Fumé' (Seyval Bl) is a commercial success.

Southern and central states

Virginia Ambitious young wine state (since '72). Acquiring status. Whites, esp Chard, lead. 46 wineries (in 6 AVAs) produce good Ries, Gewürz, Viognier, Cabs and Merlot (and newly introduced Pinot Gris and Barbera) from 1,394 acres of grapes. Monticello has some of the top producers: Prince Michel (though its good 'Le Ducq' B'x blend is made mostly with Napa grapes) and its second property, Rapidan River, Barboursville (inspired Malvaxia Reserve is Virginia's top wine), Montdomaine. Others are Horton (for Viognier and late-harvest wines), Ingleside Plantation, Linden, Naked Mountain, Meredyth, Oasis (for 'champagne'), Piedmont, Tarara and Williamsburg Winery. Ch Morrisette and Wintergreen bear watching.

Missouri A blossoming industry with 36 producers in 3 AVAs: Augusta (first in the US), Hermann, Ozark Highlands. In-state sales catching fire. Best wines are Seyval Bl, Vidal, Vignoles (sweet and dry versions). Top estate is Stone Hill, in Hermann (since 1847), with rich red from the Norton (or Cynthiana) grape variety; Hermannhof (1852) is drawing notice for the same. Mount Pleasant, in Augusta, makes rich 'port' and nice sparkling wine. To watch are Augusta Winery, Blumenhof, Les Bourgeois, Montelle, Röbler, St James.

Maryland 9 wineries and 2 AVAs. Basignani makes good Cabernet Sauvignon, Chard, Seyval. Catoctin, a mountain-v'yd boutique-winery, is developing solid, modest-priced Riesling and Chard. Elk Run's Chard and Cab can be delicious. Best-known Boordy Vineyards gets good marks for Seyval Bl (esp Reserve) and sparkling. Woodhall understands Seyval and Cab. Fiore's Chambourcin is interesting. Catoctin AVA is the main Cab and Chard area. Linganore is Second AVA.

The Southwest

Texas

In the past 15 years a brand-new Texan wine industry has sprung noisily to life. It now has over 450 growers, 26 wineries (10 in Hill Country) and five AVAs. The best wines (nearly all single-grape wines) are comparable with northern California's.

Bell Mountain Vineyards Bell Mountain AVA winery at Fredericksburg. 52 acres. Erratic but known for Cab S, Chard next.

Cap Rock (Lubbock) Since '90. Cab, Chard, Chenin, Sauv, Ries, sparkling all doing well for local medals.

Fall Creek Vineyards Consistent TEXAS HILL COUNTRY estate: fine Sauv, Chard. Also Cab S. Watch for Emerald Ries, Chenin and Carnelian.

Grape Creek Vineyards Small winery nr Fredericksburg, TEXAS HILL COUNTRY for medal-winning Chardonnay, Cabernet S and Muscat Canelli.

Hill County Cellars Nr Austin: exemplary Chard and Sauv.

Llano Estacado The pioneer (since '76); nr Lubbock with 220 acres (210 leased). Known for Chard and Cab S; good Signature red.

Messina Hof Wine Cellars Winning with Muscat Canelli grape and late-harvest Johannisberg Ries 'Angel'. Also has Pinot N.

Pheasant Ridge Lubbock estate founded '78. Now 36 acres. State leader esp for reds and now Chenin and Chard.

Sainte-Genevieve Largest Texas winery, linked with Cordier (France). V'yds (1,000 acres) owned by University of Texas. Well-made, mostly NV wines.

Sister Creek TEXAS HILL COUNTRY. Gd Pinot N, Chard, Cab S and Franc, Merlot.

Slaughter-Leftwich Tiny amount of Chard from Lubbock vineyards; the winery is near Austin.

Texas Hill Country One of 3 Hill Country AVAs (S of Lubbock, W of Austin).

New Mexico etc

New Mexico is still known for one wine, Rio Grande Valley's remarkable Gruet sparkling, but other sparklers (Dom Cheurlin) and Anderson Valley Winery varietals have proved the potential. La Chiripada is another winery doing very well, with French hybrids and port-style wine. La Viña produces good Chard (as does Gruet). There are now three AVAs and 19 wineries.

Colorado and **Arizona** are both focussing on vinifera grapes. Colorado (16 wineries) is growing rapidly, with Chard and Merlots leading the planting. Plum Creek Cellars (the largest winery, good Chard) and Grande River V'yds (recent success with Viognier) among others at Palisade are both vg. Arizona (7 wineries) is highlighting Rhône varieties (eg at Callaghan V'yds) and Pinot N and Cab from hot, high-altitude, terra rossa v'yds. **Oklahoma** and **Utah** will be the next to emerge – Utah's one winery (Arches Vineyard) sets the pace with Ries, Oklahoma's two suit sweet-toothed locals better.

South America

Chile

Chile's position has moved from primitive to tentative to mainstream in a mere ten years. Its problems were old ideas and above all old wooden vats. Stainless steel brought a revolution. Long a producer of sound healthy (at least before ageing) Cabernets, its depth and range has expanded to excellent Merlots, good Syrah and Malbec, and fresh white wines hitherto undreamed of. Conditions are ideal for vines (all irrigated) in the Maipo Valley near Santiago and for 300 miles south. The newly-planted Casablanca region between Santiago and Valparaiso offers excellent terroirs for Chardonnay and Sauvignon Blanc. Many long-time growers are no longer supplying the big bodegas but making their own wines. Principal regions, from north to south, are Aconcagua, Maipo, Rapel, Curico, Maule and southern Itata, and Bío Bío.

Aconcagua Northernmost quality wine region. Incl CASABLANCA, Panquehue.

Agrícola Aquitania ★★★ 60-acre joint venture of Paul Pontallier and Bruno Prats from Bordeaux with Felipé de Solminihac. Sole wine is Paul Bruno. First good vintage '95.

Bío-Bío Southernmost 'quality' wine region. V rainy.

Bisquertt ★★ Colchagua (RAPEL) family winery. Vg Merlot, but could be more consistent.

Caliterra ★★→★★★ Sister winery of ERRAZURIZ, now half owned by Mondavi (California). Chard and Sauv Bl improving (higher proportions of CASABLANCA grapes), reds becoming less one-dimensional. Reserva range excellent.

Canépa, José ★★→★★★ Consistently good reds incl dense, fleshy Zinfandel; CASABLANCA Sauv Bl and Rancagua Private Res Chard top white. Recent company split plus departure of talented winemaker could spell trouble.

Carmen, Viña ★★→★★★ One of oldest Chilean wineries, now under same ownership as SANTA RITA. Based in MAIPO. Ripe, fresh Special Res (CASABLANCA) Chard and deliciously light Late Harvest Maipo Sém top whites. Reds even better; esp RAPEL Merlots, Maipo Petite Sirah and Cabs, esp Gold Reserve.

Carta Vieja ★★ MAULE winery owned by one family for six generations. Reds, esp Cab and Merlot better than whites, though Antigua Selección Chardonnay is good.

Casa Lapostolle ★★→★★★ Venture incl Marnier-Lapostolle family, owners of Grand Marnier. Michel Rolland at helm. Supple oak-aged Merlot (possibly Chile's best), plummy Cab and Bordeaux-inspired Sauv.

Casablanca Cool-climate region between Santiago and coast. V little water: drip irrigation essential. Top-class Chard and Sauv; promising Merlot and Pinot N.

Casablanca, Viña ★★★ Sister winery to VINA SANTA CAROLINA. Some of Chile's best wines. RAPEL and MAIPO fruit used for some reds, Santa Isabel Estate in CASABLANCA already producing vg Sauv, Chard and Gewürz. Barrel samples of Cab and Merlot bode well.

Chateau Los Boldos ★★ Label of French-owned Santa Amalia winery at the foot of the Andes in MAULE. Cab, Sauv and some Chard for export only.

Concha y Toro ★→★★★★ Biggest, most outward-looking wine firm with bodegas and v'yds all over Chile, mainly in MAIPO and RAPEL. New Cab-Syrah is good, as are Amelia CASABLANCA Chard, premium 'Trio' red and white, chocolatey Marques de Casa Concha Merlot and Don Melchor Cab. Look out for promising Explorer range: Alicante Bouschet, Pinot N, Cab/Syrah etc.

Cono Sur ★★★ Chimbarongo winery owned by CONCHA Y TORO for vg Pinots from local and CASABLANCA fruit. Also dense fruity Cabs. Second labels Tocornal and Isla Negra.

Cousiño Macul ★★★→★★★★ Distinguished and beautiful old estate nr Santiago (MAIPO). Known for long-lived Antiguas Reservas Cab, but also: supple Merlot and old-fashioned, v dry Sém, Chard.

Domaine Oriental ★★ Good reds, esp Clos Centenaire Cab, from modern French-owned winery in MAULE Valley.

Doña Javiera, Viña ★★ Excellent first releases of Sauv and Chard from a new bodega at cooler Pacific end of MAIPO Valley.

Echeverría Boutique Curicó (MAULE) winery producing intense complex Reserve Cabs, unoaked Chard and rapidly improving Sauv.

Edwards, Luís Felipé ★★★ Beautifully situated Colchagua (RAPEL) winery making citrussy Chard and silky Reserve Cab.

Errázuriz ★★→★★★ Historic firm in Aconcagua Valley, N of Santiago, modernized and making v rich full-bodied wines, esp Merlot and Cabernet Don Maximiano and top-class whites from CASABLANCA grapes.

La Fortuna, Viña ★★ Old-est'd winery in Lontué Valley. Range of attractive varietal wines, esp Malbec, without fertilisers or herbicides.

Franciscan (★★★) New CASABLANCA-based operation of the Californian winery (qv). To follow.

Francisco de Aguirre, Viña ★★ Promising Cab and Chard from vineyards only planted in 1992 in the northerly region of Valle de Limari.

La Rosa, Viña ★★ Chardonnays, Merlots and Cabernets from this RAPEL grower-turned-wine producer are impressive. Ignacio Recabarren is consultant. Wines under La Palma and Casa Leona labels.

Maipo Oldest wine region, nr Santiago. Quite warm. Source of Chile's top Cabs.

Maule S'most top quality region. Incl Claro, Loncomilla and Tutuven Valleys.

Mont Gras ★★★ State-of-the-art winery in Colchagua Valley. Splendid debut '94 Reserve Merlot and Cabernet.

Montes ★★→★★★ Label of Discover Wines nr Curicó. Montes Alpha Cab can be brilliant, Merlot and Malbec also fine; whites more erratic.

Paul Bruno See Agrícola Aquitania.

Porta Viña, ★★ Cab and Chard specialists with Cachapoal Valley v'yds (RAPEL). Also plummy, chocolatey Merlot and gd 2nd label Casa Porta.

Portal del Alto, Viña ★★★ Small bodega with excellent Cab-Merlot blend from own v'yds in MAIPO and RAPEL.

Rapel Central quality region divided into Colchagua and Cachapoal valleys.

San Pedro ★★→★★★ Third-largest Chilean producer based at Molina, Curicó. Gato Negro and Gato Blanco: top sellers. Best wines: Castillo de Molina and Sta Helena Seleccíon de Director. Jacques Lurton of Bordeaux is consultant.

Santa Carolina Viña ★★★ Impressive old Santiago bodega making increasingly impressive and complex wines. All MAIPO Reserve wines are v gd, inc a rich limey Sauv Bl. Also excellent oak-aged Late Harvest Sém/Sauv.

Santa Emiliana ★★ A division of CONCHA Y TORO. V'yds in RAPEL and CASABLANCA. Second labels Andes Peak and Walnut Crest are v gd value.

Santa Inés ★★ Successful small family winery in Isla de MAIPO making ripe, blackcurranty Legado de Armida Cab Sauv. Also labelled as De Martino.

Santa Mónica ★★ Rancagua (RAPEL) winery; the best label is Tierra del Sol. Good Ries and Merlot under Santa Mónica label.

Santa Rita, Viña ★★→★★★ Long est'd MAIPO bodega, already gd but should be even better with new ex-CANEPA winemaker. Range in ascending quality: 120, Reserva, Medalla Real, Casa Real. Best: Casa Real Maipo Cab Sauv, but Medalla Real CASABLANCA Merlot and Chard, and Maipo Cab nearly as gd.

Segu Ollé ★★ Linares (MAULE) estate owned by two Catalan families. Cab and Merlot v gd. Labels: Caliboro and Doña Consuelo.

Tarapacá Ex-Zavala ★★ A stunning new bodega. Basic varietal wines sound; of the more ambitious wines, only Gran Reserva Chard currently succeeds.

Terra Noble ★★ Talca winery with oenologist from the Loire. Grassy Sauv and light, peppery Merlot are only wines.

Torreón de Paredes ★★→★★★ Modern RAPEL bodega. Good Reserva Cab. Attractive crisp Chard and Reserva Cabs which age better than most.

Torres, Miguel ★★★ Enterprise of Catalan family firm (see Spain) at Curicó set a modern pace for Chile but then lost its way. Back on form with fresh whites and gd reds headed by sturdy Manso del Velasco single-vyd Cab.

Undurraga ★★→★★★ Famous old MAIPO estate known for its (rather dilute) Pinot. Top wines are Reserva Chard, refreshing limey Gewürz and peachy Late Harvest Sém.

Valdivieso ★★★ An old household word in Chile for sparkling wines. New Lontué winery. French winemaker and new consultant are creating an impressive range: good Chard, Reserve Pinot N, Cab S, Cab F, Merlot, Malbec and Grange-like red wine project called 'Caballo Loco'.

Vascos, Los ★★→★★★ Owned by Lafite-Rothschild, but not one of Chile's first growths. Wines are fair but reject Chile's lovely fruit flavours in favour of firm structures.

Villard ★★★ French enterprize in CASABLANCA. Big buttery Chards, intense Sauv Bl, alluring Pinot N; good RAPEL Cab and Merlot.

Vinícola Mondragón ★★ CANEPA'S Second bodega. Labels: Rowan Brook, Peteroa, Montenuevo etc.

Argentina

The world's fifth-largest producer is at last turning its gaze to the outside world, and vice versa. Domestic demand in Argentina is still for old-fashioned tired wines, but it is dropping dramatically, while the world's buyers are moving over the Andes from Chile.

Ninety percent of vineyards are in Mendoza province (across the mountains from Santiago) – and in Salta to the north 1,700 metres (at Cafayate). Río Negro to the south is on the latitude of Hawke's Bay, NZ. All vineyards are irrigated, by flood or drip. Arid air means few diseases; phylloxera is absent. All of which means high hopes for the classic grapes as well as good things already from Argentine specialities: fleshy Malbec reds and aromatic Torrontes whites. The following are the best of the 2,000-odd bodegas.

Arizu, Leoncio ★★★ Makers of Luigi Bosca wines: Chard, Malbec, Cab and Syrah from small Mendoza (Maipu) bodega; all vg. Also promising Sauv, Pinot N and Riesling.

Balbi, Bodegas ★★★ Up-and-coming San Raphael producer making juicy Malbec and Chard and delicious Syrah rosé.

Bianchi, Bodegas ★→★★ Seagram-owned San Rafael producer, now the country's third largest bodega. Malbec and Chenin Blanc currently the best wines, experiments on 'international' varieties not as yet as successful.

Bosca, L See Arizu.

For key to grape variety abbreviations, see pages 7–13.

SOUTH AMERICA

Canale, Bodegas Humberto ★★ Premier Río Negro winery: 95 Sém and Pinot N v promising. Vg Malbec, Merlot and Cab S improving.

Catena ★★★ Dynamic Dr Nicolas Catena owns Bodegas Esmerelda which makes wines as Alamos Ridge (gd value Cab, Chard, Malbec), Catena (v gd Cab, Chard and Malbec) and Alta Catena (excellent Cab & Chard) labels. Also has a stake in LA RURAL, Libertad and WEINERT.

Esmerelda, Bodegas See CATENA.

Etchart ★★→★★★ Pernod-Ricard owned, two wineries in Salta and Mendoza. Fresh, spicy Torrontes, lively Chard and Chenin from Salta are gd, reds generally sound. Arnaldo B Etchart is vg top new blend (Salta Cab S-Malbec-Merlot).

Finca Flichman ★★ Old co with two wineries in Mendoza now owned by bank investing heavily. Range of varietals, topped by Private Reserve Cab S. Flying winemaker Hugh Ryman has been working here since 1997.

Goyenechea, Bodegas ★→★★ Basque family firm in San Rafael known for old-fashioned reds. Undergoing much-needed modernization.

H Piper ★★→★★★ Sparkling wine made under licence from Piper-Heidsieck.

La Agrícola ★★ Large privately-owned Mendoza coop producing fair-value wines under the Picajuan Peak, Santa Julia and Viejo Surco labels.

Lavaque ★★ San Raphael bodega revitalized. V sound Cab, Malbec, Pinot N.

Lopez, Bodegas ★★ Family firm best known for old-style Château Montchenot red and white and Château Vieux Cab.

M Chandon ★★→★★★ Makers of Baron B and M Chandon sparkling under Moët & Chandon supervision. '95 first Pinot N-Chard blend; huge improvement. Old-style reds and whites incl Castel Chandon, Kleinburg (w); smooth Comte de Valmont, Beltour and Clos du Moulin (r). Renaud Poirier is new varietal line for domestic consumption; Paul Galard (much better) for export.

Martins ★★ Spanish-owned (Berberana) bodega in Mendoza: sound Malbec and Merlot.

Navarro Correas ★★→★★★ Some fair reds; best Col Privada Cab S. Also reasonable whites, inc v oaky Chard and Deutz-inspired fizz.

Norton, Bodegas ★★★ Old bodega, now Austrian-owned. Good whites and v gd reds, esp chunky, fruity Malbec. Look out for results of a joint venture with Spanish bodegas Berberana and Marques de Griñon.

Orfila, Bodegas Mendoza ★→★★ Nothing to report except fair Cab S.

Peñaflor ★→★★★ Argentina's biggest wine co, reputedly the world's third largest. Bulk wines for domestic market incl Andean V'yds, Fond de Cave (Chard, Cab) labels and for finer wines: TRAPICHE.

Riojanas, Vini ★★ Salta bodega for fair Torrontes, Malbec. Best wines called SANTA FLORENTINA.

Rural, Bodegas La ★★→★★★ Now Catena-inspired. Good commercial modern wines. Best: Malbec, Merlot. Also fair Chard. Second label Libertad less intense but still gd.

San Telmo ★★→★★★ Modern winery making fresh full-flavoured Chard, Chenin Bl, Merlot and esp Malbec and Cab 'Cruz de Piedra-Maipu'.

Santa Ana, Bodegas ★→★★★ Old-est'd family firm at Guaymallen, Mendoza now controlled by Chile's Santa Carolina. Wide range incl good Syrah, Merlot-Malbec, Pinot Gr 'blush' and sparkling (Chard-Chenin) 'Villeneuve'.

Santa Florentina See Riojanas, Vini.

Torino, Michel ★★ Salta bodega linked with LAVAQUE. Good Torrontes, Chard-Torrentes blend, Chenin Bl. Best red is Malbec.

Toso, Pascual ★★→★★★ Old Mendoza winery at San José, making vg Toso Cabernet. Also Ries and sparkling wines (incl one classic-method).

Trapiche ★★→★★★ Premium label of PENAFLOR aided by French consultant Michel Rolland. Good single-grape wine range incl Merlot, Malbec, Cab, Pinot N, Chard and Torrontes. Top of the range Medalla is not cheap, Oak Cask range good value.

Vistalba, Viña y Cava ★★→★★★ (Ex Perez Cuesta) Small bodega specialising in reds. Top wine: richly smoky Barbera. Also gd Sangiovese, Malbec, Merlot.

Weinert, Bodegas ★★★ The Malbec, Cabernet and Cavas de Weinert blend (Cab-Merlot-Malbec) are among best Argentinian reds. Modernization (by CATENA) should make them even better.

Other Southern American wines

Brazil New plantings of better grapes are transforming a big and booming industry, supplying an increasing home market. International investments, esp in Río Grande do Sul and Santana do Liuramento, esp from France (eg Moët & Chandon) and Italy (Martini & Rossi), are significant and point to possible exports. The new sandy Frontera region (neighbouring Argentina and Uruguay) and the Sierra Gaucha hills (for Italian-style sparkling) are some to watch. Exports are beginning. Equatorial v'yds (eg nr Recife) can have two crops a year – or even five in two years. This is not a recommendation.

Mexico Oldest American wine industry is reviving, with investment from abroad (eg Freixenet, Martell, Domecq) and California influence via UC Davis. Best in Baja California (85% of total), Querétaro and on the Aguascalientes and Zacatecas plateaux. Top Baja C producers are L A Cetto (Valle de Guadaloupe, the largest, esp for Cab, Nebbiolo, Petite Sirah), Bodegas Santo Tomás (since 1888, Mexico's oldest), Monte Xanic (with Napa-award winning Cab), Bodegas San Antonio, and Cavas de Valmar. Marqués de Aguayo is the oldest (1593), now only for brandy.

Peru Viña Tacama near Ica (top wine region) exports some promising wines, esp the Gran Vino Blanco white; also Cab S and classic-method sparkling. Chincha, Moquegua and Tacha regions are slowly making progress. But phylloxera is a serious problem.

Uruguay Argentina has the sturdy Malbec, Uruguay has the even more rugged Tannat, a grape which amounts to a third of vinifera plantings in the country. Producers are learning to enhance the grape's rather rustic plummy flavours (and bottle it younger). Uruguay also has plantings of Cabernet Sauvignon, Merlot, Chardonnay, Sauvignon Blanc, even Viognier, but as yet the task of matching grapes to appropriate sites is in its infancy. Five different viticultural regions were established in 1992: south (Montevideo, San José, Florida), southwest (Colonia), northwest (Paysandú, Salto and Artigas), northeast (Rivera-Tacuarembo) and central (Durazno). Wineries to look out for are Stagnari (Tannat, Gewürz), Castel Pujol (Tannat, Muséo 1752) and Juanicó.

Australia

Heavier shaded areas are the wine growing regions

The influence of Australia in the modern wine world is out of all proportion to the size of its vineyards. They represent less than two percent of global production, yet Australian ideas and names are on all wine-lovers' lips. In 12 years her exports have grown from 8 to 160 million litres and the number of wineries has climbed to over 900. It is not just the climate that has done this, but radical research, uninhibited experiment and generous pooling of techniques. Even growers in the south of France listen carefully to Australian winemakers. Australia has mastered easy-drinking wine and is making some of the world's very best.

Her long-term classics are Shiraz, Semillon and Riesling wines. In the seventies they were joined by Cabernet Sauvignon and Merlot, Chardonnay, Pinot Noir and other varieties. Then in the nineties Grenache and Mourvèdre were rediscovered and embraced with the enthusiasm of a lost lover. At the same time, cool fermentation and the use of new barrels accompanied a general move to cooler areas. For a while excessive oak flavour was a common problem. It still happens, but moderation is now the fashion – and sparkling wine of startling quality is a new achievement.

The problem with Australian wines today is under-supply. A massive planting programme is underway (50,000 acres) with the aim of doubling production and trebling exports. Value for money, though, is still high.

Wine regions

Adelaide Hills (SA) Spearheaded by PETALUMA: 23 wineries at v cool, 450-metre sites in the Mt Lofty ranges.

Adelaide Plains (SA) Small area just north of Adelaide, formerly known as Angle Vale. The top Adelaide Plain winery is PRIMO ESTATE.

Barossa (SA) Australia's most important winery (though not v'yd) area; grapes from diverse sources (local, to MURRAY VALLEY; high quality cool regions: from adjacent hills, to COONAWARRA far S) make diverse wines. Local specialities: SHIRAZ, SEMILLON, GRENACHE etc. 44 wineries.

Bendigo/Ballarat (Vic) Widespread small v'yds, some of vg quality, re-creating glories of the gold rush. 24 wineries incl BALGOWNIE, JASPER HILL, HEATHCOTE.

Canberra District (ACT) 17 wineries now sell 'cellar door'. Quality is variable, as is style.

Clare Watervale (SA) Small, high quality area 90 miles north of Adelaide, best for Riesling; also SHIRAZ and CABERNET. 29 wineries spill over into new subdistrict, Polish Hill River.

Coonawarra (SA) Southernmost and finest v'yd of state: most of Australia's best CAB, successful CHARD, RIES and SHIRAZ. Newer arrivals incl Balnaves, Majella, PARKER ESTATE, PENLEY ESTATE. 23 wineries.

Geelong (Vic) Once-famous area destroyed by phylloxera, re-established mid-'60s. Very cool dry climate: firm table wines from good quality grapes. Names incl BANNOCKBURN, IDYLL, SCOTCHMAN'S HILL. 16 wineries.

Goulburn Valley (Vic) Very old (eg CHATEAU TAHBILK) and relatively new (eg MITCHELTON) wineries in temperate mid-Victoria region; full-bodied table wines. 15 wineries.

Granite Belt (Qld) High altitude, (relatively) cool region just N of NSW border; 17 wineries. Esp spicy SHIRAZ and rich SEM-CHARD.

Great Southern (WA) Remote cool area in S of state; GOUNDREY and PLANTAGENET are biggest wineries, from 25 in all.

Great Western (Vic) Temperate region in central W of state. High quality (esp sparkling). 10 wineries, 8 of relatively recent origin.

Hunter Valley (NSW) Great name in NSW. Broad soft earthy SHIRAZ and SEM that live for 30 years. CABERNET not important; CHARD increasingly so. 58 wineries.

Margaret River (WA) Temperate coastal area with superbly elegant wines 174 miles S of Perth. 45 operating wineries; others planned for Australia's most vibrant tourist wine region.

McLaren Vale (SA) Historic region on the southern outskirts of Adelaide. Big reds now rapidly improving; also vg CHARD. 52 wineries.

Mornington Peninsula (Vic) Exciting wines in new cool coastal area 25 miles south of Melbourne. 2,500 acres. 36 commercial wineries incl DROMANA, STONIERS, T'GALLANT.

Mudgee (NSW) Small isolated area 168 miles NW of Sydney. Big reds, full CHARDS; from 21 wineries.

Murray Valley (SA, Vic & NSW) Vast irrigated v'yds nr Mildara, Swan Hill (Vic and NSW), Berri, Loxton, Morgan, Renmark and Waikerie (S Aus). Principally making 'cask' table wines. Forty percent of total Australian wine production

NE Victoria Historic area incl Corowa, Rutherglen, Wangaratta. Weighty reds and magnificent sweet dessert wines. 21 wineries.

Padthaway (SA) Large vineyard area (no wineries) developed as an over-spill of COONAWARRA. Cool climate; some good PINOT N is produced and excellent CHARDONNAY (esp LINDEMANS and HARDY'S), also Chard-Pinot N sparkling wines.

Perth Hills (WA) Fledgling area 19 miles E of Perth with 13 wineries and a larger number of growers on mild hillside sites.

Pyrenees (Vic) Central Vic region with 11 wineries: rich minty reds and some interesting whites, esp Fumé Bl.

Riverina (NSW) NV Large-volume irrigated zone centred around Griffith; good-quality 'cask' wines (especially white), great sweet botrytised SEM. There are 12 wineries.

Swan Valley (WA) The birthplace of wine in the west, on the N outskirts of Perth. Hot climate makes strong low-acid table wines but good dessert wines. Declining in importance viticulturally. 16 wineries.

Tasmania 50 vineyards now offering wine for commercial sale: over 700,000 litres in all. Great potential for CHARDONNAY, PINOT NOIR and RIESLING grapes in cool climate.

Upper Hunter (NSW) Est'd in early '60s; irrigated vines (mainly whites), lighter and quicker-developing than Lower Hunter's. Often value.

Yarra Valley ('Lilydale') Superb historic area nr Melbourne: 45 wineries. Growing emphasis on v successful PINOT NOIR and sparkling.

Grape varieties in Australia

In 1996 Australia crushed a record 860, 000 tonnes of grapes which produced some 600 million litres of wine. The most important varieties are the following:

Cabernet Sauvignon (72,300 tonnes) Grown in all of Australia's wine regions, best in COONAWARRA. Flavour ranges from herbaceous, green pepper in coolest regions to blackcurrant and mulberry in Coonawarra, and dark chocolate and redcurrant in warmer areas such as MCLAREN VALE and BAROSSA. Used both on its own and blended with Merlot or more traditionally with SHIRAZ. Reaching 100,000 tonnes in '99.

Chardonnay (98,400 tonnes) Has come from nowhere since '70, with production forecast to top 170,000 tonnes in '99. Best known for fast-developing buttery, peachy, at times syrupy, wines, but cooler regions such as PADTHAWAY, S Victoria and ADELAIDE HILLS can produce more elegant, tightly structured, ageworthy examples. Oak, too, is becoming less heavy-handed.

Grenache (33,900 tonnes) As everywhere, produces thin wine if over-cropped but given half a chance can do much better. Growing interest in old Dryland BAROSSA and MCLAREN VALE plantings, with increasing amounts being diverted from fortified to table wine making.

Mourvèdre (10,400 tonnes) Called Mataro in Australia. Has fulfilled the same role and has a similar destiny to GRENACHE.

Muscat Gordo Blanco (56,000 tonnes) An up-market version of Sultana: scented spicy wine v useful in cheap table and sparkling blends but of declining importance.

Pinot Noir (15,200 tonnes) Mostly used in sparkling. Growing awareness of exciting quality of table wines from S Victoria, TASMANIA and ADELAIDE HILLS; plantings are increasing.

For key to grape variety abbreviations, see pages 7–13.

Riesling (39,900 tonnes) For long the mainstay of the quality Australian wine industry, with a special place in the BAROSSA, Eden and CLARE valleys. Usually made bone-dry; can be glorious with up to 20 years bottle-age. Newer botrytis Rieslings made sparingly but can be superb. Will hold its place in the sun.

Sauvignon Blanc (15,000 tonnes) Another recent arrival, with strong growth forecast. Usually not as distinctive as that of New Zealand, and made in many different styles from bland to pungent.

Semillon (51,000 tonnes) Before the arrival of CHARDONNAY, Semillon was the HUNTER VALLEY'S answer to South Australia's RIESLING. Traditionally made without oak and extraordinarily long-lived, but now unfortunately often an oaky Chard substitute. Far from passé; production was projected to increase to 64,500 tonnes in '99.

Shiraz (92,500 tonnes) Until the arrival of CABERNET in the '60s, Shiraz was unchallenged as Australia's red grape. Hugely flexible, with styles ranging from velvety/earthy in the HUNTER, spicy peppery and Rhône-like in central and southern Victoria; and brambly rummy sweet and luscious in BAROSSA and environs (eg PENFOLDS Grange). Recently discovered by overseas markets, with demand exceeding supply; 140,000 tonnes by '99.

Wineries

Alkoomi Mt Barker ★★→★★★ (Ries) **88' 90'** 92' 94 ' 95' (Cab S) **86' 90'** 91 94' 95 25-year veteran producing fine steely RIES and potent long-lived reds.

All Saints NE Vic ★★→★★★ Once famous old family winery bought in '92 by BROWN BROTHERS: excellent Muscat and 'Tokay'.

Allandale Hunter Valley ★→★★ Small winery without v'yds, buying selected local grapes. Quality variable; can be good, esp CHARD.

Amberley Estate Margaret River ★★→★★★ Highly successful and rapidly expanding maker of a full range of regional styles with Chenin Blanc the commercial engine, driving sales to 30,000 cases.

Angove's Riverland (SA) ★→★★ Large long-established MURRAY VALLEY family business in Adelaide and Renmark. Value-for-money whites, especially CHARD, also Colombard.

Arrowfield Upper Hunter ★★ Light CABERNET, succulent Reserve CHARDONNAY from large irrigated vineyard; also wooded SEMILLON. Majority owned by Japanese firm.

Ashbrook Estate Margaret River ★★★ Minimum of fuss; consistently makes 8,000 cases of exemplary SEM, CHARD, SAUV, Verdelho and CAB S.

Bailey's NE Vic ★★→★★★★ Rich old-fashioned reds of great character, esp SHIRAZ (formerly Hermitage), and magnificent dessert Muscat (★★★★) and 'TOKAY'. Now part of ROTHBURY group.

Balgownie Bendigo/Ballarat ★★ Once fine pioneer now owned by MILDARA BLASS: form has been variable; some recent improvement.

Bannockburn Geelong ★★★ (Chard) **87' 88' 94'** 96 (Pinot N) **90' 92' 94'** 96 Intense complex CHARD and PINOT N made using Burgundian techniques. 6,000 cases.

Basedow Barossa ★★ Reliably good range of red and white wine; especially SEMILLON 'White Burgundy'. Changes of ownership seem unlikely to help.

Bass Phillip Gippsland (Vic) ★★★→★★★★ (Pinot) **88 91' 92** 94' 95 Tiny amounts of stylish, eagerly sought PINOT NOIR in three quality grades; very Burgundian in style.

Berri-Renmano Coop Riverland (SA) ★→★★ See Renmano.

Best's Great Western ★★→★★★ (Shiraz) **88' 91** 92' 93 94' 95' Conservative old family winery in GREAT WESTERN with very good mid-weight reds, and CHARD not half bad.

Blass, Wolf (Bilyara) Barossa ★★★ (Cab blend) **86 90'** 91' 93 94 Founded by BAROSSA's ebullient German winemaker, Wolf Blass, but now merged with MILDARA. Dazzling labels, extraordinary wine-show successes, mastery of blending varieties and areas, and lashings of new oak all continue.

Blue Pyrenees Estate Great Western/Avoca ★★ (Cab S) **90 91'** 92 94 Owned by Rémy Martin. Sparkling based on CHARD and PINOT N is much improved. Also good Blue Pyrenees CAB S.

Botobolar Mudgee ★★ Marvellously eccentric little organic winery which exports successfully to the UK.

Bowen Estate Coonawarra ★★★ (Shiraz) **87 90'** 91 93' 94' (Cab) **86 90'** 91' 92 94' Small winery; intense CAB and spicy SHIRAZ.

Brand Coonawarra ★★→★★★ (Shiraz) **82 84 85** 87 90 91 92 (Cab S) **79 81 82 84** 87 90 91 92 Family estate now owned by McWILLIAMS. Fine bold and stylish CHARD, CAB and SHIRAZ under Laira label.

Brookland Valley Margaret River ★★→★★★ Superbly sited winery and restaurant doing great things with SAUV, among others.

Bridgewater Mill Adelaide Hills ★★→★★★ Second label of PETALUMA; suave wines, SAUV BL and SHIRAZ best.

BRL Hardy See Hardy's.

Brokenwood Hunter Valley ★★★ (Shiraz) **86'** 87' 91' 94' 95 (Cab) **81 83 86'** 91' 93 94 Exciting CAB, SHIRAZ since '73 – Graveyard SHIRAZ outstanding. New winery ('83) added quality CHARD, SEM; zooming to 60,000 cases.

Brown Brothers Milawa (Vic) ★→★★★ (Chard) **90 91 92** 94 (Noble Ries) **78 82 84** 85 88 90 Old family firm with new ideas: v wide range of delicate single-grape wines, many from cool mountain districts. CHARD, RIES. Dry white Muscat outstanding. CAB blend is best red. See also All Saints.

Buring, Leo Barossa ★★→★★★ (Ries) **73' 75' 79 84 86** 88 **90 91'** 94 95 96 'Chateau Leonay', old RIES specialists, now owned by LINDEMANS. Great with age (even great age), esp Show Reserve releases.

Campbells of Rutherglen NE Vic ★★ Smooth ripe reds and good dessert wines, the latter in youthful fruity style.

Cape Mentelle Margaret River ★★★→★★★★ (Zin) **90 91 92 93** (Cab) **82' 83' 86' 90'** 91' 92 93' Idiosyncratic robust CAB can be magnificent, CHARD even better; also Zin and v popular SAUV-SEM. David Hohnen also founded Cloudy Bay, NZ. Both bought in '90 by Veuve Clicquot.

Capel Vale Swan Valley (WA) ★★★ (Ries) **88' 89' 91 93'** 95' 96' (Chard) **87 91 93 95'** 96' Steadily growing and v successful with outstanding whites, incl RIES, Gewürz. Also vg CAB.

Cassegrain Hastings Valley (NSW) ★★ Relatively new winery on NSW coast: grapes from local plantings. CHARD is best, Chambourcin striking.

Chambers' Rosewood NE Vic ★★→★★★ Good cheap table and great dessert wines, esp 'Tokay'.

Charles Melton Barossa ★★★ Tiny winery with bold luscious reds, esp Nine Popes, an old-vine GRENACHE and SHIRAZ blend. To watch.

Chapel Hill McLaren Vale ★★★→★★★★ (r) **90'** 91' 92' 93 94' 95' Once tiny, now a booming estate: extra-rich fruity-oaky CHARD, SHIRAZ and CABERNET; big show successes to winemaker Pam Dunsford.

Chateau Hornsby Alice Springs (N Territory) ★ A charming aberration and magnet for tourists to Ayer's Rock.

Chateau Reynella McLaren Vale ★★→★★★★ ('Vintage Port') **75'** 77' 82 87 88 Historic winery serving as HQ for BRL HARDY group. VG 'Basket-pressed' red table wines, superb vintage 'Port'.

NB Vintages in colour are those you should choose first for drinking in 1998.

Chateau Tahbilk Goulburn Valley ★★→★★★ (Marsanne) **89 90 92'** 94 96 (Shiraz) **84'** 86 88 91' 92' 94 (Cab) **86'** 88 90 92' 94 Beautiful historic family estate: reds for long ageing, also RIES and Marsanne. Private Bins outstanding; value for money ditto.

Chateau Yaldara Barossa ★→★★ A plethora of brands incl Acacia Hill, Ch Yaldara, Lakewood and The Farms: oaky, slightly sweet, cheap – apart from eccentrically expensive The Farms.

Coldstream Hills Yarra Valley ★★★ (Chardonnay) **88 90 91** 92' 93' 94' 95 96 (Pinot N) **91 92'** 94' (Cab S) **88** 90 91' 92' 93' 94' Estate winery est'd '85 by wine critic James Halliday. Delicious PINOT N to drink young and Reserve to age lead Australia. Vg CHARD (esp Reserve wines), fruity CAB and Cab-Merlot. Acquired by SOUTHCORP mid '96.

Conti, Paul Swan Valley ★→★★ One of the doyens of the SWAN VALLEY, s'times exceptionally elegant SHIRAZ and intensely grapey Frontignac.

Coriole McLaren Vale ★★→★★★ (Shiraz) **89 90'** 91 92 94' 95 To watch especially for old-vine SHIRAZ Lloyd Reserve; best when nicely balanced by oak. Other wines are worthy.

Craiglee Macedon (Vic) ★★★ (Shiraz) **90 91'** 92 93 94' Recreation of famous 19th-C estate: fragrant peppery SHIRAZ, CHARD.

Croser Adelaide Hills ★★★→★★★★ **92 93** 94' Now Australia's top sparkling CHARD-PINOT N blend. Offshoot of PETALUMA with Bollinger as partner. Lean, fine, with splendid backbone from Pinot N.

Cullen Wines Margaret River ★★★ (Chard) **92 93'** 94 95' 96 (Cab S-Merlot) **90'** 91' 92 94' 95' Mother-daughter team pioneered the region with strongly structured (esp Reserve) CAB-Merlot, substantial but subtle SAUV and bold CHARD: all real characters.

Dalwhinnie Pyrenees ★★→★★★ (Chard) **92'** 93' 95 96' (Cab S) **86' 88** 90' 91' 92 93 94' 95' 4,500-case producer of concentrated rich CHARD, SHIRAZ and CAB S, arguably the best in PYRENEES.

d'Arenberg McLaren Vale ★★→★★★ Old firm now with a new lease of life; sumptuous SHIRAZ and GRENACHE, fine CHARDONNAY with a cascade of garrulous new labels.

De Bortoli Griffith (NSW) ★→★★★ (Noble Sem) **90 91** 92' 93' 94' Irrigation-area winery. Standard reds and whites but magnificent sweet botrytised Sauternes-style Noble SEM. See also next entry.

De Bortoli Yarra Valley ★★→★★★ (Chard) **91 92'** 93 94' 95 (Cab S) **88 90** 91 92' 94' Formerly Chateau Yarrinya: bought by DE BORTOLI and now YARRA VALLEY'S largest producer. Main label is more than adequate; second label, Gulf Station and third label Windy Peak, vg value.

Delatite Central Vic ★★★ (Ries) **90** 92 **93 94** 96 Winemaker Rosalind Ritchie makes appropriately willowy and feminine RIES, Gewurz, PINOT N and CAB from this v cool mountainside v'yd.

Devil's Lair Margaret River ★★→★★★ 100 acres of estate vineyards for opulently concentrated CHARDONNAY, PINOT NOIR and CABERNET-MERLOT. Production is 10,000 cases annually. Acquired by SOUTHCORP early '97.

Diamond Valley Yarra Valley ★★→★★★ (Pinot) **92 94** 96' Outstanding PINOT N in significant quantities; other wines good.

Domaine Chandon Yarra Valley ★★★ The showpiece of the YARRA VALLEY, leading Oz in fizz. Classic sparkling wine from grapes grown in all the cooler wine regions of Australia, with strong support from owner Moët & Chandon in France. Immediate success in UK under GREEN POINT label.

Drayton's Bellevue Hunter Valley ★★ ('Hermitage') Traditional 'Hermitage' and SEM, occasionally good CHARD; recent quality improvements after bit of a lapse.

Dromana Estate Mornington Peninsula ★★→★★★ (Chardonnay) **90 91 92 94** (Cab S-Merlot) **88 90 92** 94 Led energetically by Gary Crittenden: light fragrant CABS, PINOTS, CHARDS with sudden interest in Italian varieties.

Eaglehawk Clare ★→★★ Formerly Quelltaler. Once known for Granfiesta 'Sherry'. Recently good RIES and SEM. Owned by MILDARA BLASS.

Evans Family Hunter Valley ★★★ (Chard) **86 87 88 91 93 94 95'** Excellent CHARD from small vineyard owned by family of Len Evans. Fermented in new oak. Repays cellaring.

Elderton Barossa ★★ Old v'yds are base for flashy rich American-oaked CAB and SHIRAZ.

Evans and Tate Margaret River ★★★ (Sem) **92 93'** 95' 96 (Cab) **88** 91' 94' 95 Fine elegant SEM, CHARD, CAB, Merlot from MARGARET RIVER, Redbrook. Going from strength to strength at 100,000 cases.

Freycinet Tasmania ★★→★★★ (Pinot N) **93' 94'** 95 East coast winery producing voluptuous rich PINOT N, good CHARD.

Geoff Merrill McLaren Vale ★→★★★ (Sem-Chard) **88'** 89 **90'** 92 94' 95' (Cab) **87** 90' 92 94' 95 Ebullient maker of Geoff Merrill, Mount Hurtle and Cockatoo Ridge wines. A questing enthusiast; the best wines are excellent, others unashamedly mass-market oriented.

Giaconda Central Vic ★★★ (Chard) **88 90 91 92'** 93 94' 95 (Pinot N) **89 91 92' 93** 94' Very small ultra-fashionable winery near Beechworth: popular CHARDONNAY and PINOT N.

Goundrey Wines Great Southern (WA) ★★★ (Ries) **90 91** 92 94' 95' 96 (Cab S) **88 89 90'** 91' 94' 95 Recent expansion and quality upgrade. Now in top rank: esp good CABERNET, CHARD and SAUV BL.

Grant Burge Wines Barossa ★★→★★★ Solid output of silky-smooth reds and whites (vg CHARD 93) from the best grapes of Burge's large v'yd holdings. Burge was founder of KRONDORF. 70,000 cases.

Green Point See Domaine Chandon.

Grosset Clare ★★★→★★★★ (Ries) **88 90'** 92 93 94 95' 96' (Gaia) **86 90** 91 92 93' 94' 95 Fastidious winemaker: very elegant RIES, recent spectacular Gaia CAB-Merlot.

Hanging Rock Macedon (Vic) ★→★★★ (Shiraz) 87 **88** 90' 91' 92 93 94' Eclectic range: budget Picnic wines; huge Heathcote SHIRAZ; complex sparkling.

Hardy's McLaren Vale, Barossa, Keppoch etc ★→★★★ (Eileen Chard) **92 93'** 94 95 ('Vintage Port') **45' 51' 54 56 69 71 73 75' 81'** 87 88' Historic company using and blending wines from several areas. Best are Eileen Hardy and Thomas Hardy series and (Australia's greatest) 'Vintage Ports'. CHATEAU REYNELLA'S beautifully restored buildings are now group headquarters. '92 merger with BERRI-RENMANO and public ownership (BRL HARDY) makes this Australia's second-largest wine co.

Heemskerk Tasmania ★★★ A major commercial operation; concentrating on high-profile Jansz sparkling wine, sold to Tasmanian JAC group in '94.

Heggies Adelaide Hills ★★ (Ries) **90'** 91 **92'** 95 96' (Chard) **92'** 93 **94** 95 96' Vineyard at 500 metres in eastern BAROSSA Ranges owned by S SMITH & SONS. Excellent RIESLING and Botrytis Ries are separately marketed.

Henschke Barossa ★★★★ (Shiraz) **52 56 59 61 62 66 67 72 78 80 82 84** 86 88 **90** 91' 92' 93' 94' 95 (Cab S) **78 80 81 84 85** 86 **88** 90' 91' 92 93' 94' 95 125-year-old family business, perhaps Australia's best, known for delectable SHIRAZ (especially Hill of Grace), vg CABERNET and red blends, but Eden Valley RIESLING and SEMILLON also excellent. New high-country Lenswood v'yds on ADELAIDE HILLS add excitement.

Hill-Smith Estate Adelaide Hills ★★→★★★ Another separate brand of S SMITH & SONS, perhaps best of all; CHARD, SAUV and CAB-SHIRAZ can be vg value.

Hillstowe Adelaide Hills ★★ Recent small winery using excellent fruit for intense vivid CHARD, PINOT N; also CAB-Merlot, SAUV BL.

Hollick Coonawarra ★★ (Chard) **91 92 93** 94 96 (Cab-Merlot) 86 **90 91'** 92' 93 Hollick family plus former TOLLANA maker: gd CHARD, RIES; much-followed reds, esp Ravenswood. Terra is trendy second label.

Houghton Swan Valley ★→★★★ (Supreme) **84 86 87 89'** 91' 93' 94 95 96 The most famous old winery of WA. Soft ripe Supreme is top wine; a national classic. Also excellent CAB, Verdelho etc. See Hardy's.

Howard Park Mount Barker ★★★ (Ries) **86' 88'** 90' 91 93 94' **95'** 96 (Cab S) **86 88** 89 **90'** 91 92' 93 94' 95 John Wade (formerly of WYNNS hand-crafts tiny quantities of scented RIES, CHARD and spicy CAB S. Major winery expansion is under way with flourishing contract-winemaking business for others. Second label: Madfish Bay.

Huntington Estate Mudgee (Cab S) **81 83 84** 86 89 91' **93** 94 96 Small winery; best in MUDGEE. Fine CABS, vg SHIRAZ. Invariably underpriced.

Idyll Geelong ★→★★ Small winery making Gewürz and CAB in v individual style. A pioneer exporter.

Inglewood Upper Hunter Valley ★★ Dandy Shiraz and Chard.

Jasper Hill Bendigo ★★★ (Shiraz) **80 82 85 86 90'** 91' 92' 94' 95 Emily's Paddock SHIRAZ-Cab F blend and George's Paddock Shiraz from dry land estate are intense, long-lived and much admired. BENDIGO's best.

Jim Barry Clare ★→★★★ Some great v'yds provide good RIES, McCrae Wood SHIRAZ and convincing Grange pretender The Amagh.

Katnook Estate Coonawarra ★★★ (Chard) 86 **90 92'** 94' 95 96 (Cab S) **85 86** 90' 91' 92 93 94 Excellent and pricey CAB and CHARD; also SAUV.

Knappstein Wines Clare ★★★ Reliable RIESLING, Fumé Blanc, CABERNET S-Merlot and Cab Franc wines. Owned by PETALUMA.

Krondorf Wines Barossa ★★→★★★ Part of MILDARA BLASS group with niche market brands: Show Reserve wines are best, esp CHARD.

Lake's Folly Hunter Valley ★★★★ (Chard) **86 89** 91 92' 93' 94 95 (Cab S) **69 72 75 78 81'** 85 **87** 89 91' 92 93' 94 95 Small family winery of Max Lake. The pioneer of HUNTER CAB. Cab is v fine, complex. CHARD exciting and age-worthy.

Lark Hill Canberra District ★★ Most consistent CANBERRA producer, making esp attractive RIES, pleasant CHARD.

Leasingham Clare ★→★★★ Important medium-sized quality winery bought by HARDY'S in '87. Good RIES, SEM, CHARD and CAB-Malbec. Various labels.

Leconfield Coonawarra ★★→★★★ (Ries) **90** 91 **92** 94 (Cab S) **80 82 84** 88 90' 91' 92' **93'** 94 COONAWARRA SHIRAZ and CAB of great style. RIES and CHARD well made by former TYRRELL winemaker.

Leeuwin Estate Margaret River ★★★★ (Chard) **82' 83' 85' 86 87' 89** 90 91 92' (Cab) **79** 81 82 84 **85** 87 88 89 **90** 91' Leading W Australia estate, lavishly equipped. Superb (and v expensive) CHARD; vg RIES, SAUV and CAB.

Lenswood Vineyards ★★★ Estate now sole occupation of Tim KNAPPSTEIN making subtle SAUV BL and powerful CHARD, PINOT N.

Lindemans originally Hunter Valley, now everywhere ★→★★★ (Hunter Sem) **66 67' 70' 72 75 79'** 86 87 91 92 94 (Hunter Shiraz) **59' 65' 66' 70 73 75** 79 82 **83** 86 87 91 93 (Padthaway Chard) **85 86 87 88 90** 91 **92** 93 **94'** 95 (Coonawarra Red) **82** 85 **86'** 88 **90' 91'** 92 94 One of the oldest firms, now a giant owned by PENFOLDS. Owns BURING (BAROSSA), ROUGE HOMME (COONAWARRA), and important v'yds at PADTHAWAY. Vg CHARD and Coonawarra reds (eg Limestone Ridge, Pyrus). Pioneer of new styles, yet still makes fat, old-style 'Hunters'. Bin-number Classics can be vg. Dominant performer at wine shows.

Marsh Estate Hunter Valley ★★ Substantial producer of good SEM, SHIRAZ and CAB of steady quality.

AUSTRALIA

McWilliam's Hunter Valley and Riverina ★→★★★ (Elizabeth Sem) **79'** 80 **81 82 84' 86'** 87' 88 **89 91' 92** 94 Famous family of HUNTER VALLEY winemakers at Mount Pleasant: SHIRAZ and SEMILLON – 'Elizabeth' is the only bottle-aged (6 yrs) Sem sold, vg value. McWilliam's is also a pioneer in RIVERINA with CABERNET SAUVIGNON and sweet white Lexia. Recent show results demonstrate high standards. 'Elizabeth' (sold at 6 yrs) and 'Lovedale' (10 yrs) Sems are now Australia's best. Honest RIVERINA wines at low prices.

Mildara Coonawarra and Murray Valley ★→★★★ (Coonawarra Cab) **63' 64 70 71 78 79 80' 82 85 86'** 88 **90'** 91' 92 93 94 'Sherry' and brandy specialists at Mildara on the Murray River, also make fine CAB S and RIESLING at COONAWARRA. Now has BAILEY'S, BALGOWNIE, BLASS, KRONDORF, ROTHBURY, SALTRAM and YELLOWGLEN too, all acquired in '96 by Fosters brewing group.

Miramar Mudgee ★★ Some of MUDGEE's best white wines, especially CHARD and long-lived CAB.

Mitchells Clare ★★★ (Ries) **78' 84' 86 90'** 92 93 **94'** 95 96 (Cab S) **80' 82 84 86'** 90' 92' 93 94 Small family winery for excellent CAB and v stylish dry RIES.

Mitchelton Goulburn Valley ★★→★★★ Big modern winery, acquired by PETALUMA in '92. A wide range incl a vg wood-matured Marsanne, SHIRAZ; classic Blackwood Park RIES from GOULBURN VALLEY is one of Australia's v best value wines. Many enterprising blends and labels.

Montrose Mudgee ★★ Reliable underrated producer of CHARD and CAB blends. Now part of the ORLANDO group.

Moondah Brook Estate Gingin (WA) ★★ HOUGHTON v'yd 80km NW of Perth: v smooth flavourful CHARD, Chenin Bl, Verdelho and CAB.

Moorilla Estate Tasmania ★★→★★★ (Ries) **88** 89 90 91 93 94' 95' Senior winery on outskirts of Hobart on Derwent River: vg RIESLING (**94'** superb), Traminer and CHARD; PINOT N rather disappointing. Several recent unsettling changes of ownership.

Morris NE Vic ★★→★★★★ Old winery at Rutherglen for Australia's greatest dessert Muscats and 'Tokays'; also recently vg low-price table wine.

Moss Wood Margaret River ★★★★ (Sem) **83'** 85 **86'** 87' 91 92' 94' 95' 96 (Chard) **80 85 89 90 92** 93 95' 96 (Cab S) **77' 80' 83 86** 87 90 91 92 93 94' 95' To many the best MARGARET RIVER winery (only 29 vineyard acres). SEMILLON, CABERNET, PINOT N and CHARD, all with rich fruit flavours, not unlike some of the top California wines.

Mount Hurtle See Geoff Merrill.

Mount Langi Ghiran Great Western ★★★ (Shiraz) **86 88** 90' 91' 92' **93** 94' 95 Esp for superb rich peppery Rhône-like SHIRAZ wine, one of Australia's best cool-climate versions.

Mount Mary Yarra Valley ★★★★ (Pinot N) **78 79 82 83 85 86** 87 89 90 **91'** 92' 94' 95 96' (Cab S-Cab F-Merlot) **76 78 79 80 82 84 85 86' 88' 90'** 91' 92' 94 Dr John Middleton is a perfectionist making tiny amounts of suave CHARD, vivid PINOT N, and (best of all) CAB S-Cab F-Merlot. All will age impeccably.

Mountadam Barossa ★★★ (Chard) **82 84 87 89 90** 91 92 93 High Eden Valley winery of David and Adam Wynn. CHARD is rich, voluptuous and long. Other labels include David Wynn, Eden Ridge.

Normans McLaren Vale ★→★★★ Public listing in late '94 lifted the profile of this winery, but premium Chais Clarendon has always been excellent.

Orlando (Gramp's) Barossa ★★→★★★ (St Hugo Cab) **80 82 84 85 86 88 90** 91 92 94 Great pioneering company, bought by management in '88 but now owned by Pernod-Ricard. Full range from huge-selling Jacob's Creek 'Claret' to excellent Jacaranda Ridge CAB S from COONAWARRA. See Wyndham Estate.

Paringa Estate Mornington Peninsula ★★★ Maker of quite spectacular CHARD, PINOT N and (late-picked) SHIRAZ winning innumerable trophies with tiny output of 2,000 cases.

Parker Estate Coonawarra ★★★ Young estate making v good CAB, esp Terra Rossa First Growth.

Penfolds orig Adelaide, now everywhere ★★→★★★★ (Grange) **52' 53' 55' 62 63' 66' 67 71'** 75 76 80 **82** 83 **85** 86' 88' 90' 91' 92 (Bin 707) **64 65 66' 78 80 83 84 86' 88** 90' 91' 92' 93 94' (Bin 389) **66 70 71 82 83** 86' 87 **88'** 90' 91' 92 93 94' Ubiquitous and excellent: in BAROSSA VALLEY, CLARE, COONAWARRA, RIVERINA etc. Consistently Australia's best red wine company. Bought LINDEMANS in '90. Its Grange (was called 'Hermitage') is deservedly ★★★★. Bin 707 CABERNET not far behind. Other bin-numbered wines (eg Cab-SHIRAZ 389, Kalimna Bin 28 Shiraz) can be outstanding. Grandfather 'Port' is often excellent. The Penfolds/Lindemans group was taken over by SOUTHCORP, already owner of SEPPELT, in '90.

The taste of oak

The fashion of deliberately flavouring wine with oak began in California in the '60s and has been widely exaggerated and misused ever since. Formerly, barrels were used for their virtues as strong movable containers with enough porosity to allow very gradual oxidation of their contents. New barrels were needed for transport, but were used for storage only for the very finest, most concentrated wines, whose expected life was decades – by which time any oak flavour would be lost. The slower oak grows, the better its physical properties and the less pungent its aroma/flavour. American oak is very pungent; Baltic oak the opposite. Of the famous French oak forests, 'Limousin' (western) is relatively pungent and coarse, usable only for red wines; central 'Allier', 'Nevers', 'Tronçais' (top-grade), are most delicate, best for white or red wines; 'Bourgogne', 'Champagne', 'Vosges' (eastern) are intermediate. Barrels are put together over a fire which helps bend the staves. How much this burns (or 'toasts') the oak affects the wine as much as its origin. As cynical winemakers have long discovered, though, a handful of oak chips in a tank can create a highly profitable illusion.

Penley Estate Coonawarra ★★★ High-profile, no-expense-spared new-comer winery: rich, textured, fruit-and-oak CAB; also SHIRAZ-Cab blend and CHARD.

Petaluma Adelaide Hills ★★★★ (Ries) **79 80' 82 84** 86' 88 **90'** 91 93 94' 95' **96** (Chard) **77 86 87** 90' **92'** 93 94 **95'** (Cab S) **79 86' 88' 90'** 91 92' 93' 94 A rocket-like '80s success with COONAWARRA CAB S, ADELAIDE HILLS CHARDONNAY, CLARE VALLEY RIESLING, all processed at winery in Adelaide Hills. Red wines have become richer from '88 on, most recent vintages are outstanding. Also: BRIDGEWATER MILL. Now owns KNAPPSTEIN and MITCHELTON. See also Croser.

Peter Lehmann Wines Barossa ★★→★★★ Defender of BAROSSA faith, Peter Lehmann, makes vast quantities of wine (some sold in bulk), with v fine 'special cuvées' under own label; now public listed and flourishing. NB Stonewell SHIRAZ (tastes of blackberries and rum) and dry RIESLING.

Pierro Margaret River ★★★ (Chard) **90 91'** 93' 94 95' 96 Highly rated maker of expensive, tangy SEM, SAUV BL and sophisticated barrel-fermented CHARD.

Piper's Brook Tasmania ★★★ (Ries) **79' 82' 84' 85'** 89 91 92' 93' 94 95 (Chard) **82 84 86 87 88** 91' 92' 93 94' 95 Cool-area pioneer with vg RIES, PINOT N, excellent CHARD from Tamar Valley. Lovely labels. Second label: Ninth Island.

Plantagenet Mount Barker ★★★ (Chard) **90' 92** 94' 95 96 (Shiraz) **86 88** 90' **91'** 92 94' 95' (Cab S) **85' 86' 88** 90' 93' 94' 95 The region's older statesman: wide range of varieties, especially rich CHARD, SHIRAZ and vibrant potent CAB S.

Primo Estate Adelaide Plains ★★★ Joe Grilli is a miracle-worker given the climate; successes incl vg botrytised RIES, tangy Colombard, rich Joseph CAB-Merlot. Latest potent red: Moda Amarone.

Quelltaler See Eaglehawk.

Redman Coonawarra ★→★★ (Cab S) **69' 70 71 76 79 87 90'** 91' 92 93' 94' The most famous old name in COONAWARRA; red wine specialists: SHIRAZ, CAB S, Cab-Merlot. Quality reviving after a disappointing period.

Renmano Murray Valley ★→★★ Huge coop now part of BRL Hardy (see Hardy's). 'Chairman's Selections' value. Exceedingly voluptuous CHARD.

Reynold's Yarraman Estate Upper Hunter ★★ Former stone prison building to watch: winery of ex-HOUGHTON/WYNDHAM winemaker Jon Reynolds.

Rockford Barossa ★★→★★★ Small producer, wide range of thoroughly individual wines, often made from v old low-yielding v'yds; reds best. Sparkling Black Shiraz has super-cult status.

Rosemount Upper Hunter, McLaren Vale, Coonawarra ★★→★★★ Rich and unctuous HUNTER 'Show' CHARDONNAY is international smash. This, McLaren Vale Balmoral Syrah and COONAWARRA CABERNET lead the wide range, which gets better every year.

Rothbury Estate Hunter Valley Fell prey to Fosters/MILDARA in '96 after long bitter fight by original founder Len Evans (since departed). Has made long-lived SEM and SHIRAZ and rich, buttery, early-drinking COWRA CHARD to good effect, but the future looks doubtful. Old Evans fans should see Evans Family.

Rouge Homme Coonawarra ★★ (Shiraz-Cab S) **80 81 85 86'** 90' 91' 92 94' Separately branded and promoted arm of LINDEMANS with keenly priced CHARD and SHIRAZ-CAB leaders.

Rymill Coonawarra ★★→★★★ Descendants of John Riddoch carrying on the good work of the founder of COONAWARRA. Strong dense SHIRAZ and CABERNET esp noteworthy.

St Hallett Barossa ★★★ (Old Block) **80' 83 84' 86 87 88 90' 91' 92'** 93 94 Rejuvenated winery. 60+-yr-old vines give splendid Old Block SHIRAZ. Rest of range (eg CHARD, SAUV-SEM) is smooth and stylish.

St Huberts Yarra Valley ★★→★★★ (Chard) **90' 91'** 92' **93** 94' (Cab) **77' 86 88** 90 91' 92 94 Acquired by ROTHBURY in late '92; accent on fine dry CHARD and smooth 'berry' CAB. Now part of Fosters/MILDARA.

St Shiela's SA p sw sp **36 22 38** Full-bodied fizzer. Ripper grog.

Saltram Barossa (Merged with ROTHBURY in '94.) Pinnacle Selection is best label (esp COONAWARRA CAB); also good are Mamre Brook wines. Metala is assoc Stonyfell label for old-style Langhorne Creek Cab-SHIRAZ.

Sandalford Swan Valley ★→★★ Fine old winery with contrasting styles of red and white single-grape wines from SWAN and MARGARET RIVER areas. Wonderful old fortified Verdelho.

Scotchman's Hill Geelong ★★ Newcomer making significant quantities of stylish PINOT N and good CHARD at modest prices.

Seaview McLaren Vale ★★→★★★ Old winery now owned by SOUTHCORP. CHARD, SHIRAZ-CABERNET and single-grape CAB S frequently rise above their station in life, while the sparkling wines are among Australia's best – now based on PINOT N and Chard. Premium label: Edwards & Chaffey.

To decipher codes, please refer to 'Key to symbols' on front flap of jacket, or to 'How to use this book' on page 6.

Seppelt Barossa, Great Western, Keppoch etc ★★★ ('Hermitage') **71' 85' 86'** 90 **91'** 92 93' (Salinger) **88 90 91 92** Far-flung producers of Australia's most popular sparkling (Great Western Brut); also new range of Victoria-sourced table wines. Top sparkling is highly regarded 'Salinger'. Part of SOUTHCORP, Australia's biggest wine company.

Sevenhill Clare ★★ Owned by the Jesuitical Manresa Society since 1851; consistently good wine; reds (esp SHIRAZ) can be outstanding.

Seville Estate Yarra Valley ★★★ (Chard) **90 91 92** 94' (Shiraz) **85 86 88** 90 91 92 93' 94' Tiny winery with CHARD, SHIRAZ, PINOT N and vg CAB, acquired by BROKENWOOD in '97.

Shaw & Smith McLaren Vale ★★★ Trendy young venture of flying winemaker Martin Shaw and Australia's first MW, Michael Hill-Smith. Crisp SAUV, vg unoaked CHARD, complex barrel-fermented Reserve Chard are the 3 wines.

Southcorp The giant of the industry, despite its naff name: owns PENFOLDS, LINDEMANS, SEPPELT, SEAVIEW, WYNNS, etc, etc.

S Smith & Sons (alias Yalumba) Barossa ★★→★★★ Big old family firm with considerable verve, using computers, juice evaluation etc, to produce full spectrum of high-quality wines, incl HILL-SMITH ESTATE. HEGGIES and YALUMBA Signature Reserve are best. Angas Brut, a good-value sparkling wine, and Oxford Landing CHARD are now world brands.

Stafford Ridge Adelaide Hills ★★→★★★ 20-acre estate of former HARDY'S winemaker, Geoff Weaver, at Lenswood. V fine SAUV, CHARD, RIES and CAB-Merlot blend.

Stoniers Mornington Peninsula ★★★ (Chard) **90 91 92 93' 94'** 95 (Pinot) **91' 92 93' 94** 95 Has overtaken DROMANA ESTATE for pride of place on the Peninsula. CHARD, PINOT are consistently vg; Reserves outstanding.

Taltarni Great Western/Avoca ★★★ (Shiraz) **78 79 81** 82 **84 86** 88 89 90 91 92 94 (Cab S) **79** 81 82 84 86 88 89 90 91 92 94 Dominique Portet, brother of Bernard (Clos du Val, Napa), makes huge but balanced reds for long ageing; good SAUV and adequate sparkling.

Tarrawarra Yarra Valley ★★★ (Chard) **91'** 92 93 94' 95 (Pinot N) **88' 91** 92 94' 95 Multimillion-dollar investment: limited quantities of idiosyncratic expensive CHARDONNAY and robust long-lived PINOT NOIR. Tunnel Hill is the second label.

Taylors Wines Clare ★→★★ Large inexpensive range of table wines, now on the improve.

Tisdall Wines Goulburn Valley ★★ Went into hibernation after '93 acquisition by MILDARA BLASS; now cautiously being revived with low-key re-launch.

'Tokay' Speciality of northeast Victoria. An aged intense sweet strong Muscadelle wine; less aromatic than Muscat but at best superb. Under EC rules the name will have to go.

Tollana Barossa ★★→★★★ Old company once famous for making brandy. Has latterly made some fine CABS, CHARD and RIES. Acquired by PENFOLDS in '87.

Tulloch Hunter Valley ★ Old name at Pokolbin with reputation for dry red wines, CHARDONNAY and Verdelho. Now part of the SOUTHCORP group but a shadow of its former self.

Tyrrell Hunter Valley ★★★ (Sem Vat 1) **70 75 76 77' 79 86'** 87' 89 90 91 92' **94** (Chard Vat 47) **72 73' 76' 79' 82 84' 85 89** 90 **92'** 93 94' 95' 96 (Shiraz Vats) **73 75 77 79 80 81'** 83 **85** 87' 89' 91' 92 93 94' Some of the v best traditional HUNTER VALLEY wines, 'Hermitage' and SEM. Pioneered CHARD with big rich Vat 47 – still a classic. Also delicate PINOT N.

Vasse Felix Margaret River ★★★ (Cab S) **79** 83 **85** 88 89 91 92 With CULLEN, pioneer of the MARGARET RIVER. Elegant CABS, notable for mid-weight balance. Second label: Forest Hills (esp RIES, CHARD).

Virgin Hills Bendigo/Ballarat ★★★★ **74' 75' 78** 79 **80'** 82 **85' 87** 88' 90 91' 92 94 Tiny supplies of one red (a CABERNET-SHIRAZ-Malbec blend) of legendary style and balance.

Wendouree Clare ★★★★ **78 79 83** 86 89' 90' 91' 92' 93 94 Treasured maker (in tiny quantities) of some of Australia's most powerful and concentrated reds based on SHIRAZ, CAB S and Malbec; immensely long-lived.

Westfield Swan Valley ★→★★ John Kosovich's CAB, CHARD and Verdelho show particular finesse for a hot climate, but he is now developing a new v'yd in the much cooler Pemberton region.

Wignalls Great Southern (WA) ★★→★★★ In the far southwest corner of Austalia (near Albany), Bill Wignall makes sometimes ethereal, always stylish PINOT NOIR.

Wirra Wirra McLaren Vale ★★★ (Chard) **90 91** 92 93 (Cab S) **87' 90'** 91' 92' 94' 95 High-quality, beautifully-packaged wines making a big impact. Angelus is superb, top-of-the-range CAB, ditto RSW SHIRAZ.

Woodleys Barossa ★ Well-known for low-price 'Queen Adelaide'.

Woodstock McLaren Vale ★★ Ever-reliable maker of chunky, high-flavoured reds in regional style and luscious botrytis wines from esoteric varieties. 20,000 cases.

Wyndham Estate Branxton (NSW) ★→★★ Aggressive large HUNTER and MUDGEE group with brands: CRAIGMOOR, Hunter Estate, MONTROSE, Richmond Grove and Saxonvale. Acquired by ORLANDO in '90.

Wynns Coonawarra ★★★ (Shiraz) **53' 54' 55' 63 65 82 85 86'** 88 **90'** 91' 92 93 94' 95 (Cab S) **57' 58' 59' 60 62 82' 85** 86' 88 **90'** 91' 92 93 94' SOUTHCORP-owned COONAWARRA classic. RIES, CHARD, SHIRAZ and CAB are all very good, esp John Riddoch Cab, and Michael 'Hermitage'.

Yalumba See S Smith & Sons.

Yarra Burn Yarra Valley ★★ Estate making SEM, SAUV, CHARD, sparkling PINOT, Pinot N, CAB; acquired by BRL HARDY in '95, with changes now under way.

Yarra Ridge Yarra Valley ★★→★★★ Expanding young (70,000-case) winery, v successful CHARD, CAB, SAUV BL, PINOT N, all with flavour and finesse at modest prices. Now fully owned by MILDARA BLASS.

Yarra Yering Yarra Valley ★★★→★★★★ (Dry Reds) **78 79** 80' **81' 82' 83 84** 85 87 90 91' 92' 93' 94' 95 Best-known Lilydale boutique winery. Esp racy powerful PINOT N, deep herby CAB (Dry Red No 1) and SHIRAZ (Dry Red No 2). Luscious daring flavours in red and white.

Yellowglen Bendigo/Ballarat ★★→★★★ High-flying sparkling winemaker owned by MILDARA BLASS. Recent dramatic improvement in quality, with top-end brands like Vintage Brut, Cuvée Victoria and 'Y'.

Yeringberg Yarra Valley ★★★ (Marsanne) **90** 91' 92 93 94' 95 (Cab) **74' 75 76 79 80' 81' 82** 84 86 87 88' 90 91' 92 94' Dreamlike historic estate still in the hands of the founding family, now again producing very high-quality Marsanne, Roussanne, CHARDONNAY, CAB and PINOT N, in minute quantities.

Zema Estate Coonawarra ★★→★★★ One of the last bastions of hand-pruning and picking in COONAWARRA making silkily powerful, disarmingly straightforward reds.

For key to grape variety abbreviations, see pages 7–13.

New Zealand

Heavier shaded areas are
the wine growing regions

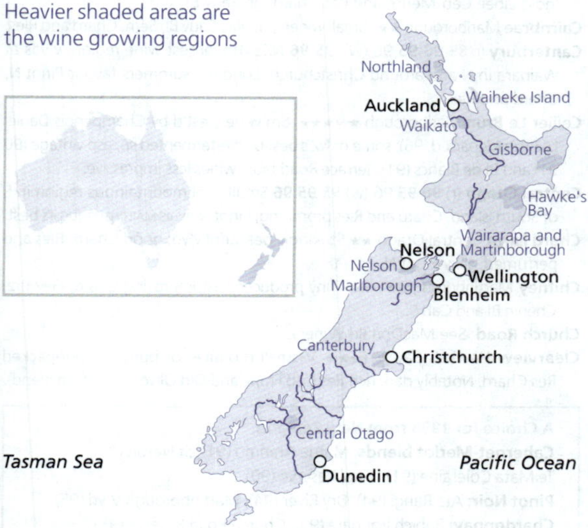

Since the mid-1980s New Zealand has made a worldwide name for wines (mainly white) of startling quality, well able to compete with those of Australia or California. In 1982 it exported 12,000 cases; in 1996 over 1.2 million. There are now over 18,000 vineyard acres.

White grapes prevail. Formerly dominant Müller-Thurgau has now been well overtaken by superior varieties. The most extensively planted grapes are: Chardonnay, Sauvignon Blanc (these two cover almost half of the national vineyard), Pinot Noir, Cabernet Sauvignon, Müller-Thurgau, Merlot (fast gaining ground) and Riesling.

Intensity of fruit flavours and crisp acidity are the hallmarks of New Zealand. No region on earth can match Marlborough Sauvignon Blanc for pungency. Chardonnay has shone throughout the country, but Riesling's stronghold is the South Island. Marlborough has also proved its worth with excellent sparkling wine. The relatively warm Hawke's Bay and Auckland regions are now succeeding with Cabernet Sauvignon and Merlot-based reds, but Pinot Noir thrives in the cooler climates of Martinborough and the South Island. The principal regions and producers follow.

Ata Rangi Martinborough ★★★ V small but highly respected winery. Outstanding Pinot N and Chard; also gd Cab-Merlot-Syrah blend (Célèbre).

Auckland (r) 89 90 **93 94** (w) 91 93 **94 95 96** Largest city in NZ. Location of head offices of major wineries. Some of NZ's top Cab-based reds. Incl Henderson, Huapai, Kumeu and Waiheke Island districts.

Babich Henderson (Auckland) ★★→★★★ Med-sized family firm, est'd 1916; quality and value. H BAY v'yds. Rare premium wines: 'The Patriarch'. Fine Irongate Chard and Cab-Merlot (single v'yd). Mara Estate varietals: value.

Brajkovich See Kumeu River.

Brookfields Hawke's Bay ★★→★★★ One of region's top v'yds: outstanding 'gold label' Cab-Merlot and Res Chard, gd Sauv Bl.

Cairnbrae Marlborough ★★ Small winery; quality Sauv Bl, Sém, Chard and Ries.

Canterbury (r) **89 90 95** 96 (w) **95 96** NZ's 4th-largest wine region; v'yds at Waipara in N and around Christchurch. Long dry summers favour Pinot N, Chard and Ries.

Cellier Le Brun Marlborough ★→★★★ Sm winery est'd by Champenois Daniel Le Brun (departed '96): some of NZ's best bottle-fermented sp, esp vintage (90 91) and Bl de Blancs (91). Terrace Road table wines less impressive.

Central Otago (r) **90 95** 96 (w) **93 95 96** Small cool mountainous region in S of South Island. Chard and Ries promising, Pinot N rivals MARTINBOROUGH's best.

Chard Farm Central Otago ★★ Strikingly beautiful v'yd; good Chard, Ries and perfumed, silky Pinot N.

Chifney Martinborough ★→★★ Tiny producer. Fast-improving Chard, Gewürz, Chenin Bl and Cab S.

Church Road See MacDonald Winery.

Clearview Hawke's Bay ★→★★★ V small producer of burly, flavour-packed Res Chard. Notably dark rich Res Cab Franc and Old Olive Block (Cab blend).

A Choice for 1998 from New Zealand

Cabernet-Merlot blends: Matua Ararimu (91), St Nesbit (89), Te Mata Coleraine (91), Vidal Reserve (90)

Pinot Noir: Ata Rangi (94), Dry River (94), Martinborough V'yd (95)

Chardonnay: Babich Irongate (95), Church Road Reserve (95), Corbans Cottage Block Gisborne (95)

Sauvignon: Cloudy Bay (96), Nga Waka (96), Villa Maria Res (96)

Chenin Blanc: The Milton Vineyard (94)

Riesling: Dry River (96), Palliser (96)

Bottle-fermented sparkling wines: Cloudy Bay Pelorus (92), Daniel Le Brun Blanc de Blancs (91), Dom Chandon Marlborough Brut (93)

Sweet wines: Ngatarawa Glazebrook Noble Harvest (94), Villa Maria Res Noble Riesling (94)

Cloudy Bay Marlborough ★★★★ Founded by W Australia's Cape Mentelle; now Veuve Clicquot principal shareholder. Thrillingly intense Sauv Bl and bold Chard. Pelorus sp also impressive. Pinot N replacing Cab-Merlot as top red.

Collard Brothers Henderson (Auckland) ★★→★★★ Long-est'd sm family winery. Whites esp Rothesay V'yd Chard and Sauv Bl, H BAY Chenin Bl, MARLB Ries.

Cooks Hawke's Bay ★→★★ Lge firm merged with McWilliams (NZ) in '84 and absorbed by CORBANS in '87. Now export brand. Good H BAY Chard and Cab S: Winemakers Res label.

Coopers Creek Huapai (Auckland) ★★→★★★ Medium-sized producer, highly successful in NZ competitions. Excellent whites and fragrant, supple reds.

Corbans Henderson (Auckland) ★→★★★ Est'd 1902, now NZ's 2nd-largest wine company. Key brands: Corbans (top wines: Cottage Block; next: Private Bin), COOKS, Stoneleigh (MARLB), Longridge (H BAY), Robard & Butler. Top GISBORNE Chards, South Island Ries and sp wines can be superb.

Cross Roads Hawke's Bay ★★ Sm winery. Satisfying Chard, Ries, Cab S, Pinot N.

De Redcliffe Waikato (S of Auckland) ★→★★ Small Japanese-owned winery; 'Hotel du Vin' attached. Good Chard, Sém blends, Ries and Sauv Bl, plain reds.

Delegat's Henderson (Auckland) ★★→★★★ Med-sized family winery. V'yds at H BAY and MARLB. Rich, robust Chard, and increasingly gd Proprietors Res Cab S and Merlot. Oyster Bay brand: deep flavoured Marlb Chard and Sauv Bl.

Deutz Auckland ★★★ Champagne firm gives name and technical aid to fine sp wines produced in MARLB by MONTANA. NV: lively, yeasty and flinty; vintage Bl de Blancs rich and creamy.

Domaine Chandon (Blenheim) ★★→★★★ One of NZ's most intense and refined sp wines made at MARLB winery by Oz subsidiary of Moët et Chandon.

Dry River (Martinborough) ★★★ Tiny winery. Penetrating long-lived Chard, Ries, Pinot Gr (NZ's finest), Gewürz (ditto) and Pinot N.

Esk Valley (Hawke's Bay) ★★→★★★ Former lge family firm, now owned by VILLA MARIA. Some of NZ's most voluptuous Merlot-based reds (esp Res label), v gd dry Merlot Rosé, oak-aged Chenin Bl, satisfying Chards and Sauv Bl.

Forrest Marlborough ★★ Small winery; fragrant, ripe Chard (non-wooded) Sauv Bl and Ries; stylish H BAY Cornerstone V'yd Cab-Merlot.

Fromm Marlborough ★★ Small winery, Swiss-founded, focussing on red wines. Fine Pinot N, esp under La Strada Res label.

Gibbston Valley Central Otago ★★ Pioneer winery with popular restaurant. Greatest strength Pinot N (esp Res, 1st vintage '95). Racy local whites (Chard, Ries, Pinot Gr, Sauv Bl). In some vintages a top MARLB Sauv.

Giesen Estate Canterbury ★→★★★ German family winery, now region's largest. Known for Ries, esp honey-sweet well-structured Res Botrytised. Grapes now from CANTERBURY except Sauv Bl (MARLB). Chard and Pinot N good esp Res.

Gillan Marlborough ★★ Small winery producing fresh, vibrant Sauv Bl and Chard, promising sparkling wine and leafy Merlot.

Gisborne (r) **89' 94 95** (w) **94 95 96** NZ's third-largest region. Strengths in Chard (typically fragrant ripe and appealing in its youth), and Gewürz (highly perfumed and peppery). Abundant rain and fertile soils ideal for heavy croppers, esp Müller-T. Reds typically light but Merlot shows promise.

Glenmark Canterbury ★→★★ Pioneer Waipara (N CANTERBURY) producer. Wide range, esp light Germanic Ries. Also berryish leafy Cab S-based Waipara Red.

Glover's (Nelson) ★→★★ V small winery producing freshly acidic Ries and Sauv Bl, muscular Pinot N and Cab S.

Goldwater Waiheke I (Auckland) ★★★ Region's pioneer Cab S-Merlot (first vintage '82) still one of NZ's finest: Médoc-like concentration and structure. Also crisp citrussy Chard and pungent Sauv Bl, both grown in MARLB.

Grove Mill Marlborough ★★ Attractive whites incl several Chards esp fully oak-ferm'd Lansdowne and vibrant MARLB Chard; good Ries, Gewürz, Sauv, Bl slightly sweet Pinot Gr. Dark chunky tannic reds.

Hawke's Bay (r) **89 90 91'** 94 95 (w) **92 94 95** 96 NZ's 2nd-largest region. Long history of table wine making in sunny climate, shingly soils. Full rich Cab S and Merlot-based reds in gd vintages; powerful rich Chard; ripe rounded Sauv Bl.

Heron's Flight Matakana (nr Auckland) ★★ Tiny producer with sturdy brambly Cab S-Merlot (esp 91 and 94).

Highfield Marlborough ★★ After hesitant start, rich oaked Chard and Sauv Bl; promising sp under premium Elstree label. Opulent Botrytised Ries. Solid lower-tier Sauv Bl, Ries, Chard and leafy Merlot.

Hunter's Marlborough ★★→★★★ Top name in intense immaculate Sauv Bl in oak-aged and non-wooded versions. Fine delicate Chard. Excellent sp. Ries, Gewürz and reds good but less notable.

Jackson Estate Blenheim ★★→★★★ Large v'yd, no winery. Rich Sauv Bl, good Chard (esp weighty Res). Outstanding debut sp (92), gorgeous sw whites.

Kemblefield Hawke's Bay ★ Sizable new American-owned winery. Initial releases (93 on) incl solid Sauv Bl, Chard, Gewürz, Merlot and Cab S-Merlot.

Kumeu River Kumeu (NW of Auckland) ★★★ AUCKLAND grapes, v rich, mealy Kumeu Chard; single v'yd Mate's V'yd Chard even more opulent. Rest of range solid. BRAJKOVICH is second label.

Kym Crawford Auckland ★★ Personal label of Coopers Creek winemaker, launched 96. Rich oaked GISBORNE Chard, robust unwooded MARLB Chard, weighty steely MARLB Sauv Bl.

Lawson's Dry Hills Blenheim ★★→★★★ Top recent arrival. Weighty wines with rich intense flavours. Distinguished Sauv Bl, Chard, Gewürz and Ries.

Lincoln Henderson (Auckland) ★→★★ Long est'd medium-sized family winery. Value sound varietals: buttery GISBORNE Chard (esp Parklands and Vintage Sel).

Lintz Martinborough ★★ Small producer. Individual wines, incl floral tangy sp Ries and treacly, botrytised Optima. Weighty oaked Sauv Bl. Chunky Pinot N, Cab S, Cab-Merlot and Shiraz.

Longridge See Corbans

MacDonald Winery Hawke's Bay ★★→★★★ MONTANA'S H BAY winery: wines under Church Road label. Rich ripe Chard (Res more oaky). Elegant Cab S-Merlot made with technical input from Bordeaux house of Cordier.

Marlborough (r) **91 94' 95** (w) **94 95 96** NZ's largest region. Sunny warm days and cool nights give intensely flavoured crisp whites. Extraordinarily intense Sauv, from sharp green capsicum to riper tropical fruit character. Fresh limey Ries. High-quality sp. Too cool for Cab S, but Pinot N and Merlot promising.

Martinborough (r) **91 94 95** 96 (w) **94' 95** 96 Small high quality area in S WAIRARAPA (foot of North Island). Warm summers, dry autumns and gravelly soils. Success with white grapes (Chard, Sauv Bl, Ries, Gewürz, Pinot Gris) but principally renowned for intensely varietal Pinot N.

Martinborough Vineyards Martinborough ★★★ Distinguished small winery, noted for one of NZ's top-ranked Pinot N (Res 91 and 94) and rich, biscuity Chard. Ries and Sauv Bl also rewarding.

Matawhero Gisborne ★→★★ Formerly NZ's top Gewürz specialist. Now has wide range (also Chard, Sauv Bl, Cab-Merlot) of varying but often gd quality.

Matua Valley Waimauku (Auckland) ★★→★★★ Highly rated middle-sized winery with lge estate v'yd. Excellent oaked Res Sauv Bl. Top wines labelled Ararimu incl fat savoury Chard and dark rich Merlot-Cab S. Numerous well-priced, attractive GISBORNE (esp Judd Chard), H BAY and MARLB wines (the latter branded Shingle Peak).

Merlen Wines Marlborough ★→★★ German-born Almuth Lorenz makes whites, notably bold fat Chard and lively appley Ries. Latest vintages best.

Mills Reef Bay of Plenty (SE of Auckland) ★★ The Preston family produces impressive wines from H BAY grapes. Top Elspeth range incl lush barrel-ferm'd Chard and Sauv Bl. Middle-tier Res range also impressive. Two quality sparkling wines: 'Mills Reef' and 'Charisma'.

Millton nr Gisborne ★★→★★★ Region's top small winery: organic. Top-flight med-sw Opou V'yd Ries. Soft, savoury Chard Barrel Ferm'd. Robust, complex Chenin Bl Dry.

Mission Greenmeadows (Hawke's Bay) ★★ NZ's oldest wine producer, est'd 1851, still run by Catholic Society of Mary. Solid varietals: sweetish intensely perfumed Ries esp gd value. Top Jewelstone range incl rich complex Chard, deep-flavoured Cab-Merlot and botrytised sw Ries.

Montana Auckland and Hawke's Bay ★→★★★ NZ wine giant, approx. 40% mkt share. Wineries in Auckland, GISBORNE, H BAY (see McDonald Winery) and MARLB. Extensive co-owned v'yds. Famous for Marlb whites, incl top-value Sauv Bl, Ries and Chard. Strength in sp, incl DEUTZ and stylish, fine value Lindauer. Elegant H Bay 'Church Road' reds and quality Chard.

Morton Estate Bay of Plenty (S of Auckland) ★★→★★★ Respected med-sized producer with v'yds in H BAY and MARLB. New owners in '95 and new winemaker in '97. Refined rich Black Label Chard one of NZ's best, but mid-tier White Label Chard also gd. Marlb wines: Stone Creek.

Nautilus (Marlborough) ★★ Small range of distributors Negociants (NZ), owned by S Smith & Son of Australia (cf Yalumba). Top wines incl classic Sauv Bl and fragrant yeasty smooth sp. Lower tier wines: Twin Islands.

Nelson (r) **94 96** (w) **94 96** Small region west of MARLBOROUGH; similar climate but little wetter. Clay soils of Upper Moutere hills and silty Waimea Plains. Strengths in whites, esp Ries, Sauv Bl, Chard. Reds can lack ripeness.

Neudorf Nelson ★★★ One of NZ's top boutique wineries. Strapping creamy-rich Chard, one of NZ's best. Fine Pinot N, Sauv Bl and Ries.

Nga Waka Martinborough ★★→★★★ Emerging star. Dry steely whites of v high quality. Outstanding Sauv Bl; piercingly flavoured Ries; robust savoury Chard.

Ngatarawa Hawke's Bay ★★→★★★ Boutique winery in old stables. Top Glazebrook range incl deep-flavoured citrussy Chard, sw Noble Harvest and v supple and attractive Cab-Merlot. Solid mid-priced 'Stables' varietals.

Nobilo Kumeu Auckland ★→★★ NZ's 4th-largest winery still family-operated (since '95 they have owned 51%). Early reputation for reds has faded. Off-dry White Cloud (Müller-T-based) international success. Gd GISBORNE Chard (in British Airways ¼ bottles). MARLB Sauv Bl is gd and sharply priced.

Okahu Estate Northland (N of Auckland) ★→★★ NZ's northernmost winery, at Kaitaia. Hot, humid climate. Reds: stuffing and warm ripe flavours. Kaz Shiraz 94 NZ's first gold medal Shiraz.

Omaka Springs Marlborough ★ Small new producer with solid Sauv Bl, Ries, Sém, Chard and Merlot.

Oyster Bay See Delegats.

Palliser Estate Martinborough ★★→★★★ One of area's largest and best wineries. Superb tropical fruit-flavoured Sauv Bl, excellent Chard and Ries. Gd Pinot N. Top wines: Palliser Estate; lower-tier: Palliser Bay.

Pask, C J Hawke's Bay ★→★★ Smallish winery, extensive v'yds. Gd, sometimes excellent Chard (esp Res). Cab S and Merlot-based reds vary from light, herbaceous to rich, complex Res releases.

Pegasus Bay Waipara (N Canterbury) ★★→★★★ Small but distinguished range, notably taut cool-climate Chard, lush complex oaked Sauv/Sém and zingy, flavour-packed Ries. Cab S-based reds: region's finest. Pinot N v promising.

Providence Matakana (N of Auckland) ★★ Since 93 James Vuletic has produced a perfumed silky Merlot-based red of v high quality and price.

Mark Rattray Canterbury ★★ Stylish Pinot N, Chard and Sauv Bl.

Rippon Vineyard Central Otago ★★ Stunning v'yd. Fine-scented v fruity Pinot N (esp Sel) and slowly evolving whites, incl steely appley Chard.

Robard & Butler See Corbans.

Rongapai Waikato (S of Auckland) ★★ Small winery using local, GISBORNE and H BAY fruit. Softly mouthfilling, ripe Sauv Bl and Chard. Renowned for botrytised sw whites, esp Res Ries and weightier Res Chard.

Sacred Hill Hawke's Bay ★→★★ Sound 'Whitecliff' varietals; gd, oaked Res Sauv Bl (Barrel Fermented and Sauvage). Gd 95 Basket Press Cab S and Cab-Merlot.

St Clair Marlborough ★★ Fast-growing export-orientated producer. Substantial v'yds. Fragrant full-flavoured Ries and Sauv Bl, fresh easy Chard. Plummy early-drinking Merlot.

St Helena Canterbury ★→★★ The region's oldest winery, founded nr Christchurch in 78. Light, supple Pinot N (Res is bolder). Chard variable but gd in better vintages. Cheap, earthy, savoury Pinot Bl is fine value.

St Jerome Estate Henderson (nr Auckland) ★→★★ Small producer of avge whites and estate-grown dark flavour-crammed tannic Cab-Merlot.

St Nesbit Karaka (S of Auckland) ★★ Top-quality Cab-Merlot in Bordeaux mould – spicy, firm, cedary. Due to replanting, 91 vintage (available '97) is final release until early 2000s.

Allan Scott Marlborough ★★ Attract Ries, Chard and Sauv Bl. Mt Riley 2nd label.

Seifried Estate Upper Moutere (nr Nelson) ★→★★ Region's only medium-sized winery, founded by Austrian. Known initially for well-priced Ries, but now also producing gd-value, often excellent Sauv Bl and Chard. Light reds.

Selak's Kumeu (NW of Auckland) ★★→★★★ Med-sized family firm. V'yds and 2nd winery in MARLB. Sauv Bl: strength, esp superb lightly oaked Sauv/Sém. Powerful yet refined Founders Chard. Reds plain; sp gd and value.

Sherwood Canterbury ★→★★ Tart, austere Ries and Chard and three Pinot Noirs, notably robust, meaty and tannic Res model.

Shingle Peak See Matua Valley.

Soljans Henderson (Auckland) ★→★★ Long-est'd small family winery. Steadily improving whites and reds, most distinctively a supple meaty Pinotage.

Spencer Hill Nelson ★★ Known for Chard (soft fragrant lemony): 1st vintage '94. 'Tasman Bay': regional blending. 'Spencer Hill': v'yd-designated and oaky.

Stonecroft Hawke's Bay ★★→★★★ Sm winery. Dark concentrated promising Syrah, more Rhône than Oz. Also v gd Cab-Merlot, Chard, Gewürz, Sauv Bl.

Stoneleigh See Corbans.

Stonyridge Waiheke Island ★★★★ Boutique winery. Two Bordeaux-style reds: Larose exceptional (esp **87 93 94**, also gd **91**); Airfield: second label (**92**).

Te Kairanga Martinborough ★→★★ One of district's larger wineries. Big flinty Chard (Res: richer), perfumed supple Pinot N (Res: complex powerful).

Te Mata Hawke's Bay ★★★★ Region's most prestigious winery. Fine powerful Elston Chard; v gd oaked Cape Crest Sauv Bl; v stylish Coleraine Cab-Merlot (89 91 94). Awatea Cab-Merlot (v gd): second label, less new oak. Cab-Merlot: third label.

Te Motu Waiheke I (Auckland) ★★→★★★ Top wine of Waiheke V'yds, owned by the Dunleavy and Buffalora families. Dark, concentrated, brambly red of v high quality, first vintage 93. Dunleavy Cab-Merlot is second label.

Te Whare Ra Marlborough ★★ Tiny producer of notably ripe high alcohol Chard, Gewürz, Ries, Sauv Bl. V gd botrytised sw whites.

Torlesse Waipara (N Canterbury) ★★ Flavour-packed tangy Sauv Bl, robust rich Chard from MARLB; zesty Ries Dry and v characterful WAIRAPA Pinot Gr.

Vavasour Marlborough ★★→★★★ Fast-expanding winery. Immaculate intense Single V'yd Chard and Sauv Bl; promising Pinot N. Dashwood: second label.

Vidal Hawke's Bay ★★→★★★ Est'd 1905 by Spaniard, now part of VILLA MARIA. Reserve range (Chard, Gewürz, Sauv Bl, Cab S, Cab-Merlot) uniformly high std. Other varietals gd and well-priced.

Villa Maria Mangere (Auckland) ★★→★★★ NZ's 3rd-largest wine company, incl VIDAL and ESK VALLEY. Top range: Reserve (Noble Ries NZ's most awarded sw white); Cellar Sel: middle-tier (less oak); third-tier Private Bin wines can be excellent and top value (esp Ries, Sauv Bl, Gewürz).

Waimarama Hawke's Bay ★★ Small producer specialising in high-quality reds; v gd Merlot, Cab S and Cab-Merlot.

Waipara Springs Canterbury ★→★★ Small N CANTERBURY producer with lively cool climate Ries, Sauv Bl and Chard; reds less distinguished.

Wairarapa NZ's fifth largest wine region. See Martinborough.

Wairau River Marlborough ★★ Small, export-orientated producer of highly flavoured Sauv Bl and succulent toasty Chard. Second label: Richmond Ridge.

Wellington (r) **89 90 91 93 94 95** 96 (w) **91 94 95** **96** Capital city and official name of the region which includes WAIRARAPA, Te Horo and MARTINBOROUGH.

Whitehaven Marlborough ★★ Emerging firm (first vintage 94); excellent wines: racy Ries, scented delicate lively Sauv Bl, flavourful easy Chard.

Wither Hills Marlborough ★★→★★★ V'yd owned by DELEGAT's winemaker, Brent Marris. Exceptional Chard and Sauv Bl since 92.

South Africa

South Africa is the seventh largest wine producer in the world, but its exports have risen so fast since the end of sanctions in 1994 that it is now importing wine for domestic (and re-export) use. There are plans for a major vineyard expansion, currently hampered by a shortage of vines to plant. Foreign investment and winery expansion is booming and dozens of new cellars will be appearing in areas where vines were not previously cultivated. Emphasis will be on the premium varieties, to balance the former preponderance of bulk and brandy grapes such as Colombard and Chenin Blanc.

South Africa's wines are also modernising rapidly with exposure to export markets and the arrival of more foreign winemakers. The trend is to softer, fruitier wines. But there is also a core of growers preserving South Africa's traditional dry, heavier style, especially in reds. Vineyard management is also improving with widespread experimentation adding to the excitement of the country's 're-entry' to international trade. Domestic consumption remains stagnant – at 8.8 litres per capita per year. Beer is still the 'staple' alcoholic beverage.

Allesverloren r ★→★★ Old 395-acre family estate, best known for 'Port' (**88 89 90**). Also hefty well-oaked but not always long-lived CAB and Shiraz (**94**) from hot wheatlands of Malmesbury.

Alphen ★ Gilbeys brand name for wines.

Alto r ★★(Cab) **89 91** Atlantic-facing mountain v'yds S of S'BOSCH. Solid CAB, Cab-Merlot, Shiraz.

Altydgedacht r w ★→★★ (Cab S) **92** Durbanville estate; also gutsy Tintoretto blend of Barbera and Shiraz. Good Gewürz dessert wine.

Avontuur r w ★★ 200-acre ST'BOSCH v'yd, bottling since '87. Soft B'x-style blend, Avon Rouge; gd 92 93. CAB, Merlot, PINOTAGE; concentrated oaky CHARD.

Backsberg r w ★★→★★★ (r) **91 92 94** Prize-winning 395-acre PAARL estate. Pioneered oak-fermented CHARD in mid-'80s, with US advice. Now leader in modern v'yd management systems. Delicious B'x blend Klein Babylonstoren is best (**91 92 94**); v reliable mid weight Chard. Also vg oaked SAUV John Martin.

Bellingham r w ★★→★★★ Big-selling, sound brand reds (**94**), popular whites, especially sweet soft CAPE RIES-based Johannisberger wines (exported as Cape Gold), CHARDONNAY, SAUVIGNON BLANC and Chard-Sauv blend 'Sauvenay'. Outstanding Cab F 95.

Bergkelder Big STELLENBOSCH company, member of Oude Meester group, making/distributing many brands (FLEUR DU CAP, GRUNBERGER), 12 estate wines.

Bertrams r ★★ (Cab) **91 94** (Shiraz) **89** Gilbeys brand of varietals, esp Shiraz, PINOTAGE. Also Robert Fuller Reserve B'x-style blend.

Beyerskloof r ★★ (Cab S) **91 93 94** Small STELLENBOSCH property, devoted to tannic deep-flavoured CAB S. Also PINOTAGE from 95.

Blaauwklippen r w ★★ (r) **89 91 94** STELLENBOSCH winery: bold reds, esp CAB Reserve. Also S Africa's top Zin (**90 91 93**); improving CHARD; good off-dry RIES.

Bloemendal r w ★★ (Cab) **89 91 93** Sea-cooled Durbanville estate. Fragrant CAB, Merlot. Good Chard CAP CLASSIQUE.

Boberg Controlled region for fortified wines, comprising PAARL and TULBAGH.

Bon Courage w sw ★→★★ ROBERTSON estate; vg dessert GEWURZ and CHARD.

Boplaas r w ★★ Estate in dry hot Karoo. Earthy deep 'Vintage Reserve Port' esp (**91 94**), fortified Muscadels. Links with Grahams in Portugal.

Boschendal w sp ★★ (Chard) **94 95** 617-acre estate nr Franschoek. Good CHARD and METHODE CAP CLASSIQUE (Chard and Pinot); also Cape's first 'blush' off-dry Blanc de Noirs. Improving Merlot (**91**). Shiraz 94 (Jean de Long label).

Bouchard-Finlayson r w ★★★ (Chard) **95 96 (Sauv) 96** (Pinot) **93 94 95** First French-Cape partnership (Paul Bouchard of Burgundy, Peter Finlayson at Hermanus, Walker Bay). Maiden release 91.

Breede River Valley Fortified and white wine region E of Drakensberg Mts.

Buitenverwachting r w sp ★★★ (Chard) **91 93 94** Exceptional, German-financed, recently replanted CONSTANTIA v'yds. Outstanding SAUV **95 96**, CHARD, B'x blend 'Christine' (**89 90 91 92** 95), CAB S (91 92). Lively clean METHODE CAP CLASSIQUE (Pinots Gr and Bl). Restaurant worthy of a Michelin star.

Cabernet Sauvignon Most successful in COASTAL REGION. Range of styles: sturdy long-lived to elegant fruity. More use of new French oak since '82 giving great improvements. Best recent vintages: **87** 89 91 94 95.

Cabrière Estate ★★→★★★ Franschhoek growers of good NV CAP CLASSIQUE under Pierre Jordan label (Brut Sauvage, CHARDONNAY-PINOT N and Belle Rose Pinot N). Also v promising 'new clone' Pinot N **94**.

Cap Classique, Méthode South African term for classic method sp wine.

Cape Independent Winemakers Guild Group of winemakers in the vanguard of quality. Hold an annual auction of progressive-style young wines.

Cavendish Cape ★★ Range of good 'Sherries' from the KWV.

Chardonnay S Africa came to Chard relatively late, beginning mid-'80s. Now offering many styles, incl unwooded and blended – with SAUV, among others. Currently nearly 200 labels, and growing; a decade ago, 3.

Chateau Libertas ★ Big-selling CAB S brand made by SFW.

Chenin Blanc Workhorse grape of the Cape; one vine in three. Adaptable, sometimes vg. KWV makes good value example. See also Steen.

Cinsaut The principal bulk-producing French red grape in S Africa; formerly known as 'Hermitage'. V seldom seen with varietal label.

Claridge r w ★★ (r) 92 94 (Chard) 93 94 96 Good barrel-fermented CHARD and CAB-Merlot from small winery at Wellington nr PAARL.

Clos Malverne r ★★ **91 93 94 95** Small STELLENBOSCH winery. Individual dense CAB S, PINOTAGE Res (**92 95**) from own v'yds and purchased grapes.

Colombard French white grape, as popular in Cape as in California. Crisp lively flowery, usually short-lived wine; often in blends, or for brandy.

Constantia Once the world's most famous sweet Muscat-based wine (both red and white), from the Cape. See Klein Constantia.

De Wetshof w sw ★★ (Chard) **91 93 94** Pioneering ROBERTSON estate. Powerful CHARD (varying oakiness: Finesse lightly oaked, Bataleur heavily) and fresh dry RHINE RIES. Also dessert GEWURZ, Rhine Ries under Danie de Wet label and own-brand Chards for British supermarkets.

Delaire Vineyards r w ★ (Chard) **94 96** (r) **93** Full-flavoured CHARD, Bordeaux blend, Barrique (**91 92**), off-dry RHINE RIES, from winery at Helshoogte Pass above STELLENBOSCH.

Delheim r w dr sw ★★ Big winery with mountain v'yds nr STELLENBOSCH. Elegant barrel-aged CAB S-Merlot-Cab F Grand Reserve (**91 92**). Value Cab (**91 92 95**), PINOTAGE, Shiraz; variable PINOT N; improving CHARD, SAUV. Sweet wines: GEWURZ, outstanding botrytis STEEN.

Die Krans Estate ★★ Karoo semi-desert v'yds making rich full Vintage Reserve 'Port'. Best are 91 **94**. Also traditional fortified sweet Muscadels.

Dieu Donné Vineyards r w ★★ Franschhoek co: CHARD **92 94**, CAB **93**.

Edelkeur ★★★★ Excellent intensely sweet noble rot white by NEDERBURG.

NB Vintages in colour are those you should choose first for drinking in 1998.

Eikendal Vineyards r w ★★ (red, Merlot) **91 93 94** (Chard) **94 96** Swiss-owned 100-acres v'yds and winery nr STELLENBOSCH. Vg CHARD; CAB S-Merlot blend Classique. Fresh whites incl semi-sweet CHENIN BL.

Estate Wine Official term for wines grown and made (not necessarily bottled) on registered estates. Regulations relaxed in '94; estates may buy in up to 40% of their production.

Fairview Estate r w dr sw ★★→★★★ (r) **91 94 95** (Chard) **94 95 96** Enterprising PAARL estate with wide range. Best are Reserve Merlot (**93 95**), blend Tower Red 95 and Charles Gerard Reserve (**90 94**), Shiraz Reserve (**90 91 93 94**). Also excellent Gamay, CHARD, plus sweet CHENIN BL. One of SA's leaders in softer, fruitier wines. Also v interesting Sémillon and PINOTAGE.

Fleur du Cap r w sw ★★★ (r) **92 94** Value range from BERGKELDER at STELLENBOSCH: good CAB (**89 91 92**) esp since '86. Also Merlot (**90 92 94**), Shiraz (**91**), fine GEWURZ, botrytis CHENIN.

Gewürztraminer Famous spicy grape of Alsace, usually made sw at the Cape.

Glen Carlou r w ★★→★★★ (r) **89 90 91 93** (Chard) **91 94 96** PAARL property. Good B'x blends Grande Classique (**90 91 93**), Les Trois, Merlot; gd CHARD Res (91 92 93). V promising 'new clone' PINOT N from '94.

> **A Choice for 1998 from South Africa**
> **Thelema Mountain Vineyards**: Sauvignon Blanc 96/97, Chardonnay 95, Cabernet 94
> **Fairview Estate**: Tower Red 95
> **Meerlust Estate**: Chardonnay 95
> **Buitenverwachting**: Sauvignon Blanc 96, Christine (Bx blend) 92
> **Warwick Estate**: Pinotage 95
> **Hamilton Russell Vineyards**: Pinot Noir 95, Chardonnay 96
> **Jordan Vineyards**: Cabernet (93)
> **Vergelegen**: Merlot (95)
> **Backsberg Estate**: Chardonnay (95)

Graham Beck Winery w sp ★★ Avant-garde ROBERTSON winery (350 acres); METHODE CAP CLASSIQUE Brut Royale NV, Blanc de Blancs; still CHARD well regarded.

Grand Cru (or Premier Grand Cru) Term for a totally dry white, with no quality implications. Generally to be avoided.

Grangehurst Wines ★★★ Among top new STELLENBOSCH wineries, buying grapes from range of suppliers. Specializing in PINOTAGE (**93 94 95**), and concentrated Res CAB-Merlot (**93 94 95**).

Groot Constantia r w ★★ Historic gov't-owned estate nr Cape Town. Superlative Muscat in early 19th C. Renaissance in progress; so far fine CAB (esp CAB-Merlot blend Gouverneur's Reserve **91 90 92 93**). Also PINOTAGE, Weisser (Rhine) RIES-GEWURZ Botrytis blend (**92**), dessert Muscat.

Grünberger BERGKELDER brand: range of dry and semi-sweet STEEN whites.

Hamilton Russell Vineyards r w ★★★ (Pinot N) **91 93 95** (Chard) **93 95 96** The pioneer. Good PINOT N 'Burgundy' vineyards and cellar. Small yields, French-inspired vinification in cool Walker Bay. Many awards. Vg SAUV BL and Southern Right label (incl PINOTAGE).

Hanepoot Local name for the sweet Muscat of Alexandria grape.

Hartenberg r w ★→★★★ STELLENBOSCH estate, recently modernized. Among Cape's top Shiraz and Merlot from 93. v individual Pontac 95 and Zinfandel 95; CAB-Shiraz blend and sw Weisser Riesling.

Jordan Vineyards ★★→★★★ Top property in SW STELLENBOSCH hills: vg SAUV BL, CHARD **94 95** 96 and Cab S **93**. Husband and wife team California-trained.

J P Bredell ★★★ Stellenbosch v'yds. Rich dark deep Vintage Reserve 'Port' from Tinta Barocca and Souzão grapes.

Kanonkop r ★★★ (r) **89 90 91** 94 N STELLENBOSCH estate with grand local status. Individual powerful CAB (89 91 94) and B'x-style blend Paul Sauer (**86 89 91 94**). PINOTAGE (**89 91 94**), oak-finished since '89 (v improved).

Klein Constantia r w sw ★★★ (r) **89 90 91** (Chard) **95** 96 Old subdivision of famous GROOT CONSTANTIA neighbour. Emphatic CHARD, SAUV (**95 96** outstanding), powerful CAB, B'x-style blend Marlbrook first released in '88 (**89 90 91**). From 86, Vin de Constance revives the 18th-C Constantia legend (annual release, now 91). Scintillating sw wine from Muscat de Frontignan.

KWV The Kooperatieve Wijnbouwers Vereniging, S Africa's national wine coop created in 1917: vast premises in PAARL, a range of good wines, esp Cathedral Cellars reds, RIES, 'Sherries', sweet dessert wines. In '92 gave up widely criticized quotas, freeing growers to plant v'yds at will.

La Motte r w ★★★ (r) **91 92** Lavish Rupert family estate nr Franschhoek. Lean but stylish reds: Merlot, B'x-style blend Millennium (**90 91 93**), among top three for Cape Shiraz (**89 91 92 93**). Racy SAUV BL.

L'Avenir ★★ Well-appointed new STELLENBOSCH property, promising CAB (**93 94**), PINOTAGE (**95 96**) and CHARD.

Laborie r w ★★ KWV-owned showpiece PAARL estate. White and red blends.

Landgoed Afrikaans for 'estate': on official seals and ESTATE WINE labels.

Landskroon r w ★→★★ Family estate owned by Paul and Hugo de Villiers. Good dry reds, esp Shiraz, CAB S, Cab F.

Late Harvest Term for a mildly sweet wine. 'Special Late Harvest' must be naturally sweet. 'Noble Late Harvest' is highest quality dessert wine.

Le Bonheur r w ★★→★★★ (r) **89 91 92** STELLENBOSCH estate often producing classic tannic minerally CAB; big-bodied SAUV BL.

Leroux, JC ★★ Old brand revived as BERGKELDER's sparkling wine house. SAUV (Charmat), PINOT (top METHODE CAP CLASSIQUE is well-aged). Also CHARD.

Lievland r w ★★→★★★ (r) **89 90** STELLENBOSCH estate: leading Cape Shiraz (**89 90 92 95**), vg CAB S, Merlot, Cab S-F-Merlot (esp **92**) and Cab S-Merlot 'DVB' **92 94**. Also whites incl intense RIES; off-dry promising Sauternes-style wine.

Long Mountain ★→★★ Pernod-Ricard label, buying grapes from coops under Australian direction (Robin Day, formerly of Orlando). CAB, CHARD, CHENIN.

Longridge Winery ★★→★★★ Quality concious STELLENBOSCH winery, purchasing grapes and wines from many sources. Incl CHARD, CAB S, Shiraz, PINOTAGE. Also good CAP CLASSIQUE sp. Winemaking consultants are Dom Jacques Prieur of Burgundy (q v).

L'Ormarins r w sw ★★→★★★ **89 91 94** One of two Rupert family estates nr Franschhoek. CAB (**86 89 91**) and vg claret-style Optima (**89 94**), also Shiraz (**91**). Fresh lemony CHARD, forward oak-aged SAUV; outstanding GEWURZ-Bukketraube botrytis dessert wine.

Louisvale w ★★→★★★ (Chard) **93 95** STELLENBOSCH winery. Attractive CHARD, also good CAB S and Cab-Merlot (from '94) and SAUV BL-Chard.

Meerlust r w ★★★ (r) **89 90 91 92 95** Prestigious old family estate nr STELLENBOSCH; Cape's only Italian winemaker. Outstanding Rubicon (Médoc-style blend **89 91 92 95**), Cab (**91**), Merlot (**89 91 93 94**), PINOT (**89 91 95**). Now CHARD too: 1st release leesy, oaky **95**. Also first SA estate grappa '96.

Middelvlei r ★★ **89 90 91** STELLENBOSCH estate: good PINOTAGE (**90 91**), CAB (**89 90 91**), Shiraz (**90**) and CHARD.

Monis ★→★★ Well-known wine co of PAARL, with fine 'Special Reserve Port'.

To decipher codes, please refer to 'Key to symbols' on front flap of jacket, or to 'How to use this book' on page 6.

Morgenhof r w dr s/sw ★★→★★★ Elaborately refurbished S'BOSCH estate. New French owner and change of winemaker (from '92). Improved reds (**93 94** Cab, Merlot); dry white, (excellent Sauv, Chard), s/sw whites; 'Port'.

Mulderbosch Vineyards w ★★★ Penetrating consistently impressive SAUV from mountain v'yds nr S'BOSCH: one oak-fermented, the other fresh bold. Also CHARD and B'x-style blend Faithful Hound (93).

Muratie Ancient STELLENBOSCH estate, esp 'Port'. Recent revival incl excellent CAB (**93 94**) and B'x blend **94**.

Nederburg r w p dr sw s/sw sp ★★→★★★★ (r) **89 91 92 93 94** (Chard) **95 96** Well-known large modern PAARL winery (650,000 cases pa; 50 different wines). Bicentenary in '92. Own grapes and suppliers'. Sound CAB, Shiraz, CHARD, RIES, blends in regular range. Limited Vintages, Private Bins often outstanding. Fresh approach with late '80s top reds: emphasis on richer fruitier flavour, more barrel-ageing. '70s pioneer of botrytis dessert wines, now benchmarks: CHENIN, GEWURZ, SAUV, Muscat, even Chard consistently gd. Stages Cape's biggest annual wine event, the Nederburg Auction. See also Edelkeur.

Neethlingshof r w sw ★★→★★★ (r) **89 90 91 93 94** Estate: replanted with classic grapes, cellar revamped at huge cost since '85. Run jointly with nearby STELLENZICHT. Vg CAB S (**89 90 93 94**), Merlot, CHARD, fresh SAUV BL, excellent GEWURZ (**93 95**) and blush Bl de Noir. Consistently judged national champion botrytis wines from RIES, and Sauv Bl. B'x-blend Lord Neethling Res **93, 94**.

Neil Ellis Wines r w ★★★ (r) **89 91 92 94** Full balanced wines from Jonkershoek Valley nr STELLENBOSCH (16 widely spread coastal v'yds). Spicy structured CAB S and Cab-Merlot; excellent SAUV; full bold CHARD.

Nuy Cooperative Winery r w dr sw sp ★★ Small Worcester coop, frequent local award-winner. Outstanding dessert wines; fortified Muscadels.

Oak Village Wines ★→★★ Export brand, blend of good coop cellar wines from STELLENBOSCH, incl CAB-Shiraz, SAUV-CHENIN BL blends.

Overgaauw r w ★★ (r) **89 90** 91 Old family estate nr STELLENBOSCH; CHARD, CAB S, Merlot (**90 91 92**), and Bordeaux-style blend Tria Corda (**89**). Also 'Vintage Port' 82, excellent 82 and 86 from Portuguese varieties.

Paarl Town 30 miles northeast of Cape Town and the surrounding demarcated district. Headquarters of KWV, SA's largest cooperative.

Paul Cluver w ★★ Label launched '92. Good SAUV, RHINE RIES, CHARD: grapes from cool upland Elgin Coastal region.

Pinot Noir Like counterparts in California and Australia, Cape producers struggle for fine, burgundy-like complexity. They are getting closer. Best are CABRIERE, BOUCHARD FINLAYSON, HAMILTON RUSSELL, MEERLUST and GLEN CARLOU.

Pinotage S African red grape cross of PINOT N and CINSAUT, useful for high yields and hardiness. Can be delicious but overstated flamboyant esters often dominate. Experiments/oak-ageing show potential for finesse.

Plaisir de Merle r w ★★★ New SFW-owned cellar nr PAARL producing its first reds from own v'yds in '93: CAB-Merlot and Merlot are outstanding, supple, also CHARD. Paul Pontallier of Château Margaux is consultant.

Pongracz ★★ Successful value non-vintage sp METHODE CAP CLASSIQUE from PINOT N (75%) and CHARD, produced by the BERGKELDER.

Premier Grand Cru See Grand Cru.

Rhebokskloof r w ★→★★ **90 92 95** 200-acre estate behind PAARL mountains: sound small range. CAB is promising.

Rhine Riesling Produces full-flavoured dry and off-dry wines but reaches perfection when lusciously sweet as 'Noble Late Harvest'. Generally needs 2 yrs or more of bottle-age. Also called Weisser Riesling.

Riesling S African Ries (actually Crouchen Bl) is v different from RHINE RIES, providing neutral easy-drinking wines. Known locally as Cape Ries.

Robertson District inland from Cape. Mainly dessert wines (notably Muscat); white table wines on increase. Few reds. Irrigated v'yds.

Roodeberg ★→★★ Red KWV blend including PINOTAGE-Shiraz-Tinta Barocca-CAB. Can age well (76 in '96!): sweetish porty, 'typical old Cape red style'.

Rooiberg Cooperative Winery ★ Successful big-selling ROBERTSON range of more than 30 labels. Good CHENIN BL, COLOMBARD and fortified dessert wines.

Rozendal r ★★★ (r) **89 91 92 93 94** Small STELLENBOSCH v'yd: excellent CAB-Merlot.

Rust en Vrede r ★★→★★★ Well-known estate just E of STELLENBOSCH: red only. Good CAB (**89 90 91**), Shiraz (**89 90 91**), Rust en Vrede blend (**89 91**).

Rustenberg r w ★★★ (red except Pinot N) **82 84 86 91 92 93 95** Old STELLENBOSCH estate, founded 300 yrs ago, making wine for last 100. Extensively renovated; also SA's first New Zealand winemaker. Fresh start from '96: modern fruitier wines, initially under Brampton label. Formerly Rustenberg Gold CAB (**89 91**), Médoc-style blend. Also lighter Cab-CINSAUT-Merlot and Cab (**89 91**).

Sauvignon Blanc Has adapted well to SA conditions. Widely grown. In both wooded and unwooded styles. Also v sweet.

Saxenburg Wines r w dr sw ★★★ (r) 91 92 93 94 STELLENBOSCH v'yds and winery; recently prize-winning. Distinctive powerful reds under Private Collection labels; robust deep-flavoured PINOTAGE; CAB (**91 92**), Shiraz (**91 92 93 94**). Also Merlot (94), CHARD and SAUV BL.

Simonsig r w sp sw ★★→★★★ (r) **90 91 92 93** (Chard) **95 96** Malan family S'BOSCH estate with a wide range: vg CAB, Shiraz (**91 95**), CHARD, PINOTAGE (**92 93 95**), dessert-style GEWURZ (**90 92**). Cab-Merlot Tiara (**90 91 92 93**). First Cape METHODE CAP CLASSIQUE (esp **91 93**).

Simonsvlei r w p sw sp ★ One of S Africa's best-known coop cellars, just outside PAARL. A prize-winner with PINOTAGE under 'Reserve' label.

Steen S Africa's commonest white grape, probably a clone of CHENIN BL. It gives tasty lively wine, sweet or dry: short-lived if dry, lasts better when off-dry or sweet. Normally better than S African RIES.

Stein Name often for commercial blends of s/sw white. Not to be despised.

Stellenbosch Town and demarcated district 30 miles E of Cape Town (2nd oldest town in S Africa after Cape Town). Heart of wine industry, with the 3 largest companies. Most top estates, esp for reds, are in mountain foothills.

Stellenbosch Farmers' Winery (SFW) The world's fifth largest winery, South Africa's biggest after KWV: equivalent of 14M cases pa. Range incls NEDERBURG; top is ZONNEBLOEM. Wide selection of mid-/low-price wines.

Stellenryck Collection r w ★★★ Top-quality BERGKELDER range. RHINE RIES, Fumé Blanc, CAB (**89 91 92**) among S Africa's best.

Stellenzicht ★★★ Recently replanted STELLENBOSCH v'yds; outstanding wines now, across wide range: B'x blend (**94**), Cab (**94**), Syrah (94), SAUV, Sém Res; outstanding noble late harvest botrytis dessert wines.

Swartland Wine Cellar r w dr s/sw sw sp ★→★★ Vast range of wines from hot, dry wheatland: big-selling and low-price, esp CHENIN and dry, off-dry or sweet, but (recently) penetrating, SAUV, also big no-nonsense PINOTAGE.

Talana Hill r w ★★ (r) 88 89 (Chard) **93 95** STELLENBOSCH winery: good CHARD and St-Emilion-style CAB F-Merlot blend Royale (**91 92 94**).

Tassenberg Popular red blend (CINSAUT, Carignan, PINOTAGE and CAB S) by SFW, fondly called 'Tassies'. Trad student and braaivleis (barbecue) wine. Oom Tas, a dry Muscat, is white equivalent.

Thelema r w ★★★★ (Cab S) **89 90 91 92 93** 94 (Chard) **93 94 95** 96 Heavy-hitting v'yds and winery at Helshoogte, above S'BOSCH. Impressive, individual fruity-minty CAB and B'x blend (starting with vg **91**) and Merlot (since '92). Excellent CHARD, and unoaked SAUV. American v'yd advice is giving winemaker Gyles Webb (festooned with awards) fab fruit.

Theuniskraal w ★ TULBAGH estate: whites incl S Afrian RIES, GEWURZ.

Tulbagh Demarcated district N of PAARL best known for white THEUNISKRAAL, TWEE JONGEGEZELLEN and dessert wines from DROSTDY. See also Boberg.

Twee Jongegezellen w sp ★★ Old TULBAGH estate, helped pioneer cold fermentation in '60s, night harvesting in '80s; still in Krone family (18th-C founder). Esp whites, best known: popular dry TJ39 (mélange of a dozen varieties), Schanderl off-dry Muscat-GEWURZ. METHODE CAP CLASSIQUE Cuvée Krone Borealis Brut (CHARD, PINOT N) with Champagne's Mumm.

Uiterwyk r w ★ Old estate W of S'BOSCH. CAB 'Carlonet' (**89 90**), Merlot, whites.

Uitkyk r w ★★ (r) **89 90 92 94** Old estate (400 acres) W of STELLENBOSCH esp for Carlonet (big gutsy CAB, **89 90 93**), Carlsheim (SAUV) white. Recently CHARD.

Van Loveren r w sw sp ★★ Go-ahead ROBERTSON estate: range incl muscular CHARD (**95**), good Pinot Gr; scarcer Fernão Pires, Hárslevelü.

Veenwouden ★★ Promising Merlot (**93 94**), dense B'deaux blend '94 from PAARL property owned by Geneva-based opera tenor, Deon Van der Walt.

Vergelegen w (★★★) One of Cape's oldest wine farms, founded 1700. Long neglected, now spectacularly restored. From '95, excellent Merlot, CAB S CHARD Res. Also vg SAUV.

Vergenoegd r w sw ★→★★ Old family estate in S S'BOSCH bottling CAB S, Shiraz. New B'x-style blend 'Reserve' (**89 90 92**).

Villiera r w ★★→★★★ PAARL estate with popular NV METHODE CAP CLASSIQUE 'Tradition'. Top SAUV BL (**95 96**), good RHINE RIES, fine B'x-style blend CAB-Merlot 'Cru Monro' (**90 91 92**). Recently exceptional Merlot (**91 92 94**).

Vredendal Cooperative r w dr sw ★ S Africa's largest coop winery in hot Olifants River region. Big range: mostly white.

Vriesenhof r w ★★→★★★ (Cab) **91 92 93** (Chard) **95 95** Highly rated CAB and B'x blend Kalista (**89 91 93**). Vg CHARD. Also Pinot Bl and vg PINOTAGE under Paradyskloof label.

Warwick r w ★★→★★★ STELLENBOSCH estate run by one of Cape's few female winemakers. Vg Médoc-style blend Trilogy (**92 93 94**), Cab F (**92 94 95**). One of top SA PINOTAGES (**94 95**) from 22-yr-old untrellised bush vines. CHARD (95 96).

Weisser Riesling See Rhine Riesling.

Welgemeend r ★★→★★★ Boutique PAARL estate: Médoc-style blends (**90 92 94**). Also Duelle a Malbec, CAB, Merlot blend (95).

Weltevrede w dr sw ★→★★ ROBERTSON estate. Blended, white, fortified. Good CHARD (**95 96**), GEWURZ (**94 95**), White Muscadel.

Wine of Origin The Cape's appellation contrôlée, but without French crop yield restrictions. Demarcated regions are described on these pages.

Woolworths Wines Best S African supermarket wines, many specially blended. Top are CHARDS, young reds incl Merlot, B'x-style blends.

Worcester Demarcated wine district round BREEDE and Hex river valleys, E of PAARL. Many coop cellars. Mainly dessert wines, brandy, dry whites.

Yonder Hill ★★ Small STELLENBOSCH mountainside property, with vg Merlot and CAB-Merlot blend (**93 94**).

Zandvliet r ★★ Estate in ROBERTSON area making fine Shiraz (**94 95**) and CHARD (96) and CAP CLASSIQUE sparkler.

Zevenwacht r w ★★ STELLENBOSCH. Vg WEISSER (**96**), fresh SAUV BL (**96**) and CHARD (**96**). Reds incl CAB-Merlot, Pinotage improved from 96.

Zonnebloem r w ★★ (Cab S) Good quality range from SFW incl CAB S, Merlot (**88 91 92 93**), Bordeaux-style blend Laureat (**90 91 93**), Shiraz, PINOTAGE (**91 92**), SAUV BL and CHARD (**95 96**) and, new '94, a Sauv-Chard blend. Bl de Bl is among best dry Chenins of the Cape – drink young.

A little learning...

A few technical words

The jargon of laboratory analysis is often seen on back-labels of New World wines. It has crept menacingly into newspapers and magazines. What does it mean? This hard-edged wine-talk, unsympathetic as it is to most lovers of wine, is very briefly explained below.

The most frequent technical references are to the ripeness of grapes at picking; the resultant alcohol and sugar content of the wine; various measures of its acidity; the amount of sulphur dioxide used as a preservative; and occasionally the amount of 'dry extract' – the sum of all the things that give wine its character.

The **sugar** in wine is mainly glucose and fructose, with traces of arabinose, xylose and other sugars that are not fermentable by yeast, but can be attacked by bacteria. Each country has its own system for measuring the sugar content or ripeness of grapes, known in English as the '**must weight**'. The chart below relates the three principal ones (German, French and American) to each other, to specific gravity, and to the potential alcohol of the wine if all the sugar is fermented.

Sugar to alcohol: potential strength

Specific Gravity	°Oechsle	Baumé	Brix	% Potential Alcohol v/v
1.065	65	8.8	15.8	8.1
1.070	70	9.4	17.0	8.8
1.075	75	10.1	18.1	9.4
1.080	80	10.7	19.3	10.0
1.085	85	11.3	20.4	10.6
1.090	90	11.9	21.5	12.1
1.095	95	12.5	22.5	13.0
1.100	100	13.1	23.7	13.6
1.105	105	13.7	24.8	14.3
1.110	110	14.3	25.8	15.1
1.115	115	14.9	26.9	15.7
1.120	120	15.5	28.0	16.4

Residual sugar is the sugar left after fermentation has finished or been artificially stopped, measured in grams per litre.

Alcohol content (mainly ethyl alcohol) is expressed in percent by volume of the total liquid. (Also known as 'degrees'.)

Acidity is both fixed and volatile. **Fixed acidity** consists principally of tartaric, malic and citric acids which are all found in the grape, and lactic and succinic acids which are produced during fermentation. **Volatile acidity** consists mainly of acetic acid, which is rapidly formed by bacteria in the presence of oxygen. A small amount of volatile acidity is inevitable and even attractive. With a larger amount the wine becomes 'pricked' – to use the graphic Shakespearian term. It starts to turn to vinegar.

Total acidity is fixed and volatile acidity combined. As a rule of thumb for a well-balanced wine it should be in the region of one gram per thousand for each 10°Oechsle (see above).

pH is a measure of the strength of the acidity, rather than its volume. The lower the figure the more acid. Wine usually ranges from pH 2.8 to 3.8. Winemakers in hot climates can have problems getting the pH low enough. Lower pH gives better colour, helps stop bacterial spoilage and allows more of the SO_2 to be free and active as a preservative.

Sulphur dioxide (SO_2) is added to prevent oxidation and other accidents in winemaking. Some of it combines with sugars etc and is known as **'bound'**. Only the **'free' SO_2** that remains in the wine is effective as a preservative. **Total SO_2** is controlled by law according to the level of residual sugar: the more sugar, the more SO_2 needed.

A few words about words

In the shorthand essential for this little book (and often in bigger books and magazines as well) wines are often described by adjectives that can seem irrelevant, inane – or just silly. What do 'fat', 'round', 'full', 'lean' and so on mean when used about wine? Some of the more irritatingly vague and some of the more common 'technical' terms are expanded in this list:

Acid
To laymen often a term of reproval, meaning 'too sharp'. But various acids are vital to the quality and preservation of wine (especially white) and give it its power to refresh. For those on the advanced course, malolactic, or secondary, fermentation is the natural conversion of tart malic (apple) acid to lactic, replacing the immediate bite of a wine with milder, more complex tastes. The undesirable acid is acetic, smells of vinegar and is referred to as 'volatile'. Too much and the wine is on the way out.

Astringent
One of the characters of certain tannins, producing a mouth-drying effect. Can be highly appetizing, as in Chianti.

Attack
The first impression of the wine in your mouth. It should 'strike' positively, if not necessarily with force. Without attack it is feeble or too bland.

Attractive
Means 'I like it, anyway'. A slight put-down for expensive wines; encouragement for juniors. At least refreshing.

Balance See Well-balanced.

Big
Concerns the whole flavour, including the alcohol content. Sometimes implies clumsiness, the opposite of elegance. Generally positive, but big is easy in California and less usual in, say, Bordeaux. So the context matters.

Bitterness
Another tannic flavour, usually from lack of full ripeness.
Much appreciated in N Italy but looked on askance in most regions.

Body
The 'weight', the volume of flavour and alcohol in wine. See Big and Full.

Botrytis See page 100.

Charming
Rather patronizing when said of wines that should have more impressive qualities. Implies lightness and possibly a slight sweetness. A standard comment regarding Loire Valley wines.

Corky
A musty taint derived (far too often) from an infected cork. Can be faint or blatant, but is always unacceptable.

Crisp
With pronounced but pleasing acidity on the palate; fresh and eager.

Deep/depth
This wine is worth tasting with attention. There is more to it than the first impression; it fills your mouth with developing flavours as though it had an extra dimension. (Deep colour simply means hard to see through.) All really fine wines have depth.

Earthy
Used of a sense that the soil itself has entered into the flavour of the wine. Often positive, as in the flavour of red Graves.

Easy
Used in the sense of 'easy come, easy go'. An easy wine makes no demand on your palate (or your intellect). The implication is that it drinks smoothly, doesn't need maturing, and all you remember is a pleasant drink.

Elegant
A professional taster's favourite term when he or she is stuck to describe a wine whose proportions (of strength, flavour, aroma), whose attack, middle and finish, whose texture and whose overall qualities call for comparison with other forms of natural beauty.

Extract
The components of wine (apart from water, alcohol, sugar, acids etc) that make up its flavour. Usually the more the better, but 'over-extracted' means harsh, left too long extracting matter from the grape skins.

Fat
Wine with a flavour and texture that fills your mouth, but without aggression. Obviously inappropriate in eg a light Moselle, but what you pay your money for in Sauternes.

Finesse See Elegance.

Finish See Length.

Firm
Flavour that strikes the palate fairly hard, with fairly high acidity or tannic astringency giving the impression that the wine is in youthful vigour and will age to gentler things. An excellent quality with high-flavoured foods, and almost always positive.

Flesh
Refers to both substance and texture. A fleshy wine is fatter than a 'meaty' wine, more unctuous if less vigorous. The term is often used of good Pomerols, whose texture is notably smooth.

Flowery
Often used as though synonymous with fruity, but really meaning floral, like the fragrance of flowers. Roses, violets etc are some of those specified.

Fresh
Implies a good degree of fruity acidity, even a little nip of sharpness, as well as the zip and zing of youth. All young whites should be fresh: the alternative is flatness, staleness. . . ugh.

Fruity
Used for almost any quality, but really refers to the body and richness of wine made from good ripe grapes. A fruity aroma is not the same as a flowery one. Fruitiness usually implies at least a slight degree of sweetness. Attempts at specifying *which* fruit the wine resembles can be helpful. Eg grapefruit, lemon, plum, lychee. On the other hand writers' imaginations freqently run riot, flinging basketfuls of fruit and flowers at wines which could well be more modestly described.

Full
Interchangeable with full-bodied. Lots of 'vinosity' or wineyness: the mouth-filling flavours of alcohol and 'extract' (all the flavouring components) combined.

Heady
The sense that the alcohol content is out of proportion.

Hollow
Lacking a satisfying middle flavour. Something seems to be missing between the first flavour and the last. Characteristic of wines from greedy proprietors who let their vines produce too many grapes. A very hollow wine is 'empty'.

Honey
A smell and flavour found especially in botrytis-affected wines, but often noticeable to a small and seductive degree in any mature wine of a ripe vintage.

Lean
More flesh would be an improvement. Lack of mouth-filling flavours; often astringent as well. Occasionally a term of appreciation of a distinct and enjoyable style.

Length
The flavours and aromas that linger after swallowing. In principle the greater the length, the better the wine. One second of flavour after swallowing = one 'caudalie'. Twenty caudalies is good; 50 terrific.

Light
With relatively little alcohol and body, as in most German wines. A very desirable quality in the right wines but a dismissive term in eg reds where something more intense/ weighty is desired.

Maderized
Means oxidized until it smells/tastes like Madeira. A serious fault unless intentional.

Meaty
Savoury in effect with enough substance to chew. The inference is lean meat; leaner than in 'fleshy'.

Oaky
Smelling or tasting of fresh-sawn oak, eg a new barrel. Appropriate in a fine wine destined for ageing in bottle, but currently often wildly overdone by winemakers to persuade a gullible public that a simple wine is something more grandiose. Over-oaky wines are both boring and tiring to drink.

Plump
The diminutive of fat, implying a degree of charm as well.

Rich
Not necessarily sweet, but giving an opulent impression.

Robust
In good heart, vigorous, and on a fairly big scale.

Rough
Flavour and texture give no pleasure. Acidity and/or tannin are dominant and coarse.

Round
Almost the same as fat, but with more approval.

Structure
The 'plan' or architecture of the flavour, as it were. Without structure wine is bland, dull, and won't last.

Stylish
Style is bold and definite; wears its cap on its ear.

Supple
Often used of young red wines that might be expected to be more aggressive. More lively than 'easy' wine, with good quality implications.

Well-balanced
Contains all the desirable elements (acid, alcohol, flavours etc) in appropriate and pleasing proportions.

The Options Game

Like-minded wine-lovers who enjoy discussing wines together to improve their knowledge cannot do better than to play the Options Game. The game was devised by the MC of the wine world, Australian Len Evans of Rothbury Estate. It is played during a meal and needs only a chairman who knows what the wine is, and any number of players who don't. Each player is given a glass of the same wine. The chairman asks a series of questions: one choice is the truth.

For example: 'Is this wine from California, France or Australia?' France is correct. Any player who has said France collects a point. 'Is it from Bordeaux, the Rhône or Provence?' Bordeaux is correct; another point. 'Is it from St-Emilion, Graves or the Haut-Médoc?' Haut-Médoc is correct; another point. 'Is it from Pauillac, St-Julien or Margaux?' Pauillac is right; another point. 'Is it a first, second or fifth growth?' Fifth is right; another point. 'Is it Grand-Puy-Lacoste, Lynch-Bages or Batailley?' Grand-Puy-Lacoste is right. 'Is it from 1982, 1983 or 1985?' The answer is 1985: the wine is identified.

Each time a player answers correctly he or she scores a point. There is no penalty for being wrong. So you can start by believing it was a California wine and still be in at the kill. There are many possible variations, including a knock-out version which can be played with a ballroom full of guests, who stand so long as they are answering correctly, and sit when they drop out. 'Options' is a great game for the competitive, and a wonderful way to learn about wine.

What to drink this year in an ideal world

Red Bordeaux
Top growths of 91, 85, 83, 81, 79, 78, 75, 70, 66, 61, 59
Other crus classés of 92 89, 88, 87, 86, 85, 83, 82, 81, 79, 70, 66, 61
Petits châteaux of 96, 95, 94, 93, 90, 89

Red Burgundy
Top growths of 92, 90, 89, 88, 87, 85, 83, 82, 80, 79, 78, 71, 69, 66, 64
Premiers Crus of 94, 93, 92, 90, 89, 88, 87, 85, 83, 78
Village wines of 95, 94, 93, 92, 90, 89

White Burgundy
Top growths of 94, 93, 92, 90, 89, 88, 86, 85, 83, 79, 78
Premiers Crus of 95, 94, 93, 92, 91, 90, 89, 88, 86, 85, 83, 78
Village wines of 96, 95, 94, 93, 92, 90, 89, 88

Rhône reds
Hermitage/top northern Rhône reds of 91, 90, 88, 86, 85, 83, 82, 79, 78, 71
Châteauneuf-du-Pape of 93, 90, 89, 88, 86, 85, 83, 82, 81

Sauternes
Top growths of 90, 89, 88, 86, 85, 83, 82, 81, 79, 78, 76, 75, 71, 70, 67
Other wines of 90, 89, 88, 86, 85, 83, 82, 81, 79, 76, 75

Alsace
Grands Crus and late-harvest wines of 92, 90, 89, 88, 85, 83, 78, 76, 67
Standard wines of 95, 94, 92, 91, 90, 89, 88, 85

Sweet Loire wines
Top growths (Anjou/Vouvray) of 93, 90, 88, 86, 85, 78, 76, 75, 71, 64

Champagne
Top wines of 86, 85, 83, 82, 79, 76, 75

German wines
Great sweet wines of 92, 90, 89, 88, 86, 85, 83, 76, 71, 67
Auslesen of 93, 92, 90, 89, 88, 86, 85, 83, 76, 71
Spätlesen of 95, 94, 93, 92, 91, 90, 89, 88, 86, 85, 83, 76
Kabinett and QbA wines of 95, 94, 93, 92, 91, 90, 89

Italian wines
Top Tuscan reds 93, 91, 90, 88, 86, 85, 82
Top Piedmont reds 91, 90, 89, 88, 87, 86, 85, 83, 82, 79

California wines
Top Cabs, Zins, Pinot N of 92, 91, 87, 86, 85, 84, 82, 81, 80, 79, 78, 77, 76, 75
Most Cabernets etc of 95, 94, 93, 90, 89, 87, 86, 85
Top Chardonnays of 95, 94, 90, 89
Most Chardonnays of 96, 95, 94

Australian wines
Top Cabs, Shiraz, Pinot N of 91, 89, 88, 86, 84, 82, 80, 79, 75
Most Cabernets etc of 95, 94, 91, 90, 89, 88, 87, 86
Top Chardonnays of 95, 94, 92, 90, 89, 88, 86
Most Chardonnays of 96, 95, 94, 93, 92, 91
Top Semillons and Rieslings of 94, 92, 90, 86, 78

Vintage Port
83, 82, 80, 70, 66, 63, 60, 55, 48, 45...

And the score is...

It seems that America and the rest of the world will never agree about the idea of scoring wines. America is besotted with the 100-point scale devised by Robert Parker, based on the strange US school system in which 50 = 0. Arguments that taste is too various, too subtle, too evanescent, too wonderful to be reduced to a pseudo-scientific set of numbers fall on deaf ears. Arguments that the accuracy implied by giving one wine a score of 87 and another 88 is a chimera don't get much further.

America likes numbers (and so do salesmen) because they are simpler than words. When it comes to words America likes superlatives. The best joke of 1997 – at least I hope it was a joke – was the critic who came up with a 150-point scoring system. He argued that if 50 was no score at all you needed 150 to reach 100. Logical, but if it catches on there will be chaos. It might just ridicule the whole unreal business to death.

The Johnson System

Very cautiously, therefore, I offer an alternative way of registering how much *you* like a wine. The Johnson System reflects the enjoyment (or lack of it) that each wine offered at the time it was tasted or drunk with inescapable honesty. Here it is:

The minimum score is 1 sniff

One step up is 1 sip

2 sips = faint interest

A half glass = slight hesitation

1 glass = tolerance, even general approval

Individuals will vary in their scoring after this (they do with points systems, too). You should assume that you are drinking without compunction – without your host pressing you or the winemaker glowering at you.

Two glasses means you quite like it
(or there is nothing else to drink);
three glasses – you find it more than acceptable;
four – it tickles your fancy;
one bottle means thorough satisfaction;
two, it is irresistible. The steps grow higher now:
a full case means you are not going to miss out on this one... and so on.
The logical top score in the Johnson System is, of course, the whole vineyard.

The right temperature

No single aspect of serving wine makes or mars it so easily as getting the temperature right. White wines almost invariably taste dull and insipid served warm and red wines have disappointingly little scent or flavour served cold. The chart below gives an indication of what is generally found to be the most satisfactory temperature for serving each class of wine.

		°F	°C	
		68	20	
		66	19	
Room temperature		64	18	Best red wines
		63	17	especially Bordeaux
	Red burgundy	61	16	
	Best white burgundy	59	15	Chianti, Zinfandel
	Port, Madeira	57	14	Côtes du Rhône
		55	13	*Ordinaires*
		54	12	Lighter red wines
Ideal cellar	Sherry	52	11	eg Beaujolais
	Fino sherry	50	10	
	Most dry white wines	48	9	Rosés
	Champagne	46	8	Lambrusco
Domestic fridge		45	7	
		43	6	Most sweet white wines
		41	5	Sparkling wines
		39	4	
		37	3	
		35	2	
		33	1	
		32	0	

Quick reference vintage charts

These charts give a picture of the range of qualities made in the principal 'classic' areas (every year has its relative successes and failures) and a guide to whether the wine is ready to drink or should be kept.

I	drink up	—	needs keeping
/	can be drunk with pleasure now, but the better wines will continue to improve	⊼	avoid
		0	no good
		10	the best

France

	Red Bordeaux		White Bordeaux		Alsace	
	Médoc/ Graves	Pom/ St-Em	Sauternes & SW	Graves & dry		
96	6–9 —	5–8 —	7–9 —	7–10 |∠	6–9 |∠	96
95	6–9 —	6–9 —	6–9 —	5–9 V	5–8 |∠	95
94	5–8 —	5–9 —	4–6 —	5–8 V	4–8 |∠	94
93	4–7 ∠	5–8 ∠	2–5 /	5–7 /	6–8 V	93
92	3–7 ∠	3–5 ∠	3–5 ∠	4–8 V	7–9 V	92
91	3–6 V	2–4 V	2–5 V	6–8 /	5–7 V	91
90	7–10 ∠	8–10 |∠	7–10 |∠	7–8 V	7–9 V	90
89	6–9 |∠	7–9 |∠	7–9 |∠	6–8 V	7–10 V	89
88	6–9 |∠	7–9 |∠	6–10 |∠	7–9 V	8–10 V	88
87	3–6 I	3–6 I	2–5 ⊼	7–10 V	7–8 ⊼	87
86	6–9 V	5–8 V	7–10 |∠	7–9 I	7–8 I	86
85	7–9 V	7–9 V	6–8 V	5–8 I	7–10 V	85
83	6–9 V	6–9 I	6–10 |∠	7–9 I	8–10 ⊼	83
82	8–10 V	7–9 I	3–7 V	7–8 I	6–8 ⊼	82
81	5–8 V	6–9 I	5–8 V	7–8 I	7–8 I	81
79	5–8 V	5–7 I	6–8 V	4–6 ⊼	7–8 ⊼	79
78	6–9 V	6–8 I	4–6 I	7–9 ⊼	6–8 I	78
76	6–8 I	7–8 I	7–9 V	4–8 ⊼		76

	Burgundy			Rhone		
	Côte d'Or red	Côte d'Or white	Chablis	Rhône (N)	Rhône (S)	
96	7–9 —	7–9 ∠	7–9 /	5–7 —	4–6 —	96
95	7–9 ∠	5–8 ∠	5–8 /	6–8 —	6–8 —	95
94	5–7 ∠	5–8 ∠	6–8 /	6–7 ∠	5–7 |∠	94
93	6–9 |∠	4–6 V	4–7 V	3–6 I	4–9 |∠	93
92	4–7 V	6–8 V	5–8 V	4–6 I	3–6 V	92
91	5–7 V	4–6 I	4–6 I	6–9 |∠	4–5 I	91
90	7–10 |∠	7–9 |∠	6–9 V	6–9 |∠	7–9 |∠	90
89	6–9 |∠	6–9 V	7–10 V	6–8 ∠	6–8 |∠	89
88	7–10 |∠	7–9 V	7–9 V	7–9 |∠	5–8 V	88
87	6–8 V	4–7 ⊼	5–7 I	3–6 V	3–5 I	87
86	5–8 I	7–10 V	7–9 I	5–8 V	4–7 V	86
85	7–10 V	5–8 V	6–9 I	6–8 V	6–9 I	85
83	5–9 V	6–9 I	7–9 I	7–10 |∠	7–9 I	83

Beaujolais 96 and 95 Crus will keep, 93 vg, 91 drink up. **Mâcon-Villages** (white) Drink 96 and 95 now or can wait. **Loire** (Sweet Anjou and Touraine) best recent vintages: 96, 95, 93, 90, 89, 88, 85; Bourgueil, Chinon and Saumur-Champigny: 96, 95, 93, 90, 89, 88. **Upper Loire** (Sancerre and Pouilly-Fumé): 96 and 95 vg; 94 and 93 good now. **Muscadet** 96 vg: DYA.

	Germany		Italy	USA (California)		
	Rhine	Mosel	Tuscan reds	Cabs	Chards	
96	7–9 /	6–8 /	6–8 —	5–7 —	6–8 ∠	96
95	7–10 /	8–10 /	4–6 —	4–6 ∠	4–6 ∠	95
94	5–7 /	6–10 |∠	6–8 ∠	6–9 ∠	4–7 V	94
93	5–8 |∠	6–9 |∠	7–9 V	5–7 /	5–8 I	93
92	5–9 V	5–9 V	3–6 V	7–9 V	6–8 I	92
91	5–7 V	5–7 V	4–6 V	8–10 ∠	5–7 I	91
90	8–10 |∠	8–10 |∠	7–9 V	8–9 |∠	6–9 I	90
89	7–10 V	8–10 V	5–8 V	6–9 I	5–9 I	89
88	6–8 V	7–9 V	6–9 I	4–6 V	6–8 ⊼	88
87	4–7 I	5–7 I	4–7 I	7–10 /	7–9 I	87
86	4–8 I	5–8 I	5–8 I	5–8 V	6–8 ⊼	86
85	6–8 I	6–9 V	7–10 I	7–9 V	7–9 ⊼	85
83	6–9 I	7–10 V	5–7 I	4–8 ⊼	4–7 I	83